Defending Irene

Lauren,

Kristin Wolden Nitz

KRISTIN WOLDEN NITZ

PEACHTREE

ATLANTA

Published by
PEACHTREE PUBLISHERS
1700 Chattahoochee Avenue
Atlanta, Georgia 30318-2112

www.peachtree-online.com

Jacket design by Loraine Joyner
Book design by Melanie McMahon Ives

Manufactured in United States of America

10 9 8 7 6 5 4 3 2 1
First Edition

Library of Congress Cataloging-in-Publication Data

Nitz, Kristin Wolden.
  Defending Irene / written by Kristin Wolden Nitz.-- 1st ed.
    p. cm.
  Summary: A thirteen-year-old American girl plays on a fiercely competitive
boys' soccer team during the year her family spends in Italy and experiences
culture clashes both on and off the field.
  ISBN 1-56145-309-9
  [1. Soccer--Fiction. 2. Sex role--Fiction. 3. Americans--Italy--Fiction. 4.
Italy--Fiction.] I. Title.

PZ7.N6433De 2004
[Fic]--dc22
                                    2003018677

For Calvin, Sara, and Gretchen

Acknowledgments

Grazie mille to the players, coaches, parents, and support staff at U.S. Sinigo for giving me a window on the world of Italian soccer. Another thousand thanks to Marina, Tina, and Mara for their additional insights to the culture of the South Tyrol. This project could not have been completed without the help of Gretchen, Sara, and Calvin Nitz—my able team of in-house research assistants—or my husband Kurt who gave me encouragement, time to write, and the chance to live in the Alto Adige for three years. The generosity of other writers helped me over the rough spots. Jeanie, Debbi, Terrie, Pat, Tovah, and Julia followed Irene every step of the way. Darcy and Terrie talked me through the ending one night in Arkansas. Stephanie, Donna, and Sue checked out the big flick issues. Erin, Vicki, and Sondy provided unrelenting support and key insights into the writing process. Gary taught me about generating conflict. Isi, Dorothy, and Lisa helped me off the ground at the beginning of my writing journey. And thanks finally to my editor, Lisa Banim, who asked, "Why don't you send me what you've got?"

Contents

1

Calcio (CAL-cho)

Soccer

I should have known something was wrong when the woman's eyes moved quickly past me to my five-year-old brother, Max. The wrinkles around her eyes deepened as she smiled and ruffled his hair. "So, you want to enroll yourself in soccer?" she asked.

Max bounced on his toes and nodded.

The woman turned to my mother and handed her a white piece of paper. "His group finished five minutes ago, but they'll meet again tomorrow."

From the way Mom's lips twitched, I could tell she wanted to say something but couldn't find the words. I stepped forward.

"We're also here to enroll *me* on your girls' team," I announced.

The woman blinked. "There isn't one."

What she actually said—I suppose I should mention—was "*Non c'e,*" which in Italian means about the same thing. If this conversation had taken place back in the States, in English, my mother probably would have launched into a speech on equal opportunity for girls. But now we were in Merano, a small city in the Italian Alps, so all she could do was stand there and look horrified.

And to tell you the truth, even though I am almost fluent in Italian, that's about all I could do, too.

The woman studied me for a moment, from my tight, businesslike French braids down to my black cleats. "How long have you played soccer, *cara?*"

"Eight years," I replied.

"And what grade do you frequent?"

"The second year of middle school."

"One moment, please. I must speak with someone." She nodded and walked briskly around the corner of the yellow stucco clubhouse.

I stared after her in disbelief. "When Dad and I made a search on Yahoo Italia, there were lots of girls' teams," I said to Mom.

"Near Milan and Turin, maybe," Mom said. "This isn't the big city, Irene. Here in Merano, things might be a little more—conservative."

Mom could read, write, and understand Italian. But sometimes, especially when the conversation took an unexpected turn, she couldn't always speak it very well. She says it's much harder to pull a word up out of your brain than to hear it spoken or to read it on a page.

I wouldn't know. My dad's first words to me were "*Ciao, bimba. Come stai?*" Hi, baby girl. How are you? And from that moment on, he had spoken to me almost exclusively in Italian. Somehow, a baby can easily separate languages into different boxes. It's a lot harder for grown-ups.

"Don't worry," Mom said. "You'll play. I'll make that clear to whoever's in charge."

"But Mom, if the teams here are all boys…"

"That never stopped you back home," Mom reminded me.

"Yeah, but that was just around the neighborhood. Half those guys don't play competitively. What if…" I bit my lip.

"Yes?" Mom prompted.

I rubbed my palms against my shorts. "What if I can't keep up?"

"You will, honey," Mom assured me. "But maybe you'll have to work even harder this season. It'll be good for you."

Sure, I thought. Just like having a cavity filled.

A man wearing dark blue pants and a white polo shirt rounded the corner. "*Buona sera,*" he said, greeting us. He must have overheard us talking because he switched to English. "I am the manager, Giacomo Corona. You are Americans, no?"

"Yes," my mother said.

"Signora Martelli tells me your daughter wants to play at *calcio* with us?"

"Yes."

He smiled. "We are glad. And she speaks a little Italian?"

"She speaks a lot of Italian," Mom said. "My husband was born in Milan, er, Milano."

"Ah. *Molto bene.* Very good. I must tell you that there are no other girls of her age in our program, but we are happy she is here. Very happy." He turned to me. "What is your name?"

"Irene Benenati."

Unlike every coach I'd ever had in America, he did not ask me to repeat my first name, "ee-RAY-nay." There's no such thing as a silent *e* in Italian.

"A pleasure, Irene. You meet with your squad at four o'clock, Monday and Thursday. September to November and

March to May. Six months, yes? It is a hundred euro to the year. That is not too much?" He glanced at my mother.

The corners of her mouth turned down. She was probably trying not to smile. The outrageous fee she'd had to pay for my select team last winter was more than four times that.

"No. It is not too much at all," Mom said and reached for her purse.

Signor Corona waved his hand. "No, no. Not today. Next week."

Next week? For all his smiles and pleasure at meeting me, maybe he was hoping that I wouldn't be around next week—that if they didn't take our money it would be easier to get rid of the girl. But no, a smiling Signora Martelli appeared a few seconds later. She was carrying a white T-shirt, navy blue shorts, matching sweats, and an official backpack. I took the pile she handed me, fighting the urge to shove it back at her and make a terrified break for the parking lot. Did I really want to do this?

"Her team already begins five minutes ago," Signor Corona said, pointing in the direction of the soccer field.

My fingers tightened around the clothing. "Five minutes ago?" I asked, switching to Italian.

"*Sí,*" Signora Martelli said. "You can change clothes in the bathroom around the corner. Take a left and then another left. I will tell the *mister* that you are here."

Late to practice on my first day? My new coach, or the *mister* as they called him here, would not be impressed.

My hands shook as I locked myself into the bathroom. I changed into my uniform, trying to tell myself there was no reason to be nervous.

No reason at all, a voice inside me mocked. After all, these boys only practiced six months out of the year from first grade on up. They only watched soccer on TV every chance they got. Soccer was only Italy's national pastime, its national passion.

I leaned heavily on the sink, my fingers clutching its porcelain sides. I rocked back and forth with my eyes closed. What could I do?

Dad had passed his passion for soccer along to me. I loved it. I loved the sound and feel of the ball exploding off my foot for a shot on goal. And I certainly didn't want to fall behind in my training during my family's yearlong stay in Italy. But to go from being one of the top players on the squad to the last substitute lingering on the bench… How could I stand it?

A fist thudded against the door.

"Die, Irene! Die!"

2
Mister (MEE-stair)
Coach

I rene, die!" Signora Martelli's voice repeated. "Die" is what the word would have sounded like to American ears. And since I had been thinking in English right then, I didn't recognize the Italian word, *dai*. She was telling me to "Come on," or "Hurry up!"

"I'm almost ready." I stuffed my shorts and T-shirt into the equipment bag, snapped it shut, and opened the door.

"I told Marco Fornaio, the *mister,* that you were here," Signora Martelli said. "Give me your backpack. I'll put it in the room with the others." Her smile was encouraging, but it still made me nervous.

"Thanks," I said.

"It's nothing. *Dai.*"

I ran down to the field of powdery brown dirt. The *mister* was leading the players in a slow trot around the chalked boundary. The line was straight and the spaces between the players were all the same. They were even jogging in time. Right. Left. Right. Left. I fell in behind the last boy.

He wore black shorts and a long-sleeved gray shirt instead of the white and blue uniform. The goalie, I guessed. He must have heard my footsteps because he glanced over his shoulder.

"*Madonna!*" he exclaimed in surprise. Then, without stopping his forward motion, he spun around to get a good look at me. In the process, he nicked the heel of the player in front of him.

"Hey, watch out, Luigi," the second player called. Then he saw me and made the same spinning move as his teammate. The news of my arrival kept drifting up the line, destroying its organization and rhythm.

Only the *mister* did not turn to look at me. "No talking!" he snapped. "Follow me." He switched from a jog to a sideways gallop.

Another team slowly circled the other half of the field. I kept my eyes fixed on the six-thousand-foot-high mountain peaks rising sharply behind them, but my peripheral vision told me that they were staring at me too. I hadn't had so much attention paid to me since...well, never.

Boys did not make a habit of falling at my feet—not unless I tripped them during a pickup game after school. My hair is either dark blonde or light brown, depending on whom you ask. My curves are small. My long, thin face boasts a complexion that has its good days and bad days. My smile shows slow and painful improvement with every visit to the orthodontist.

The *mister* blew his whistle and changed from the sideways gallop to an exaggerated skipping motion. His arms swung in large arcs. He drove his knees high into the air.

"Maybe the *mister* skips for the girl," the goalie joked.

Snorts and suppressed laughter followed that remark.

"Nothing to laugh at!" the *mister* snapped.

And so we skipped. This sight took the attention away from me. The other team grinned, pointed, and chuckled until their *mister* made them start skipping too.

The muscles in my calves and thighs began to tighten. I carefully controlled my breathing so no one would catch me sucking air during the warm-ups. I was relieved when the coach stopped and arranged us in three lines for the stretches.

We started with our necks and worked our way down to the Achilles tendons. The slight tugs on my triceps, quads, and hamstrings all felt familiar and reassuring.

When we finished, the *mister* emptied a mesh bag full of black and white soccer balls onto the ground. All the other players surged forward to get one. I hung back until the end.

"Irene?" the *mister* asked as I stepped up. A deep dent appeared between his black eyebrows.

"*Sí.*"

"Watch well the others. Do that which they do. Pay attention. *Dai!*"

I took the ball the *mister* handed me and joined the team in what my coach in the U.S. called the dribbling drill. Each of my teammates dribbled the ball at his own speed, choosing his own direction. They moved faster than a jog but slower than a run. There was one exception.

A boy with curly black hair, surprisingly blue eyes, and a determined chin was dribbling at top speed. He dashed at players head-on and then cut left or right. I heard boys call out his name in protest: "Matteo!" He was as graceful and gorgeous as Bernini's statue of David, but he could move like a racehorse.

My new teammates, with the exception of Matteo, continued to check me out, undoubtedly wondering whether the girl knew how to handle the ball. And so I found myself focusing on the ball and the way it made the dirt puff up behind it.

"Don't look at the ball! Don't look at the ball!" the *mister* roared. I flinched. Undoubtedly, the *mister's* bad first impression of me had only gotten worse. Then he blew the whistle. Everyone stopped for a ball-handling drill. We each bounced our ball off of our thighs, ankles, and feet, keeping it in the air for as long as possible. I counted my touches: one, two, three, four, five, six, seven, eight...

Another whistle blast and we were off again. My thighs felt as though someone had strapped sandbags to them. It was tough to get my breath. After five minutes of this, even Matteo had slowed to a steady jog. But again, the familiarity reassured me. My American coaches had stressed conditioning at the earliest practices.

Finally, the *mister* told us to form two lines near the center circle and sent Luigi to the goal. Matteo stood at the front of the line with his right foot resting on the ball, waiting for the signal.

"*Dai,* Matteo!"

Matteo kicked the ball to the *mister* and bounded forward a few steps. He bounced on his toes until the *mister* returned the ball. Matteo dashed to intercept it. With a one-touch pass, he sent it directly back to the *mister,* who tapped it toward the goal.

Matteo sprinted toward the ball again. The tilt of his body, his angle of approach, the way he held his head—each promised that he would kick it to the right. Instead he buried the ball in the far left corner of the goal.

"*Bravo,* Matteo!" the *mister* said.

Matteo retrieved his ball and dribbled it to the end of a line—my line. Even though I was taller than he was, he still managed to stare down his nose at me. Every inch of his body seemed to ask: "How dare you set foot on the same soccer field as ME?" But all he settled for was a contemptuous "How do you call yourself?"

"Irene," I told him.

"From where do you come?"

"The United States. Near St. Louis."

His eyes widened. "You're an *Americana?* Really?"

"*Sí.*"

His upper lip curled. "Girls really play soccer over there?"

I clenched my jaw. Matteo probably did not know or would not care that the American women's national team was one of the top three in the world, so I merely said, "*I* do."

His lip curled in silent disapproval, but before he could say anything, the *mister* called: "Stop talking! Stay attentive!"

Soccer was obviously serious here, not a social event. Matteo took a step back.

I faced forward and studied the goalkeeper, Luigi, as he caught, kicked, or batted away almost every shot. His moves had a grace of their own, a living, full-color illustration in a book on how to defend the goal.

My turn came. I had done this thousands of times before, and I could do it now. Why was I more nervous today than I had been at any game back home—even the tournaments?

I kicked my ball toward the *mister*. He returned it to me. Instead of a fancy one-touch pass, I controlled the ball and booted it back to him. After a few more passes, he sent the ball spinning toward the goal with a "*Dai,* Irene."

The ball rolled across the chalk line and into the penalty area faster than any other pass during the entire drill. Was this a gift for the girl? I wondered. But that didn't matter. I charged forward.

Instead of coming out to challenge me, Luigi stayed in the goal. Something about his stance reminded me of Matteo. He obviously didn't expect much from me.

I decided to change his mind.

3

Portiere (por-tee-AIR-ay)
Goalkeeper

The ball exploded off the instep of my left foot with a satisfying thud. It sailed a few inches past Luigi's outstretched fingertips and hit the net.

"*Brava,* Irene!" the *mister* called. "Luigi, don't fall asleep in the goal!"

Yes! I thought triumphantly, but I showed no outward signs of celebration. Maybe the *mister* had used me to give a wake-up call to the goalkeeper. I didn't care. At least Luigi would have to take me seriously now.

I only scored on him one more time, but that was okay. He didn't relax when my turn came. I could tell. And that was the important thing.

After a few more drills, the *mister* sent us to the clubhouse for a short break. I had yet to see a water fountain in Italy. They didn't seem to believe in them here. Fortunately, Dad had warned me, so I took a long drink out of my water bottle and then ducked my head under the enormous sink in the hallway to cool off. As I straightened and brushed the water out of my eyes, I saw that someone was waiting for me.

I remembered from the *mister's* shouts that the boy's name was Emi. The top of his head reached the bottom of my nose.

Thin, dark, and fast, he could control the ball almost as well as Matteo, but he lacked the other boy's King-of-the-Field attitude.

"What do you call yourself?" he asked.

"Irene."

"I'm Emi," he volunteered. "From where do you come?"

"The United States."

"Really? Wow!" He actually did say "wow," or at least the Italian variation. It's spelled differently and you can hear a lot more "oooh" at the beginning and the end. "*Uaou!*" he repeated. "You live here?"

"*Sí.* My dad is working here for a year."

"*Bello!*"

I hoped Emi's "Beautiful!" meant he was glad I was staying an entire year, rather than happy I would be leaving so soon.

I heard a growing buzz behind him. Fifteen players from both our team and the other one had gathered there. Even though they seemed more curious than hostile, I felt trapped.

"What is your phone number?" Emi continued.

"Oooh!" said a fifteen-member chorus.

"Emi plus Irene!" someone called out. His left hand hovered palm-down at waist level while his right hand shot up above his head to exaggerate the difference in our heights.

If my face hadn't already been red from running, I would have blushed.

The goalie, Luigi, dropped to his knees, clasped his hands and looked up at me. In an almost perfect imitation of Emi's voice, he said, "How *bella* you are, Irene! How tall! I love you!"

Emi only grinned and shook his head. "No. No. I ask this

for my twin sister, Giulia. It would please her to meet you, Irene."

"*Ma dai!*" someone complained. "What if Giulia comes back?"

"*Two* girls on the team? How gross!"

Emi crossed his arms. "Don't worry. Giulia will not return." He looked back at me expectantly.

"I don't know my number yet. We just moved in."

"Then I will tell you ours. It is very simple: twenty-one, twenty-one, twenty-one. Please call her. It would please her very much. Really."

"Thank you," I said. "I will."

Emi grinned. "Very good. Well, let's go before the *mister* calls us."

Luigi scrambled to his feet. He lowered his voice to imitate the *mister*'s bellow: "*Dai, ragazzi!*" Come on, guys!

"*Dai* is the *mister*'s favorite word?" I asked.

"Look out. The *Americana* learns fast," Emi said.

"How *bella,* tall, and intelligent, you are, Irene," Luigi murmured.

I ignored him and joined the group trotting back down to the field from the clubhouse. I was starting to feel a part of things now, despite the earlier comments from some of the boys that playing with two girls would be gross. I thought back to my last team in the U.S. We had been like family. In other words, we fought all the time. Maybe playing soccer with these boys would be that way, too.

The *mister* rattled off names and positions for the scrimmage against the other team. Luigi trotted off to the goal. Matteo and Emi, both of them forwards, headed for the center. And I—for the first time in my life—was left on the sidelines. I had a vision of the games to come. Instead of playing the whole game and pushing myself to the limit, I would be standing, watching, waiting.

Waiting a long time. The other two substitutes went in before I did. The *mister* paced the sidelines, chanting "*Dai, dai, dai!*" He told his players to pass, spread the field, lengthen their legs, and not be afraid of the ball. At one point, he noticed me. I saw an unhappy, unguarded look flicker across his face, and I knew that he didn't want me there any more than Matteo did. I could tell. I wasn't one of his players so much as an unwelcome problem. His eyes left me and returned to the field. He watched the action for a moment, shouted *dai* a few more times, and then asked me, "So Irene, what position do you play?"

"Attack. Sometimes midfield."

"Hmmm." Then he nodded. "First, we will try you on defense."

Defense? A place where I would do the least damage? With a good goalkeeper behind me to stop anyone who made it past me? But I knew better than to complain to this coach. He didn't act like someone's dad or a friendly, enthusiastic college student. From the way the other players responded to him, I could tell he was used to being obeyed promptly and without question. If I argued, he might keep me on the sidelines even longer. So I studied the way the defense moved up and down the field and the way they covered for each other if a boy was pulled out of his area. Finally, when the ball rolled out of bounds, the *mister* sent me in.

I moved up and down the field as my team controlled the ball. And then one of the other team's forwards broke free at midfield and charged down my side of the field with the ball.

Defending Irene

I felt strange. I wasn't used to challenging someone who was making a breakaway down the field.

My legs were fresh. He was tired. I matched speeds, staying between him and the goal and forcing him down the sidelines. In a foot race, he would have beaten me, but he had to control the ball. A tackle—stealing the ball—wasn't an option. The forward was protecting it too well. If I could put the ball out of bounds, the rest of the team could catch up with us.

The *mister* seemed to agree. "Put it out! Put it out!" he roared. The slight note of alarm in his voice told me that the other team had more people attacking the goal than we had defending it.

"Center it! Center it, Montegna!" the *mister* from the other team called to my opponent, confirming my suspicions.

That meant Montegna's teammates were probably behind me in the penalty area, staying behind the ball and the defense to avoid the offsides call. I told myself to go after the ball, to ignore the fear. As long as I was going for the ball, no one would call a foul on me. Before Montegna could reach the penalty area, the large chalked-in area in front of the goal where a foul by the defense results in a free kick on the goal, I made my move. Our legs tangled. I went down.

Montegna's cleats struck my thigh and upper arm. As the first intense pain faded, I could feel the bruises forming. Blood trickled down my leg. Back in the U.S., I might have spent a few seconds on the ground to recover. Here I couldn't. What if the *mister* decided to take me out of the scrimmage? I had only played for three or four minutes.

Don't pull me. Don't pull me, I thought as I rolled onto my knees and stumbled to my feet.

4

Schifo (SKEE-foe)
Disgusting

And so then she galloped off, bruised and bleeding, pretending nothing had happened," Mom told Dad. We were still sitting in the kitchen after dinner, having one of our bilingual family discussions. (The muddle of Italian and English always seemed to fascinate people seated near us in a restaurant.) I wanted to escape from Mom's analysis of my performance at practice, but I was stuck in the middle of the U-shaped bench that ran along three sides of a matching rectangular pine table. When we'd moved in, I thought the built-in furniture with its old-fashioned alpine design was charming. Now it felt like a cage.

"I didn't try to trip him," I insisted. "It was an accident. I was going for the ball."

"There was no whistle?" Dad asked in Italian.

I shook my head. "No. Nothing."

Dad nodded. "Good. You must be careful. A free kick is too dangerous near the goal. You know, Irene, I think it will be good for you to play on defense here. It will make you a complete soccer player. After all, everyone must play defense from the very second that the other team takes the ball. No?"

"*Sì,*" I grumbled. "But it is impossible to make any goals from the wrong side of the center line."

"You're both missing my point," Mom cut in, moving the conversation back into English. "Irene could have been hurt. Some of these boys are bigger than she is."

"Yeah, like Emi." I held my hand palm-down at chin level.

"You know what I mean. Maybe this wasn't the best idea," said the same woman who less than four hours ago had insisted the experience would be good for me.

"Aren't you the one who plays co-ed softball?" Dad asked her.

"Softball isn't a contact sport."

Dad grinned. "Really? I've seen you slide over home plate."

Mom turned to me. "How did it really go out there? And don't just tell me 'fine' the way you usually do."

What could I say? That I hated being stared at? That I hated being stuck on defense and—even worse—the side-lines? That my coach didn't want me there? That the only time I really wanted to keep playing was when somebody wanted me to quit? Like right now.

"It *was* fine," I insisted. "I mean, not everyone is happy that I'm there, but some of the guys are nice. One even gave me his phone number."

"Ooooh!" said Max, my younger brother.

"—so I could call his twin sister, Giulia," I finished, glaring at him. He crossed his eyes and stuck out his tongue.

"*Fantastico!*" Dad said, looking suspiciously relieved. Did he feel a sneaking sympathy for these boys who were stuck with a girl on their team? A romance at practice? How gross. How disgusting. How...*schifo.* The Italian word seemed to say it best.

"Julia?" Mom said. "That doesn't sound like an Italian name."

"No, it's Giulia. G-I-U-L-I-A."

"She could be a friend for you," Mom said. "Would you like to give her a call right now?" Without waiting for an answer, she slid off the bench in order to let me past.

I wasn't ready to call Giulia right then. Not with an audience. I hadn't thought of a single thing to say to her other than "Your brother told me to call you." But at least it was a way to escape more questions about the soccer team.

I picked up the phone, punched in the city code, and then the number Emi had given me: twenty-one, twenty-one, twenty-one.

The phone rang. Once. Twice. Three times.

"*Pronto,*" a voice greeted me. It sounded like Emi, but I couldn't be sure.

"Is Giulia there?" I asked.

"Irene?" It *was* Emi.

"*Sì.*"

"*Ciao,* Irene! One moment. I'll get her."

I heard a woman's voice complaining in the background.

"I know, Mamma," Emi said, his voice distant. "But it is Irene, the *Americana* I told you about."

I heard a *thump, thump, thump.* Then a breathless voice spoke: "*Ciao,* Irene? This is Giulia. Emi told me about you. I'd like to meet you, but tonight I'm in a rush. We're going out for the birthday of my grandma. Tomorrow, I am also busy. I'm sorry. But listen, do you know where the middle school is on Via Roma?"

She talked fast, but I was pretty sure I had followed everything she said. "*Sì,*" I answered.

"All right. Can you meet me there the day after tomorrow? At two?"

"One moment." I covered the mouthpiece with my hand, but before I could even ask the question, Mom nodded enthusiastically and gave me the thumbs-up sign.

"I can come," I told Giulia.

"Very good! We'll meet each other at the steps where there's a bit of shade. Until Wednesday. *Ciao!*"

"*Ciao,*" I echoed.

"See? Wasn't that easy?" Mom beamed at me. It was the same expression she'd worn when I stepped off the bus on the first day of kindergarten. "And you were so worried about making new friends. What will you and Giulia do together?"

"Oh, she's planning on jumping off a bridge, so I probably will too."

"No, really," Mom said.

"We're just going to hang out at the middle school after lunch the day after tomorrow. That's all." I walked back to the table and started piling silverware onto a serving platter. The sooner I could clear the table, the sooner I could get away.

Instead of continuing the interrogation, Mom told Max to help me. My brother and I dodged around each other in the narrow space between the table and polished granite countertops, murmuring insults in Italian. The kitchen was half the size of the one back home, and so was the fridge. Fortunately, the dishwasher was full size. I managed to load most of the pots and pans instead of having to scrub them by hand.

While we worked, Dad talked to Mom about his first few days in the plant as the new manager from corporate headquarters. Mom told Dad about our trip to the grocery store and how the cereal took up a scant six feet of shelf space while pasta had almost an entire aisle. Eventually, their conversation drifted back to soccer: the fields, the lights, the clubhouse, the coaches, and the low price. By the time Mom reached the absence of concession-stand duty and fund-raisers, she sounded much more positive.

"Irene can even ride to practice on her bike. I won't have to drive her to the field and watch her being run over by the other players. And there's even a team van that takes them to away games."

"I want to go to all the games," Dad said.

And so on.

I left quickly, sliding my stocking feet along the polished wooden hallway all the way to my tiny room. At least I had a room of my own. A lot of Italian kids didn't. We were very lucky that my dad's company had been able to find us this three-bedroom, furnished apartment. It took up the entire fourth floor of a late–nineteenth century house. The stone walls were two feet thick, covered with a smooth yellow stucco on the outside and plaster on the inside. It was a big change from my two-year-old house in Missouri with plastic siding on the outside and plasterboard on the inside.

I dodged my cleats, which were lying in the middle of the floor, and tumbled onto my bed. The wrought iron bedstead rattled, but held. The only other pieces of furniture in my room were an old, slightly scratched desk of inlaid wood and a wardrobe for my clothes. It must have been assembled where it stood because it would have been too large to fit through the door. Faded prints of local landmarks and people wearing old-fashioned dirndls and woolen jackets hung on the walls. My bulletin board, with its bright color photos of

Lindy, Dorothy, Jeanie, and my other friends and teammates, filled what had been a bare spot over the desk. It looked so out of place. Like me on the soccer field this afternoon? Maybe. Probably. Definitely.

I closed my eyes and covered my face with my hands. Why did we have to come here? I blamed Mom as much as Dad. At least Dad had been worried about pulling Max and me out of school for a year. But Mom had swept aside every objection. Wouldn't it be good for us to immerse ourselves in our Italian heritage? Wouldn't it be wonderful for Max and me to see the *nonni,* our Italian grandparents, once every few months instead of once every few years? And just how would Dad explain turning down the job to his mother? The last question had put an end to the discussion. Now I had to live with the consequences.

At least my chance to meet Giulia was a bright spot. Would she be a friend? Or maybe even a teammate?

5

Impossibile

(im-poh-SEE-bee-lay)

Impossible

Giulia. Friend and teammate? Neither friend nor teammate? Even a potential enemy? These thoughts worried me as I walked to the school on Via Roma. Emi had seemed nice enough, but what if this was some double-edged prank designed to get both me and his sister? What might Giulia be expecting of the *Americana?* Someone straight from MTV? If so, she would be disappointed by my soccer camp uniform.

My stomach had an uncertain, empty feeling as I walked down the chestnut-lined street toward the middle school. The buildings I passed all told me that I wasn't in Missouri anymore. A hundred-year-old Liberty-style building sat next door to a modern five-story apartment house with a distinctly Italian air in its flowers and balconies. Next came a miniature castle complete with towers, an enormous, solid-looking door, and the red and white shutters that meant the building had once belonged to the minor Tyrolean aristocracy. Maybe it still did. Curious, I peered through the wrought-iron fence at the twining ivy, ancient pine trees, and massive rhododendrons.

Defending Irene

Procrastinating. I was procrastinating. I checked my watch: 1:55 P.M. Five minutes and a few hundred meters separated me from my meeting with Giulia.

Why was I so worried? Giulia had seemed very happy to hear from me, just as Emi had promised. But we hadn't had time to talk much.

Minutes later, only the long shiny leaves of a laurel hedge hid the grounds of the middle school from my view. My steps slowed. I took a deep breath, straightened my shoulders, and then picked up my pace as I turned the corner. I had to look confident even if I wasn't.

I saw movement under the shadows of an enormous tree. A small dark figure with the unmistakable bounce of an athlete darted down the steps and stepped into the light. A barrette held thick, black hair away from her face. The rest of it fell six inches below her shoulders.

"Irene? You're here! *Ciao!* I'm Giulia. A pleasure to meet you! Emi described you to me. Come and sit down. It's much cooler on the steps."

I blinked at the rapid flood of words and Giulia's keen interest. Maybe I looked confused, because she continued more slowly, "You understand me? Was I talking too fast?"

"No. I understood you perfectly. A pleasure to meet you," I echoed. I followed her to the steps. The gray stone was cool and welcoming.

Giulia sat down cross-legged and rested her elbows on her knees. "How do you speak Italian so well? And with such a good accent? Did you study it in school?"

I shook my head. "My *papá* is Italian. From Milan. He met my mother at the university in America."

"Really?"

Impossibile: **Impossible**

"He was a graduate student studying materials sciences, but they asked him to teach a few Italian classes. My mother was teaching German literature. One day in the office, they started complaining about their first-year students and that was it."

"Ah. How romantic. And why do you live here now?"

I explained how my dad was doing some work for the Italian branch of his company and my mom was taking a year off of teaching high school German to live among German-speakers and study the local dialect.

Giulia immediately pounced with another question—a whole series of them, actually. How old was I? What class would I frequent? Who was my favorite music group? Had I heard of Eros Rammazzotti? Did I really have every single one of his CDs? What did I think of the *mister,* of Emi, of Luigi, of Matteo?

Our conversation finally stopped sounding like a magazine interview when Giulia began slipping a few facts about herself into the stream of talk. We exchanged our favorite soccer stories about last-second goals, blind referees, unreasonable coaches, difficult opponents, and even more difficult teammates. I learned, for example, that when they started soccer seven years ago, Matteo had been the last kid on the team to learn how to tie his shoes. At every practice, the grandfatherly coaches had knelt at his feet and tightened his laces. Matteo had stared off into the distance with the attitude and confidence of the great Brazilian soccer player, Ronaldo.

"Matteo is so full of himself," I complained. "He acts like no one belongs on the field with him."

Giulia's upper lip curled. "No one is worthy to be on the same field as Matteo. Not even Matteo."

"No one is worthy to tie his shoes," I said. "Too bad he can't do it either."

Giulia giggled. "Well he can now."

"Are you sure? Maybe his *mamma* does it for him at home."

"Ah, we are making his ears whistle today," Giulia said with satisfaction. "The other girls don't understand the Dr. Jekyll and Mr. Hyde of soccer."

"He's different at school?"

"Oh, *sì*. The girls are crazy for him. Some of them have his photo on a key chain with the English words 'I love you!' Really! It is too funny. It pleases me to meet someone who understands."

"Agreed," I said, finally seeing the perfect opportunity to ask my big question. "So, would you like to play soccer with me this year?"

Giulia jerked away from me, her fingers closing into fists. "No! Never! It is *impossibile.*"

"Why?" The word slipped out before I could stop it.

Giulia uncrossed her legs and hugged her knees to her chest. "Of course, it would be possible. It is very simple to ask Signora Martelli for a practice uniform. But wait, I do not even have to ask. My old one is not too narrow for me yet. And my *papá* would pay. It would not please him that I play soccer with the boys. It never pleased him. Soccer is not for girls, he thinks. But since Emi plays, he could not say I was too busy with school."

"Giulia, I'm so sorry. I wish I hadn't asked."

"No, no. It is nothing. I'm glad that you asked me. It means you wish to be friends, no? If only you had come earlier, Irene. I had already been the only girl for years. I knew I would never make the traveling team. I am a good player, better than many of the boys who quit before me. But now, it's not worth the trouble." She stopped and shook her head. "Maybe I played so long just to annoy Matteo."

I snorted.

"I wasn't joking."

"I know."

"I have lost a year, Irene. You will leave next summer, and I would have to quit again." She paused and tilted her head to the side. "Of course, Matteo would hate it..."

I let the silence between us lengthen, hoping that she might change her mind. Instead, she closed her eyes and shook her head. "I cannot. I'm sorry."

"It's nothing. Don't worry yourself. So, now it is my turn to annoy Matteo."

Giulia's shoulders straightened. "Very good! I will come to the games to watch him suffer, and you can come to my volleyball games. Unless..."

"What?"

Giulia leaned forward. "Unless you'd like to quit soccer and play volleyball with me. I am learning to play. I am too short to spike or block, but you are tall. That is an advantage in volleyball, no?"

If I switched to volleyball, it would be an honorable escape from a team that didn't want me to a team that would. People might smile when I walked into practice instead of wishing I'd go away and never come back. I might lose a year, but I wouldn't lose all my conditioning. And I was sure that Giulia would be more than happy to kick the soccer ball around with me for fun.

I found myself staring at her. I could see traces of Emi in

her nose and high cheekbones. She had his wavy hair, dark eyes, and warm enthusiasm. Had this been Emi's plan all along—having his sister tempt me away from soccer with volleyball?

"No. It can't be," I whispered.

"No?" Giulia asked, frowning.

What had we been talking about? Height. Volleyball. Advantage. "Er, *sì*. In volleyball, it is an advantage to be tall. But no, I can't play volleyball."

"Mmmmm. I see. Emi told me that you are a good player. Well, enough of soccer. Listen. Let's go into the center. We'll eat some ice cream. I know the best place."

"Where is it? On the promenade by the theater bridge?"

"No. Pfff! That one is for tourists. I will bring you to the best. And maybe tomorrow we go to the pool with my friends?"

"Perfect. No, wait. There's soccer."

"But Irene, the pool is only two steps from the field."

"I know. I saw. But I cannot be dead tired for practice."

"Ah, *sì*. You're right. Then how about the day after tomorrow?"

"I'll ask my mom. But without doubt, she will say yes."

The next day I thought longingly of the pool as I sat on a wooden bench outside the clubhouse and changed into my cleats. Dead-tired or completely baked: which was worse? My T-shirt was already damp, and I hadn't done anything more strenuous that day than pedal my bike slowly to practice.

The calm, hazy air was thick with pollution and humidity. But relief was in sight. Literally. Dark, threatening clouds hid the mountain peaks to our north; but while they shifted and changed shape, they did not move into the valley.

Impossibile: Impossible

A herd of sweaty munchkins limped past me. Max's team of first graders.

"Look! A girl!" one of them shouted.

There were plenty of girls who had been dragged along to practice to pick up their brothers, so I assumed by the note of surprise that the kid was pointing me out. I was right.

"*Uaou!*" said another. "She plays at soccer with the guys? How strange!"

"How *schifo!*" put in a third.

"True," said a voice I recognized. "She is my sister."

"Really? Poor you!"

Ha! I love you too, Max, I thought. The next time he wanted me to kick the ball around in the garden I would say no. Or at least make him beg. I glared at my brother from under my eyelashes as I finished tying my shoe. He grinned at me and stuck out his tongue.

I leaped to my feet and took a step toward him. He bolted, shrieking happily. Most of his teammates dashed after him. But two girls at the end of line moved more slowly, looking up at me in wonder.

I checked out the glass case on the wall with its collection of schedules and photos. One notice proclaimed that my group, the *Esordienti I* of Merano, had a game scheduled for this Saturday afternoon. I glanced at the first three names on the list:

M. D'Andolo

E. DeChechi

L. Fornaio

Matteo, Emi, and Luigi? The goalie and the top two forwards? Naturally, they would be first. I scanned the rest of the list for my name—I. Benenati. It wasn't there. Not even with the substitutes. I checked again. Nothing. Had I been forgotten or left out on purpose?

I don't remember making a noise, but I must have, because Signora Martelli appeared at my elbow. "*Ciao, cara.* There is a problem?"

"My name isn't there," I whispered, not trusting my voice.

"Ah." She nodded. "There are only enough places in the van for fourteen. Thirteen players and the *mister.*"

"My *papá* could bring me."

Signora Martelli shook her head. "I'm sorry, but we do not do it like that. This time, it is you who stays. The other times you will go. Everyone plays at home games unless they annoy the *mister.*"

"Oh. Uh, thanks."

"It's nothing. Good work, *cara,*" she said.

I nodded and faked a smile. I couldn't complain—much. The plan made sense. I was the newcomer, the foreigner, the girl. Three strikes and I was most definitely out. Not that anyone would have the first clue about softball around here.

Whump! Somewhere, out of my line of sight, someone's foot connected with a soccer ball. It had to be one of my teammates. I doubted that any of the munchkins could put that much energy on the ball. I felt like kicking something myself, so I left my blue and white duffle on the bench and trotted down to the field.

The *mister* stood with his feet planted on the white line. The mesh bag of soccer balls rested at his feet. His arms were crossed as he studied Luigi, the only player on the field so far. The man nodded at me as I pulled a ball out of the bag. "Irene."

I nodded back at him. A "*ciao*" would have seemed too

friendly, and the formal "*buona sera,*" good afternoon, didn't seem right for the soccer field.

I dribbled my ball onto the dirt field while Luigi positioned his at the corner of the penalty area. He took a few steps back before booming it into the goal. I could imagine it sailing just above the gloved hands of a goalkeeper, leaping to attempt a save. Luigi didn't have the quickness of Emi or Matteo, but he certainly had a good leg.

I accelerated and charged forward, dribbling the ball at my top speed. A few steps after crossing into the penalty area, I slammed the ball into the goal. Luigi and I both arrived to bend down and pull our balls out of the neon orange netting at the same moment.

Luigi raised his eyebrows. "You're here."

"Of course. Where else?" I asked lightly, determined not to take offense at his obvious surprise.

He shrugged. "In the shade. At the pool."

My chin dropped in outrage. Did he think I'd skip practice just because a sauna would be a cooler, drier place to work out?

"Everyone else will arrive at four-thirty on the dot," Luigi continued calmly before I had a chance to say a word. "Not early. Not late. It's too hot today."

"Oh," I said, feeling foolish. "But you're here."

"Ah, but my *papá...*" Luigi jerked his head in the direction of the *mister.* Then he stopped himself. "No, I mean to say, I must work now. I stand around during half the scrimmage."

"It's the same for me," I observed. "At least you get to stand on the field."

Luigi's lips twitched and then widened to a smile. He opened his mouth, but a roar from the sidelines stopped him.

Defending Irene

"Don't chatter! *Dai*, Luigi!"

I pressed my lips together, annoyed that the *mister* had yelled at my teammate. Practice hadn't even started yet. Even worse—and this is going to sound completely stupid—he hadn't yelled at *me*. What kind of coach would treat two players so differently? He sounded more like a father yelling at his son. And then it hit me: Fornaio. Luigi Fornaio. The *mister* was Luigi's dad. I should have guessed it earlier. Luigi had practically said so. But to me, Luigi had seemed so much more like a fresh wad of Silly Putty than a chip off the old block of granite that I hadn't been able to see it.

This was still just a guess, and I had to know for sure. I waited a few minutes before timing my ball to fly into the orange netting a few seconds before that of Luigi's.

"The *mister* is your *papá?*" I asked Luigi in a voice I hoped would not carry.

"Of course. This surprises you? Everyone says we are as alike as two drops of water."

Not to my eyes.

I defended myself. "At the first practice, you called him 'the *mister.*'"

Luigi shrugged. "My older brother Renzo did the same. My *papá* has coached the *Esordienti* for years. It pleases me to play on his squad finally." He broke off and pointed. "Look! Here come the others. Like I said: neither early nor late."

Eleven boys trotted onto the field. Matteo led the group with an easy loping stride. It hit me again just how gorgeous he was with his black curly hair and eyes of startling blue. The *mister* dumped half the balls onto the ground and kicked them one after another toward his players.

Impossibile: Impossible

The boys raced each other for a chance at the balls, laughing, pushing, and tripping each other. This friendly competition continued between them as we practiced shooting into an unguarded net. But no one touched my ball. It and I could have been invisible except that everyone stayed well out of my way. I felt like a magnet in a school science experiment, repelling rather than attracting the charged metal filings.

Then, after four or five minutes of this, Emi darted in front of me. With a friendly "*Ciao,* Irene," he tackled my ball and made off with it. I grinned.

Practice was certainly taking on a confusing Alice in Wonderland air. I was happy when someone stole my ball and upset when the coach didn't yell at me.

I wiped the sweat off my forehead with the back of my hand. It felt good to have a short rest. My heart pounded in my chest. The same fast beat pulsed in my throat. I took a few deep breaths. One. Two. Three. Luigi was defending the goal now and returning as many balls as possible back to the attackers. I tensed my muscles and made a break for a nearby loose ball.

Before I could reach it, someone slammed into me, knocking me to the ground.

6
Goal (gōl)
Goal

I pushed myself onto my elbows and blinked. The mister was standing with his back to the field, talking to Signora Martelli. "Excuse me, Irene! I did not see you!" Matteo's blue eyes were wide with well-faked sincerity. Ah, I thought. While the cat's away, the mice dance. He held out his hand: an offer of help.

I wanted to slap it away, but that was exactly what he wanted. And if I ignored him completely, he'd probably like that too. So I took his hand and let him pull me up. He braced his feet and grunted.

"How strong and kind you are. A thousand thanks," I murmured, batting my eyelashes for good measure.

Matteo let go. I was ready for that, so I stayed on my feet instead of falling back into the dirt. He pointedly wiped his hand on his shorts. Afraid of girl germs?

"This is not a sport for a *ragazza* here," Matteo hissed. "Do you want to make us lose?"

"No, I want to help us win. I am not so terrible."

"There are better places to meet boys, you know. No one will fall in love with you here."

Goal: Goal

I put my hand to my heart. "Thank heaven! You have reassured me so much."

Matteo muttered something. It sounded like one of the Italian words that Dad had always refused to teach me.

A whistle sounded, a long blast followed by two short ones. Matteo whirled to face the *mister*. I half-expected the man to yell at Matteo for chattering, but instead, he spoke to the entire team:

"Leave the balls and come here."

We all did as he ordered except for one boy, who began tapping the abandoned balls into the empty goal as he slowly worked his way toward the *mister*.

"Federico! I said leave them!"

Federico jerked in surprise. His right foot hung in the air above a ball, and he only narrowly managed to stop himself from kicking it. Then, head down, he sprinted to the line forming behind the *mister*. I tried not to smile.

Something told me that Federico was as new to the *Esordienti* team as I was. He was taller than Emi, but there was a suggestion in his rounded face and the way he moved that he was a younger player—a good younger player with lots of promise. Had he been promoted ahead of the others his age?

We all followed the *mister* along the sideline at a brisk trot, making a sharp right at the centerline to stay on our half of the field we shared with the other team.

Practice had just started and I was already hot and tired. It had been impossible to pace myself with Luigi practicing at one hundred percent. I lifted my eyes to the massive cloudbank hiding the mountaintops. It sent out a few shifting tentacles, but otherwise, it hadn't moved. There would be no relief from that direction.

On our second lap, just as the *mister* turned the corner toward the opposite goal, a boy dashed down the small hill leading from the clubhouse. He slipped through the gate and onto the field, falling into line two spots ahead of me. He seemed to be trying to sneak onto the field without the *mister* noticing.

"Dah-vee-day! Where were you?" someone whispered.

Davide shook his head. His hair was wet, almost dripping. A scent like that of a freshly cleaned bathroom followed him. I sniffed. Chlorine? Had Davide lost track of time at the pool? His head and shoulders drooped and his steps dragged by the time we finished the fifth lap. Yes, I decided.

The *mister* left off the skipping that afternoon, as well as the exhausting dribbling drill. Instead we took turns shooting against an empty net for a while. Then Luigi entered the goal for a new drill.

The *mister* called out pairings: Matteo against Emi, Gianlucca against Roberto, and so on. After matching me with Davide, the *mister* placed the ball on the chalked line surrounding the penalty area and stepped back. Emi and Matteo sat on the ground a few steps away from the center-line with their hands in the air. The whistle sounded. Both scrambled to their feet and pelted toward the ball. Emi had a quicker start, but Matteo won the race to the ball. When he slowed down in order to control it, Emi caught up and tackled, tripping Matteo and sending him somersaulting across the dirt.

The whistle blew. "Foul, Emi," the *mister* called. "A penalty shot for the other team. Too costly." Then he put the second ball down and blew the whistle for the next pair to come forward. Emi and Matteo trotted to the end of the line.

I watched as my teammates took their turns. It became clear that whoever reached the ball first would be on offense while the other person became the defender.

My turn arrived. The whistle sounded. My legs tangled as I scrambled to my feet. Davide beat me to the ball by three strides. Luigi deflected his shot easily.

As I waited for my next turn, I studied the other players, trying to figure out the best way to get to my feet. Davide braced his hands against his knees and panted.

Our second turn came. I sat down a few feet away from Davide, my knees bent and my feet flat on the ground. I held up my hands and waited.

Tweeeet!

The heels of my hands drove into the ground behind me, pushing me forward. I made it to my feet ahead of Davide and reached the ball first. I would be the forward, the attacker.

Luigi positioned himself by the near post, ready to block any shot. In a game, I would have looked to pass the ball. But now I sent the ball slicing across the penalty area. Luigi dove forward, trying to cut it off. He missed. It crossed the white chalked line only inches from the far post.

Goal!

Luigi plucked the ball out of the net and flung it to the *mister*—his father. I could still hardly believe it.

"Nice shot, Irene!" Emi said as I passed him on my way to the end of the line.

"*Buona notte!*" Matteo protested. "Good night! Luigi must be in love with her to let her score like that."

"Clearly," said Matteo's shadow, Giuseppe. "Irene plus Luigi."

"Irene Fornaio," Davide muttered, giving me Luigi's last name instead of my own.

My surge of pride disappeared. Protests flashed down out of my brain and onto my tongue. But I clamped my lips shut. Don't answer. Don't answer. Don't answer. Any reply to that rat could only make things worse.

I had three more respectable shots on goal, but I still found myself on the sidelines as my teammates lined up on the field for the scrimmage. At least Davide had joined Federico and me, the two newest members of the *Esordienti*. He lay spread-eagled on the ground nearby, but he sat up at the kickoff as Emi passed the ball to Matteo. The two forwards drove ball down the field.

"*Bello!*" Federico said, turning to me. "They play so well. You do too. That surprises me."

"Oh, thank you," I said. Someone else could have turned the same words into an insult, but Federico had all the sincerity, enthusiasm, and grace of a St. Bernard puppy.

"What class do you frequent?" he asked.

"The second year of middle school. And you?"

"I am in the fifth class in the elementary school. Or at least I will be next Tuesday."

So he was younger.

"My friends in the United States started school two weeks ago," I told him.

"No! In August? The month of vacation?" For a brief moment, Federico pulled his eyes away from the game to look at me. "I cannot imagine it. August is…well, August."

I knew what he meant. Half of Italy shut down for vacation in August.

"Well, we finished on the last day of May," I explained. "This is the longest summer vacation of my life."

"Really? Very interesting. What do you think of—" Federico broke off and shouted, "*Dai,* Matteo. *Dai!*"

Matteo had broken away from the defenders in the penalty area. He shot the ball. It hit the crossbar and bounced out. Matteo got the rebound and tried again. The goalkeeper dove and fell on top of the ball. He wound his arms around it to protect it from Matteo, who stood above him looking for a third chance.

"*Uaou!* Matteo is such a good player." Federico sighed with delight and envy.

"I know."

At a break in the action, the *mister* put Davide in for a midfielder. Within five minutes, Davide was clutching his side and moving no faster than a trot.

"Lengthen your legs, Davide! *Dai!*" the *mister* shouted.

Davide ran a few steps and then slowed to his old pace. At the next whistle, the *mister* pulled Davide and put Federico in the game.

Davide stumbled off the field. The *mister* was there to meet him. "What's wrong today?"

"Nothing," Davide said.

"You are already dead tired. Without breath. Are you sick?"

"No."

There was a short pause before the *mister* continued, "Tell me, why were you late?"

Davide mumbled something and studied his dusty cleats.

"What? Louder please."

"I forgot the time."

"Really? And where were you?"

"At the pool."

"Ah, I see. There's a game Saturday, you know."

"I know."

"Is it right that you should go?"

Davide hung his head.

I held my breath, waiting. Would a space open up in the van? I had come early. He had come late. I had scored in the drill when we'd faced each other. He had not. Wasn't that worth something? I bounced on my toes, feeling hopeful.

The *mister* pressed his lips together. He glanced away from Davide. And our eyes met. His right eyebrow lifted in surprise. His nostrils flared. Oh, no. My face and ears burned as I turned away. I knew better than to watch a coach chewing out a player on the sidelines.

The *mister's* silence stretched for several seconds. "You can come as a substitute, Davide. Do not expect to start."

"Thank you, Mister."

The man raised his voice. "Irene!"

"What?" I turned.

"Go two times around the field. Not too fast. Jogging only. Then I will put you in."

Laps? Davide had gone to the pool. Davide could barely stand on his legs. And *I* was being punished with laps? Not fair. Not fair at all.

7

La gara (la GAH-rah)
The Game

It's not fair. It's not fair. The chorus repeated itself in my brain. Thunder rumbled in agreement, the echoes bouncing back and forth across the Adige River valley until it sounded exactly like a bowling ball spinning down an alley.

I was sitting in a white plastic Adirondack-style chair on our covered balcony with my feet propped up on the wrought iron bars. Since our apartment didn't have air conditioning, the coming storm made it fifteen degrees cooler outside than in my room. I found it a much more comfortable place to sulk after soccer practice.

The wind danced through the purple leaves of an enormous hundred-year-old tree, whose highest branches were even with my fourth-floor balcony. But not a breath of air touched me. The wind came from the other side of the building, from the mountains. The storm, which had threatened for the entire practice, was finally arriving.

The leading edge of rain swept past trees and buildings, blurring their edges before hiding them completely. And then, with the sound of a hundred cats racing across a ballroom, it rolled past me, wrapping around my balcony. Privacy.

For a minute or two. Then the door to the balcony swung open and Dad stepped outside.

"*Ciao,* Irene." He lowered himself into the chair next to mine and sighed. "What a long day."

"*Davvero,*" I agreed, thinking about my second soccer practice. "True."

"I know why you're out here," Dad continued.

My head snapped around. Had Dad started reading minds? I hadn't said anything to Mom, and I certainly hadn't said anything to Max.

But Dad was staring at the branches whipping in the wind. "*Bello.* Truly *bello,*" he went on. "I have never seen a storm like this one in Missouri. Or such a view."

I leaned forward, pretending to peer through the mist, and said in a puzzled voice, "I don't see anything."

"*Ma dai!* You know that which I meant. To live here is to live in a botanical garden. Don't you think?"

"Sure."

I must not have been enthusiastic enough because Dad frowned. "Everything all right? How did soccer go today?"

"Well enough," I said.

Two dents appeared between Dad's eyebrows. "What happened? Tell me."

Dad couldn't read minds, but he could read my face. Lying wasn't an option. I took a deep breath. "There's a game Saturday."

Dad's face brightened. "Where? At what time?"

"Scena. At two o'clock."

La gara: The Game

"Good. I know that town. It isn't too far from here. I can come. Write it on the calendar."

"It's not necessary. I'm—I'm not going." My voice quivered.

The dents deepened. "Why not?"

"There are only fourteen seats in the van."

Dad seemed to know there was more to the story. He said nothing, waiting for me to break the silence.

I did. I told him about what Signora Martelli had said and about the coach letting Davide go in spite of his poor performance in practice. When I finished, Dad rubbed his forehead with his fingertips. "Maybe it is better that you do not play this game, *cara.*"

"How?"

Dad tilted his head. "You don't believe me? Listen, if Davide hadn't been allowed to go, he would have blamed you instead of himself. Can't you imagine it? I think it is already difficult enough for you at soccer."

"*Davvero.* But I still wanted to go to the game. You know, soccer was supposed to be the easy part about living here."

"I'm sorry, *cara.* I did not expect this. Other problems, but not this." He leaned back in his chair. "But wait. I have an idea. We will go to the game and watch it together."

"No! I meant to play. I already watch them enough."

Dad nodded, but he wasn't agreeing with me. "Yes. We will go. We'll watch them warm up to prepare you for next time. It is a good idea, no?"

"No," I said again. I could hardly think of a worse one. Watching from the sidelines was always bad enough, but from the bleachers? How could I stand it?

So when I met Giulia outside the pool entrance the next day, I expected some sympathy. Instead, she exclaimed: "It is so *bella* that your *papá* wants to help you. Like a dream in a box."

A daydream? More like a nightmare. But luckily, before I could say that, I remembered how Giulia's dad was less than enthusiastic about her playing. So I said, "But it is a bit strange, isn't it?"

"More than a bit," Giulia said. "No one has ever done it. Never."

I groaned.

"But you are an *Americana*. The people do not expect normal things from you."

"My *papá* is Italian."

Giulia shrugged. "*Sí.* But how many years has he lived in the United States? This is very good. Matteo and his friends will not find it so easy to push you off the team."

"Were you pushed off the team?"

She shrugged her shoulders. "No, not really. I made the decision to quit."

Not really? There was a story there. I was sure of it. Giulia was gazing over my shoulder, a look of indecision on her face. Then her expression brightened. "Look! Barbara has arrived. Bar-bah-ra! *Ciao!* Over here!"

Barbara waved frantically at us before weaving her bicycle through the crowded racks.

I smiled and waved back, still nervous despite the girl's enthusiasm. I could tell from the way that Giulia spoke about her that Barbara was her *amica del cuore,* her friend of the heart, her best friend. Giulia said that the two of them had been in the same class together since preschool. Their families even went on vacation together.

"*Ciao,*" I said to Barbara after Giulia introduced us. "A pleasure."

Barbara grinned. "A great pleasure, Irene! *Uaou.* So tall. Too bad that you don't wish to play at volleyball. We have need of another spiker. Giulia sets, you know."

"But I haven't played very often."

"*Sì.* But you are the sporting type. For you, it would be very simple to learn. I used to do gymnastics. Now I am too tall to be a serious gymnast."

"So Barbara makes somersaults whenever possible at volleyball," Giulia murmured.

Barbara rolled her eyes. "Giulia is so jealous. Let's go."

We paid at the window and walked through the brown stucco bathhouse before stepping back into the sunshine. Barbara led the way around the Olympic-sized pool to a set of three empty wooden deck chairs on the other side. As we walked, I looked around. A pair of gigantic water slides emptied into a smaller pool. Down the hill and past some trees, there was a big wading pool.

The atmosphere seemed much more laid-back than an American pool. Lifeguards chatted instead of gazing intently into the water. The shallow end wasn't roped off. People swam just about anywhere they wanted except in an unmarked, open spot in front of the three diving boards. One lifeguard supervised at the top of the slide; no one watched at the bottom.

Following Giulia's example, I kicked off my shoes and spread my towel on the deck chair.

"First the *trampolino?*" Barbara asked, waving at the diving boards.

Giulia squinted. "The lines are not too long. Okay."

Barbara headed right for the three-meter springboard. When Giulia and I fell into line behind her, she turned to me.

"All right, Irene. Giulia tells me that in the United States you have parties at school during the evening. It's true?"

"*Sì.*"

"With music and dancing and lights? Like a disco?"

I wrinkled my nose. "A little. Except it's in the school cafeteria."

"But there are lights and dancing and *ragazzi* all the same. Right?"

I nodded.

"*Bello.* And a DJ?"

"*Sì.*"

"*Uaou!* You have danced with boys at the party?"

"A few." I blushed, remembering the way my friend Lindy used to pressure one of the boys I liked into asking me to dance. It had been very embarrassing.

"Really? Tell me everything. Oh, wait. It's my turn." Barbara bounced up the ladder.

"I'm sorry, Irene," Giulia whispered. "Barbara is crazy about boys. But otherwise, she is a good friend. You can count on her."

"*Sì, sì,*" I said.

Barbara paced down the diving board like a dancer, her shoulders back and head erect. She took one bounce of the end and rose almost straight into the air before bending at the middle for a jackknife. She entered the water in a straight line with pointed toes. An "ooh" of approval went up from the lines at both diving boards. She swam to the ladder in a fast, smooth front crawl-stroke.

My turn came next. I waited for the board to stop vibrating before stepping cautiously along its rough surface. By the time I had reached the end it had started bouncing again. So I waited again. Once it stopped I made the simplest of dives and splashed over to the side of the pool. Barbara was waiting for me, ready to start in with the questions again.

I distracted her by asking her about the boys at school. Her analysis was detailed. Luigi was cute, but a clown. Montegna was quiet and intelligent and *molto bello.* Very good-looking. Matteo was fascinating and *molto, molto, molto bello.* I finally got her off the track by telling her about malls and multiplexes. (There were only two movie screens in Merano. One was German, the other Italian. But both showed American movies.)

An unofficial diving competition started between Barbara and a few of the boys. Style meant nothing to them; only height, splash, and number of spins, bounces, or twists mattered. Giulia and I didn't even try to compete.

Finally, Barbara walked very slowly to the end of the diving board. Once the gentle bounce had faded away, she put her palms down on the edge of the board and did a handstand. Her body made a straight line from her pointed toes to her wrists. She held the pose for five long seconds. Then she pushed off with power and dropped straight down. Her forehead, nose, and chin skimmed past the end of the diving board. Her shoulders, hips, knees, and toes safely followed.

"Point!" Giulia whispered.

Two turns later—after the boys had failed to come up with

a new challenge—Barbara observed that the lines were too long. How about some volleyball?

We used a lightweight plastic ball. Laughing, we bumped, set, and spiked the ball at each either. A chubby three-year-old hovered on the edge of the pool deck, eager to chase any ball that came his way.

Take some athletic girls. Add water. Bake in the sun for four hours. Instant friendship. Why couldn't it have been like this on the soccer field? The long list of reasons depressed me.

On Saturday afternoon, I tried to think of Giulia's positive attitude as Dad and I walked across the parking lot in Scena and past the enormous, empty, white team van. My neck hunched down between my shoulders. An invisibility cloak—that's what I needed.

I don't think anyone on the field noticed us as we found a place on the bleachers—they were too busy stretching their hamstrings. But it was just a matter of time.

For the next twenty minutes, Dad and I watched the warm-up. While the *mister* shouted instructions, encouragement, and praise, Dad dissected everyone's playing style and likely position. He took pictures with a digital camera and promised that I could send Lindy pictures of all my new teammates.

"Matteo is marvelous," he told me. "Playing with him will make everyone better."

I shrugged and looked over at the other team. The coach roared at his players in German. To me, the hard consonants and nasal sounds of German against the rhythms and pure vowels of Italian sounded strange. But such a match-up was common here. I knew from all of the tourist brochures Mom had thrown my way that the Adige River valley had belonged to Austria's South Tyrol until the end of World War I. While the signs, stores, and government forms were all bilingual, the local German-speakers had their own schools and their own soccer teams.

If I had been down on the field, any rude remarks about a girl playing would have flown right over my head. Of course, I could think of someone who would be more than happy to translate every insult and even make up a few of his own.

Dad stood up. "I want two words with the *mister.*"

"Please, no." I grabbed his arm.

Dad grinned. "Ah, Irene, do not have fear. I will not be one of those crazy American parents who ask of the *mister:* 'Why isn't my daughter playing?'"

Dad clambered down the bleachers. I watched as he attracted the *mister*'s attention, introduced himself, and waved a hand in my direction.

The *mister* smiled. I hadn't thought that he could. More surprising still, he laughed at something Dad said. Luigi and his father. Alike as two drops of water? For the briefest of moments, yes.

My back straightened. I leaned forward. But I could only hear their voices and not their words. Before long, they shook hands and my father bounded back up the bleachers.

"What did he say?" I asked. "Why did he laugh?"

"Oh, it was nothing. A small joke. The *mister* pleases me," Dad announced. "He has organized the team very well. His players respect him."

Or else they were all afraid of him. Even Luigi. Or was it especially Luigi?

Defending Irene

"What joke?" I persisted.

"A small one. So small, I have already forgotten it," Dad told me.

Frowning, I turned my attention back to the field. The game was starting. I meant to watch it quietly and not draw attention to myself. But the action was exciting and Dad was so enthusiastic that I found myself cheering for Emi, Luigi, and yes, even Matteo. I was on my feet as he broke away from the defenders and scored his second goal.

At the end of the first period, my teammates sat on the bench or sprawled at full-length on the ground near it. I avoided looking in their direction. It was easy since Dad was happily reconstructing the best and worst plays of the game and telling me what I should have done if I'd been out there.

By the end of the second period, everyone had started to slow down. In the third period, when free substitution of players was allowed, my teammates were really dragging. Matteo still had his bursts of speed but otherwise had dropped to a trot or even a walk. Luigi made several great saves: falling on balls, diving catches, and even punching the ball up and over the goal. But a rash of corner kicks and our team's inability to push the ball past midfield left him vulnerable.

"I am sure the *mister* wishes that he had you in the game now," Dad murmured after Scena scored their second goal. "Everyone is tired. It goes this way very often in the first game of the season. On Monday, you will run."

My team managed to hang onto a one-point lead. After another diving save, Luigi had sent the ball sailing down the field as the final whistle blew. I was ready to dash out of the stands and into the car, but Dad was deep in conversation with a local on how we could find the remains of a Roman road somewhere just past Castle Thurnstein.

My teammates gathered around the *mister* for what looked and sounded like a lecture. It had been an ugly win. When the huddle broke up, one figure broke away from the group and ran to the foot of the bleachers. Matteo.

"Irene! *Ciao!*" He smiled at me, a heart-melting smile of peace on earth and good will to all. Then he motioned for me to come down.

I smiled, waved, and shook my head. I didn't trust him.

Dad elbowed me. "*Dai,* Irene."

I stood up. It was not the time for explanations, even though I knew it could be a trap. But 'hope is a thing with feathers'—at least according to a poem I'd read in Communication Arts last year. I could feel the feathers tickling my spine and stomach. Could Matteo have changed his mind? Had my coming to the game made him realize that I was a dedicated teammate who would work just as hard as he did?

I looked over Matteo's shoulder as I descended. Over half the team was watching us. Emi raised his chin in a subtle hello. Luigi gave me an ironic, lopsided smile and lifted his eyebrows.

"*Ciao,* Matteo," I said. "Good game."

"I am so happy to see you here, Irene," he said. His tone, bright and warm, sounded almost enthusiastic.

"Oh?" I smiled at him cautiously.

"Enjoy yourself?"

"*Sì.*"

"Super." Matteo said the English word with a German inflection before switching back to Italian. "I think you have found the perfect place to watch our games. Understand?"

Games. Plural. The thing with feathers flew away. "I understand you very well," I said. "But we are not in agreement. I prefer to play."

Matteo's mask slipped. "It is no wonder that the Americans have no soccer tradition if they must play with girls. It is ridiculous...enough to make the chickens laugh."

I decided against telling Matteo that boys and girls usually played on different teams after third grade. It might give him ideas. "I don't care about the chickens," I said, even though I recognized the Italian expression.

"And our opponents too. They will fall down laughing."

"Then it will be so much easier to make goals, no? *Ciao,* Matteo."

"*Ciao,* Irene. We'll see each at school on Tuesday," the Dr. Jekyll and Mr. Hyde of soccer called cheerfully.

"Don't forget soccer on Monday," I said. Then I turned around before Matteo could try another verbal shot on goal.

"So nice!" Dad murmured as I sat down beside him. "It is good to have Matteo on your side."

I crossed my forearms. "It would be."

"What?" Dad asked.

"Nothing."

This time Dad did not say *dimmi*—tell me. And this time the widening silence did not make me spill my guts.

"You will show him," Dad finally said. "It may take time, but he will become accustomed to you."

"Mmm," I said. I had my doubts.

8

Ciao (chow)
Hi or Good-bye

I eased myself into the desk behind Giulia's. Air whistled between my clenched teeth as every muscle in my legs, arms, and shoulders complained. The hard wooden seat made me glad this would only be a ninety-minute orientation instead of a full day of school.

"You seat yourself like my grandmother," Giulia observed. "How did soccer go yesterday?"

"Well enough," I said. "The other team passed, we ran. The other team worked on shooting, we ran. No one even touched a ball until the scrimmage except Federico."

"Ah, Federico is the new boy from the elementary school, right? Emi has told me about him. What did he do?"

"He jumped out of line to kick a few loose balls back to the other team. The *mister* told him to leave them alone. Twice."

"Two times? The boy is crazy. The *papá* of Luigi terrifies Emi."

"The third time the *mister* made Federico do twenty sit-ups, ten push-ups, and then catch up to us." I shook my head. "Maybe Federico finds the ball irresistible. He cannot help himself."

Defending Irene

"*Sì*. It calls him: 'Federico. Federico. Come kick me. Please.'"

We giggled.

A thin woman with a lined face stepped to the front of the buzzing classroom. Her eyes were made up with all the care of a *Vogue* magazine model. Her silk blouse and tailored slacks had a casual elegance. I was almost sure the distinctive shade of her short red hair came from a bottle—Italy had millions of unnatural redheads—but on her, it looked right.

"Good day, class," she said. "Are you ready to begin the new scholastic year?"

A few groans answered her.

"Ohhh," she said with mock pity. "The vacation was too short? I believe you. Too bad. There is much to do today. But first, I must present myself to Irene Benenati, our new student from the United States. I am Professoressa Trevisani. Welcome, Irene." She waved a hand in my direction.

Heads swiveled. Everyone picked me out with ease, even though my walking shorts and T-shirt seemed to blend in with what everyone else was wearing. But it was a very small school with ninety students per grade. I might have been the only unfamiliar face.

"The principal has told me that Irene speaks Italian very well. Now, for Irene and for those who have forgotten everything they learned during the vacation, I will review some of the rules from last year. First, I am not the *mamma maestra* of the elementary school; I am the *professoressa*, the *prof.* You will address me in that way. You will not give me the *'tu.'* You will always say *'lei.'* You will demonstrate respect to all the teachers in this way."

I pressed my lips together. This part had me worried. "*Tu*" is how Italians say the word "you" to children, friends, and family. "*Lei*" is for almost everyone else. We always used the familiar "*tu*" forms at home. Dad had gone over the long list of exceptions and the proper grammar for the polite forms with Mom and me before we came to Italy. There is nothing in English quite like this.

"With your first mistake, you receive extra homework," the *professoressa* continued. "The second time, we send a note home to your parents; on the third, suspension."

Harsh. I couldn't imagine anyone back home being suspended for using the wrong pronoun and verb conjugation to a teacher.

"Irene, please remain after class. We will speak of how it will go with you."

I nodded.

During the hour that followed, teachers came and went, discussing their plans and expectations. Except for art, gym, music, and science, the teachers would come to us. I wrote down the varying times and days for those subjects as well as Italian, English, German, mathematics, history, and religion in my student diary. We all took religion. Separation of church and state is not an Italian concept.

I understood almost everything that was said. Some words were unfamiliar, but then Dad and I never talked about the Pythagorean Theorem, the Second Law of Thermodynamics, or the Counter-Reformation at home. I would have to learn a lot of new definitions for old concepts. How hard could it be? English would be a boring breeze, but there was a gleam in the teacher's eye when she looked at me that suggested I would be helping to teach the class.

Then the German teacher, Professorin Schneider, walked

in. I got lost after *"Guten Morgen, Klasse"* and *"Willkommen, Irene Benenati."* She spoke in clear, almost conversational-speed German. Everyone else laughed at her jokes.

Toast. I would be complete toast in this class.

For five minutes I listened intently and picked out some words that were close to their English counterparts: *Buch,* book; *studieren,* to study; *Minuten,* minutes. But eventually, my thoughts drifted as the incomprehensible waterfall of syllables washed over me.

Glancing at my watch, I wondered what my friends were doing back home. It was nine thirty-four. Second period would have just ended at my old middle school. I could picture Lindy, Kristi, and Deb chatting in the crowded, noisy hallways, slamming their locker doors shut or cramming for a quiz during those five minutes between second and third periods.

No. Wait. It was only two thirty-four A.M. at home. My friends would all be sleeping. It would be hours before their hands reached out from under their covers to slap the snooze alarm for five more crucial minutes. With the bright, morning sun shining in through the windows, it was hard to imagine that darkness still hung over my old corner of the world.

In an attempt to fight back a wave of homesickness, I looked down at my schedule. The basic school day ran from 7:55 A.M. to 13:10 (1:10 P.M.), Monday through Saturday. Yes, Saturday. After an hour and a half for lunch—Italians would consider my old American schedule of getting twenty minutes to scarf down cafeteria food at 10:27 A.M. to be cruel and unusual punishment—students could return at 14:40 (2:40 P.M.) for remedial instruction, special language courses, computers, sports, music, or other non-academic activities.

Professoressa Trevisani returned at the end of the hour to hand out a list of school supplies we would need. "We begin tomorrow," she said. "*Arrivederci.*"

The room emptied quickly.

"We'll see each other at the paper shop after you finish with the *professoressa,*" Giulia said. "Barbara and I will collect everything you need. You have enough money?"

"I think so."

"I hope so," Giulia said. "I do not want to go there two times today. It will be chaos. Absolute chaos."

From what Giulia had told me earlier, hundreds of parents and their children were ready to descend on the neighborhood paper shops scattered throughout the city to buy everything that they needed for the next day.

"Thanks for helping me," I said.

"It's nothing. *Ciao.* I must hurry."

As Giulia dashed out the door, the *professoressa* motioned me to a chair near the front of the room. "So, Irene, the principal tells me that you actually have two mother tongues: Italian and English."

I smiled. "*Sì.* But at home, we say that Italian is my father tongue."

"Ah, very good," she nodded with appreciation at my family's small joke. "This will still be a difficult year for you. You will have much to learn about the written language. It is different, you know."

"Yes, I've seen it. My grandparents always send me books for Christmas."

"Really? Then it could be worse. By the end of the year, you will be able to write Italian in the 'remote past' and 'past anterior' as well as read it." She sounded confident. I must have looked less so, because she laughed. "Don't worry yourself. Your classmates must work hard on the same thing."

The *professoressa* glanced down at her sheet of paper and continued, "Naturally, you give each other the *'tu'* at home. It seems that there is no way to speak formally in English. True?"

I nodded.

"Not even to the President or a senator?"

"Not even for them."

She shook her head. "A strange language, English. Now, let us check your understanding of the polite forms. Talk. Ask me a question."

Slowly and carefully, I asked if she could loan me a pencil, if she planned to give us much homework, if she thought I was using the proper pronoun and verb forms.

"*Brava!*" Professoressa Trevisan said when I finished. "Perfect."

"But I'm not used to it," I said, panicked. "I must think."

"Ah, Irene, to think is a good habit. Hmmmm. You may practice until the first week of October. We will allow you five punishments before sending a note to your parents. Your teachers will have much patience with you. If you always use the formal pronoun, your *professori* will merely corect any mistakes with your verbs. They will not give you a punishment. Do not have fear of asking for help with this and other things."

Professoressa Trevisani looked down at her notes again.

"Let's go on. You will remain in class when the other students study German. Given that everyone else began studying it six years ago, your grade will be based on your effort and ability. Do not expect an *ottimo* or *distinto.* Until you are proficient, you will receive *buono* at the maximum."

I nodded. Optimum, Distinctive, and Good were the A, B, and C of the Italian report card.

"I recommend that you buy a dictionary and a grammar book to help you. Do not worry yourself. Since you already speak two languages, you may learn the third quickly. It would be easier for you down in Italy. Students start with English in elementary school instead of German."

"Down in Italy?" I repeated.

The *professoressa* smiled. "People say that here. The Alto Adige is in Italy; but it is not Italy. It belonged to the Austro-Hungarian Empire until the end of World War I. You have seen the architecture. It is more like Innsbruck and Salzburg than Verona or Venice. In the city, half the people speak German at home and the other half speak Italian. We have German schools and Italian schools. I could spend an hour telling you why. But your friends are waiting for you, true?"

"*Sí,* at the paper shop."

The woman closed her eyes and shivered theatrically. "By good luck, I need not go there today. Come to me with any problems or questions, Irene. Until tomorrow."

"*Ciao,*" I said.

"*Arrivederci, professoressa,*" she corrected me.

"Sorry."

"This will take time. It will be hard and frustrating. But you will learn."

I smiled, nodded, and stood up. My muscles, which felt fine as long as I wasn't moving, had tightened. My first steps would have made Giulia's grandma look lively.

"Irene, have you hurt yourself?" Professoressa Trevisani asked.

"No. It's nothing," I told her. "The *mister* made us run at soccer yesterday."

"You play soccer? With the boys?" For the first time that morning, my teacher showed surprise. Her eyes traveled from my sandals to my ponytail.

"*Sì.*"

"This is normal in the United States?"

"No. I had my own team there. All female."

The left corner of her mouth lifted. "Maybe school will not be so difficult and frustrating for you as I thought. Good luck, Irene."

"Thank you. *Arrivederci, professoressa.*"

"*Brava,* Irene."

I escaped.

I walked the two blocks to the nearest paper shop, squeezed through the door and pushed my way past the people already making a line in front of the counter. As I made my way to the back of the store, I met Giulia and Barbara struggling to the front with their arms full of notebooks, pencils, and drawing pads. They had an extra stack of things for me: a pencil case, a pair of scissors, a protractor, a compass, and a box of watercolor paints.

Giulia grinned at me. "See. We arrived in time. There are not too many people yet."

As we stood in line and other kids from the middle school pushed past us, I heard my name and nationality repeated in soft voices. That's why it didn't surprise me that, by the end of the first full day of school, everyone knew my name. I was Irene, the *Americana* Who Played Soccer.

"Does she really play soccer with you?" I overheard a boy ask Matteo the next day.

"No."

"But I heard—"

Matteo sniffed. "Oh, she comes to soccer. I do not call what she does playing."

After lunch on Thursday, when the fifth person asked me the same question, I finally snapped. "*Sì.* I do it. Shall I demonstrate it to you?"

The boy blinked in surprise. Then his lips pulled back in a Matteo-like smile. "That would please me—please us." He waved his hand at the two boys who stood behind him.

I turned to Giulia beside me. "Ready, Giulia?"

Her eyes asked a silent question: Do you really want to do this, Irene?

I gave a tiny nod.

She grinned. "Oh, *sì.* Barbara?"

"No!" Barbara answered. "I will watch."

I scanned the courtyard for another recruit and saw a familiar form bounce down the gray stone steps. "Luigi, come here!" I said. It was not a request.

A small, calm corner of my brain noted that I should have asked instead of ordered. But instead of calling "Why?" or "No!" Luigi joined us, his eyes bright with curiosity.

"What is it?"

"I need you in the goal. We're playing soccer."

Luigi crossed his arms, thrust out his lower lip and complained, "But *mister,* I am always in the goal."

"Poor Luigi," Giulia said, playing along with his imitation of a whiny first grader. "You can change with me after five minutes."

"Okay," Luigi said. His expression suddenly looked very much like my brother Max when he managed to get his own way.

I turned back to my questioner. "Find a ball and meet us at the basketball court."

We had finished setting up a pair of goals inside the rusting chain link fence when our opponents arrived.

"*Ciao, ragazze!*" one of them shouted.

An insult. Luigi's face stayed blank even though the *e* on the end of *ragazze* labeled him as one of the girls. With thousands of girls and one boy, it would still be appropriate to use the masculine form and say *ragazzi*.

"Giulia, I forget. When did those idiots quit playing soccer?" he asked in a low voice. It was the same voice his father had used to speak to Davide about arriving late to practice.

"Oh, four or five years ago."

"Very good. Very, very good," Luigi said with an evil smile.

So what happened? The three of us rocked! We cleaned the court with them. As I raced up and down, I thought about how wonderful it would be to stomp Matteo in the same way. Once. Just once. He would need some kind of handicap, though. A bad cold? A twisted ankle? A mild case of salmonella poisoning from a slice of tiramisu pastry that had been left out on the counter too long?

A small but growing audience cheered every goal we scored. Or, to be more precise, they taunted our opponents for every ball we put past them. I recognized the difference. Ten minutes into this shellacking, some of the *ragazzi* who had been hanging on the outside of the chain link fence had either grown tired of our opponents' performance—or taken pity on them—and asked if they could play too.

"What do you think, Alessandro?" I asked. That was the name of the boy who had asked me if I really played soccer. I had learned his name while he and the rest of his friends yelled at each other about improving their defense.

"It's okay," he muttered, shrugging. He turned away, his lips a thin line. Giulia and I had probably hurt his and his friends' poor masculine feelings. Well, so be it. It was worth the trouble. I probably wouldn't have liked him anyway. At least this demonstration would put an end to the questions about whether or not I could really play.

And Giulia! Her performance made me wonder again exactly why she had quit. Maybe she wouldn't have made it into the *Terza Categoria,* the 16-years-and-up traveling team. But she could have lasted easily through this year and maybe the next one. It was true that male hormones were already at work, giving the guys an unfair advantage. But the honor of being the first girl in town to wear an *Esordienti* uniform should have belonged to her. Instead, on Saturday, it would be mine.

9

In difesa (een de-FAY-za)
On Defense

Irene!" the mister snapped.

"Here I am," I said. I felt a rush of energy. A light breeze made the soft, smooth, almost slippery fabric of my game uniform flutter against me.

"Stay by me, Irene," the *mister* said, his eyes still locked on the game. "At the beginning of the second period, I must put you in the game for Giuseppe. You will be *terzino*…or *terzina?*" He shrugged. "I don't know. In any case, it is the same. You will be a wing on defense. Understand?"

"*Sì.*"

"If a player gets past you, do not chase him. Run to the nearest goalpost and you will find yourself between him and the goal. Okay?"

I nodded.

"Watch well the Lana player Number 44. He is very fast. If he is in your area, mark him. Stay with him. If it is safe and appropriate, do not hesitate to kick a ball back to Luigi. Don't worry yourself. He can stop any pass from you."

"Without a doubt," I said. For the first time, the *mister's* eyes left the game and focused on me. The left corner of his mouth lifted in a half-smile, giving his face an expression that I could not read.

My stomach lurched. Had I been disrespectful? Or did he think I had complimented Luigi to get on his good side?

"Without a doubt," he echoed. The barest hint of smile defrosted the other side of his face. "All right, Irene. Watch and wait."

I nodded. Watching and waiting had been my job, and I was becoming very good at it. My legs and arms had stopped demanding "Put us in! Put us in!" when I stood on the sidelines. It was an adjustment, though—one of the many that I had made that week.

At the beginning of the second period, I trotted onto the field with my hair braided tightly against my head. It seemed less conspicuous than a ponytail. I had thought seriously about having it all cut off, so I would blend in more with my teammates.

"*Forza,* Irene!" Giulia cheered from the stands. "Come on, get tough!"

Werner, a tall, solid boy with light brown hair, smiled at me as we ran onto the field together. "Listen to me and Manuel. We will tell you what to do."

Werner usually played in the middle of the defensive line. There he was allowed to dash into our opponents' territory, break up a play, and go deep into their penalty area for a corner kick. As the tallest player on the field, he had a chance to head the ball into the goal. It had taken me a few practices to figure out that Werner was part of the local German-speaking population. He usually didn't say much to me beyond "Go forward" or "Come back," and when he did, it was without an accent.

Defending Irene

I didn't have much to do at first. Werner, Manuel (the other wing), and the midfielders kept knocking the ball down to Matteo and Emi. Since most players tend to drive toward their right, I knew that Manuel and Werner would see most of the action. There was no better place to put a weak player than where I stood.

So I watched the red uniforms from Lana work against my Merano teammates in blue, adjusting my position every time things moved in my direction. I tried not to wish that the ball would head toward our goal. That wouldn't be good for the team. Still, it was only a matter of time before someone decided to test me: the girl, the tempting target. Maybe I should have worn the ponytail.

Finally, trouble arrived. With a beautiful fake, Number 44, the player the *mister* had warned me about, drove past Manuel.

"*Dai,* Mendichela, *dai!*" his coach shouted.

Werner rushed to cut him off, and I sprinted back into the penalty area to help.

Thirty feet from the goal, Number 44 dropped his eyes and shot the ball. Luigi batted it away with two hands.

Like any good player, Mendichela followed his shot in, looking for another chance if the first one failed. He and I raced to the ball. I heard footsteps behind us. My teammates or his? It didn't matter. Not yet anyway.

This sprint felt like that drill I had done against Davide at the second practice. The first person to reach the ball would be on offense. I had one or two steps on Mendichela. I reached the ball first and kicked it straight at the goal.

A gasp of surprise went up. My stomach dropped. Was my aim off? Was it too hard? No. The ball sailed right to Luigi.

In difesa: On Defense

He caught it and wrapped his arms around it.

He took only a second to scan the field before racing to the right hand in order to punt the ball. The low, hard kick made the other team scramble back on defense.

"So, trying to score on me, Irene?" Luigi asked.

"No!"

"Only joking. Well done. And *grazie,* eh?" He retreated to the goal.

When our opponents moved the ball back down the field toward Luigi, I backed into the penalty area. But then I saw Number 44 again, Mendichela. He was standing alone on my side of the field. Danger.

I pelted back toward him. His teammate passed him the ball. He must not have seen me coming. Or if he did, he must have assumed I wouldn't be a problem. He was wrong. I intercepted the ball and sent it spinning to the sidelines. Since none of my teammates were there, I chased after it. A pass isn't complete until it reaches a target.

Players converged on me, cutting off the pass to the center, so I dribbled the ball down the field instead, protecting it as best I could. A player caught up to me and knocked the ball out of bounds.

I glanced back at the *mister.* He pointed his linesman flag in my direction—the direction of our opponent's goal. Our ball. I picked it up for the throw-in.

"No, Irene!" the *mister* shouted.

"What are you doing?" Matteo asked. He did not add the word *idiota,* but I could still hear it in his tone.

"Have you forgotten your place, Irene?" asked a third voice I barely recognized. It was snotty with distinct overtones of Matteo. Not Federico? But it was, and he wasn't joking.

Defending Irene

My face burned. Yes, I had forgotten my place. Or at least I hadn't realized I was twenty feet over the centerline. No one could criticize me for bringing the ball down the field and staying with it. But picking up the ball for a throw-in? A definite mistake.

I jogged backwards to my spot, so I could keep an eye on the action. When I arrived, Werner smiled at me. "I would prefer to play midfielder too, you know," he said.

"Me too," Manuel added. "But we are on defense. We are the brutes."

"We do not score. We only stop the enemy before he can do so," Werner went on.

"Hey, sometimes we score. I had one goal last year," Manuel interrupted.

"And I had two. All right then. *Sometimes* we—"

"Pay attention, defense!" the *mister* shouted. "Don't chatter!"

My neck muscles tightened. People seemed to talk on the field when I was around. The *mister* would not consider that a good thing. No coach would.

I was still thankful to Werner and Manuel. They knew how it felt to be back on defense instead of getting the chance to score. A brute, huh? I rather liked the idea.

We, the brutes, worked together well. We stopped Number 44, Mendichela, like a pride of lions taking down a lone antelope.

Time ticked away. We kept a narrow 1–0 lead into the third and final period. For five tense minutes, Luigi, Manuel, Werner, and I had more action that we would have liked as the other team controlled the ball on our half of the field. We barely managed to get the ball to the centerline before they forced it back in the direction of Luigi and the goal.

In difesa: On Defense

In what must have been the fifth or sixth attack, Mendichela swept past Manuel with another of his convincing fakes. Instead of dribbling closer to the goal, he decided to shoot the ball. It rocketed into the air. If I hadn't been directly in the ball's path, I could have done nothing to stop it. But since I was, it slammed into the bottom of my ribcage, forcing the breath out of my body.

My mind urged me to stay with the ball—to pass it to safety. My lungs said no. I dropped to my knees. If the ball had hit an inch or two lower, I would have been flat on my back.

Whump!

It was not the sound of someone taking a shot. More like a high pass spinning twenty feet above the field. I glanced up. Manuel? I wanted to cheer, but only a choked squeak came out.

A hand touched my shoulder. "Irene. Irene? You have hurt yourself?" Luigi asked.

"No. Mendichela has done it," I whispered.

Luigi snorted. "Do we need to call a time-out for you?"

"Where's the ball?"

"Far away, or I would not be here."

"I'll be okay. Only a second."

"*Brava.*" His fingers tightened briefly on my shoulder.

I lurched to my feet and made it back to my area with about twenty seconds to spare before the next attack. One of Lana's forwards dribbled the ball up the sideline on Giuseppe's side of the field.

"Put it out! Put it out!" our *mister* roared. Mendichela and another forward were waiting in the center of the field for a crossing pass from their teammate.

Defending Irene

Giuseppe put it out. The whistle blew. With a sideways gallop, I made my way into the penalty area to join the fight for the ball. But the mister called me: "Irene, come here. Federico, you too."

Reluctantly I went.

"Everything all right?" Werner asked as our paths crossed.

"*Sì,*" I said.

"*Gut,*" he said, switching to German. He sounded relieved.

"How do you feel, Irene?" the mister asked.

"Fine," I said.

"Well done, Irene. *Bravo,* Federico," the mister said. Instead of taking us aside and commenting on our play, he was already looking past us to the action on the field.

Federico was the one person who didn't seem interested in my health. He stared right past me, as if I didn't exist. Matteo had gotten to him. I was sure of it.

Between a punt from Luigi and a header by Davide, the ball finally moved back down to our forwards. Emi and Matteo managed a few more shots on the other team's goal before a long blast on the whistle signaled the end of the game. Another win.

Federico pumped his fists in the air. He turned to me, his face bright with enthusiasm. His mouth opened to say something. Then it closed to a tight, horrified O when he realized his near mistake. He spun around.

Mom and Dad waved from the stands. Dad's wide smile told me that he would have a lot to say when I met him at home. Most of it positive.

In the locker room, the mister distributed a few compliments and a lot of criticism. He was greatly disappointed by our lack of stamina. We did not pass well. We did not play our positions. He made his way around the circle for personal remarks, but skipped right over me. When he finished, I grabbed my blue backpack with our team name and sponsor stenciled on it and headed for the bathroom to change.

Three people were standing in line when I came out. But they weren't waiting to use the bathroom. They were waiting for me.

"*Poverina,*" Matteo said softly. "How are you?"

I glanced back over my shoulder, as if looking for the "poor little girl." Then I stood up as straight as possible. Even though I had changed into tennis shoes and Matteo still wore his cleats, I was taller than he was.

"To whom are you speaking, Matteo?" I asked.

He shook his head. "I fear it is too dangerous for you here. I saw how that ball knocked you to the ground. *Poverina,*" he repeated. "And I heard what the *mister* said to you after the game."

"He didn't say anything."

"Exactly." Matteo smiled.

"Maybe there is too much for you to remember here in Italy, Irene," Giuseppe said. "If you are on defense, you must stay in your area."

Federico smirked from his spot behind Matteo. "Or did you forget you were on defense, Irene? You tried to score on Luigi."

"That's not true!" I shouted. A mistake. Now they knew they were getting to me. I kept my voice even. "I *passed* the ball to Luigi."

Matteo laughed. "Luigi said that the only time he was afraid during the game was when you 'passed' him the ball."

"It's true," Federico said. "I heard him say it."

Defending Irene

Not Luigi too? For an instant, my brain froze. Fortunately, my mouth did the same thing. No, not Luigi. He had even told me that he was scared for a moment, but then he had thanked me. I had done the right thing. I had done what the *mister* told me to do. I took a deep breath, ready to tell them so.

"*Ciao,* Irene." Giulia appeared at my side and tugged at my elbow. "Let's go."

"Okay," I said.

"*Ciao, ciao, ciuccio,*" Giuseppe said.

Bye, bye, baby pacifier? I stiffened. The *ch* sound, which started every syllable he spoke, landed on my ears like a series of slaps.

"*Ciao, ciao, cucciola,*" Matteo added.

The different meanings of *cucciola* ran through my brain: kitty, puppy, little darling. This was definitely not a compliment.

I was ready to turn and face them, but Giulia said softly, "*Dai,* Irene. Don't listen to them."

"I am not a *cucciola,*" I said through clenched teeth. "I am a brute. Werner said so."

Giulia giggled. "Werner would know. But I like him. He's fair."

"Agreed."

So many people were being fair to me: Werner, Luigi, Emi, Manuel, and maybe even the *mister.* So how could three idiots ruin everything for me? Or was it just one idiot—one extremely talented idiot?

10
Uaou! (oo-WOW-oo)
Wow!

The story traveled through the middle school of how I had tried to put the ball into my own goal. I smiled a patient smile and told everyone how I was feeding it to the goalie. Hadn't they ever seen a defensive player do that on television? Yes? Well then, they understood.

Luigi overheard me repeating my explanation to a group of popular girls. I had picked them out quickly in the first few days by their hair, nails, clothes, and tendency to travel in packs. He promptly stepped between Giulia and me and into the conversation. His voice took on the rhythm of an announcer doing a play-by-play:

"Both Mendichela and Irene Benenati race for the ball. My heart beats in my chest. I know the signs. The crazy *Americana* plans to shoot the ball into her own goal—my goal."

"It was a pass," I said.

Luigi ignored me. "Irene's eyes drop. She brings her foot back. *Puuut!* The spectators gasp. Mendichela gasps. The ball comes directly to me—to my chest. It is a pass. I know it. But I am still afraid. Will it knock me backward into the goal?"

Luigi paused. His eyes slid sideways to look at me, offering me a chance to protest. I did not take it.

"But no!" Luigi continued, gesturing widely. "I pull the ball into my arms. For now, it is safe from Mendichela and his team."

"*Uaou!*" said one of the girls. "How *bello! Brava,* Irene!"

Luigi grinned at me.

"But Luigi, isn't it dangerous for Irene to play with the boys?" a girl named Elena asked. As far as I could tell, she tended to do most of the talking for her group.

"Weren't you listening to me?" he asked. "It is *my* head that is in danger."

"If only," I said.

"Monte Catino at Merano 2000 is more dangerous, Elena," Giulia pointed out. "And you ski down that like a crazy woman."

"Monte Cattivo," someone else said, which could be translated as "Bad Mountain."

Elena smoothed down the front of her shirt, looking pleased. "*Sì.* But the trees and course markers don't move themselves on the mountain. Matteo told us how the ball hit you in the stomach and the *mister* called you off the field. Matteo was so worried."

Oh, yes. Worried that I might get up again. Worried that I would keep getting up no matter what.

"It was so cute," another girl cooed. "Maybe Matteo has fallen in love with you."

"Ha!" I said. The syllable jumped out of my mouth before I could stop it. Giulia snorted. Luigi covered his ears with his hands.

Uaou!: Wow!

"*Madonna!*" he said. "Has Matteo asked for your phone number too?"

"Too?" echoed an appreciative crowd.

"No." I said, trying to sound calm. "Emi asked for my phone number so I could meet Giulia. Matteo promised me that if I wanted a boy to fall in love with me, I was in the wrong place."

"Too bad," someone murmured. "Or I would start to play soccer."

"And be a *maschiaccio?*" a girl named Sonia asked. "Not I. It's not worth the trouble."

Ma-ski-AH-choh? I didn't recognize the word, but the "choh" sound at the end almost guaranteed it was not a compliment.

Elena frowned at Sonia. "Don't worry, Irene. Maybe it is like an American film. A man and a woman—they do not like each other when first they meet. Then everything changes. Love!"

Denials crowded through my brain so thick and fast they paralyzed my vocal cords.

Giulia stepped in before the silence ran too long. "In this case I think not," she said.

"But this morning, I heard him say to Irene, 'How are you, *cucciola?*'" another girl said.

This brought on another round of giggles. And horror of horrors, I blushed.

"Oooh!"

"Enough!" ordered Elena. "I have a favor to ask of Irene. There is an American song that really pleases me, and I want to know what it means. Will you help me?"

Defending Irene

"Certainly," I said. Now it all made sense why Elena was being so nice. Apparently she didn't want the walking, talking, English/Italian dictionary to get mad and stomp away before doing a few translations.

Elena sang a few lines. Her pure Italian vowels made it difficult to understand the words, but I recognized the melody.

"*Love?*" Luigi picked out the English word with horror. "I must go. Really. I cannot stand this chatter about love anymore. See you later, Irene. I am so glad I could help you explain what happened at the game."

"Help me again and your head will really be in danger," I told him.

"You're welcome," he said. His grin told me that he wasn't particularly worried.

I spent the next five minutes singing and explaining lyrics. Elena and her friends were entranced.

"*Uaou,* Irene. You sound just like the radio!" Sonia said. Was that her apology for implying that I was a *maschiaccio?* (Whatever that meant.) If so, I had a feeling it was directed at Elena more than me.

"What is a *maschiaccio?*" I asked Giulia after the bell rang. She blinked. "You don't know?"

"No."

"Hmm. After school someday, I must teach you the words that you should never repeat at home. Otherwise, your *papá* will tell your *mamma* that I am not a good girl to know."

"Is *maschiaccio* that bad?" I asked.

"No. But it is not very…polite. You have never heard it? Not even as a joke?"

I shook my head. "What does it mean?"

"It is a girl who does that which a boy does. Not in a positive way."

Yes. I could see it now. Changing *maschio,* which means male, to *maschia* and tacking on *-cio,* an ending signifying that something was awful or brutal, made *maschiaccio* into a very negative Italian word. Something worse than tomboy, I suspected. In Italy that would be a huge insult.

"There's so much I don't know. What would I do without you, Giulia?"

"Become a friend of Elena?" Giulia tilted her head and looked up at me.

"No thanks," I said. "She reminds me of Matteo. Nicer, maybe but...I don't know. I prefer you and Barbara."

Giulia laughed. "Elena is not so bad. I remember once when we were angry with a boy in elementary school, we sent Elena to punch him for us. For her, it was safe."

"Really? Why?"

"Almost all the *ragazzi* had fallen in love with her. And those who weren't in love with her were afraid of the others."

"Does she still punch guys? I could send her after Matteo."

Guilia shook her head. "She would not believe you about Matteo. She never believed me."

11
Brutta strega
(BROO-tah STRAY-gah)
Ugly Witch

The clock was winding down in our third game. But how much time was left? Three seconds? Thirty seconds? More? I only hoped that the whistle blasts signaling the end of the game would come before the team from Appiano erased our one-point lead. I was tired. Our team was tired. The air, thick with pollution and humidity, was difficult to breathe. Low clouds hid the four old castles that perched a few hundred feet above the river valley.

The Appiano team attacked again. Giuseppe challenged the forward, who dribbled down his sideline. I backed toward the penalty box. My attention shifted between the ball and the players pounding up the field. When would the crossing pass to the middle come?

Instead, the ball spun out of bounds. I couldn't tell whether Giuseppe had touched it or the player from Appiano had lost control.

With the action stopped, both of the coaches sent in their substitutes.

Werner, who had been out for a short rest, loped onto the field. I trotted toward him, knowing that I was being replaced.

Brutta strega: Ugly Witch

"No! Stop yourself, Irene!" the *mister* called. "Giuseppe, come here."

I was still in the game? In the last critical seconds? *Me?* I felt a rush of unexpected energy.

Giuseppe, who had been resting the heels of his hands against his lower thighs, straightened. His mouth opened and closed like a fish. A protest? Or a complete lack of air? He walked to the sidelines, his head down, his hands clutching his sides, his cleats kicking up swirls of dirt.

The *mister* put a hand on Giuseppe's shoulder and said a few quiet words. Giuseppe shook his head. The *mister* spoke again, patted Giuseppe's back and gently shoved my teammate in the direction of the bench.

In the meantime, Appiano finished rearranging itself for the throw-in. The referee handed the ball to one of Appiano's midfielders, Number 10. He held the ball above his head with both hands. His eyes flicked up and down the field, looking for an open player.

Werner marked Appiano's best forward, matching the shorter, thinner player almost step for step. He looked almost as fresh as when he started the game. That couldn't last long, but all we needed was another minute or maybe two. But not three. Please, not three.

Number 10 threw in the ball to a midfielder who had been hanging back by the centerline. The boy drilled the ball downfield into an empty space on the field ten feet in front of me.

This was not the time to move the ball slowly up the field. A booming kick with plenty of power—that's what was needed.

A midfielder from Appiano was closing rapidly, but I was

sure I'd have time to launch it over his head. I planted my right foot. My left foot swung forward, catching the ball with the top and side of my shoe to give it lift and plenty of forward momentum. *Whump.*

But I miscalculated. The ball slammed into the midfielder's face like a cannonball that didn't make it over the castle wall. He staggered back a step or two as the ball ricocheted off his forehead—no, his nose, I realized as a burst of crimson stained his jersey.

I kept going and played it off his face the way I would have played it off a cement wall. I could make sure he was all right once the ball was safely on the other side of the centerline. Again came that satisfying *whump.* A successful takeoff this time. The ball's flight lacked the height and distance of one of Werner's better efforts, but as the ball came down, our side of the field emptied.

Davide positioned himself under the ball. It bounced up and off his head like a flat rock skipping across a glassy pond. This was not just a lucky move. It was a skillful one known as *fare il ponte,* making the bridge. The ball sailed over a line of defenders and landed at Matteo's feet.

Matteo dribbled rapidly down the field. Only one defender stood between him and the goalkeeper. The others streamed behind him, trying to catch up. Emi and Federico were also charging hard down the field to force Appiano to defend against a possible pass. Not that Matteo would give up the ball if he had a chance to score. So why did I find myself shouting "*Dai,* Matteo, *dai!*" with the rest of them?

I don't know whether Matteo heard the footsteps behind him. But instead of taking the ball all the way in, Matteo kicked it from just over the chalked line of the penalty area.

Brutta strega: Ugly Witch

The goalkeeper lunged, but he wasn't even close. The orange netting stretched taut.

"Goal!" shouted our team and our fans. They actually used the English word—although the *o* was rounder and from further back in the throat.

I was only one touch away from an assist, I realized. The closest I had come all season. The ball would have never made it near Matteo, of course, without Davide's header.

"*Bravo,* Davide!" I shouted. "You have made a beautiful bridge!"

He had been jumping up and down, pumping his fist, and cheering Matteo. When he heard my voice, he stopped and looked at me. His mouth twisted in a grimace of some sort. Anger? Outrage? No, pretended pain. He rubbed his head, grinned at me, and gave me a thumbs-up. It was the first friendly gesture he'd shown me since I watched the *mister* lecture him for coming to practice late.

I smiled and gave him a thumbs-up in return.

The midfielder from Appiano stood next to me, clutching his nose and looking a bit wobbly.

"Everything all right?" I asked.

"*Brutta strega,*" he said.

Ugly witch. Well, I had been called worse. And given that we had just scored, I suppose my question hadn't been phrased in the most diplomatic way possible. But then he added another word, one that Giulia had taught me after school.

I searched my new, small collection of words for something appropriate to say back to him. Then Werner appeared from one direction and Luigi from another. The boy from Appiano stalked off, still pinching his nose.

Defending Irene

"Well done, Irene! We have taught you many things, no?" Werner said proudly. "Ah, the things you will show your friends in America."

"*Dai,* Irene," Luigi murmured. "Must you try to take off the head of someone at every game?"

"I didn't mean to do it."

"At least this time, it was not my head," he said. He brushed the back of his hand across his forehead.

"Oh, it pleases Irene to do that?" Werner asked. "I will stay attentive."

I just grinned at him.

The celebration was ending now on the other end of the field. Luigi backpedaled to the goal before the *mister* could complain about our chattering. I took my place in one of the straight, evenly spaced lines for the kickoff.

The team from Appiano looked determined, but all the determination in the world can't make a dent in a two-goal lead with ten seconds left in the game. The whistle blew three times.

Our fans—parents, brothers, sisters, grandparents, and a few kids from school—cheered. I looked up into the stands for my family. Dad sat near a cluster of other parents, but I didn't see everyone else. My grandparents were supposed to arrive by train from Milan a few minutes before my game started. Dad didn't look worried, though, so everything must have been all right. Maybe their train was late. Or they might have missed a connection.

As usual, the *mister* focused on the negatives: poor passing, lack of hustle, lack of energy. Oh, yes, he told us, we were happily standing on the sidelines with a final score of three to one, but how close had we come to letting Appiano score? How could we start so strongly and finish so very poorly?

Something—it might have been a slight change in our faces or our breathing—told him we felt that we had actually finished the game rather well.

The *mister* snorted. "Matteo never would have scored if Appiano had not been so aggressive. They were pressing us very hard and keeping nothing in reserve. Thanks to heaven that Giuseppe, Werner, and Irene stopped them. *Bravo,* Davide, you have done well the bridge. Until Monday."

We scattered before he could think of anything else to say. Leaving the circle, I found Matteo on my right and Giuseppe on my left. Someone else was directly behind me, breathing on my neck and stepping on my heels like an eager puppy. Federico? Matteo's new shadow.

"Let me give you some good advice, *cucciola,*" Matteo said. "Maybe in America, you kick the ball into the face of another player. But here in Italy, we think it works better to kick it over his head."

"Were you angry with him?" Giuseppe asked. "Did he call you something?"

"No. Nothing," I said. Not until afterwards anyway. "It was an accident."

"An accident," Giuseppe echoed. "So you admit that you cannot control the ball?"

"If you could have done better," I said, showing all my teeth, "the *mister* would have left you in the game."

Giuseppe's nostrils flared. A low blow, I guess. But I hadn't started this. I was tired of it. I had proved myself repeatedly as a hardworking substitute. Polite answers to rude remarks had done nothing. Here they were again, hoping to make the little puppy, the *cucciola,* yap and snap at them. Well, I wouldn't bark, but my words might bite.

"And you, Matteo," I added. "I have heard you tell Federico that you have scored in every game for the last two years. Right, Federico?" I stopped abruptly and turned around. The boy bounced off my shoulder and backed away.

"*Ehm...sí.*"

"Matteo is marvelous, right, Federico? You think so, I think so, and it is absolutely certain that Matteo thinks so. But without my pass and without the bridge that Davide made, that streak would have ended. Enough." I dusted off my hands, an Italian gesture meaning "And that's that."

My quiet attack had taken them completely off their script. Good. I'd had the last word, and I meant to keep it, so I strode forward to meet Giulia who was standing at the gate. Matteo the Egotistical could run after me if he wanted to.

Giulia's eyes sparkled. "What did you say to Matteo?" she asked.

I told her.

"*Bella. Molto, molto bella,*" she said. "But be careful. He can be tricky."

"*Ciao,* Irene. Giulia," my dad called. He examined me. The right corner of his mouth lifted. "You are very dirty today, Irene."

"I know," I said, glancing down. The dust of the field coated my arms and legs like an uneven tan.

"If you wash your face and hands—" he broke off. "No. That won't work. You have need of a shower."

"I know," I said. "Where are the grandparents?"

"At home. Your *nonna* was, uh, too tired after the trip. And as for your *nonno,* well. His back hurts him. To seat himself on a hard bench after spending the entire morning on the train—it was not a good idea."

"Too bad. It was an exciting game, no?" Giulia said. "They would have enjoyed themselves."

Dad pressed his lips together, looking uncomfortable. "The *mister* found it a bit too entertaining at the end, I think. But you did well, Irene. My *papá* would have cheered."

"And Nonna?" I asked.

"*Ópla!*" Dad exclaimed. "Oh my! It's better to tell you the truth, *cara.* Your *nonna* loves you well, but she does not think you should play soccer."

"What? But I've always played soccer. She knows that."

Dad shrugged. "But now you're doing it in Italy with the boys. That makes it…different."

Giulia nodded. "That does not surprise me. She and my *nonna* are in agreement."

"She loves you well, Irene," Dad repeated. "But…" His search for the right thing to say seemed unsuccessful.

"It's nothing," I said. "Don't worry yourself."

"Are you sure?" He frowned.

"Of course."

"Listen, Irene. It could be best if we do not speak of the game when you arrive home. Then all will go well, I'm sure."

I was sure too. If I could handle Matteo, I could certainly handle my *nonna.*

12
Gentile (jen-TEE-lay)
Polite or Proper

As I rode my bike home, I replayed the end of the game in my head: my big kick, Davide's header, Matteo's breakaway. Yes, my *nonno* probably would have cheered. In his opinion, soccer was the perfect game, and everyone should spend as much time as possible either playing it or watching it. So "everyone" might even include his granddaughter.

But my grandfather hadn't come to my game. My *nonna* would never make a scene, but I had an idea of what happened when Dad picked them up at the train station:

Dad: We must go in a hurry. The soccer game starts
　　soon.
Nonno: Excellent!
Nonna: But Max, you should be at the field already.
Max: Not me. Irene is the one who is playing. Her team is all boys. They all hate her.
Mom: Now that's not true, Max.
Max: Okay, most of them hate her.
Mom: Massimiliano!
Nonna: I'm sorry, but I cannot go to this game. Who

could sit for an hour on a hard bench after passing
all those hours on the train?

Nonno: But—

Nonna: Your back hurts you, *caro.* It is better that we
go to the apartment and get some rest.

I reached the gate and pressed our doorbell.

"*Sì?*" Mom's voice came from the intercom.

"I'm home," I said.

Without a word, she buzzed me in. I pushed open the gate
and eased my bike through.

A second well-timed buzz greeted me at the dark, heavy,
carved wooden door. I crossed the small ceramic-tiled entry-
way and wrestled my bike down a half flight of stairs to the
cantina, the basement, where we had a small storage room.

Tack. Tack. Tack. My cleats clacked against the stairs as I
trudged up to the fourth floor. Mom had left the door slightly
ajar.

The smell of lemon oil and bleach still lingered in the air
from Mom's heroic cleaning efforts of the past few days.
Almost every surface in the house had been mopped,
scrubbed, or dusted. Everyone and everything had to be as
neat and clean as possible whenever Nonna came to visit.

Even though I had washed my face and hands in the clubhouse sink, I was well below the usual standards. Maybe I
should slip into the shower before anyone saw me.

But Nonna stood waiting for me in the hallway, a smile of
welcome on her face. Petite, wrinkled, and white-haired, she
wore a silk blouse, pressed slacks, and matching chunky gold
jewelry at her ears, throat and wrist. Something about the
set of her shoulders made me cringe. "It's a trap!" a small,

panicked voice inside me chanted. "Run away! Run away!"

"Ah. Here you are, Irene. *Ciao,*" Nonna said.

"*Ciao,*" I echoed.

She held out her hands and raised her face to mine for the double kiss of welcome, a difficult maneuver if you weren't sure which way to lean. I had watched Mom bump chins and eyeglasses with people many times. This would be my first attempt ever. As I leaned forward, I caught the scent of lavender. Nonna's lips touched my left cheek and then my right. I wound up kissing mostly air.

"I have heard your *papá* tell your *mamma* that you won your game. Congratulations." She stepped back, still holding onto my hands.

"Thank you. I must take a shower now." I tried to edge away.

Nonna did not let go. "No, wait. I have a present for you."

"Bait! It's bait!" shrilled that small voice again. "Don't take it. Run away!" I needed backup. Lots of backup.

"Uh, what about Max?" I asked.

"Max has already opened his. He could not wait."

He *could* have waited. But Nonna was not the woman to make him. She couldn't spoil us enough. A snack? It would not ruin our dinner. Dessert? So what if Max didn't clean his plate. Bedtime? They can certainly stay up a few more minutes—a few more hours.

I followed her into the study. Not a paper was out of place. Every single stray box had finally been cleared away. And no sign of Nonno or Dad. I was on my own. Nonna plucked her purse and a small package off a neat line of luggage in the corner before continuing out onto the balcony.

She eased herself onto one of the white Adirondack chairs

and crossed her legs at the ankles. "Here. Open it."

I eased off the bow, an elaborate work of art surrounded by a mass of curling ribbons. I pulled a small, green box out of the wrapping paper and flipped it open. Inside, I found a gold herringbone necklace.

"Oh, Nonna," I breathed. "It's beautiful. A thousand thanks."

"It's nothing. Try it on."

When I finished fastening the necklace, Nonna handed me a small mirror that she'd pulled out of her purse. I gazed at my reflection. The chain hung from a neck streaked with dirt. Untidy wisps of hair, which had escaped from my ponytail, framed a red face streaked with mud. I quickly handed the mirror back.

"I was not expecting to find you such an elegant, well-educated *ragazza* when you arrived here last month," Nonna began. "I bought the necklace for her...for you."

A great, echoing "but" hung between us. I waited.

"Irene, you know I love you well," my grandmother began. "I would prefer that it was not necessary to say this to you, my treasure, but your parents have not done it, therefore I must."

"What, Nonna?" I asked.

"Soccer is not a feminine sport." She could have been repeating the latest pronouncement from the Pope in Rome.

"In America, *sí,*" I insisted politely. "As many girls play it as boys."

"The young women here have good reason not to play it. It is not graceful. No. It is dangerous. It is brutal. You cannot deny it."

Hmm. Shouting and kicking and bloody noses.

Defending Irene

"Ah! We are in agreement," Nonna said, pouncing on my hesitation. "I can read it in your face. Listen, I know that you are the sporting type, *carissima,* but there must be something else that would please you. Swimming? Skating?"

I shook my head.

"Volleyball? Basketball?"

My jaw dropped. "Basketball is fine, but soccer no?"

"Basketball and soccer are different," Nonna said.

Not the way I played. "How?" I asked.

She crossed her arms. "They just are. Mmmm. What about tennis? Would tennis please you? There is a club here. I saw the signs."

I shook my head again. "No. It's too expensive."

Nonna leaned forward, her hands clutching the armrests of her chair. "If you quit soccer, your *nonno* and I would pay for lessons."

I had picked the wrong excuse. "No thank you," I said. "Soccer is my favorite sport. I must continue to play."

"Your team accepts you?"

I hesitated again. "Some of them."

"And the rest?"

The rest of them would be cheering my *nonna* on.

"This is a small town, Irene," she continued. "Who will be a friend to a—a *maschiaccio?*"

I grinned. I could tell that Nonna hated to even use the word, much less have her granddaughter actually be such a thing. "Another *maschiaccio,*" I answered. "She is called Giulia."

"Another girl plays with you?"

"No. She quit a year ago."

"Why?" Nonna asked triumphantly.

"There are no teams for girls here. She had no future in soccer. I do."

"What about the present?" Nonna's voice rose in frustration. "Has my son taught you nothing of the *bella figura?*"

"Appearances are everything" was Mom's rather cynical definition of that Italian concept.

"Does the *bella figura* mean to stop something you have already started?" I asked.

"If you should not have started it at all, *sì.*" Nonna pounded her fist on the arm of the chair. "Truly."

"We do not agree, Nonna. If I stopped now, I would seem stupid and weak. Everyone would say—"

"That you are gracious, *gentile,* well educated, not afraid to admit a fault," Nonna cut in. "You are such a charming girl, Irene, until you step onto the field." She wrinkled her nose and held out the mirror. "Look at yourself now. Dirty. Smelly. Hair like Medusa."

I stood up. My calves knocked the chair backwards. Impolite words and gestures, both English and Italian, were dancing through my head. I had to leave before one of them escaped, before I pitched the necklace and the box and its beautiful bow off the balcony.

"*Grazie,* Nonna. You're right." I waited just long enough for hope to blossom on her face before adding, "I certainly must take a shower. But no, I will not quit soccer. I'm sorry."

She shook her head. "*Povera.* It is all the fault of my son. He is mad for the game. If Max had been born five years earlier, we would not be having this discussion."

I pressed my hand to the bottom of my ribcage and whispered, "That's not true."

Or was it? No. I would not—could not—believe that Dad

had just been making do with me. He would have coached my teams and kicked the ball around with me in the backyard just the same. I was sure of it.

I stumbled across the balcony and back into the suddenly blurry study.

"Maria Pia!" Nonna called, her tone halfway between a plea and an order. "I'm sorry. Come here, *cara.*"

Maria Pia was the name of my youngest and most independent-minded aunt, not mine. I would not answer to it. I passed the living room. Dad was describing our view, telling Nonno what he would be able to see if the air was clear. Tall and angular with the same lift to their shoulders, they were as alike as two drops of water.

I snatched a pair of shorts and a flowered shirt off my bed. Nonna had given them to me as a welcoming gift when we arrived in Milan a few weeks ago. Since my grandmother always liked seeing me wear the things she had bought for me, I had laid them out before the game. Now I wanted to grind them under my dirty cleats, crumple them into a ball and shove them into a drawer. After a week or so, the stains would set and never come out.

Instead, I carried them and the golden chain to the bathroom. I would show her. I would be gracious, *gentile,* well educated, and not afraid to admit a fault. If playing soccer was a fault, well then, I was guilty.

I could have stayed under the stream of hot water all day. There was no tank to empty. Every drop was heated as it flowed rapidly through the *riscaldamento.* But natural gas was expensive, much more expensive than in the U.S. When most of my anger had swirled down the drain with the water, I reached for a towel.

Gentile: Polite or Proper

I wondered what might have happened if Nonna and I had had that conversation about soccer in Milan when we arrived. I might not have been able to stand up to her without the prospect of having to explain to my team why I quit—without having the vision of a wildly celebrating Matteo to stiffen my backbone. I might have wound up with a closet full of tennis outfits, a coach to help me with my backhand, and a determined rationalization that tennis would be a wonderful opportunity for cross-training. I wouldn't be struggling in a game that I used to dominate. No one would be trying to force me off the tennis court just because I was a girl.

And there was also the real possibility that I might have become an enthusiastic member of the I-Love-Matteo club. I wouldn't have known any better. And I might have been desperately trying to fit in with Elena's group instead of being myself with Giulia. No soccer. No Emi. No Giulia.

Over the high-pitched whir of the hair dryer, a knock sounded. I pretended not to hear. A second knock followed, this one more insistent.

"Who's there?" I asked in Italian.

"Me," Mom said in English. "Let me in."

I unlocked the door and pulled it open.

Mom scanned me. "So you decided to get cleaned up before saying hello to your grandma. A good idea."

"Um, not exactly," I said, fingering the gold chain that was hanging around my clean neck.

"Oh no." Mom came in and shut the door. I saw that she was wearing makeup, jewelry, and a silk blouse that Nonna had given her. "I had hoped to catch you before she did. We had a little, uh, discussion before you came home. Your dad told her to leave you alone—that you were his *bella, brava calciatrice.* That you'd made your decision and stuck with it."

"Nonna thought I'd be more reasonable."

"And?"

I sighed. "I wasn't."

"What happened?" Mom demanded. Something in her eyes told me that mentioning Nonna's theory—how Max could have saved me from becoming a *maschiaccio* if only he had been born a few years earlier—would be a really bad idea. I shook my head.

Mom crossed her arms. "Your father needs to have another talk with your *nonna.* Or maybe I will. You're making a real difference here in Merano. You should see the way the little girls on Max's team watch your every move. You're their role model."

"No. It's okay. Really. I guess I understand how Nonna feels." Mom looked unconvinced, so I decided to pull out the big guns. "I mean, how would you feel if I told you I wanted to be a cheerleader?"

Mom's eyes widened. She cleared her throat. "Um, they don't have those in Italy, do they?"

"No. I mean when we go back to the U.S."

"You're just saying this to make a point, right?"

I smiled.

"All right. I won't say a word about soccer, and neither will your father."

It was a good plan. Too bad Max and my *nonno* weren't in on it.

13
Calcio al'angolo
(CAL-cho all AHN-go-low)
Corner Kick

I know you were too tired to come to the Irene's game, Nonno," Max said at dinner that same Saturday night. "But will you come to watch me play soccer on Monday?"

I stiffened. Mom grimaced. Dad hissed through his teeth. Nonna's fingers tightened around her knife and fork.

"Gladly," Nonno said, completely oblivious to the whole only-boys-play-soccer thing. "It interests me to see your team."

"Nonna?" Max turned his enormous brown eyes on my grandmother and blinked twice.

"Ah, if only I had such eyelashes," Nonna said. She laid down her knife and reached out to pat Max's cheek.

"Please?" Max begged.

How much did Max know? How much had he heard? My rat of a little brother always had a better understanding of what was going on than anyone ever gave him credit for.

"Certainly. It would please me to go," Nonna said, smiling.

Max's face was at its most innocent as he continued, "Irene's team follows mine on the field, you know."

Nonna's smile froze. "Really. One after the other?"

"There is a short break between them. But Irene always plays with *Luigi* then," Max said, batting his beautiful eyelashes at me. From the way he said my teammate's name, anyone would think that I had plastered "Luigi plus Irene" all over my notebooks and bulletin board.

I smiled calmly. Max the Manipulator wouldn't get a reaction this time. "Luigi and I both stand around a lot during the scrimmage. He is our goalkeeper."

Nonno nodded. "Mmm, good idea to practice during the break. So dedicated. All right, how many hours of soccer on Monday afternoon?"

"Three and a half," Mom answered.

"I fear that is too much for your back, *caro,*" Nonna said.

"You could go to half of one and half of the other," Mom suggested with an air of polite helpfulness.

"A good plan!" Nonno said. "*Va bene.*"

On Monday afternoon, a bank of clouds had once again settled over the mountains surrounding the town. A light mist was falling, but Mom and the *nonni* sat in the stands just the same. Nonno had joked in the car on the way to the field that if he hadn't seen postcards of Merano, he would never have believed we had a mountain view.

Mom had insisted that I ride with the family. She didn't like me biking on wet, crowded streets. But instead of joining the others in the stands to watch Max, I sat in the car writing about just how stupidly all the characters were behaving in

Calcio al'angolo: Corner Kick

I promessi sposi, a classic novel that every Italian student learns to know and hate. I didn't know how I would ever make it all the way through this long boring love story set in the 1600s. Mom's Italian grammar handbook lay on the seat beside me to help with the special verb tenses Professoressa Trevisani had warned me about.

The clock on the dashboard read 16:09. Almost ten after four. Time to go. I stuffed my essay, grammar, and *I promessi sposi* into my backpack and stepped out of the car.

I peered over the laurel hedge at the two fields below. My brother's group was playing on the smaller one, which was covered by a pale green artificial turf. Carpet, they called it here. The players' damp hair and identical uniforms made it difficult for me to spot Max. In contrast, the lone girl on his team, with her long, dark braid, was easy to find. I wondered what had happened to the other two. Maybe the wet weather had kept them at home.

A grandfatherly *mister*, whose sweats matched those of his players, supervised. He coached, refereed, and sometimes even played. A broad grin lit up his face each time he trotted stiffly to the ball for a demonstration of precision passing.

I studied him suspiciously, watching for signs of sexism or favoritism. Did he leave the girl out? Did he ignore her? Did he criticize her more than the boys? Less?

I saw almost no difference in the way the way he treated her except that his smile seemed to broaden and soften each time she handled the ball. The *cucciola* effect? Yes. Add seven or eight years to her age and a foot or so to her height, and the effect would not be so adorable. I knew.

According to Giulia, it had been this way for years. Girls

from the first, second, and even third class of the elementary school would play with the boys. Eventually, they dropped out for dance, swimming, volleyball, basketball, figure skating, riding lessons, or tennis. At least they did here in Merano. It was different in other parts of Italy.

The ball popped out of the cluster of players and rolled toward the sidelines. The *mister* reached it first. Instead of letting the ball roll out of bounds, his foot connected with it for a kick that Werner would have been proud to claim. It sailed directly to midfield where the girl stood waiting near the centerline.

"*Dai,* Angelica," he shouted to her.

I grinned. Dad used to reward players for staying in position in the very same way. Most kids seemed to hover near their teammates instead of sticking with their assigned positions. The herd instinct was hard to overcome. Little kids couldn't seem to help chasing after the ball instead of sticking with their assigned areas.

Angelica's braid flicked back and forth as she ran to meet the ball. Her pace slowed as she dribbled the ball upfield.

"*Dai,* Angelica! *Forza, forza, forza!*" the *mister* called. Only one defender stood between her and the goalie. Instead of coming forward to challenge her and slow her down, the boy backed up a few steps into the penalty area. Led by Max, the herd was gaining. They streamed after her in a wide V, like a flock of geese.

Angelica might have heard footsteps, because she decided to take a shot. The goalkeeper lunged to the left just as the ball nicked the defender's shin and rolled to the right— straight into the goal.

"*Brava,* Angelica!" the girl's *mister* and I shouted in unison.

Calcio al'angolo: Corner Kick

"Have you taught her to do that, Irene?" asked a voice at my shoulder.

I turned to frown at Luigi. "What do you mean?"

"To kick the ball at someone. She missed his head. But she is still young. It takes time to learn such things."

I started walking toward the clubhouse. "Ha, ha. You are so comical, Luigi."

The sarcasm in my voice was unmistakable. But he smiled, put his hand over his heart and said in English, "T'ank you."

"It's '*thhhh*ank you,'" I corrected. "Put your tongue under your teeth. Thhhhh."

"Thhhhhh—ank. Thhhhhh—ank. Thank. Thank." On the final repetition, he plugged his nose to convert his British accent into an American one.

"*Perfetto,*" I said.

"Thank you," Luigi answered. He let go of his nose and switched back to Italian. "It is difficult, you know. Almost as difficult as another small word…oh, how do you say it?"

"The?" I suggested.

"Exactly. A short word, but difficult," Luigi agreed.

"At least English only has 'the' instead of eight or nine words that mean the same thing. Sometimes my mother only knows that she has chosen the wrong one when she reaches the end of the noun."

"And you? I have not heard a mistake from you."

"I have been speaking Italian as long as you. It is automatic. But German! *Ai, ai, ai.*"

"*Der, die, das, und den.*" Luigi listed some of the German translations for "the" using the voice of Professorin Schneider.

"Irene. Luigi," the *mister* interrupted. The nearness and

unexpectedness of his voice at my back made me jump. "Before the others arrive, both of you can take turns in the goal."

I swallowed a protest and coughed.

"What is it, Irene?" the *mister* asked.

"Nothing. But I have not played goalkeeper for many years—since the fourth class."

"Don't worry yourself. A goalie without much experience is better than an empty net, no?"

No. At least not if I had to be the goalie, allowing ball after ball to rocket past me with Nonno watching and Matteo due to show up at any minute.

"Luigi, give Irene your gloves," the *mister* said, not waiting for me to disagree.

Luigi peeled them off and handed them to me. I pulled them on and flexed my fingers. Their dry warmth felt good.

It occurred to me as I trotted across the field that I had played keeper at Giulia's house ten days ago in a game of two-on-two against Emi and one of their neighbors. But it was different on an official pitch with a regulation net behind me.

Luigi dribbled the ball out to the centerline. Then he started forward with a smooth, steady acceleration. Fast, but in control. If I stayed in the net, he could put the ball any-where he wanted. So I raced out to meet him.

I positioned myself in front of Luigi. My arms stretched out a few inches from my sides, palms facing forward. I shuf-fled to the right as he changed direction. Ready... Ready.

My left leg shot out in time to nick the ball. It changed direction. But Luigi followed it and buried it. The way he grinned reminded me of Max's *mister* kicking the ball to Angelica.

Calcio al'angolo: Corner Kick

Where a good keeper would have caught more of Luigi's shots and pulled them into her body, I felt lucky to punch them up and over the net with my closed fist or slap them wide where Luigi couldn't get an easy rebound.

My brother's group finished their penalty shots and streamed past me on their way to the clubhouse.

"It's not fair," I heard Max complain to one of his teammates as they passed behind the net. "The *mister* is in love with Angelica. He always passes her the ball and lets her play *attaco.*"

"It is too fair," I told Max in English. "Angelica is a good forward who stays in her position. She doesn't play herd ball like a brother of mine."

"What has your sister said?" Max's teammate asked.

"Um, she does not agree," Max said in Italian.

"*Brutta strega.* She gives ideas to Angelica. Can't you make her quit?"

"No one can. Not even my *nonna.*"

"*Uaou.* Too bad."

A flash of movement caught my eye. I turned my attention back to the field. Luigi, who had brought the ball out to the centerline again, had begun his charge to the goal. He put another one past me, but it hit the crossbeam and bounced back out. I flung myself forward just as Luigi arrived and brought his foot back in preparation for another try. I had an airborne view of a black leather cleat with gold and white stripes on a collision course with my face. Luigi hesitated. I fell on the ball and tucked my chin into my chest.

"*Dai,* Luigi!" the *mister* roared. "Irene is not made of porcelain."

A compliment? I raised my head.

"I'm so sorry, Irene," Luigi murmured. "The next time I will smash you. Ready to change?"

"Almost. Two more times." I didn't want my last memory to be Luigi's shoe headed toward my face.

Still, it was a relief to leave the net. I attacked Luigi from a half a dozen different ways: long shots, short shots, left-footed, right-footed, from the right, from the left. The second time he left the net to challenge me I chipped the ball over his head in a lazy floater that drifted two feet over his out-stretched arms. It bounced toward the net. Luigi pelted after it, but lost the race to the white line.

"*Brava,* Irene!" boomed a voice from the stands.

"Who cheers for you, Irene?" Luigi squinted at the line of three—no, four—umbrellas. Max must have joined them.

"My *nonno.*"

"He lives here?"

"No. Milano. He is staying with us for a few days."

"Ah. That is why I have not seen..." Luigi paused. "...or heard him before this."

Luigi stayed in front of the net when Davide and Werner arrived. When he deflected one off to the sidelines, I chased after it.

"*Ehi!*" I called. "Davide, Werner! Corner kick."

They took up positions in the box while I dribbled the ball down to the orange flag marking the corner of the field. I set the ball down and took a deep breath.

Whump! I sent the ball sailing across the field. High enough to make it over any imaginary defender. Low enough that Davide or Werner would have a chance to make a play on the downward arc. Far enough away from the goal so that

Calcio al'angolo: Corner Kick

Luigi could not make a play on the ball. Close enough that he would not have much time to react. In short: perfect.

Davide shuffled his feet to get in position. He snapped his head forward and connected with the ball right at his hairline. Luigi didn't have a chance.

"*Brava! Bravi!*" my *nonno* roared, his first cheer for me and the second for Davide and me.

Davide glanced at the stands. Luigi said something. Werner and Davide nodded. I hunched my shoulders. I couldn't expect Nonno to watch us in silence. He always yelled at the players, officials, and announcers when we watched soccer on TV.

Luigi punted the ball back to me. "Another."

My next one was not so pretty. But it was a decent crossing pass—a challenge to Luigi. More players arrived: Giuseppe, Federico, Emi, and Manuel. But the *mister* did not hand out any more balls. Instead, he filled the penalty area with people.

Three or four minutes later, Emi dribbled the ball toward me. I knew what he wanted. Corner kicks were usually his job.

"My turn," he said, smiling.

I shrugged and said lightly, "You're the expert."

He lowered his voice. "*Dai,* Irene. With such trees as Manuel and Werner in the box, I am too short for this. You have a better chance to make a goal than I do. Please?"

"Certainly. Send the ball my way a few times."

So I joined the jostling crowd in the box. Emi lofted ball after ball into the penalty area. Finally, a good one came my way. I tensed my muscles and shuffled my feet to get under it.

I jumped, bringing my head and shoulders forward. But as I hit the ball, something hit me. I lost all sense of where the ground was until it reached up to smack me.

My eyes squeezed shut on impact and stayed shut as I mentally checked to make sure my arms, legs and head were all still connected to my body.

"Foul," someone said.

"*Gelbe Karte,*" Werner muttered in German. I recognized the words from my remedial German class. *Gelbe* was yellow. What was *Karte*? Map? Yes, but it could mean card too. Yellow card? Any player who received one from the official was one flagrant foul away from being ejected from the game. My eyes popped open.

Matteo lay on the ground a few feet away from me. He pushed himself up onto his elbows. "I'm sorry, Irene. I was watching the ball."

"It's nothing," I said, even though I didn't believe that he was A) watching the ball or B) sorry.

"Irene is not made of porcelain, you know," Luigi said from his place in the circle of faces staring down at us. He twitched his eyebrows at me and held out his hand. I let him hoist me to my feet.

The *mister* pushed through the crowd. "All right," he said briskly. "A penalty kick for Irene and then we start."

He motioned Luigi toward the goal and arranged the ball on the penalty spot. As I stepped back, everyone else moved out of my way.

I leaned my weight on my back foot, hesitating, trying not to overthink the play. Luigi waited for me, his feet a little over shoulder-width apart, his arms spread for balance.

I ran forward, fists clenched. My body tilted to the right.

Calcio al'angolo: Corner Kick

My left foot, my kicking foot, came back and swung forward. I connected with my laces and instep, coming in under the ball to give it some lift. But not too much. I followed through, landing on my kicking foot. The ball curved toward the upper-left corner of the net.

No pole. No crosspiece, I begged silently. Then I revised my plea. Either would be better than catching empty air. Luigi lunged and then—

"*Goal! Perfetto! Bravissima!*" roared my newest, loudest, and maybe even my biggest fan.

A few of the latecomers' heads turned in surprise. A quiet mumble let them know whose relative was so strange as to cheer at a practice.

Instead of running, we started on a series of drills: dribbling, juggling, passing, shooting. Anyone not working hard enough to suit the *mister* was sent off to do three or four laps.

When we took our usual break, three umbrellas followed us in the direction of the clubhouse. A fourth stayed in the bleachers. My *nonno* had decided not to go home. Throughout the scrimmage that followed, he cheered for us all: a breakaway by Matteo, a beautiful save by Luigi, a header by Davide, a sliding tackle from Werner, a corner kick by Emi.

Afterwards, Nonno limped stiffly toward me with his arms outstretched and a closed umbrella in one hand. "*Brava! Bravissima!* I have never seen a *ragazza* like you on the field. Never. *Complimenti!*"

"No one plays like our Irene," Matteo said. He sounded sincere—almost proud. What was going on? Had our collision knocked some sense into Matteo's head?

Nonno beamed. "With such a team, it does not surprise me that you have not lost a game yet. *Bravi,* both of you."

Matteo ducked his head, waved his hand, and walked on.

Nonno turned back to me. "I have heard good things about the American women. Listen, you have dual citizenship. You can play soccer for America, and in the off-season you can be a model for Versace? Would that please you?"

I rolled my eyes. "Oh, sure. Or else I will have my own line of clothing."

"Even better. But truly, you are a *brava calciatore. Calciatrice,* I mean. Your *nonna* thought so too."

"Really?"

"*Mamma mia. Mamma mia.*" She said it many times. Nonno chuckled.

There was no doubt that my performance had made an impression on Nonna, but I suspected that she was more horrified than proud. I could just imagine our next private conversation.

14
Calciatrice
(cal-cha-TREE-chay)
Female Soccer Player

Do you have much homework today, *cara?*" Nonna asked when I came home from school on Tuesday. "Not too much," I said.

"Very well. Your *mamma* and I saw such darling clothes this morning. Let's go into the center to shop."

"In the rain?"

"It is no more than a mist. *Dai*, Irene, you played at soccer for ninety minutes in worse weather, true?" She tilted her head and raised her eyebrows.

"Uh, true. What about Max and Nonno?"

She sniffed. "They do not have enough patience to stand around in a store while you try on clothes. Besides, I leave tomorrow and I have not yet heard about your school and your friends."

Of course she hadn't. I had successfully avoided being alone with Nonna since Saturday afternoon. This time no little voice screeched that this was another trap. It only whispered, "Bribe."

"Please, Irene. Come with me, and we will eat ice cream." Nonna blinked twice and peered at me over her glasses.

That was all it took.

"Oh, Nonna, that's not necessary," I said quickly. "I'll go voluntarily—if Mamma says it's all right."

"*Va bene.* Ask her."

I did.

"Of course, you can go." Mom answered. "But if you don't want to…"

"No, I do," I said.

Mom nodded. "Good girl. I think your *nonna* wants to buy you a present to apologize. I'll move dinner back an hour. I imagine ice cream is on her agenda."

A fifteen-minute walk took Nonna and me to the Via Portici, a seven-hundred-year-old street that looked like something out of *The Sound of Music.* The stucco buildings, orange tiled roofs, shuttered windows, and iron signs all reflected the town's long Tyrolean history. But once we slipped into the sheltered portico, things around us were more varied: up-to-the-minute styles from Milan were featured next door to shops with the traditional clothes—loden cloaks, boiled wool jackets, dirndls, and lederhosen. A pizzeria shared a wall with a restaurant featuring the local specialties: *Spätzle, Speck,* and *Schlutzkrapfen.* Little dumplings, bacon, and ravioli filled with spinach and cheese.

The clerks all recognized Nonna as she sailed in through the door. They addressed her as *signora,* effortlessly using the formal language that I was struggling with in school. They produced the items that she had left behind the counter earlier in the day. Everything was exactly my color. Everything fit perfectly. Everything was very, very expensive.

"Thank you, Nonna. Um, have we finished?" I asked a little nervously after we left the fourth store with yet another bag.

Calciatrice: Female Soccer Player

"Don't worry yourself. Your *mamma* saw everything this morning."

"But she probably didn't think that you were going to buy it all," I said.

Nonna laughed. "Ah, but your *nonno* wants his favorite *calciatrice* to be well-dressed. And I agree. Shall we go? We go," she concluded, answering her own question.

When we finished with the last shop on the end of the Via Portici, I told Nonna about the best ice cream place in town. She seemed interested until she discovered that we would have to order cones from the counter.

"Today, no," she insisted. "We'll find a place more elegant."

So a few minutes later, I found myself sitting on a padded wicker chair protected from the rain by a green and white striped awning. The restaurant was right on the *passegiata,* a wide walkway running along the top of the twenty-foot-high embankment that protected Merano from the waters of the Passirio. The first time I'd seen the river, it was clear and no more than two feet deep. Today, it was a rushing brown torrent.

Nonna bent over the menu and pointed out desserts to me. Each seemed to have at least five or six scoops of ice cream and masses of whipped cream. "You can eat them without trouble. You are almost too thin. Soccer helps you stay in shape, no?" She sighed and shook her head. "At least I understand why you cannot quit soccer now."

"Really?"

"The goalkeeper—he is called Luigi, no?"

"*Sí,*" I said, puzzled.

Nonna patted my arm. "You have a weakness for him, I think."

"*What?*"

"You have fallen in love with him," Nonna explained, as if I didn't understand the Italian phrase.

I stared at her. What could my sharp-eyed grandmother have seen yesterday to give her such an idea? Luigi almost kicking me in the face, blocking over eighty percent of my shots on the goal, helping me to my feet...? No. This was all Max's fault. He had put the idea into her head.

"I suppose that you want to be near him," she continued. "He will only think of you as a good friend. A *calciatrice*. Or worse, a *calciatore*. But maybe that is better. You are too young to become serious."

"Nonna, I have not fallen in love with Luigi."

"As you wish, *cara.*" Her eyes gleamed. She obviously did not want to believe me.

The next morning, I told Giulia about the new theory of my *nonna* while we stood in the courtyard before school started. She laughed so hard she nearly dropped her umbrella.

Barbara, who had been skimming my homework for spelling errors, looked up. "*Tranne* has two *n*'s, not one," she told me, pointing to the Italian word for "except." "What is so funny?"

"Nothing." I took my paper from Barbara and corrected the word while Giulia continued to laugh.

"What?" Barbara asked, looking from Giulia to me and back again. "What have I missed?"

"Irene is only playing soccer because she loves Luigi," Giulia whispered.

Barbara blinked. "Really?"

"No! Absolutely not!" I glared at Giulia. "My *nonna* thinks so."

"Why?" Barbara asked.

"It my brother's fault," I grumbled. "He told her how we play soccer together before the others arrive."

Giulia snorted. "The *nonna* prefers that her granddaughter be a *ragazza romantica* instead of a *maschiaccio.*"

Barbara shrugged. "Makes sense to me. I meant from the point of view of your *nonna,* Irene. But it is funny. Luigi will laugh."

"No!" Giulia cut in before I could. "Do not tell Luigi!"

"Why not?" Barbara asked. "It's a beautiful joke."

"Playing soccer is already difficult enough," I said. "Believe me, Barbara. It's not a good idea."

"Irene is right," Giulia said, her voice serious. "Leave it, Barbara."

Barbara stuck out her lower lip. "*Ma dai!* Both of you. So. Why do you play soccer, Irene? Why not play volleyball with us?"

"*Ciao,* Irene," a voice cut in.

"*Ciao,*" I said instinctively. A heartbeat later, I realized who had spoken.

"*Ciao,* Giulia. Barbara," Matteo continued. Tiny droplets of rain shimmered in his black curly hair.

"*Ciao,*" Barbara said. Giulia pressed her lips together and crossed her arms.

"Soccer pleases your *nonno* very much, Irene," Matteo observed.

"True," I said and waited.

"My *nonno* was like that too. He died last year."

I wasn't prepared for that. "Oh, I'm sorry." I said.

"Me too." He lifted his chin. His blue eyes stared into mine. "But I was glad to think of him yesterday. Thank you."

I blinked. "It was nothing."

"Thank you just the same. Well, I must find Gianlucca before school begins. We'll see each other later, Irene. *Ciao,* Barbara. Giulia."

"*Ciao,*" Barbara echoed.

Neither Giulia nor I answered. I was too shocked by this sudden outburst of friendliness, and, judging by her narrowed eyes and tight lips, Giulia was too suspicious.

"Ohhhh," Barbara sighed once Matteo disappeared into the crowd. "So open. So sad. So *bello.*"

Giulia pulled down on her eyelid with her pointer finger, a gesture that meant sneaky, clever, *furbo.* "I don't trust him," she said.

"I don't either," I said. But I wanted to.

"He seemed so sincere," Barbara protested. "Remember how—"

"Ha," Giulia said. "He only pretends. I know him. Enough."

Barbara shrugged. "All right. What were we talking about?"

"How many *n*'s there are in *tranne,*" I said.

"*Sí,*" Barbara said. "And one other thing. But…we'll leave it."

Instead of "it," did she mean "him"? In Italian, the pronoun could mean either one. Barbara's eyes gleamed in an echo of my *nonna*'s expression. She didn't believe me either.

Calciatrice: Female Soccer Player

What did they think I saw in Luigi? I wondered as I sat next to him on the team van on the way to Bolzano the following Saturday. I studied his face as he told me the strengths and weaknesses of our next opponents. Luigi had a strong chin, but an equally strong nose. His light brown eyes had a slightly darker band of brown around the iris. His black eyebrows were in danger of growing together someday. His teeth were even and relatively straight without the artificial perfection a few years with braces would...

"What are you looking at? Is there something in my teeth?" Luigi asked. He ran his tongue back and forth a few times, curled back his lip, and asked, "Better?"

"Oh, *sì.*"

"All right. What was I talking about?"

"The team from Bolzano?" I said, hoping he hadn't switched topics.

"Exactly. I told you about Antonio Russo? How he is left-footed?"

I nodded. The name did sound familiar.

"You must stay attentive. Of course, it is possible that the *mister* will put you on the other wing. Russo is very danger-ous. Very. Very."

"Okay."

"Russo?" Davide cut in from Luigi's other side. "He scored three goals against us last spring."

"Three?" I said. "No one has made that many goals against us all year."

"Eduardo Gozzi was our goalkeeper in that game," Luigi said. "I was sick."

"I don't know him. Did he quit?" I asked.

"No. He plays with the *Giovanissimi* this year. He is too old for the *Esordienti.*"

"So players change levels depending on their age here?"

"Age and ability," Luigi said. "For example, Federico came up early this fall. The *mister* will ask for a few more *pulcini* in the spring. Then a big group will come up next fall."

Luigi's explanation of the system made me think of just how strange the names for the various Italian soccer categories were. We were part of the *Esordienti,* the beginners. Even though the *Giovanissimi* were older than we were, their name meant "the youngest." But the *Pulcini* had it worst of all. They were the freshly hatched chickens, the "chicks."

"Do you think that Russo still plays for Bolzano?" Davide asked.

"I'm certain. The *mister* has heard stories."

"Tell me," Davide said.

Luigi never needed a second invitation to talk. In other parts of the van, similar conversations were going on. I could feel the energy, the bottled excitement.

Outside, it was dreary. The light rain continued. Volvos, BMWs, Audis, and the occasional Mercedes Benz blew past us, sending fine bursts of spray across the windshield of the van. Low clouds still hung over the valley. The long rows of apple trees on either side of the *autostrada* faded into the mist.

Visibility didn't improve when we reached Bolzano. I knew from an earlier trip that the Castel Marreccio—Schloss Maretch to the German speakers—was just a few hundred yards away. If it was clear, would the orange tile roofs of its towers be visible through the trees? I couldn't remember.

The Talvera River roared past us. The grassy playing fields

were in no danger. Not yet. But if the rain continued for another week, that could change.

As usual, I watched the opening kickoff from the sidelines. Matteo tapped the ball to Emi and both of them surged forward into a sea of yellow and white uniforms. Even without Luigi's warning, I would have known to study Russo. Like Matteo, he was a player who drew the eye. When the *mister* put me in during the second period, I knew that I wouldn't be able to stop him. My job would be to get between him and the goal, slow him down, and wait for reinforcements. If I played him too closely, he would be able to throw me off-balance with one of his beautiful fakes just as he had with Manuel, Werner, and Davide.

Our teams were evenly matched: both of us were still undefeated. I could sense Bolzano's growing frustration on the field as the score stayed zero to zero. Luigi had said in the van that our opponents were used to getting an early lead and then holding it. There was some bumping going on—some words being exchanged. But then a player deliberately smashed into Davide just as he was coming down from a header, "making the bridge." Davide skidded a few inches on the wet grass before hitting the ground hard.

The *mister* shouted—a wordless cry of outrage. My dad, our one fan who came to all the games, echoed it.

Davide sat up, tried to stand, and then fell back with a stifled cry, clutching his ankle. The *mister* handed me his purple and green linesman's flag and trotted onto the field.

The referee reached into his pocket, pulled out a yellow card, and held it over his head. It was the first I'd seen since I'd left the U.S.

Defending Irene

Roberto, the other substitute who stood a few feet away from me, shook his head. "Davide is not an actor. He is not pretending."

The player who committed the foul stepped forward and opened his mouth. Two of his teammates dragged him back, muttering in his ear. No doubt reminding him what a red card would mean—his removal from this game, leaving his team a player short.

Davide continued to lie on the wet ground. The *mister* knelt beside him, talking quietly. Finally, Davide nodded and sat up. At a motion from the *mister*, Matteo and Gianlucca stepped forward to lift him up under his armpits. With their help, Davide hopped over to the sidelines. Roberto hovered by the white line, waiting to go into the game. But the *mister* had a different idea.

"Gianlucca, play midfield. Irene, take the spot of Gianlucca on attack."

Attack? Me? The last time I'd played forward was back in the U.S.

Squerch. Squerch. Squerch. I trotted through the soggy grass onto the field and joined players from both squads in the penalty area.

Werner stepped up to the ball. It was a direct kick, but he was so far away from the goal that it was unlikely that he could put it in. He could, however, loft the ball into the penalty area. I was taller than Roberto. Was that why the *mister* had put me in?

The ball didn't come anywhere near me then or for the next few minutes. Then Gianlucca passed me the ball. I turned upfield.

From the defender's smile, anyone would think that he

116

had already stolen the ball from me and sent it sailing down toward Luigi. He closed rapidly. Too rapidly. He had too much forward momentum to stop himself when I kicked the ball past him down the sidelines to the empty corner. Full of energy from all the time on the bench, I caught up with it.

"Center it! Center it!" the *mister* yelled. "Pass, pass, pass!"

I sent a line drive of a kick into the penalty box. Without waiting to see how Matteo would handle it, I raced to the box myself. An assist. Maybe I would get an assist. My first since I'd left Missouri.

Matteo's shot sliced through the air toward the goal. The keeper dove with both hands extended and deflected the ball right to me. He hit the ground and rolled to his feet. But he didn't have time to fully extend his body before I smashed the ball over his head, just a foot or so below the crossbar. Not an assist. A goal!

"Yes! Yes!" I shouted in English. With my fists raised over my head, I sprinted back to midfield.

"*Bravo,* Irene!" the *mister* roared. "*Brava!*" he corrected himself. But the damage was done. For a moment, I was a full-fledged member of the team. Not the *ragazza.* Not the *calciatrice.* A player.

Luigi waved wildly from the goal and gave me two thumbs up. Manuel thumped me on the back. Werner hugged me. Then he stepped back, but kept his hands on my shoulders. "I understand now," he said. "You are not a defender. You are an attacker. You have always been an attacker."

"Not always."

"Oh, you also played midfielder in the United States, too." He shook his head. "Come, Manuel. We go on defense."

"Without a doubt, I'll join you in the second half. It was a trick of the *mister,*" I said.

A trick that had worked really well. The other team looked bewildered. The defender, whose lack of respect for me had made the play possible, stood slump-shouldered in the corner while his coach yelled.

I ran to my spot near the centerline. Some of my teammates waited there to give me five: Gianlucca, Emi, and Matteo.

But instead of a passing slap, Matteo's fingers wrapped around my hand. Our thumbs entwined. "Let's do it again," he said.

"Okay," I said.

But the Bolzano goalkeeper wasn't quite in on our plan. Instead of deflecting Matteo's next shot, he let it go past him without even putting a fingertip on the ball.

As I predicted, when the third period started, I returned to my spot on the defense, replacing Giuseppe. While Luigi finally let one of Russo's blistering shots past him, midway through the third period, we held on to win 2–1.

A goal. I had scored a goal. In the U.S., that had been an exciting but fairly regular event. Here, it was just short of a miracle. And Matteo had spoken to me like I was one of his teammates. Had I finally earned his respect? I didn't need all of the reindeer to love me. I only wanted them to let me join in some of those reindeer games without being called a *cucciola.*

15
Furbo (FOOR-bo)
Tricky

I stood alone in the school courtyard, studying the strange behaviors of irregular German verbs for the afternoon remedial class I attended twice a week. At the bottom of the list, I had written a quote from Professorin Schneider: "German is a very logical language." My mother would probably agree with that, but the eight of us who had to struggle with things like strong and weak verbs did not.

"*Ciao,* Irene," Matteo said. "How's it going?"

"Fine. And you?"

"Well enough. But I'm so tired of the rain."

"Me too."

"And now there isn't soccer today," he grumbled.

"Really?"

"Signora Martelli has not called you yet?"

I shook my head. "No."

"She said that it's too wet—that we would destroy the field. Can you believe it?"

That made sense. The ground probably couldn't absorb another drop. I remembered the skid marks that our feet had already made in the field. And yet....

"No. You do not believe me. I understand." The right

corner of Matteo's mouth twisted. He scanned the courtyard and then shouted, "*Ehi,* Nicolo!"

Nicolo Montegna, the forward from the other Merano team who had run me over on the first day of practice, turned around. "What?"

"We'll beat you at soccer today."

"Today, no. Soccer is cancelled. Hadn't you heard?"

"Oh, thanks. Wait for Thursday then."

Matteo turned back to me. "There," he said. "A message probably waits on your answering machine. So, what are you studying? German?" He peered at my notebook.

"It's difficult," I said. "Everyone knows more than I do."

"Patience. It takes time. Everything takes time."

Including Matteo's acceptance of me as a teammate? It seemed that way. But things between us seemed to be improving just a little.

I had trouble keeping my mind on German that afternoon, even though Professorin Schneider spoke much more slowly and simply in our class than she did in my regular one. We took notes, played games, and read simple stories. Or at least the other students did. I only managed to pick out a few simple words: and, but, is, you, they, then.

We broke up into groups of two to talk about our families. For the other kids it was a review. I had to have notes in front of me. I sat across from Wei, whose family owned one of the Chinese restaurants in town. She spoke slowly, using easy German words, so I would be sure to understand.

"My grandmother lives in China. She calls herself Wu

Anling. My grandfather lives in China. He calls himself Wu Shilong. My aunt and uncle live here in Merano. My cousin calls himself Maurizio. He is Italian."

"Oh, is your aunt Italian?" I asked.

"No."

"Your uncle?"

"No." Her eyes sparkled.

"I do not understand."

"Maurizio is born here. He speaks Italian perfectly. He says, 'I am not Chinese. I am Italian.'" She giggled.

"*Interessant,*" I said. It was a surprisingly long word for my limited Germany vocabulary, but it was one of my mother's favorites.

Professorin Schneider clapped her hands and said something. I managed to recognize the words for "minute" and "write" as she waved her hands at the clock and the white board. It was clear what she wanted. We had another set of strong verb conjugations to copy.

The bell rang before I finished, but for once there was no need for me to scribble frantically, toss things into my backpack, and hurtle out the door. There was no soccer practice today. I had plenty of time.

As I walked down the hall a few minutes later, a voice said, "*Buona sera.*" Professoressa Trevisani, my Italian teacher, stood in the door to her classroom, holding a wooden recorder in one hand and a folder full of music in the other. In the cold, wet weather even she had switched over to jeans and her eye makeup was much simpler.

"*Buona sera,*" I said.

"So, Irene," she asked. "You have almost finished your first month with us. How goes it?"

"Very well," I said. "I must study a lot, of course. It isn't easy."

"You have impressed me. You even know some words that many of your classmates do not. For example, you gave me the best definition for irony yesterday."

"There is a similar word in English," I said. "I guessed that they were about the same."

"Mmmm. That makes sense. And your other classes?"

"Well, math is math," I began, shrugging. "But—"

Just then, Professorin Schneider stepped out of her room and closed the door behind her.

"Ah!" Professoressa Trevisani said. "The proper person to ask about your progress in German. Tell me, Professorin, how is Irene doing?"

"Very well. Very, very well. Her pronunciation and accent are very good. Her homework is correct much of the time."

"Um, my mother helps me a bit," I admitted. "In the United States, she teaches German at the high school."

Professorin Schneider touched her hand to her stomach. "Ah, then you heard the language before you were born. That explains much. Listen, Irene. Some friends and I have started a book club. Would it please your mother to join us? Or perhaps our opinions would not interest her."

"No. Please. It would interest her very much," I said quickly before my teacher could take back the invitation. I had never thought of my mom as shy, but I knew that she had been lurking in cafés taking notes on the Tyrolean dialect instead of actually talking to people. Since we went to Italian schools, she was finding it more difficult to meet people from the German half of the population.

I reached into my backpack, tore a piece of paper out of

my notebook and scribbled down our number and my mother's name. "Please call her. For my mother, it would be a pleasure."

Two minutes later, I bounced out of the sheltered courtyard of the school onto the sidewalk along Via Roma. I had done a good deed for the day. My teachers thought I was doing well. There was no need to race home and choke down a snack before spending a wet ninety minutes on the pitch.

I recognized Luigi through the scratched plastic of the bus stop's shelter and knocked. "*Ciao,*" I said.

"Hello, Irene. How are you?" he asked in English—an English with long, pure vowels, strong diphthongs, rolling *r*'s and a slight British accent.

"Fine," I said.

"Tomorrow will be a nice day," he continued in English.

"Really? Will the rain stop?" I replied, putting small spaces between each word so that he could follow me better.

"Stahp?" Luigi repeated.

"*Stop,*" I said, giving the word its Italian pronunciation. I waved toward the red and white traffic sign on a nearby corner.

"Ah. I understand. No. The rain will stahp never."

I giggled. "We say 'never stop' in America. Are you waiting for a bus?"

Luigi considered my question a moment before answering. "No. I wait my father. He brings me to—how do you say it...?"

"Home?"

"No. There is a word in German. Ah, yes. Football. He brings me to football."

"Football? You mean soccer? *Calcio?*"

Defending Irene

"*Sí, calcio.*" Luigi slid back into Italian. "Have you forgotten today is Monday?"

"But Matteo and Montegna said—" I stopped myself.

"The Passirio would have to run over its banks and through the practice field before our *mister* would cancel. We play upon the carpet today." Luigi stopped and frowned. "What have Matteo and Montegna said?"

Telling the coach's son was a lot like telling the coach.

"Nothing." I backed away. "I've got to go. Don't want to be late. We'll see each other in a bit. *Ciao,* Luigi. *Ciao.*"

It would have been much more dignified to wait until I had turned the corner before launching into a trot. But I didn't have time for dignity. I tightened my grip on the strap to my backpack to keep it from bouncing against me.

Stupid, stupid, stupid. How could I have been so stupid? I had never expected a romantic ending to my troubles with Matteo: my Miss Elizabeth Bennet to his Mr. Darcy, my Meg Ryan to his Tom Hanks. His friendly words to my *nonno,* his sad words about his *nonno,* the high five after my goal—they were all just part of his plan to gain my trust. Not that he had. Not quite. I wouldn't have believed him except for Montegna. And why did I believe Montegna? Because I was stupid. Stupid, stupid, stupid.

The chorus repeated itself as I jogged three blocks uphill past hundred-year-old houses and fences covered in ivy. My calves burned. My shins vibrated every time my thick-soled boots hit the pavement. But when I reached the final—and thankfully flat—two blocks leading to my house, I accelerated into a run.

When I reached our gate, I leaned hard on the buzzer.

"*Sí?*" Mom asked an eternity later.

"It's me. I'm late for soccer!" I yelled.

Without a word, she buzzed me through the gate. Another long buzz was waiting for me when I made it down the flag-stone walk. I plowed into the massive door with my right shoulder and made it up a flight of stairs before it slammed shut behind me with an echoing boom. I cringed. The family on the ground floor had a new baby who liked late afternoon naps.

The door leading to our apartment stood open. I kicked off my shoes and dumped my backpack on the floor. My jacket followed.

Mom came out of the study with my practice T-shirt in one hand and blue shorts in the other. "They're a little damp," she apologized. "I put them on the drying rack first thing this morning. It's so wet in here, but it's against the law to turn on the heat until next week."

"That's okay. They'll be soaked soon anyway." I snatched them out of her hand and raced down the hallway to my room.

Mom's voice followed me. "I would have put them by the electric heater, but Max's practice was cancelled."

"Didn't you just say we can't turn on the heat?" I shouted through the closed door.

"They don't use infrared goggles to check up on people, but smoke from the chimney would be a dead giveaway."

I finger-combed my hair into a ponytail and wound a black rubber band around it to hold it in place. When I came out, Max was standing in the hallway with his arms crossed, glaring up at Mom.

"Can't I stay here by myself while you take Irene to soccer?" he asked.

"No," she said.

"Why not? You let Irene do it all the time."

"Irene has six more years than you."

"Irene *is* six years older than me," Max corrected.

"You know what I meant. Find your shoes." Mom's eyes flicked up in the direction of the hall light. "All this Italian is affecting my English."

With the rain, the streets were empty of pedestrians and cyclists, but full of cars. There were long lines at all of the traffic circles as cars waited for their turn to enter. We finally reached the bridge over the Passirio.

"*Uaou!*" Max said. "Look at the water!"

The river was the highest I had ever seen. It had climbed halfway up the stone retaining wall. The muddy water with its flecks of dirty foam battered the willow trees that grew along the banks. I could hear its roar through the closed windows and over the hum of the engine.

I offered to jump out and run the rest of the way along the river walk. Mom shook her head.

"Be patient. I want to make sure that you have practice. What if the fields are flooded?"

So we moved in a slow line toward Piazza Mazzini's traffic circle. We waited for the commuter train to clatter by.

When we finally arrived, I peered over the fence. Only eight players shared two balls. It looked like Montegna, at least, had told the truth. His team didn't have practice. But mine did. I ran down to the field. The squeaky hinges of the chain link door complained.

The *mister* turned to look at me.

"Welcome, Irene. Luigi told me you would be late."

"I'm sorry," I said.

The *mister* waited, as if expecting an explanation. When I didn't provide one, he shrugged his shoulders and motioned for me to join the others.

Squerch. Squerch. Squerch. A thin layer of water lay on the springy, pale green carpet. My socks were dry now, but not for long.

Giuseppe tapped Matteo's shoulder and whispered in his ear. Matteo's head snapped around to look at me. I stared back at him.

He smiled and waved. And then he did the unthinkable: he passed me the ball.

I ran forward to meet it and slammed it into the empty goal. For a moment, I was confused. Could I have imagined the conversation between Matteo, Montegna, and me? Could I have misinterpreted it somehow?

No.

But the passes continued and the compliments started.

"*Brava,* Irene!"

"*Bravissima!*"

Anyone else—the *mister,* for example—might believe that Matteo had finally accepted me as a teammate. But to me, each pass and every enthusiastic word seemed to say: "Ha! I caught you! Are you stupid enough to step into my trap a second time?"

Drill followed drill. We concentrated on shooting and passing and moving. It was a good thing that the *mister* didn't allow chatting in line. I would have snarled at anyone who spoke to me.

During the break, I didn't feel like joining the crowd making a break for the bathrooms and drink bottles. I wasn't thirsty. Instead, I circled the field by myself, chilled and hot at the same time. When everyone came back, I joined them at the center line.

Trickles of water ran down the *mister*'s face. "Today is a beautiful day for soccer." He grinned. "But every day is a beautiful day for soccer. All right, we have only ten today."

"Nine," Matteo cut in.

"Ten." The *mister* touched his open palm to his collarbone, indicating that he was joining the game. "So we are like Garibaldi conquering Italy. Without a plan. Without organization. Let me see. Emi and Matteo: goalkeepers. There and there. Manuel and Irene are attackers. Gianlucca and Roberto, you defend." He motioned the four of us to the side in front of Matteo. "Werner and Luigi, you attack. Federico and I will defend... No midfielders today. Let's go."

Everyone was switched around from their normal positions: attackers in the goal, midfielders and the *mister* on defense, and defenders attacking. Everyone was getting a new perspective on the field. Except for me. I was back in my old familiar territory. It felt right to see the field from my old perspective as Manuel and I kicked off.

Fortunately, Matteo's position in the goal put him as far away from me as possible. But each moment of accomplishment—scoring a goal, making an assist, and once even faking out the *mister*—was ruined by Matteo's phony applause.

The wind picked up. It would have sent my hair and shirt fluttering if the rain hadn't already plastered them down. And then it started to pour so hard that I couldn't see Matteo on the other side of the field. A definite improvement.

"Enough!" the *mister* bellowed finally. "Let's go! No penalty shots today!"

Players cheered this announcement. The *mister* was first to the gate. After he pushed it open, he stood there counting players as we went by.

Once I reached the sheltered overhang of the clubhouse, I stopped to wring out my hair and wait for Matteo. I confronted him as he came up the steps. Federico, his shadow, was right behind him.

"You lied to me," I said.

"*Ma dai!* Maybe the *Americana* doesn't understand Italian as well as she thinks."

"Ha! I've been speaking it just as long as you. Probably longer, *ciuccio.*"

"Ooh," Matteo said with a smirk. But I could tell that the babyish nickname had gotten to him.

"Why did you lie to me?"

His mask dropped. "Do you know what others call us? The *ragazze.* The females. That is not right. It's all your fault."

"What did you used to be called: the team of Matteo? Of course you prefer that. You are so full of yourself."

"You are a *maschiaccio* who is too stupid to know when to leave. You ruin the game."

"Why is it so horrible that I play?"

"Girls should not play soccer."

"Women fill stadiums at their World Cup. Ronaldo's wife played for the club of Perugia."

That stopped Matteo for a moment. Mentioning the great Brazilian player Ronaldo was like invoking a saint. "At least she plays with other women," he said.

"There's no team for girls here," I snapped. "It doesn't please me to play with you either."

"Then quit. When you are there, it's like playing with ten instead of eleven."

"Ha! I scored a goal Saturday."

"Anyone could have scored that goal: your little brother, a baby, or even Federico."

From his position behind Matteo, Federico inhaled sharply.

"I scored a goal today too," I pointed out.

Matteo changed the subject. "Who ruined our vacation from you? Probably Luigi. The *mister* told him to be nice to you."

All the air rushed out of my lungs. "I don't believe you. I will never believe you again. Never."

"Excuse me, Irene," Emi cut in. "I have an important message for you from Giulia. Very important...and private. Come with me."

"In two seconds," I snarled.

"No, now. It's very, very important. Come."

"*Dai,* Irene," Matteo drawled, waving me away as if we were having an unimportant chat about the weather. "I'll go." He headed toward the clubhouse door with a satisfied bounce to his step. Head down, Federico waited five seconds and then followed.

I glared at Emi. "The message?"

"There isn't one. I'm sorry, Irene. But when I heard you screaming at Matteo—"

"I wasn't screaming," I said. But my throat was sore and my voice was shaking. "You came to save me? Next time, protect Matteo."

Emi held up his hand to shield his face. "Okay. Okay. I'm sorry. What happened?"

"Matteo told me that soccer was cancelled."

"You believed him?"

"No. But then Montegna agreed."

Emi's face smoothed out. "Ahh. I understand."

"Then Matteo pretends that nothing happened. He smiles at me, passes me the ball, cheers for me."

Emi nodded. "I saw it. It reminded me of the plan of Matteo to make Giulia quit soccer."

"What?"

"He pretended to be in love with her."

16

Basta! (BAH-stah)
Enough!

I sat in the warm, bright kitchen, twirling spaghetti carbonara around my fork. Yes, warm. Dad had come home with the news that due to the unseasonably cold, wet weather, the province had announced that everyone could go ahead and turn on their heaters.

My feet were dry, but my hair was still wet. Rug burns from the soccer carpet throbbed on my right knee and elbow. I felt tired, too—more tired than after a normal practice. Sure, playing five on five in the rain was tough, but I knew there was more to it than that.

Until a few hours ago, I had almost felt as if I had made a place for myself on the team. But I had been about as successful as a person trying to dig a hole in water. Matteo would never change his mind about me. And Luigi was only being nice to me because his father the *mister* had told him to.

I felt empty inside, but not hungry. The irregular cylinder of pasta I had twisted around my fork was almost two inches in diameter. I slid the noodles off my fork and started twirling them around it again.

"You should have warned me, Irene," Mom said.

I looked up blankly. "What?"

"That you gave my number to Vanessa."

"Who?" I asked. Reality sank in. "Oh, wait a minute. I'm sorry. You mean Professorin Schneider? She called already?"

Mom laughed. "Earth to Irene. What have I been talking about for the last five minutes? Her book club sounds like a fascinating experience. I think it's so admirable the way the Germans are hanging onto their language in the South Tyrol."

Dad snorted. "They are not German. They are Italian. They have been Italian since the end of World War I."

"No, they have lived in Italy. That does not make them Italian. Why shouldn't an oppressed minority hang onto their heritage?"

"Oppressed?" Dad repeated. "Now hold on! Who is oppressing whom in the Alto Adige? Italians who come from outside the province must wait several years before they're allowed to vote. That is the law. That is official. But the unofficial is worse. My new colleague from Torino finds an apartment for sale. He makes an offer. Suddenly, the place is taken off the market. The owners say, 'We have decided not to sell.'"

"Well, that could happen," Mom said.

"*Four* times? The Germans who live here do not want to sell to Italians. It is bad in town, but it is nearly impossible in the mountains. An Italian cannot buy land there. Is this right? Could it happen in America?"

Mom shook her head. "Not unless someone wanted to get slapped with a lawsuit."

I rolled my eyes across the table at Max. Our parents were always getting into political discussions. But Max wasn't paying much attention. He was gulping down pasta two forkfuls at a time.

"And the parents are teaching it to their children," Dad said.

Defending Irene

"Remember what those little boys who threw sand at Max said? *'Geh nach Hause, Italiener. Du kannst mit uns nicht spielen.'*"

The English words flashed across my brain like a subtitle in a movie theater: Go home, Italian. You can't play with us.

"That's awful!" I said. "When did that happen?"

Dad's eyes widened. He looked at Mom and raised one eyebrow.

"Oh, dear. Vanessa did say that Irene's German was really coming along," Mom murmured.

"What? What did the boys say?" Max asked. "Mom wouldn't tell me."

"Never mind," I told him. Max opened his mouth in what was sure to be a protest, so I continued quickly, "Not everyone is like that, you know. Werner is German. He decided to play on an Italian team. Or his parents decided for him. And he's one of the nicest guys there."

"Ooh! Irene plus Werner," Max said.

The pity I'd felt for my little brother only twenty seconds earlier evaporated. "Shut up, Max!"

But Max didn't shut up. "Dad said Werner gave you a hug after you scored that goal. Luigi must be so jealous."

"Stop it!" My voice rose in pitch and volume.

"*Basta!*" Dad said. "Enough, both of you."

"You're out of line, Max," Mom cut in. "And Irene, you're overreacting."

"Me? Haven't you been listening to the little toad?"

Mom held up a hand. "If you can't calm down, Irene, you'll have to clean up the kitchen by yourself."

"Fine! Having Max help in the kitchen is like having no help at all."

"And after you finish, maybe you'd like to go straight to bed?" Mom continued.

"Even better!" I snapped.

"Then we have a plan," Dad said.

I bent down over my plate and plunged my fork into the pile of pasta. That was the end to conversation for the rest of dinner.

Half an hour later, I checked over my work. Wooden floor? Swept. Granite counters? Wiped. Dishwasher? Loaded. Drying rack? Full of pots and pans.

"Hey, it looks great in here," Mom said. She sounded cheerful and slightly apologetic. "Let me finish up, honey. You've got an e-mail in your inbox that you can read before bed."

"Thanks," I said.

"Everything okay?"

"No," I said in a burst of honesty.

"Do you want to talk about it?"

"No."

Mom's eyebrows pulled together. "Maybe tomorrow then."

I sighed. "It'll be okay. I'm just tired."

"If you say so," Mom replied doubtfully. "Get a good night's sleep, honey." Her face looked troubled, but the last thing I needed was her calling the manager or the *mister* in a useless attempt to make soccer a warm and cozy place for me to be.

I went into the study, dropped into the office chair in front of the computer, and clicked open my inbox. A message was waiting for me from Lindy. I smiled. I had sent her some pictures weeks ago from dad's digital camera.

Defending Irene

E-Ray,

Whazzup?

Sorry I didn't write U back sooner. School is 2 D-pressing. Homework takes 4ever. Pre-algebra makes absolutely no sense. I hate the letter x. Y isn't much better.

How R your classes?

Guess what? We made it to the semifinals of a tournament in Columbia even though we were missing our #1 striker. And who would that be? No 1 else but U! Duh. But, hey! I scored a goal. Go me!!!!

Send more pix of Matteo. He is so cute! What's it like playing with him?

Luv ya!

Lindy

What was it like? Ha! The tears that had been threatening for hours spilled over my eyelids. I wanted to retreat to my room with the cordless phone, call Lindy, and tell her everything the way I always used to. But even if Mom and Dad let me make an international phone call, there was a seven-hour time difference between Italy and Missouri.

I shut down the computer and sneaked back to my room so no one would see my red eyes and wet cheeks. I was so tired I went straight to bed, but I was "2 D-pressed" to sleep. A steady rain would have been soothing. The heavy drops that slammed against my window were not. I replayed the scene with Matteo twenty times, some just as it had happened and others with a new script that gave me all the best lines. I finally drifted off sometime after midnight.

The next morning, I woke up before my alarm. Something

was different. Brighter. I turned my head to look out the window. Was that blue sky? I swung my legs out of bed and staggered across the room.

Snow covered the treetops high on Monte San Virgilio. The sparkle was dazzling. It seemed like a promise that things would get better.

I sorted through the books and papers in my backpack to make sure I had everything I needed for school. By that time, Max had gotten out of bed, so we had a quiet breakfast together. He didn't tease me about Werner or Luigi. I didn't call him a toad.

Then it was back to my bedroom. I looked out the window again. This time, instead of snow sparkling in the sunshine, the top of the mountain was shrouded in clouds. The banks of swirling white grew before my eyes as the water changed state from snow to vapor.

So much for things getting better.

The intercom buzzed. I wondered who it could be at this hour. It was too early for the men who sold socks, towels, and tablecloths door to door.

"Irene, Giulia's downstairs!" Mom called.

"Thanks," I called back. I pulled on a jacket and slipped my backpack onto my shoulder.

But Mom blocked the door. "Our house isn't exactly on her way to school, Irene."

"No."

"Did you two have a fight yesterday? Is that what was bothering you?"

"No." I smiled at her. "Nothing like that."

But Guilia and I did have a few things to talk about.

17

Passo a passo

(PAH-so ah PAH-so)

Step by Step

"*Ciao*, Irene. How's it going?" Giulia asked from the other side of the wrought iron gate.

"*Ciao*, Guilia. You mean Emi has not told you?" I buzzed myself out and joined her on the sidewalk of black tar.

"A bit. I wanted to talk to you without Barbara. She is my friend of the heart, but she does not know Matteo. Not like we do."

I nodded. "She would make excuses and say 'Maybe you did not understand him.'"

Guilia nodded. "That is true. So tell me. What happened?"

As we walked to school, I told Giulia about Matteo's trick and our argument outside the clubhouse. But I didn't mention what Emi had said about her and Matteo.

Giulia brought up the subject herself. "So. Emi told you of Matteo's plan as well?"

"A bit."

"I'm sorry, Irene," Giulia whispered. "I wish that I had told you myself, but I never even told Barbara what happened. She could not have understood. So what happened to you yesterday was my fault."

Passo a passo: Step by Step

My voice dropped an octave. "It was not your fault, Giulia. It was the fault of Matteo, no one else. You prepared me well. He lied to me. He set a trap for me. I did not believe him until Montegna…"

"But for Nicolo Montegna, the practice was cancelled, true?" Giulia's lips twitched. "Now I sound like Barbara. But Nicolo never gave me trouble. Never. I'm so sorry, Irene."

"Please don't worry," I said. "It's nothing."

"Ha! That's a lie. But listen. I'll tell you everything now."

I was about to say she didn't have to, but something in Guilia's eyes made me stop.

"Two years ago," she said, "the other squad began to talk about us. Every time we lost a game, they would jeer at us. 'We know why they lost,' they'd say. 'A *ragazza* plays with them.' They called us 'the *ragazze*,' 'the girls.' This did not please Matteo, so he asked Emi when I would quit. My brother said, 'Maybe never.' Matteo bet Emi twenty euro that he could make me quit. Emi said, 'Ha! I'll take your money.' Then Matteo made Emi promise he would not say a word to me or else the bet would not be fair."

"What happened?"

Giulia closed her eyes. "Matteo talked to me at school. He walked me home. In December, we went to the Christmas Market together. In February, we went to the *passeggiata* together for *carnivale.* He gave me a necklace for Christmas. A Diddl with a heart for Valentine's Day."

"A Diddl? Oh, you mean that stuffed mouse with enormous feet on your dresser? You kept it?"

The right corner of Giulia's mouth lifted in a sly smile. "What happened was not the fault of the Diddl, Irene. Only Matteo."

"True," I said, smiling.

Finally, a week before soccer began in the spring, Matteo asked me if I planned to play again. I told him, 'Naturally.' He said that I should watch him play with the *Esordienti* instead—that he was afraid I would get hurt. I told him not to worry. Finally, he agreed. Maybe he thought I'd change my mind later. But I went to the first day of soccer, and that was the end of our big romance. At school, Matteo did not even look at me—did not speak to me. Then Emi explained it all to me. He said he was sorry." Giulia sniffed. "He tried to give me the twenty euro he had won from Matteo."

"*Ai, ai, ai,*" I said. "That's horrible."

"At least Emi tried to warn me many times. 'Why do you like him?' he asked. 'He never pleased you before. You always laughed at him.' But no one else said anything. Everyone on the squad knew about the bet. And nobody told me. I hated them all."

"Luigi knew also?"

"Maybe yes. Maybe no. He is the son of a *mister*, you know. He is always the last to hear." Giulia looked up at me through her eyelashes. "Your *nonna* was right, Irene. You do have a weakness for Luigi."

I didn't deny it. It was true. I could hardly lie to Giulia after the story she had just finished telling me.

"Soccer and love do not mix well," Giulia said.

"I know." We were silent for a few steps before I went on, "Giulia, do many players quit after November?"

"A few. But not as many as in the summer. Everyone must pay for the whole year in autumn. Why?" Giulia's eyes widened and she answered her own question. "*Madonna!* You're not going to quit because you have fallen in love with Luigi?"

Passo a passo: Step by Step

"No! I'll miss playing with Luigi. But I can't stand five more months of soccer with Matteo. It's not worth the trouble."

"Not worth Luigi?" Giulia grinned.

"Enough." I crossed my arms. "Listen, I am very glad that you feel better, but please don't take me in circles like that."

"I'm sorry. Listen, I have a good idea. When soccer finishes, you will start to play volleyball with me. In January or in February, I will tell Emi that volleyball pleases you so much that you don't wish to play soccer in the spring."

"Matteo won't believe it."

"Who cares what Matteo thinks?"

"I do, unfortunately. How could you stand playing with him for so long?"

"Step by step. Game by game."

"That sounds like a plan." I sighed. "Let's talk about something else."

"Certainly. Let's see. Let's go over all the regions and their capitals for our test today."

We worked our way from the northwest region of Piedmont all the way south to Calabria and Sicily.

Elena greeted us as we stepped into the courtyard. "*Ciao,* Irene. Giulia. How's it going?"

"Fine," I lied.

"I heard that you made a goal last Saturday. *Complimenti.*"

"Thank you."

"I also heard that many players gave you a hug afterwards," Elena's eyes sparkled. "Also Matteo?"

Her chorus of friends all said, "Oooo."

"No. He gave me a high five. Nothing more." I wanted to sound casual, but I couldn't.

"Ahh. Matteo has done something to make you angry?

Have no fear. It will pass."

"No, it won't," I growled. "He's a pig. I hate him."

Elena blinked. "Why? What happened?"

"Ask Matteo. He'll lie to you too. Excuse me."

"Wait. Irene—"

Instead of waiting, I pivoted sharply and slammed right into Montegna. He must've been hovering right behind me.

"*Ópla!*" he said and grabbed at my hands to keep me from falling. Elena's crowd murmured appreciatively. Once I regained my balance, he let go.

Montegna swallowed and said, "Can I speak two words with you, Irene?"

"Okay."

"Come with me." Montegna led me a few steps away to the corner of the courtyard. "Listen," he said in a low voice. "I'm so sorry. I heard about what happened yesterday. For me, soccer was cancelled. I didn't mean to trap you. I forgot that your *mister* is crazy and makes his team play in all kinds of weather."

"It's nothing." That common response to an apology leapt to my lips even though it wasn't entirely true.

"What Matteo did was not right," Montegna continued. "It is not so completely horrible to play with you. You are here only for one year, true? And you don't cry...." Montegna's rather weak defense of my right to be on the soccer pitch wound down into silence.

"A thousand thanks," I said.

"I'm sorry," he repeated, stepping back. "*Ciao,* Irene."

"*Ciao,* Montegna," I said.

I heard a buzz from the group of girls behind me.

"Montegna? She calls him by his last name?"

Passo a passo: Step by Step

"I should play soccer. All the guys are falling in love with her."

Falling in love with me? Ha! Barely tolerating me was more like it. I walked quickly away. How was I going to stand soccer for six more weeks?

Game by game. Day by day. Step by step. And the first step would be practice on Thursday.

The sky was a cloudless blue. The snow on the mountains had melted except for a few patches above 6,000 feet. The river was still high and brown as the water drained from the mountainsides into the valley. The air was warm, but I carried my sweat suit in my backpack to wear home from practice.

As I turned into the gravel parking lot, the light dimmed as though someone had flipped a switch. I braked and looked up. Not a cloud in the sky. But no sun either. It had just dipped behind the Monte San Virgilio.

I looked over my shoulder. The valley behind me was still in sunshine. I felt like spinning round and chasing the light back along the road, across the railroad bridge and into town.

Instead I continued toward the clubhouse and locked my bike to the rack. After changing into my cleats, I stopped in front of the glass case to check our roster for the game up in Naturno. My eye dropped down to the list of alternates: My name wasn't there.

I would be left off the van? Not fair! Everyone should have to take a turn. Not Luigi, Emi, Werner, or Matteo, of course. But the rest of us.

I stared at the two substitutes' names again: G. Bergamo

and F. Vaccari. Giuseppe and Federico. I felt like walking back to my bike, ripping off the lock with my bare hands, and heading home. Instead I jumped onto the wide wooden bench and paced back and forth. My being left off the roster was beyond unfair. I had come to every single practice—early.

I skidded and narrowly kept myself from falling backwards. If I broke my wrist, my season would be over. I clenched my fists and hated Matteo all the more for driving me to this point.

"Irene, what's wrong?" Luigi was looking up at me.

"Nothing," I snapped.

"You sounded like a pot of boiling water." Luigi made a series of sputtering noises in order to demonstrate. "What happened? Tell me."

"All right. Look at the roster for our next game."

Luigi studied it for a moment. "Okay. I've read it."

"Understand now?"

"No."

I waved at the board. "Don't you see? It's not fair. I've already missed one game."

"What does that matter?"

"What does it matter? But of course you can't understand. You play every minute of every game."

Luigi stared at me. Could he fake such a look of utter confusion? "The *mister* has written your name wrong?"

"Written my name wrong? What?" I jumped down from the bench and looked at the board again.

Nothing had changed. F. Vaccari and G. Bergamo were still the substitutes. Then, about halfway down the list, a familiar grouping of letters caught my eye: I. Benenati.

"*Santo cielo!* Good heavens! I'm starting. I'm starting!" I spun around in a circle, my cleats pounding against the cement.

Luigi shook his head. "*Madonna!* You are truly a mad cow, Irene."

I peered through the glass to read my name again. "*Uaou!* I'm starting! I can't believe it. It's not possible!"

"If you want, I can change it," a deep voice informed me. My stomach dipped. "No. No. Thank you, *mister.*"

He swung the bag of balls off his shoulder and pulled one out for me and another for Luigi. "*Va bene.* Enough chattering, both of you. *Dai!*"

I retreated down the steps with the ball tucked under my arm. My legs shook from a double dose of adrenaline.

"Don't worry yourself. He was joking," Luigi said.

"Oh, sure. It's clear where you get your sense of humor."

Luigi grinned. "Yes, everyone says so."

Excitement came creeping back. I was actually starting a game! How had this happened? The answer came to me: Davide. D. Leonardi was not one of the names on the list.

"Luigi, how is Davide?"

"His ankle is healing. He returns on Monday. Davide will be missed by us on Saturday."

And he was. Especially by me. The first game that I started was the first game that we didn't win. Matteo was quick to point out that fact after the game.

"*Ecco,* Irene. Look. You played the entire game and we ended in a tie. Zero to zero. What does that mean to you?"

"Your series of making a goal in every game has ended," I said. "I'm so sorry."

Matteo's nostrils flared. "It's clear you could not take the place of Davide."

"Agreed." (I had spent the second half of the game in the

midfield.) "But no one on our team could do that. Not even you, Matteo."

In the weeks that followed, Matteo and I had similar charming conversations before, during, and after soccer. When he charged off on a breakaway with his usual speed and grace, I watched without cheering. When he scored, I walked back to my spot in silence. His whispered insults and shouts of false praise seemed to twist every one of my successes into failure.

One good thing that resulted from that supposedly cancelled, rainy practice was that Federico had suddenly moved out of Matteo's orbit. Now he was following Emi. In a few weeks, the youngest of the *Esordienti* had turned back into the friendly, enthusiastic boy of the second practice.

I still wished that Matteo would twist his ankle, sprain his wrist, or come down with a mild case of salmonella poisoning from a bad piece of tiramisu. Just for one practice—or better yet, a game.

I don't know if I would have made it through October and into November without Giulia. She sympathized. She let me vent. She let me whine. And she never told me that I was being unreasonable. But sometimes, I wondered: How stupid was it for me to let one person poison my entire experience? Two, if I counted Giuseppe.

Well, picture a drink of two parts sewer sludge and twelve parts water. Shake it up. Fill it with ice. Sound refreshing? Feel thirsty?

But practice followed practice, and game followed game. I crossed the dates off on my calendar until there were only four more practices and two more games.

18
Un bel' scherzo
(oon bell SKERT-zo)
A Good Joke

I stood in the goal, defending it from Luigi. Above our heads the four massive stadium lights brightened slowly. Full dark wouldn't arrive until midway through the practice, but ever since daylight savings time had ended, Signora Martelli always had them turned on by the time I arrived.

"Ready?" Luigi asked from the centerline. Without waiting for an answer, he drove forward. I watched him, my knees bent, my arms extended, and my feet shuffling to adjust for his every change in direction.

Stay in the goal or charge forward to meet him? That was the question. It was always the question. This time I waited, coming only a few steps out in order to make the goal look smaller.

Luigi dropped his head, a clear signal that he was about to shoot. He brought his right leg back and kicked the ball from the top of the penalty area. *Whump!* In a great curving hook, it flew toward the upper-left corner. I dove, but it was hopeless. I didn't even get a fingertip on it.

Still, I was improving. A little practice as goalkeeper might come in handy someday. I only hoped it wouldn't be in Italy. Other than Matteo and Emi's turns on that rainy Monday over a month ago, I had never seen anyone but Luigi in the goal. Going into the game as his backup was my worst nightmare, one that I actually had a few times. The game never ended until my alarm clock rang. On those mornings, I didn't hit the snooze bar.

As I rolled over to pick up the ball, the air around me brightened. Beams of light slanted across the valley to the north and struck Dorf Tyrol, a small town three hundred meters above the soccer field. It had been in shadow too until the sun had moved far enough northwest to shine through a gap in the mountains.

Footsteps thudded to a stop beside me. "Goal!" Luigi said. "The sky applauds."

"Ha!" I said, and tossed him the ball.

"*Molto bello,*" Luigi said, looking north. "Very pretty, like a painting, no? Ready to change?"

"*Sí.*" I peeled off the goalkeeper's gloves and handed them to him. Then I pulled off my jacket and threw it behind the net.

I started by taking a few shots from close in. Luigi caught most of them and whipped the ball back to me. But a few found their way into corners. Players from the other team started filtering onto the field.

"*Ciao,* Montegna," Luigi called. "It was very entertaining on Saturday, no?"

I rolled my eyes. On Saturday, we had beaten Montegna's team, our regular scrimmage partners, in an official game.

Montegna stared past Luigi, but waved at me. "*Ciao,* Irene."

"*Ciao,*" I echoed.

Un bel' scherzo: A Good Joke

Ever since that day I had crashed into him in the school courtyard, Montegna had made a point of saying a few words to me at every practice: greetings, observations on the scrimmage, even a few compliments.

"Luigi, that was not very nice," I whispered.

Luigi's eyes glinted. "I know. It was revenge. You did not hear what his team said when they won last spring."

Emi and Federico came through the gate next. For once, the *mister* was not standing over the bag of balls with his arms crossed and his face an unreadable mask. So Emi and Federico pulled a pair of balls out of the bag themselves and dribbled them over to us.

"*Ciao,* Luigi. Irene," Federico said. "I have a joke."

Luigi stepped out of the goal. "Tell me."

Emi rolled his eyes. "It is not very good. He made it up himself."

"It is a beautiful joke," Federico protested. "Listen, what can Matteo do at any time except during a game?"

"I don't know," I said.

"Luigi?" Federico asked.

"Wait. I must think a little." After a few seconds, Luigi shook his head. "I don't know either. Tell me."

"Pass the ball."

I giggled. "That's not a joke. It's the truth."

Luigi snickered. "Matteo can do it, you know."

"I have seen it," Emi said. "One or two times."

"I have not seen it ever," Federico said.

"Me neither," I added.

"It is a beautiful joke. Eh, Irene?" Federico cocked his head at me.

"Agreed."

"Uh oh! The *mister* comes," Federico said. He darted away.

By four-thirty, our entire team had arrived for practice. But only ten players were warming up on the other side of the field.

"They are embarrassed to show their faces here after Saturday," Luigi whispered.

"*Dai,* Luigi. We won by only one goal," I pointed out. "It was a good game."

It had actually been a very good game, with a larger audience than normal. Parents, brothers, sisters, and classmates, including Elena and about half of her giggling followers, had come to watch the *Esordienti* of Merano I take on the *Esordienti* of Merano II.

"*Brava,* Irene! But how dangerous!" Elena had said, hugging me. "You are the craziest girl. I don't know how you do it."

During the pause between the drills and the scrimmage, I learned why so many on the other team were absent. "Some of my players are home sick today," I heard their *mister* tell ours. "Will you give me a *calciatore?*"

"Let me see…" Luigi's father was silent for a moment. "I'll give you a *calciatrice.*"

"*Va bene.*" I could hear amusement in the other man's voice.

"Irene!" the *mister* called.

I turned and blinked, as if I had heard nothing.

"You'll play with the other squad today. They don't have enough players."

"Okay," I said.

The other *mister* motioned to me. "Come with me, Irene, and we'll talk."

Un bel' scherzo: A Good Joke

I followed him to the other side of the field. A circle gathered around us.

The Merano II coach began with me. "We'll put you on defense, Irene. You have watched our system?"

I nodded.

Montegna put a hand on my shoulder. "Remember, Irene: Matteo is the enemy."

"That will not be difficult to remember," I said.

I heard snorts of muffled agreement. It appeared that my feud with Matteo was more public than I had realized.

A grin spread across the coach's face. "Ah, *sí*. I have an idea. Irene, you mark Matteo. Everyone else play zone. If Matteo gets past you, Irene, don't worry. Someone will help you. If it doesn't work, we will change things. All right. Venturi, Beccari, Montegna: attackers. Gasperi, Corte, Sartoi: midfield. Tedeschi, Zanella, Ritter: on defense. Irene, what is your last name?"

"Benenati," I said.

"*Va bene,* Benenati. You have D'Andalo. Is everyone ready? *Dai!*"

I found a place in front of the three defenders but behind the midfielders. I wouldn't shadow Matteo until after the kickoff. The whistle blew and the scrimmage began.

Montegna and Venturi pushed the ball forward about twenty feet across the centerline before Gianlucca tackled and lofted the ball to Matteo.

Instead of running forward to meet the ball, Matteo went off on an angle to match speeds with it. No one would be near him, he must have reasoned. No one usually was.

But I darted in front of him. With a one-touch pass, I sent the ball flying back toward Montegna.

Defending Irene

Matteo walked up the field and to the right. I trotted after him. He looked over his left shoulder, saw me, grimaced, and moved again. Grinning, I followed. This might be fun.

"What are you doing, Irene?" Matteo asked.

"Nothing."

He bolted left, sprinted two-thirds of the way across the field, and stopped. I jogged after him. Montegna still had control of the ball, so there wasn't any immediate danger. I took up my position behind Matteo's right shoulder this time.

"Leave me alone," he said through his teeth.

"No."

"*Stupida!* You're not playing midfield."

"Today, no," I said with no further explanation. Matteo was smart. He would realize soon enough that no one was yelling at me for being out of position.

I continued to shadow Matteo up and down the field, staying between him and the goal. He was fast; I was completely outclassed. But all I had to do was slow him down and make things as difficult for him as possible until Tedeschi, Zanella, or Ritter came along to help out.

He broke away from me every chance he got. Once I let him go and even drifted a few steps in the other direction. Emi sent a crossing pass into the box and Matteo slammed it in for a goal.

Matteo held up his fists and swung around to face me.

A whistle blew. "Offsides," Luigi's father called.

"No!" Matteo mouthed. He stomped off to midfield to await a free kick from the spot of the penalty.

Tedeschi, Zanella, Ritter, and I came together to exchange high fives. Then I struck out after Matteo.

Overall, the plan seemed to work fairly well. Matteo only

scored once. During the last ten or fifteen minutes of the scrimmage, Matteo walked with his hands on his hips. His bursts of speed were shorter and less frequent. The rest of my usual team, Merano I, didn't look much livelier. They might have been suffering from letdown, but Merano II—led by Montegna with two goals—had something to prove. When six o'clock arrived, the informal score was 2 to 1.

"*Brava,* Irene. You stopped Matteo," Montegna said as we walked over to the goal nearest the clubhouse for the usual round of penalty shots.

I would have loved to take the credit for shutting Matteo down, but I couldn't. "No. He stopped himself."

Montegna's eyes narrowed. "Maybe he is coming down with the influenza. It could be. Several others in our class are out sick."

Montegna's guess was right. Tuesday morning, Matteo left class midway through third period. Wednesday, he did not come to school. Thursday brought the practice I had dreamed about: a Matteo-free zone. Giuseppe was present but silent.

Federico took over the center forward position. Emi and I played on either side of him. The *mister* yelled at me almost the entire time: "*Dai! Dai! Dai!* Lengthen your legs. Pass, pass pass. Center it! Make the cross!" But it was the same way that he would have yelled at Emi, Luigi or Matteo. I couldn't ask for anything more. Except to score a goal or two. That didn't happen, but at least I made the goalkeeper work, and Emi scored off a rebound from one of my shots.

The *mister*'s closing lecture was a bit different from his usual one. "Wash your hands often," he told us. "Drink lots of water and juice. Avoid sick people. Get plenty of sleep. We will see each other at fourteen-thirty, not later. Until Saturday."

I turned to go with the rest of the team. Then the *mister* called me back. "Wait, Irene. I have a question. When does your family move back to America?"

"In June. After school finishes," I told him.

"Fine. You are able to play with us next spring." It was a more of a statement than a question.

Able to play: yes. Want to play: no. But I had planned to slink away between the fall and spring seasons, not announce my plan to the *mister*. I had two seconds to pull together an answer.

"*S-s-sí*, I can."

The *mister* made a mark on his clipboard. "Thanks. It is going well. We'll see each other Saturday."

I smiled, nodded, and felt like I was about to throw up. Step by step, week by week, game by game, I had nearly made it to freedom. How could I have committed myself to three more months of Matteo?

Go ahead, a small voice inside my head dared me. Turn around. Tell the *mister* that you can play but you won't. Tell him you've been counting the days until soccer was over.

But I couldn't.

I expected sympathy from Giulia on Friday morning. Instead, she laughed.

"*Ehi!*" I protested. "It's not funny."

"I know," she said and continued to giggle.

"There's nothing to laugh at. This is serious!"

"I know. But fortunately, you want to play soccer."

"When I return to America, yes, I want to do it. But here…no."

Un bel' scherzo: A Good Joke

Giulia shook her finger at me side to side like a metronome. "You're wrong. You enjoyed yourself this week, true?"

"Of course. Matteo was absent yesterday."

"Don't forget Monday. You enjoyed yourself Monday."

"*Sí*, but—"

"*Dai*, Irene. Think. Matteo said all the same things as usual, but they did not bother you."

"It was different."

"How?"

"We were not on the same team."

Giulia tilted her head and waved her hands in encouraging little circles. "What else?"

I looked up at the bare tree limbs for inspiration. "I don't know."

"That's clear."

I changed the subject. "I haven't seen Matteo yet this morning."

"Maybe he is still sick."

"If only. Too bad the team has need of him." A worse thought struck me. "Where is Luigi?"

This was the first sign that my dream (no Matteo) and my nightmare (no Luigi) were about to collide.

19

Portiera (por-tee-AIR-ah)
Female Goalkeeper

On Saturday afternoon, the mister stood waiting for me outside the bathroom. He held out Luigi's gloves and the goalkeeper's jersey. "Here, Irene."

I took them between my thumb and pointer finger.

"Don't worry yourself, Irene," the *mister* said. "They are clean. They should not make you sick."

That was not the reason I wanted to hand the shirt and gloves right back to him. A familiar lift to his eyebrows—the one Luigi used when he was teasing—suggested that the *mister* knew that.

"How is Luigi?" I asked.

"This morning he told us he was fine and even dressed himself for school. But he had a fever of 37.8°. *Ai, ai, ai.*" The *mister* shook his head.

That translated to a temperature of over 102° Fahrenheit.

"Poor Luigi," I said out loud. Poor me, I added silently to myself. It was going to be a long game.

Five minutes later, we began our warm-up in the usual way: jogging around the field evenly spaced, in step and single-file. My ponytail streamed behind me like a banner. For the first time in weeks, I wished that I'd chopped my hair off. I knew the other team had noticed me, the girl in the gray and blue goalkeeper's shirt.

After stretching, we took turns shooting into an empty goal. But as I pulled my fourth or fifth shot out of the orange netting, the *mister* held out his hand. "Stay there, Irene. Emi, *dai!*"

Emi dribbled forward with the ball, his legs a blur of motion. He booted the ball diagonally across the penalty area. It bounced off the pole and across the white line: a goal. Werner came next. He lacked Emi's speed, but could put a lot of power and swerve on the ball. It hooked into the upper-right corner of the goal.

I unclenched my fingers and shook them out. I needed to stay loose. I hadn't faced a line of shooters since the end of fourth grade. But as person after person attacked, I learned which shots I could catch, which ones I should block, which ones I should punch over the net, and which ones were hopeless. Terror kept me focused.

When everyone else moved on to a passing drill, the *mister* motioned to a figure leaning against the fence. The person came forward with a familiar walk. My heart contracted. I recognized Luigi's nose, his chin, his hair. But the height was wrong.

"Irene, this is Renzo. He will help you prepare yourself while I work with the others." The *mister* nodded at us both before walking away.

"A pleasure," Renzo said, looking down at me. "I have heard much about you, Irene. Every evening after soccer, it goes like this: 'Irene has done this. Irene has done that.' And that is just the *mister.* Luigi is worse. Much, much worse."

Defending Irene

If Renzo had been six instead of sixteen, I think he might have launched into a chorus of "Luigi plus Irene." Instead, he merely said, "Let's go."

He started with soft kicks and easy throws. I caught the ball and threw it back to him. He sent other shots bouncing across the penalty area. I charged forward to fall on top of those and wrap them in my arms. The shots came faster and harder. My percentage of saves dropped. I didn't even touch the last six balls he sent me. Finally, he had me punt the ball downfield a few times. Then it was time to go back to the clubhouse until just before game-time.

As we sat on the built-in wooden benches, the *mister* warned us about various players, pointed out our weaknesses from past games, and told us what we must do well in order to win. I bounced up and down, full of nervous energy.

Federico leaned over to whisper in my ear. "Stay calm, Irene. Emi and I will make goals. You will stop them." He dusted off his hands as though that would be that. I wished I could be so confident.

"All right," the *mister* said. "We have only eleven players. I want to finish with eleven. But please tell me if you do not feel well—if you cannot continue. Irene is our goalkeeper. Protect her. If they put it in the box enough times, they will score. But don't forget: if we put it in their box often enough, we will score."

For most of the first period, Werner, Manuel, and Giuseppe kept the ball away from me. It rolled into the penalty area a few times when a booming kick overshot the fastest forwards. Each time, I ran out, scooped up the ball, and punted it down the field. I started to relax.

Halfway through the middle of the second period, the

team from Ora had its first breakaway. No one stood between me and Number 17.

"*Schnell, schnell, schnell!*" shouted their *mister* in German. "Fast!"

"*Dai,* Werner, *dai!*" shouted ours in Italian.

Werner was gaining. He pounded after the player, his arms pumping, his long strides covering the ground.

The forward must have heard Werner's footsteps getting closer. Instead of bringing the ball all the way in, he made a blistering shot from the corner of the penalty area. I managed to punch it up and over the crossbar. For a horrible second I wondered whether it would have gone over all by itself. If so, our team would be setting up for a goal kick to send the ball flying away from me instead of facing a corner kick.

No second-guessing, I told myself firmly. It was always better to be aggressive.

Players poured into the penalty area. Manuel took up his position next to the post. A player from Ora placed the ball in the corner next to the orange flag and stepped back.

The kick went up with plenty of lift and power. An orange-shirted form launched himself into the air. His head snapped forward. His forehead connected with the ball. A goal.

His teammates celebrated. I called myself a few bad names and reached down to pick up the ball.

"Don't worry, Irene," Werner said. "Luigi could not have stopped that one either."

Not from where I was standing he couldn't have. But he might have judged it in the air better.

Luigi would have definitely stopped Ora's second goal. Instead of knocking down the first shot as I barely managed to do, he probably would have caught it. The second player would never have had the chance to tap in the rebound.

Stay calm. Stay calm, I told myself as I paced back and forth. Don't panic.

Right. Even though I might wind up being personally responsible for our first loss. Even though I could almost hear Matteo say that leaving the goal empty would be just as good as having me in there.

Fortunately, Federico made a move to hold up his end of his whispered deal when he and Emi made a break of their own. Emi sent Federico a beautiful crossing pass. Federico ripped a shot from about five meters out.

Goal!

Federico jumped up and down, shaking his fists above his head in celebration. Then he picked Emi up and spun him in a circle. I think it was our youngest player's first official goal as a member of the *Esordienti*.

A few minutes after the kickoff, the referee's whistle stopped play when the ball hit Giuseppe in the wrist: a hand-ball. Since the illegal use of the hands happened in the penalty box, Ora was awarded a penalty shot. The only defender would be me.

As I expected, Number 17 stepped forward. The referee placed the ball on the penalty spot and stepped back. I stood with my legs just over shoulder-width apart and my arms out to the side. Which way would he go? The left corner? The right? Or straight at me?

Number 17 stood for a moment with his right leg behind his left. Then he made his move. His right leg came back. The angle of his body suggested the ball was going to my right. He made contact. I lunged. My fingertips struck the ball, but it was only enough to change the ball's angle of flight, not stop it. Another goal. The score was 3 to 1.

But Emi and Federico were ready to answer. Federico intercepted a slow-rolling pass at midfield and passed it to Emi. Emi drove down the right side of the field and faked out the other team's keeper for another goal, making the score 3 to 2.

Less than a minute later, two whistle blasts signaled the end of the second period. We trotted to the bench, feeling energized. The game wasn't out of reach. Not yet. Only Gianlucca walked.

"*Dai!*" the *mister* shouted at him. The boy ran a few steps and then settled back into a slow motion jog.

"I'm sorry, *mister,*" Gianlucca gasped. "I don't feel well."

"Do you need to lie down?"

"No, but..." Gianlucca's voice trailed off.

"I understand. Those in the midfield must run every moment. All right. Seat yourselves." The *mister* pressed his fingers to his lips. Then his gaze came to rest on me.

"Irene..."

Free at last! My hands reached down and crossed to grasp the hem of my goalkeeper's shirt, ready to rip it off. Eleven males ducked their heads or covered their eyes.

I stopped.

"No. No, Irene," the *mister* said, still gazing away from me. "I changed my mind. Continue as goalkeeper."

"But I'm wearing my jersey underneath," I said.

I meant to explain why I could change in public, but it came out like I was questioning his decision. No one ever did that to the *mister.* I hunched my shoulders, waiting for him to roar.

Instead, one of his rare half-smiles appeared. "That is not

the problem. What if Gianlucca faints in the goal, and no one sees it until Ora shoots the ball?"

Gianlucca made a face but said nothing.

"Gianlucca, you are on defense. Remain near the penalty area. Do not go to the centerline with the others. If you cannot continue, fall down. The referee will call time out and we can organize ourselves. Werner, Manuel, and Giuseppe, go forward a little. Keep it on their side. It's possible to win this game. It's possible. The other team can change players. We cannot, but you have strength, energy, the *forza vitale.*"

The vital force. I tried to imagine my coach in America using a phrase like that.

The *mister* motioned to the other team, who had already stepped onto the field. "They are tired, weak, desperate. They know you can win, as I do. Look at them. Four on defense. Four in midfield. Only two attackers. You can do it. *Dai!*" He held his hand out. We scrambled to our feet, formed a circle, and put our hands in the middle.

"*Uno, due, tre…forza!*" the *mister* told us.

We echoed his count and cheer at a yell: "*Uno, due, tre…FORZA!*" Our hands flew up above our heads on the last word.

We can win this game, I thought as I ran toward the goal. I could feel it—especially if my teammates could keep the ball away from me.

They started well. The ball stayed on the other side of the centerline.

Eventually, Gianlucca took a knee in order to save energy. His head and shoulders stayed straight and tall, only swaying occasionally. Any time that Ora pushed the ball to midfield, Gianlucca stood up. When one of our defenders sent it back to the opposite goal, Gianlucca sank down again.

Then Werner headed the ball into the goal on a corner kick from Emi. I cheered. Gianlucca, who had stood up to watch, jumped up and down. *Uaou!* Three goals by three different players. We were more than just a supporting cast for the Matteo/Luigi show.

Two minutes later, Davide scored in a booming kick from the top of the penalty area. Four goals by four different players. Now we had the lead and we intended to keep it.

The coach from Ora yelled at his team in a flood of angry German. I couldn't understand a single word.

It was Ora's turn to throw everything possible forward. It was absolute chaos in the penalty area as players tackled and retackled. The ball rolled free into an empty space to my right. Giuseppe and I both raced toward it.

"Mine!" I called in English and dove onto the ball.

Giuseppe might not have understood. Or maybe he couldn't stop himself. Whatever happened, as I came down, the toe of his cleats struck my ribs.

"*Ahi!*" I curled up like a hedgehog, my arms wrapped around the ball. I knew I should get up, dash to the corner of the penalty area, and punt the ball downfield. Maybe in the fast turnaround Emi or Federico could score again to put the game out of reach. But all I could do was lie there, temporarily frozen by pain. Tears squeezed out of the corner of my eyes. Matteo knew it would happen someday. I could almost hear him chanting: "*Calciatore* don't cry. *Calciatrice, sí.*"

But his voice would have been drowned out completely by Giuseppe's: "I'm sorry, Irene. I did not mean to do it. I'm sorry. It was an accident."

Giuseppe was no actor. I believed him.

Someone else may not have. "It was an accident," I heard him insist.

"Irene, how are you?" the *mister* asked.

"Less bad," I choked. "Only a moment."

I breathed in and out a few more times. My lungs still seemed to be working fine. The pain faded enough for me to move. I uncurled and released the ball.

"All right. Where does it hurt?"

I placed my hand on the bottom of my ribcage.

The *mister* frowned. "Can I check it?"

I nodded.

His fingers gently moved over the area. "A bad bruise, I think." he said. "Nothing broken."

"Thanks to heaven," I heard Giuseppe murmur.

"Cough," the *mister* ordered.

I did.

"Again."

I coughed a second time. It hurt, but I didn't flinch like my Uncle Frank had when he'd broken a rib in a car accident.

"*Benissimo.* Very good. Ready to get up?"

"*Sì.*" I stood up gingerly.

Players and fans from both teams applauded. I took a step toward the goal.

"No," the *mister* said. "Come with me, Irene. For you, the game is finished."

"But *mister*—"

"No. You can watch. Nothing more. At least I'm not sending you to the hospital. Davide, come here. Irene, you can take off that shirt now. Do you need help?"

I shook my head and peeled off the gloves. I never thought I would be so reluctant to give them up. Davide's eyes were filled with concern as he took them. I wanted to snap: "It doesn't hurt that much." But considering the way I hissed through my teeth as I eased the shirt over my head, it was just as well that I didn't.

The *mister* walked beside me as I left the field. So much for his hope that we finish with eleven. But maybe he had made the right decision. Watching the action from the bench suddenly seemed like a really good idea.

Thirty seconds later the whistle blew three times.

Yes! We won! To celebrate our victory, I sat on the bench and smiled.

"Irene, how are you?" Giulia whispered from behind me.

"Better," I said.

"Oh," she growled. "When I saw Giuseppe kick you, I was outside myself. But I'll adjust him. Elena will help me."

"No. No. It was an accident."

"Are you sure?"

"*Sì, sì.*"

"*Va bene.* We'll see each other afterward." Giulia patted my shoulder and headed back up into the stands.

When everyone else made it back to the bench, the *mister* gave us his shortest post-game speech ever. "Well done. I am very proud of you. Go home and rest yourselves."

Was he too proud for words or coming down with the flu himself? I leaned toward the second option: he was holding his head up in the same way that Gianlucca had.

I spent the rest of the afternoon on the couch, feeling completely drained. It felt like I had been playing midfielder, not goalkeeper. Mom felt my head, brought me juice, and offered me a choice of movies.

Dad paused *You've Got Mail* about halfway through. He

held the cordless phone out to me, his hand covering the receiver. "Your *nonno* wants to talk to you. I told him about the game."

I moaned and covered my face with my right hand.

"*Ma dai,*" Dad said. "You did well. I have told you so many times. Take it."

I did. "*Ciao,* Nonno."

"How are you, Irene?"

"Better," I said.

"What a *brava calciatrice!* I heard how you held onto the ball when someone kicked you."

"Thanks. But Papá has told you the score?"

"It's nothing. Only three goals."

"In one period."

"Ah, *poverina.* Tomorrow, you will feel better. You will know that you did well. Listen, I have heard that your last game is next Saturday. At least until spring, right?"

"*Ehm...si.*" If I hadn't been committed to playing soccer in the spring before, I was now.

"Very well. Anyway, your *nonna* has wanted to visit the Advent Market in the Alto Adige for years. Now, we can see your game and the market. A good idea, eh?"

I could just picture Matteo making up rude remarks about my loud, enthusiastic grandfather. Well, let him try.

"We'll see each other Saturday," I told my *nonno.* "That would please me very much."

20
Come stai?

(CO-may STAH-ee)
How Are You?

L uigi and I arrived early to soccer on Monday afternoon. But answering the question "How are you?" took so long that we drifted over to a bench to sit down instead of going out onto the field.

"A very interesting game on Saturday, I heard," Luigi said.

I leaned my head against the wall of the clubhouse. "Too interesting for me."

Luigi laughed, but the laugh turned into a cough that lasted more than twenty seconds. Finally, he straightened and wiped his eyes.

"All well?" I asked.

"*Sí.*" He coughed a few more times, held his breath for five seconds, and was finally able to speak. "You surprised Renzo, you know. Especially when you held onto the ball after Giuseppe kicked you. Why didn't you tell Giuseppe that you wanted the ball?"

"I did. But in English. My fault."

Luigi snorted. "The *Americana* still plays soccer in English after three months in Italy?"

"Only when I am the *portiera.*"

"Ah. I understand. All right. We must get up now." But Luigi didn't move.

"Agreed," I said, not moving either.

"We sit like a pair of old people who have gone into retirement twenty years ago," Luigi observed.

"True. Let's go." I stood up.

It wasn't one of our normal pre-practice sessions. Luigi stopped to cough every minute or two. I trotted stiffly. My bruise, which had turned a deep purple, hurt every time my cleats struck the ground and every time I swung my arms.

But Luigi and I were not alone. Over half our team looked like they ought to be getting plenty of rest and fluids instead of running and kicking. The cold air made most of them cough. Matteo only had enough air for one wheezing insult the whole time: "*Brava,* Irene. Luigi allows three goals in the last seven games, and you allow three in one period?"

Montegna and the rest of Merano II had ended their season last Saturday and had stopped practicing. We had a make-up game. Instead of a scrimmage, we worked on throw-ins, corner kicks, and crossing passes.

"How are you, Irene?" the *mister* asked when we finished.

"Well enough."

"Your ribs still hurt you?"

"Not too much." I glanced at the clipboard that the *mister* carried. Attached to it was the roster for our final game in Bolzano.

I could imagine where this was leading. The *mister* was about to tell me that there wouldn't be room in the van for me during the final game of the season—when my grandparents were making a special trip to watch me play. It made sense. Should I have worked harder during practice?

"Not your fault, *cara,*" my *nonno* would say. The reaction of my nonna would probably be a whispered, "Thanks to heaven!"

"Listen," the *mister* continued. "I know that your *papá* has been to every game—even the one in which you did not play. It takes time to drive into Bolzano, but would he take you to the game? Then we can have fourteen players instead of thirteen. It would be much better."

"Of course," I said, knowing that Dad would drive a lot farther to make sure I could play.

"It goes well. I will explain the situation to Roberto on Thursday. Thank you, Irene." The *mister* lowered his clipboard. I watched him write Roberto's name in as the third substitute.

I found my name among the starters. Well, this would be all right. I was helping Roberto, helping the team, and even helping my *nonna.* Now she had a great excuse to avoid watching me play. There was not room in the car for six people. But I would have to explain the situation to Dad. I decided to wait until after dinner to avoid annoying comments from Max.

When I cornered Dad in front of the computer to tell him what happened, he tilted back in the black office chair to listen. When I finished, he covered his mouth in an unsuccessful attempt to hide a smile. "What were you thinking, Irene?" he finally asked. "You have been starting for over a month."

My left hand touched my ribs. "This seemed like a good excuse for the *mister* to leave me behind."

"A good excuse to leave behind one of his most versatile players? *Dai,* Irene. But it will please Roberto. No one wants to miss the last game of the season."

At dinner Friday night, Nonno felt happy for Roberto

too, but it was my *nonna* who came up with a plan. "The *calciatori* will take the car," she announced. "They must arrive early. The others can take the bus." (The plural feminine ending on the word "others" meant that she was talking about my mom and herself.)

"Good idea," Mom said. "I'll check the bus schedule."

"After the game, we will visit the Advent Market together. Maybe see Ötzi the Iceman at the museum." Nonna turned to me. "Don't forget to bring another outfit, *cara*. Let's select it together? After dinner?"

"I have to clean the kitchen first," I said.

"I'll do it," Max offered.

"*Che carino,*" Nonna crooned. "How sweet. A thousand thanks, Massimiliano."

My brother blinked twice and smiled angelically. I wondered if he was up to something. He might not have realized that Nonna had given up on trying to make me quit soccer. But it seemed as though her other campaign was still going strong. If I was determined to look and act like a *maschiaccio* on the field, the least she could do was make sure I looked elegant off of it. It didn't seem fair. Max probably would have been allowed to parade all over Bolzano in his soccer uniform. Still, at least my *nonna* was coming to my game, instead of insisting that she would be perfectly happy checking out the smaller local Advent Market with my mom. That was progress.

It took fifteen minutes of going through every scrap of clothing in my old wooden wardrobe before Nonna announced: "The blue sweater together with your gold chain please me most."

"Agreed," I said quickly, before she could change her mind. Mission accomplished.

But she wasn't done yet. Nonna reached for the bag that she had left on my desk. "All right, Irene. Now that you are older, you must learn to respect your skin. To run outside is bad for it. Also, too much sun. My cosmetologist recommends these for the young." Nonna pulled out tubes of cleanser and moisturizer and handed them to me. "These will also prevent acne. A good thing, no?"

"*Sí.* Thank you."

"We also discussed your coloring," Nonna continued. She reached into the bag and pulled out blush, lip gloss, eye shadow, fingernail polish. "Let's try them. If they seem *bella* enough, you can wear them tomorrow."

"Not during the game?" I said, horrified.

"No. How silly, Irene. After the game, *carissima*. After. But I do have a plan for your hair...."

Before I left for the game on Saturday afternoon, Nonna braided my hair so tightly against my head that not a single strand would be able to escape. A way to minimize the Medusa effect? My scalp still hurt ninety minutes later as I waited on the field for the game to begin.

The only parts of my body exposed to the chill, autumn air—my hands, face and knees—were cold. But that would change once we started to play. I liked the view from where I stood—and I wasn't talking about the vineyards rising up the steep slopes of the valley, the people in loden cloth jackets taking a walk, or the bluffs rising high above Bolzano. I liked playing *terzina,* the left defensive wing. It was a thousand times better than being the goalkeeper, but there was more to it than that. I liked working with Werner and Manuel. I liked hearing our opponents' grunts of disappointment when we stole the ball and sent it back to the midfielders.

The referee blew his whistle. Matteo kicked the ball to Emi. The game began.

For the first ten minutes Matteo played with all of his usual speed, style, and selfishness. He took two blistering shots off of two gorgeous crossing passes from Emi. The goalkeeper caught the first one and deflected the second one out of the penalty area. But as the minutes ticked down for the end of the first period, Matteo's pace slowed. The ball seemed to give him energy. When he had it, he could run. Otherwise, he walked.

During the short break between the first and second periods, the *mister* rearranged us. First, he sat down two tired midfielders who looked grateful rather than annoyed to come out of the game.

"Giuseppe, you take the place of Irene. Irene, you attack from the left wing. Gianlucca, move from attack back to midfield. You have a lot of energy still, no? It goes well. Federico, you go in for Matteo. Matteo, seat yourself. We'll have need of you in the third period."

Matteo crossed his arms and bent his head. Except for the game he missed, I couldn't remember Matteo ever being out of the game. The *mister* had pulled Matteo to talk to him for a few minutes during a scrimmage or two, but he had always sent him right back in at the next opportunity.

Since I had scored my one official goal of the season

against the other team from Bolzano, I didn't expect anyone to underestimate me. They didn't.

The ball moved up and down the field. There was plenty of action—throw-ins, goal kicks, free kicks, high headers, floating passes—but no one scored. There weren't even that many shots on goal.

Midway through the period, Emi stole the ball and made a break down the right sideline. Federico sprinted up the center while I made my way up the left side of the field.

One of Bolzano's defenders caught up to Emi and did his best to force my teammate out of bounds. Under pressure, Emi lost control of the ball. It sailed down into the empty corner and rolled to a stop, still inbounds. Emi put on a burst of speed and won the race to the ball. He sent a high-crossing pass into the penalty area where Federico and I were waiting.

I knocked it to the ground with my chest. A defender raced to put himself between me and the goal. With my instep, I passed the ball to Federico. He drilled the ball past the helpless goalie and into the net.

No whistle. No flags waving to signal offsides. A goal!

"*Bravi!*" my *nonno* roared. "*Brava!*"

Federico ran toward me with his arms outstretched. I think that he had every intention of picking me up and spinning me around, even though I was five inches taller than he was.

"No, no!" I waved him away with my left hand and pressed my right one protectively against my ribs.

Federico settled for pounding me on the back. "Thanks! A thousand thanks. What a beautiful pass! Two beautiful passes!" he added as Emi arrived. "*Bello, bello, bello.*"

We wrapped our arms around each other's shoulders in a

mini-huddle and grinned. But Federico couldn't hold still for more than a few seconds. He broke away from us and bounded across the field in a spinning gallop.

Emi rolled his eyes. I murmured, "*Bello,*" and we trotted up the field after him.

The score was 1–0. If we could keep Bolzano II from scoring, that might be all we would need.

But Bolzano attacked hard. A few minutes later, Manuel was marking Number 22—a strong, fast, dangerous player—when their legs tangled. They both went down. The referee blew his whistle and play stopped.

Manuel had been called for unintentional tripping. That meant a direct kick and not the more dangerous penalty kick—as long as the foul had happened outside the penalty area. Yes. The referee was placing the ball a few feet outside the white line.

I ran downfield. As one of the tallest people on our team, I would be part of the group forming a wall between the spot of the foul and the goal.

We stood shoulder to shoulder. The rest of our team arranged themselves in the penalty area to guard the other players.

Number 22 stood a few steps back from the ball, waiting for the referee's signal. It came. The boy rushed forward and kicked the ball. Our wall jumped, even though it was well over our heads. I turned just in time to see the ball sail into the far left corner of the goal.

The score was now one to one. It stayed that way through the end of the second period.

Davide was limping slightly as he walked off the field. The

mister stood waiting for him on the sidelines. "You have hurt your ankle, Davide?"

"A minute ago. It's nothing."

The *mister* crossed his arms. "The same ankle as before?"

"*Sí,* but only a bit."

"Really?"

Davide nodded.

The *mister* reached for his first aid kit. "All right, come with me. I want to check the ankle and maybe wrap it. Everyone else rest."

I noticed Matteo sitting on the bench, his head down between his knees. A shiver ran across his back. Then another. A cough shook him. His fist covered his mouth as he half sat up. Then he leaned back down, pillowing his head on his crossed forearms.

I glanced over at the *mister.* He was easing the shoe off of Davide's foot. Giuseppe stood in a huddle with Werner and Manuel discussing strategies for stopping Number 22. Gianlucca, Emi, and Federico were waving their arms at each other and talking about our breakaway.

Matteo shivered again. He could have just been cold from sitting out the second period. But what if he were having some kind of relapse? I couldn't remember the last time I had started a conversation with Matteo, but I couldn't leave him like that without making sure he was all right.

I bent down. "Matteo, how are you?"

He didn't answer me.

21

Amica donna mia

(a-MEE-ca DON-ha MEE-ah)

My Lady Friend

Was Matteo ignoring me or too sick to say anything?

"Matteo, all well?" I said.

"Tell me," Matteo growled.

"What?" I asked, confused.

"That which you want to tell me. *Dai.*"

"*Ehm,* if you don't feel well, my parents have brought extra blankets."

Matteo sat up and glared at me. He hadn't been sick; he had been sulking. From his open-mouthed outrage it looked like asking him about his health was the worst insult I could have offered him—far worse than any of the dozen slams that Giulia and I had thought up together. My concern evaporated in a hot rush of satisfaction, like the flow of lava that had swept down Mount Vesuvius and destroyed Pompeii.

"A thousand thanks, Irene," Matteo snarled. "So sweet. So polite. Now I know how it is to be a girl on the field: weak, slow, terrible."

"Ha! Obviously, you were not watching me. I can do something during a game that you cannot."

Matteo stood up. "*Impossibile!*"

"No. It's *possibile*. And it is something important. Everyone agrees."

"You have divided the squad. You have ruined soccer for me this year."

I could have spat the words back in his face, but I would not give him the satisfaction. I kept my voice calm and low. "I can pass the ball. You, no."

"Pffff. I can do it too."

"Really? How many assists do you have this fall?"

Matteo's eyes flickered upward, a sign that he was scanning his memory.

"Zero," I told him. "It's true that you are our center forward, our striker. But sometimes, even for you, it is a good idea to pass the ball. How strange that a *ragazza* who spent most of her time on defense has an assist and you don't. But there's still one period left. You have the opportunity to make a tie."

"Irene, the *mister* comes," Federico whispered.

At that moment, I realized that my face and Matteo's were inches apart. I loosened my clenched fists, took a step back, and nodded at him. "Good luck."

As I turned away, I caught sight of my entire family staring at me from the stands. They'd seen me arguing with Max enough to recognize the signs. Nonna's hands covered her mouth. I could imagine what she was thinking. It was bad enough for her granddaughter to be on the field without fighting with her own teammate. Pretending that nothing was wrong, I waved. *La bella figura.* Appearances are everything.

"All right," the *mister* said. "Davide can continue, but must rest a bit first. The game recommences soon. Listen well." He held up his clipboard and rattled off a list of people and their positions. Davide, Roberto, and I were not on it.

That was okay. It gave me a chance to get my breath back. I sat down and arranged my sweatpants on top of my legs like a blanket.

Davide paced back and forth without the smallest sign of a limp. "I'm fine, Irene," he said as he passed me. "My ankle only hurt me for ten seconds before the end of the period. Ten seconds. It's nothing. Absolutely nothing."

"Patience. Don't worry yourself. Within five minutes, you'll return."

It only took four. Then it was my turn to pace. My muscles had begun to tighten up in the cold air. I walked and waited. Roberto went in for Manuel, and still I waited.

The *mister* finally turned to me. "Irene, at the next throw-in, you go in for Emi. But I want you on the left wing and Federico on the right. Clear?"

"*Sì.*"

But the ball stayed in the field of play. I bounced on my toes and jogged in place. Finally, one of Bolzano's forwards lost control of the ball, and it rolled out of bounds. I came in, Emi came out, and Federico moved over.

Every time the ball moved into the third of the field closest to Luigi, I had to fight the urge to go down there and help. But that wasn't my job. I had to stay wide in order to be ready for a pass, so the defenders could clear it out of the dangerous zone. But the defenders for Bolzano II seemed to feel the magnetic pull of the ball. They drifted across the centerline.

A shot went up toward Luigi, hard and fast. Extending his arms, he caught the ball and pulled it in. He raced a few steps to his left up the field, found a small clear area, and punted the ball downfield—to me.

A defender rushed to meet me. I faked to the inside and then drove left. With that, the player was behind me and I launched into my first breakaway of the year. His *mister* probably hadn't studied me the way opposition coaches used to in Missouri. He hadn't been told: "Attention! The girl prefers to drive to the left."

Not a single yellow-shirted player stood between me and my destination. The goalie wore black.

"*Forza,* Irene, *forza!*" Nonno roared from the stands.

"Lengthen the legs, Irene! *Dai! Dai! Dai!*" the *mister* yelled.

I drove my arms, clenched my teeth and dribbled the ball downfield. This was my chance to score. Under the shouts and cheers from both teams, I could hear footsteps behind me.

"*Dai,* Irene, *dai!*" Matteo shouted. It sounded like honest encouragement, but he was probably just letting me know he wasn't far behind. Good. If the goalkeeper deflected my shot, someone would be there to tap in the rebound.

The goalkeeper stayed in front of the net. With two of us pounding down the field toward him, he wouldn't come out and commit to me too soon. Would he come out at all? Well, if he stayed there, I could put the ball anywhere I wanted.

"*Dai, dai, dai,* Irene!" Matteo shouted. He was somewhere to the right of me, somewhere just behind the range of my peripheral vision, so he wouldn't be offsides in case I wanted to pass him the ball. Dreamer.

Finally, the goalkeeper made his move, rushing forward like a spider. Decision time. I could loft it over his head with a chip shot, smash it into the right corner, or fake my way past him. But there was one more option: a way to take the goalkeeper out of the play and give our team its best chance to score. I passed the ball to the right, to Matteo. He surged into view. With grace, speed, and an almost unimaginably light touch, he shot the ball into the empty net.

"*Goal!*" Nonno shouted, his voice carrying above the crowd. "*Brava! Bravi!*"

"*Brava!*" The shout came from my teammates all around the field. "*Bravo!*"

I walked over to congratulate Matteo. It was a matter of *la bella figura*. Not to mention a chance to show my *nonna* that I was gracious and my *nonno* that I was a good sport. At least it would look that way from a distance.

I smacked my right palm against his and asked, "Two assists to zero. Did that pass please you, Matteo? Want another one? Maybe in March when we begin again."

"No. I will never play with you anymore. Never. I have finished with the *Esordienti*. I promise you."

That stopped me. My eyebrows pulled together. Nothing I said had been that awful, had it? A few snotty comments from me should not have been enough to drive a player with a future like his off the team. But I choked back questions. I had once made a promise of my own: that I would never believe Matteo again. Something wasn't right. This wasn't the U.S., where he had tons of other options. Somehow I couldn't see him joining a local German club. How could he give up soccer just to avoid three months on a team with me? The answer was…he couldn't. And then, I understood.

"Ah, you go on to the *Giovanissimi* in the spring. *Complimenti.*"

Amica donna mia: My Lady Friend

Federico arrived just in time to hear my guess. "Really, Matteo? What good news. Without you, I will start every game."

Matteo looked like a boy whose lit firecracker had landed in a puddle. "Without me, you will lose every game."

I shrugged and started my walk back to the centerline. "We did not have you last week."

Matteo stayed even with me. "Others will probably move on too: Emi, Manuel, Werner, Davide, Luigi."

My smile slipped. I would still see Emi, Manuel and Luigi in school, but not Werner or Davide.

"*Poverina.* But how darling," Matteo crooned in a sarcastic falsetto. "Irene and the *piccoli pulcini.*"

Irene and the little chicks.

I straightened my shoulders. "Someone must give them a good example. I will miss my friends. But I will not miss you. Not even if we lose every game."

"Irene!" the *mister* shouted. "On defense, Irene. You will be the stopper."

I nodded. While the other defenders would go up to the centerline, I would stay back in the penalty area to keep the other team from making a breakaway like mine. Like mine. I shivered, but not from the cold. On the way to my new position, I collected *complimenti* from Davide, Werner, and my other tired teammates, who had decided to save their energy instead of coming forward for the celebration.

My new position was so far back that Luigi stepped out of the goal to meet me. "So, Irene, why didn't you take off the head of the goalkeeper?"

I grinned at him. "It was more important that someone make a goal. Even Matteo."

Defending Irene

"*Amica donna mia!*" He hugged me. I hugged him back, not worrying about my bruised ribs or what Nonna, Max, or Matteo might say later. Luigi's words, taken separately, meant "friend, lady, my." But together they were the title to a song by my favorite Italian singer, Eros Ramazzotti, about a girl who wouldn't let anyone stop her. She would change the world because she knew what she wanted. I had never gotten a better compliment.

Luigi thumped my back twice and pulled away. "All right. Now we must stop them. And it will be the best season the *mister* has ever had. Ever. Even better than that of Renzo."

Bolzano attacked, but we didn't let anyone, not even Number 22, close enough to shoot. The final whistle sounded, ending the best season the *mister* ever had. And ending a lot of other things too.

After we shook hands with the other team, the *mister* called us around him.

"I could tell you about a hundred different mistakes. But today, no. I am very proud of you. I am proud of how you worked together. I am proud of your energy and determination. And this came after injuries and influenza. *Complimenti!*" He paused to take a breath. We applauded ourselves and cheered.

"*Brava*, Irene," the *mister* continued. "Two assists!"

More cheers. Hands patted my head and shoulders and tugged at my braids.

"*Bravo*, Matteo, we are very glad you could catch up to Irene on the breakaway. In such a case, two are always more dangerous than one. It pleased me to see you work together so well.

Amica donna mia: My Lady Friend

"I think about this season and see two things that make it different from all the others. First, we had a fan—a fan who came to every game. Rain, wind, cold—nothing has stopped him. Because of him, we had fourteen on the field today. It was important. A thousand thanks to the *papá* of Irene." The *mister* stepped out of the circle and waved his hand at my dad. "Hip hip—"

"Hurrah!" we said like a well-trained chorus.

Dad rubbed his forehead and shook his head. My *nonno* grinned.

The *mister* turned back to us. "All right. There is a second difference between this season and all the others: You have not lost a game!"

Whoops and applause.

"You have not won every game, but one tie is not so bad, eh? To tell you the truth, I don't know how you did it. Certainly, it was not always *bella.* But you were determined and stubborn. *Bravi!* Well done."

The *mister* let us applaud ourselves one more time. Then he waved us to silence. "All right. Enough. It's cold. Dress yourselves. Soccer is finished, but I still don't want you to become sick. *Dai.*"

Shoulder to shoulder with my teammates, I dug through the pile of sweat suits for my jacket and sweatpants. I couldn't stop smiling. We had won. I had two assists. Matteo was leaving. And having me, a *calciatrice,* on the team had not made the *mister's* list of things that made this season unusual.

By the time I had changed clothes and collected everything, my family had already walked on without me. I was grateful that I could be part of the team for a few more minutes instead of having my *nonna* rush me over to the Advent Market. The hand-carved manger scenes, ceramic angels, and blown-glass ornaments could wait.

Luigi, Manuel, Werner, and I walked together, analyzing the game and describing the plays to each other. Was this really for the last time? Since not trusting Matteo was one of my policies, I waited for an opening to ask: "So, who else besides Matteo goes on to the *Giovanissimi* in the spring?"

"Matteo already knows?" Manuel shook his head. "Typical."

"Matteo thinks the three of you will move on too," I said.

"I hope so," Manuel said.

Werner nodded. "Me too."

"For me, it depends," Luigi said. "If Antonio Verdi moves onto the *Allievi,* the *Giovanissimi* will have need of a good goalkeeper. Otherwise, no. It would please me to play for the *mister* one last time."

That would have definitely pleased me too, but I said: "Even if you do not play every game, you would improve more with tougher players, no?"

Luigi tilted his head. "I have Renzo at home in the garden. It's enough."

"I believe you," I said, remembering the scorching shots from Luigi's older brother before our last game.

"Not only that, but if the weather is nice enough, the friends of Renzo come to play a couple of times a week during the winter."

"*Bello,*" I said.

"You are invited," Luigi said. The Italian word he used, *invitata,* was singular and feminine. Before Manuel's lips could finish curving for the inevitable "Oooooo!" Luigi added, "All of you are invited."

"That would please me," Werner said.

Manuel nodded. "Me too."

"I will come. Thanks," I said.

"It's nothing. We must stay in shape."

"Agreed," I said. "Without all of you, we *Esordienti* must work hard."

"*Ma dai,* Irene," Werner said. "Maybe you will go on too."

I shrugged. "The *mister* already asked, 'Are you playing with us next spring?'"

"Has he said 'with me' or 'with us?'" Luigi asked.

I thought back. "With us."

"*Madonna!* With us means with the club, not just the *Esordienti.* Maybe you'll go on. We'll see."

We reached the van. The *mister* had already unlocked the doors and most of our teammates had piled inside. My family stood waiting on the sidewalk nearby.

"*Ciao,* Irene," Federico said. He leaned toward me, holding up his hand. I gave him five.

Other blue-sleeved arms reached out. I slapped their hands too, climbing halfway into the van to finish the job. Matteo sat in the backseat with his arms crossed.

"*Ciao,*" I said. "We'll see each other later."

"Until Monday, Irene. *Ciao.*" Luigi pulled himself into the front seat, humming. As he slammed the door shut, I recognized the song by Eros Ramazzotti.

Yours will be the right step—the new way.

Amica donna mia.

NORAGAMI
STRAY GOD

ADACHITOKA

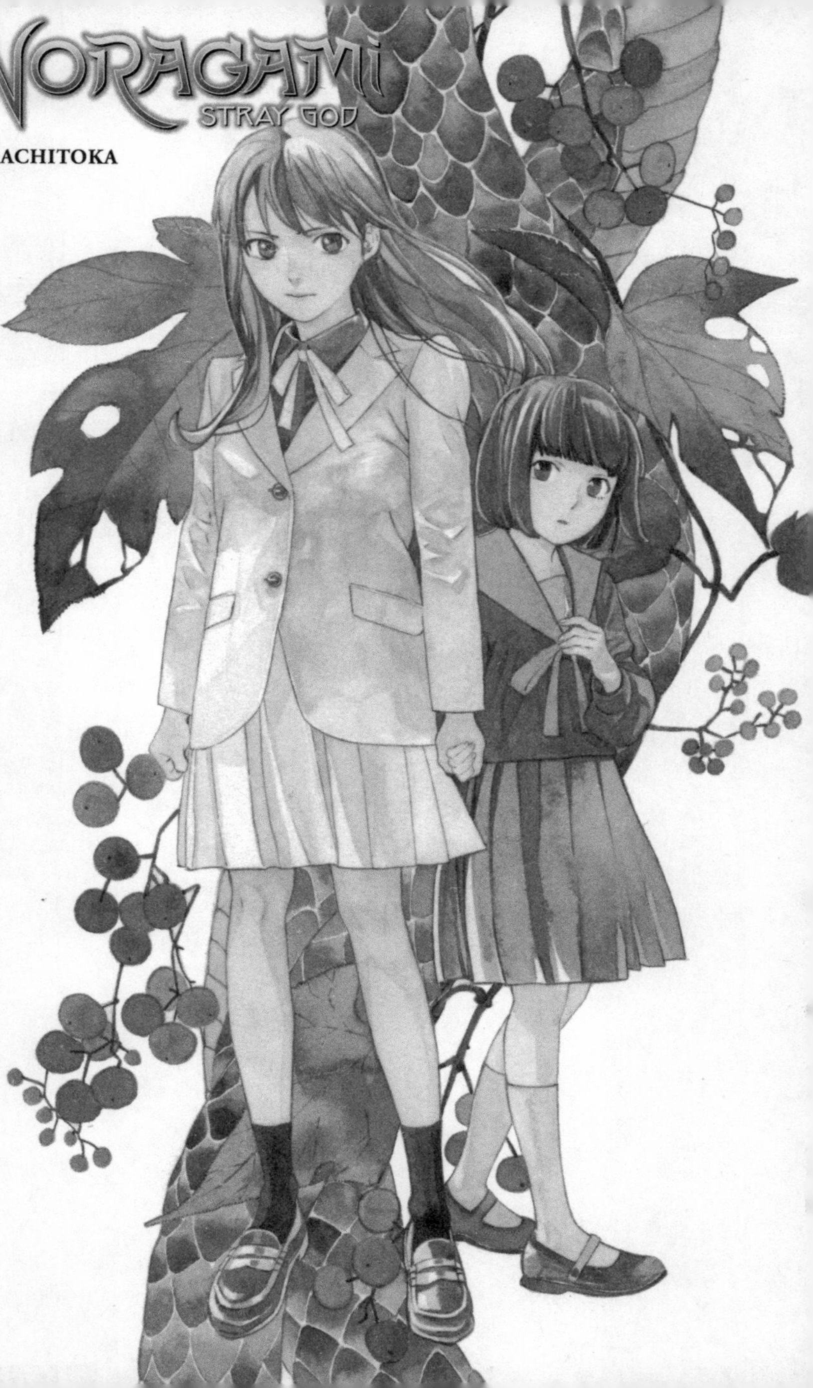

characters

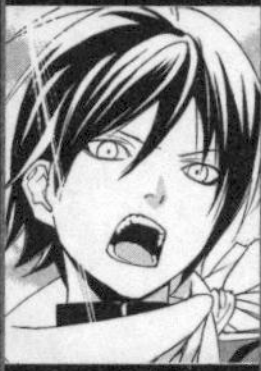

YATO

A minor deity who always wears a sweatsuit.

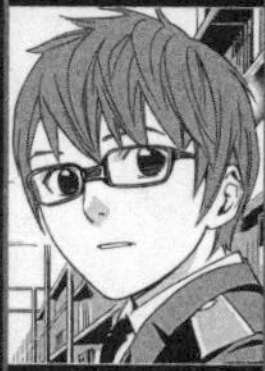

KAZUMA/ KAZUNÉ

Bishamon's shinki who now works for Yato.

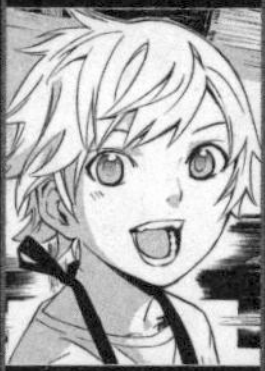

YUKINÉ/ HAGUSA

Yato's shinki who turns into swords.

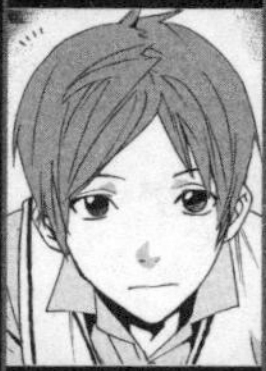

KÔTO FUJISAKI

The crafter who disrupts the world order. Yato's father.

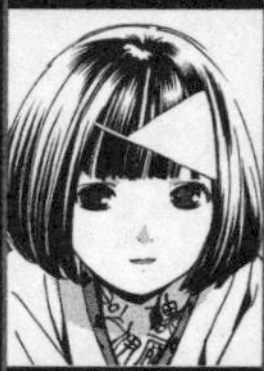

STRAY

A shinki who serves an unspecified number of deities.

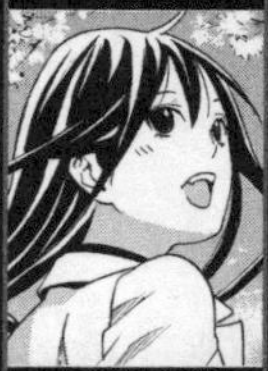

HIYORI IKI

A high school student who has become half ayakashi.

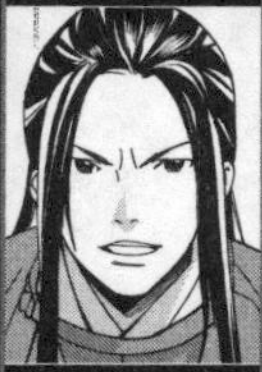

TAKE-MIKAZUCHI

A warrior god who causes Brave Lightning to strike the earth.

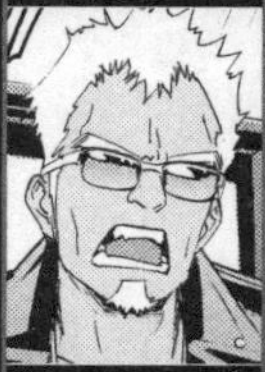

ÔKUNI-NUSHI (DAIKOKU-TEN)

Number one of the Seven Gods of Fortune.

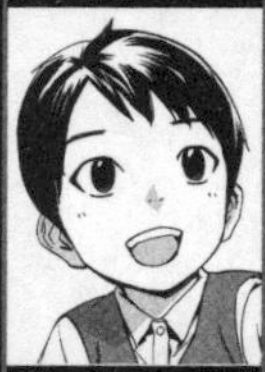

EBISU

A business-god in the making, one of the Seven Gods of Fortune.

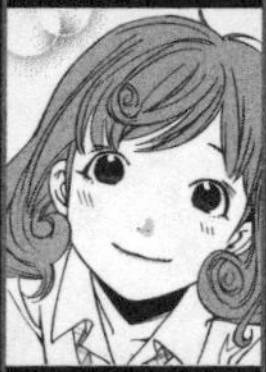

KOFUKU

A goddess of poverty who calls herself Ebisu after the god of fortune.

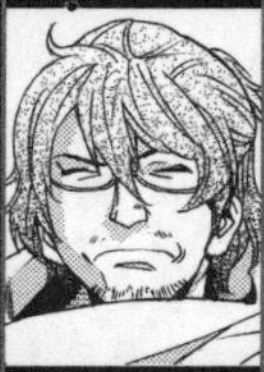

ARA-HABAKI

A god of the indigenous peoples of the north who was once struck down by the Heavens.

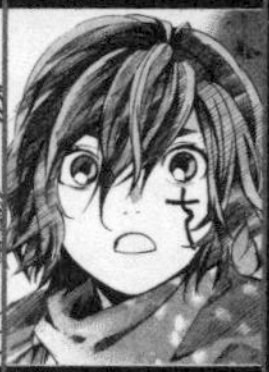

NANA

A burial vessel who was sealed away by the Heavens.

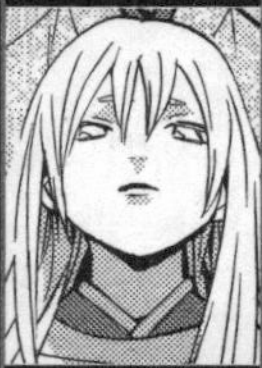

AMA-TERASU ÔMIKAMI

The god who rules all under the sun.

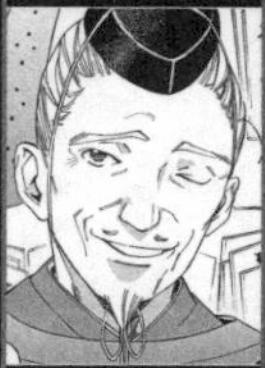

TENJIN

The god of learning, Sugawara no Michizane.

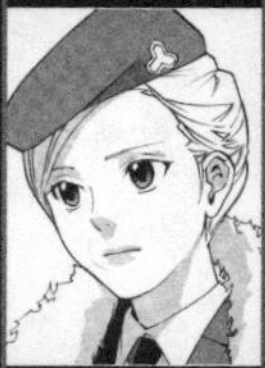

BISHAMON-TEN

A powerful warrior god, one of the Seven Gods of Fortune.

野

曼

師

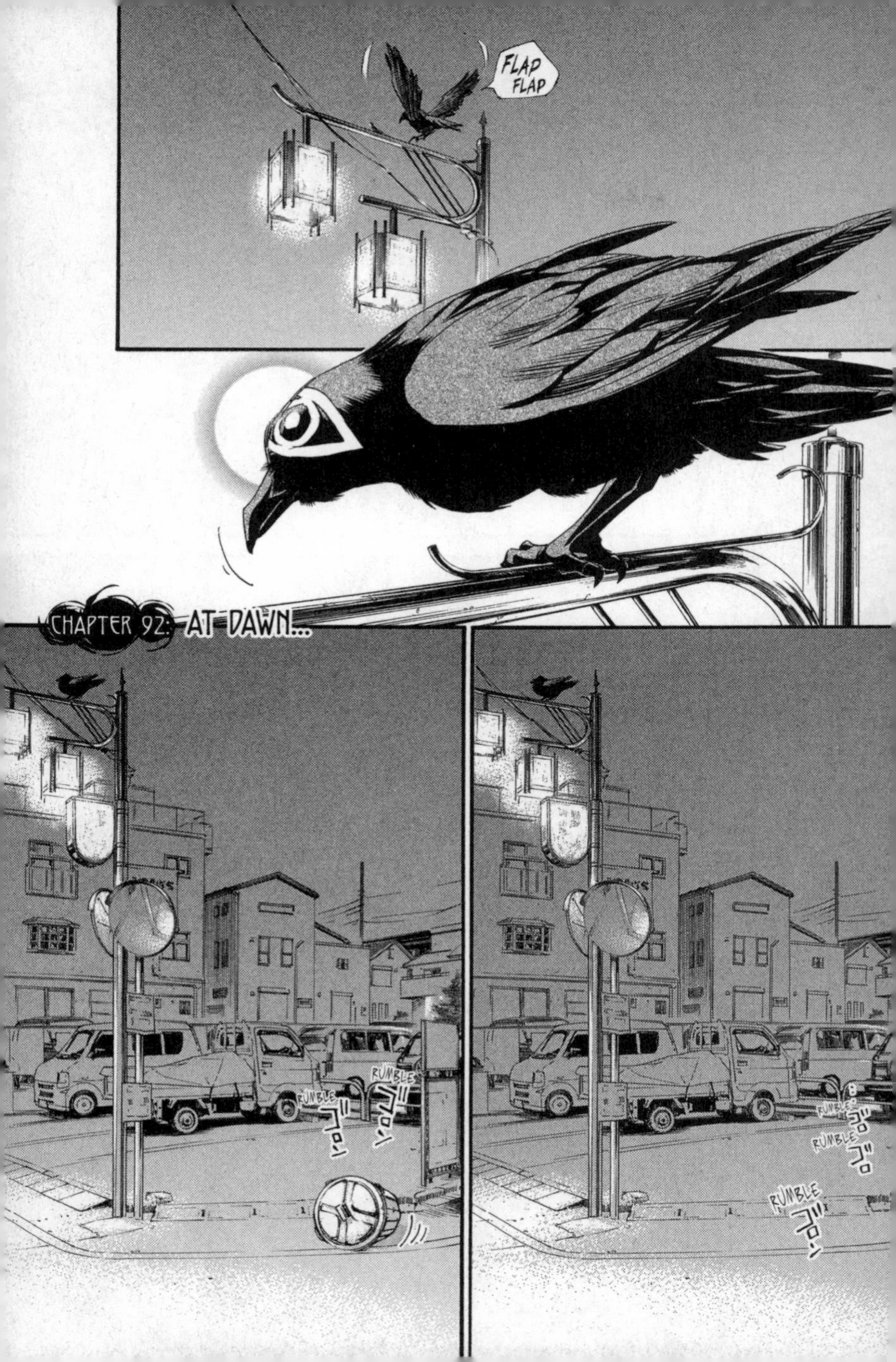
FLAP FLAP
CHAPTER 92: AT DAWN...
RUMBLE
RUMBLE
RUMBLE
RUMBLE
RUMBLE

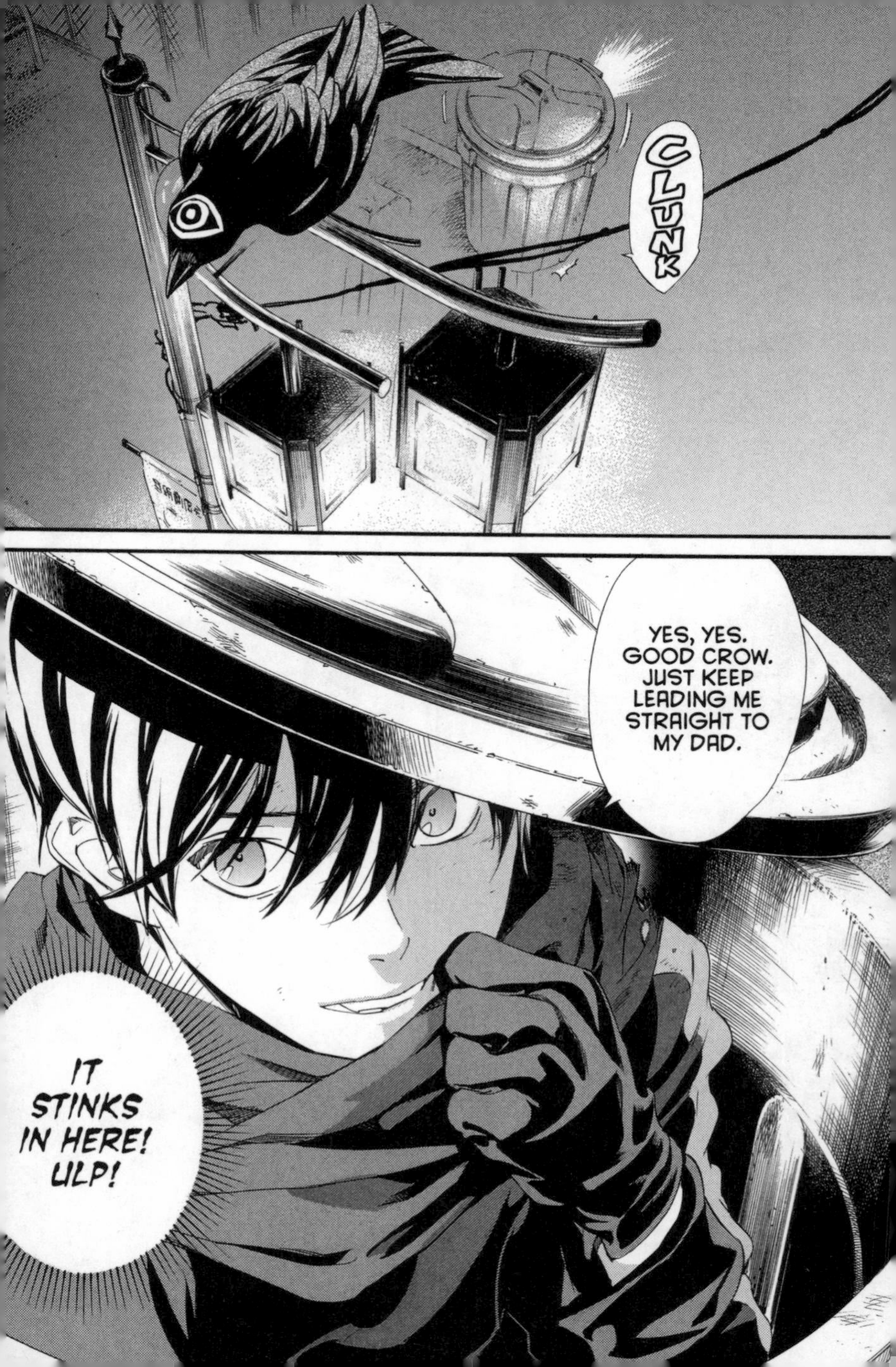
CLUNK
YES, YES. GOOD CROW. JUST KEEP LEADING ME STRAIGHT TO MY DAD.
IT STINKS IN HERE! ULP!

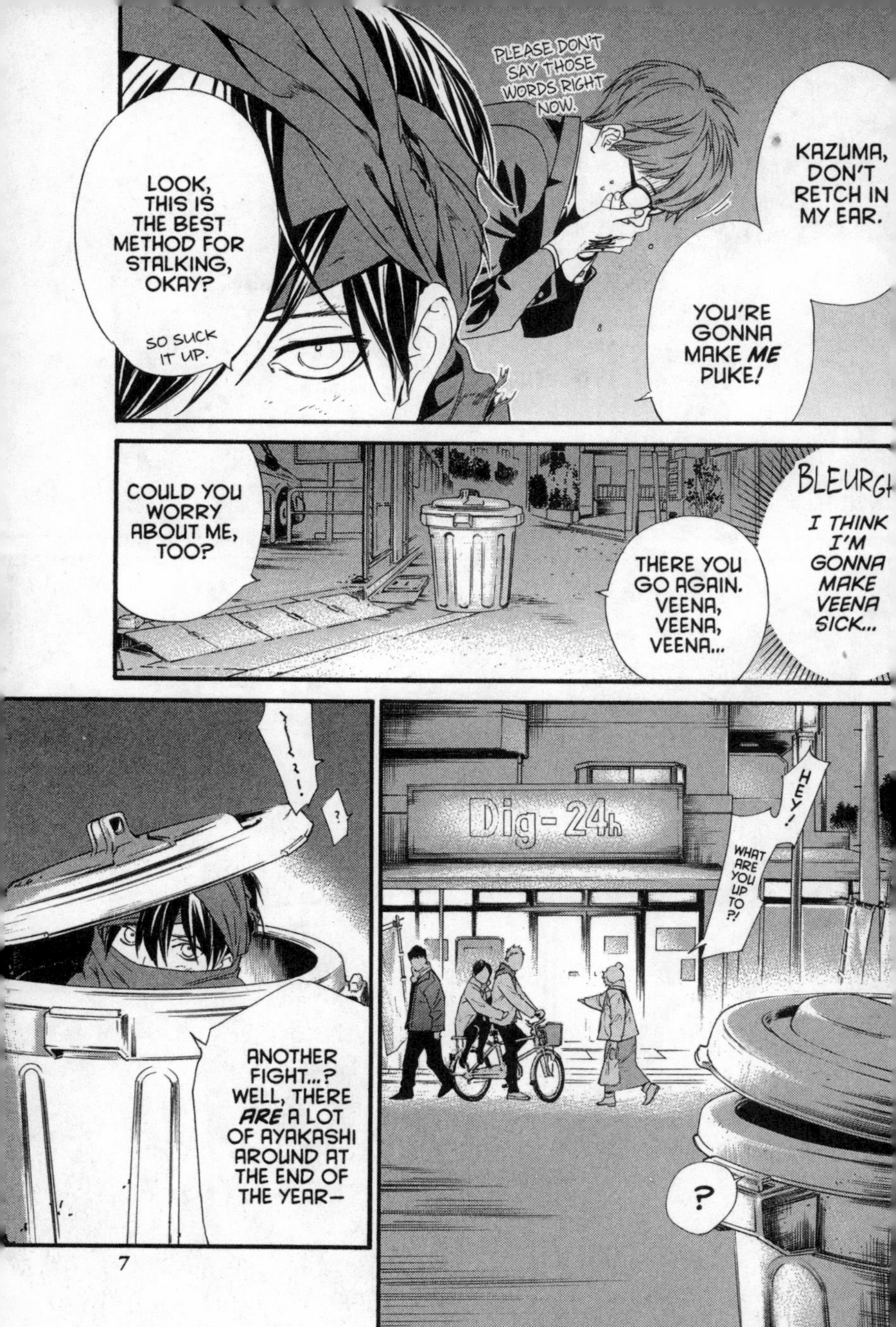
KAZUMA, DON'T RETCH IN MY EAR.
YOU'RE GONNA MAKE *ME* PUKE!
PLEASE DON'T SAY THOSE WORDS RIGHT NOW.
LOOK, THIS IS THE BEST METHOD FOR STALKING, OKAY?
SO SUCK IT UP.
BLEURGH
I THINK I'M GONNA MAKE VEENA SICK...
THERE YOU GO AGAIN. VEENA, VEENA, VEENA...
COULD YOU WORRY ABOUT ME, TOO?
HEY!
WHAT ARE YOU UP TO?!
Dig-24h
?
!?
?
ANOTHER FIGHT...? WELL, THERE *ARE* A LOT OF AYAKASHI AROUND AT THE END OF THE YEAR—

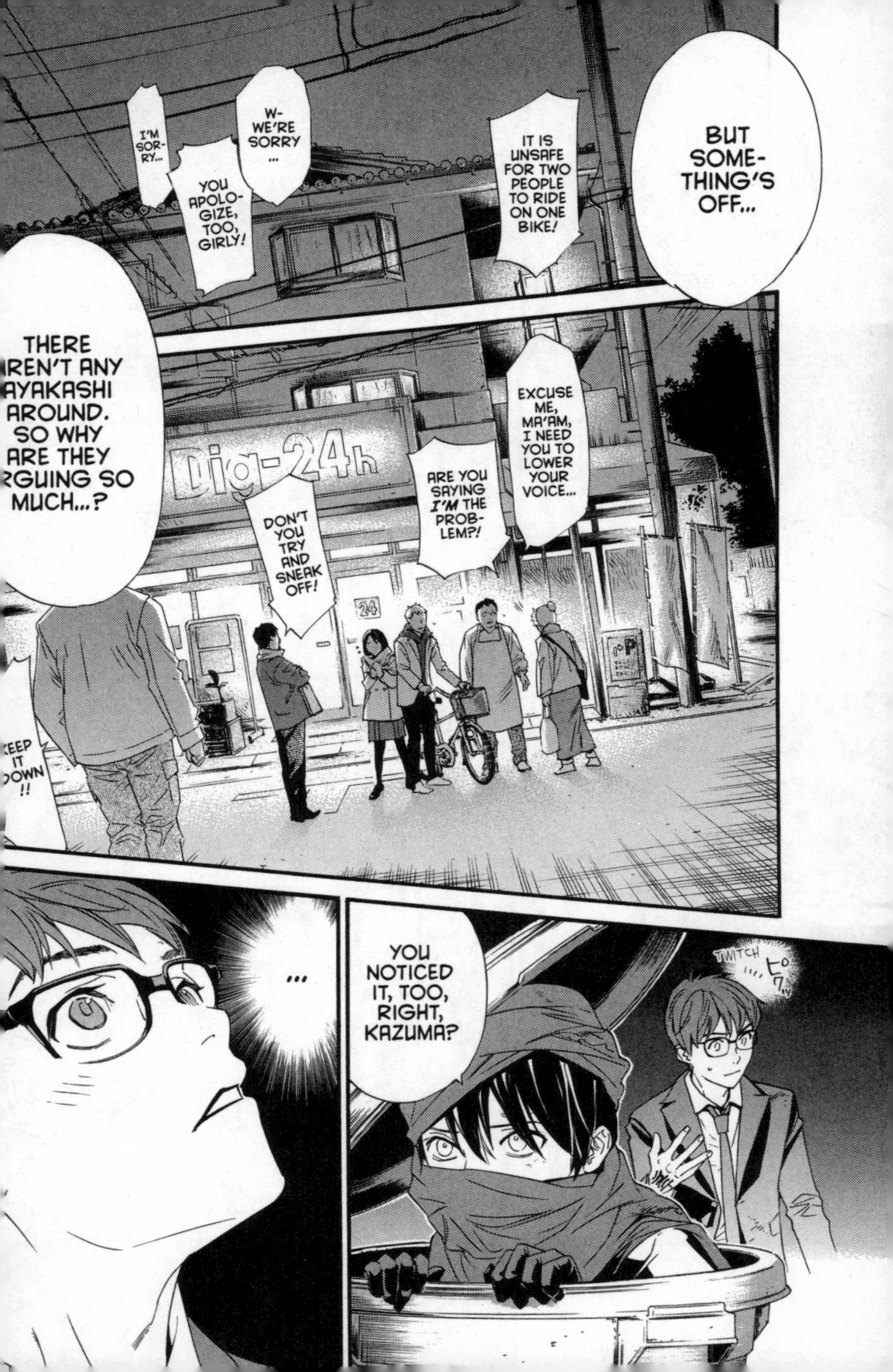
BUT SOMETHING'S OFF...
IT IS UNSAFE FOR TWO PEOPLE TO RIDE ON ONE BIKE!
W-WE'RE SORRY ...
YOU APOLOGIZE, TOO, GIRLY!
I'M SORRY...
EXCUSE ME, MA'AM, I NEED YOU TO LOWER YOUR VOICE...
ARE YOU SAYING *I'M* THE PROBLEM?!
DON'T YOU TRY AND SNEAK OFF!
THERE RENT ANY YAKASHI AROUND. SO WHY ARE THEY RGUING SO MUCH...?
EEP IT OWN!!
TWITCH
YOU NOTICED IT, TOO, RIGHT, KAZUMA?
...

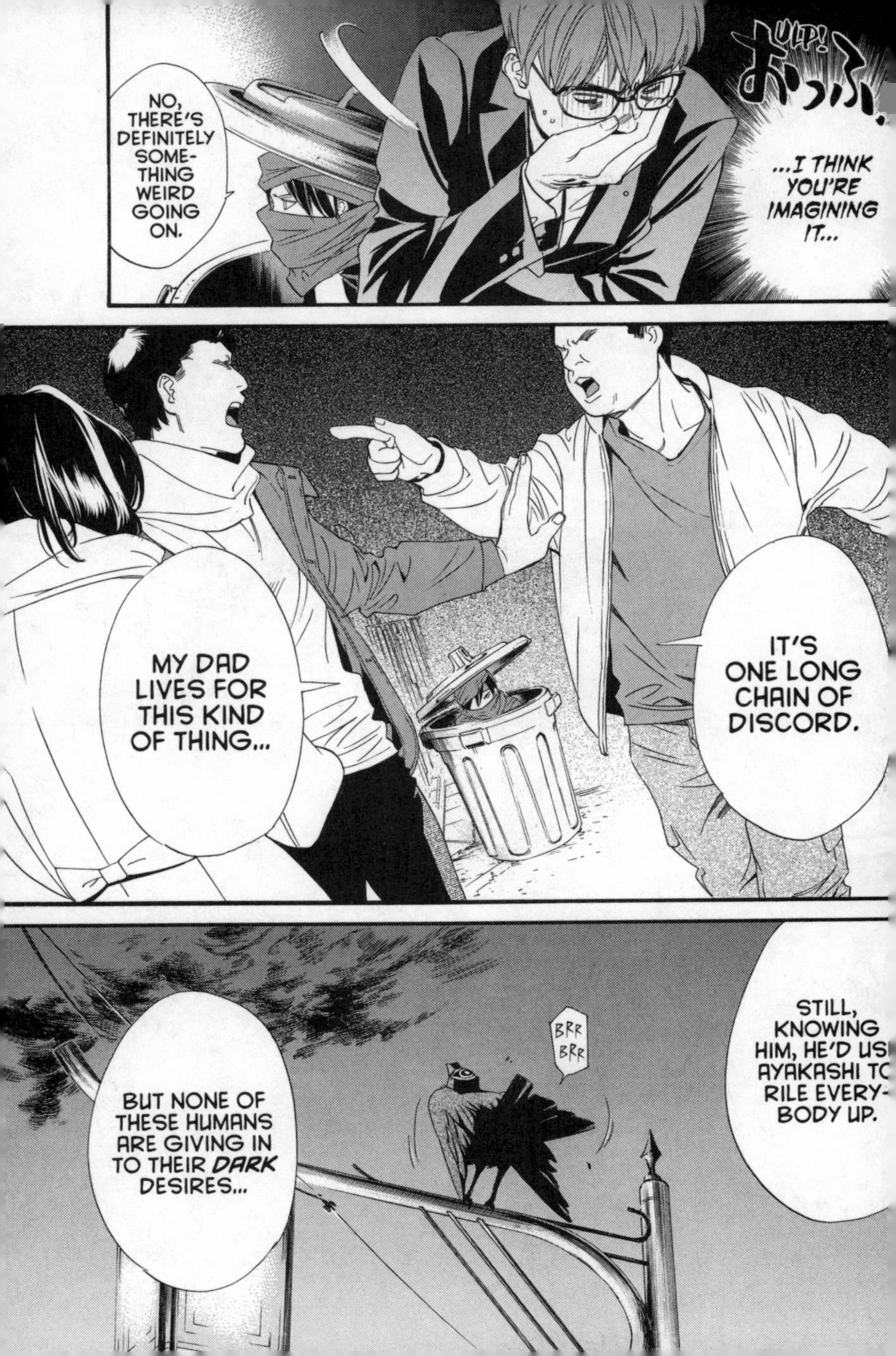
ULP!
おっふ
...I THINK YOU'RE IMAGINING IT...
NO, THERE'S DEFINITELY SOMETHING WEIRD GOING ON.
IT'S ONE LONG CHAIN OF DISCORD.
MY DAD LIVES FOR THIS KIND OF THING...
STILL, KNOWING HIM, HE'D USE AYAKASHI TO RILE EVERYBODY UP.
BRR BRR
BUT NONE OF THESE HUMANS ARE GIVING IN TO THEIR *DARK* DESIRES...

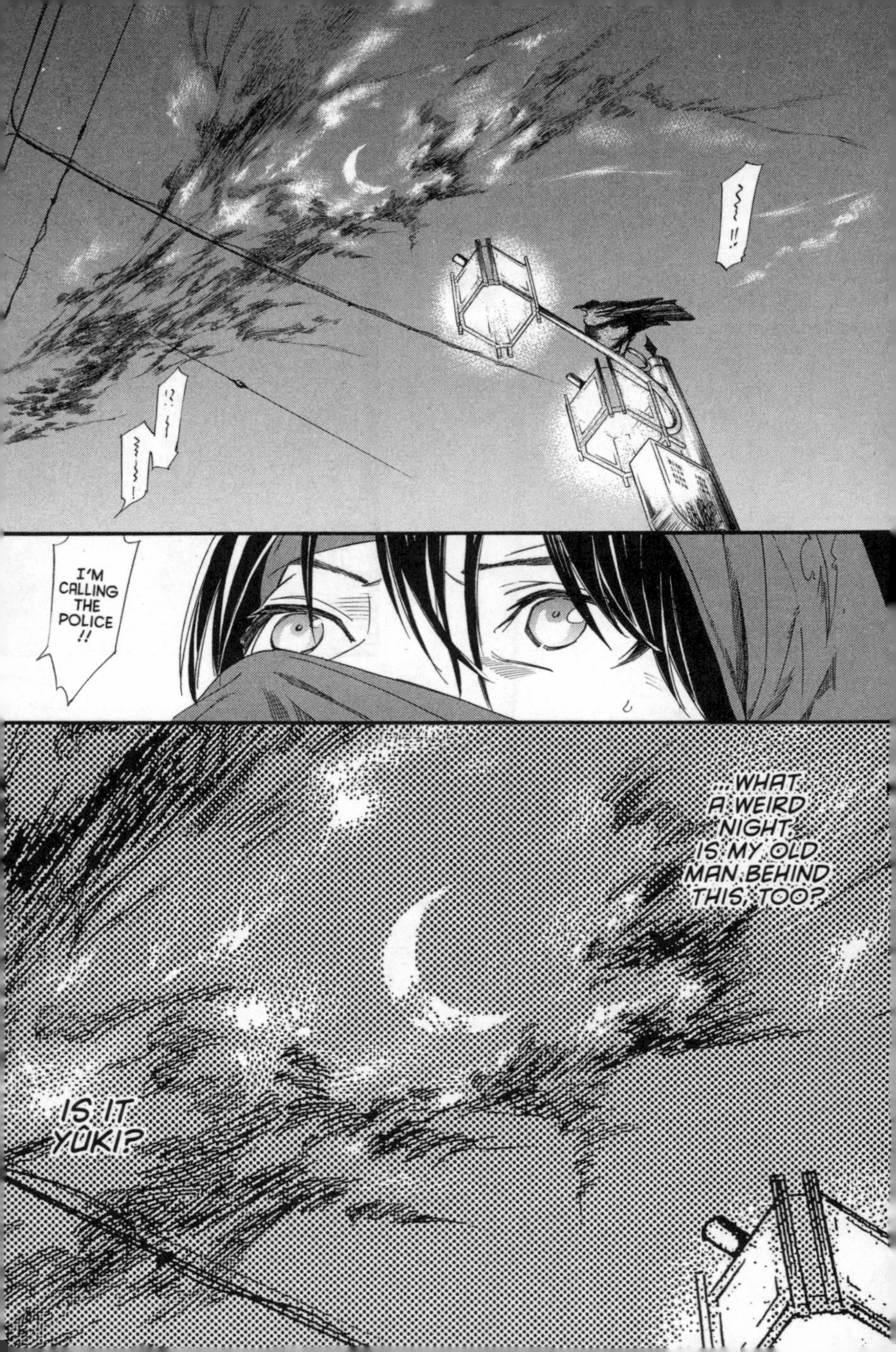
~~!!
!?~~~!
I'M CALLING THE POLICE!!
...WHAT A WEIRD NIGHT. IS MY OLD MAN BEHIND THIS, TOO?
IS IT YUKI?

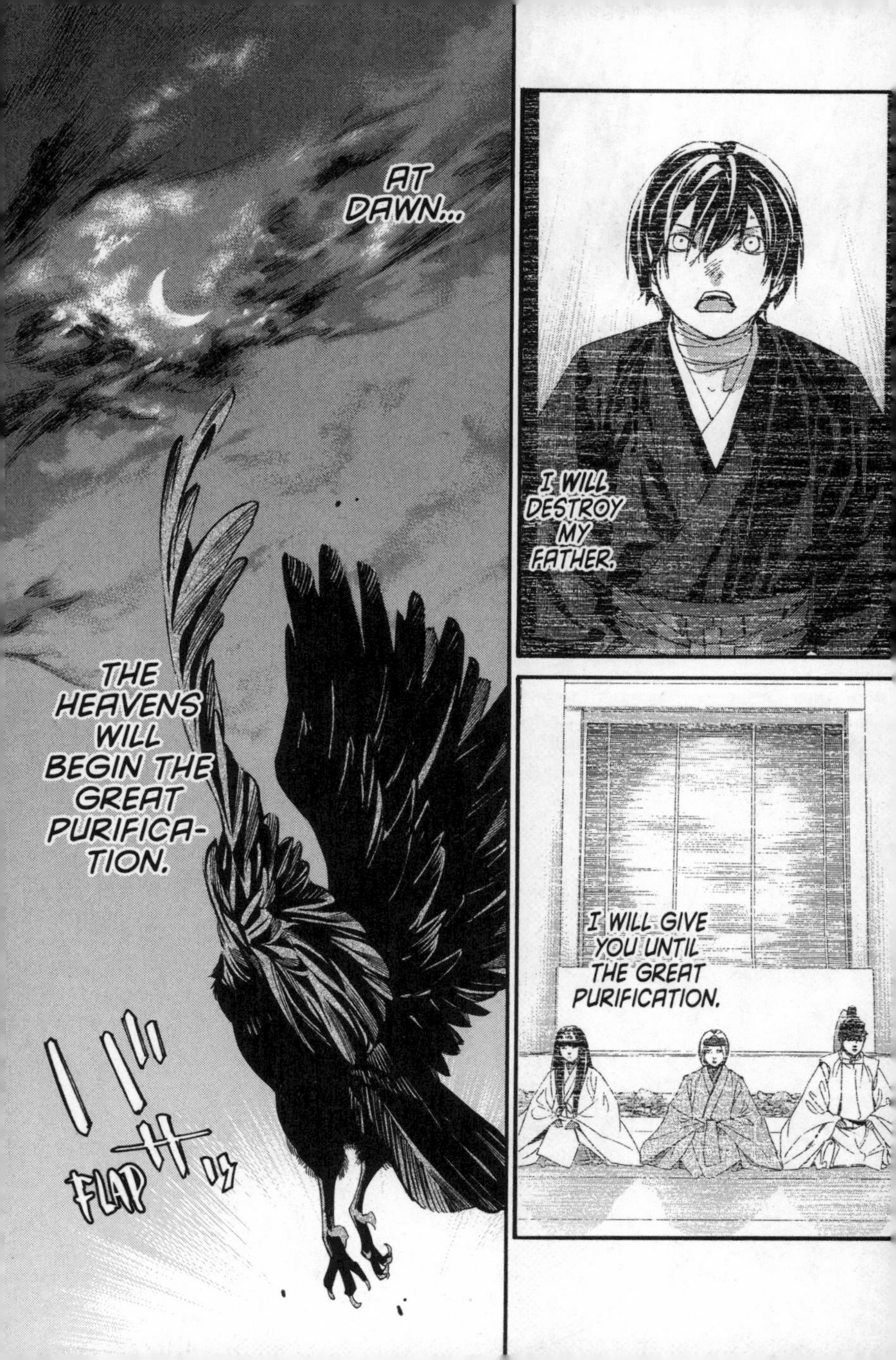
I WILL DESTROY MY FATHER.
I WILL GIVE YOU UNTIL THE GREAT PURIFICATION.
AT DAWN...
THE HEAVENS WILL BEGIN THE GREAT PURIFICATION.
FLAP

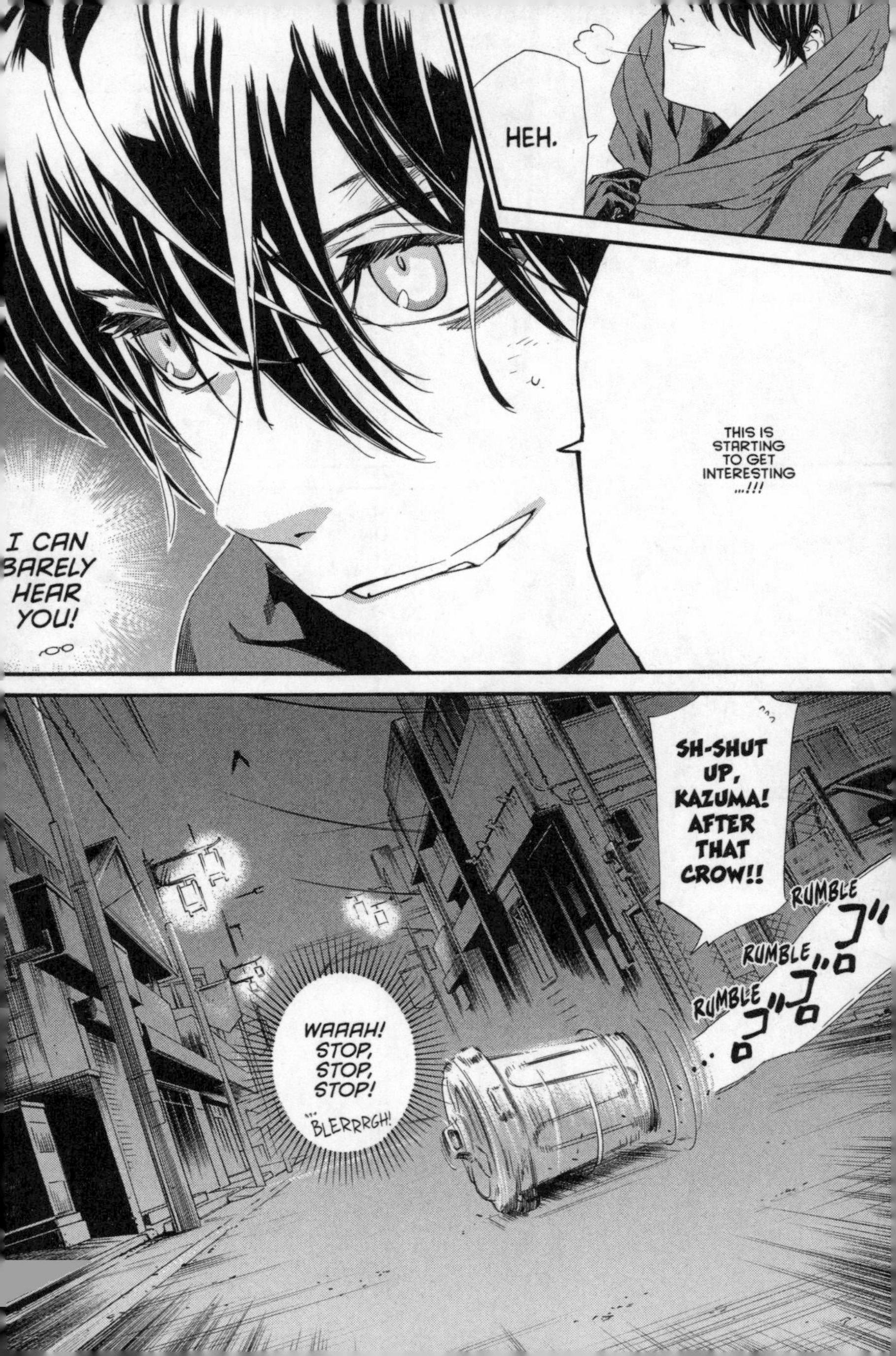
HEH.
THIS IS STARTING TO GET INTERESTING ...!!!
I CAN BARELY HEAR YOU!
SH-SHUT UP, KAZUMA! AFTER THAT CROW!!
RUMBLE
RUMBLE
RUMBLE
WAAAH! STOP, STOP, STOP!
BLERRRGH!

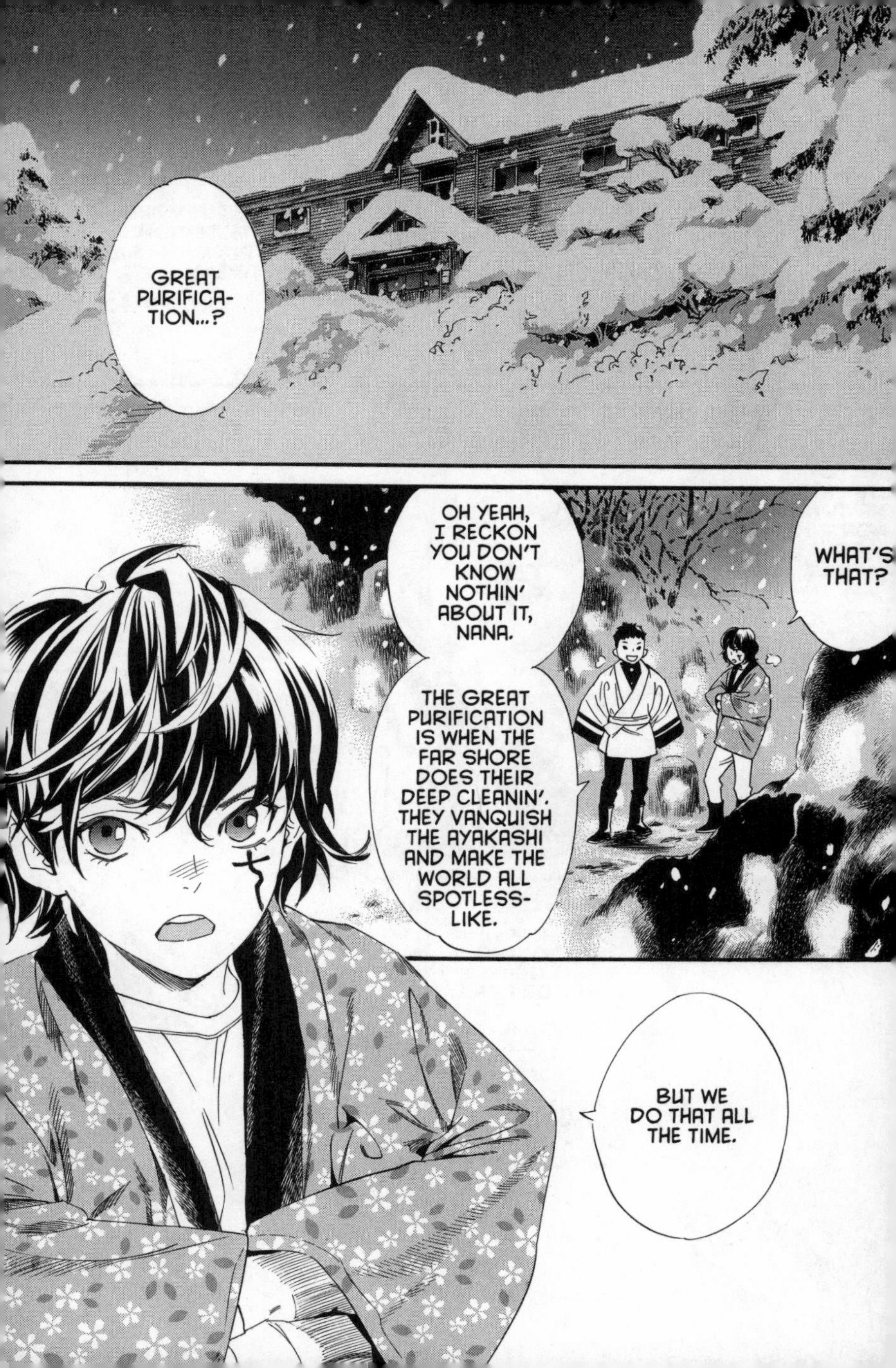
GREAT PURIFICA-TION...?
WHAT'S THAT?
OH YEAH, I RECKON YOU DON'T KNOW NOTHIN' ABOUT IT, NANA.
THE GREAT PURIFICATION IS WHEN THE FAR SHORE DOES THEIR DEEP CLEANIN'. THEY VANQUISH THE AYAKASHI AND MAKE THE WORLD ALL SPOTLESS-LIKE.
BUT WE DO THAT ALL THE TIME.

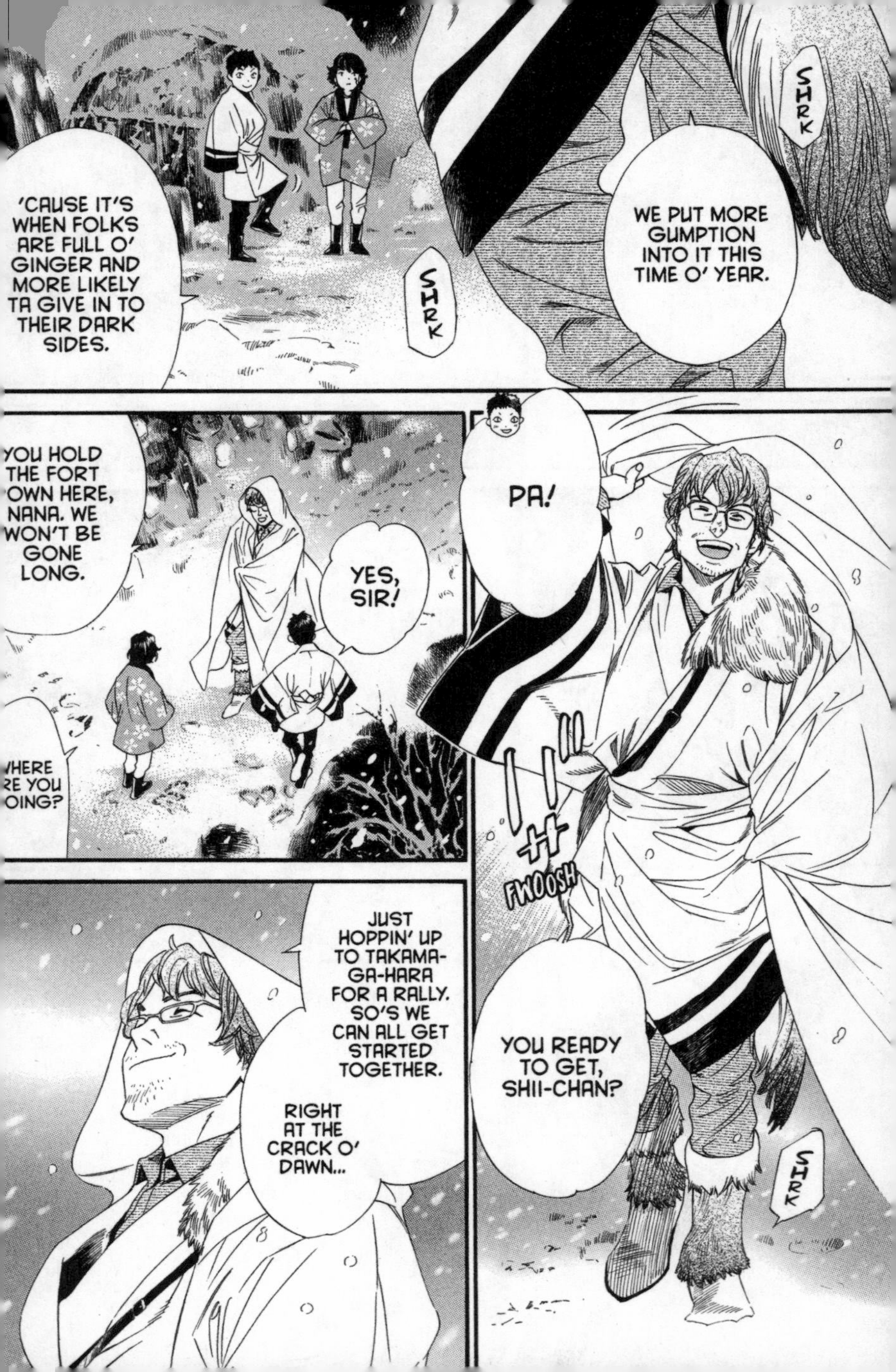
SHRK
WE PUT MORE GUMPTION INTO IT THIS TIME O' YEAR.
SHRK
'CAUSE IT'S WHEN FOLKS ARE FULL O' GINGER AND MORE LIKELY TA GIVE IN TO THEIR DARK SIDES.
PA!
FWOOSH
YOU READY TO GET, SHII-CHAN?
SHRK
YOU HOLD THE FORT OWN HERE, NANA. WE WON'T BE GONE LONG.
YES, SIR!
WHERE RE YOU OING?
JUST HOPPIN' UP TO TAKAMA-GA-HARA FOR A RALLY. SO'S WE CAN ALL GET STARTED TOGETHER.
RIGHT AT THE CRACK O' DAWN...

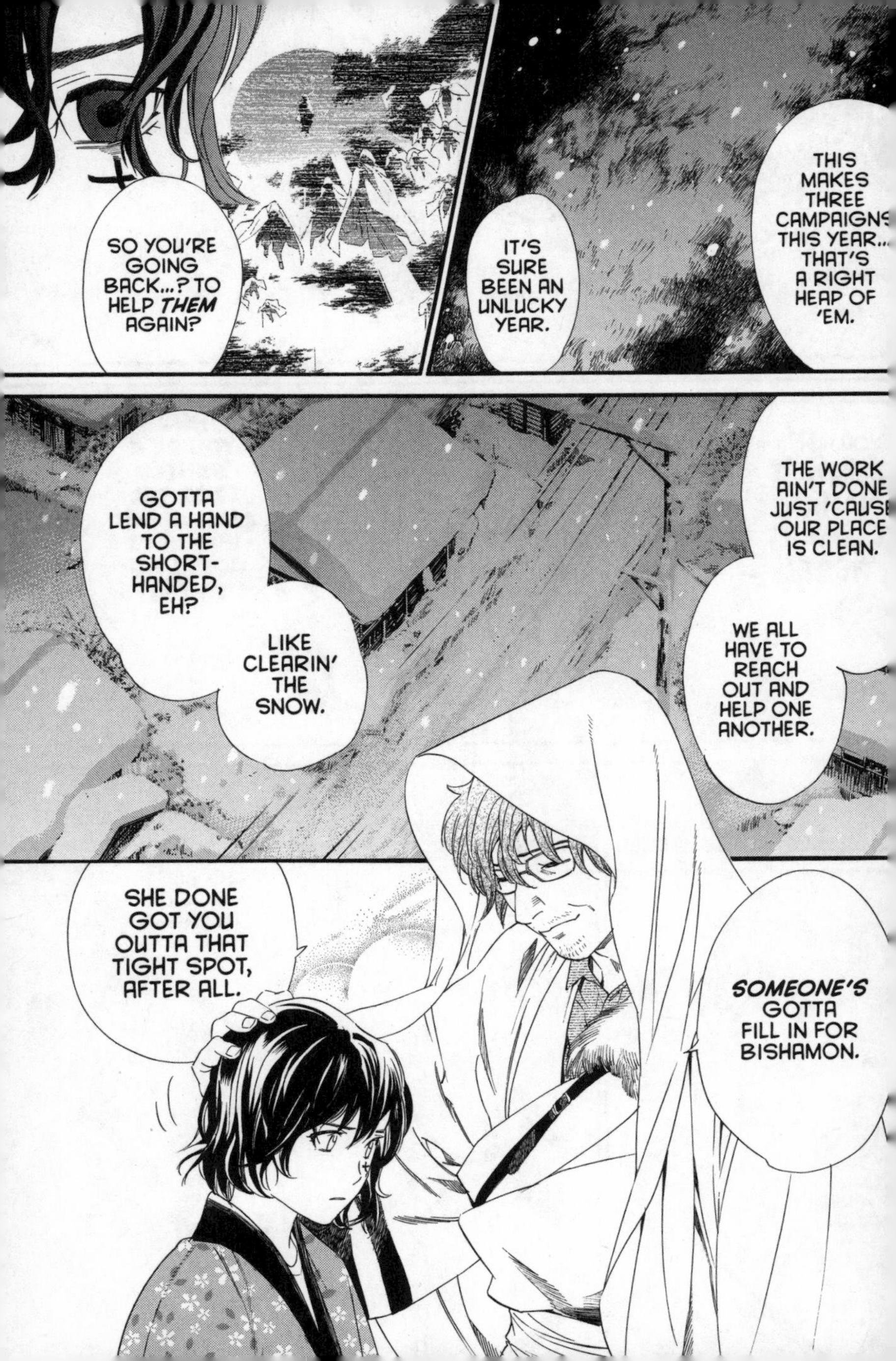
THIS MAKES THREE CAMPAIGNS THIS YEAR... THAT'S A RIGHT HEAP OF 'EM.
IT'S SURE BEEN AN UNLUCKY YEAR.
SO YOU'RE GOING BACK...? TO HELP *THEM* AGAIN?
THE WORK AIN'T DONE JUST 'CAUSE OUR PLACE IS CLEAN.
WE ALL HAVE TO REACH OUT AND HELP ONE ANOTHER.
GOTTA LEND A HAND TO THE SHORT-HANDED, EH?
LIKE CLEARIN' THE SNOW.
SOMEONE'S GOTTA FILL IN FOR BISHAMON.
SHE DONE GOT YOU OUTTA THAT TIGHT SPOT, AFTER ALL.

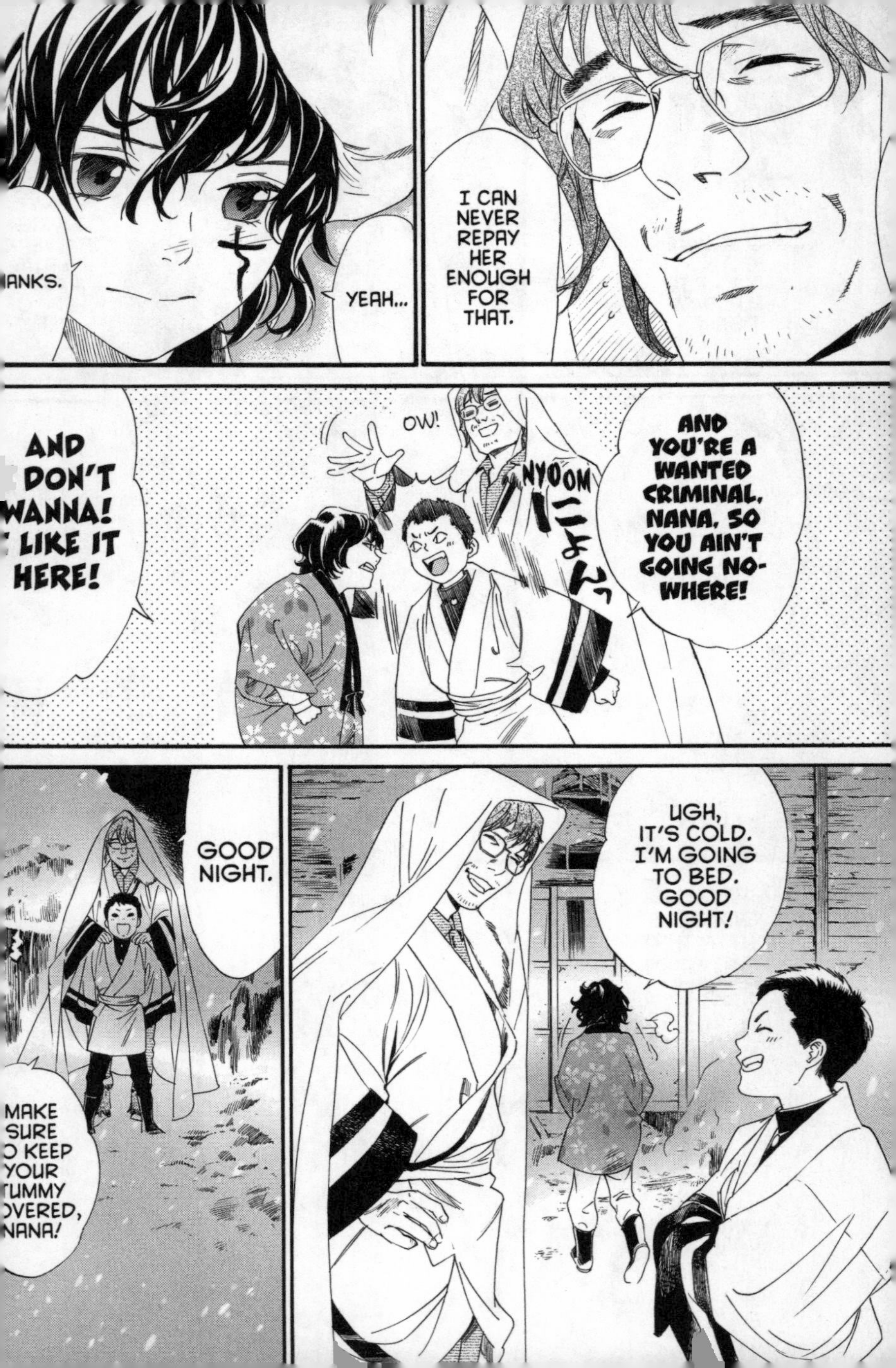
I CAN NEVER REPAY HER ENOUGH FOR THAT.
YEAH...
ANKS.
AND YOU'RE A WANTED CRIMINAL, NANA, SO YOU AIN'T GOING NO-WHERE!
NYOOM
こよんっ
OW!
AND DON'T WANNA! LIKE IT HERE!
UGH, IT'S COLD. I'M GOING TO BED. GOOD NIGHT!
GOOD NIGHT.
MAKE SURE O KEEP YOUR TUMMY OVERED, NANA!

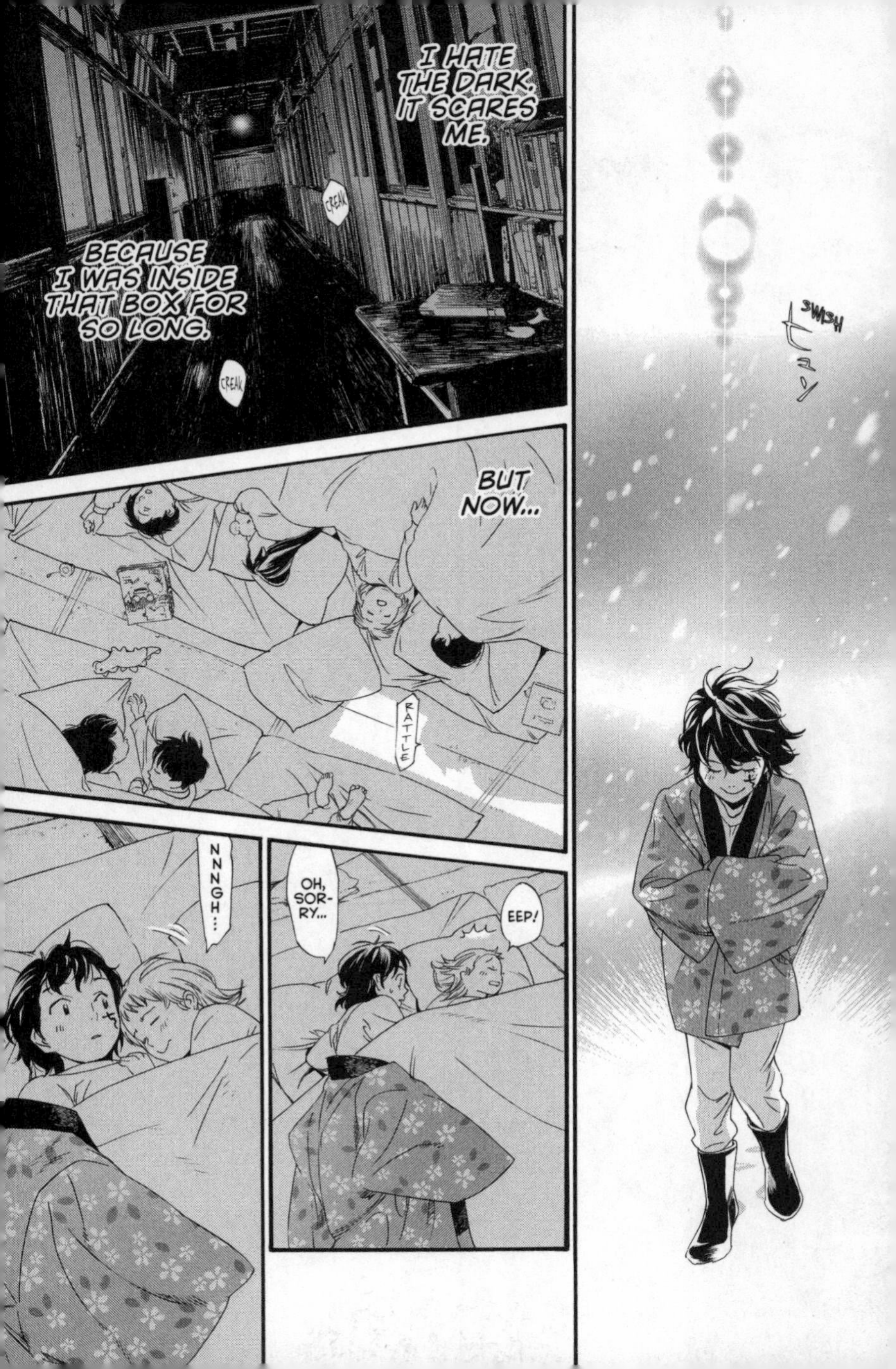
SWISH
ヒュン
I HATE THE DARK. IT SCARES ME.
CREAK
BECAUSE I WAS INSIDE THAT BOX FOR SO LONG.
CREAK
BUT NOW...
RATTLE
EEP!
OH, SORRY...
NNNGH...

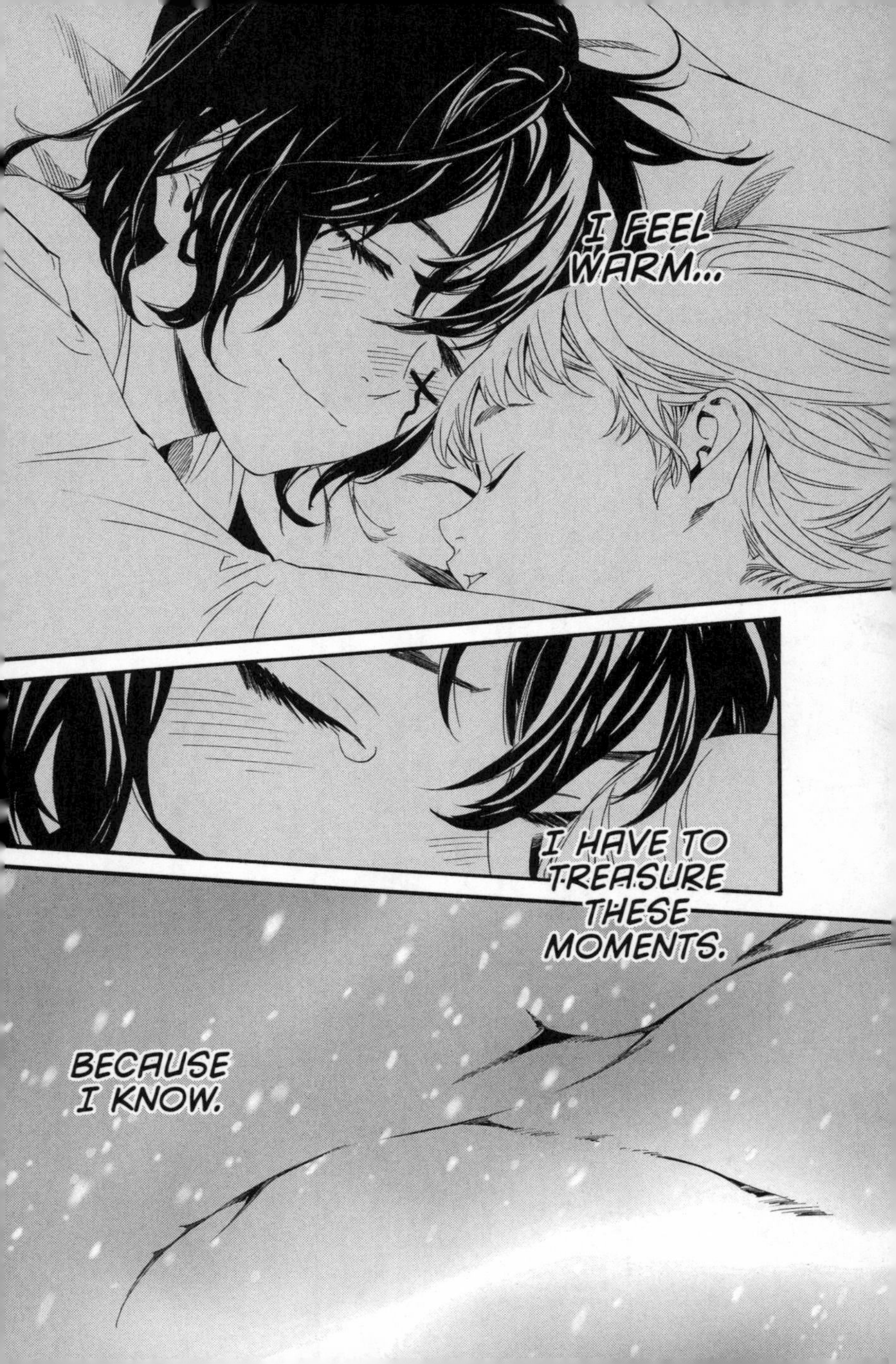
I FEEL WARM...
I HAVE TO TREASURE THESE MOMENTS.
BECAUSE I KNOW.

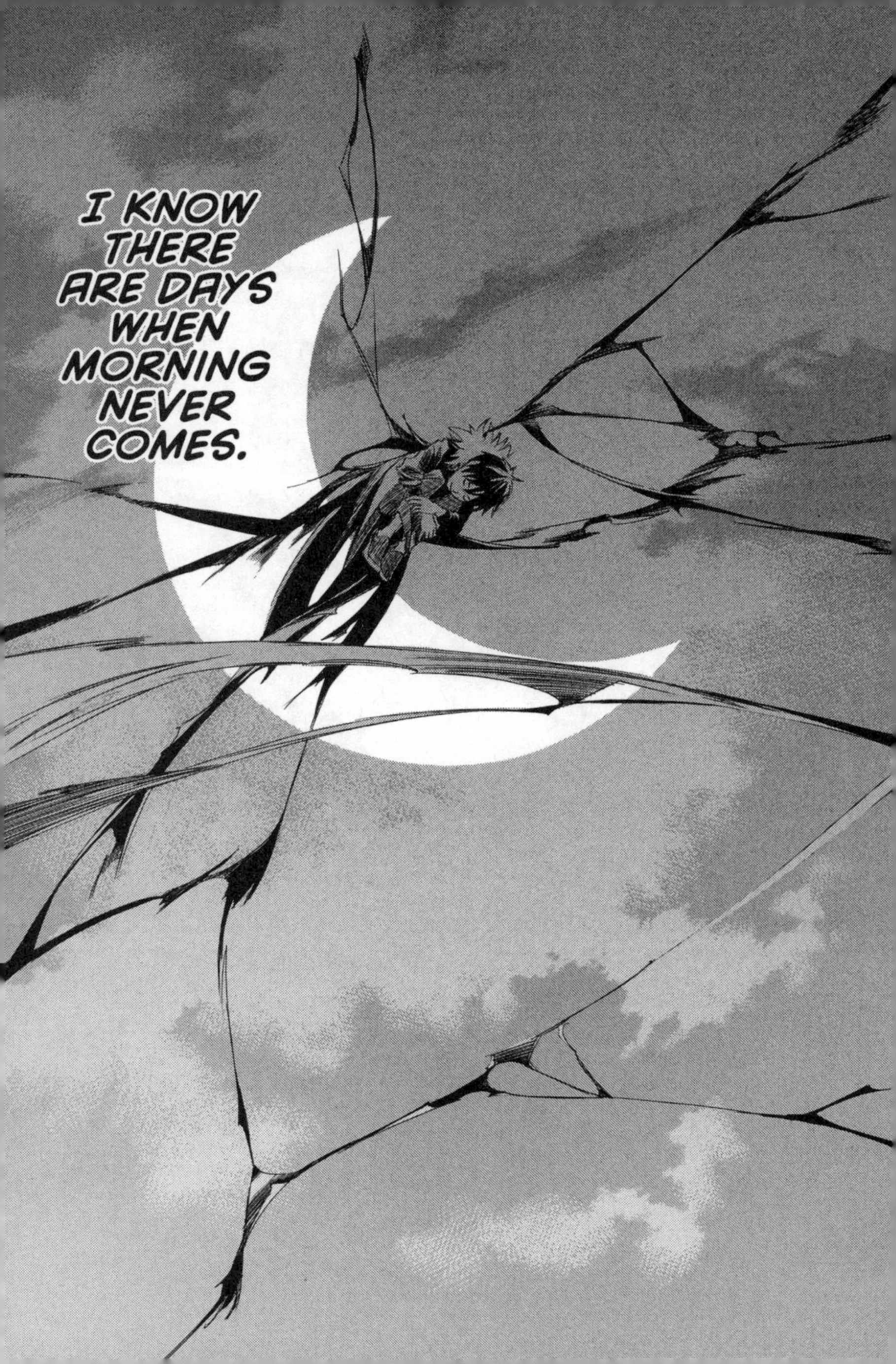
I KNOW THERE ARE DAYS WHEN MORNING NEVER COMES.

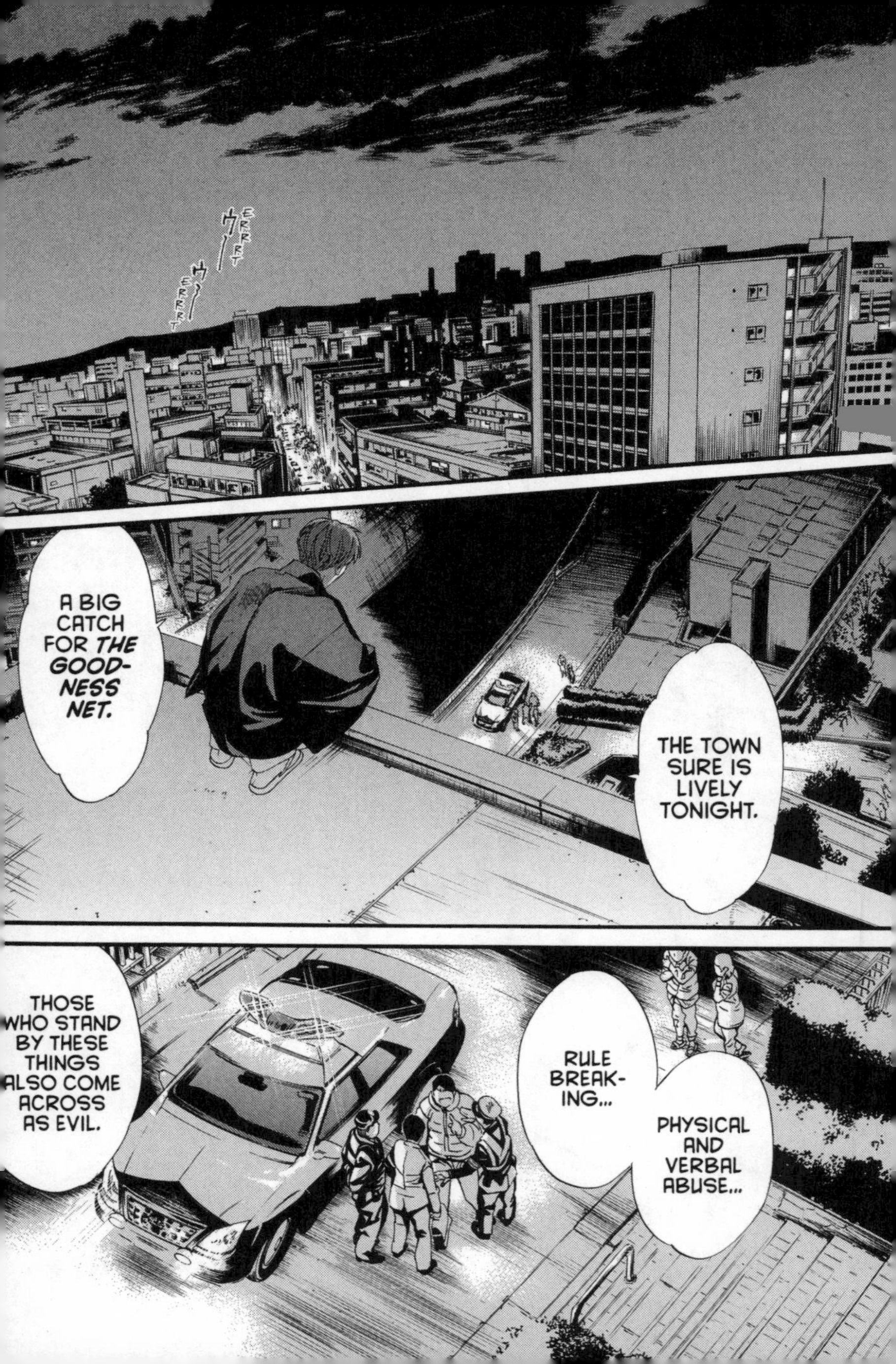
ERRRT
ERRRT
THE TOWN SURE IS LIVELY TONIGHT.
A BIG CATCH FOR *THE GOODNESS NET.*
RULE BREAKING...
PHYSICAL AND VERBAL ABUSE...
THOSE WHO STAND BY THESE THINGS ALSO COME ACROSS AS EVIL.

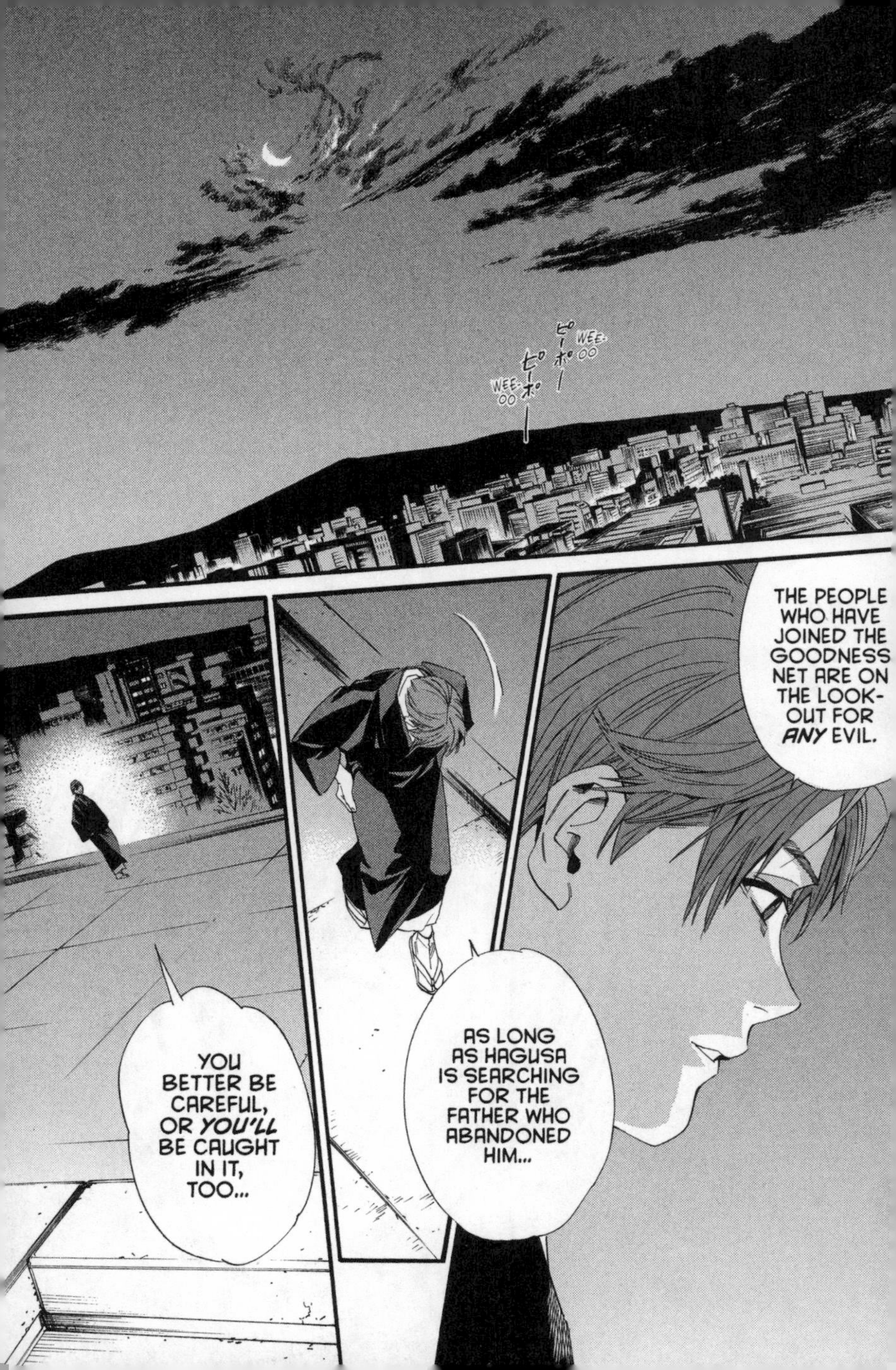
ピーポー
WEE-OO
ピーポー
WEE-OO
THE PEOPLE WHO HAVE JOINED THE GOODNESS NET ARE ON THE LOOK-OUT FOR *ANY* EVIL.
AS LONG AS HAGUSA IS SEARCHING FOR THE FATHER WHO ABANDONED HIM...
YOU BETTER BE CAREFUL, OR *YOU'LL* BE CAUGHT IN IT, TOO...

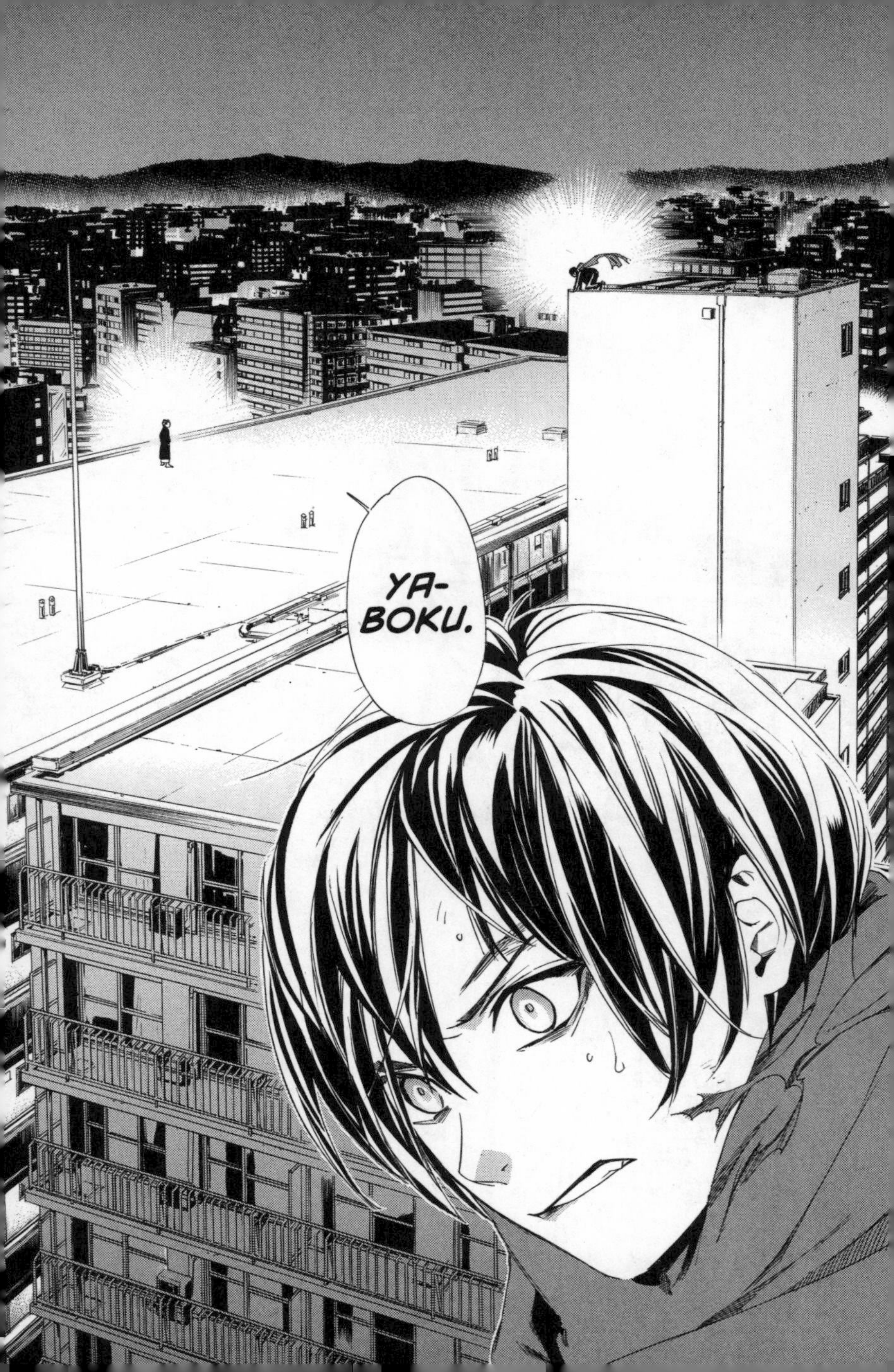
YA-
BOKU.

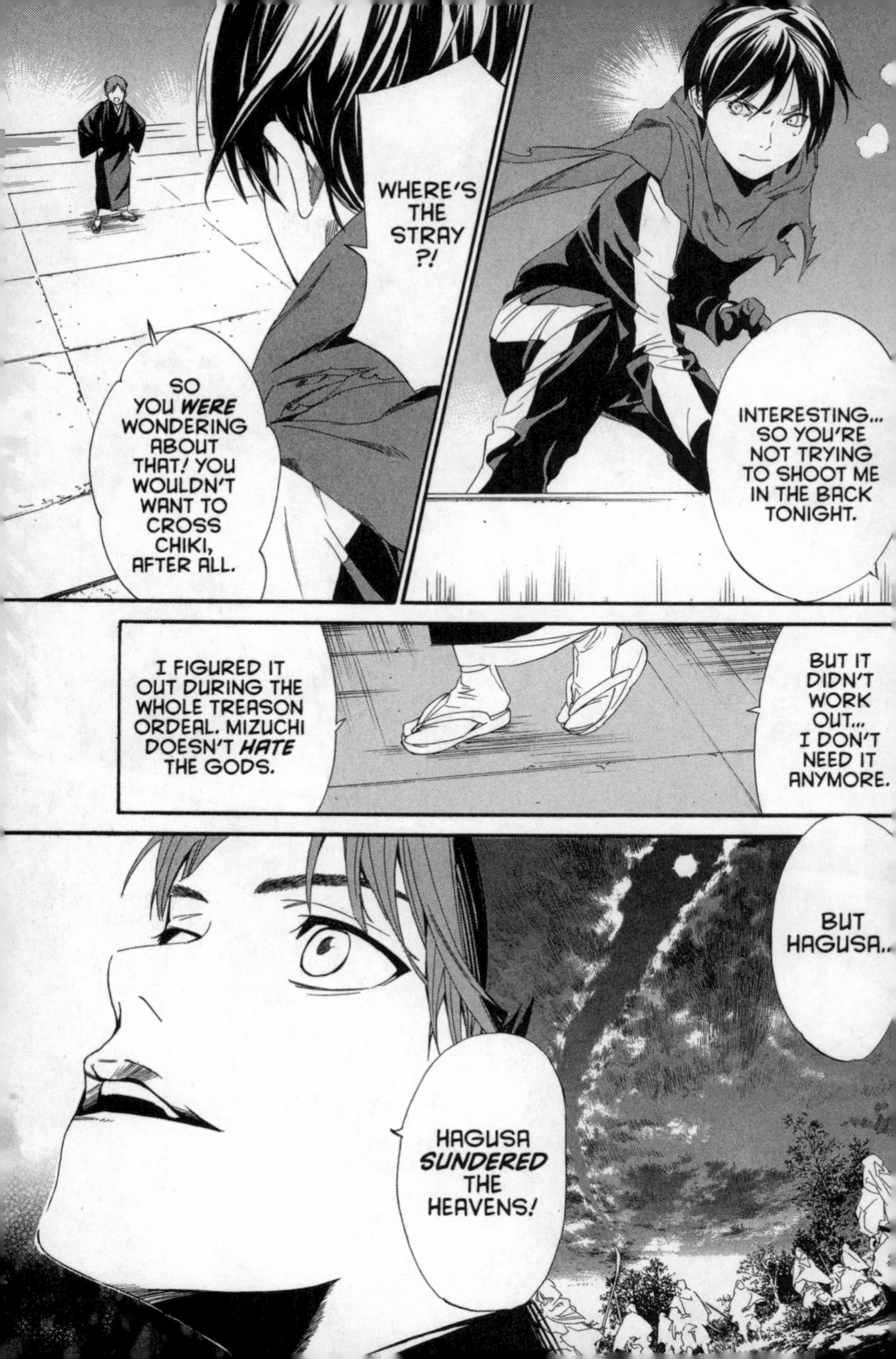
INTERESTING... SO YOU'RE NOT TRYING TO SHOOT ME IN THE BACK TONIGHT.
WHERE'S THE STRAY ?!
SO YOU *WERE* WONDERING ABOUT THAT! YOU WOULDN'T WANT TO CROSS CHIKI, AFTER ALL.
BUT IT DIDN'T WORK OUT... I DON'T NEED IT ANYMORE.
I FIGURED IT OUT DURING THE WHOLE TREASON ORDEAL. MIZUCHI DOESN'T *HATE* THE GODS.
BUT HAGUSA..
HAGUSA *SUNDERED* THE HEAVENS!

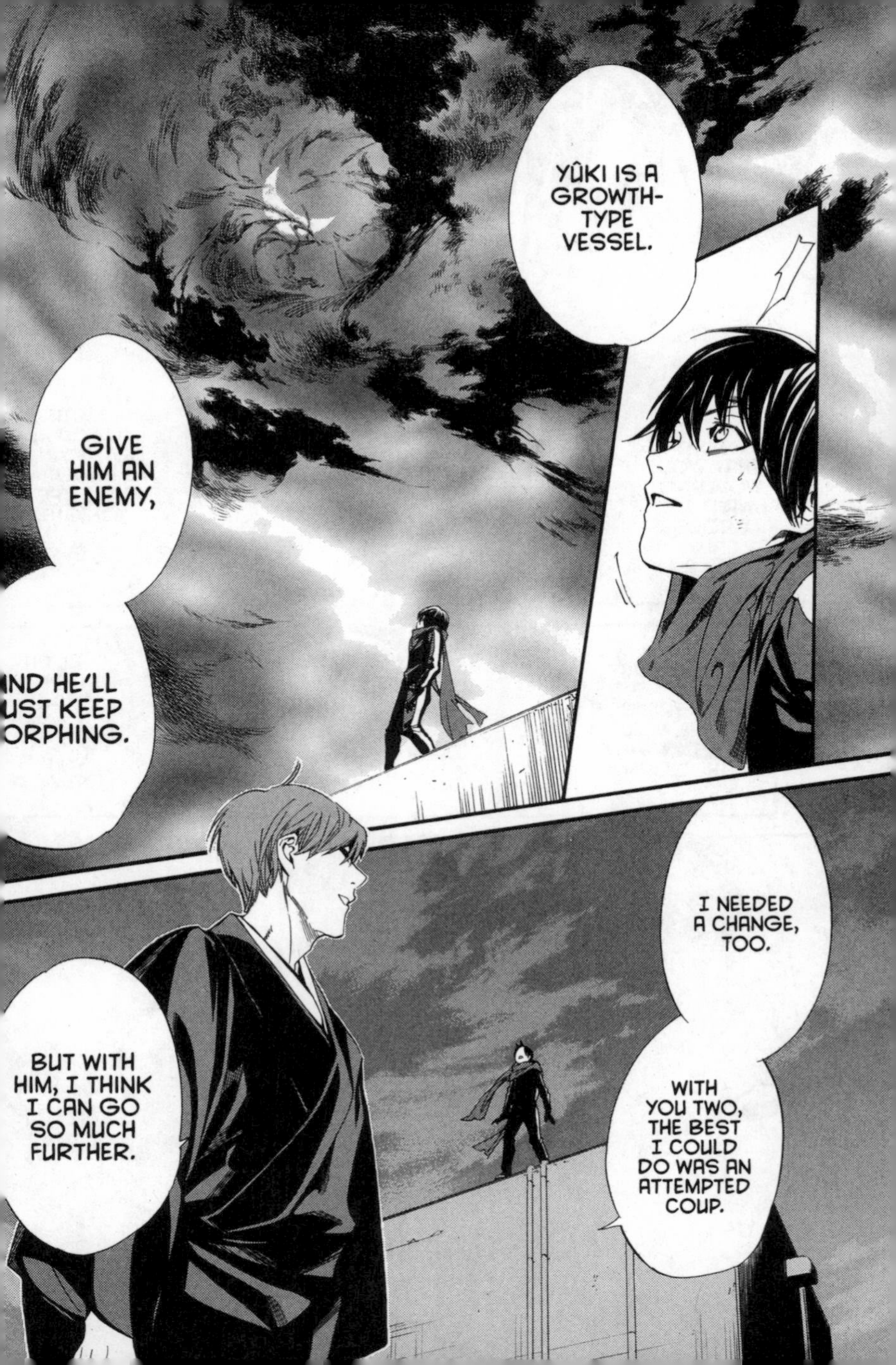
YÛKI IS A GROWTH-TYPE VESSEL.
GIVE HIM AN ENEMY,
ND HE'LL UST KEEP ORPHING.
I NEEDED A CHANGE, TOO.
WITH YOU TWO, THE BEST I COULD DO WAS AN ATTEMPTED COUP.
BUT WITH HIM, I THINK I CAN GO SO MUCH FURTHER.

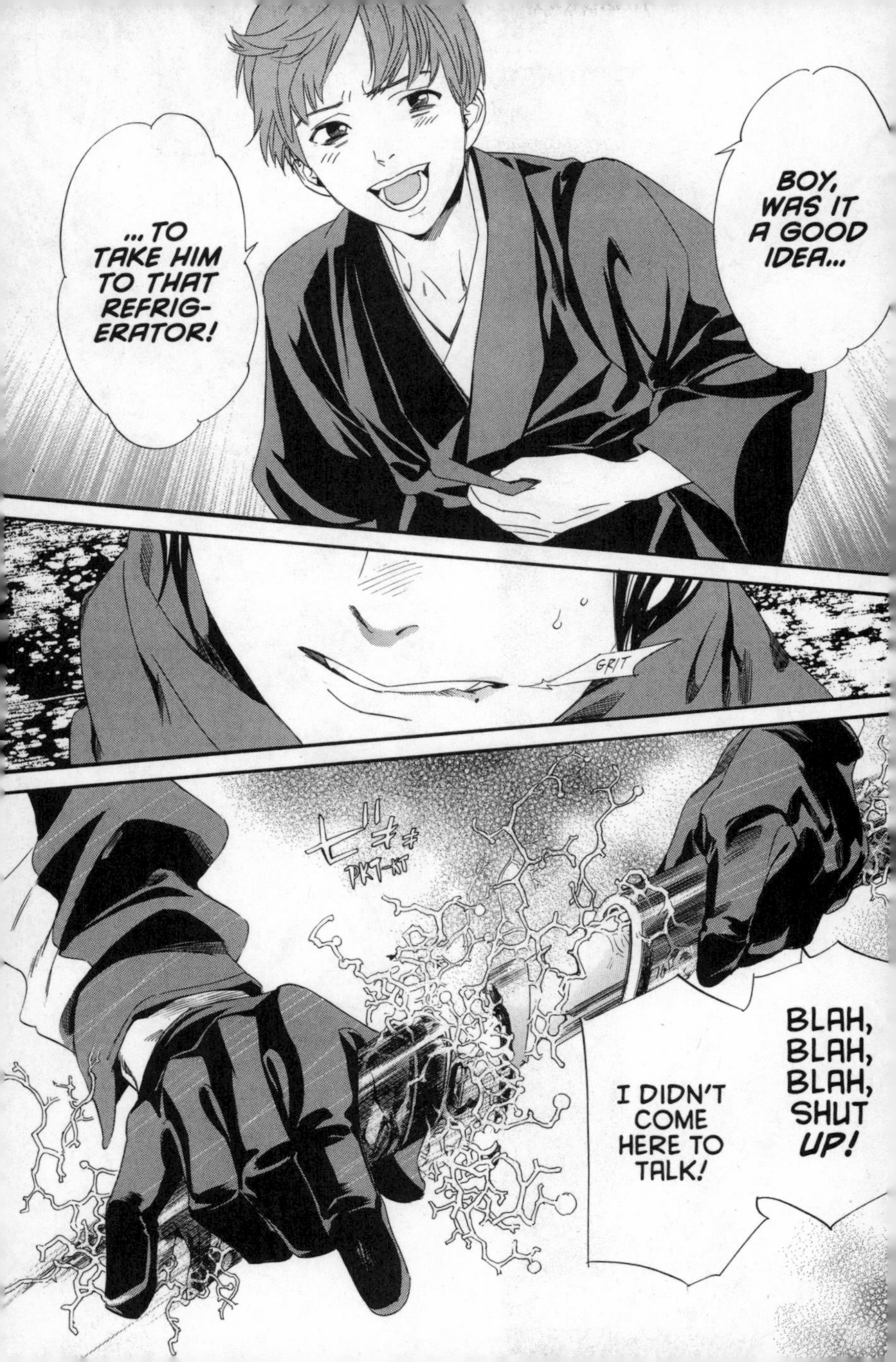
BOY, WAS IT A GOOD IDEA...
...TO TAKE HIM TO THAT REFRIG-ERATOR!
GRIT
PKT-KT
BLAH, BLAH, BLAH, SHUT UP!
I DIDN'T COME HERE TO TALK!

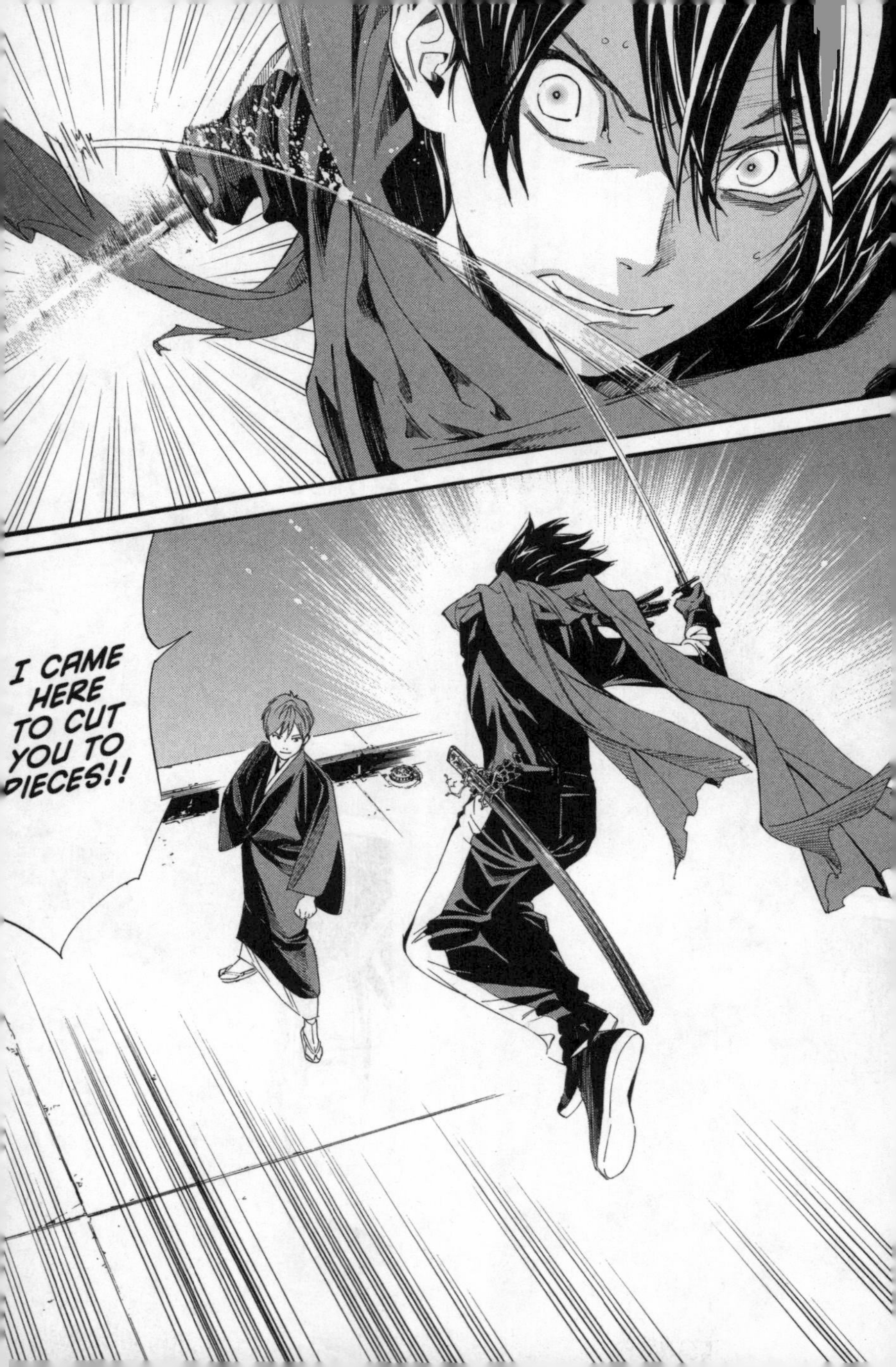
I CAME HERE TO CUT YOU TO PIECES!!

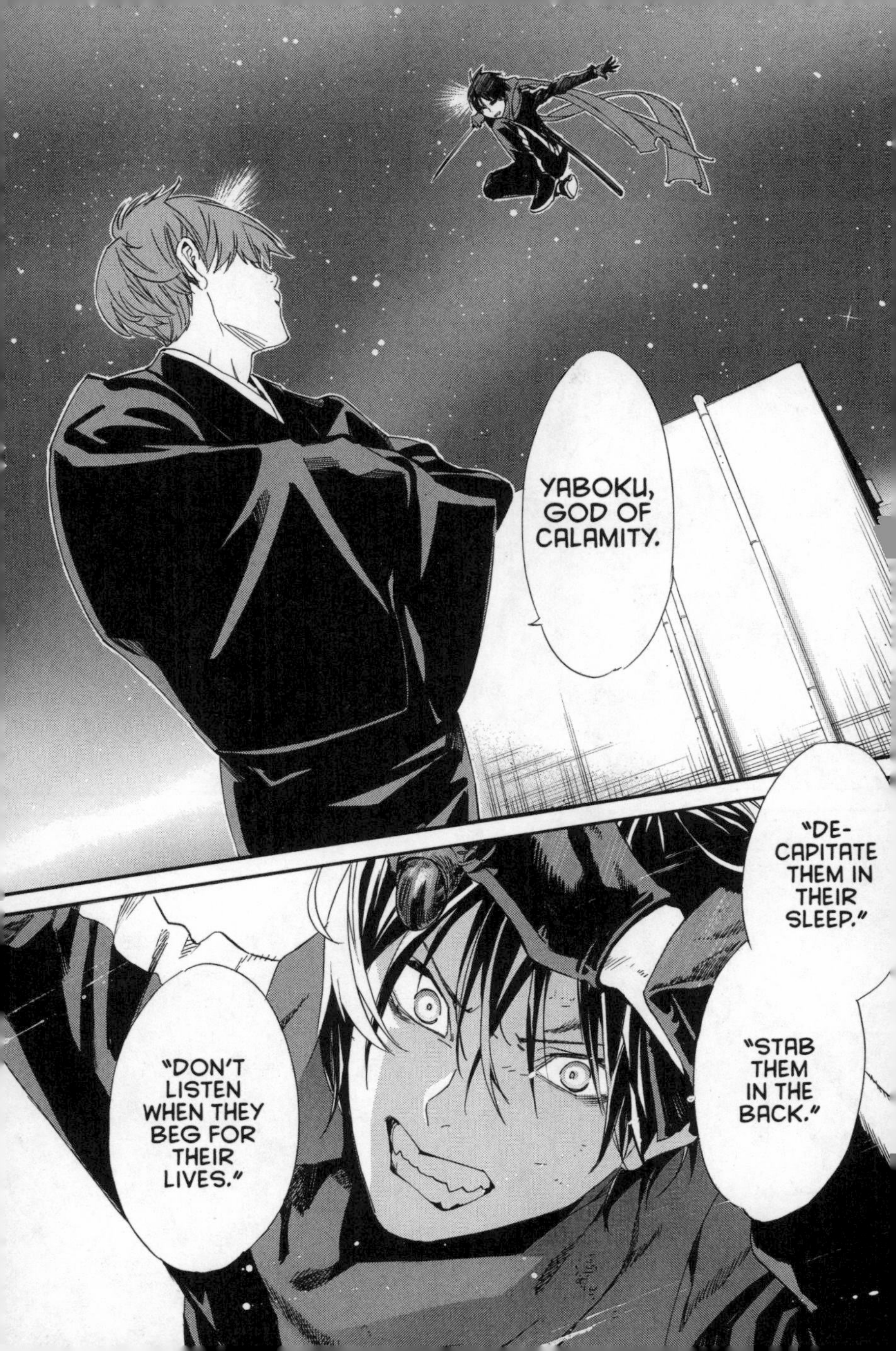
YABOKU, GOD OF CALAMITY.
"DE-CAPITATE THEM IN THEIR SLEEP."
"STAB THEM IN THE BACK."
"DON'T LISTEN WHEN THEY BEG FOR THEIR LIVES."

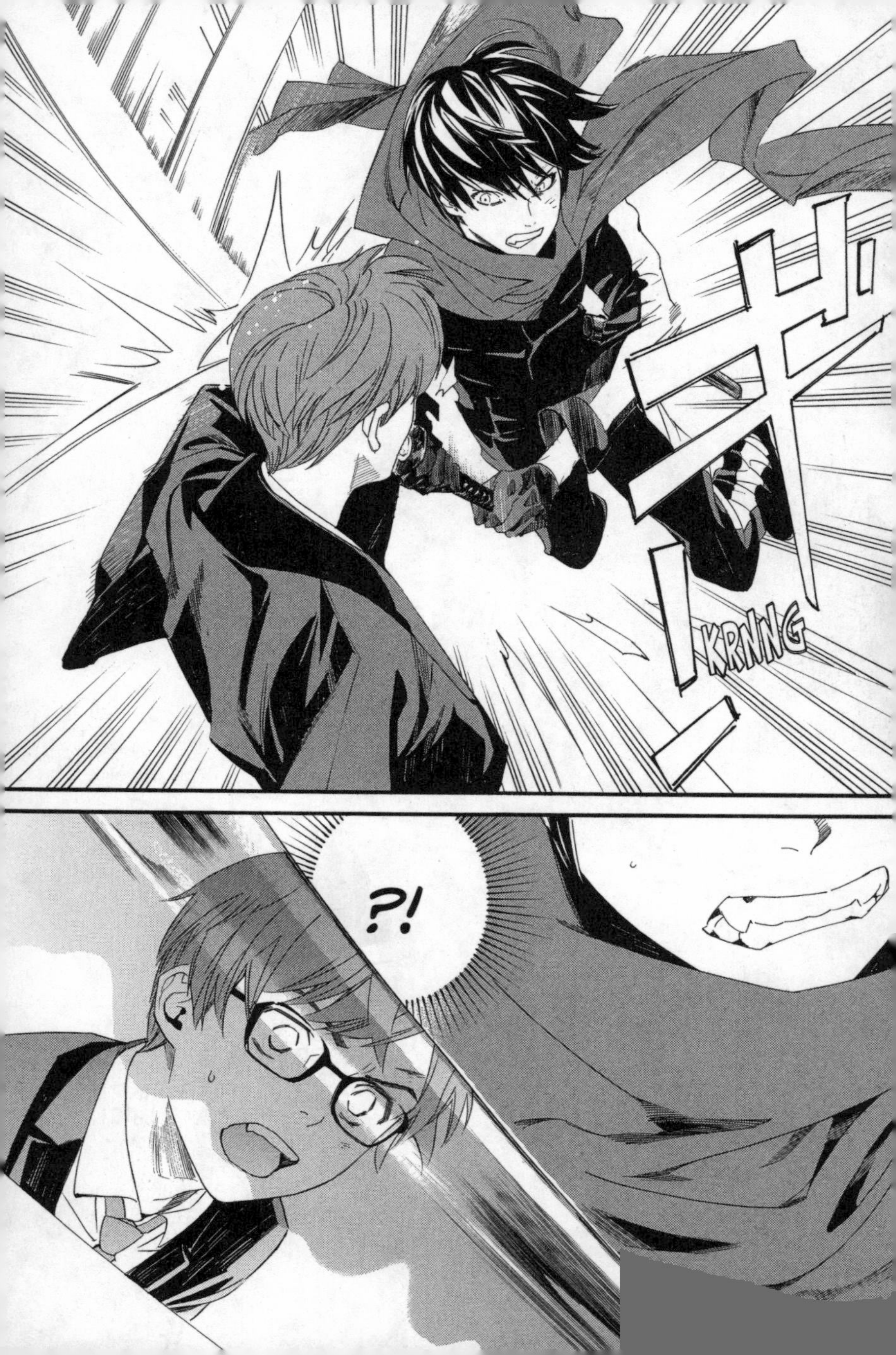
KRNNG
?!

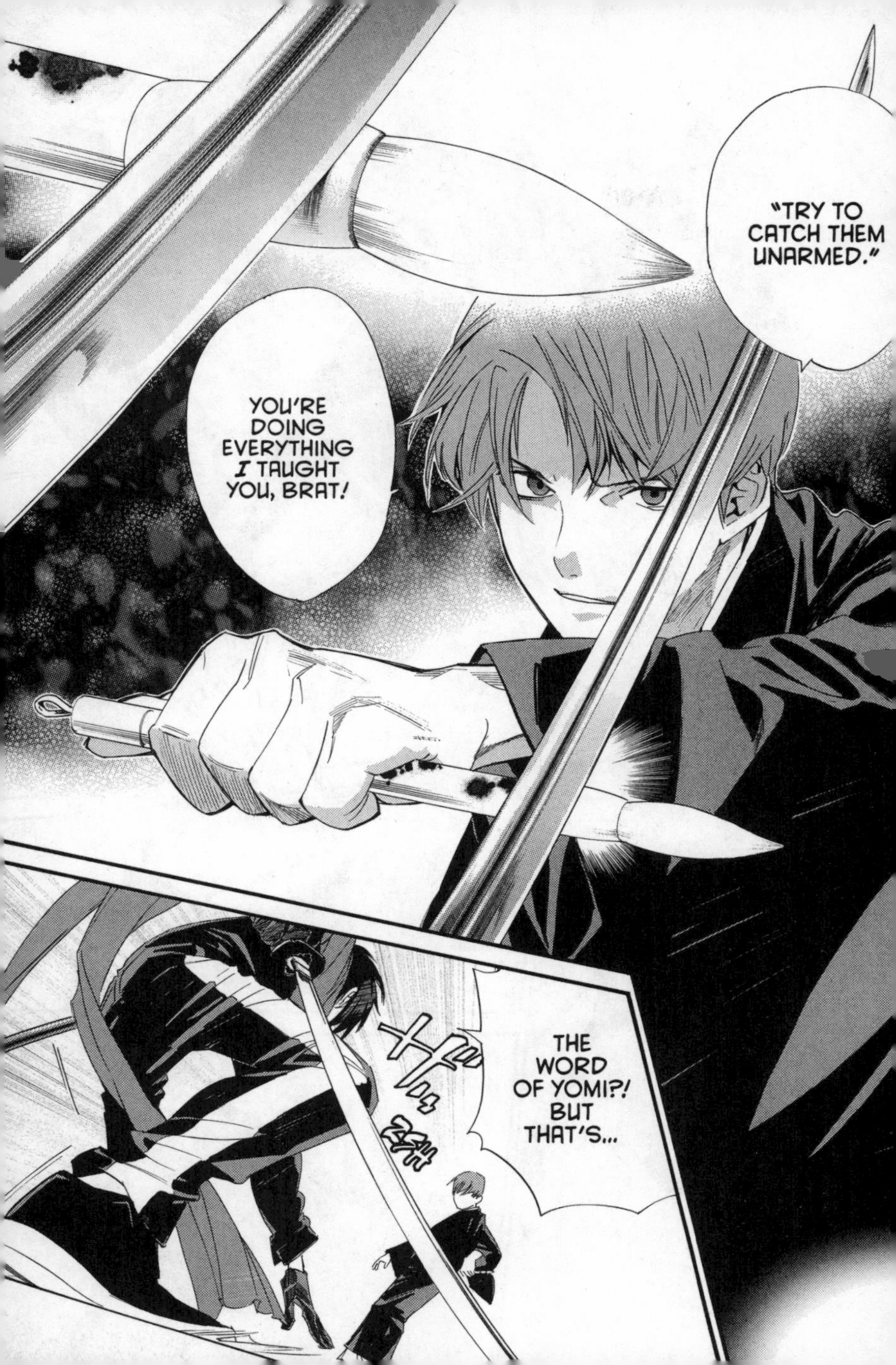
"TRY TO CATCH THEM UNARMED."
YOU'RE DOING EVERYTHING *I* TAUGHT YOU, BRAT!
THE WORD OF YOMI?! BUT THAT'S...

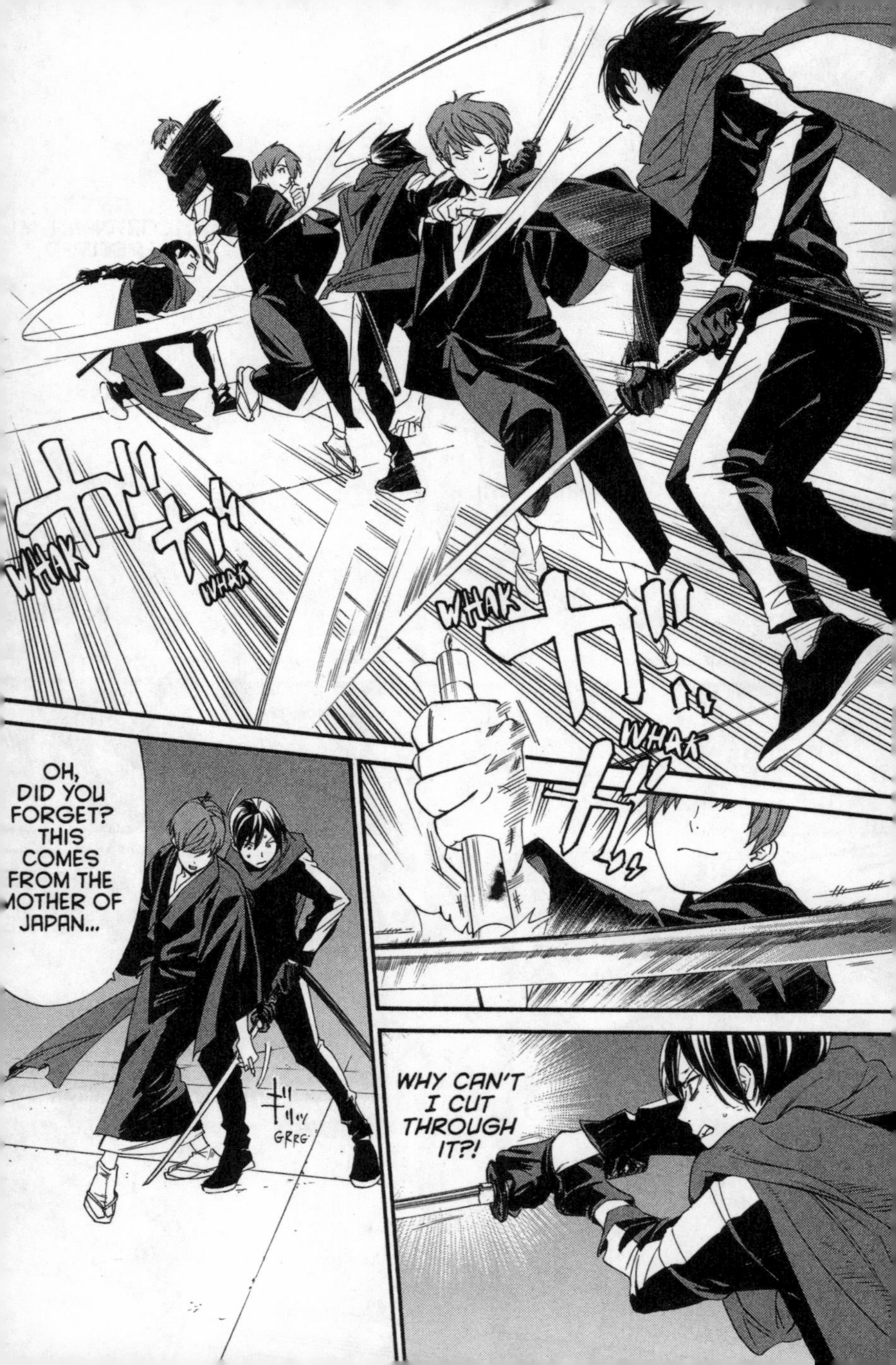
WHAK
WHAK
WHAK
WHAK
WHY CAN'T I CUT THROUGH IT?!
OH, DID YOU FORGET? THIS COMES FROM THE MOTHER OF JAPAN...
GRRG

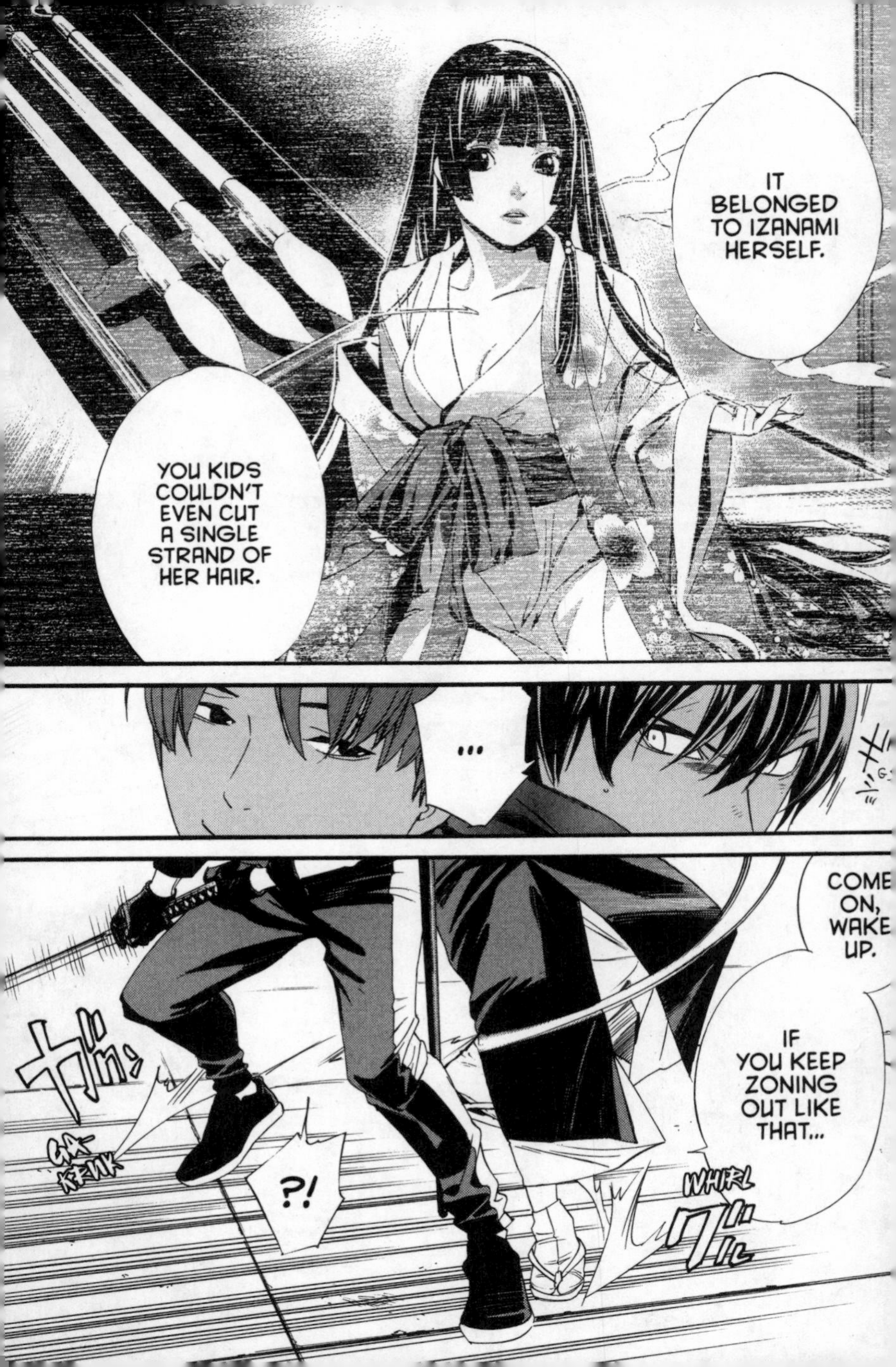
IT BELONGED TO IZANAMI HERSELF.
YOU KIDS COULDN'T EVEN CUT A SINGLE STRAND OF HER HAIR.
...
COME ON, WAKE UP.
IF YOU KEEP ZONING OUT LIKE THAT...
WHIRL
?!
GA-KRUNK

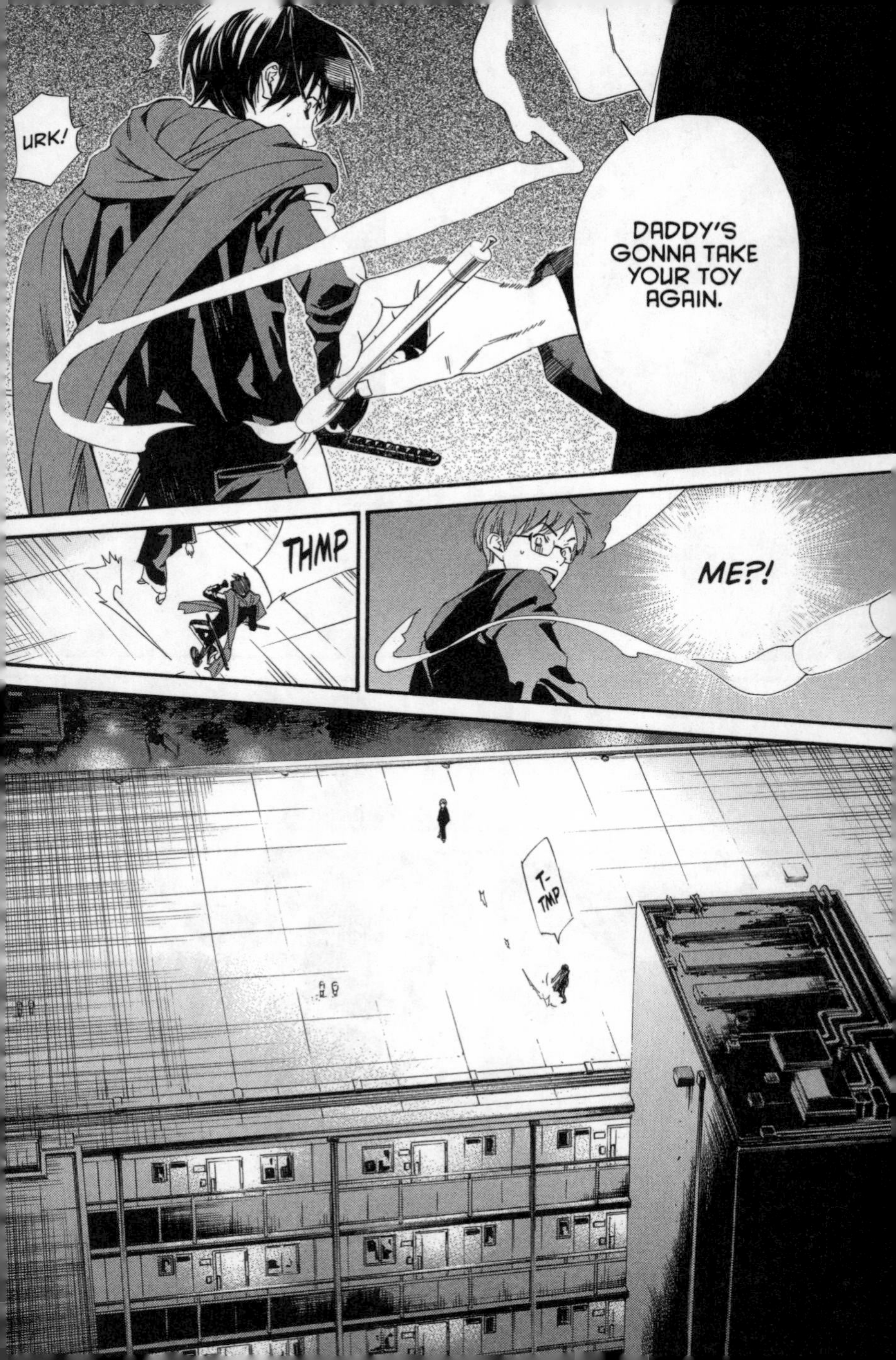
DADDY'S GONNA TAKE YOUR TOY AGAIN.
URK!
ME?!
THMP
T-TMP

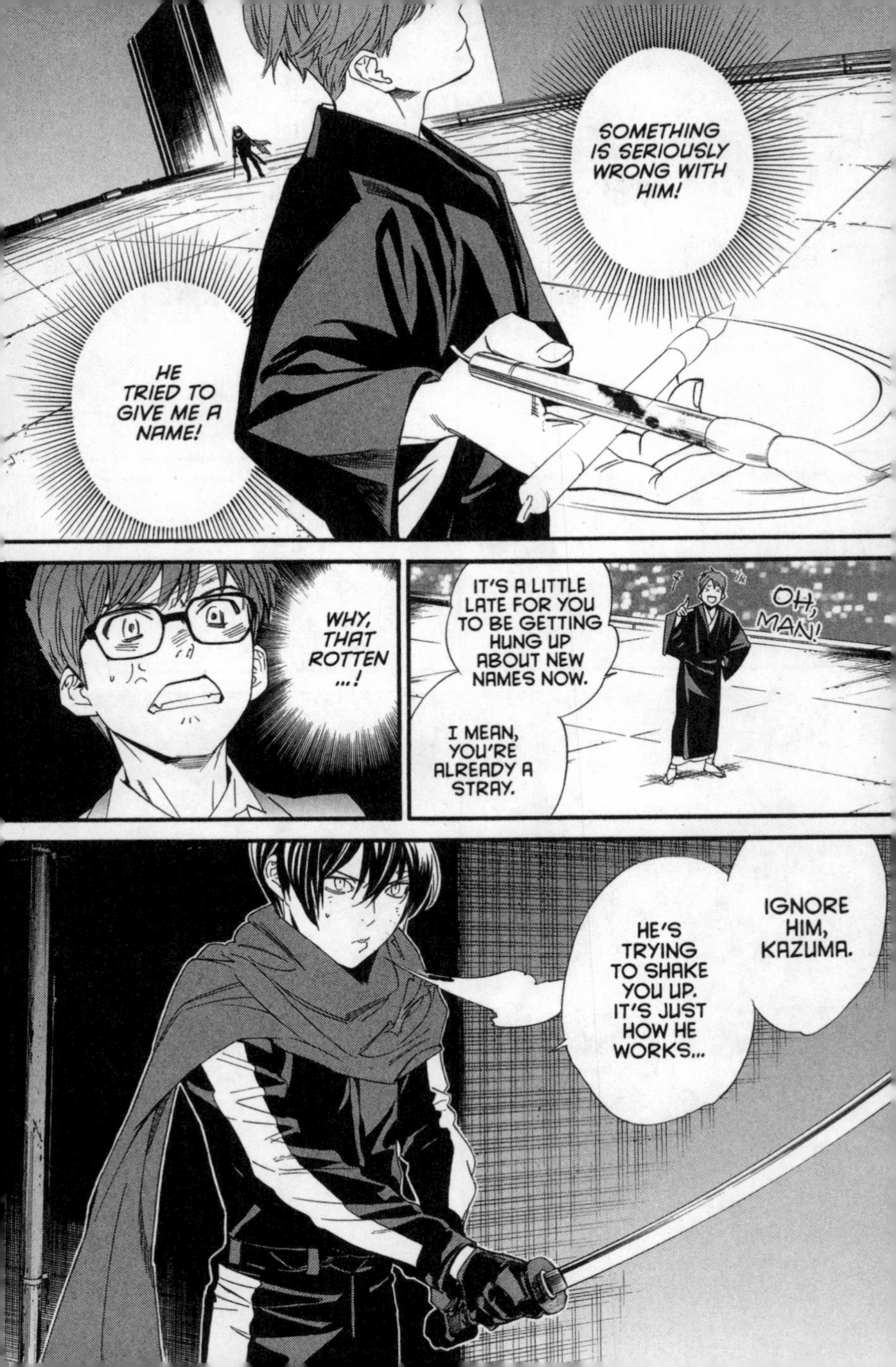
SOMETHING IS SERIOUSLY WRONG WITH HIM!
HE TRIED TO GIVE ME A NAME!
IT'S A LITTLE LATE FOR YOU TO BE GETTING HUNG UP ABOUT NEW NAMES NOW.
OH, MAN!
I MEAN, YOU'RE ALREADY A STRAY.
WHY, THAT ROTTEN ...!
IGNORE HIM, KAZUMA.
HE'S TRYING TO SHAKE YOU UP. IT'S JUST HOW HE WORKS...

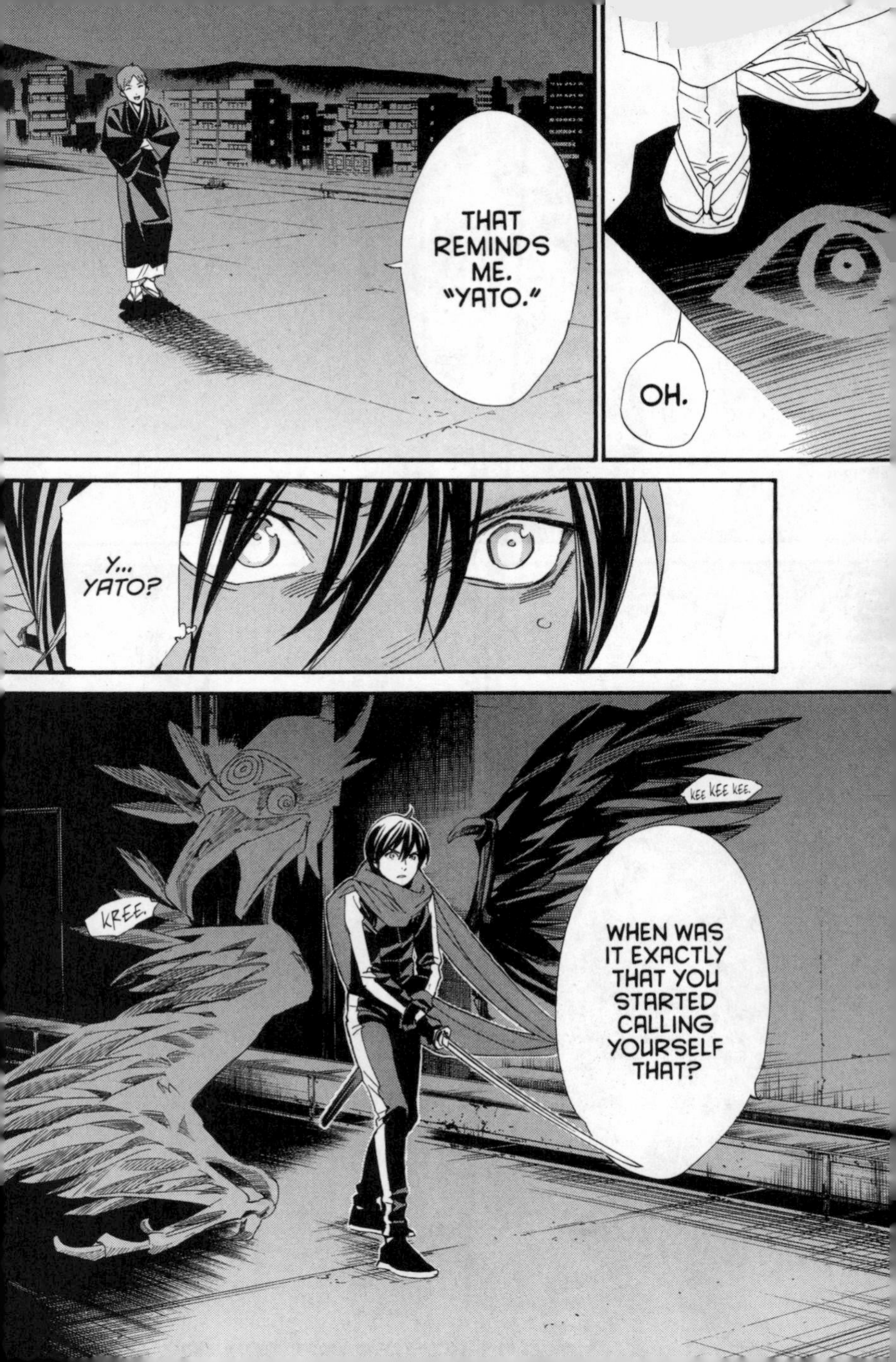
OH.
THAT REMINDS ME. "YATO."
Y... YATO?
KEE KEE KEE.
WHEN WAS IT EXACTLY THAT YOU STARTED CALLING YOURSELF THAT?
KREE.

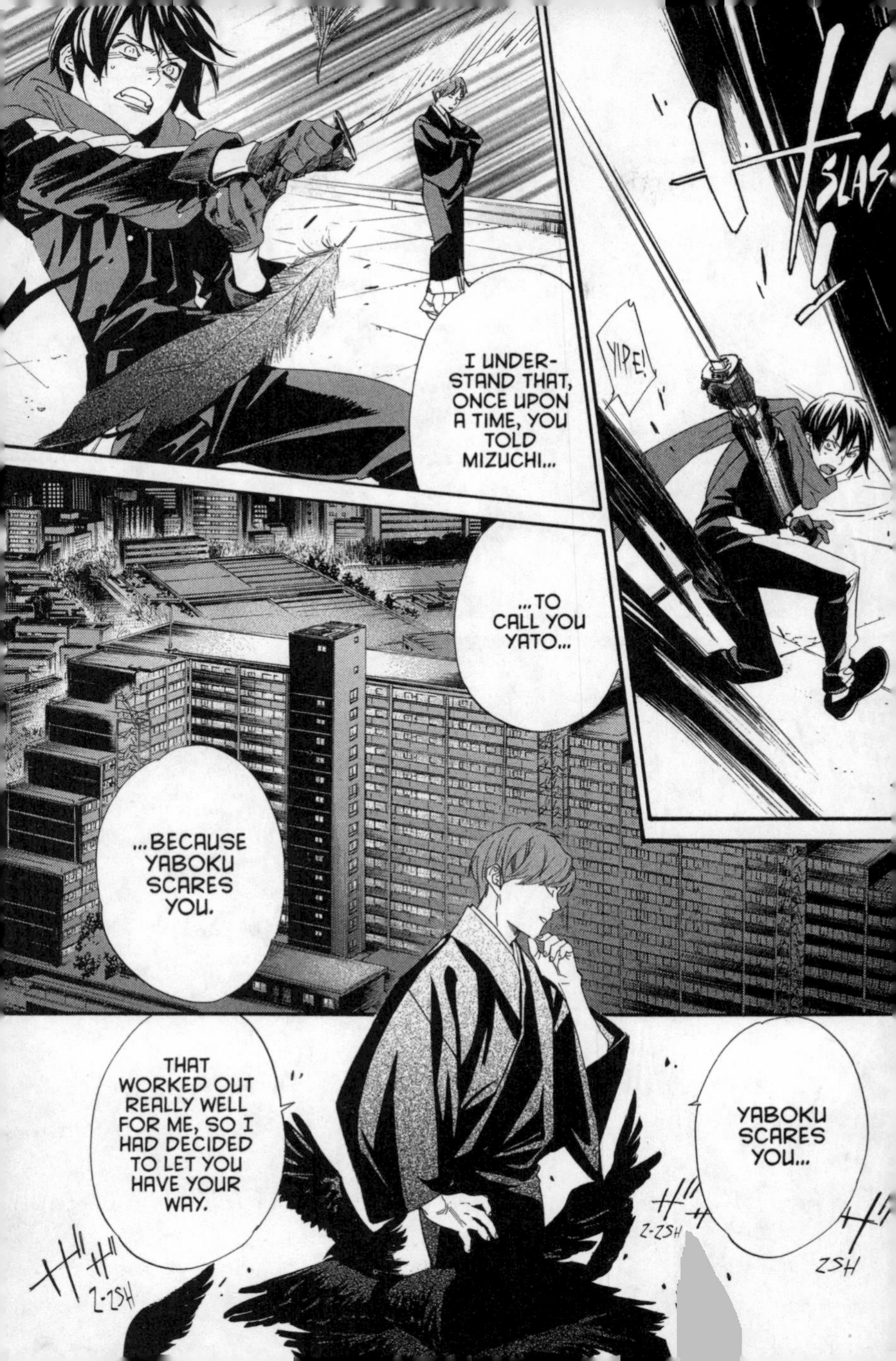
SLAS
YIPE!
I UNDERSTAND THAT, ONCE UPON A TIME, YOU TOLD MIZUCHI...
...TO CALL YOU YATO...
...BECAUSE YABOKU SCARES YOU.
YABOKU SCARES YOU...
Z-ZSH
ZSH
THAT WORKED OUT REALLY WELL FOR ME, SO I HAD DECIDED TO LET YOU HAVE YOUR WAY.
Z-ZSH

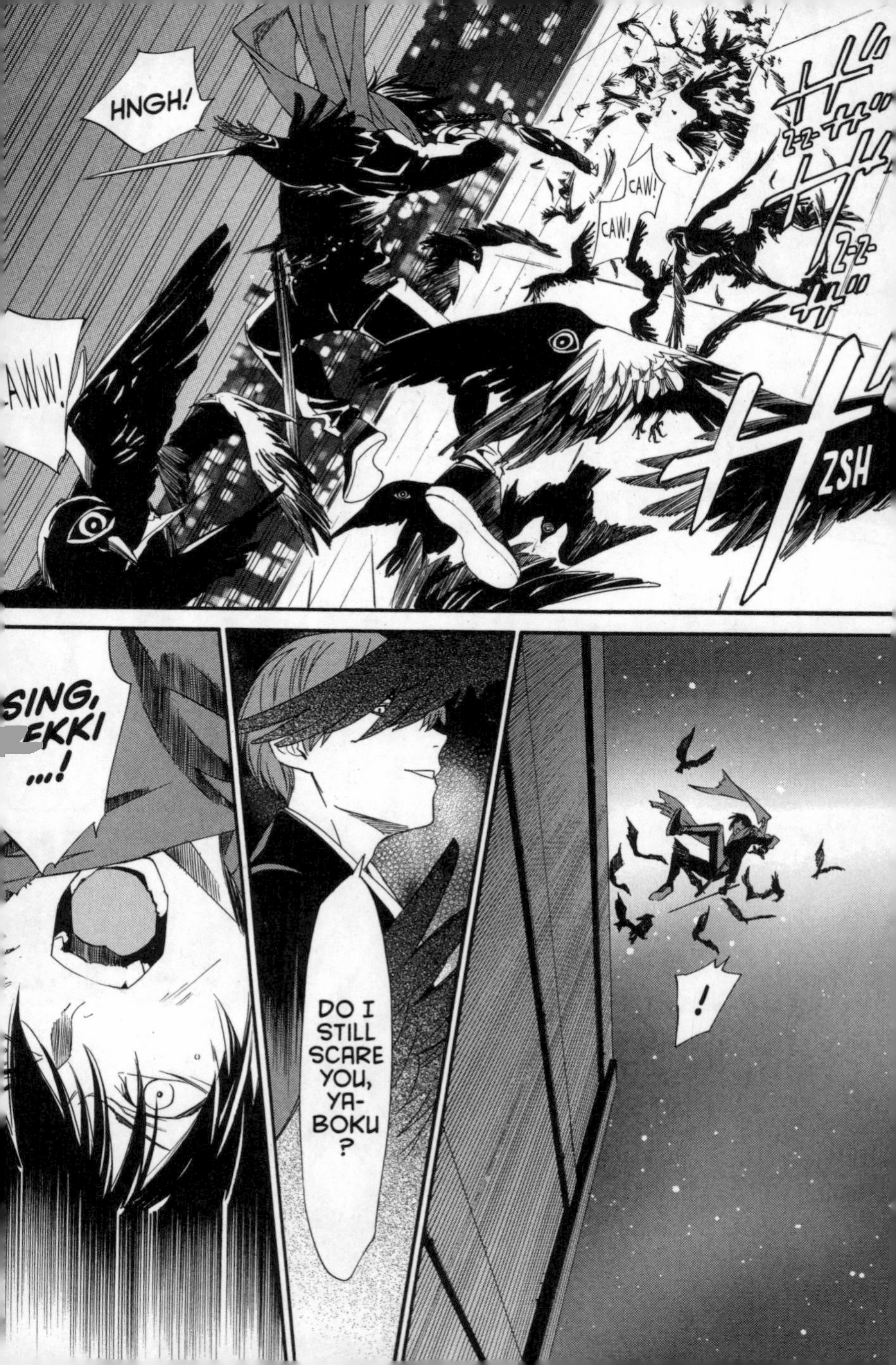

ZSH
CAW!
CAW!
HNGH!
AWW!
!
DO I STILL SCARE YOU, YA-BOKU?
SING, EKKI ...!

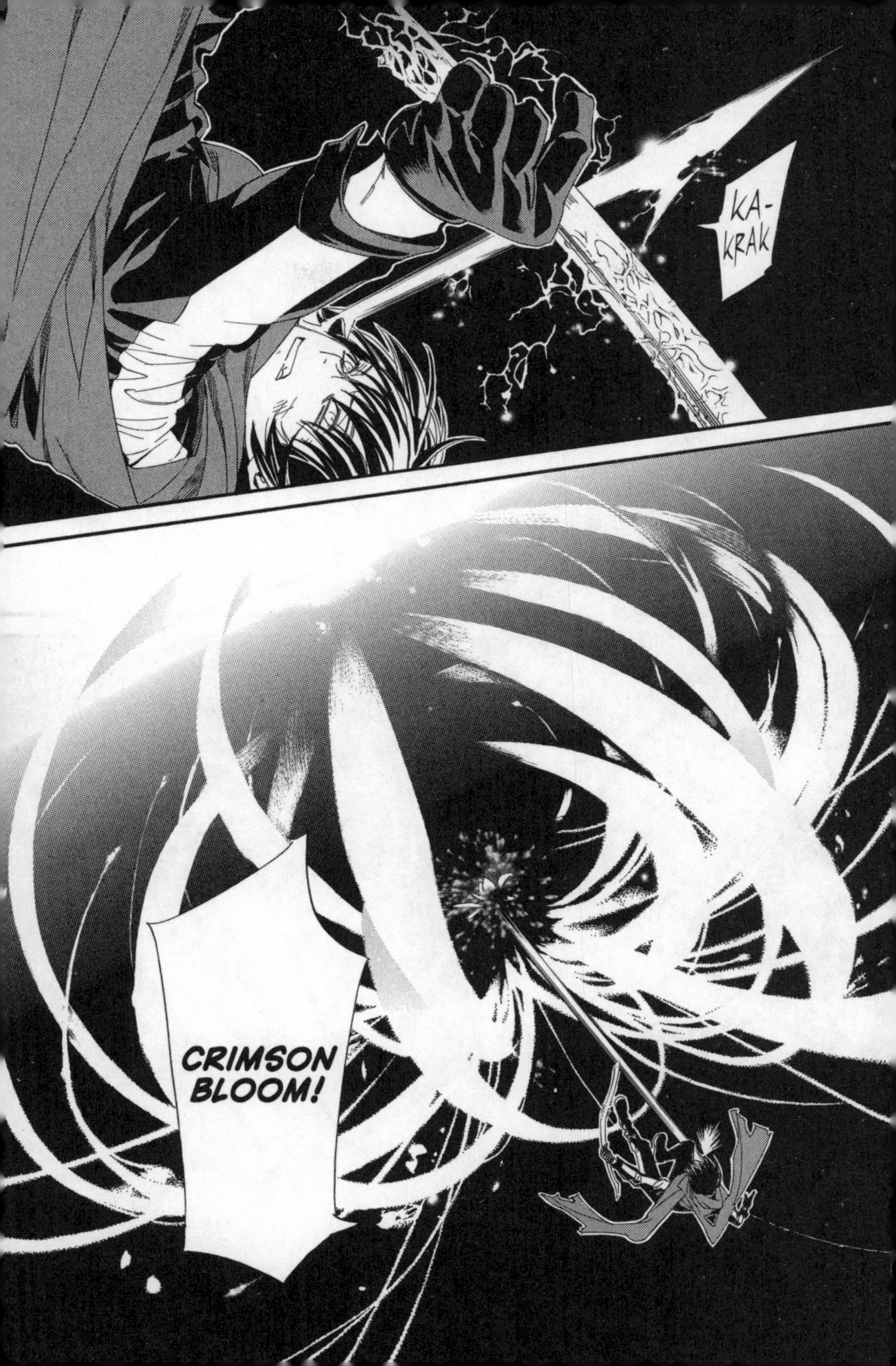
KA-
KRAK
CRIMSON
BLOOM!

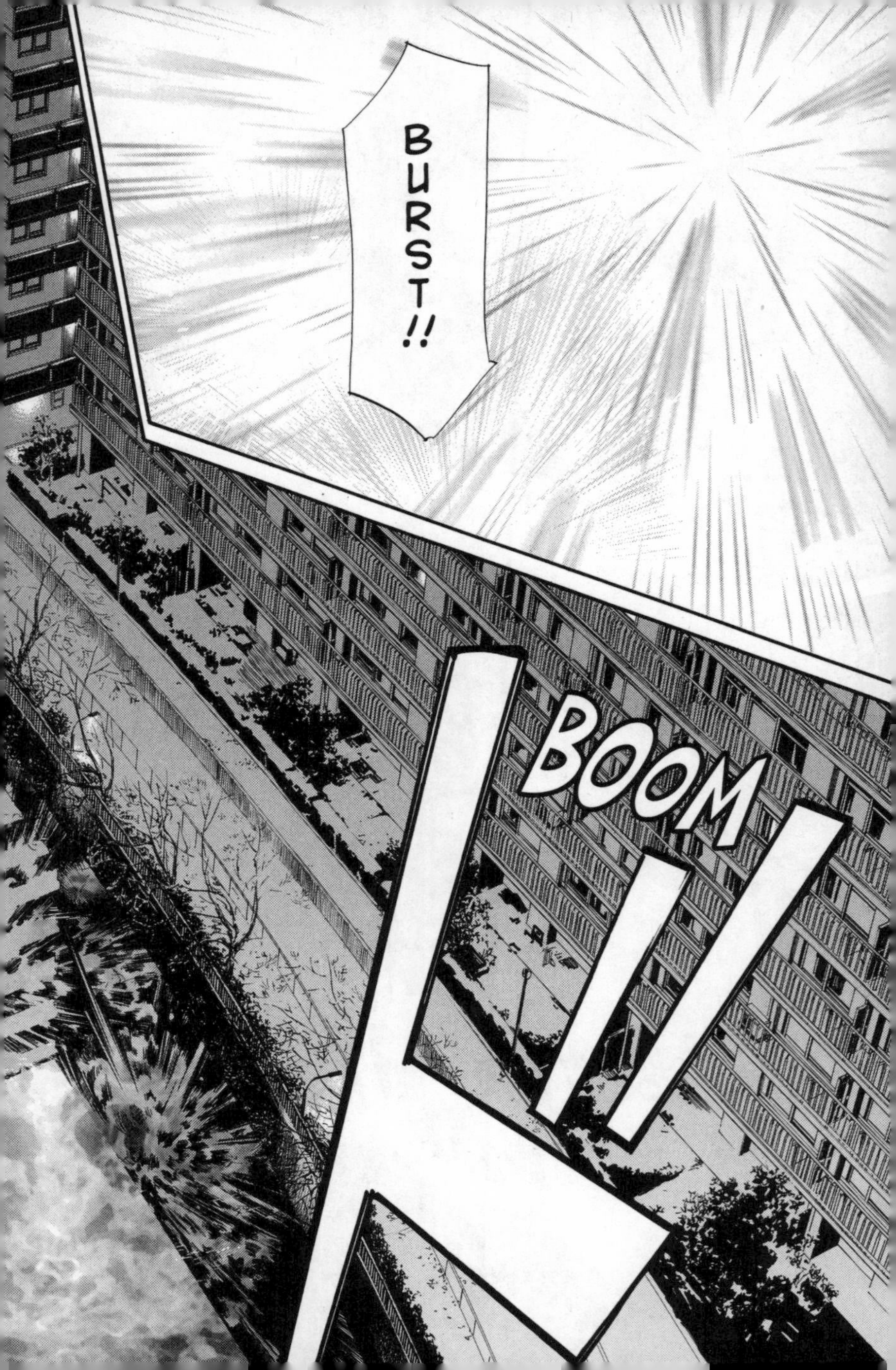
BURST!!
BOOM

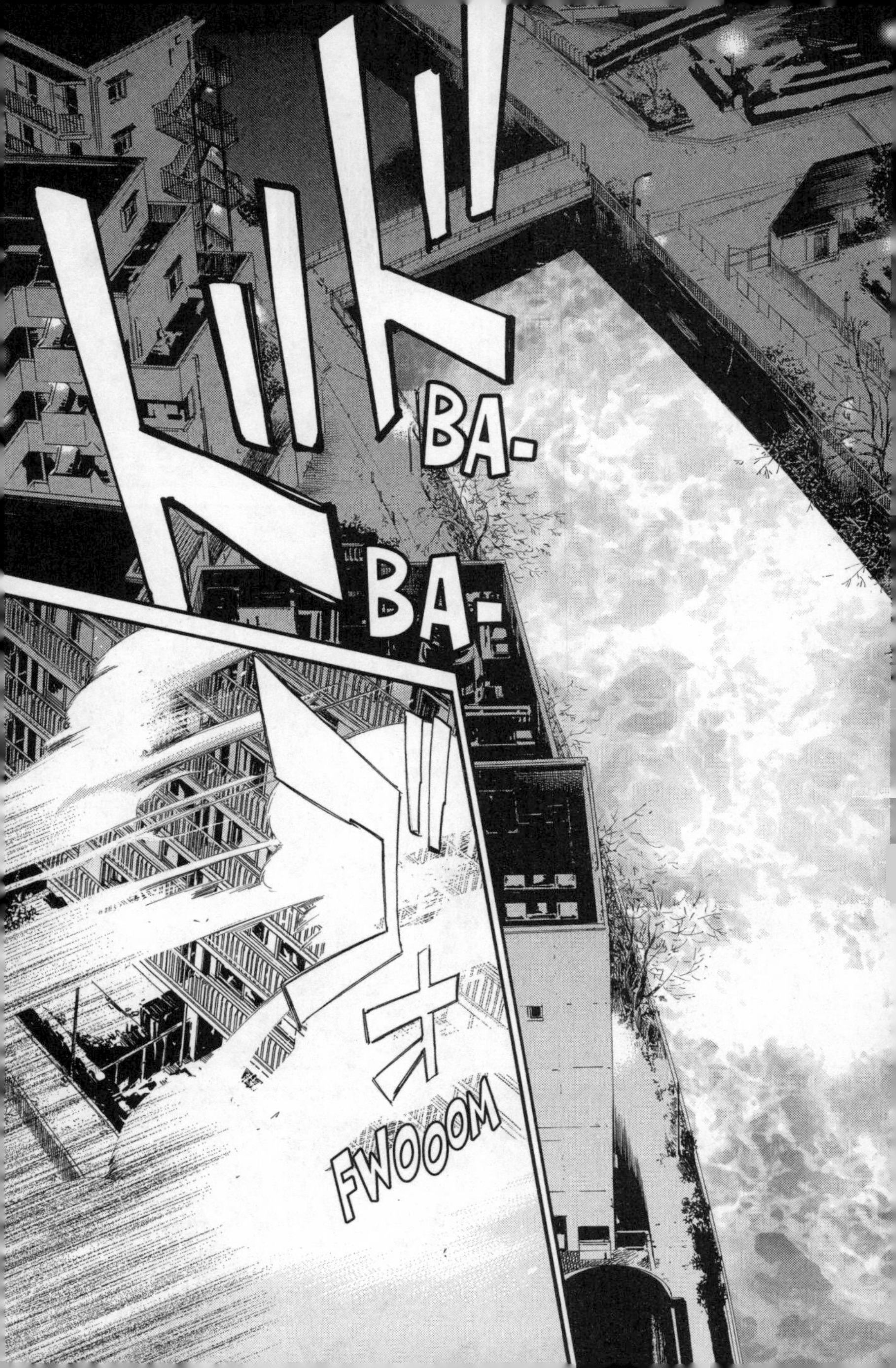
ドバーッ
BA-
BA-
ゴオ
FWOOOM

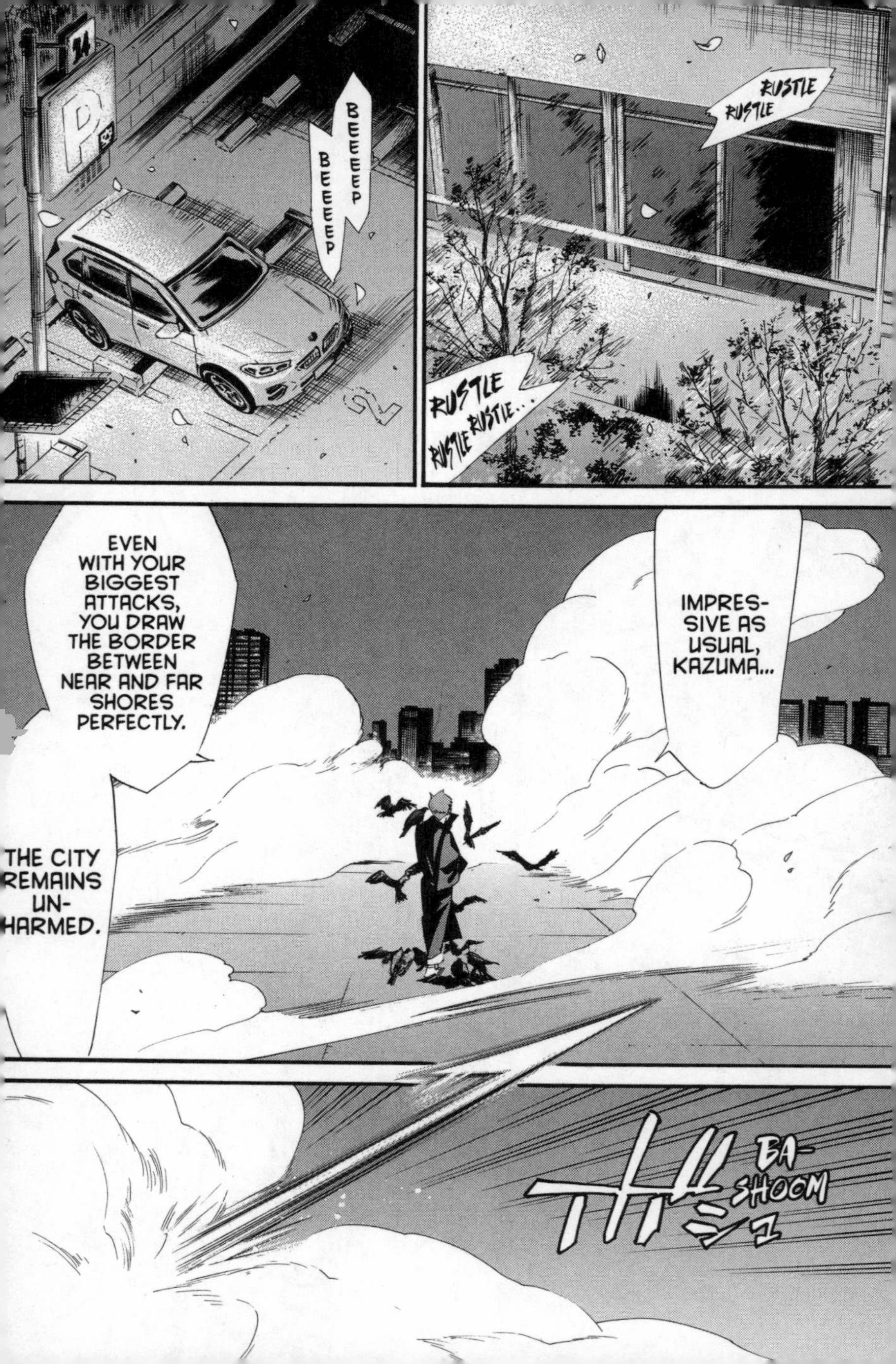
RUSTLE
RUSTLE
RUSTLE
RUSTLE RUSTLE...
BEEEEP
BEEEEEP
IMPRES-
SIVE AS
USUAL,
KAZUMA...
EVEN
WITH YOUR
BIGGEST
ATTACKS,
YOU DRAW
THE BORDER
BETWEEN
NEAR AND FAR
SHORES
PERFECTLY.
THE CITY
REMAINS
UN-
HARMED.
BA-
SHOOM

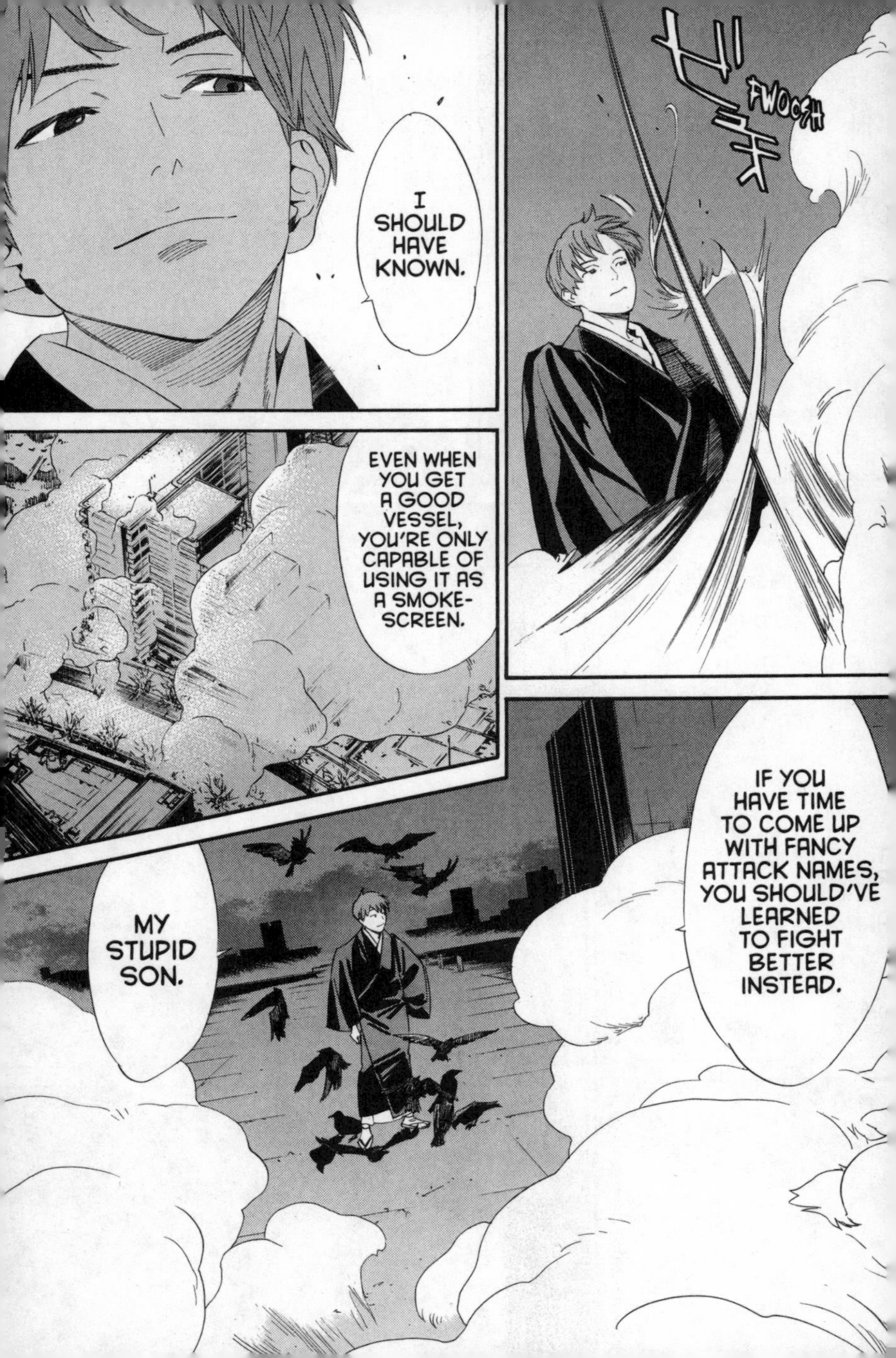
FWOOSH
I SHOULD HAVE KNOWN.
EVEN WHEN YOU GET A GOOD VESSEL, YOU'RE ONLY CAPABLE OF USING IT AS A SMOKE-SCREEN.
IF YOU HAVE TIME TO COME UP WITH FANCY ATTACK NAMES, YOU SHOULD'VE LEARNED TO FIGHT BETTER INSTEAD.
MY STUPID SON.

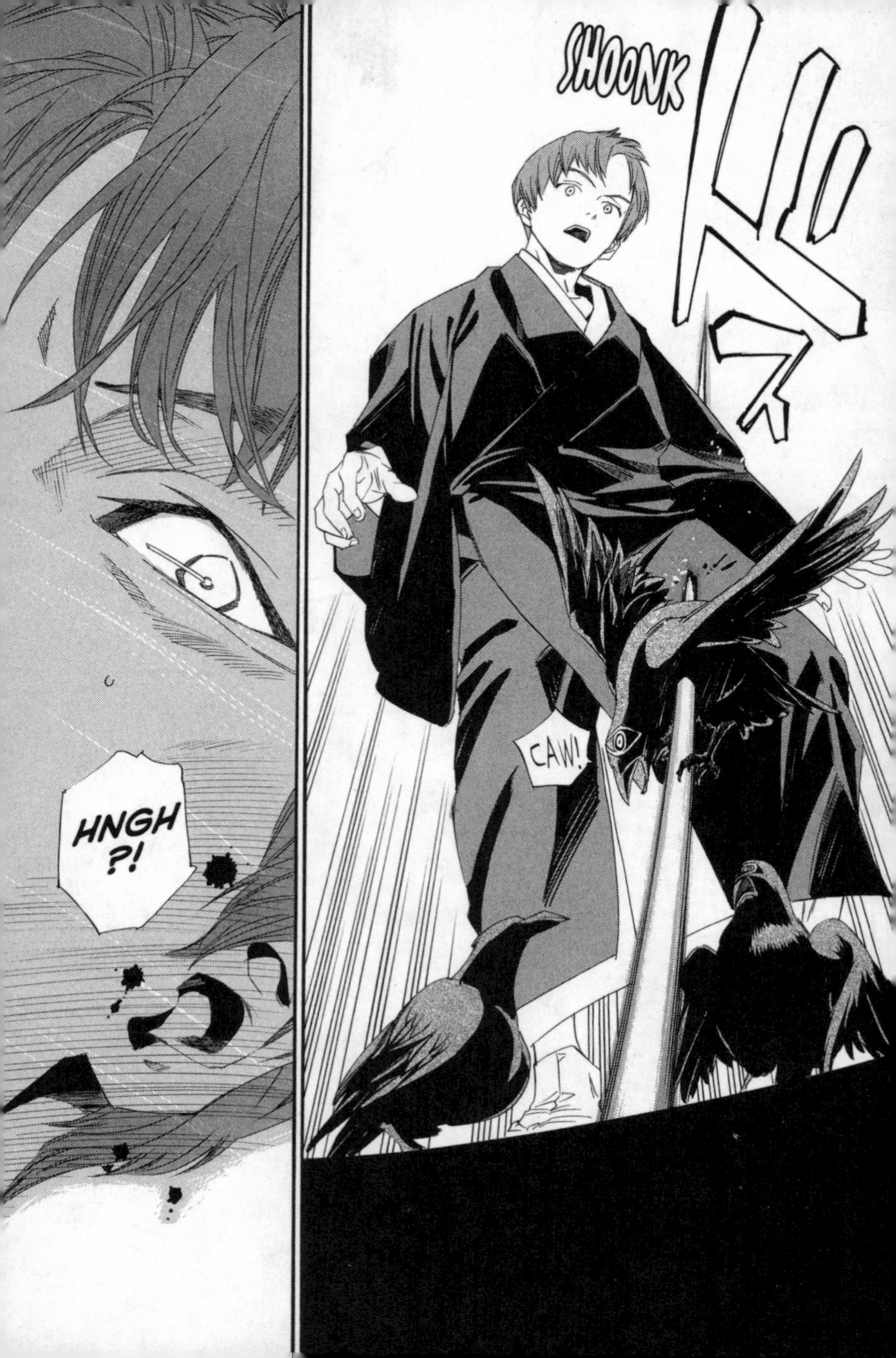
SHOONK
CAW!
HNGH ?!

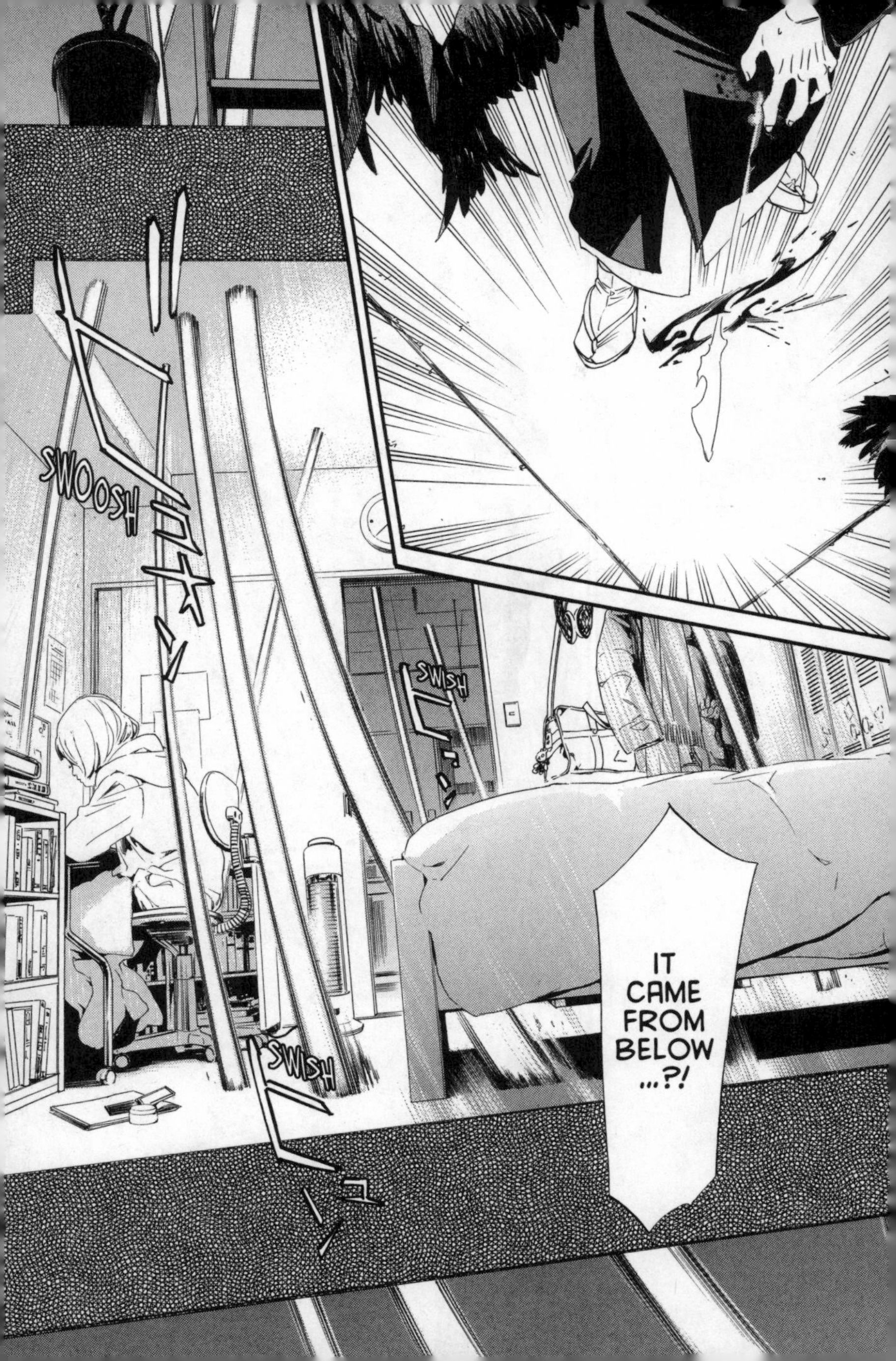
SWISH
IT CAME FROM BELOW ...?!
SWOOSH
SWISH

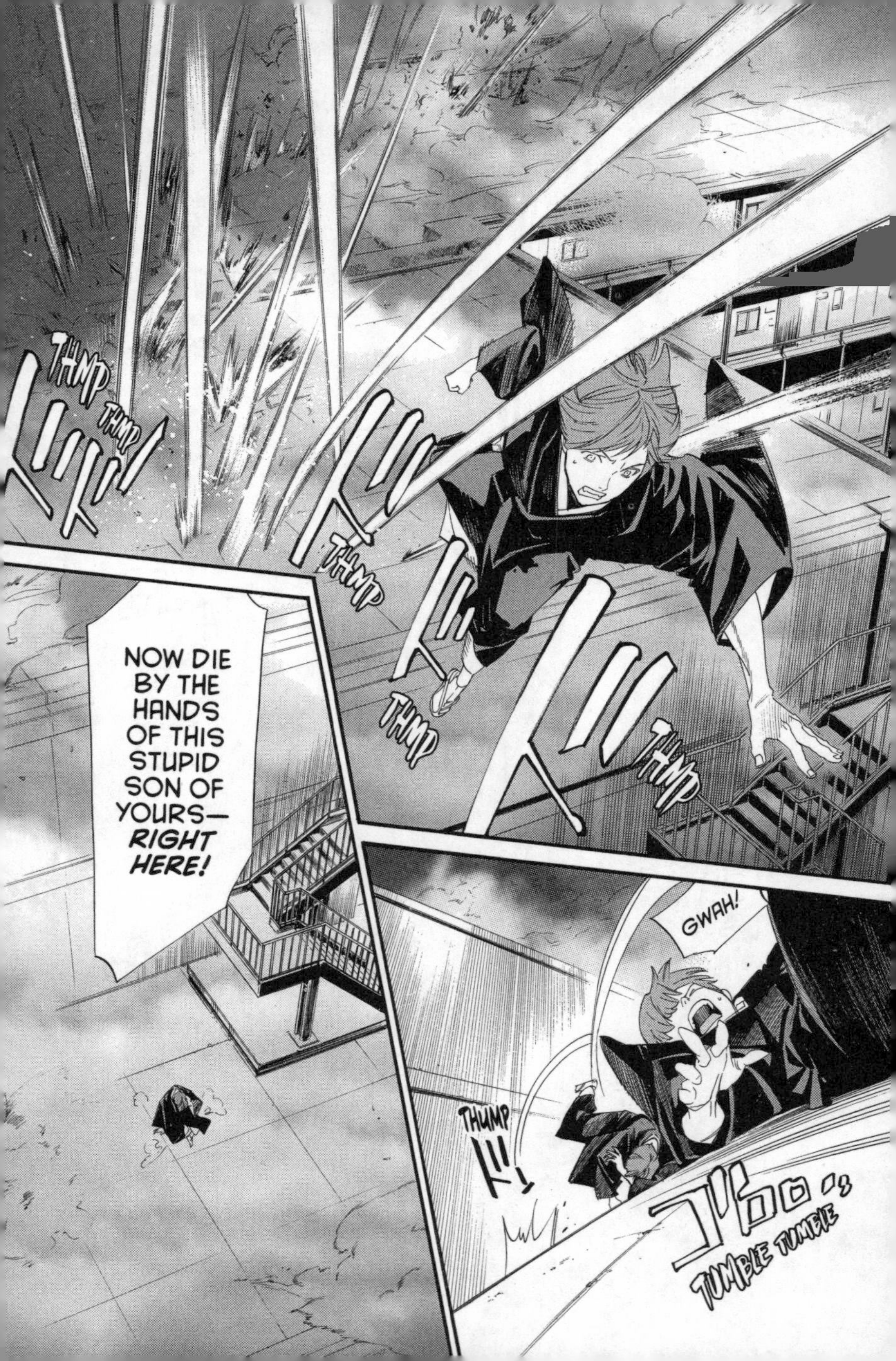
THMP
THMP
THMP
THMP
THMP
NOW DIE BY THE HANDS OF THIS STUPID SON OF YOURS—RIGHT HERE!
GWAH!
THMP
TUMBLE TUMBLE

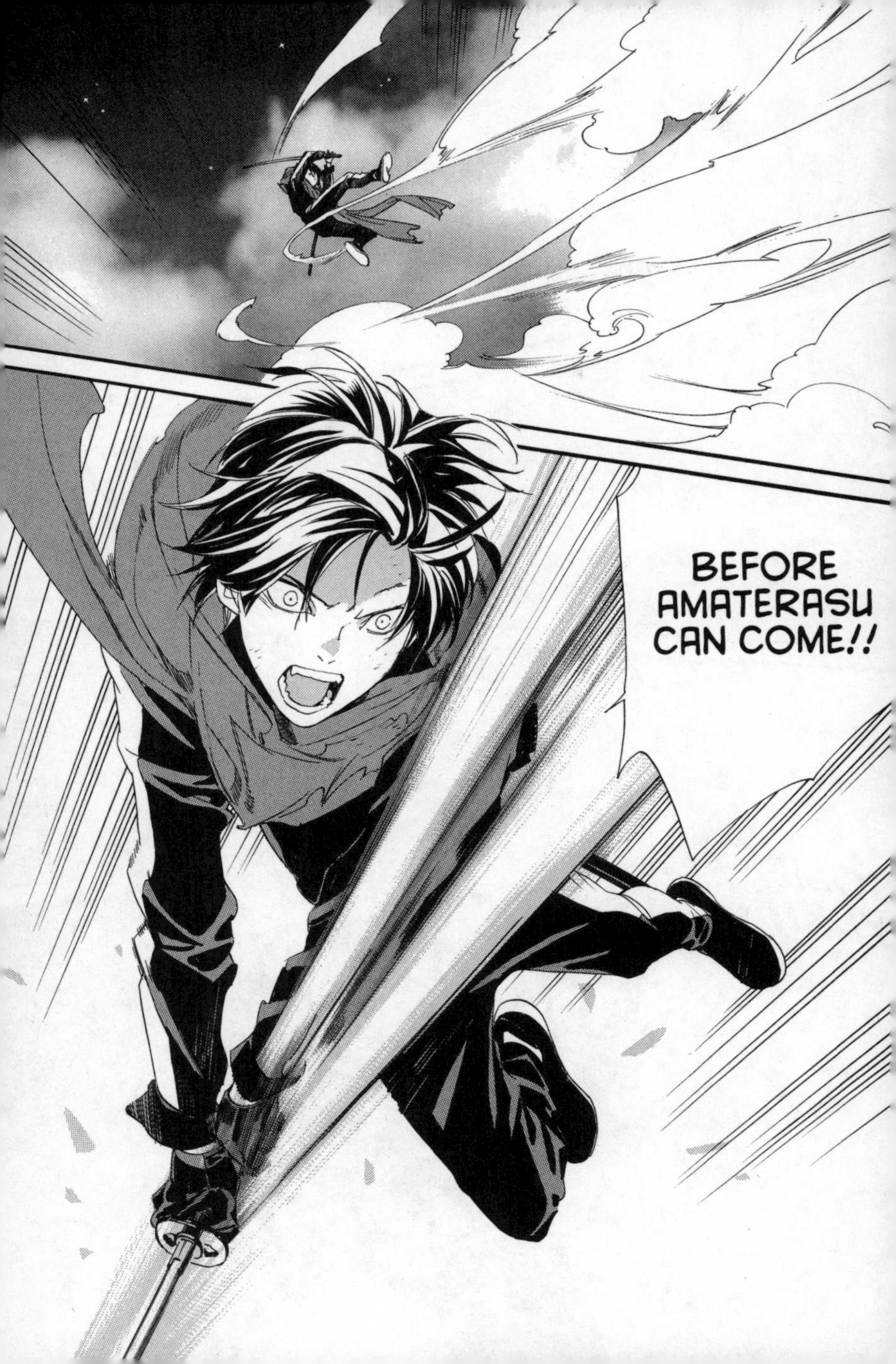
BEFORE AMATERASU CAN COME!!

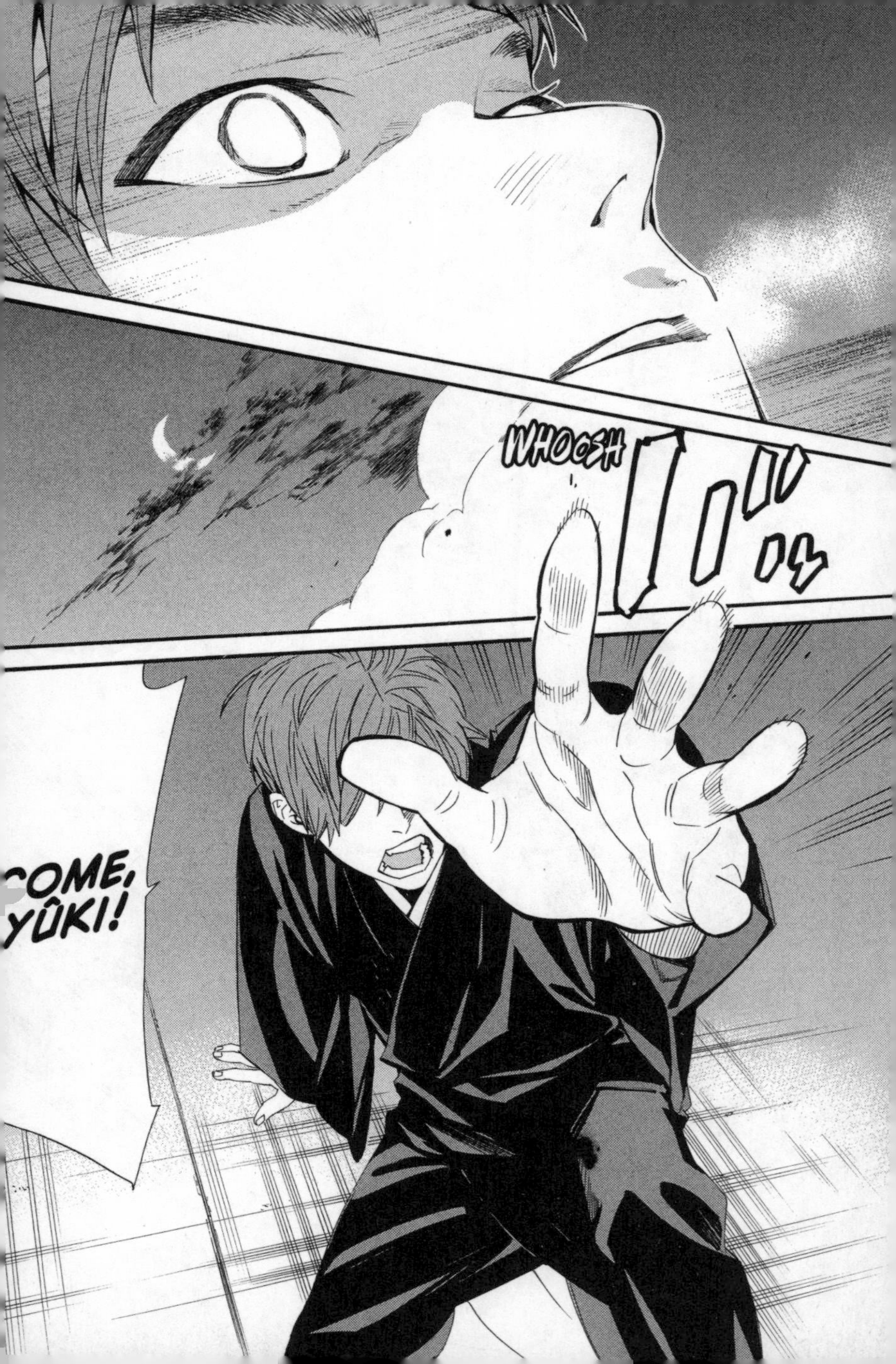
WHOOSH
COME, YÛKI!

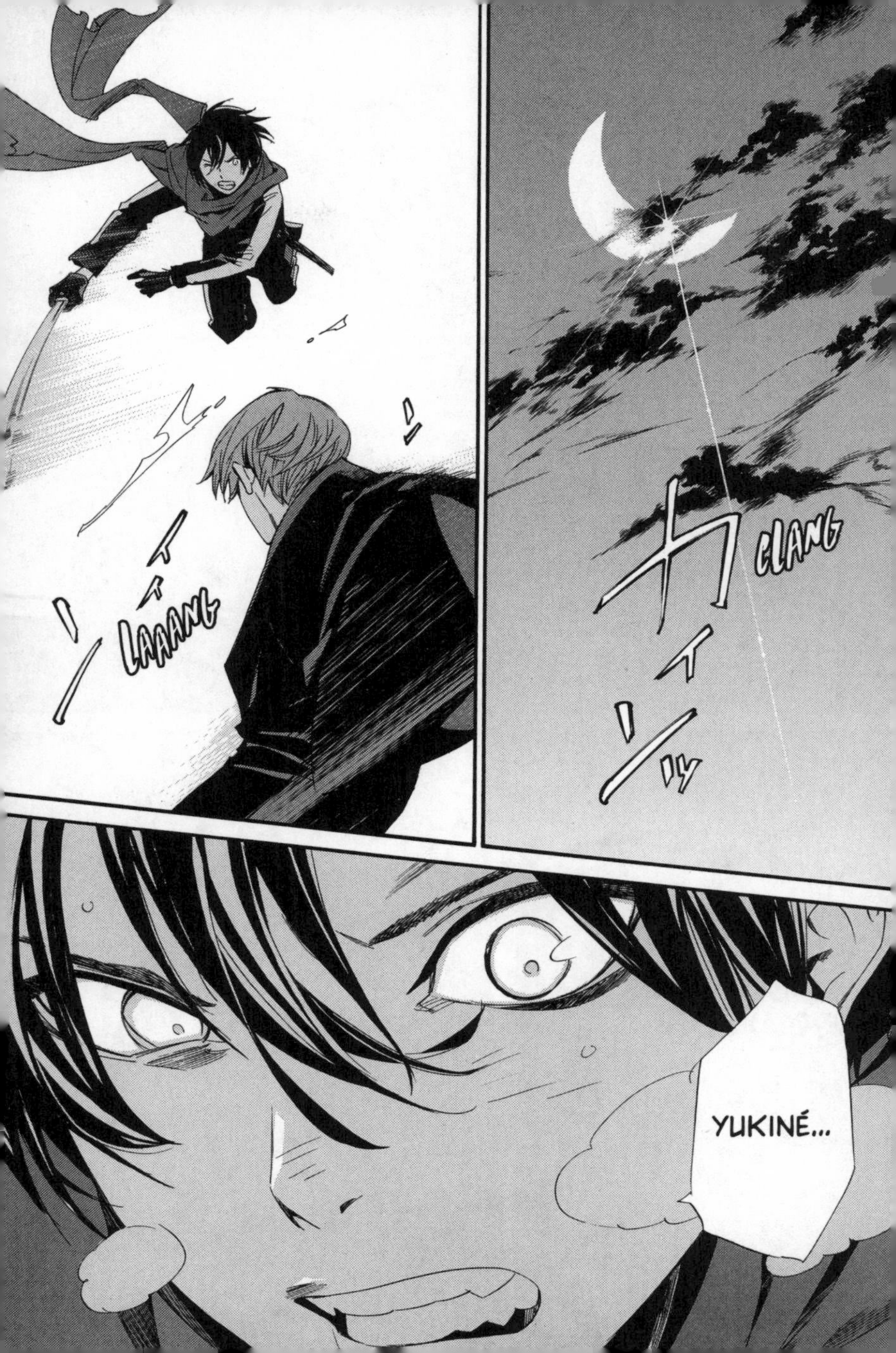
CLANG
LAAANG
YUKINÉ...

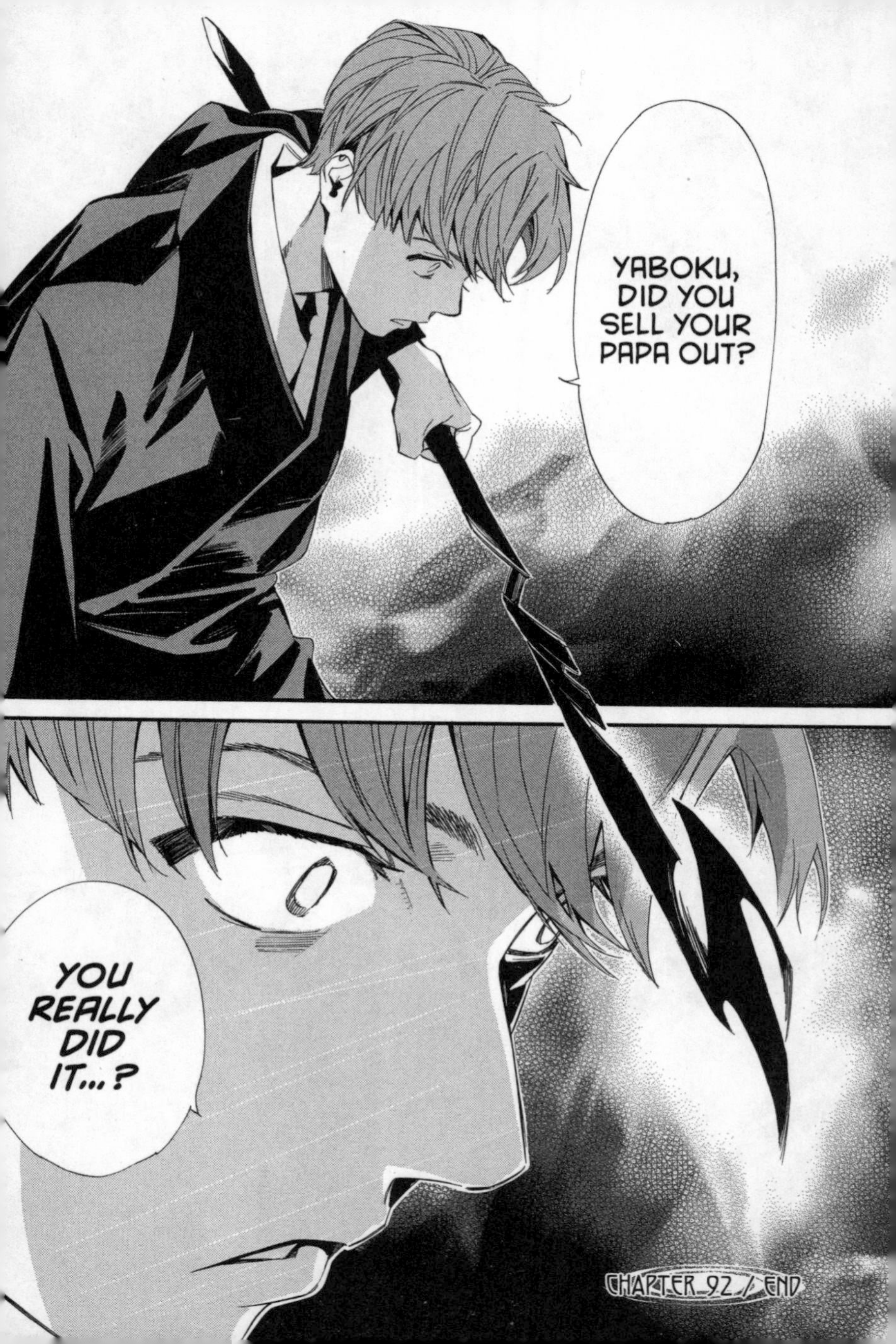
YABOKU, DID YOU SELL YOUR PAPA OUT?
YOU REALLY DID IT...?
CHAPTER 92 / END

野

良

神

CHAPTER 93: FACINGS

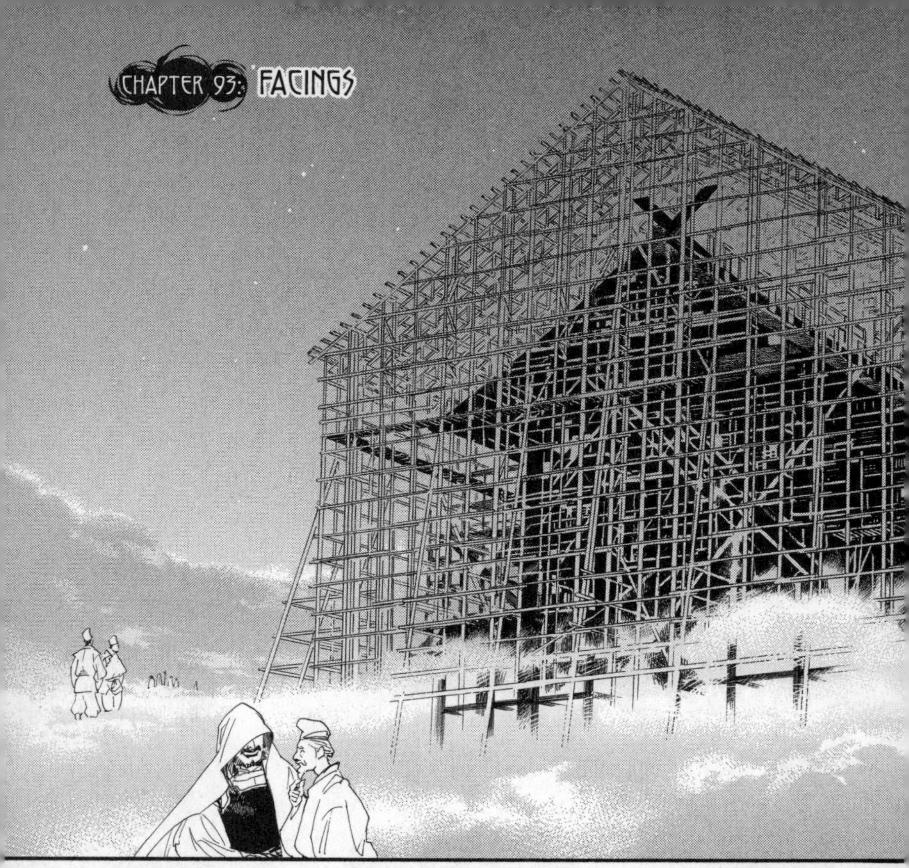

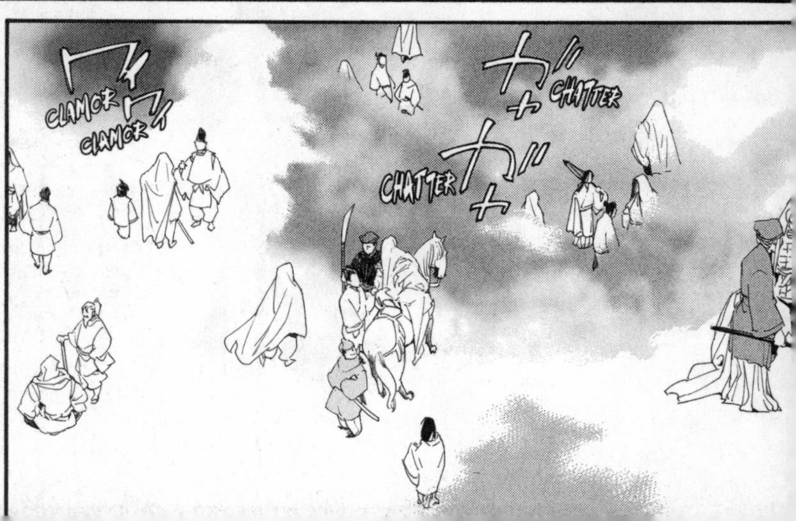
ガヤ CHATTER
ガヤ CHATTER
ワイ CLAMOR
ワイ CLAMOR

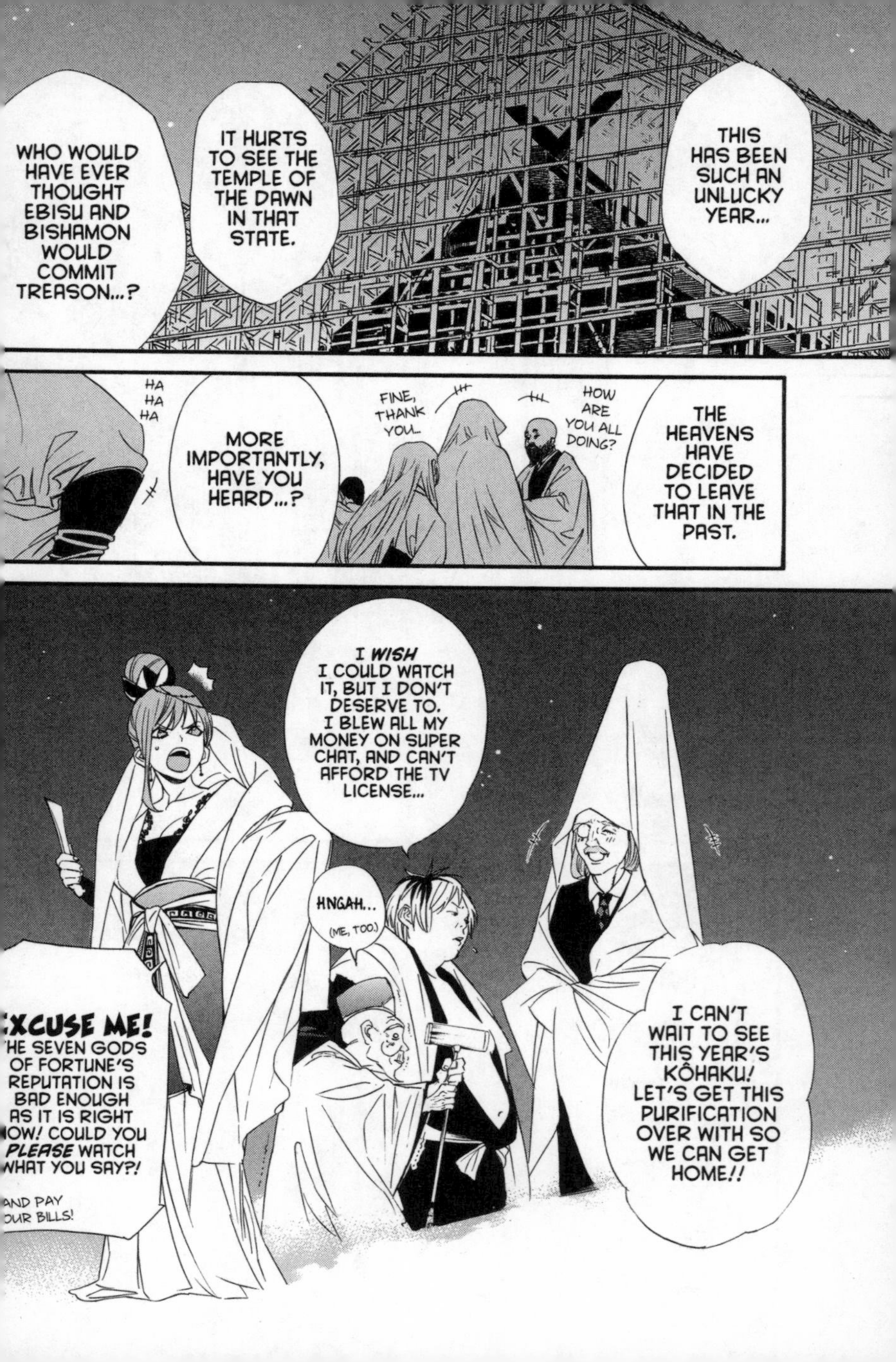
THIS HAS BEEN SUCH AN UNLUCKY YEAR...
IT HURTS TO SEE THE TEMPLE OF THE DAWN IN THAT STATE.
WHO WOULD HAVE EVER THOUGHT EBISU AND BISHAMON WOULD COMMIT TREASON...?
THE HEAVENS HAVE DECIDED TO LEAVE THAT IN THE PAST.
HOW ARE YOU ALL DOING?
FINE, THANK YOU..
MORE IMPORTANTLY, HAVE YOU HEARD...?
HA HA HA
I CAN'T WAIT TO SEE THIS YEAR'S KÔHAKU! LET'S GET THIS PURIFICATION OVER WITH SO WE CAN GET HOME!!
I *WISH* I COULD WATCH IT, BUT I DON'T DESERVE TO. I BLEW ALL MY MONEY ON SUPER CHAT, AND CAN'T AFFORD THE TV LICENSE...
HNGAH...
(ME, TOO.)
XCUSE ME! THE SEVEN GODS OF FORTUNE'S REPUTATION IS BAD ENOUGH AS IT IS RIGHT OW! COULD YOU *PLEASE* WATCH HAT YOU SAY?!
AND PAY OUR BILLS!

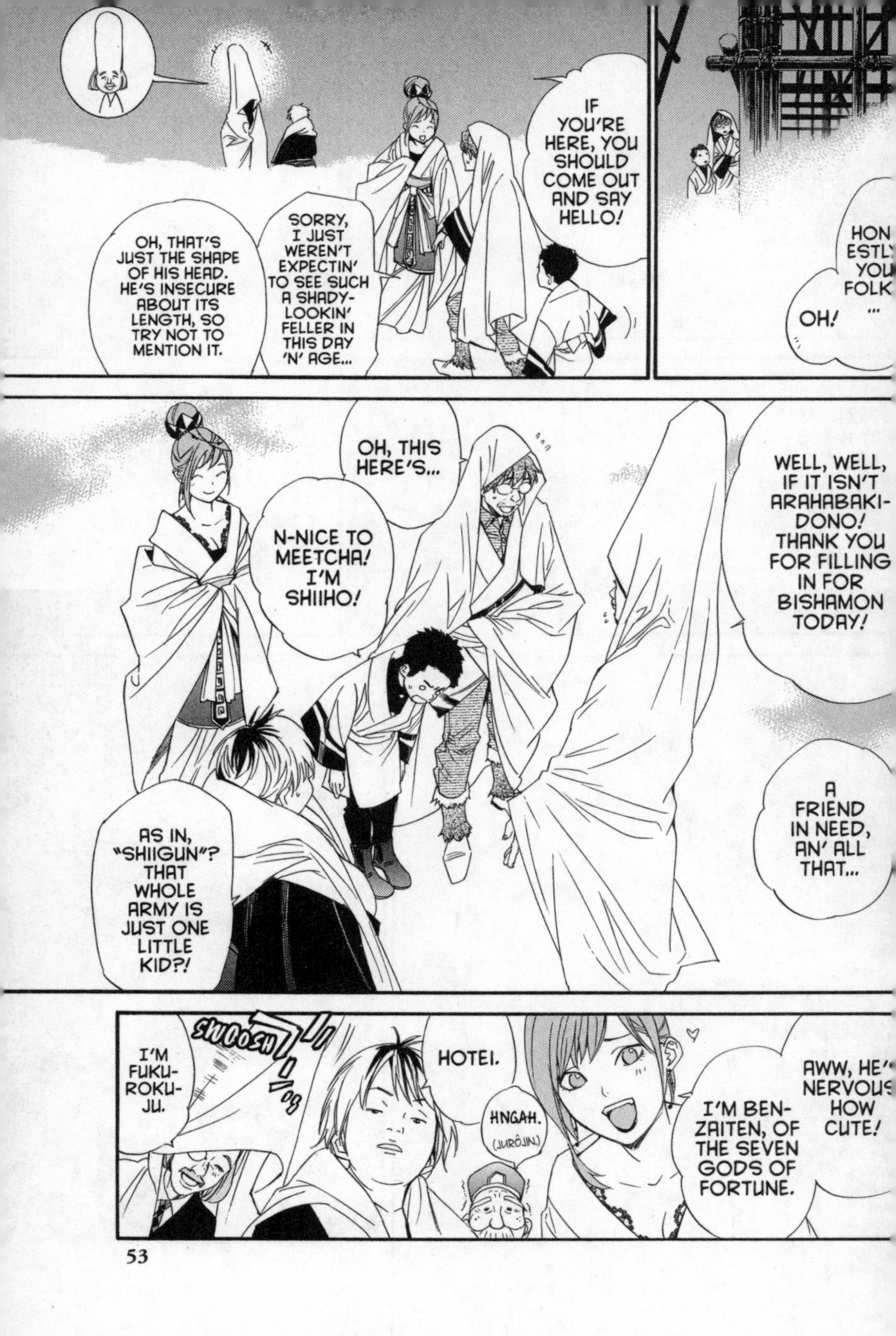
HON ESTLY YOU FOLK ...
OH!
IF YOU'RE HERE, YOU SHOULD COME OUT AND SAY HELLO!
SORRY, I JUST WEREN'T EXPECTIN' TO SEE SUCH A SHADY-LOOKIN' FELLER IN THIS DAY 'N' AGE...
OH, THAT'S JUST THE SHAPE OF HIS HEAD. HE'S INSECURE ABOUT ITS LENGTH, SO TRY NOT TO MENTION IT.
WELL, WELL, IF IT ISN'T ARAHABAKI-DONO! THANK YOU FOR FILLING IN FOR BISHAMON TODAY!
A FRIEND IN NEED, AN' ALL THAT...
OH, THIS HERE'S...
N-NICE TO MEETCHA! I'M SHIIHO!
AS IN, "SHIIGUN"? THAT WHOLE ARMY IS JUST ONE LITTLE KID?!
AWW, HE' NERVOUS HOW CUTE!
I'M BEN-ZAITEN, OF THE SEVEN GODS OF FORTUNE.
HNGAH.
(JURÔJIN)
HOTEI.
I'M FUKU-ROKU-JU.

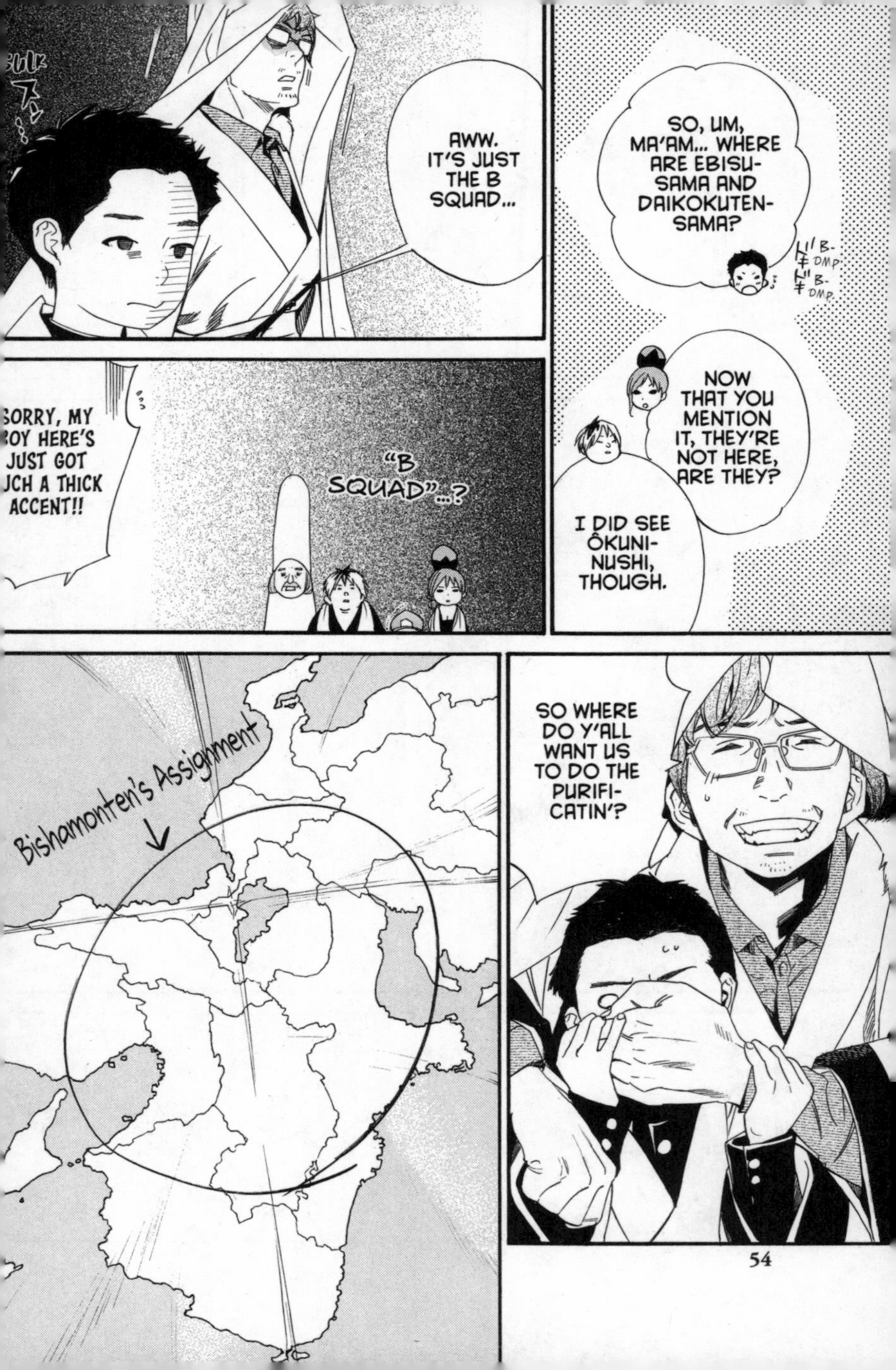
AWW. IT'S JUST THE B SQUAD...
SORRY, MY BOY HERE'S JUST GOT SUCH A THICK ACCENT!!
"B SQUAD"...?
SO, UM, MA'AM... WHERE ARE EBISU-SAMA AND DAIKOKUTEN-SAMA?
B-DMP B-DMP
NOW THAT YOU MENTION IT, THEY'RE NOT HERE, ARE THEY?
I DID SEE ÔKUNI-NUSHI, THOUGH.
SO WHERE DO Y'ALL WANT US TO DO THE PURIFI-CATIN'?
Bishamonten's Assignment

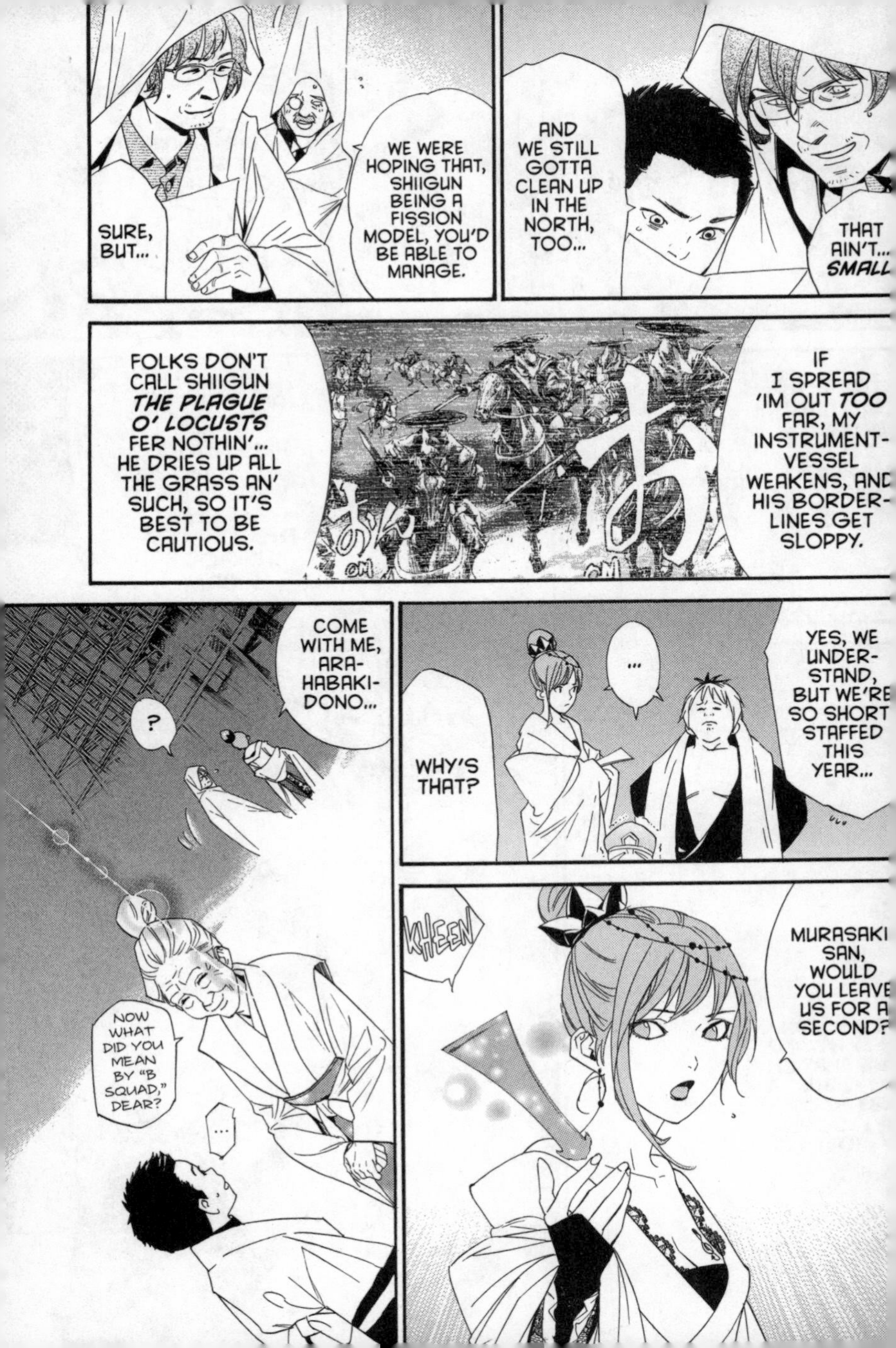
THAT AIN'T... *SMALL*
AND WE STILL GOTTA CLEAN UP IN THE NORTH, TOO...
WE WERE HOPING THAT, SHIIGUN BEING A FISSION MODEL, YOU'D BE ABLE TO MANAGE.
SURE, BUT...
IF I SPREAD 'IM OUT *TOO* FAR, MY INSTRUMENT-VESSEL WEAKENS, AND HIS BORDER-LINES GET SLOPPY.
OM
OM
FOLKS DON'T CALL SHIIGUN ***THE PLAGUE O' LOCUSTS*** FER NOTHIN'... HE DRIES UP ALL THE GRASS AN' SUCH, SO IT'S BEST TO BE CAUTIOUS.
YES, WE UNDERSTAND, BUT WE'RE SO SHORT STAFFED THIS YEAR...
...
WHY'S THAT?
MURASAKI SAN, WOULD YOU LEAVE US FOR A SECOND?
KHEEN
COME WITH ME, ARA-HABAKI-DONO...
?
NOW WHAT DID YOU MEAN BY "B SQUAD," DEAR?
...

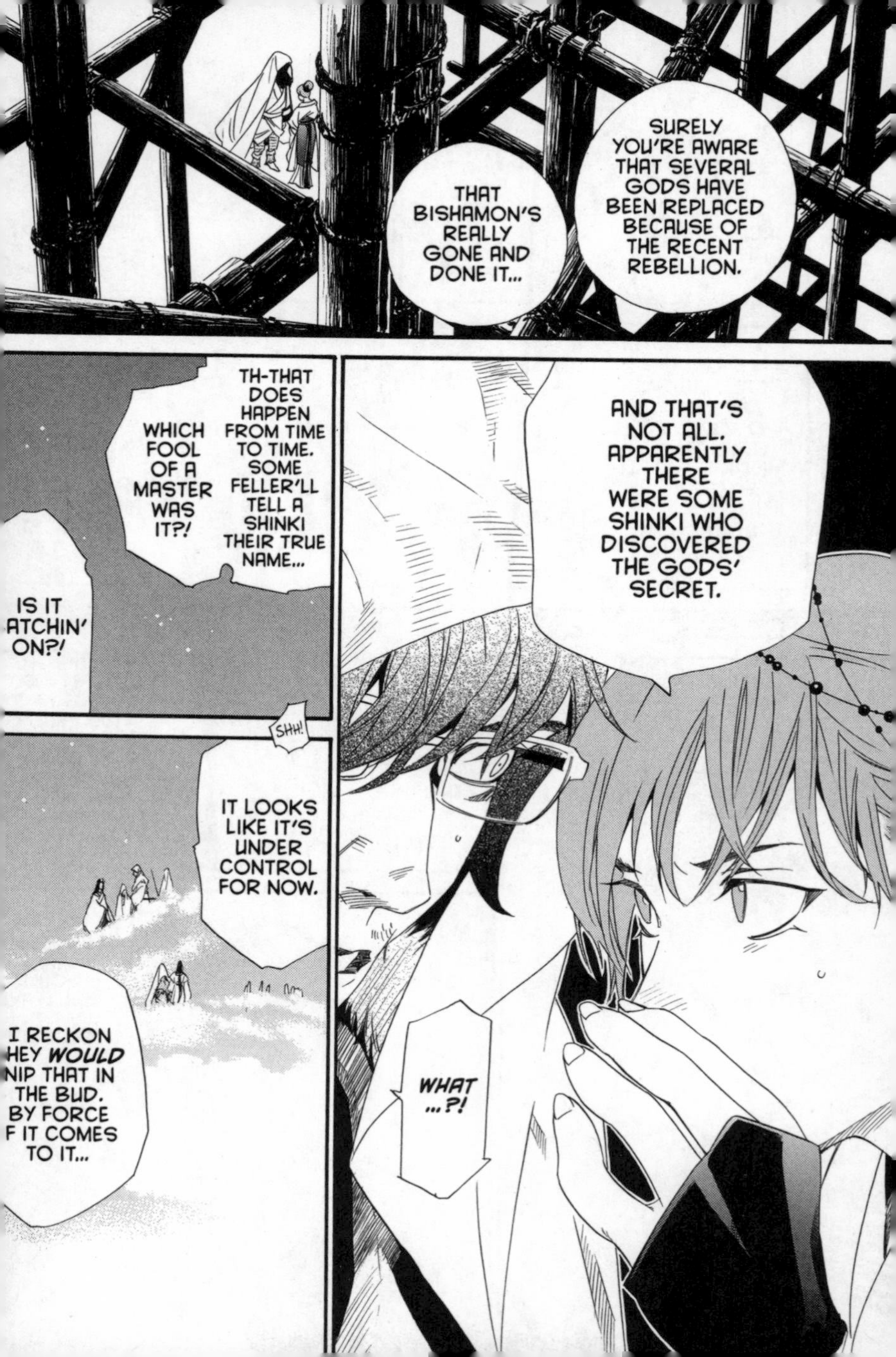
SURELY YOU'RE AWARE THAT SEVERAL GODS HAVE BEEN REPLACED BECAUSE OF THE RECENT REBELLION.
THAT BISHAMON'S REALLY GONE AND DONE IT...
AND THAT'S NOT ALL. APPARENTLY THERE WERE SOME SHINKI WHO DISCOVERED THE GODS' SECRET.
WHAT ...?!
TH-THAT DOES HAPPEN FROM TIME TO TIME. SOME FELLER'LL TELL A SHINKI THEIR TRUE NAME...
WHICH FOOL OF A MASTER WAS IT?!
IS IT ATCHIN' ON?!
SHH!
IT LOOKS LIKE IT'S UNDER CONTROL FOR NOW.
I RECKON HEY *WOULD* NIP THAT IN THE BUD. BY FORCE F IT COMES TO IT...

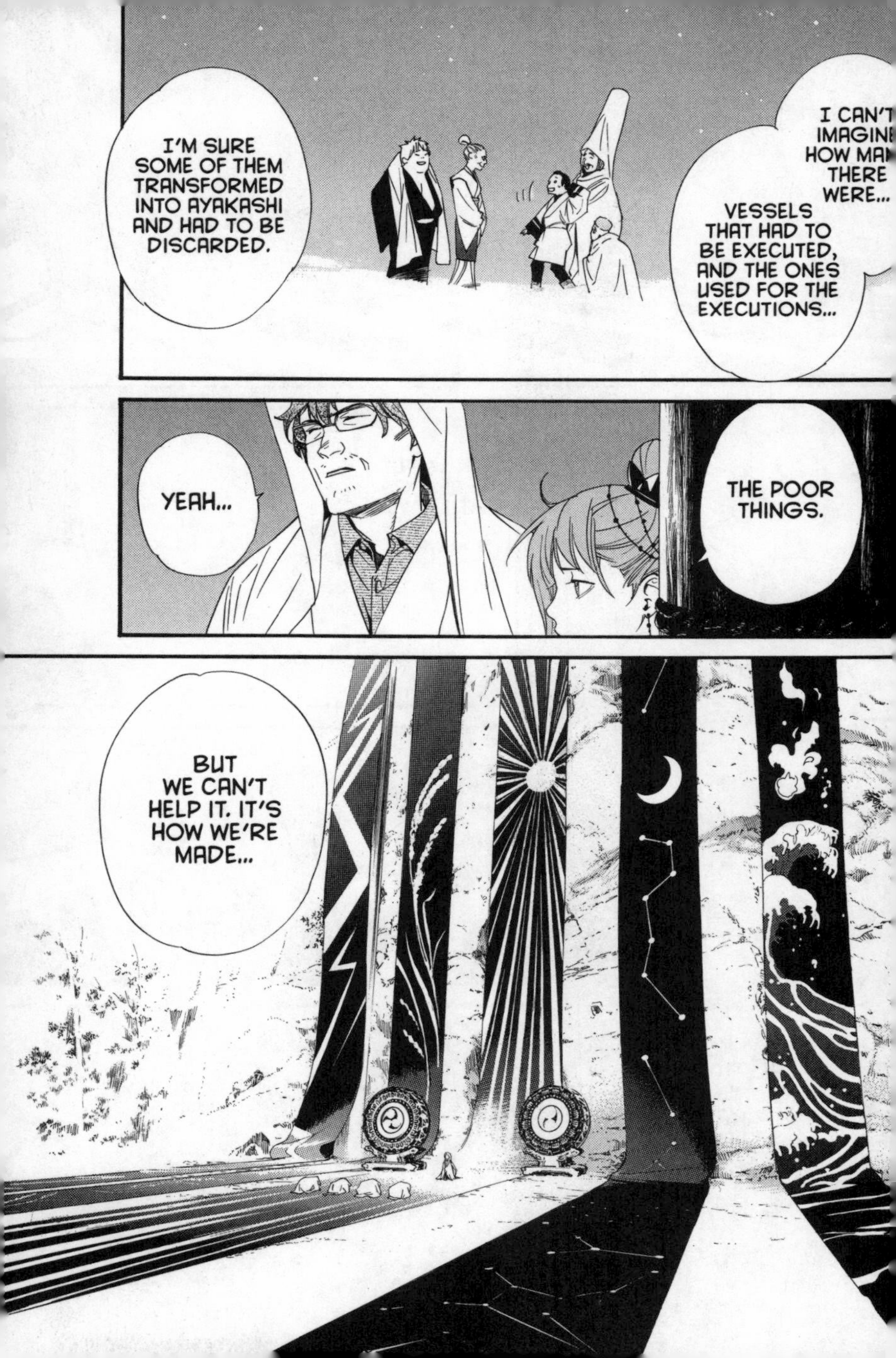
I CAN'T IMAGINE HOW MA THERE WERE... VESSELS THAT HAD TO BE EXECUTED, AND THE ONES USED FOR THE EXECUTIONS...
I'M SURE SOME OF THEM TRANSFORMED INTO AYAKASHI AND HAD TO BE DISCARDED.
THE POOR THINGS.
YEAH...
BUT WE CAN'T HELP IT. IT'S HOW WE'RE MADE...

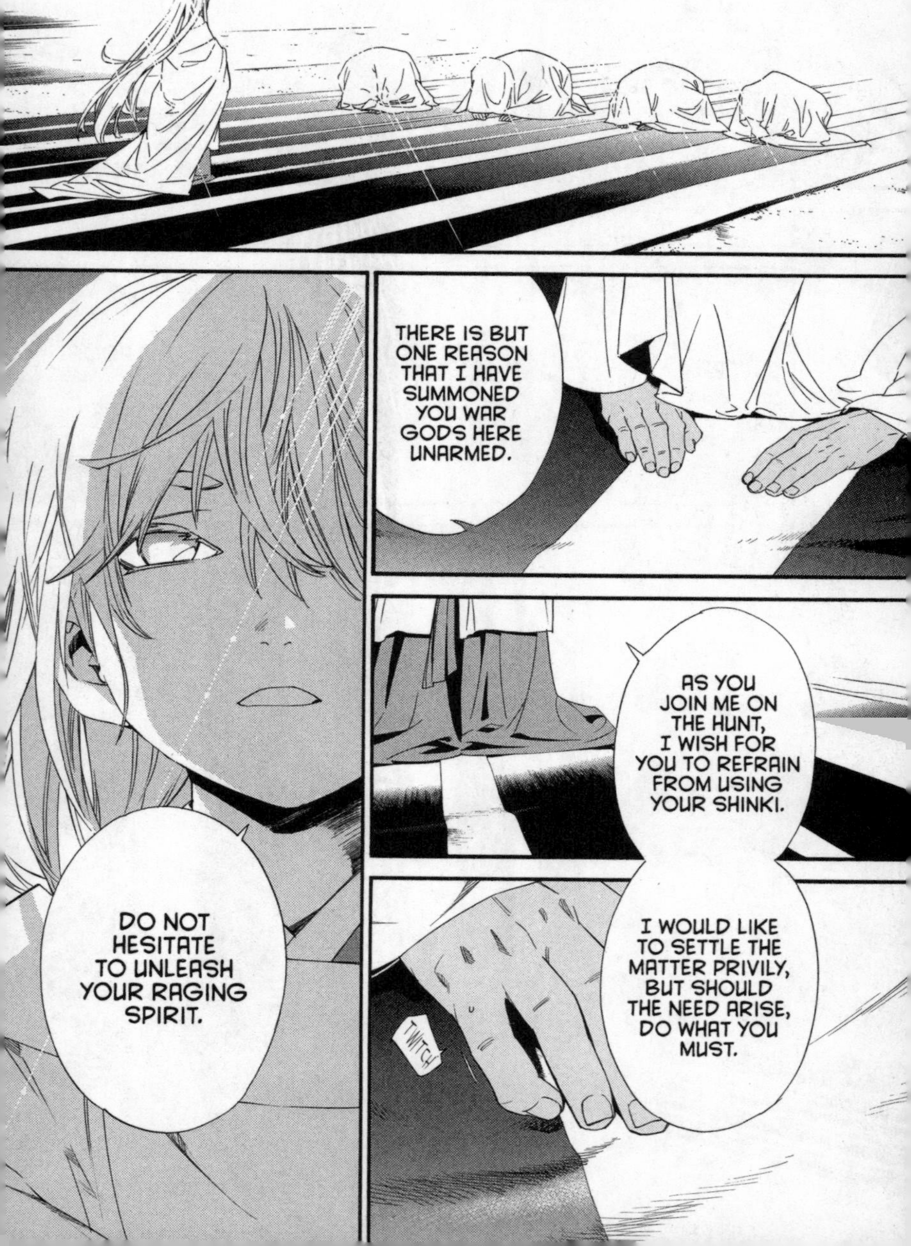
THERE IS BUT ONE REASON THAT I HAVE SUMMONED YOU WAR GODS HERE UNARMED.
AS YOU JOIN ME ON THE HUNT, I WISH FOR YOU TO REFRAIN FROM USING YOUR SHINKI.
I WOULD LIKE TO SETTLE THE MATTER PRIVILY, BUT SHOULD THE NEED ARISE, DO WHAT YOU MUST.
TWITCH
DO NOT HESITATE TO UNLEASH YOUR RAGING SPIRIT.

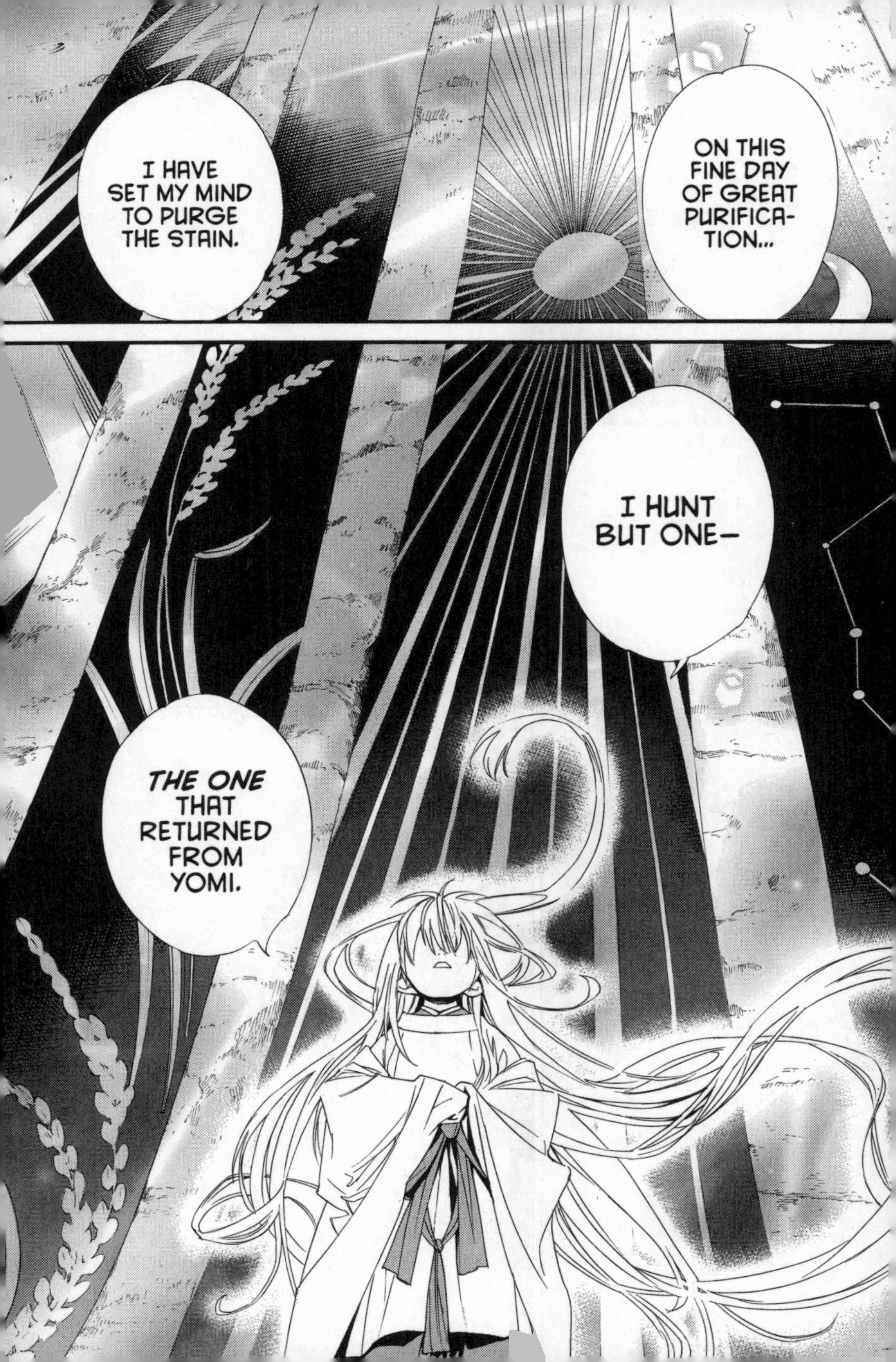
ON THIS FINE DAY OF GREAT PURIFICATION...
I HAVE SET MY MIND TO PURGE THE STAIN.
I HUNT BUT ONE—
THE ONE THAT RETURNED FROM YOMI.

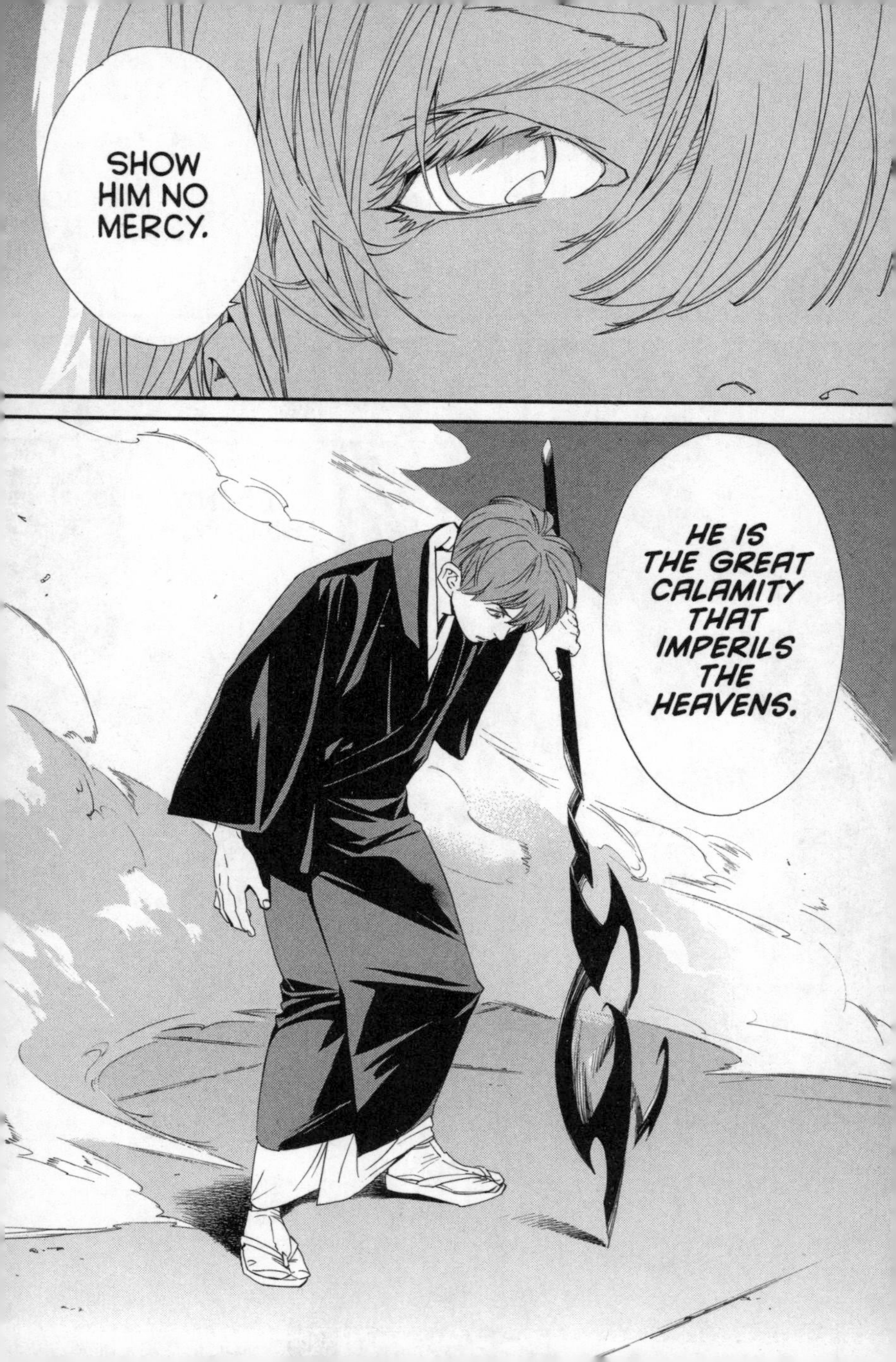
SHOW HIM NO MERCY.
HE IS THE GREAT CALAMITY THAT IMPERILS THE HEAVENS.

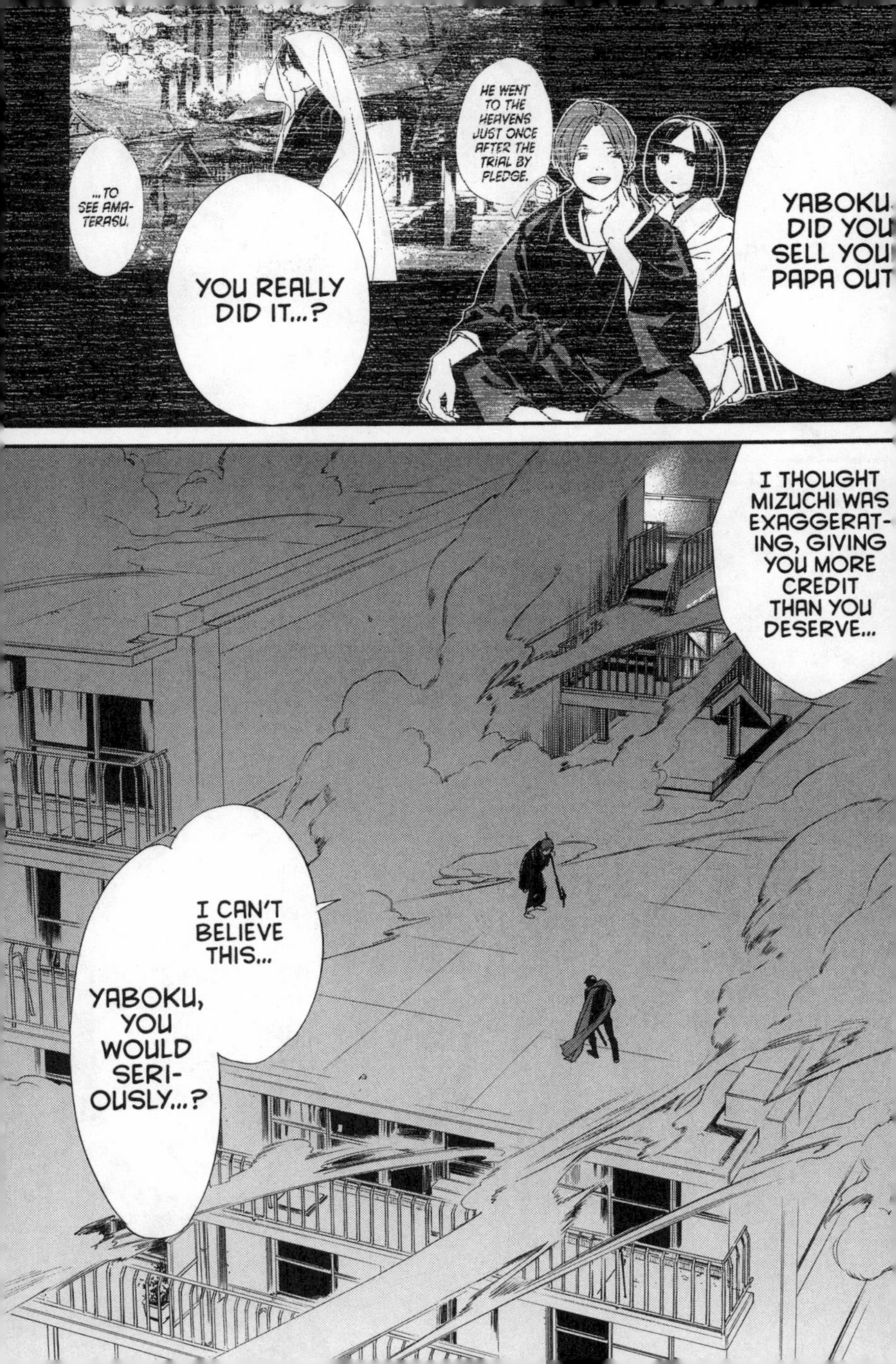

YABOKU. DID YOU SELL YOU PAPA OUT
HE WENT TO THE HEAVENS JUST ONCE AFTER THE TRIAL BY PLEDGE.
...TO SEE AMA-TERASU.
YOU REALLY DID IT...?
I THOUGHT MIZUCHI WAS EXAGGERAT-ING, GIVING YOU MORE CREDIT THAN YOU DESERVE...
I CAN'T BELIEVE THIS...
YABOKU, YOU WOULD SERI-OUSLY...?

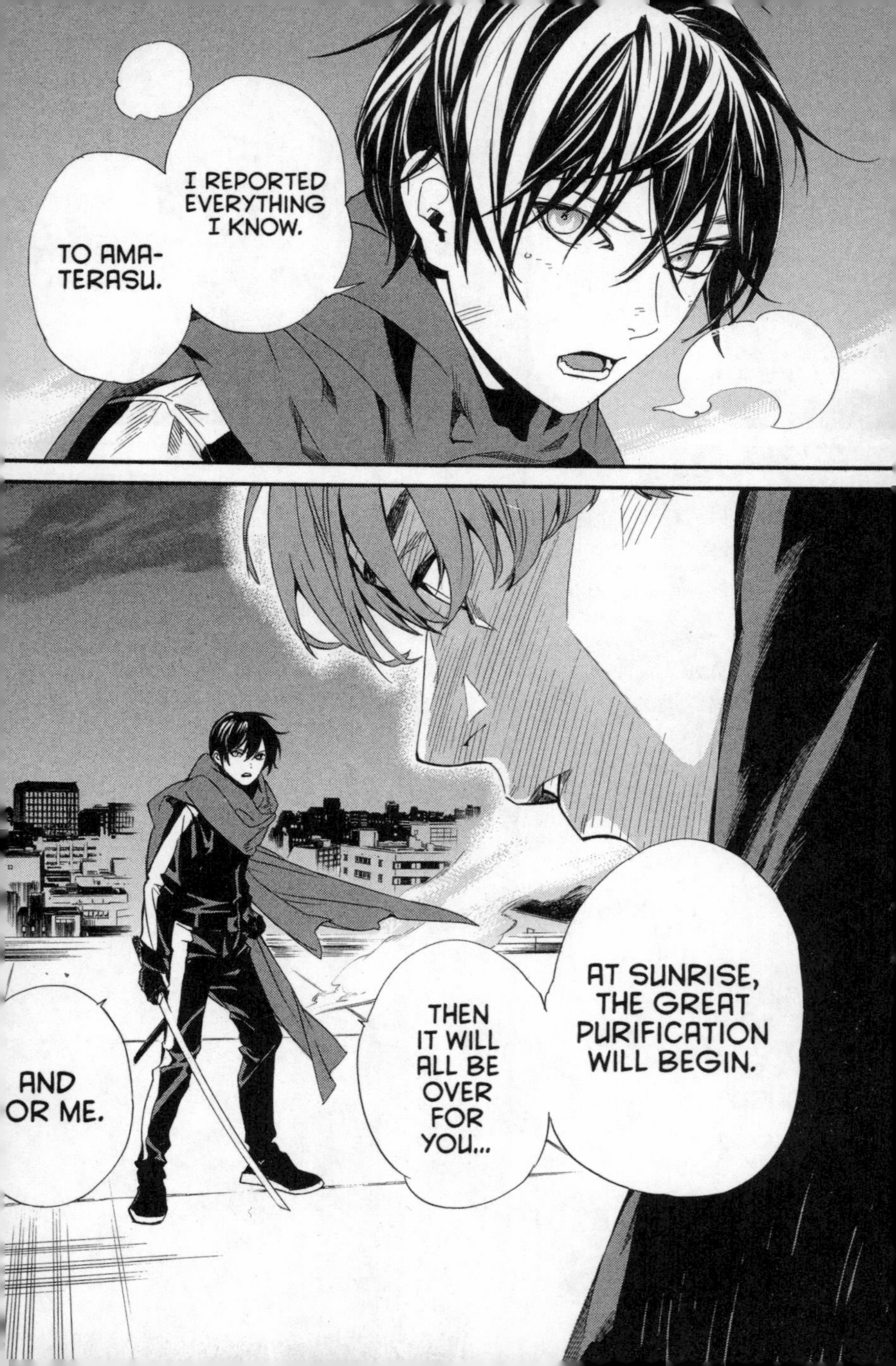
I REPORTED EVERYTHING I KNOW.
TO AMA-TERASU.
AT SUNRISE, THE GREAT PURIFICATION WILL BEGIN.
THEN IT WILL ALL BE OVER FOR YOU...
AND
OR ME.

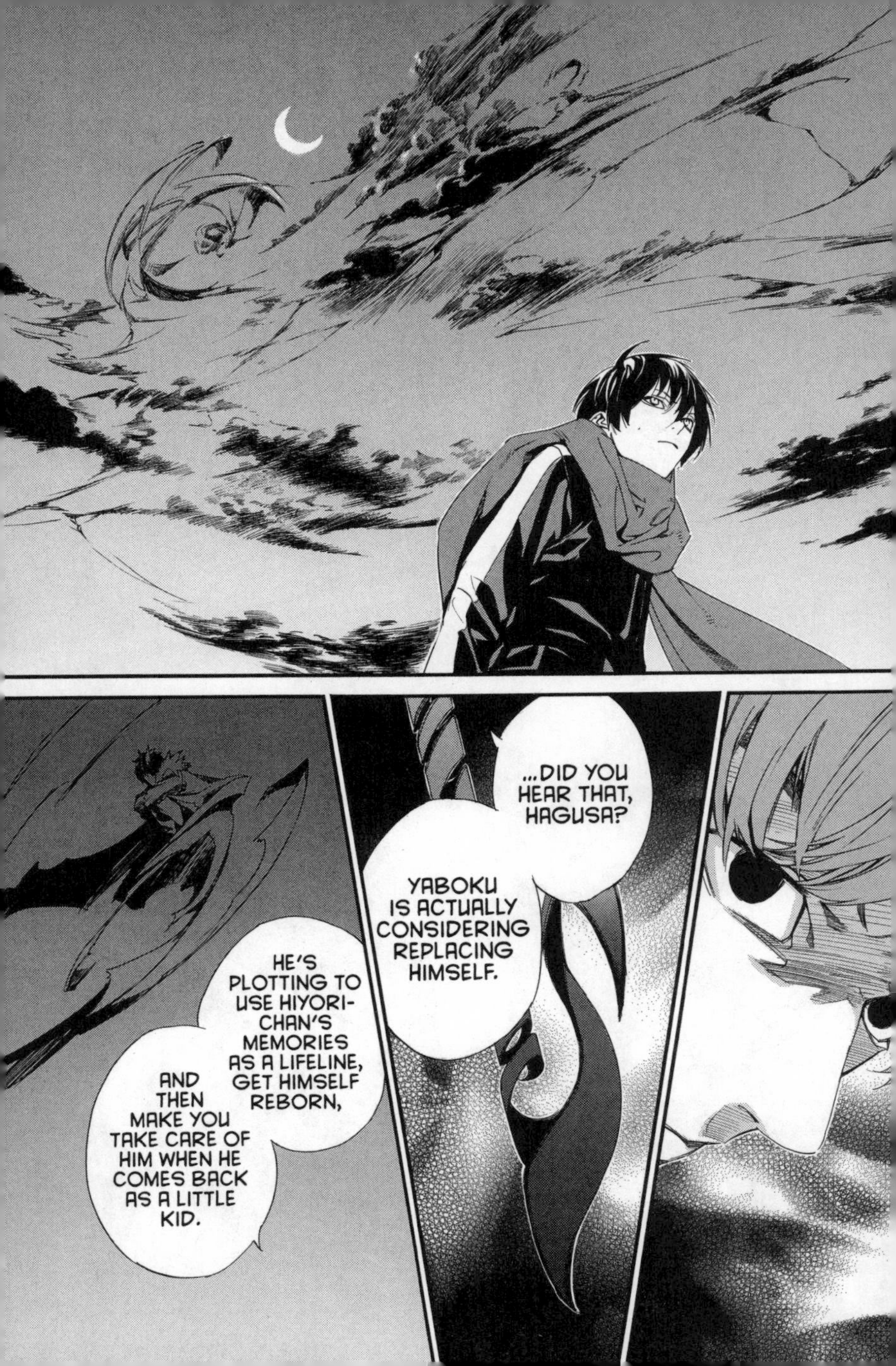
...DID YOU HEAR THAT, HAGUSA?
YABOKU IS ACTUALLY CONSIDERING REPLACING HIMSELF.
HE'S PLOTTING TO USE HIYORI-CHAN'S MEMORIES AS A LIFELINE, GET HIMSELF REBORN,
AND THEN MAKE YOU TAKE CARE OF HIM WHEN HE COMES BACK AS A LITTLE KID.

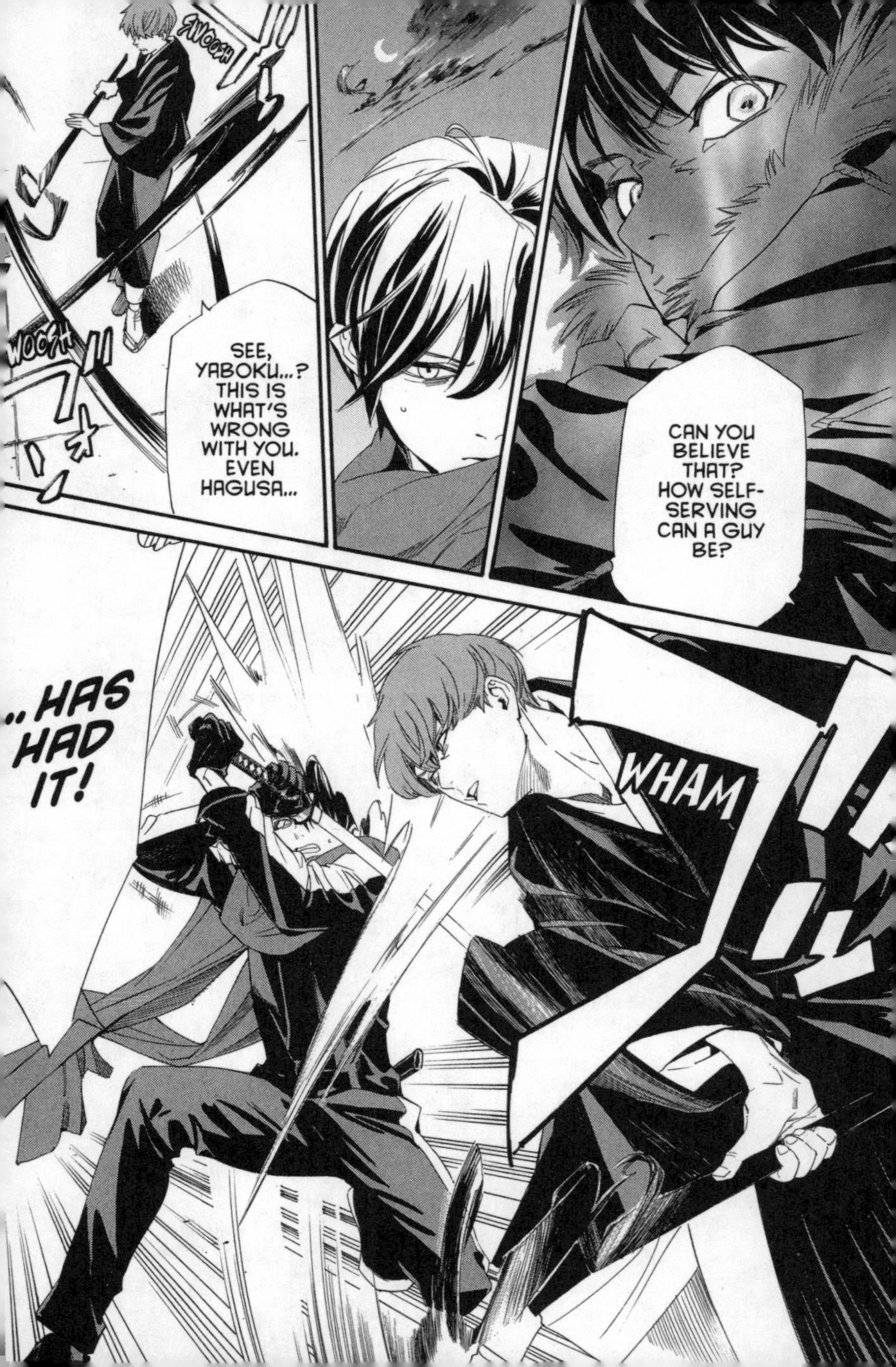
CAN YOU BELIEVE THAT? HOW SELF-SERVING CAN A GUY BE?
SEE, YABOKU...? THIS IS WHAT'S WRONG WITH YOU. EVEN HAGUSA...
SWOOSH
WOOSH
WHAM
..HAS HAD IT!

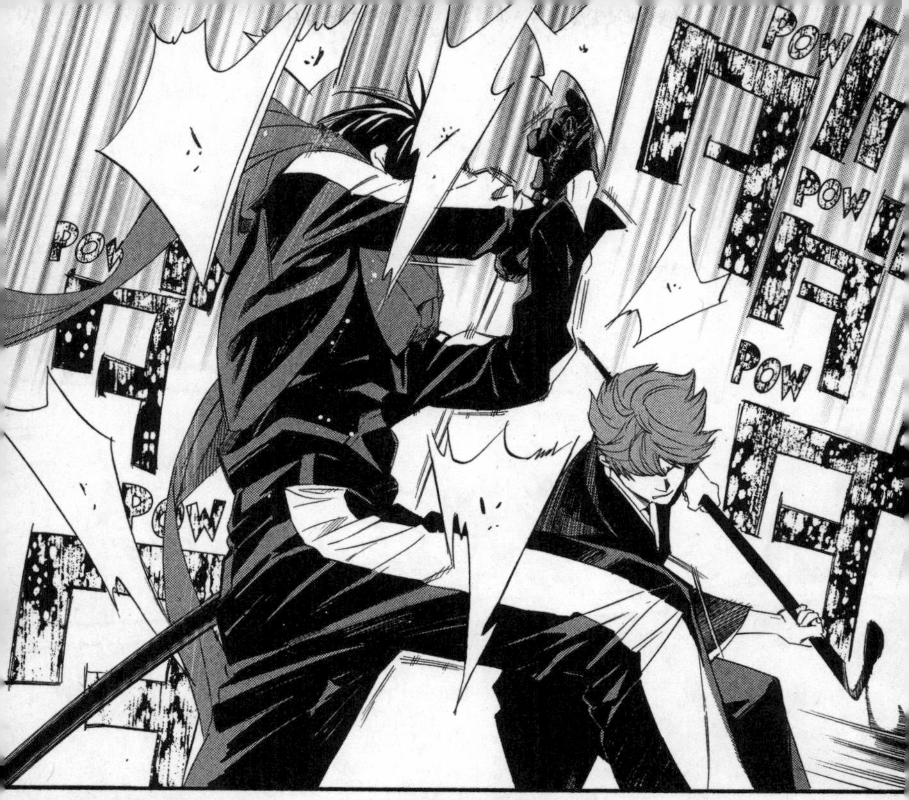
POW
POW
POW
POW
POW
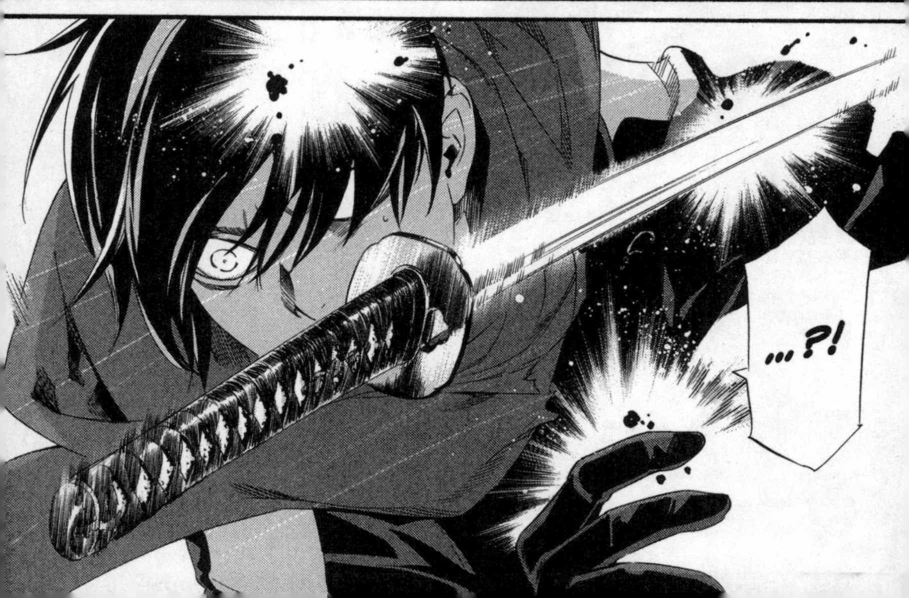
...?!

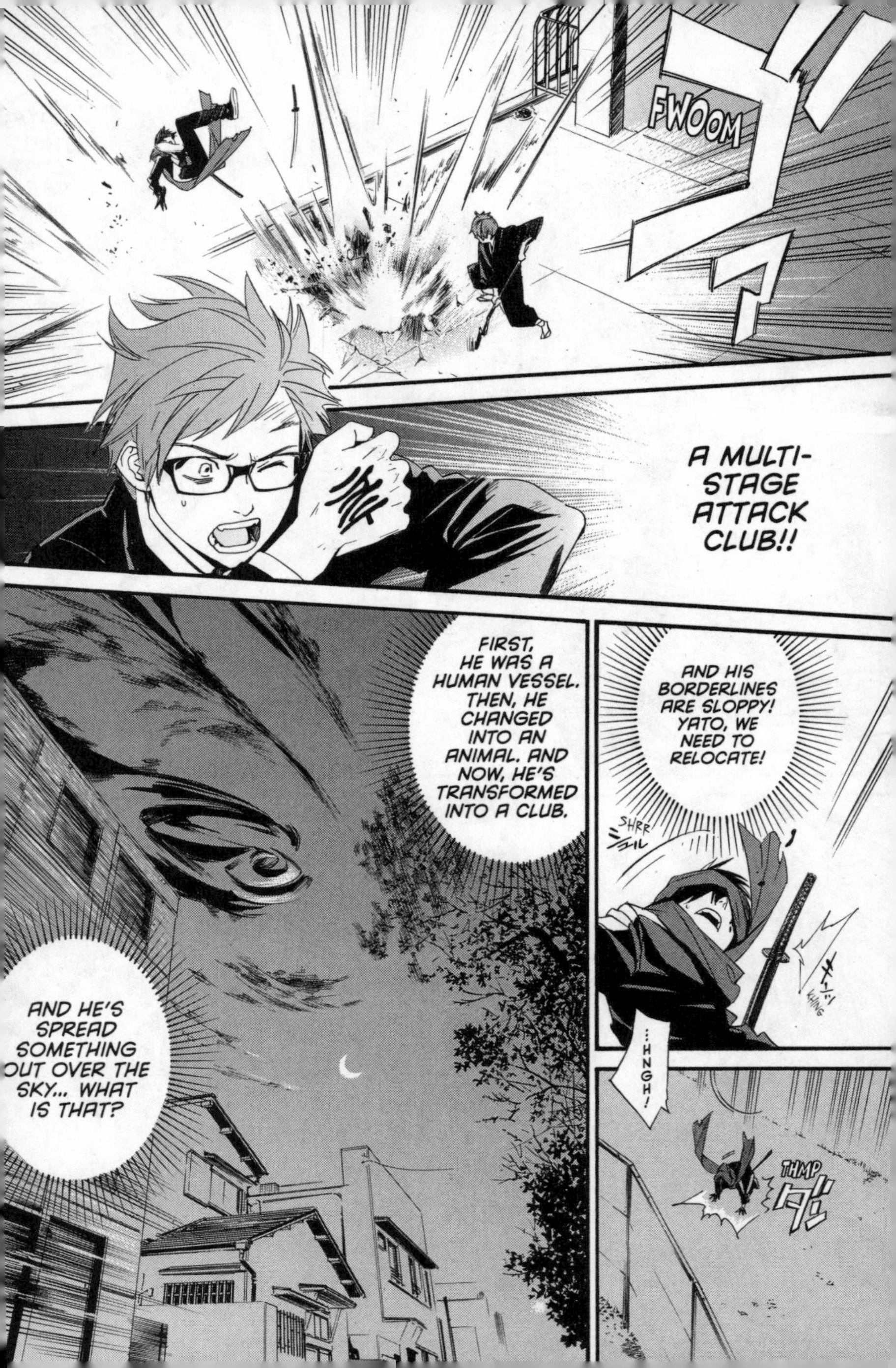
FWOOM
A MULTI-STAGE ATTACK CLUB!!
FIRST, HE WAS A HUMAN VESSEL. THEN, HE CHANGED INTO AN ANIMAL. AND NOW, HE'S TRANSFORMED INTO A CLUB.
AND HIS BORDERLINES ARE SLOPPY! YATO, WE NEED TO RELOCATE!
SHRR
KHING
...HNGH!
THMP
AND HE'S SPREAD SOMETHING OUT OVER THE SKY... WHAT IS THAT?

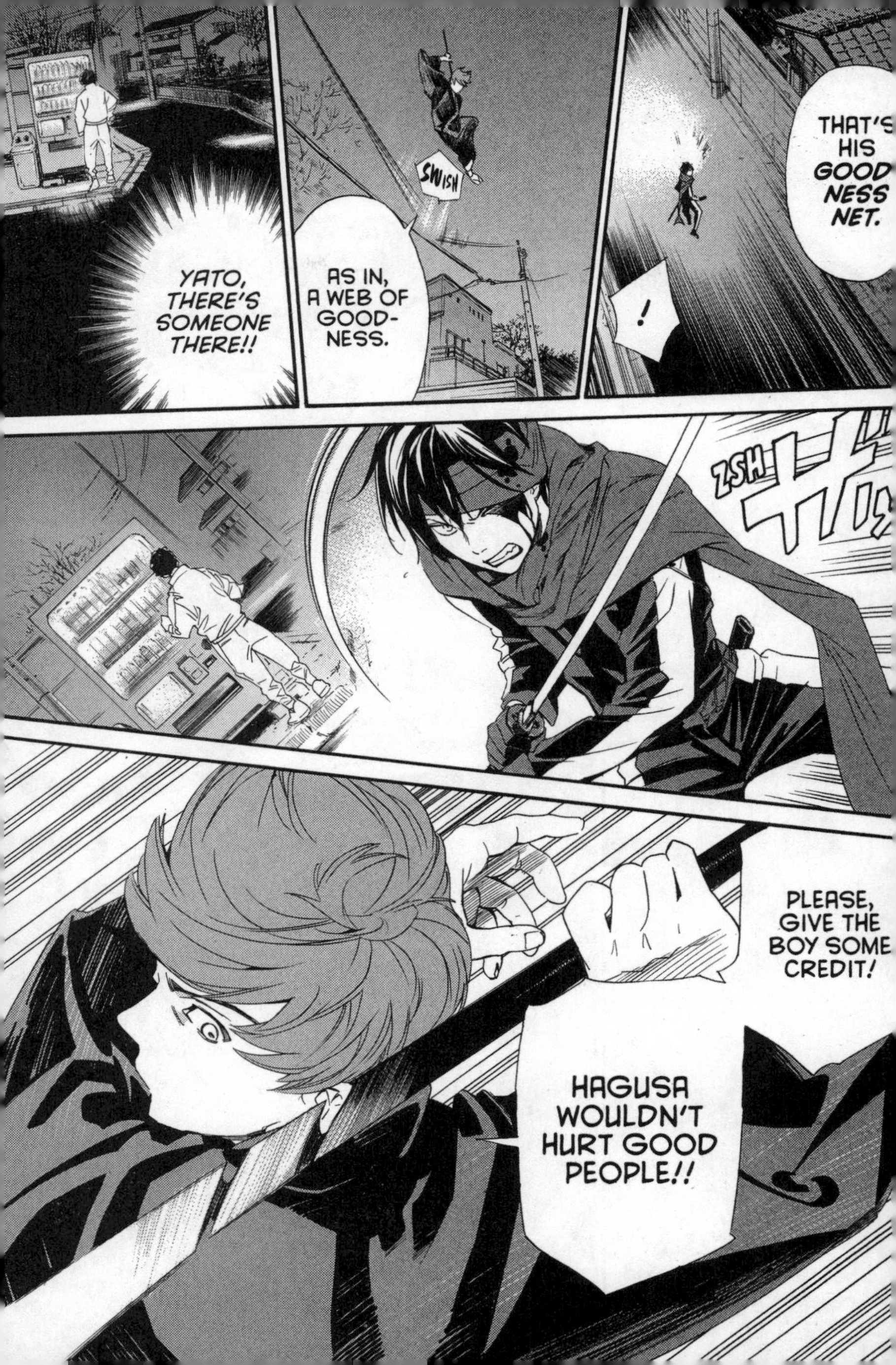
THAT'S HIS GOODNESS NET.
!
SWISH
AS IN, A WEB OF GOODNESS.
YATO, THERE'S SOMEONE THERE!!
ZSH
PLEASE, GIVE THE BOY SOME CREDIT!
HAGUSA WOULDN'T HURT GOOD PEOPLE!!

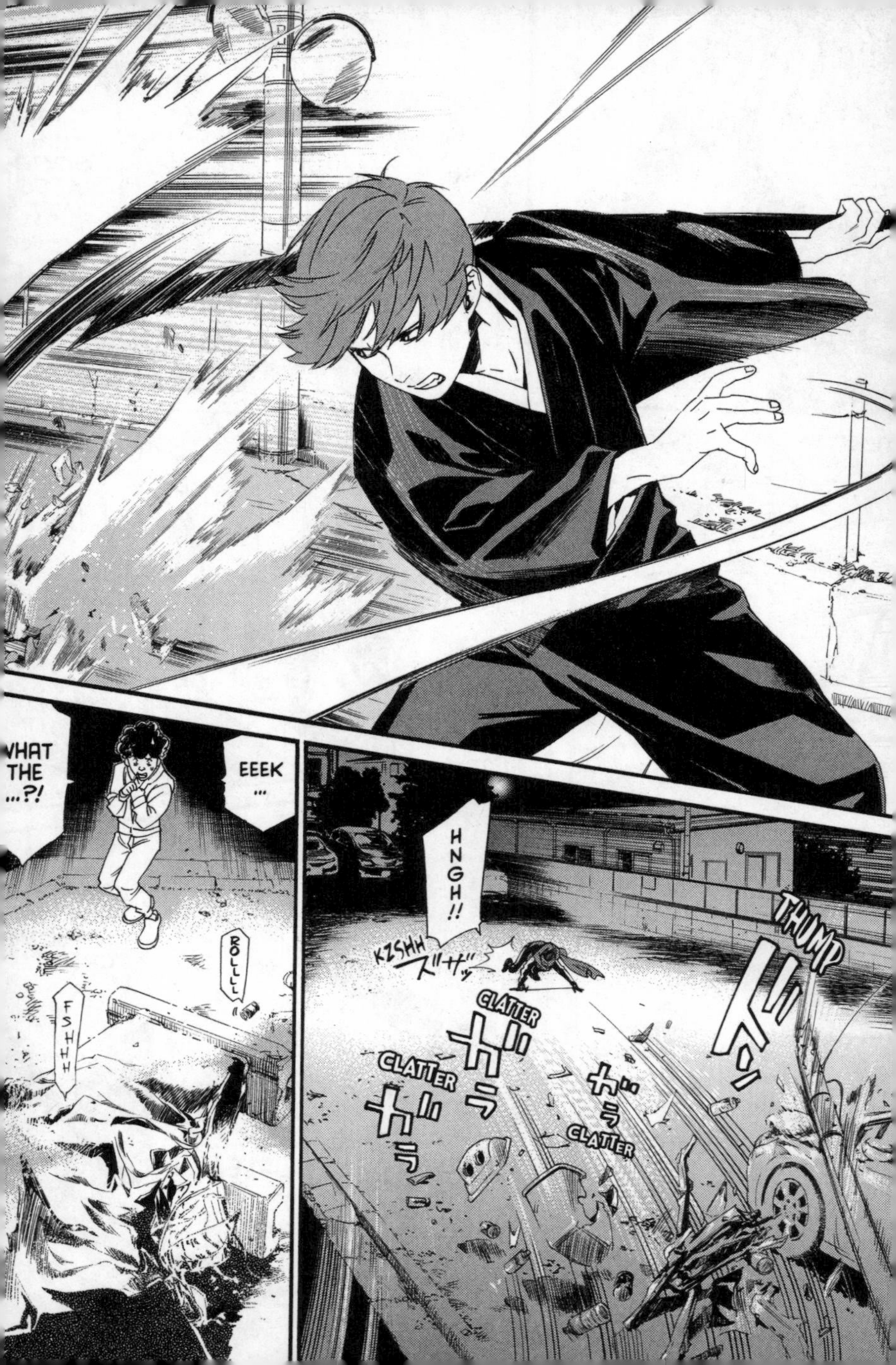
THUMP
HNGH!!
KZSHH
CLATTER
CLATTER
CLATTER
EEEK ...
WHAT THE ...?!
ROLLLL
FSHHH

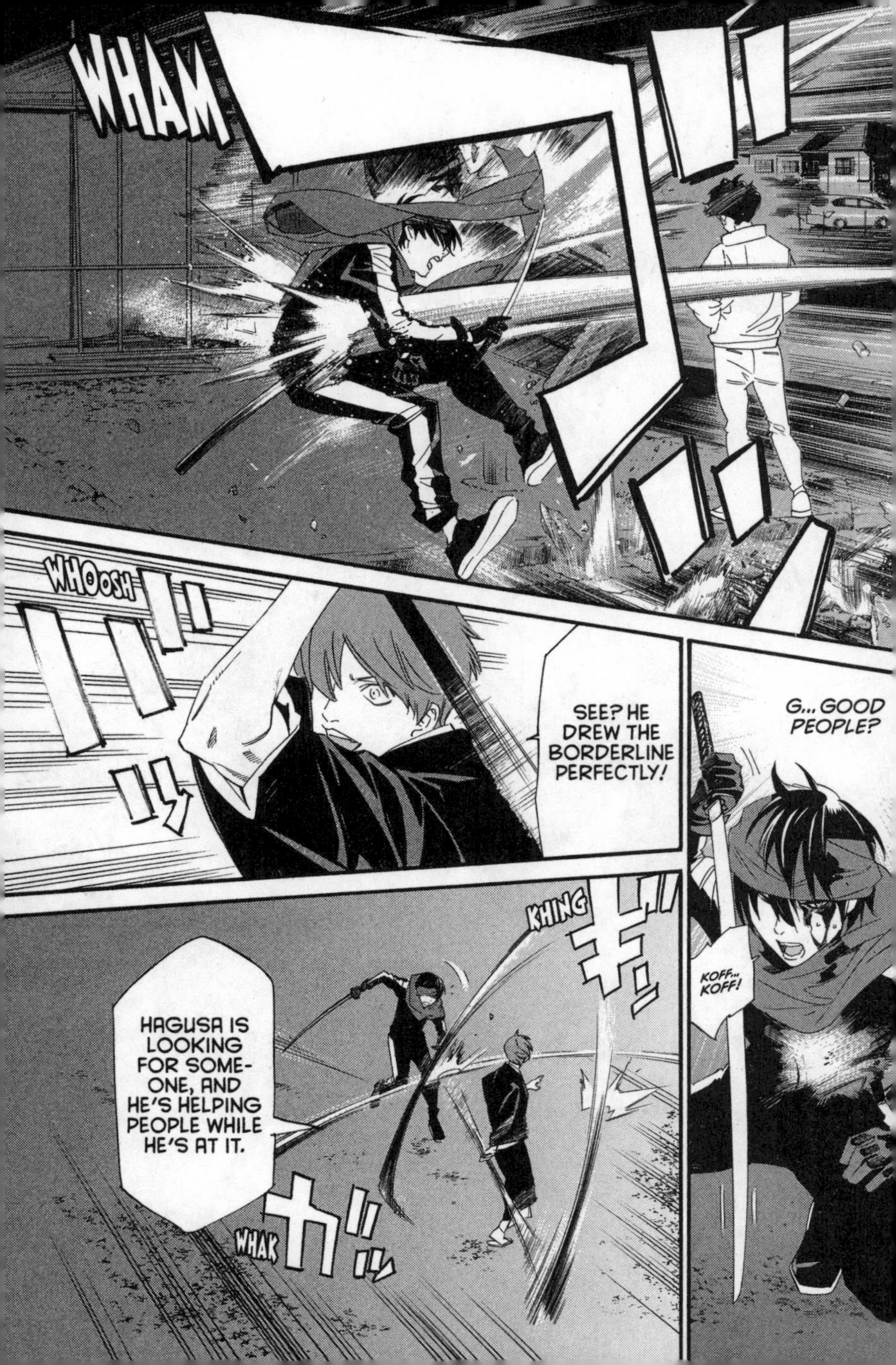
WHAM
G... GOOD PEOPLE?
KOFF... KOFF!
WHOOSH
SEE? HE DREW THE BORDERLINE PERFECTLY!
KHING
HAGUSA IS LOOKING FOR SOME-ONE, AND HE'S HELPING PEOPLE WHILE HE'S AT IT.
WHAK

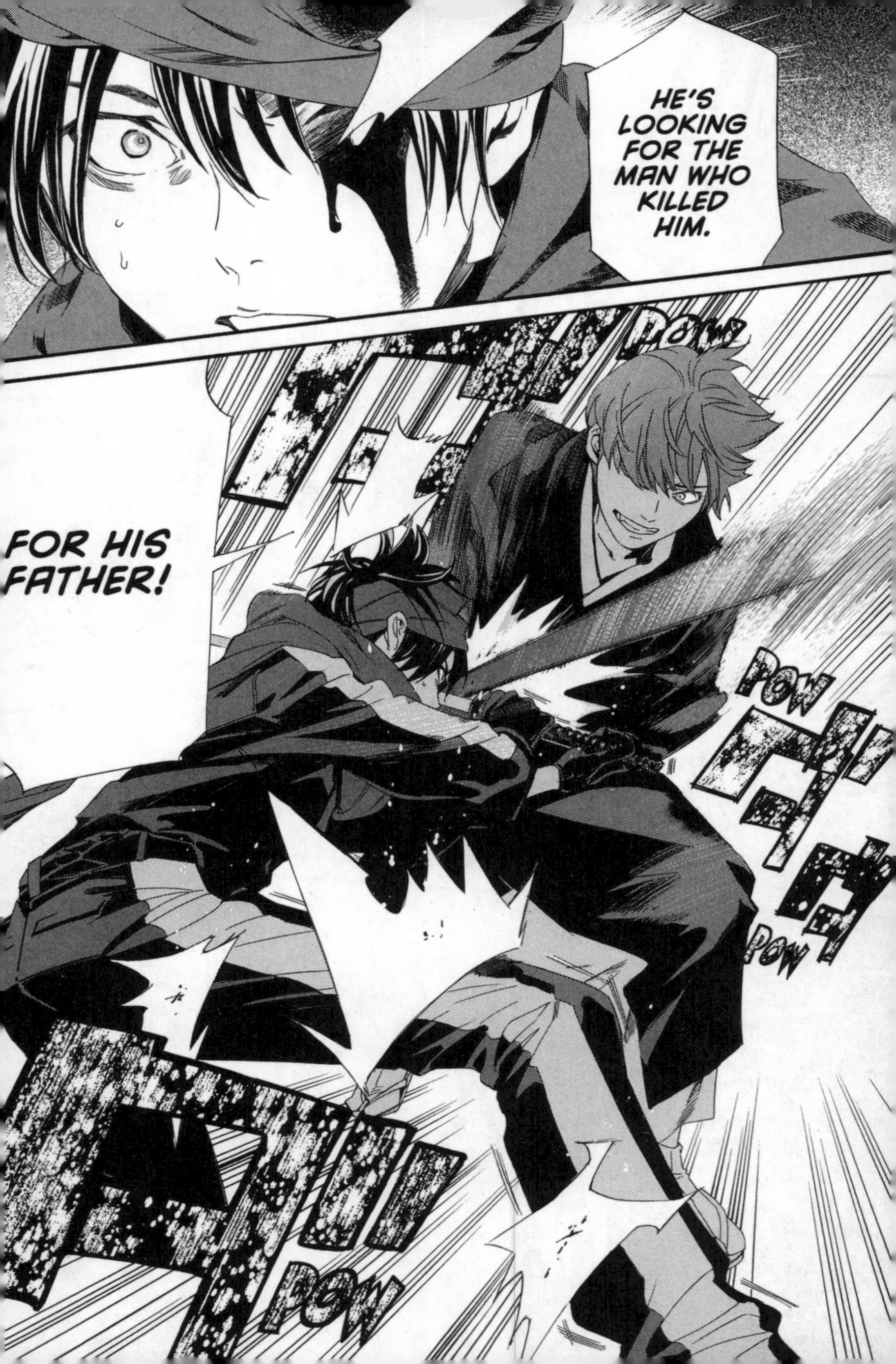
HE'S LOOKING FOR THE MAN WHO KILLED HIM.
POW
POW
POW
FOR HIS FATHER!
POW

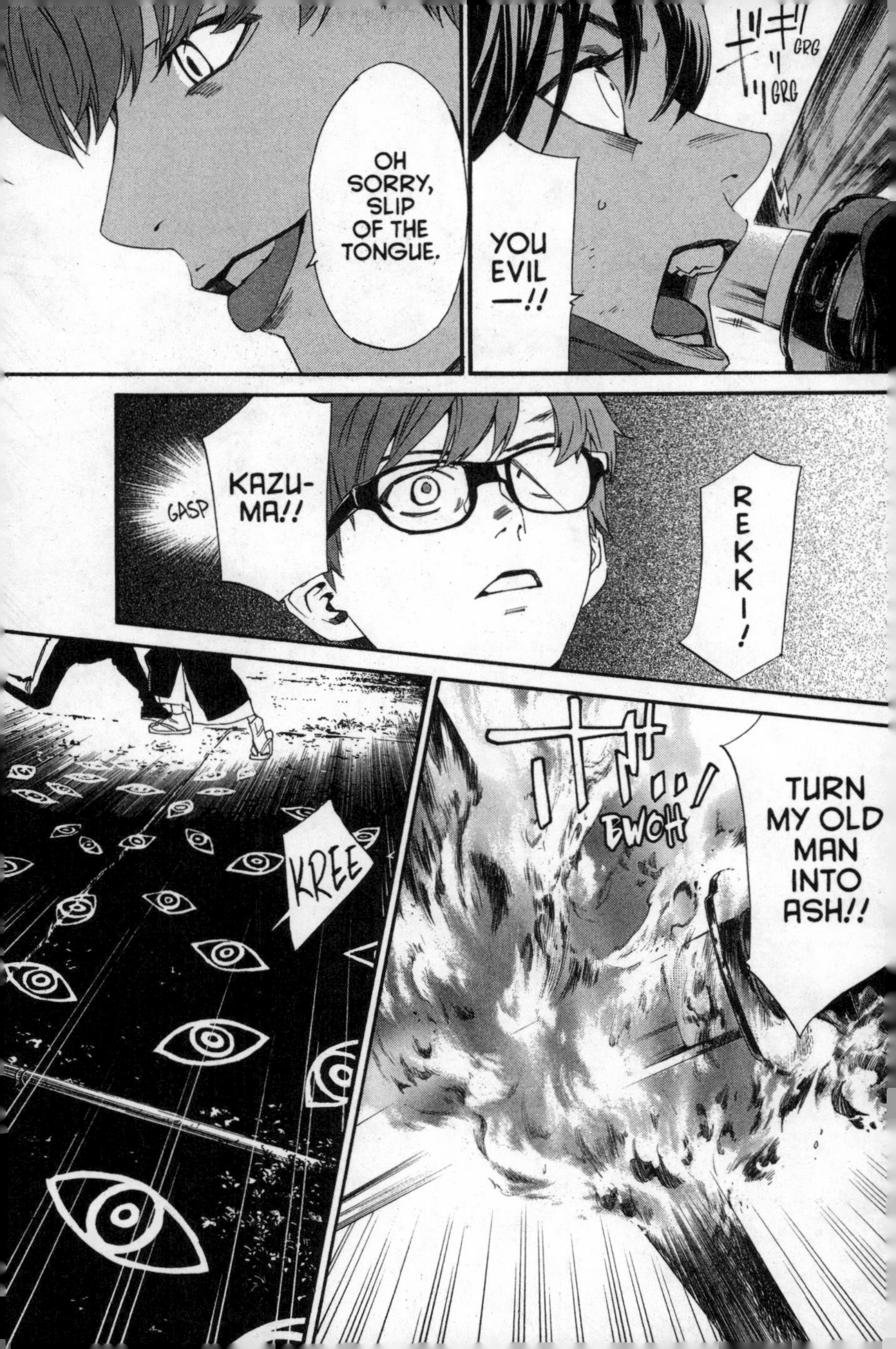
GRG
GRG
YOU EVIL —!!
OH SORRY, SLIP OF THE TONGUE.
REKKI!
KAZUMA!!
GASP
TURN MY OLD MAN INTO ASH!!
BWOH
KREE

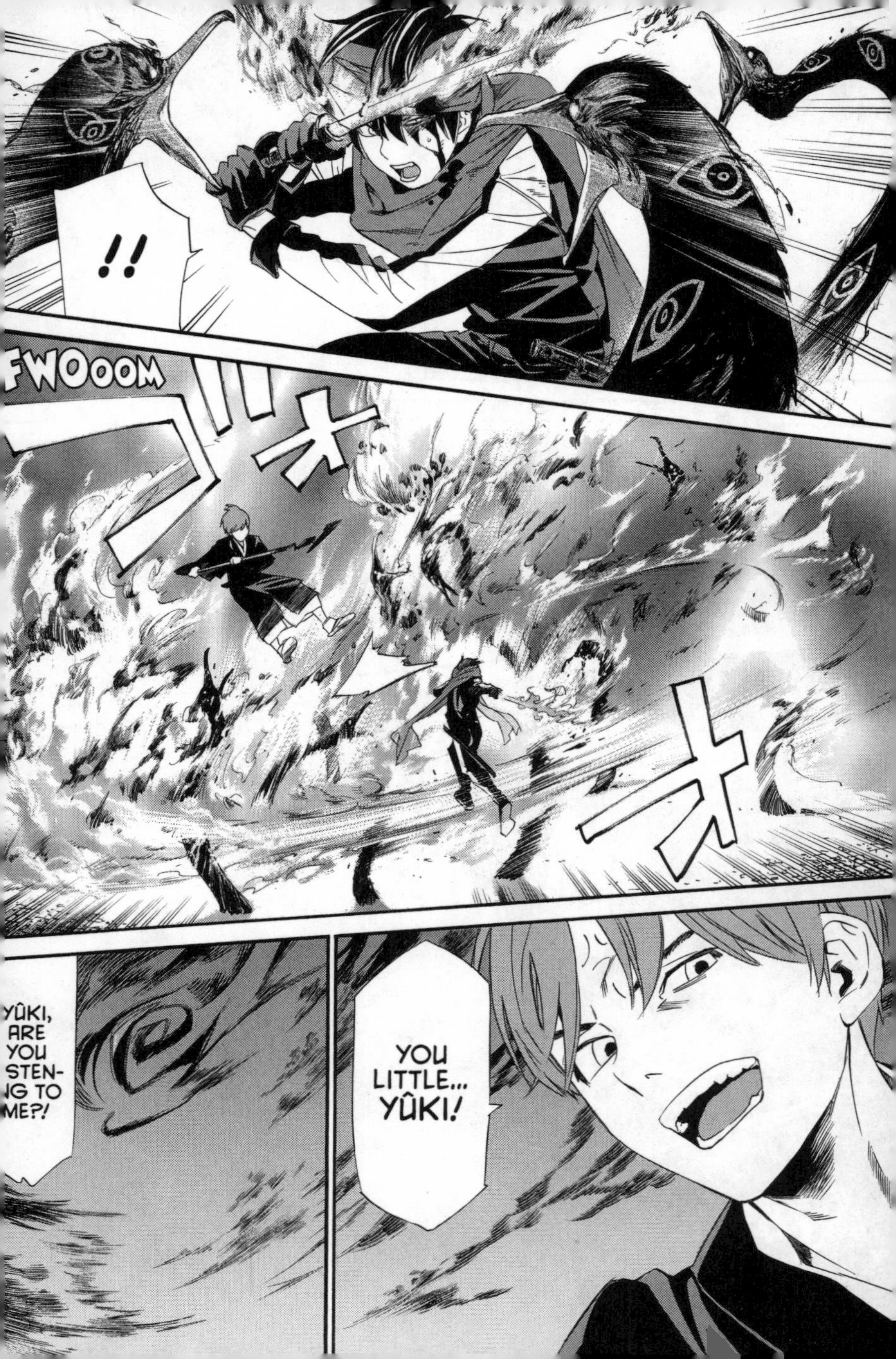
!!
FWOoom
YOU LITTLE... YÛKI!
YÛKI, ARE YOU
STEN-
IG TO
ME?!

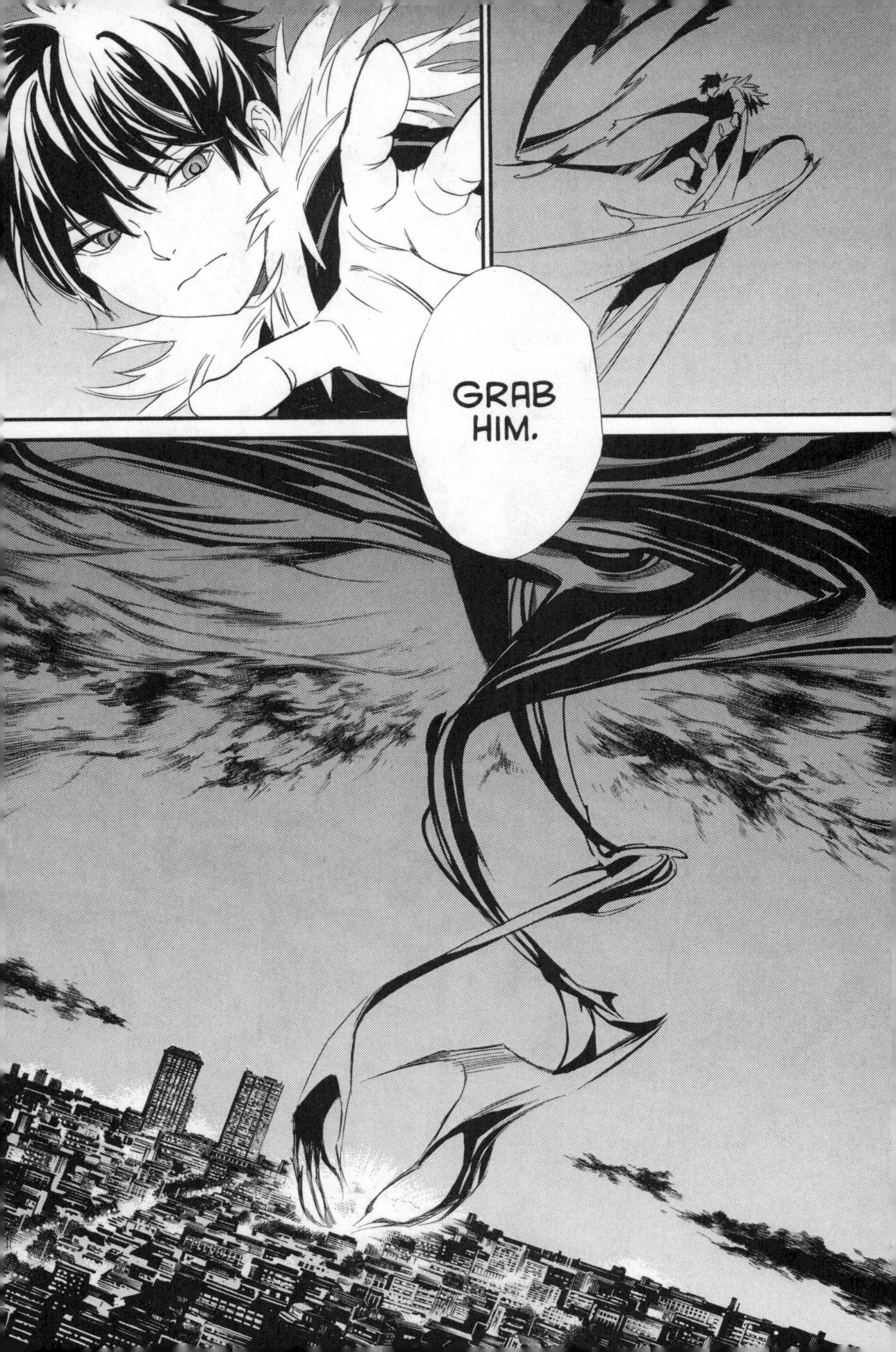
GRAB HIM.

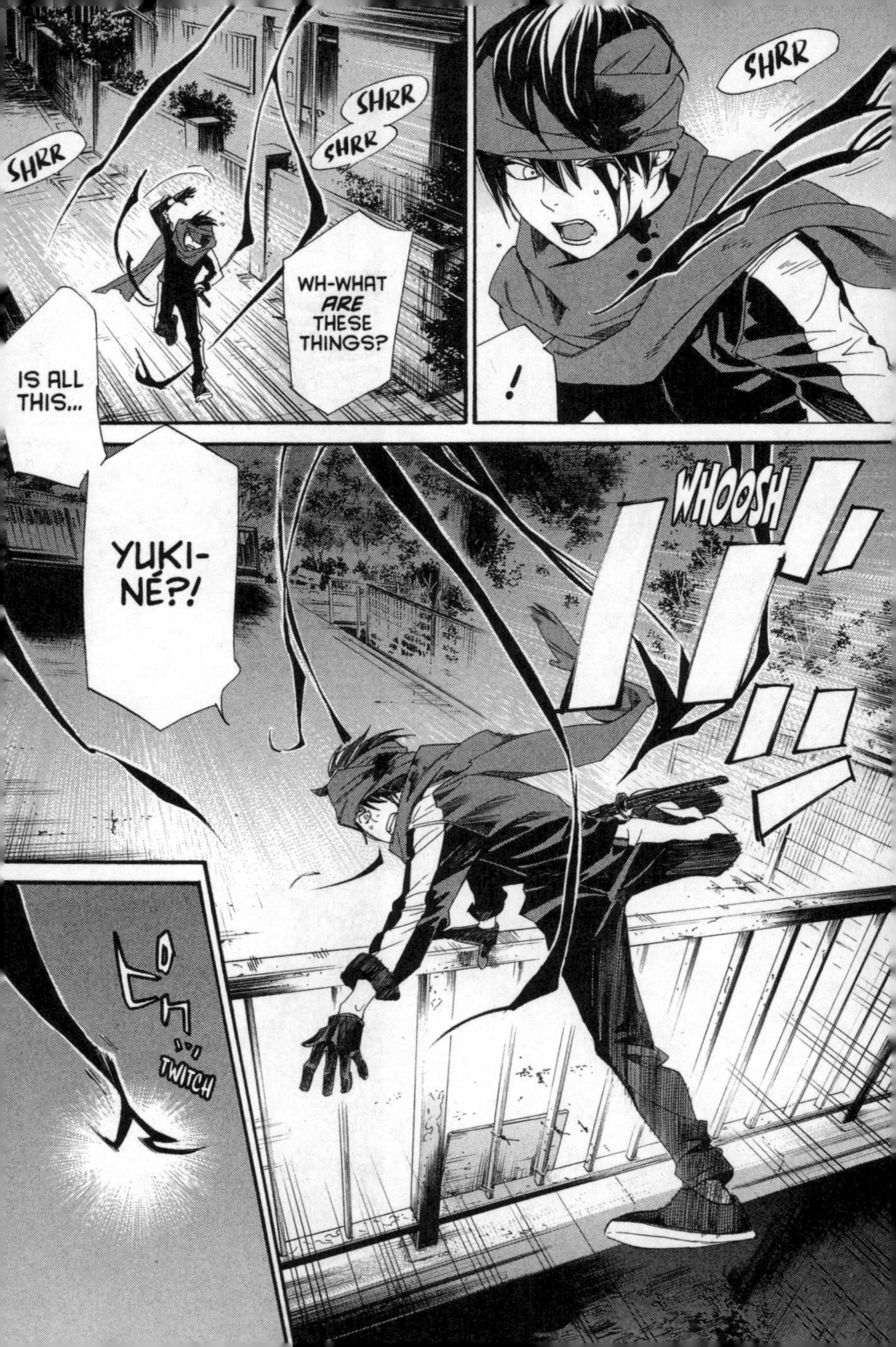
SHRR
!
SHRR
SHRR
SHRR
WH-WHAT *ARE* THESE THINGS?
IS ALL THIS...
YUKI-NÉ?!
WHOOSH
TWITCH

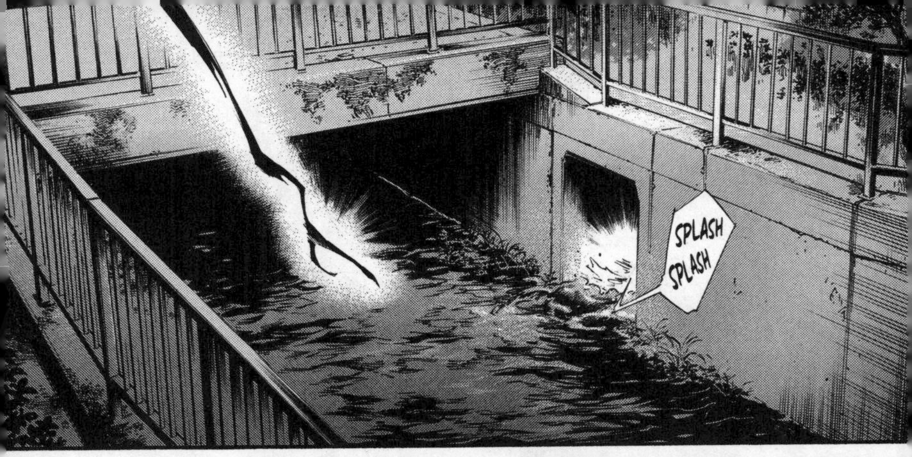
SPLASH
SPLASH
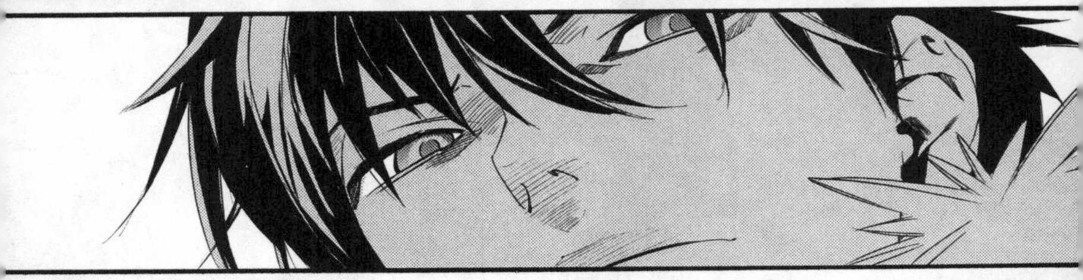
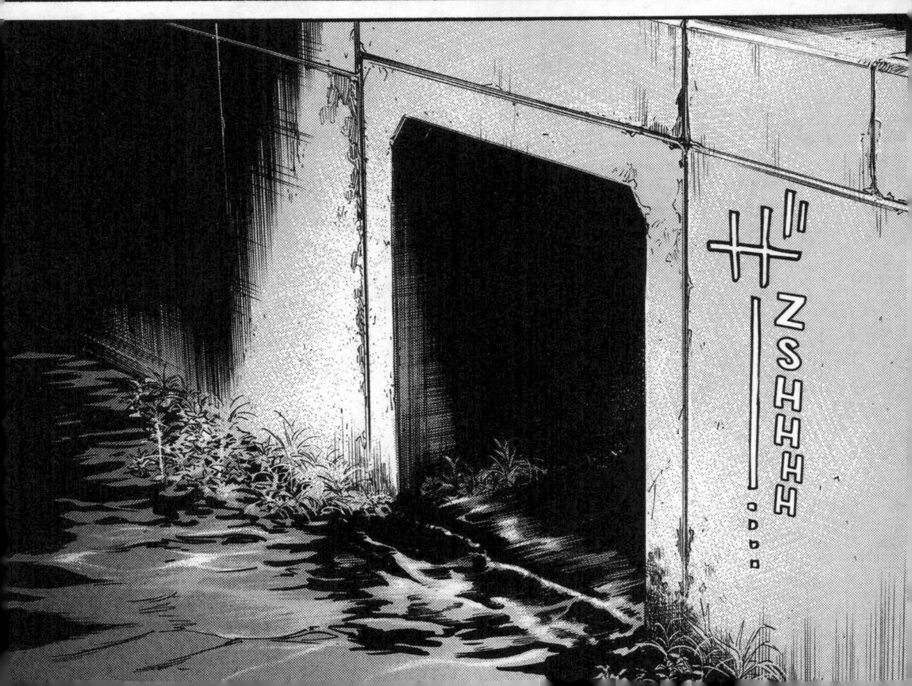
ザー
ZSHHHH...

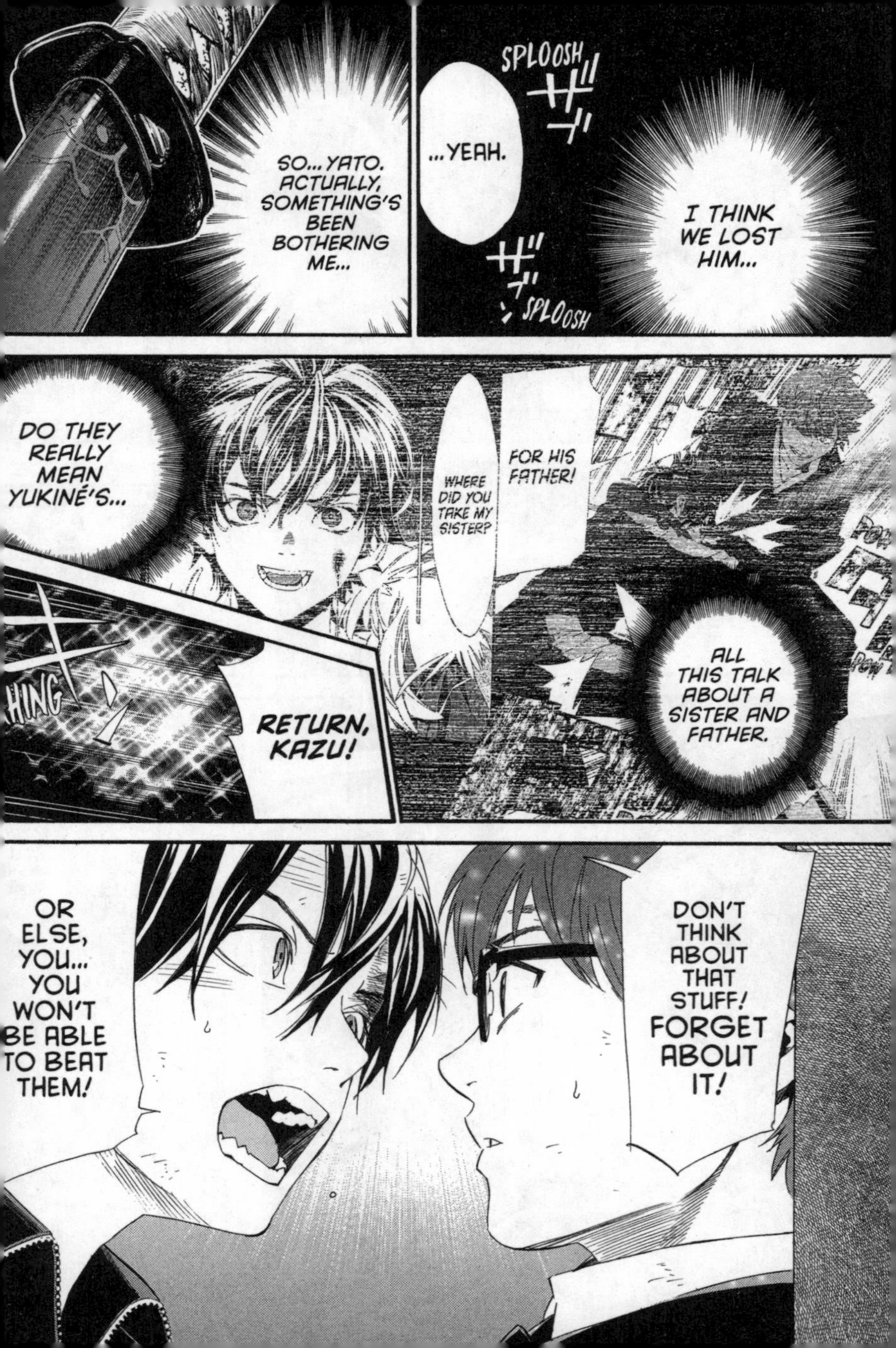
SPLOOSH
I THINK WE LOST HIM...
...YEAH.
SPLOOSH
SO...YATO. ACTUALLY, SOMETHING'S BEEN BOTHERING ME...
ALL THIS TALK ABOUT A SISTER AND FATHER.
FOR HIS FATHER!
WHERE DID YOU TAKE MY SISTER?
DO THEY REALLY MEAN YUKINÉ'S...
RETURN, KAZU!
HING
DON'T THINK ABOUT THAT STUFF! FORGET ABOUT IT!
OR ELSE, YOU... YOU WON'T BE ABLE TO BEAT THEM!

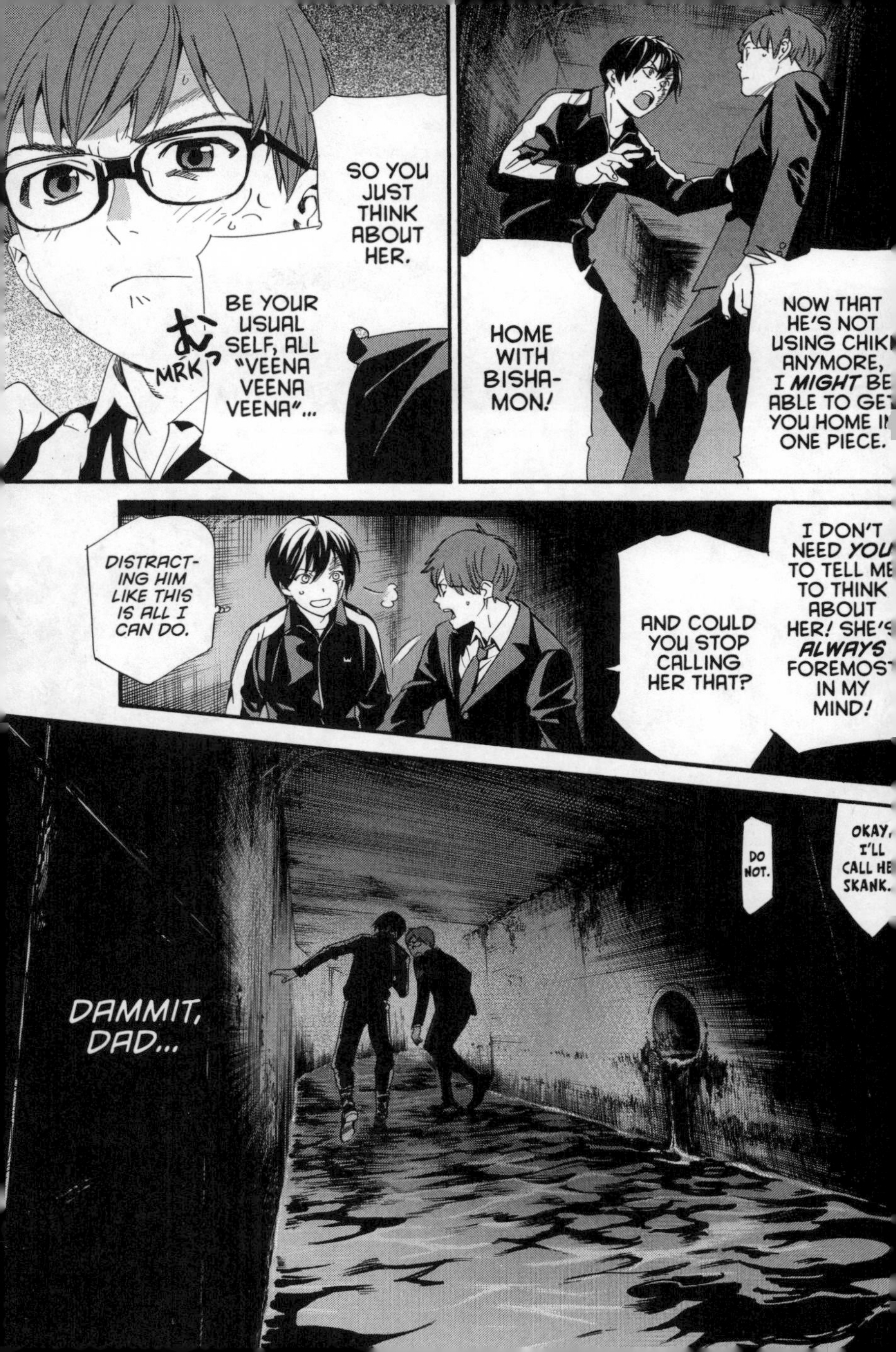
NOW THAT HE'S NOT USING CHIKI ANYMORE, I *MIGHT* BE ABLE TO GET YOU HOME IN ONE PIECE.
HOME WITH BISHAMON!
SO YOU JUST THINK ABOUT HER.
BE YOUR USUAL SELF, ALL "VEENA VEENA VEENA"...
MRK
I DON'T NEED *YOU* TO TELL ME TO THINK ABOUT HER! SHE'S *ALWAYS* FOREMOST IN MY MIND!
AND COULD YOU STOP CALLING HER THAT?
DISTRACTING HIM LIKE THIS IS ALL I CAN DO.
OKAY, I'LL CALL HER SKANK.
DO NOT.
DAMMIT, DAD...

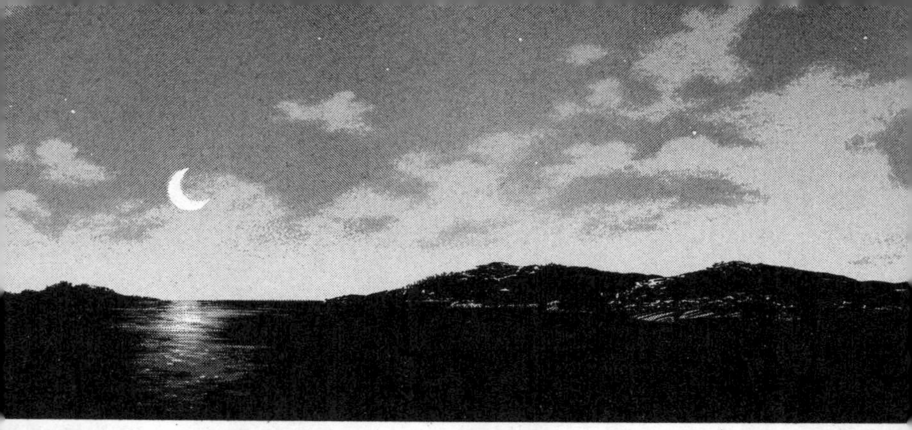

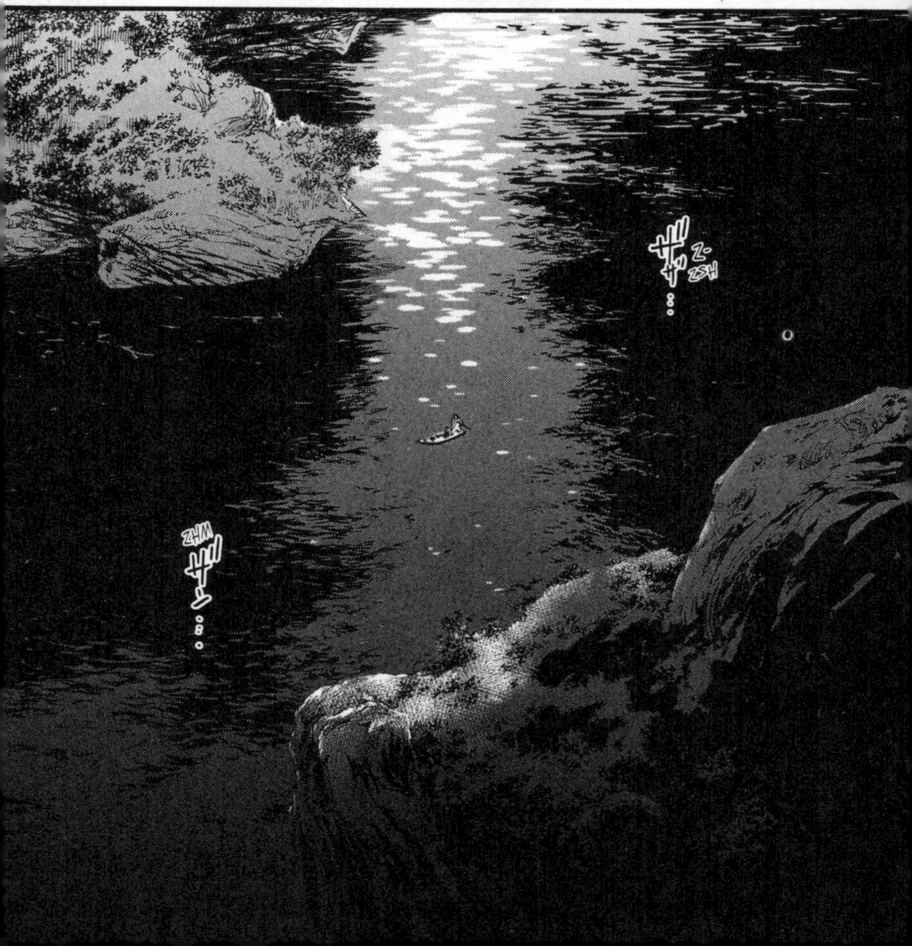
Z-ZSH
WHZ

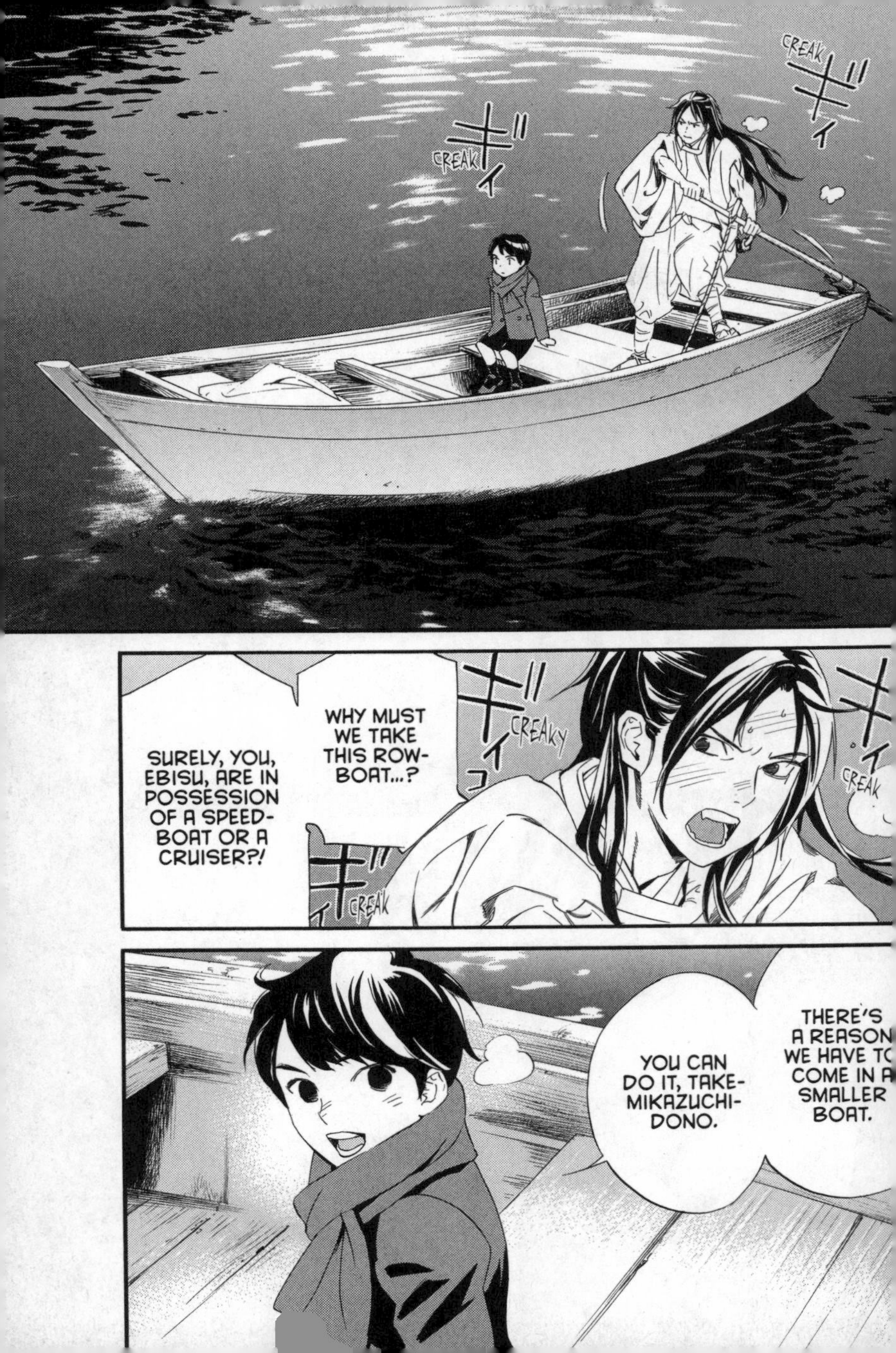
CREAK
CREAK
WHY MUST WE TAKE THIS ROW-BOAT...?
SURELY, YOU, EBISU, ARE IN POSSESSION OF A SPEED-BOAT OR A CRUISER?!
CREAK
CREAKY
CREAK
THERE'S A REASON WE HAVE TO COME IN A SMALLER BOAT.
YOU CAN DO IT, TAKE-MIKAZUCHI-DONO.

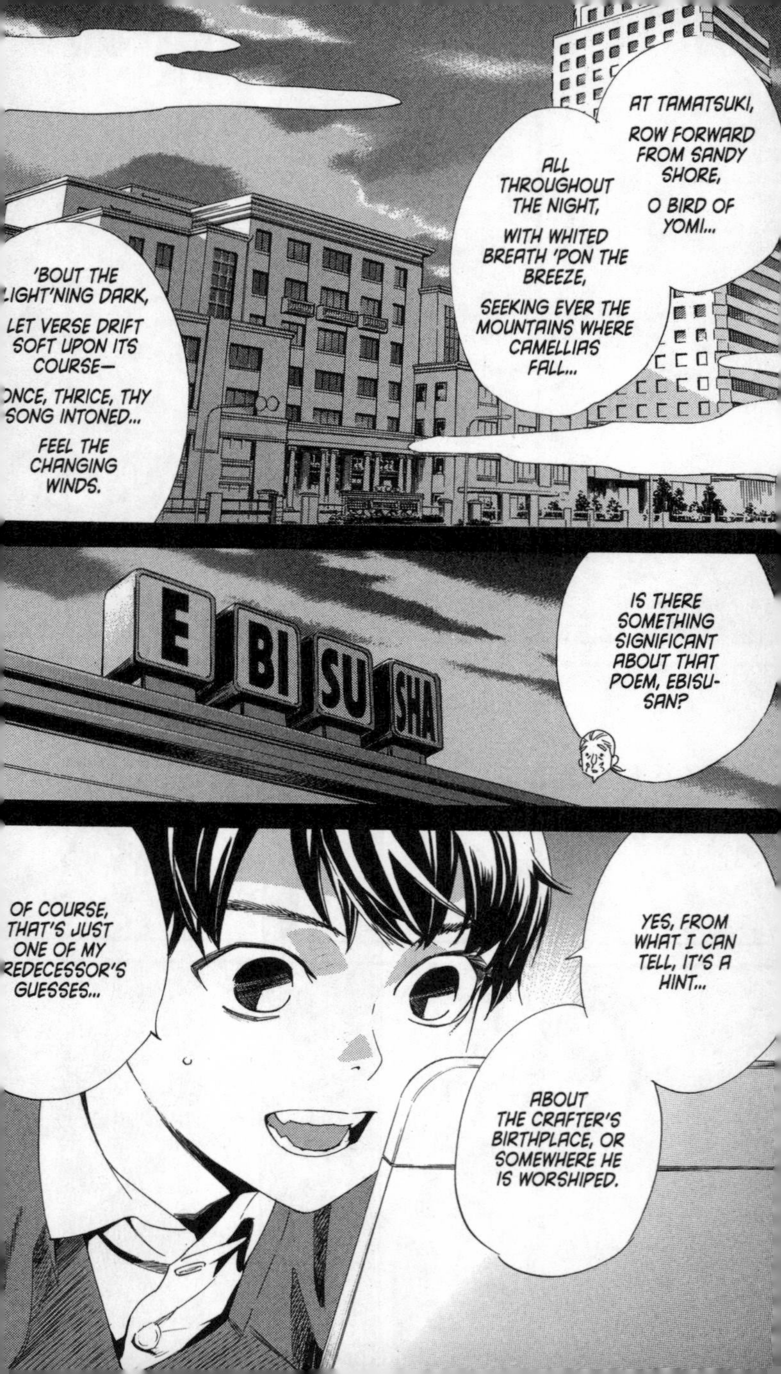
AT TAMATSUKI, ROW FORWARD FROM SANDY SHORE, O BIRD OF YOMI...
ALL THROUGHOUT THE NIGHT, WITH WHITED BREATH 'PON THE BREEZE, SEEKING EVER THE MOUNTAINS WHERE CAMELLIAS FALL...
'BOUT THE LIGHT'NING DARK, LET VERSE DRIFT SOFT UPON ITS COURSE— ONCE, THRICE, THY SONG INTONED... FEEL THE CHANGING WINDS.
E BI SU SHA
IS THERE SOMETHING SIGNIFICANT ABOUT THAT POEM, EBISU-SAN?
YES, FROM WHAT I CAN TELL, IT'S A HINT...
ABOUT THE CRAFTER'S BIRTHPLACE, OR SOMEWHERE HE IS WORSHIPED.
OF COURSE, THAT'S JUST ONE OF MY PREDECESSOR'S GUESSES...

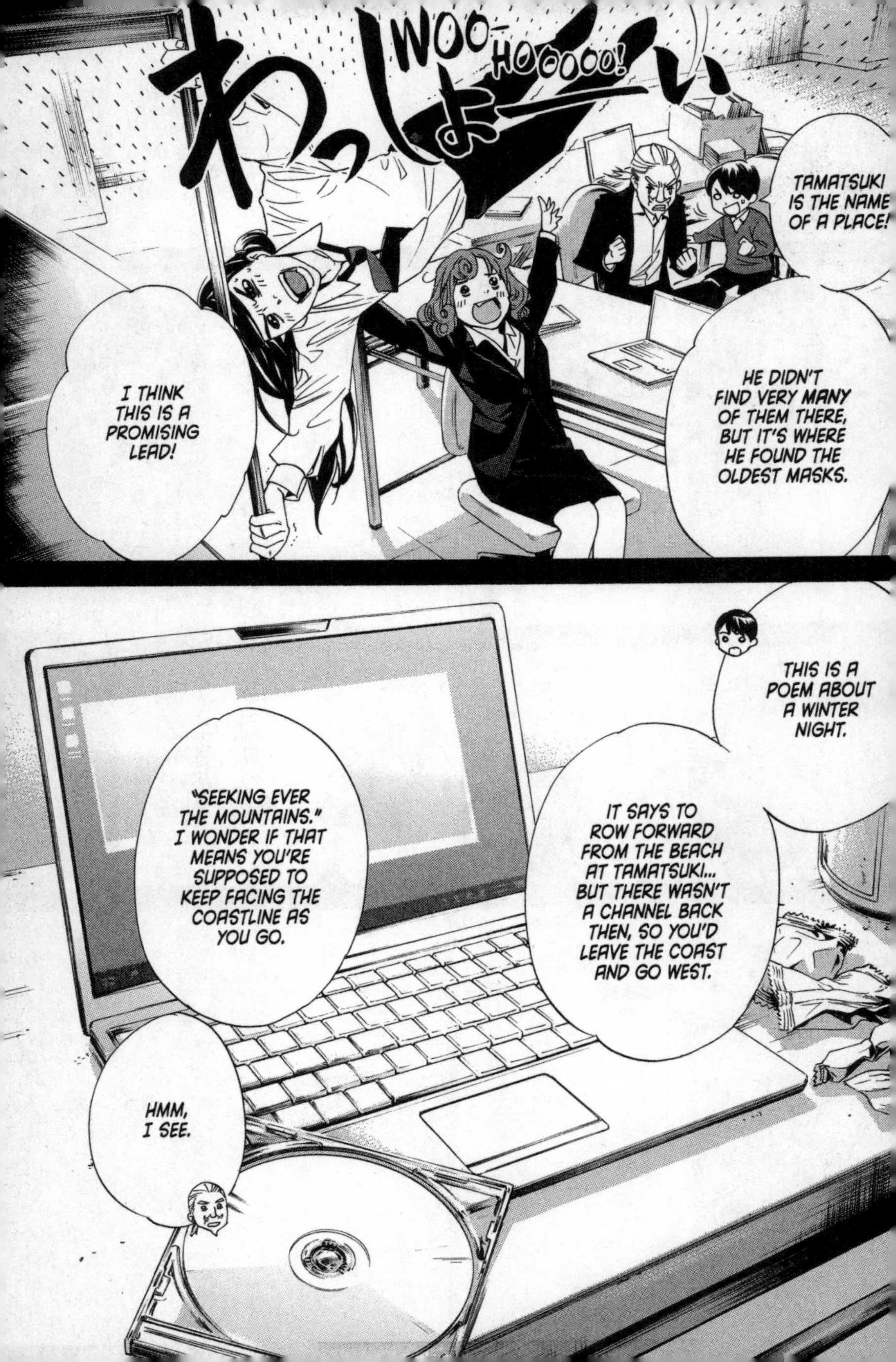
わっしょーい
WOO-HOOOOOO!
TAMATSUKI IS THE NAME OF A PLACE!
HE DIDN'T FIND VERY MANY OF THEM THERE, BUT IT'S WHERE HE FOUND THE OLDEST MASKS.
I THINK THIS IS A PROMISING LEAD!
THIS IS A POEM ABOUT A WINTER NIGHT.
IT SAYS TO ROW FORWARD FROM THE BEACH AT TAMATSUKI... BUT THERE WASN'T A CHANNEL BACK THEN, SO YOU'D LEAVE THE COAST AND GO WEST.
"SEEKING EVER THE MOUNTAINS." I WONDER IF THAT MEANS YOU'RE SUPPOSED TO KEEP FACING THE COASTLINE AS YOU GO.
HMM, I SEE.

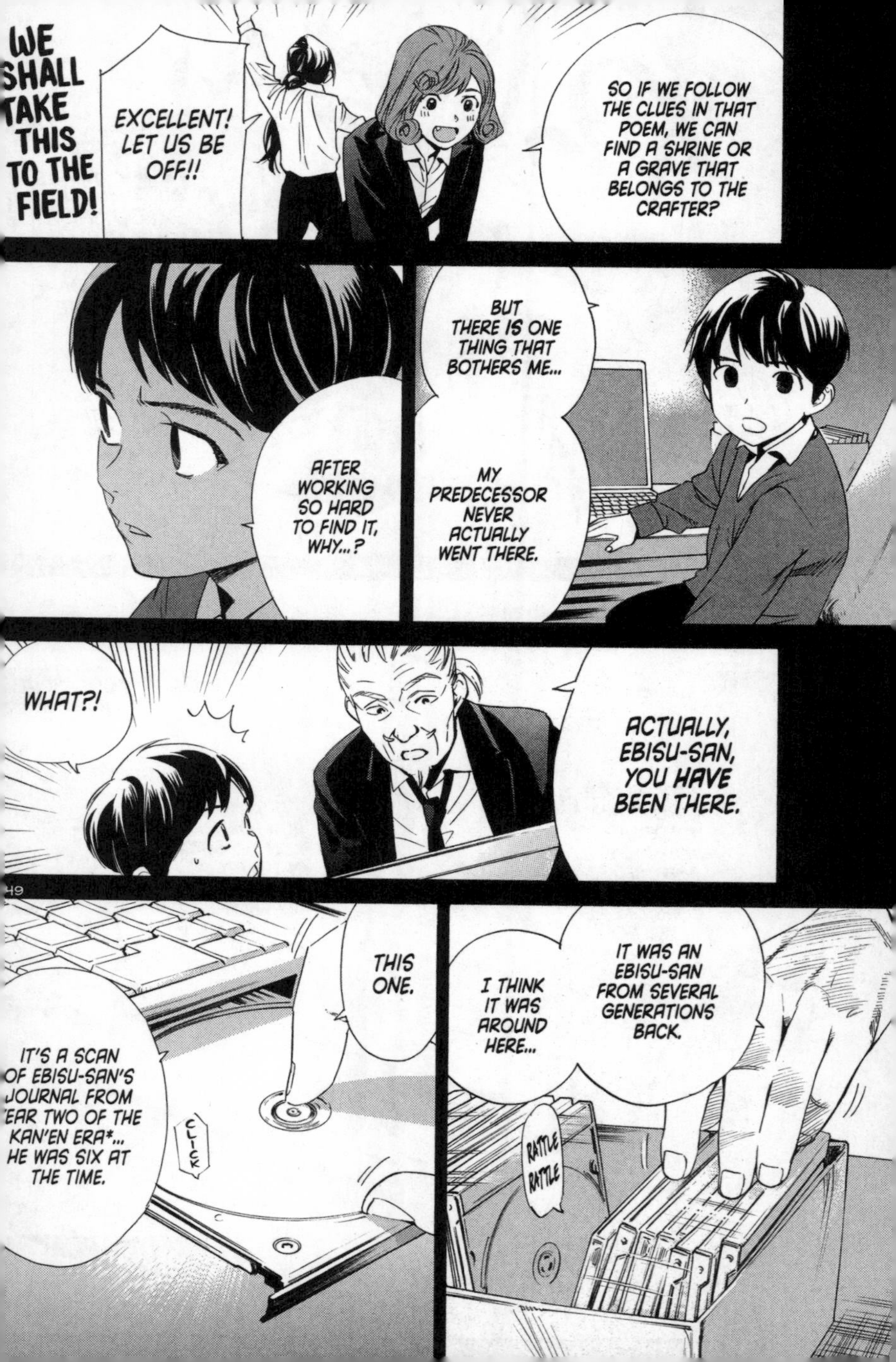
SO IF WE FOLLOW THE CLUES IN THAT POEM, WE CAN FIND A SHRINE OR A GRAVE THAT BELONGS TO THE CRAFTER?
EXCELLENT! LET US BE OFF!!
WE SHALL TAKE THIS TO THE FIELD!
BUT THERE IS ONE THING THAT BOTHERS ME...
MY PREDECESSOR NEVER ACTUALLY WENT THERE.
AFTER WORKING SO HARD TO FIND IT, WHY...?
ACTUALLY, EBISU-SAN, YOU HAVE BEEN THERE.
WHAT?!
IT WAS AN EBISU-SAN FROM SEVERAL GENERATIONS BACK.
I THINK IT WAS AROUND HERE...
RATTLE RATTLE
THIS ONE.
CLICK
IT'S A SCAN OF EBISU-SAN'S JOURNAL FROM EAR TWO OF THE KAN'EN ERA*... HE WAS SIX AT THE TIME.

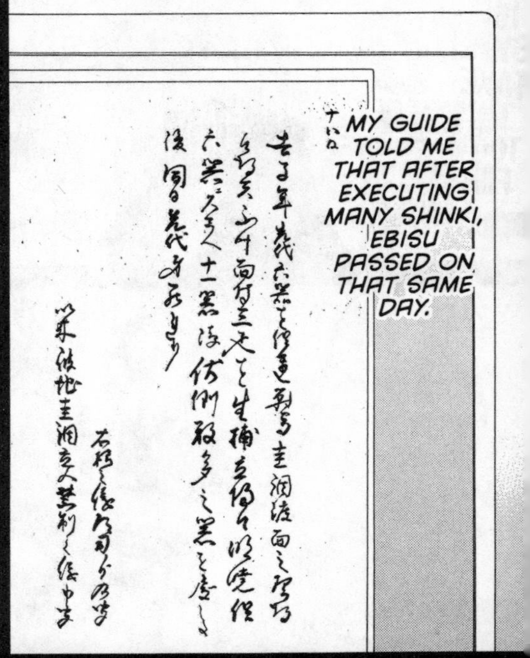
MY GUIDE TOLD ME THAT AFTER EXECUTING MANY SHINKI, EBISU PASSED ON THAT SAME DAY.

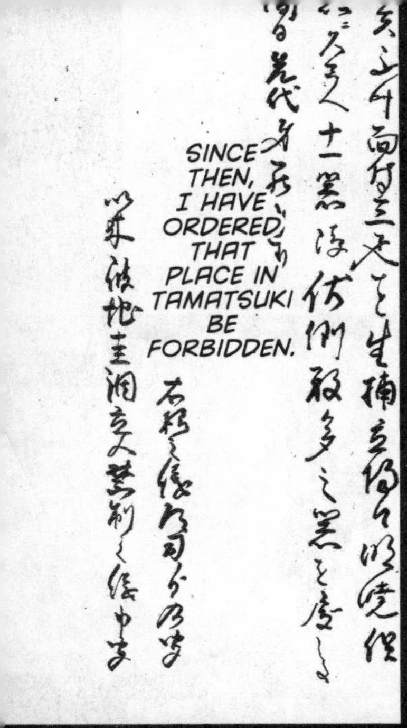
SINCE THEN, I HAVE ORDERED THAT PLACE IN TAMATSUKI BE FORBIDDEN.

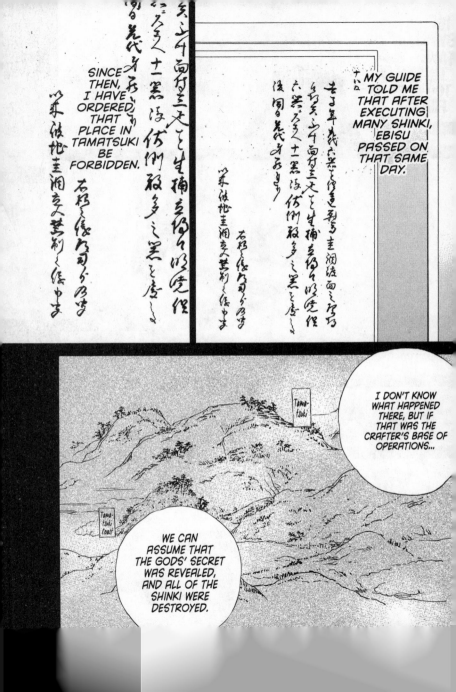

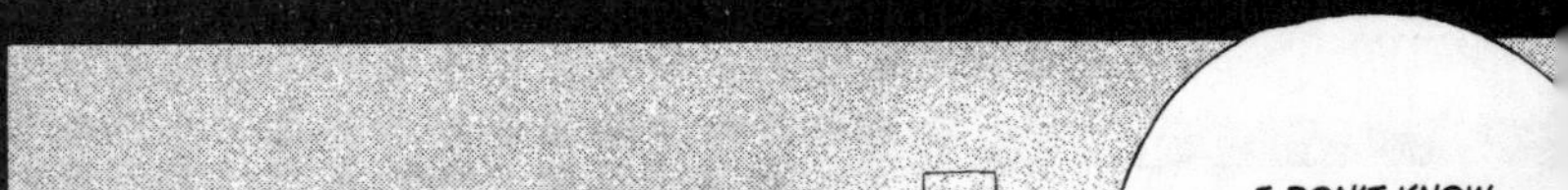
I DON'T KNOW WHAT HAPPENED THERE, BUT IF THAT WAS THE CRAFTER'S BASE OF OPERATIONS...
Tama-tsuki
Tama-tsuki Coast
WE CAN ASSUME THAT THE GODS' SECRET WAS REVEALED, AND ALL OF THE SHINKI WERE DESTROYED.

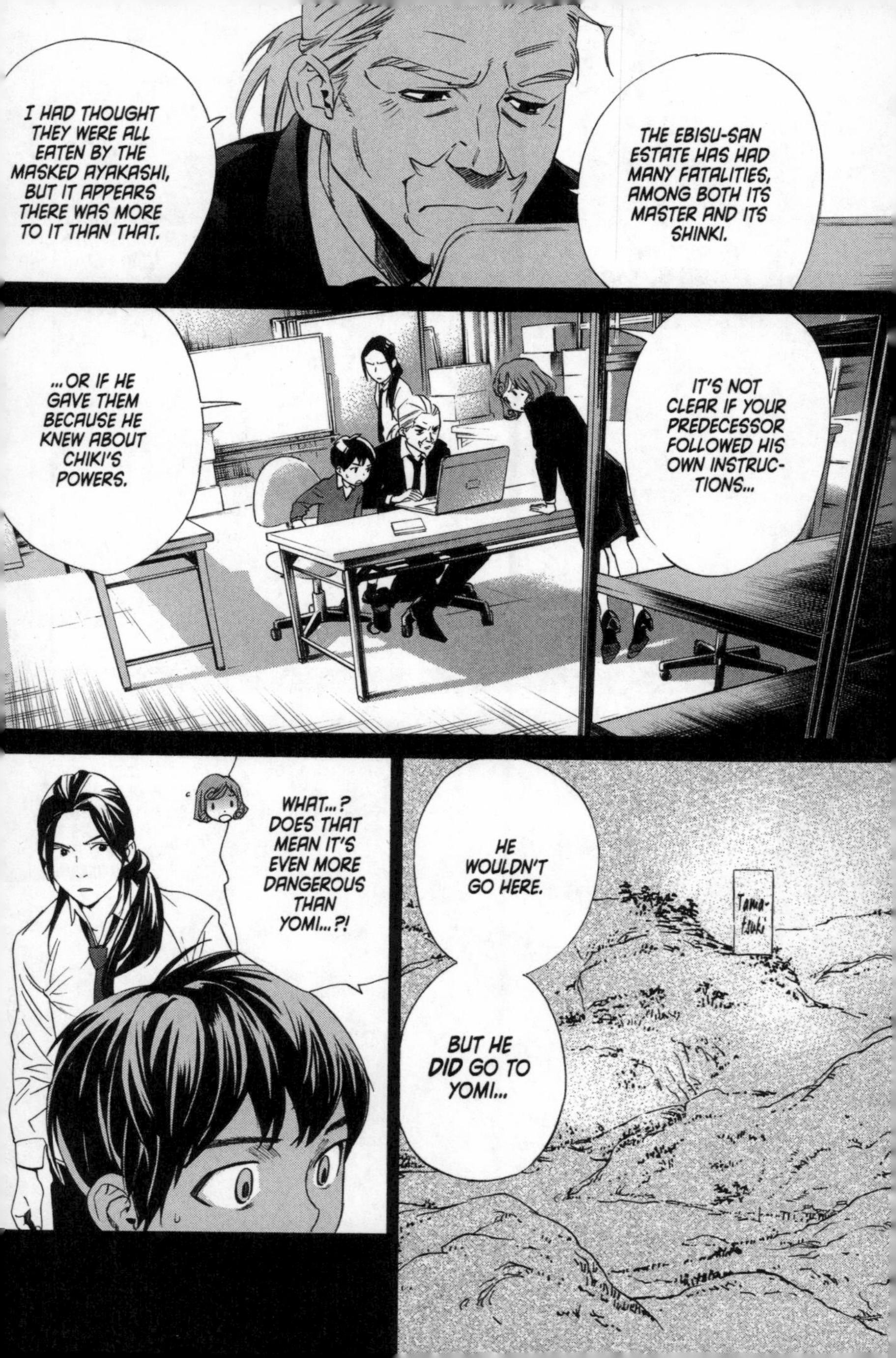
THE EBISU-SAN ESTATE HAS HAD MANY FATALITIES, AMONG BOTH ITS MASTER AND ITS SHINKI.
I HAD THOUGHT THEY WERE ALL EATEN BY THE MASKED AYAKASHI, BUT IT APPEARS THERE WAS MORE TO IT THAN THAT.
IT'S NOT CLEAR IF YOUR PREDECESSOR FOLLOWED HIS OWN INSTRUCTIONS...
...OR IF HE GAVE THEM BECAUSE HE KNEW ABOUT CHIKI'S POWERS.
HE WOULDN'T GO HERE.
Tama-tsuki
BUT HE DID GO TO YOMI...
WHAT...? DOES THAT MEAN IT'S EVEN MORE DANGEROUS THAN YOMI...?!

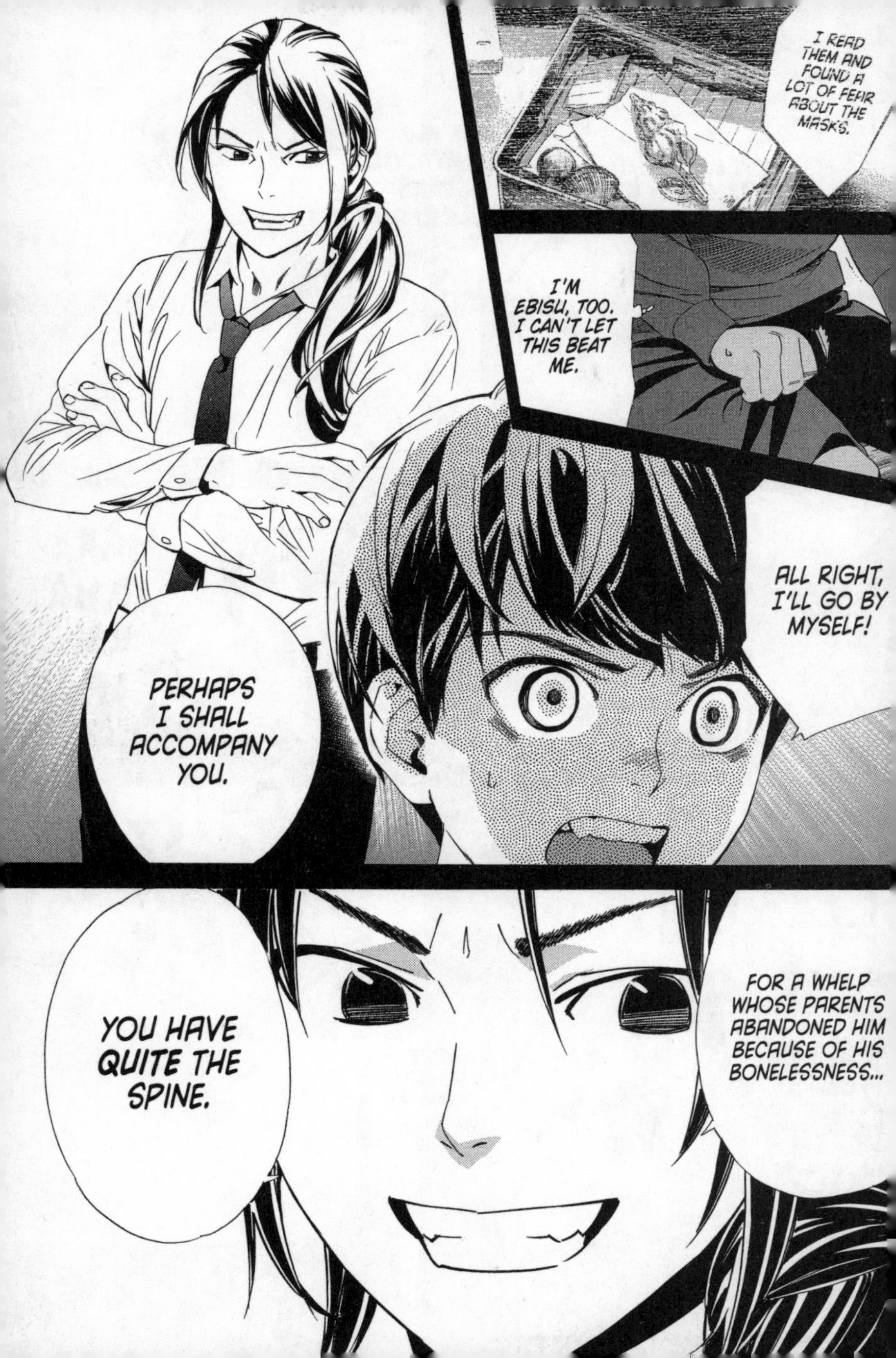
I READ THEM AND FOUND A LOT OF FEAR ABOUT THE MASKS.
I'M EBISU, TOO. I CAN'T LET THIS BEAT ME.
ALL RIGHT, I'LL GO BY MYSELF!
PERHAPS I SHALL ACCOMPANY YOU.
FOR A WHELP WHOSE PARENTS ABANDONED HIM BECAUSE OF HIS BONELESSNESS...
YOU HAVE QUITE THE SPINE.

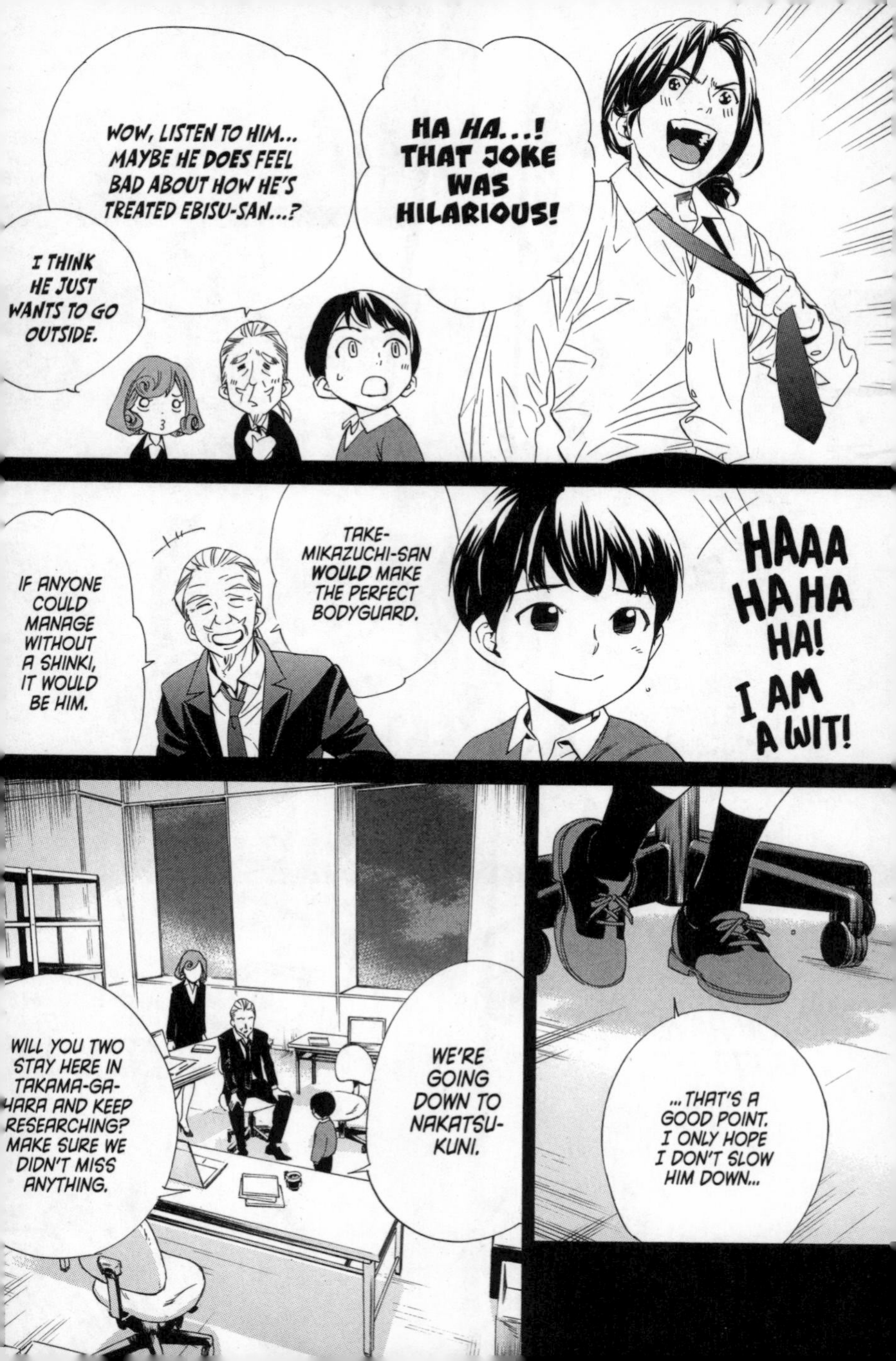
HA HA...! THAT JOKE WAS HILARIOUS!
WOW, LISTEN TO HIM... MAYBE HE DOES FEEL BAD ABOUT HOW HE'S TREATED EBISU-SAN...?
I THINK HE JUST WANTS TO GO OUTSIDE.
HAAA HA HA HA! I AM A WIT!
TAKE-MIKAZUCHI-SAN WOULD MAKE THE PERFECT BODYGUARD.
IF ANYONE COULD MANAGE WITHOUT A SHINKI, IT WOULD BE HIM.
...THAT'S A GOOD POINT. I ONLY HOPE I DON'T SLOW HIM DOWN...
WE'RE GOING DOWN TO NAKATSU-KUNI.
WILL YOU TWO STAY HERE IN TAKAMA-GA-HARA AND KEEP RESEARCHING? MAKE SURE WE DIDN'T MISS ANYTHING.

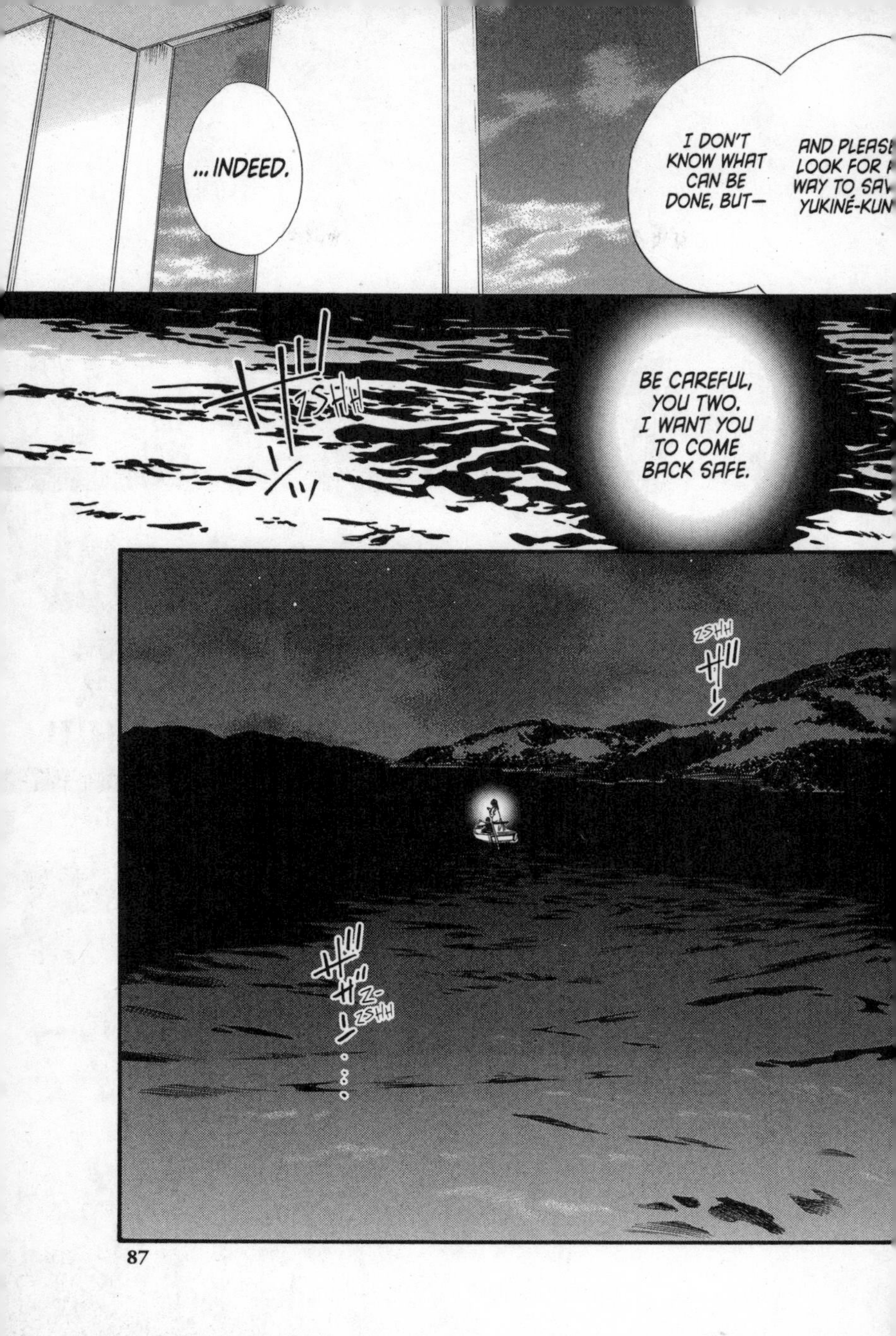
AND PLEASE LOOK FOR WAY TO SAV YUKINÉ-KUN
I DON'T KNOW WHAT CAN BE DONE, BUT—
...INDEED.
BE CAREFUL, YOU TWO. I WANT YOU TO COME BACK SAFE.
ZSHH
ZSHH
Z-ZSHH
...

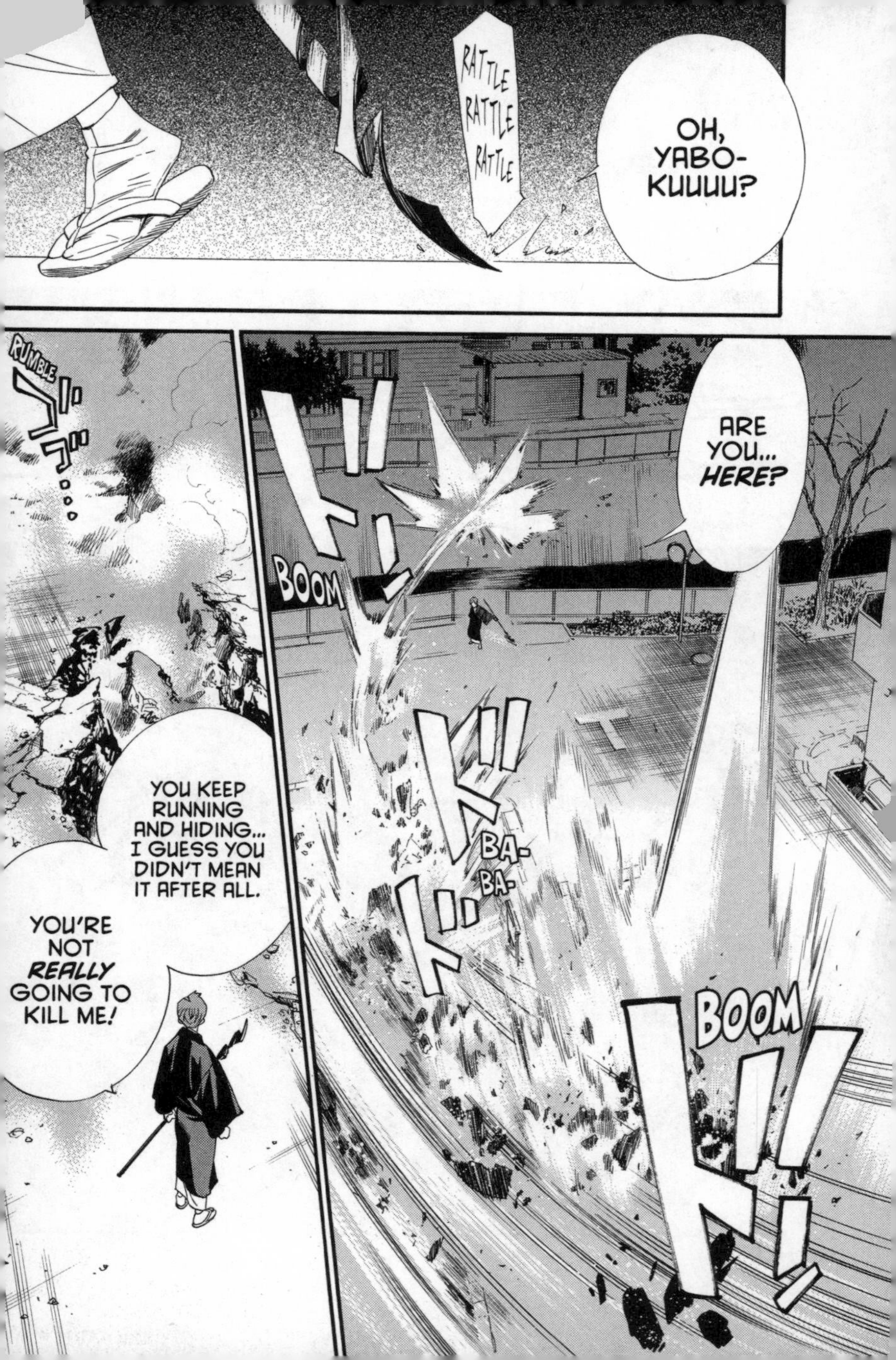
OH, YABO-KUUUUU?
RATTLE RATTLE RATTLE
ARE YOU... *HERE?*
BOOM
BA-BA-
BOOM
RUMBLE
YOU KEEP RUNNING AND HIDING... I GUESS YOU DIDN'T MEAN IT AFTER ALL.
YOU'RE NOT *REALLY* GOING TO KILL ME!

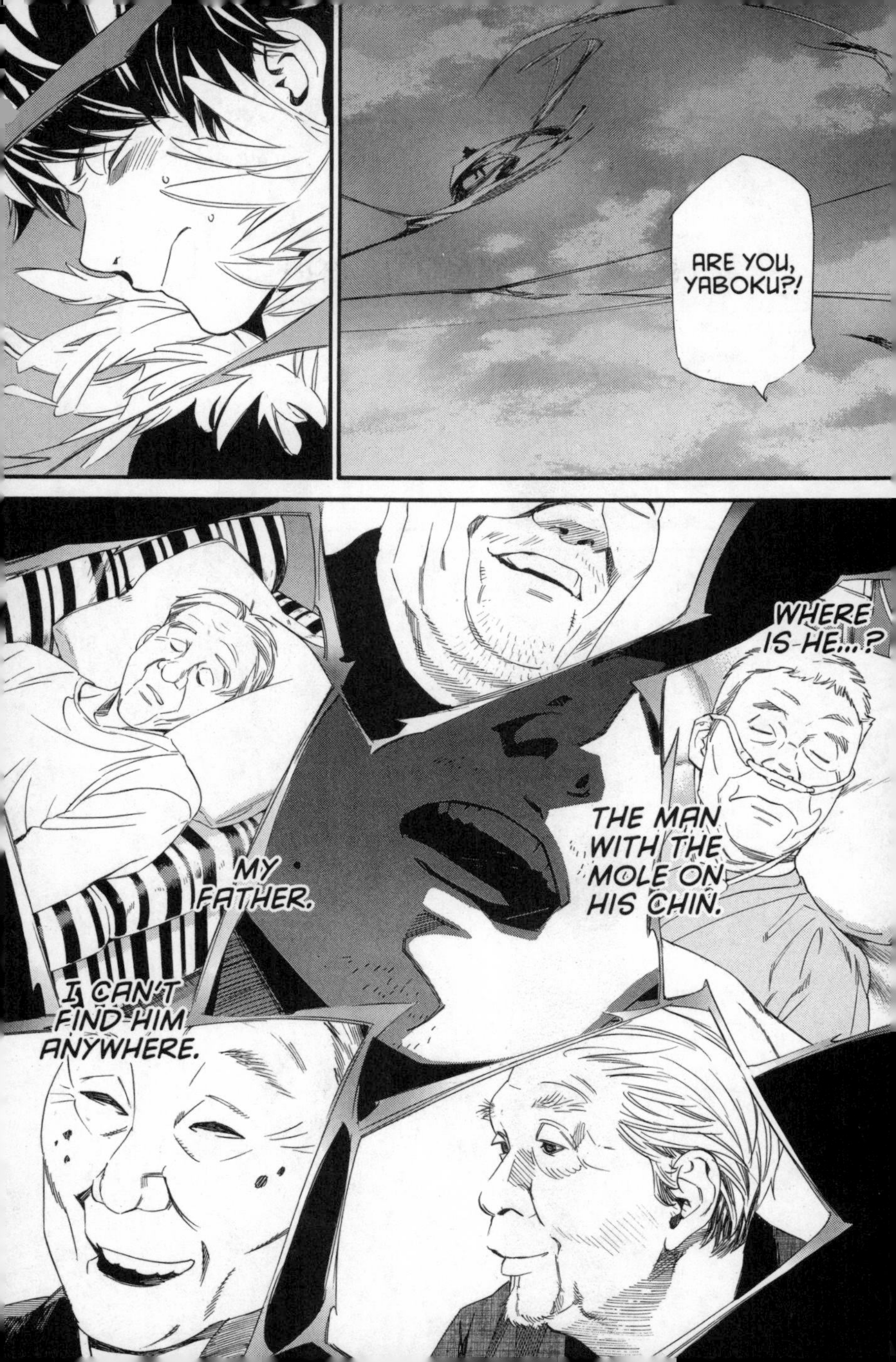
ARE YOU, YABOKU?!
WHERE IS HE...?
THE MAN WITH THE MOLE ON HIS CHIN.
MY FATHER.
I CAN'T FIND HIM ANYWHERE.

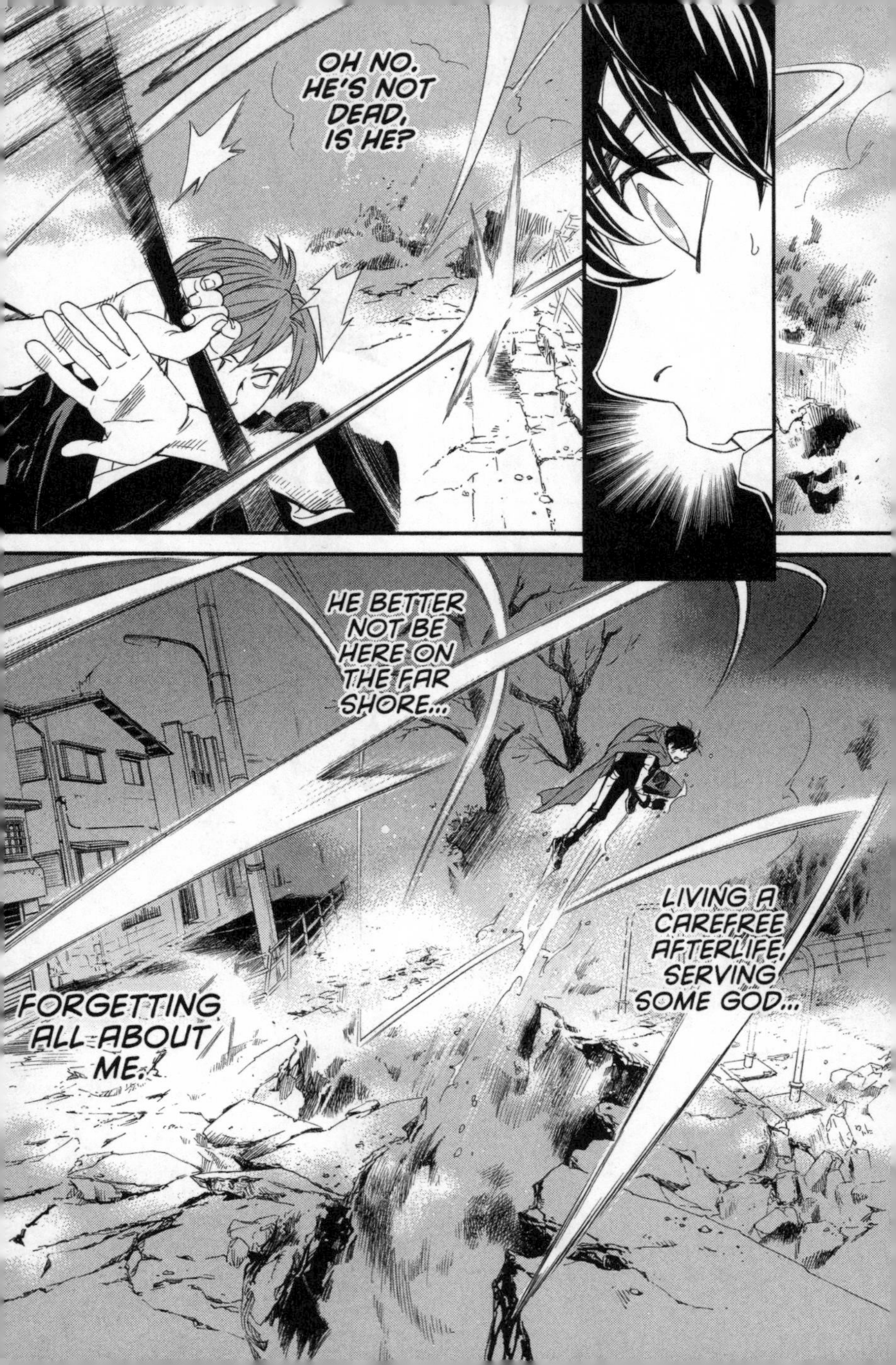
OH NO. HE'S NOT DEAD, IS HE?
HE BETTER NOT BE HERE ON THE FAR SHORE...
LIVING A CAREFREE AFTERLIFE, SERVING SOME GOD...
FORGETTING ALL ABOUT ME.

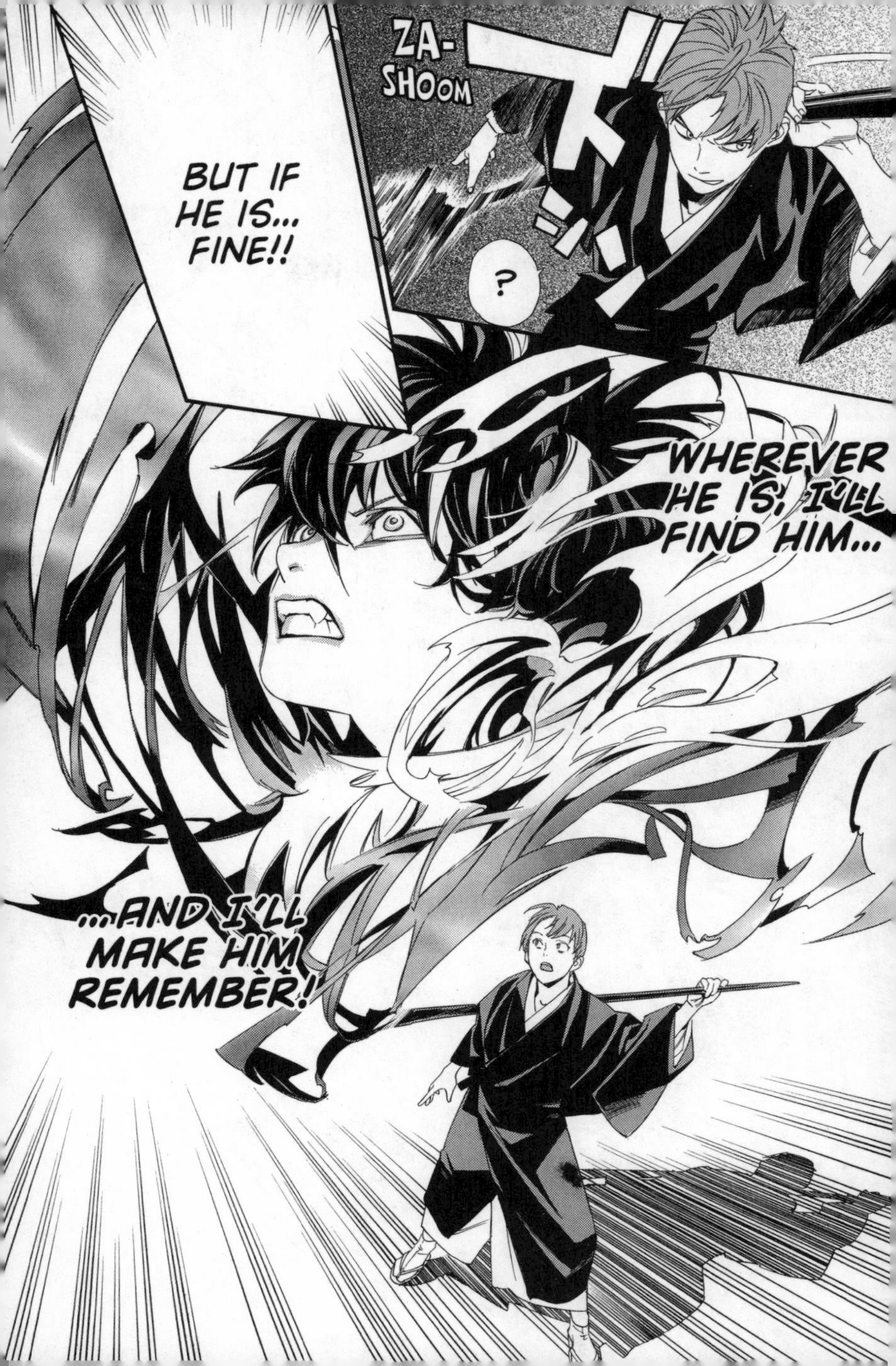
ZA-SHOOM
?
BUT IF HE IS... FINE!!
WHEREVER HE IS, I'LL FIND HIM...
...AND I'LL MAKE HIM REMEMBER!

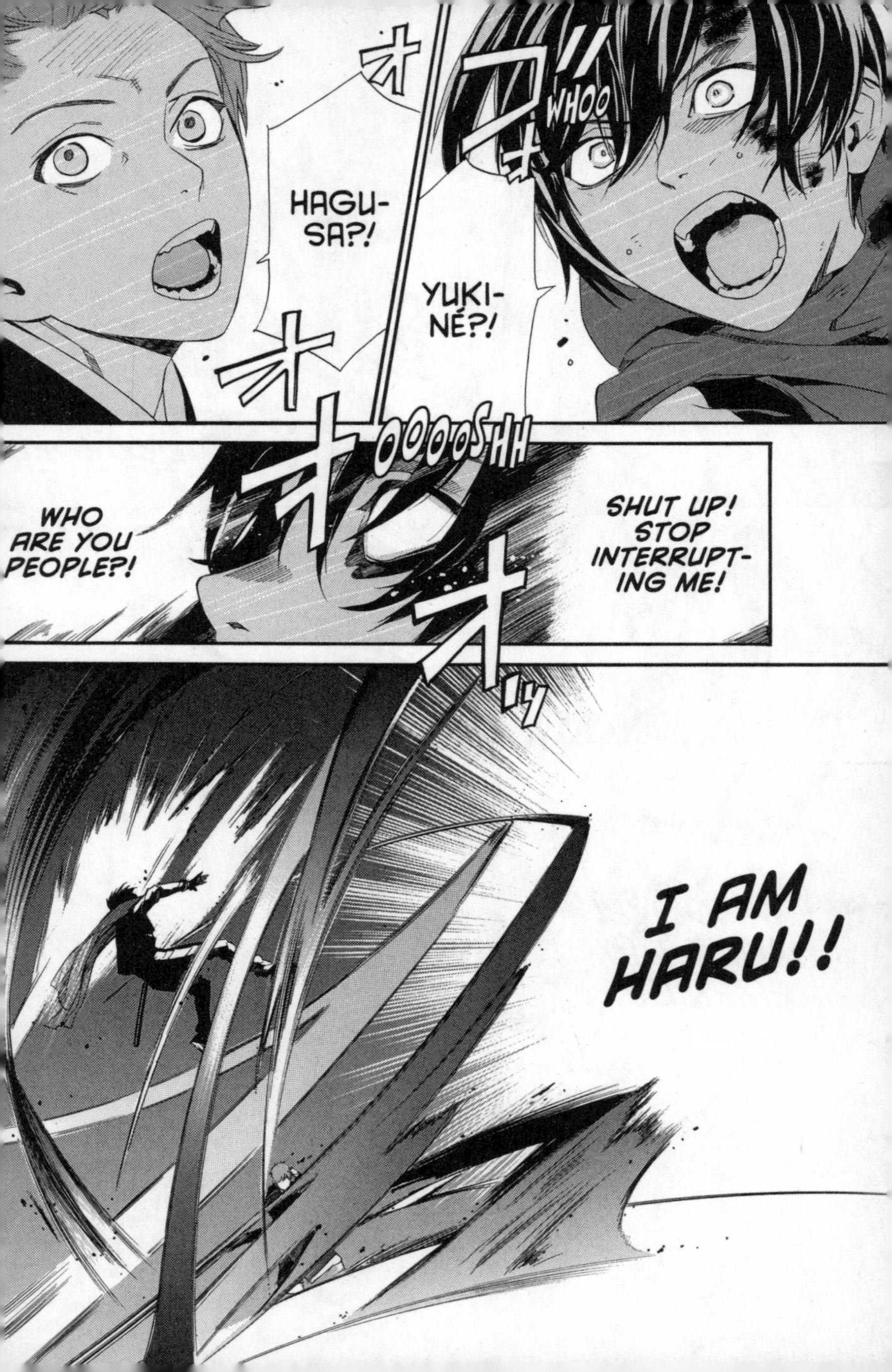
WHOO
YUKI-NÉ?!
HAGU-SA?!
OOOOSHH
SHUT UP! STOP INTERRUPT-ING ME!
WHO ARE YOU PEOPLE?!
I AM HARU!!

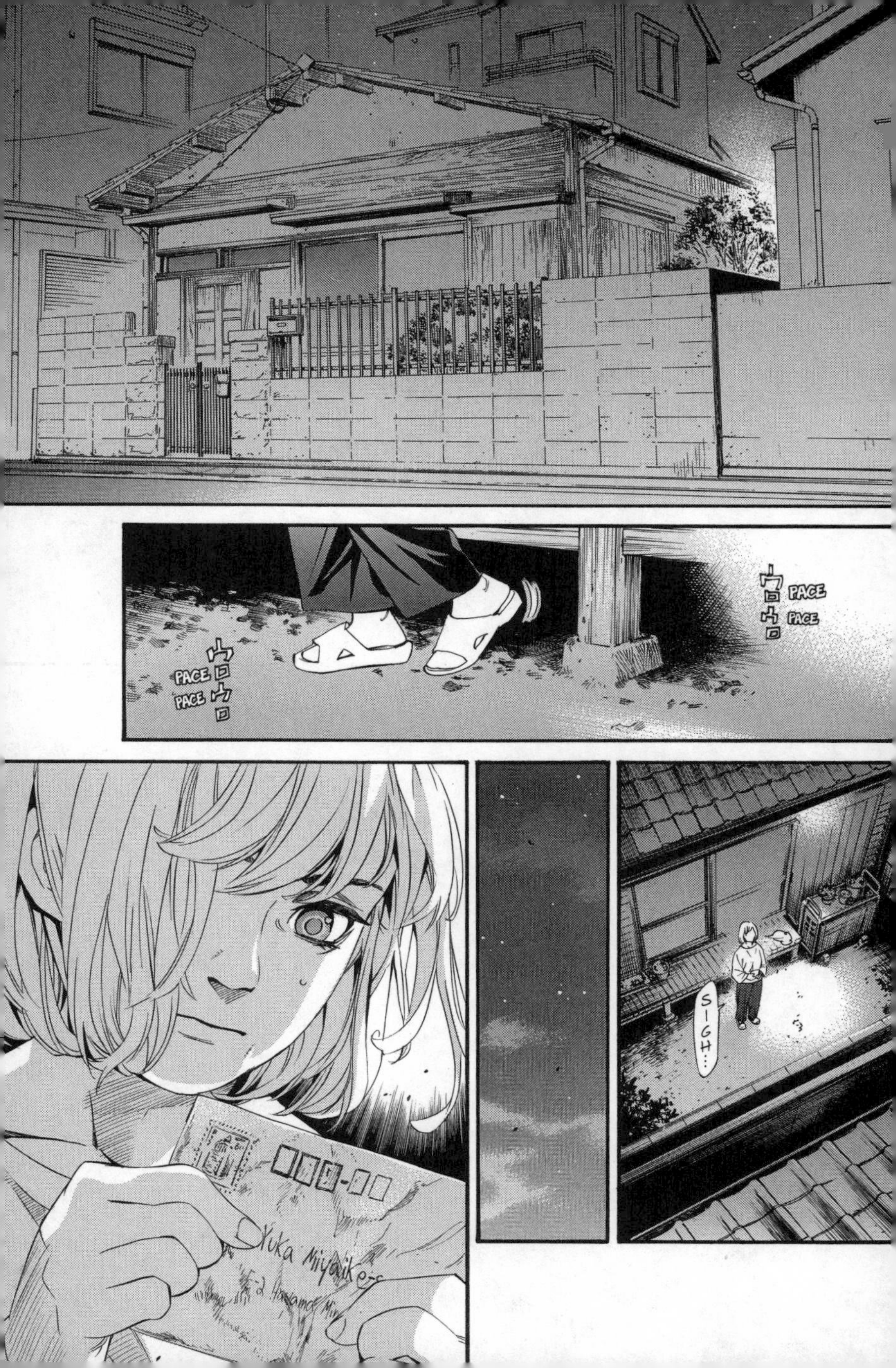
PACE
PACE
PACE
PACE
SIGH...
Yuka Miyaike-s

RUSTLE

Haruki Tajima
Inn ~ Takeuchi Inn
5-2 Hatishi Nishitoyo

CHAPTER 93 / END

野

良

神

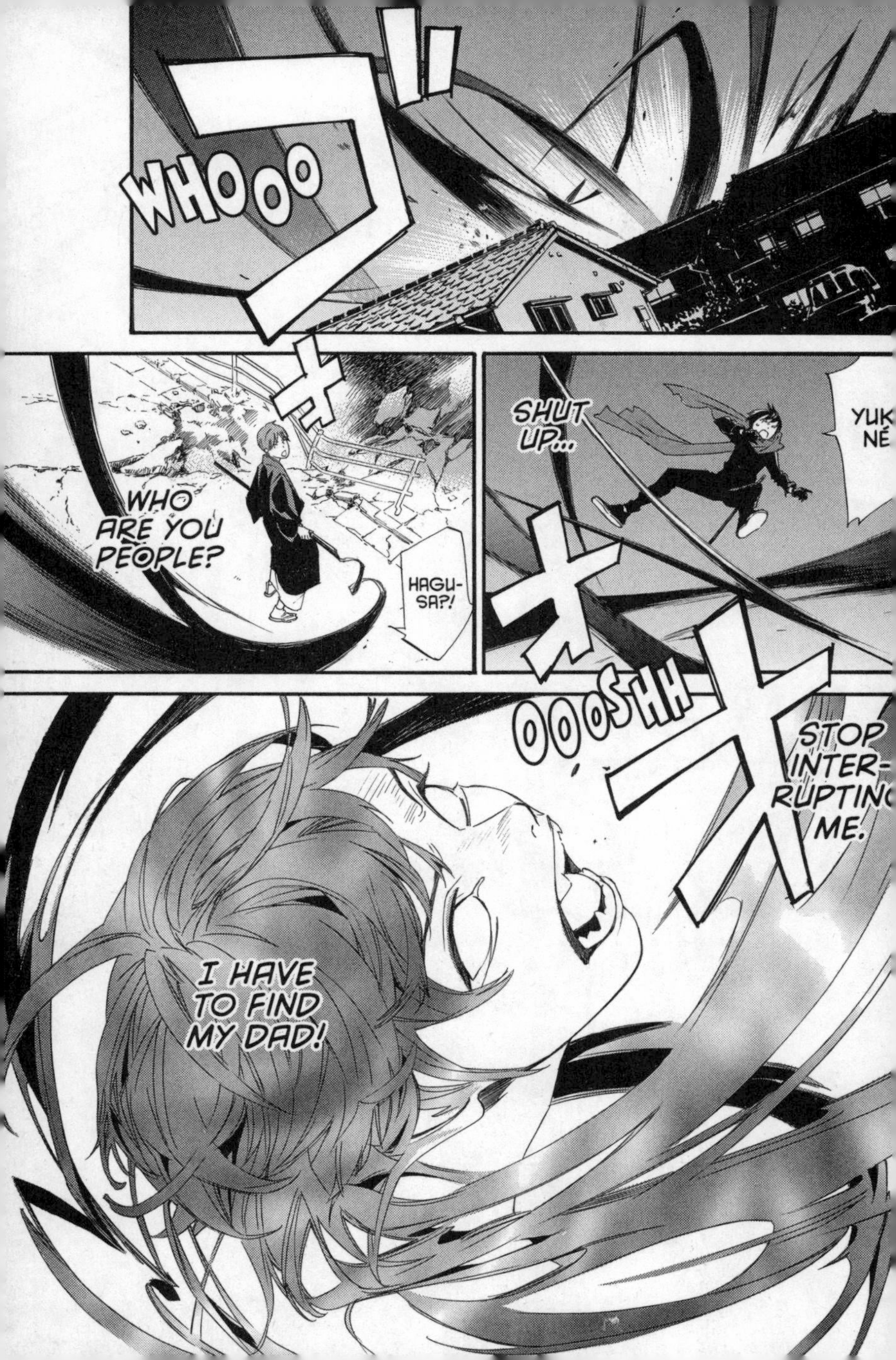
WHOOO
YUK
NÉ
SHUT UP...
HAGU-SA?!
WHO ARE YOU PEOPLE?
OOOSHH
STOP INTER-RUPTING ME.
I HAVE TO FIND MY DAD!

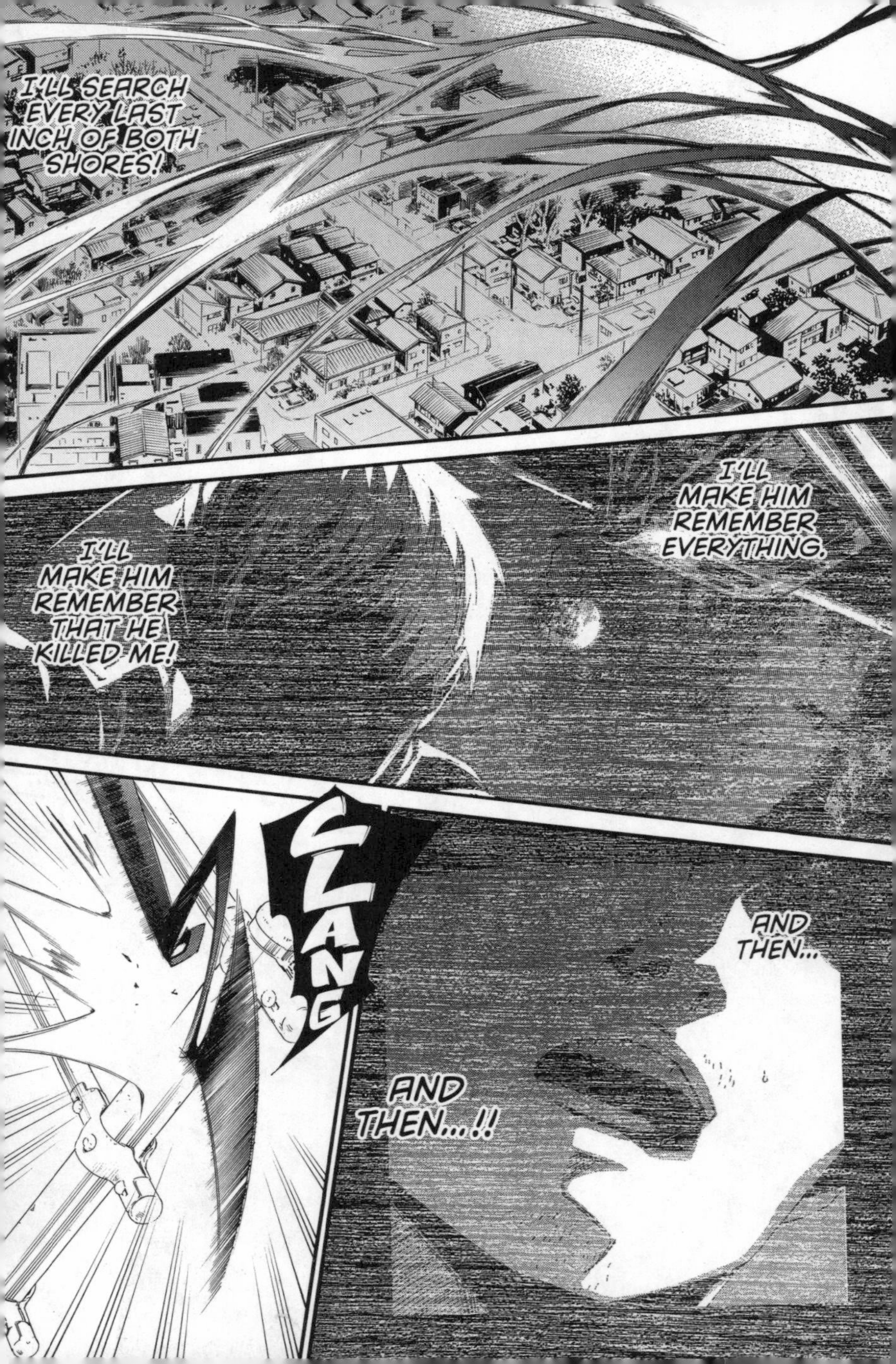
I'LL SEARCH EVERY LAST INCH OF BOTH SHORES!
I'LL MAKE HIM REMEMBER EVERYTHING.
I'LL MAKE HIM REMEMBER THAT HE KILLED ME!
AND THEN...
AND THEN...!!
CLANG

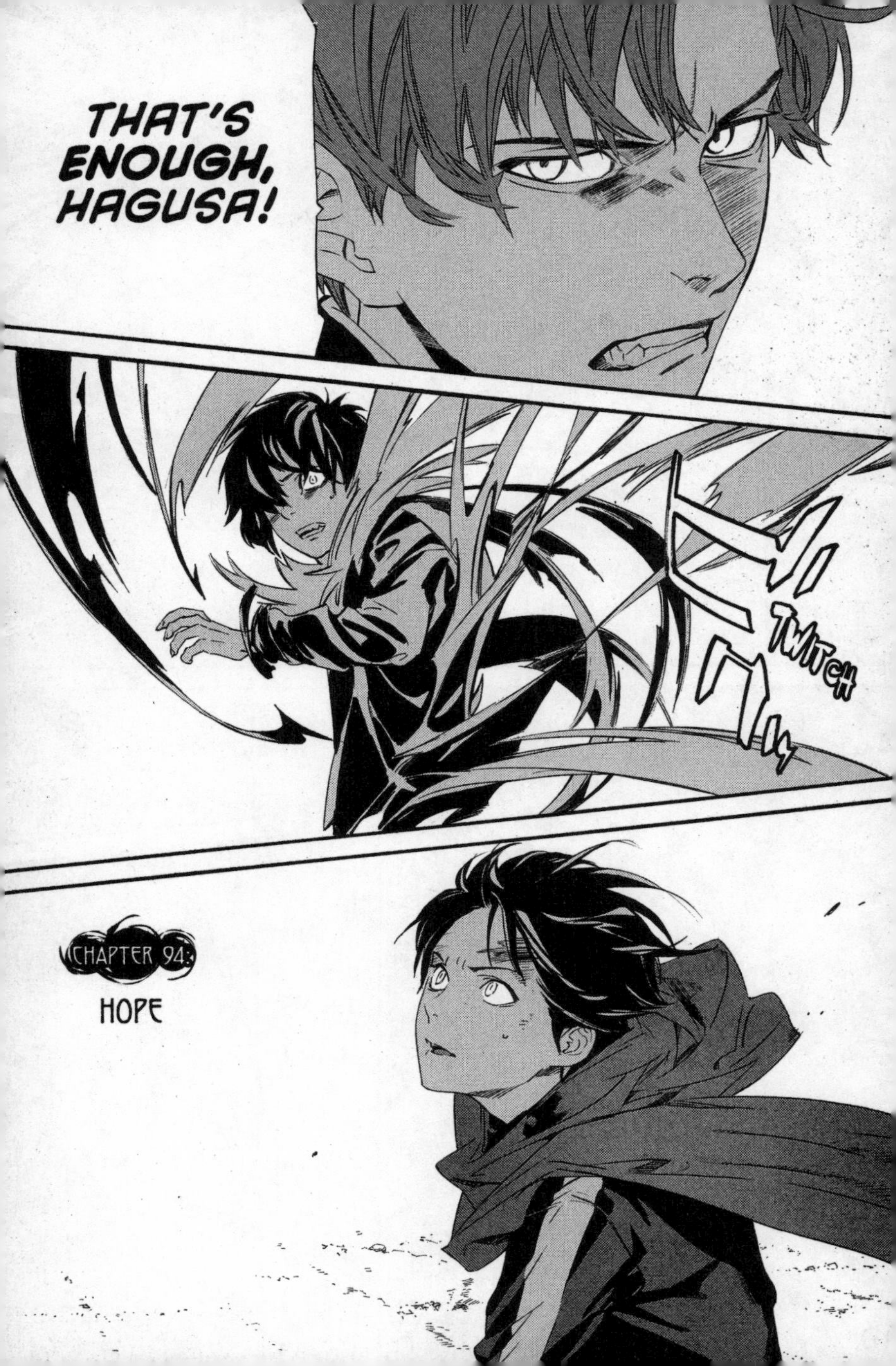
THAT'S ENOUGH, HAGUSA!
TWITCH
CHAPTER 94:
HOPE

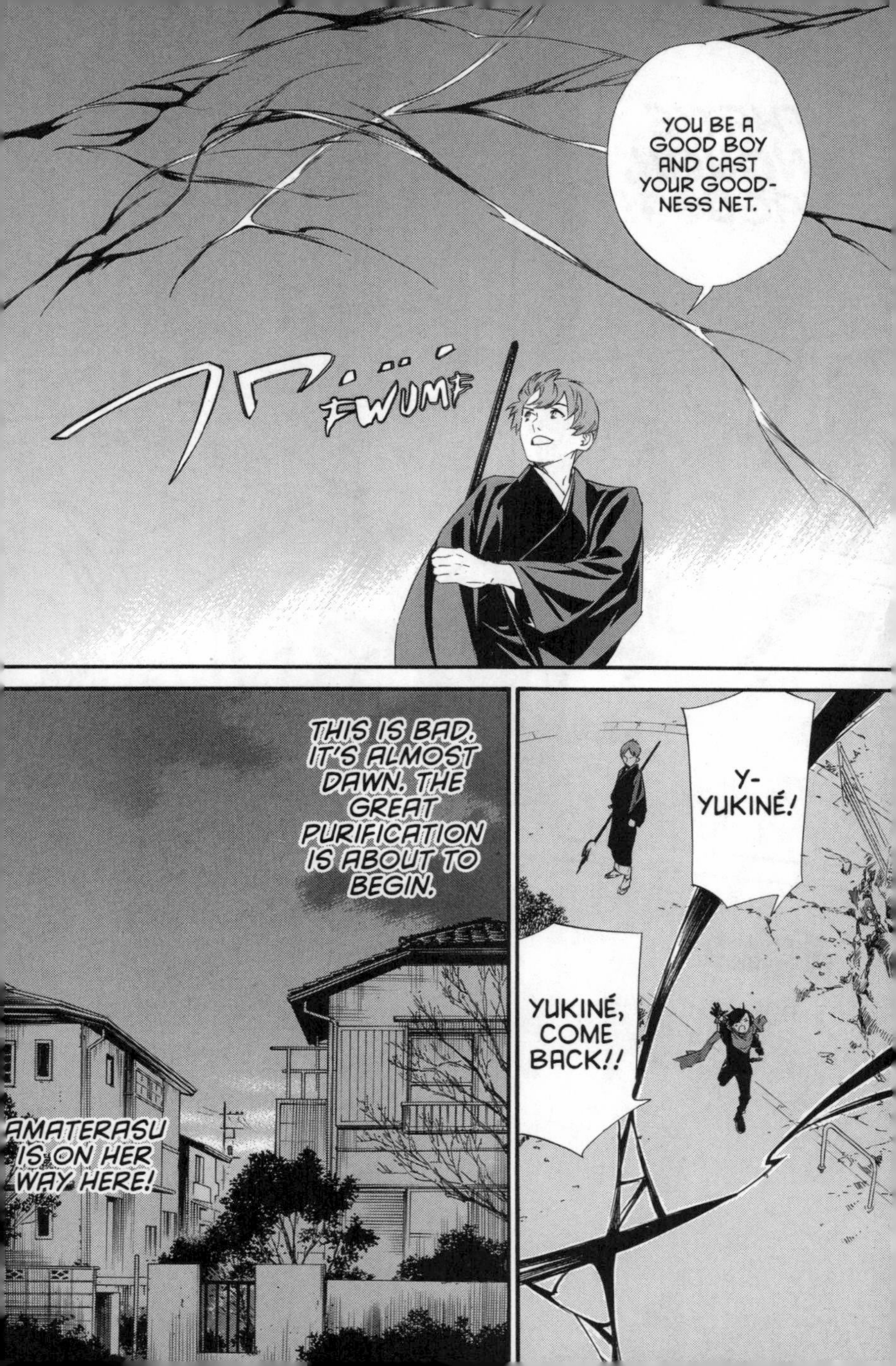
YOU BE A GOOD BOY AND CAST YOUR GOOD-NESS NET.
FWUMF
Y-YUKINÉ!
YUKINÉ, COME BACK!!
THIS IS BAD. IT'S ALMOST DAWN. THE GREAT PURIFICATION IS ABOUT TO BEGIN.
AMATERASU IS ON HER WAY HERE!

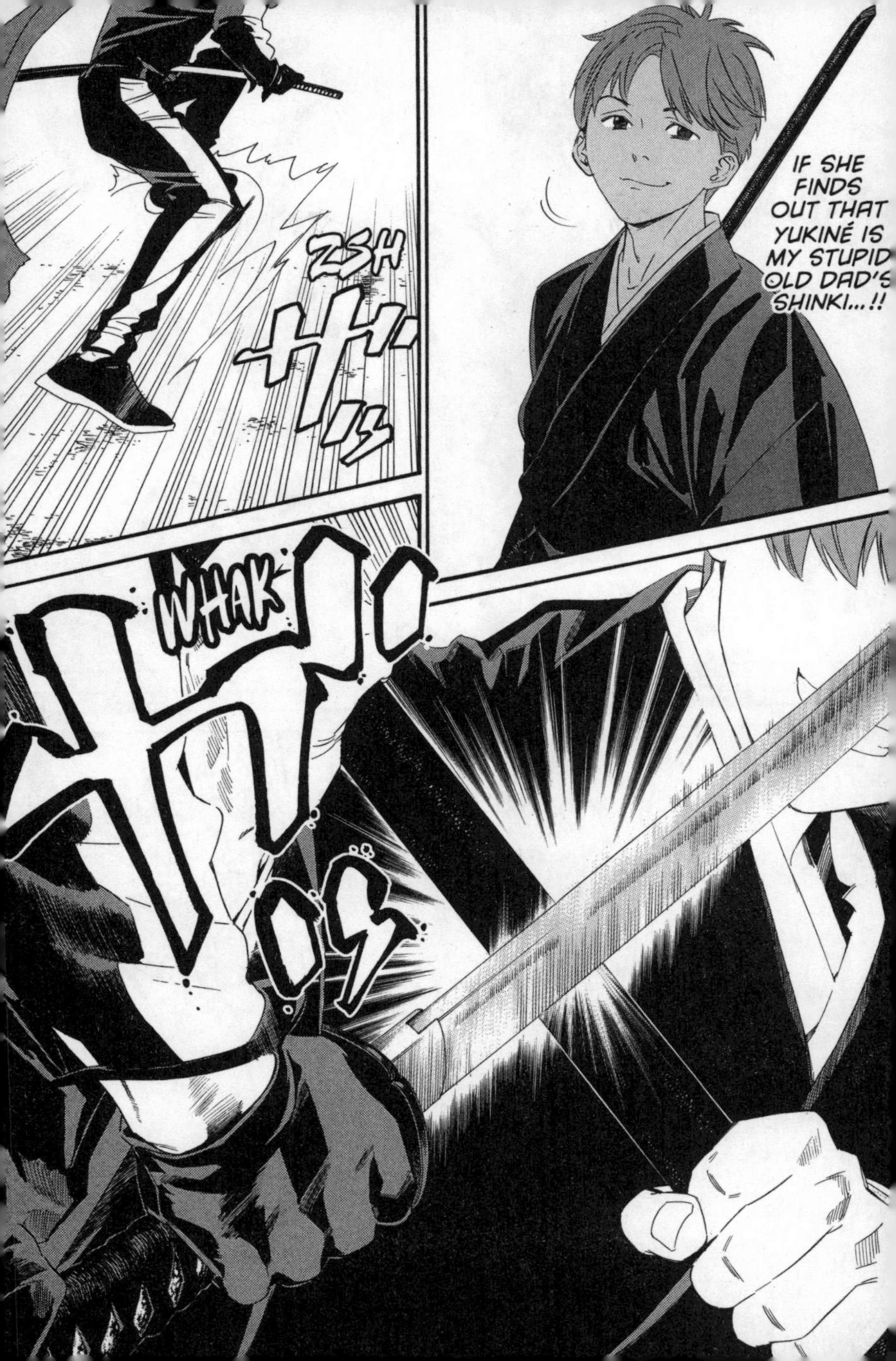
IF SHE FINDS OUT THAT YUKINÉ IS MY STUPID OLD DAD'S SHINKI...!!
ZSH
WHAK

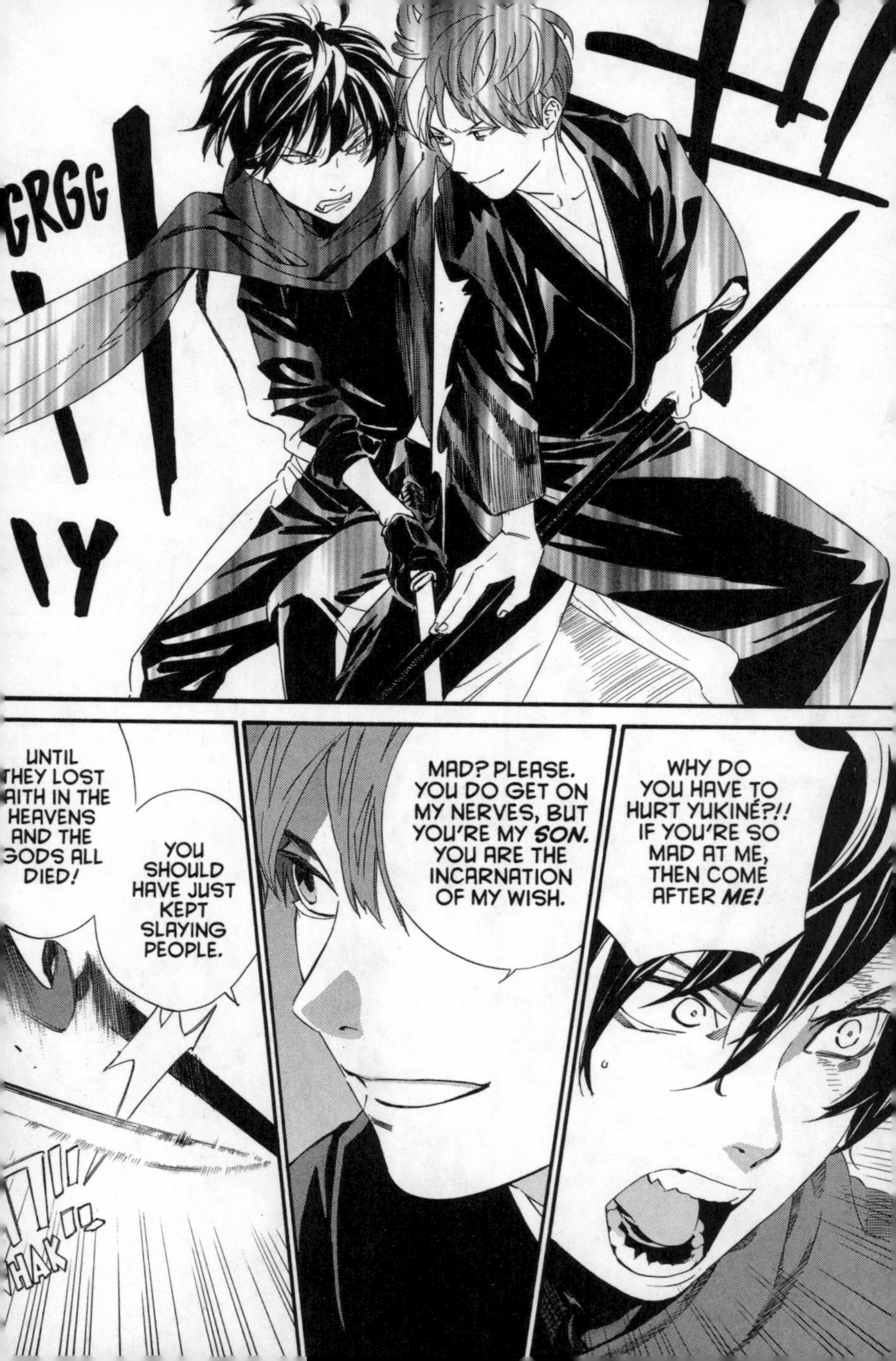
GRGG
WHY DO YOU HAVE TO HURT YUKINÉ?!! IF YOU'RE SO MAD AT ME, THEN COME AFTER *ME!*
MAD? PLEASE. YOU DO GET ON MY NERVES, BUT YOU'RE MY *SON.* YOU ARE THE INCARNATION OF MY WISH.
YOU SHOULD HAVE JUST KEPT SLAYING PEOPLE.
UNTIL THEY LOST AITH IN THE HEAVENS AND THE GODS ALL DIED!
HAK

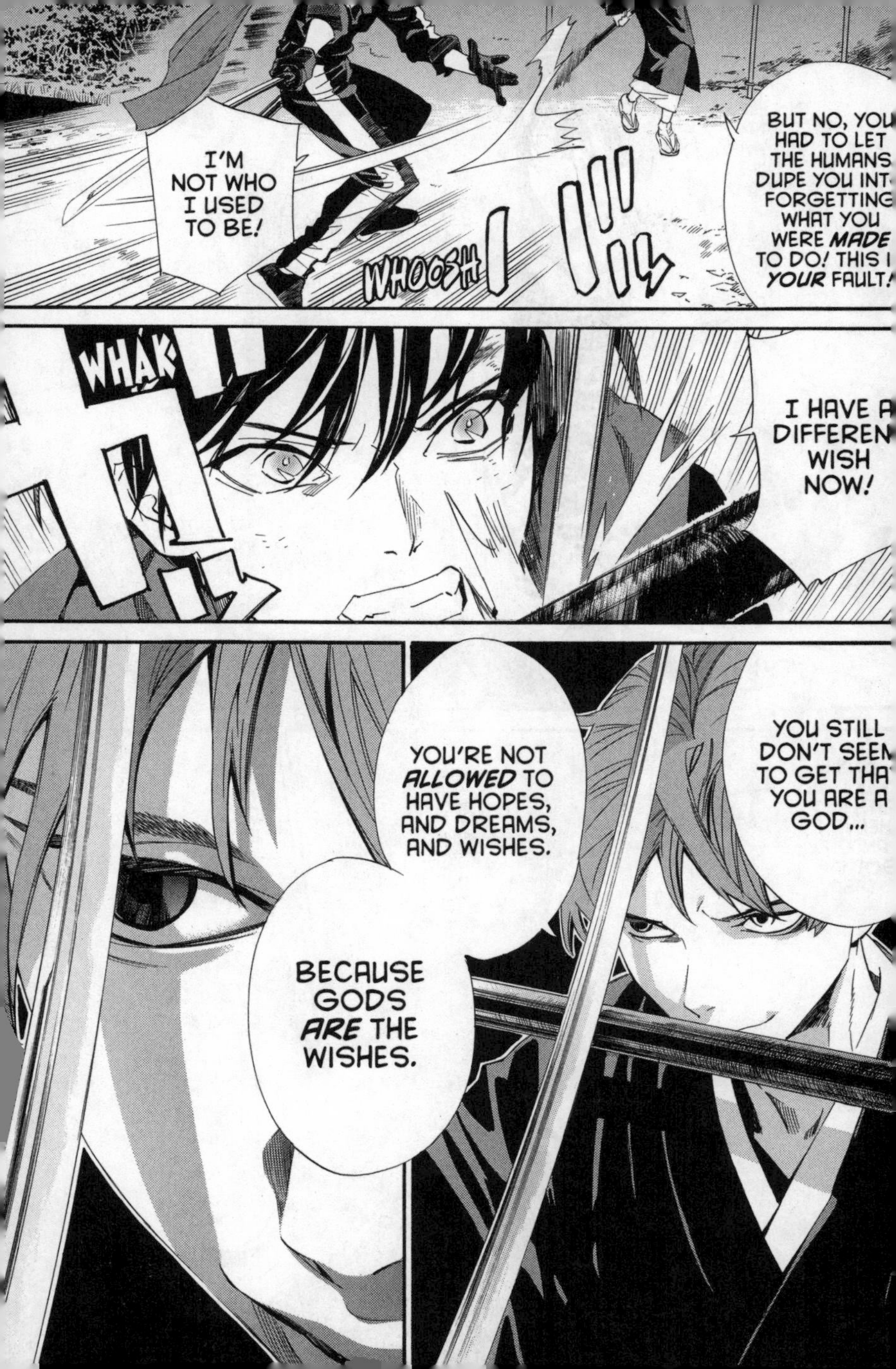
BUT NO, YOU HAD TO LET THE HUMANS DUPE YOU INTO FORGETTING WHAT YOU WERE *MADE* TO DO! THIS IS *YOUR* FAULT!
WHOOSH
I'M NOT WHO I USED TO BE!
I HAVE A DIFFERENT WISH NOW!
WHAK
YOU STILL DON'T SEEM TO GET THAT YOU ARE A GOD...
YOU'RE NOT *ALLOWED* TO HAVE HOPES, AND DREAMS, AND WISHES.
BECAUSE GODS *ARE* THE WISHES.

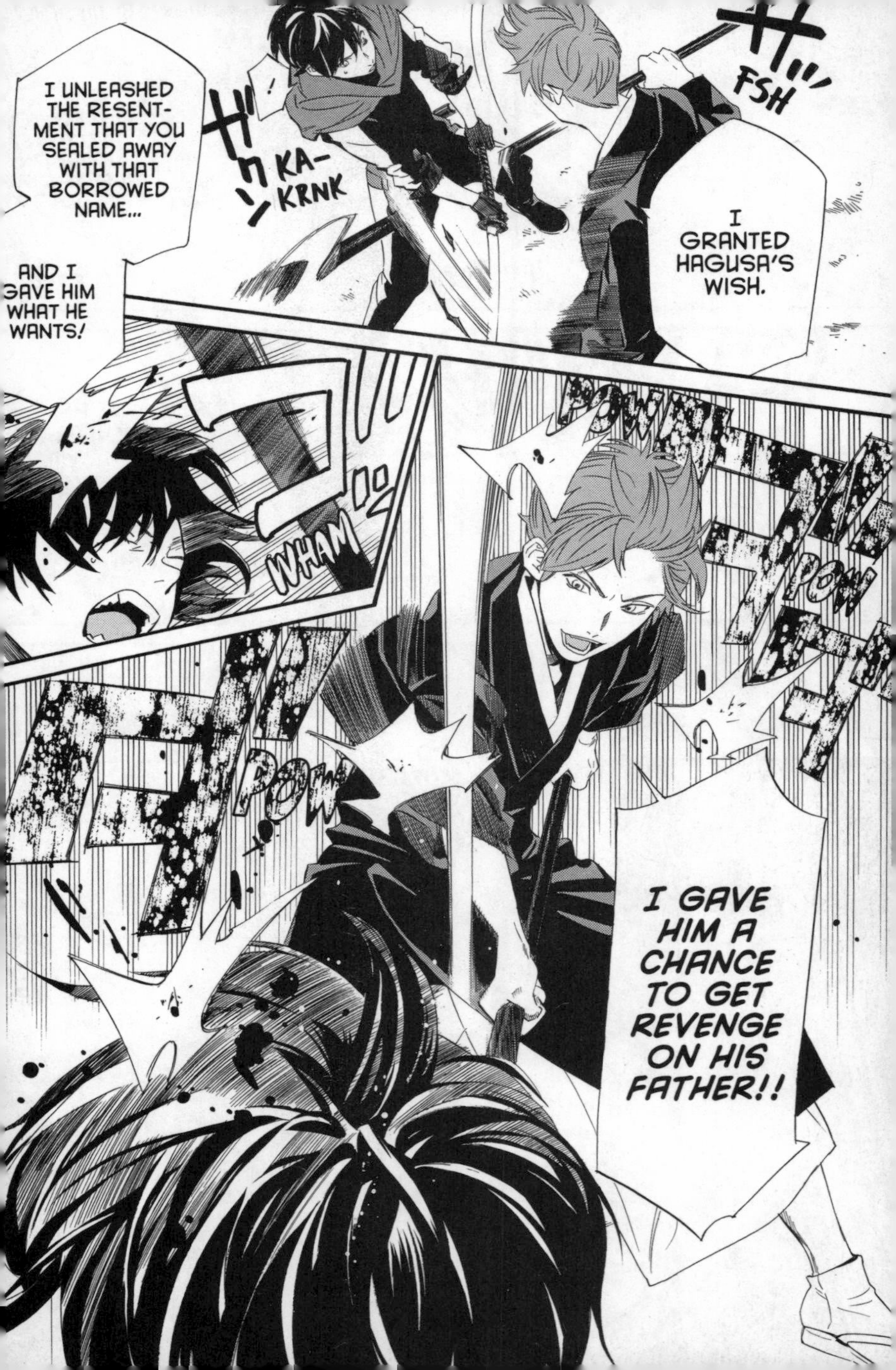
FSH
I GRANTED HAGUSA'S WISH.
I UNLEASHED THE RESENTMENT THAT YOU SEALED AWAY WITH THAT BORROWED NAME...
KA-KRNK
AND I GAVE HIM WHAT HE WANTS!
POW
POW
I GAVE HIM A CHANCE TO GET REVENGE ON HIS FATHER!!
POW
WHAM

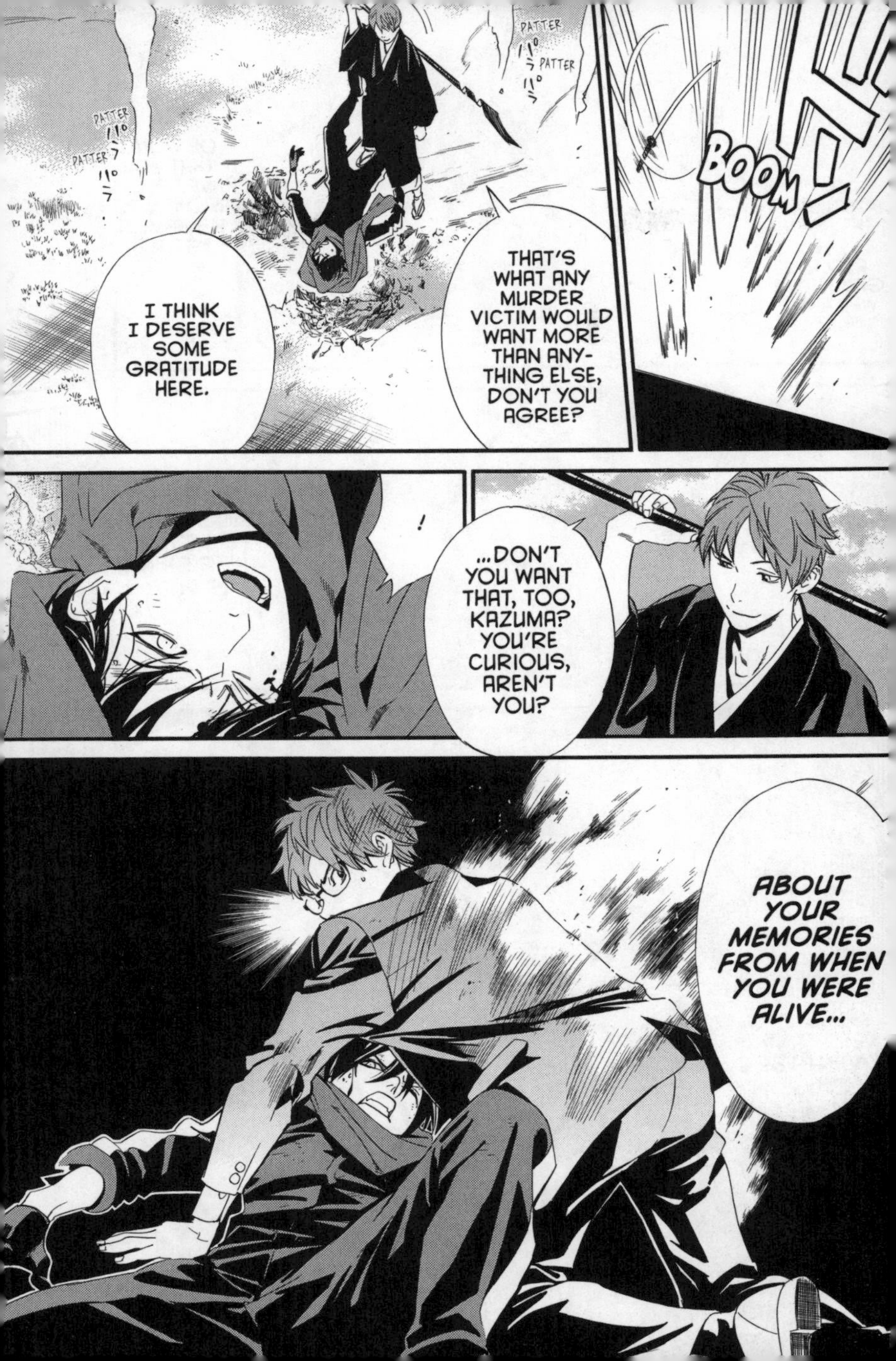
BOOM!
PATTER PATTER
PATTER PATTER
THAT'S WHAT ANY MURDER VICTIM WOULD WANT MORE THAN ANY-THING ELSE, DON'T YOU AGREE?
I THINK I DESERVE SOME GRATITUDE HERE.
...DON'T YOU WANT THAT, TOO, KAZUMA? YOU'RE CURIOUS, AREN'T YOU?
!
ABOUT YOUR MEMORIES FROM WHEN YOU WERE ALIVE...

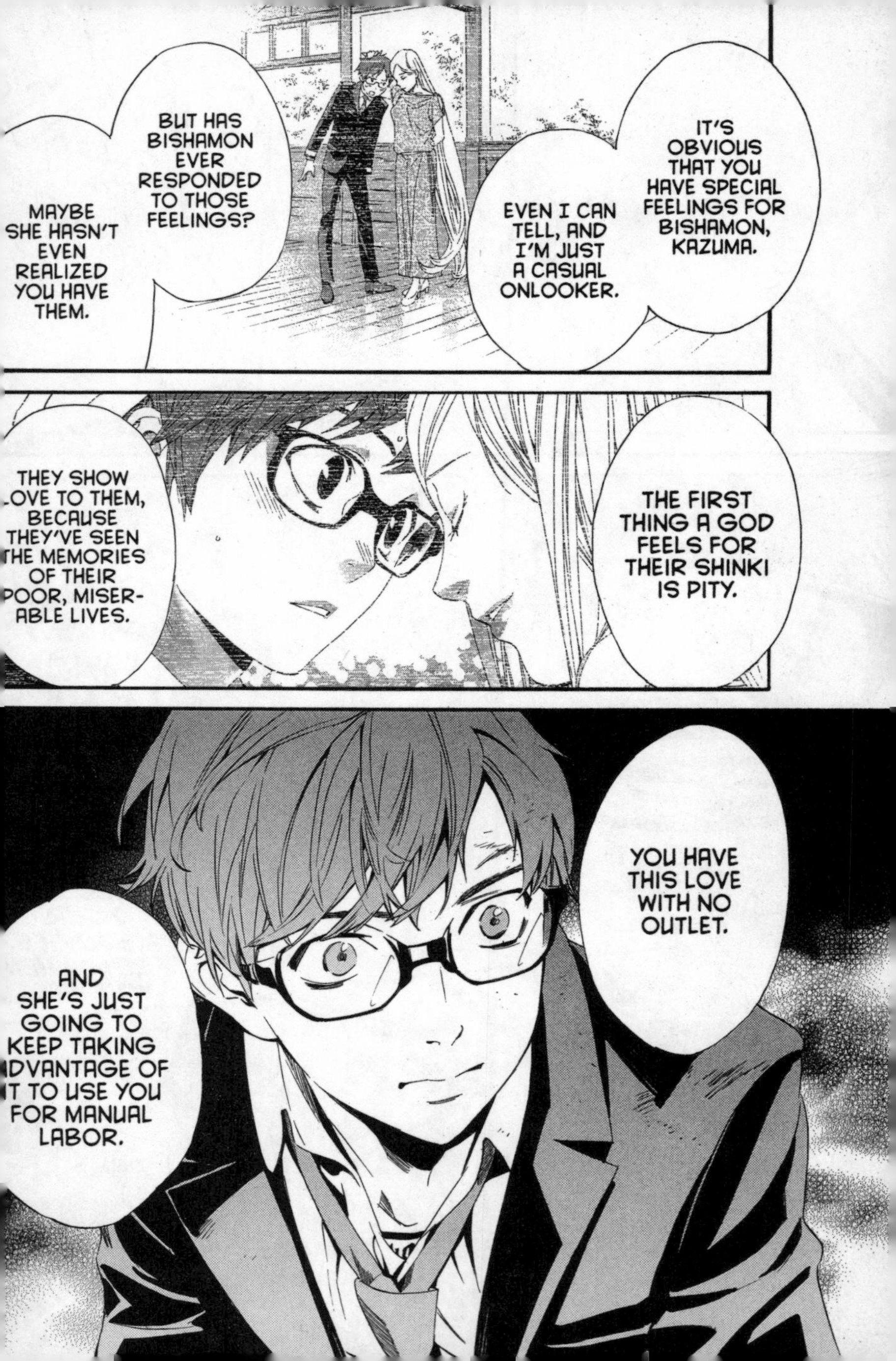
IT'S OBVIOUS THAT YOU HAVE SPECIAL FEELINGS FOR BISHAMON, KAZUMA.
EVEN I CAN TELL, AND I'M JUST A CASUAL ONLOOKER.
BUT HAS BISHAMON EVER RESPONDED TO THOSE FEELINGS?
MAYBE SHE HASN'T EVEN REALIZED YOU HAVE THEM.
THE FIRST THING A GOD FEELS FOR THEIR SHINKI IS PITY.
THEY SHOW LOVE TO THEM, BECAUSE THEY'VE SEEN THE MEMORIES OF THEIR POOR, MISER-ABLE LIVES.
YOU HAVE THIS LOVE WITH NO OUTLET.
AND SHE'S JUST GOING TO KEEP TAKING ADVANTAGE OF IT TO USE YOU FOR MANUAL LABOR.

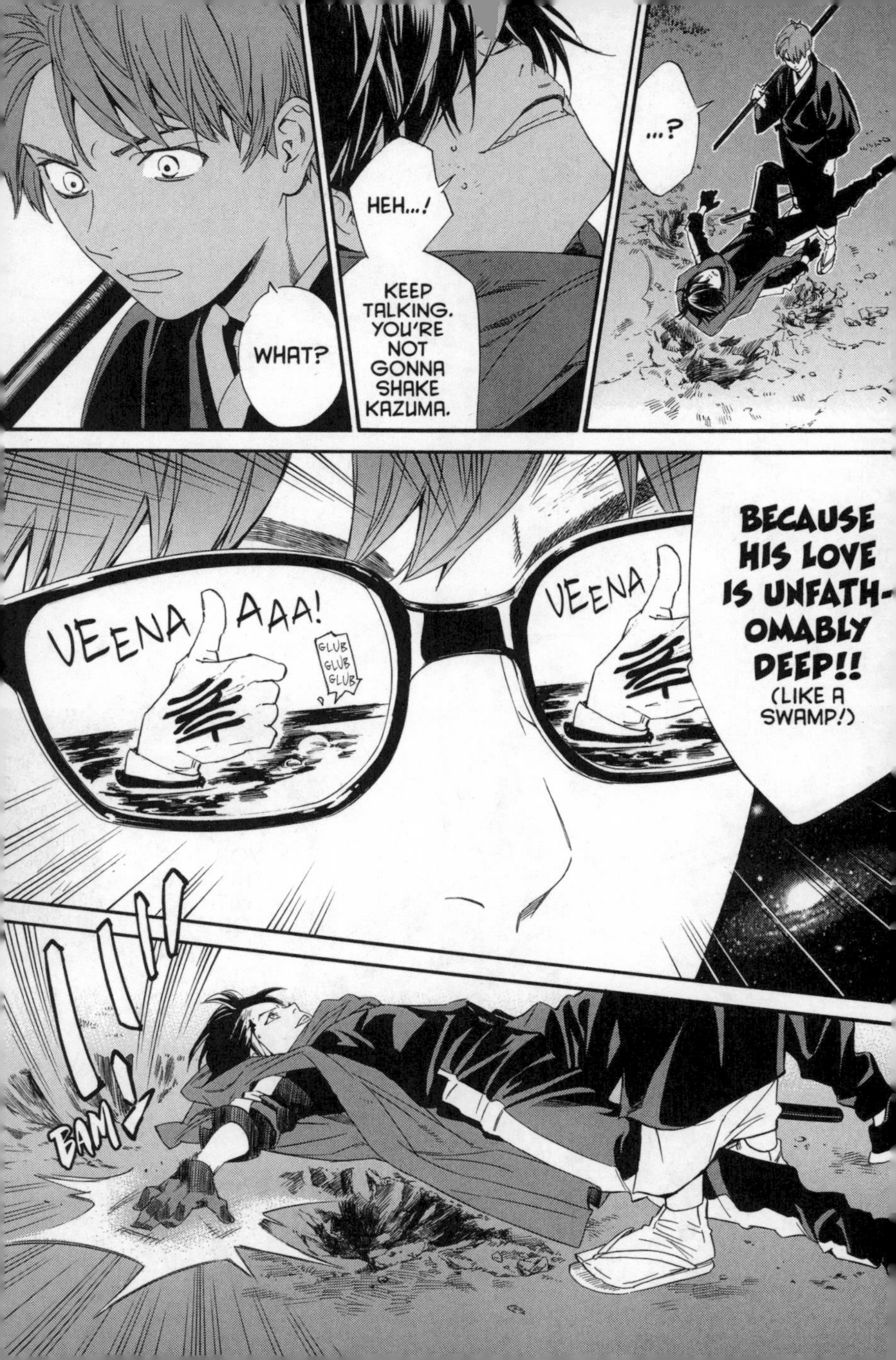
...?
HEH...!
KEEP TALKING. YOU'RE NOT GONNA SHAKE KAZUMA.
WHAT?
BECAUSE HIS LOVE IS UNFATHOMABLY DEEP!!
(LIKE A SWAMP!)
VEENA
VEENA AAA!
GLUB GLUB GLUB
BAM

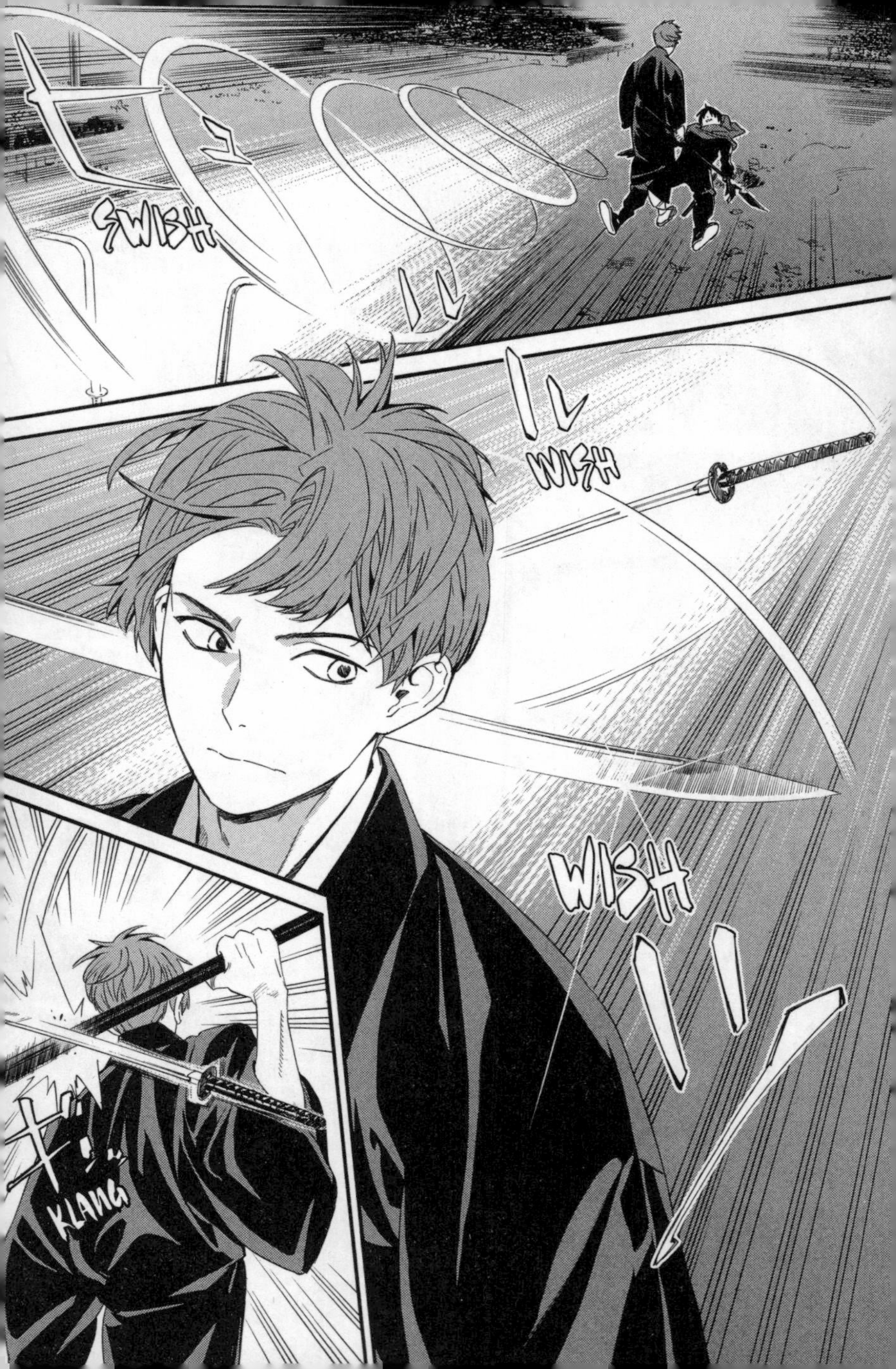
SWISH
WISH
WISH
KLANG

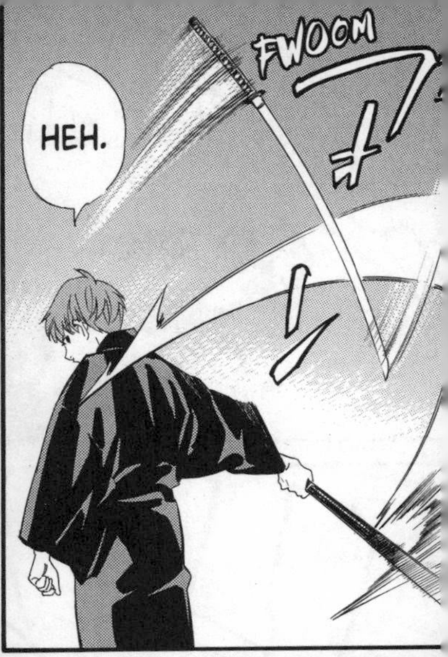
FWOOM
HEH.

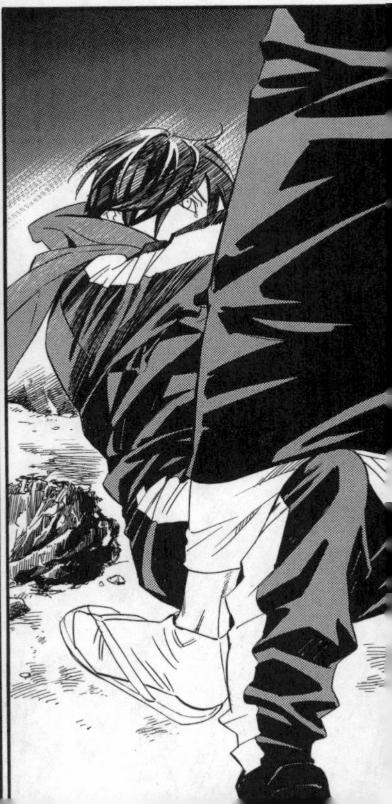

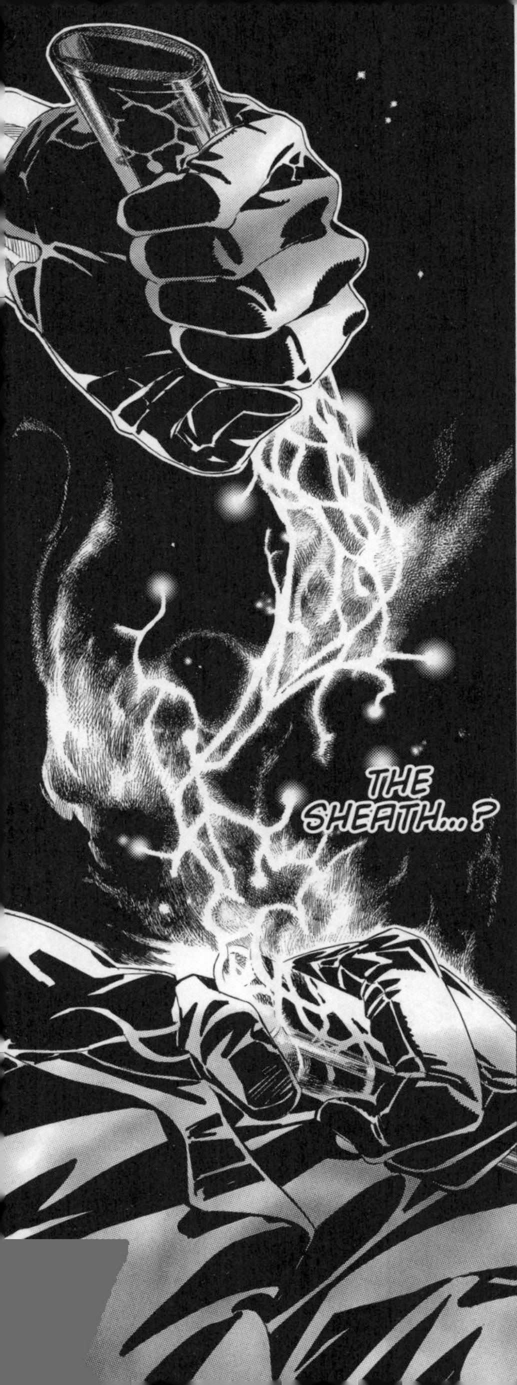
THE SHEATH...?

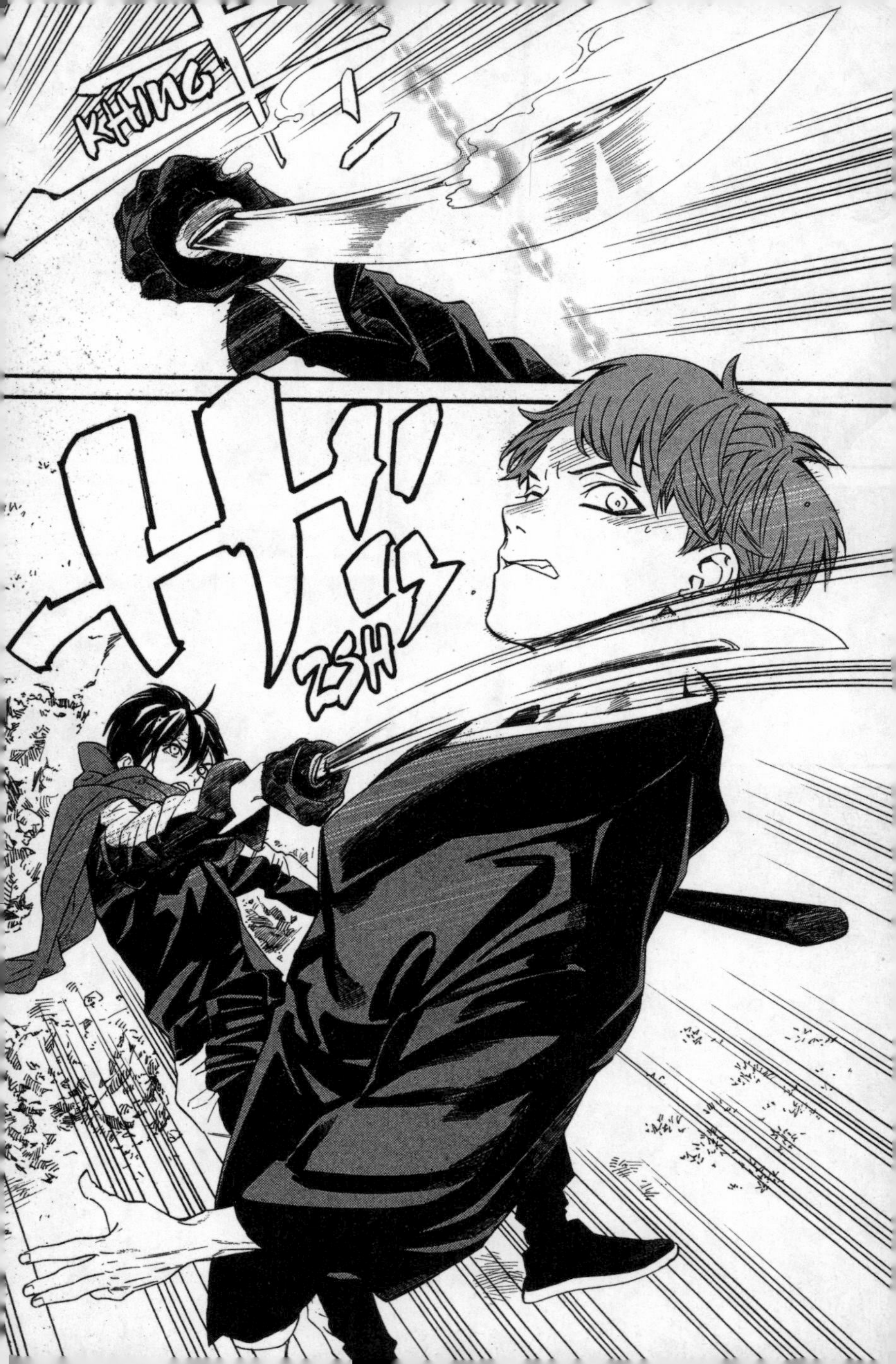
KHING
ZSH

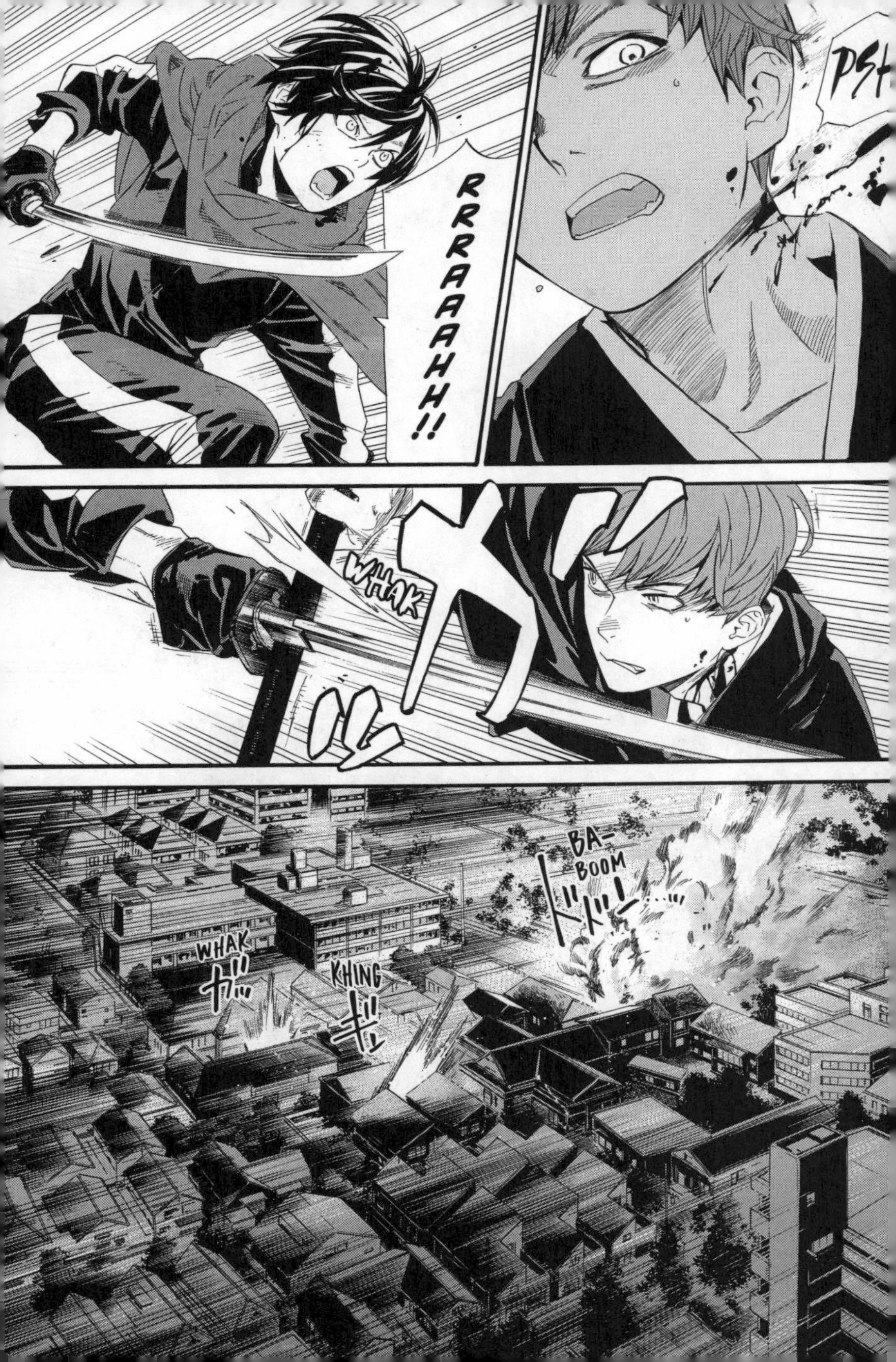
PSH
RRRAAAHH!!
WHAK
BA-BOOM
ドドー……
KHING
ギン
WHAK
ガッ

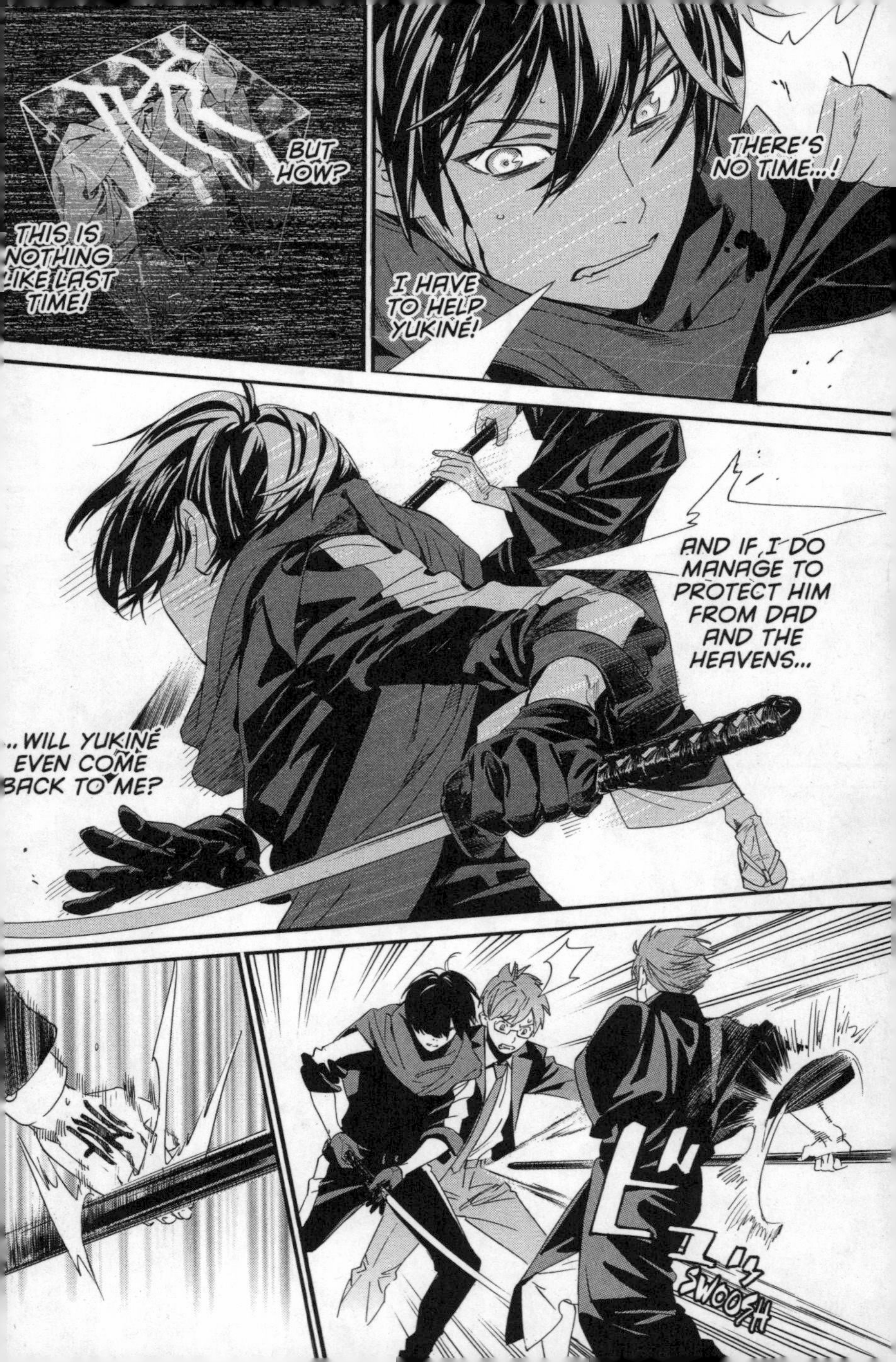
THERE'S NO TIME...!
I HAVE TO HELP YUKINÉ!
BUT HOW?
THIS IS NOTHING LIKE LAST TIME!
AND IF I DO MANAGE TO PROTECT HIM FROM DAD AND THE HEAVENS...
...WILL YUKINÉ EVEN COME BACK TO ME?
SWOOSH

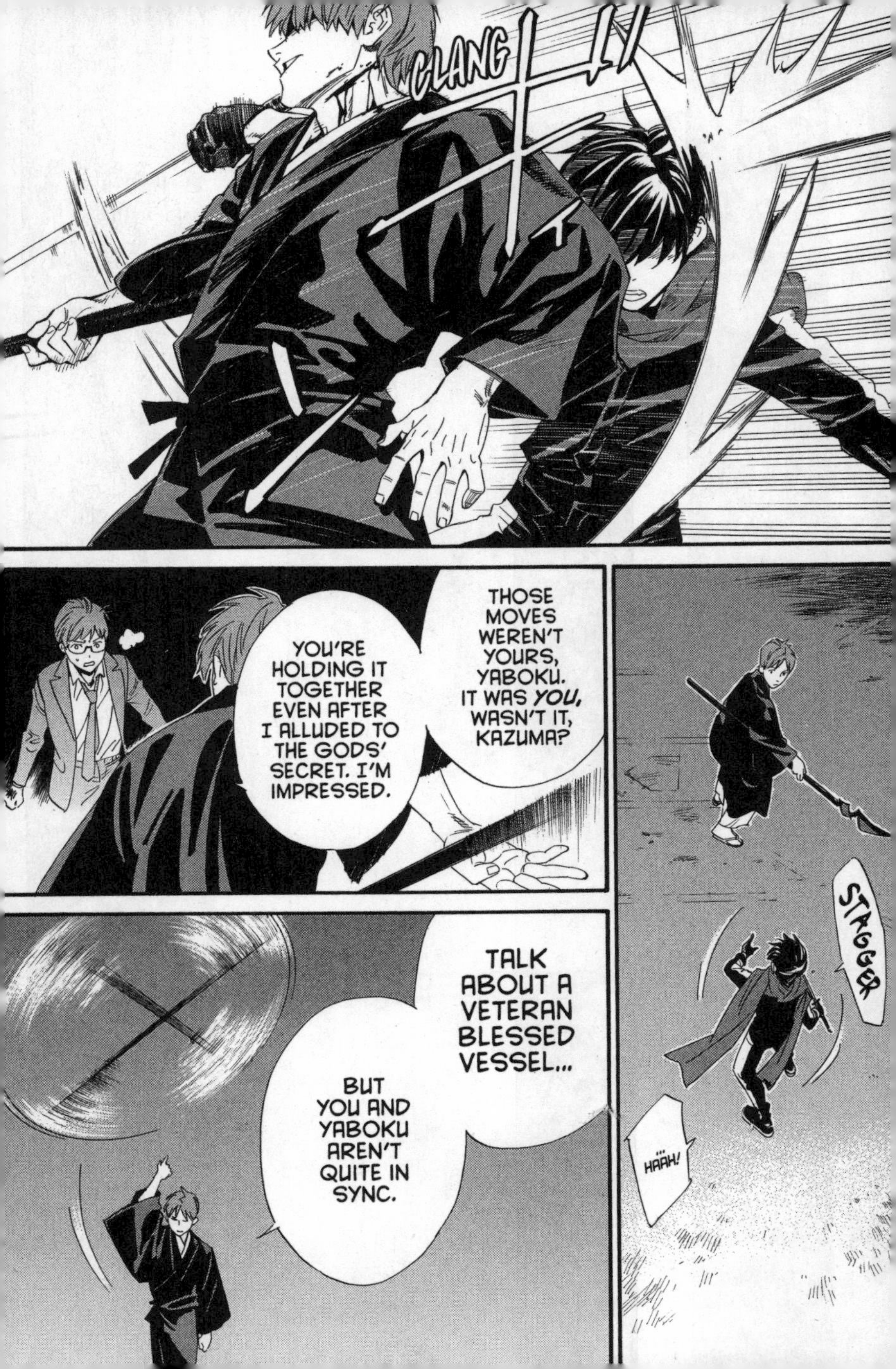
CLANG
STAGGER
... HÄÄH!
THOSE MOVES WEREN'T YOURS, YABOKU. IT WAS *YOU*, WASN'T IT, KAZUMA?
YOU'RE HOLDING IT TOGETHER EVEN AFTER I ALLUDED TO THE GODS' SECRET. I'M IMPRESSED.
TALK ABOUT A VETERAN BLESSED VESSEL...
BUT YOU AND YABOKU AREN'T QUITE IN SYNC.

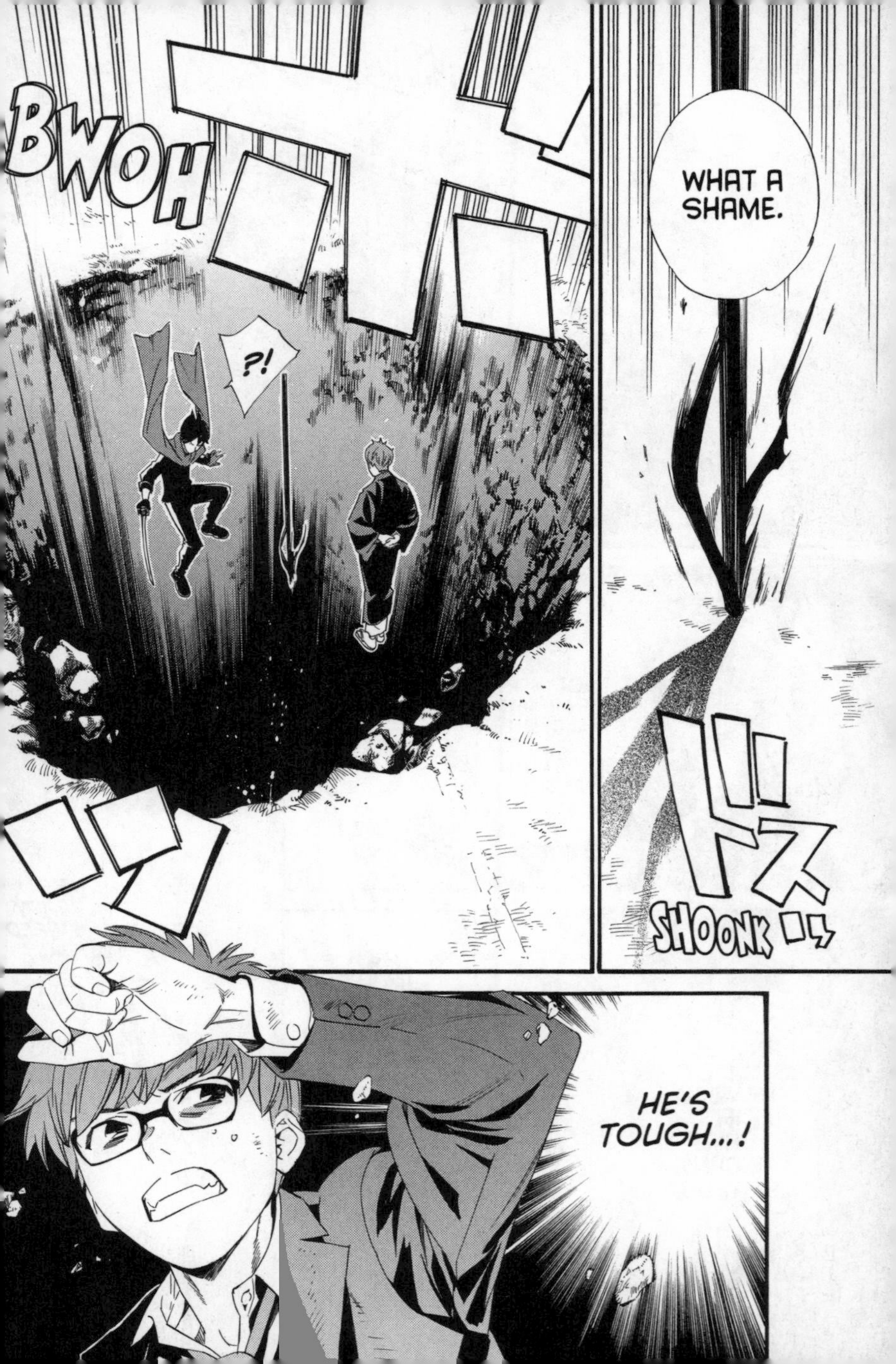
WHAT A SHAME.
ドス
SHOONK
BWOH
?!
HE'S TOUGH...!

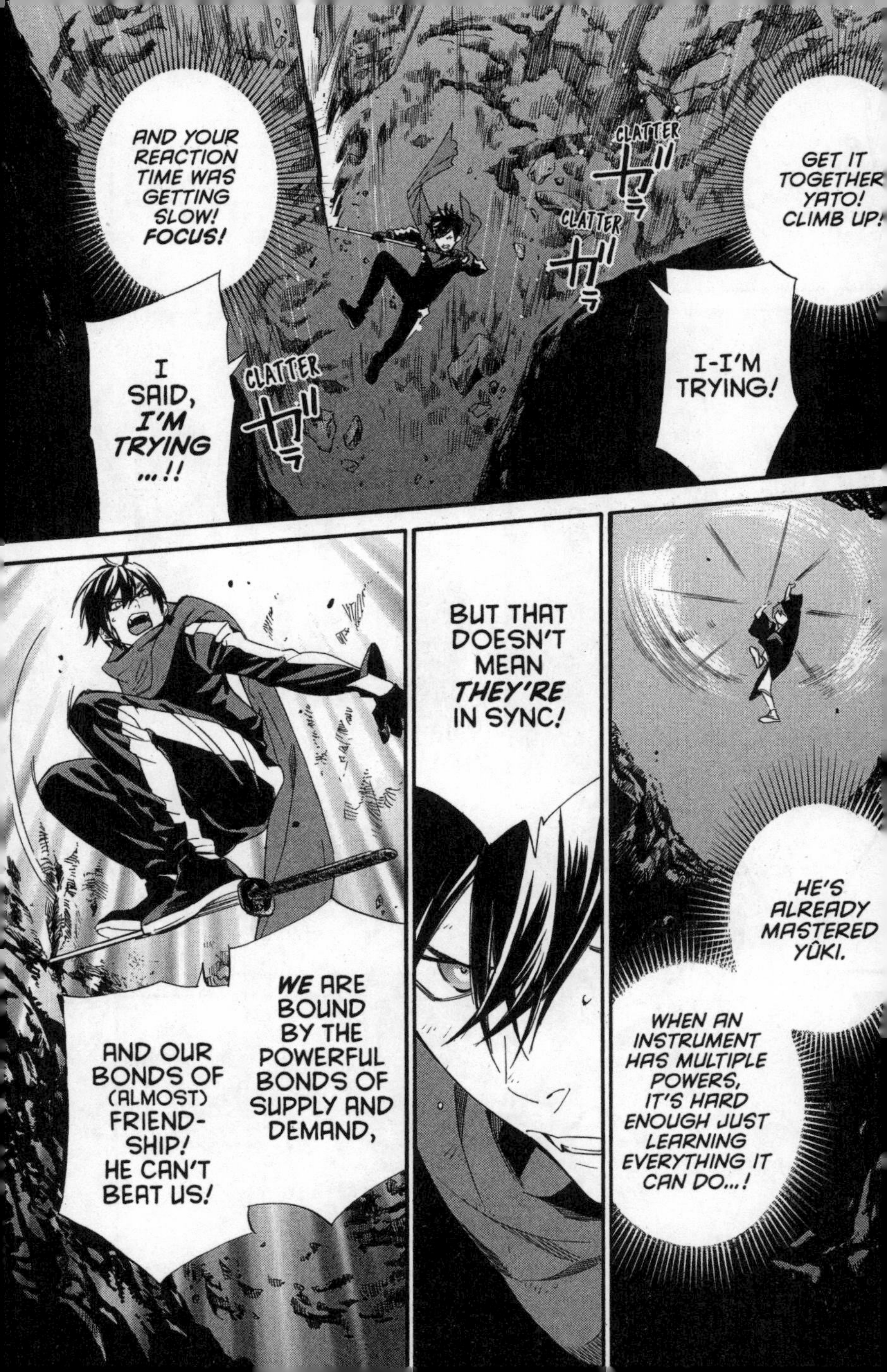
GET IT TOGETHER YATO! CLIMB UP!
CLATTER
CLATTER
AND YOUR REACTION TIME WAS GETTING SLOW! FOCUS!
I-I'M TRYING!
CLATTER
I SAID, I'M TRYING ...!!
HE'S ALREADY MASTERED YÛKI.
WHEN AN INSTRUMENT HAS MULTIPLE POWERS, IT'S HARD ENOUGH JUST LEARNING EVERYTHING IT CAN DO...!
BUT THAT DOESN'T MEAN THEY'RE IN SYNC!
WE ARE BOUND BY THE POWERFUL BONDS OF SUPPLY AND DEMAND,
AND OUR BONDS OF (ALMOST) FRIEND-SHIP! HE CAN'T BEAT US!

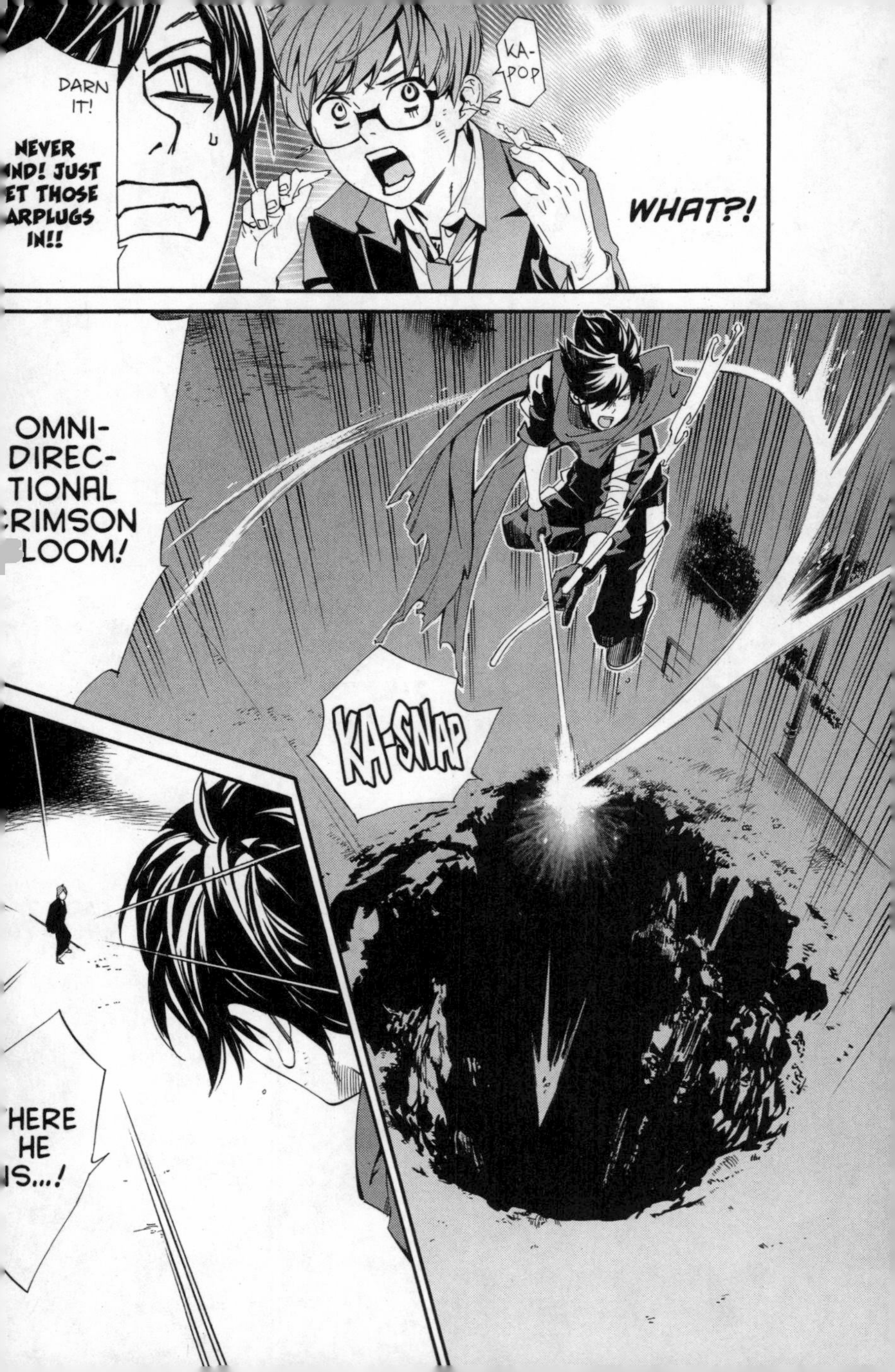
KA-POP
WHAT?!
DARN IT!
NEVER
ND! JUST
ET THOSE
ARPLUGS
IN!!
OMNI-DIRECTIONAL
RIMSON
LOOM!
KA-SNAP
HERE HE
IS...!

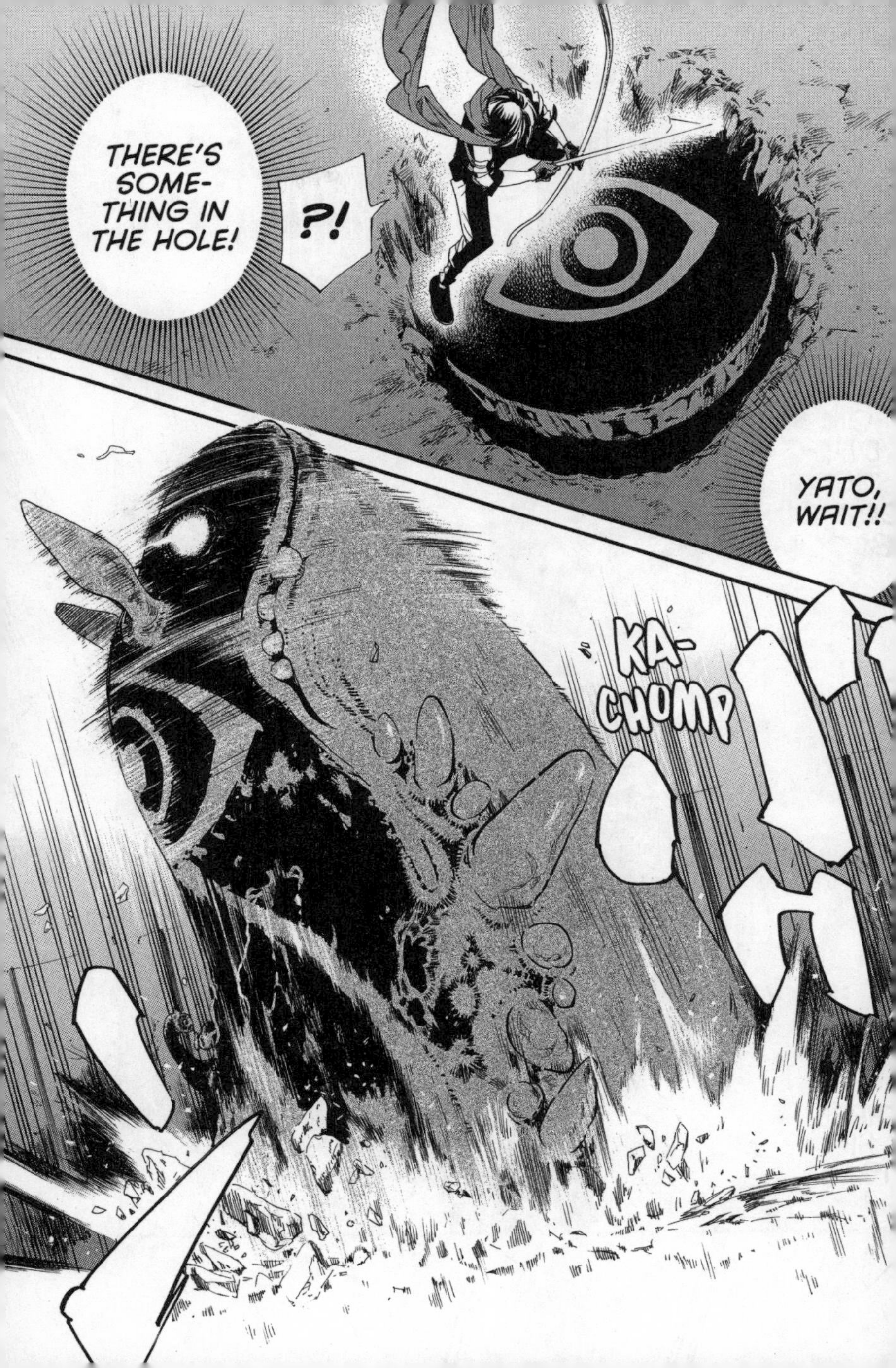
?!
THERE'S SOME-THING IN THE HOLE!
YATO, WAIT!!
KA-CHOMP

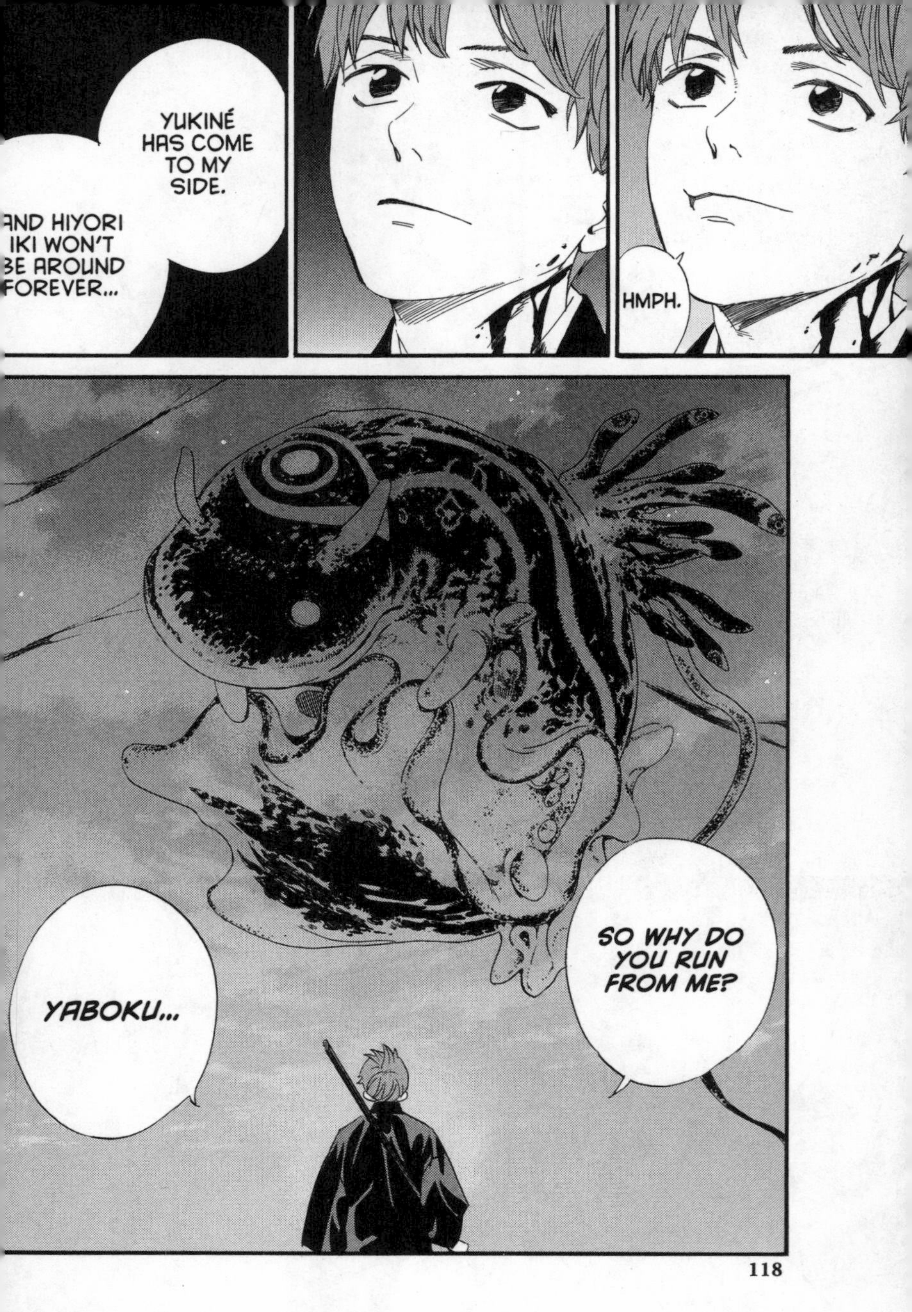
HMPH.
YUKINÉ HAS COME TO MY SIDE.
AND HIYORI IKI WON'T BE AROUND FOREVER...
SO WHY DO YOU RUN FROM ME?
YABOKU...

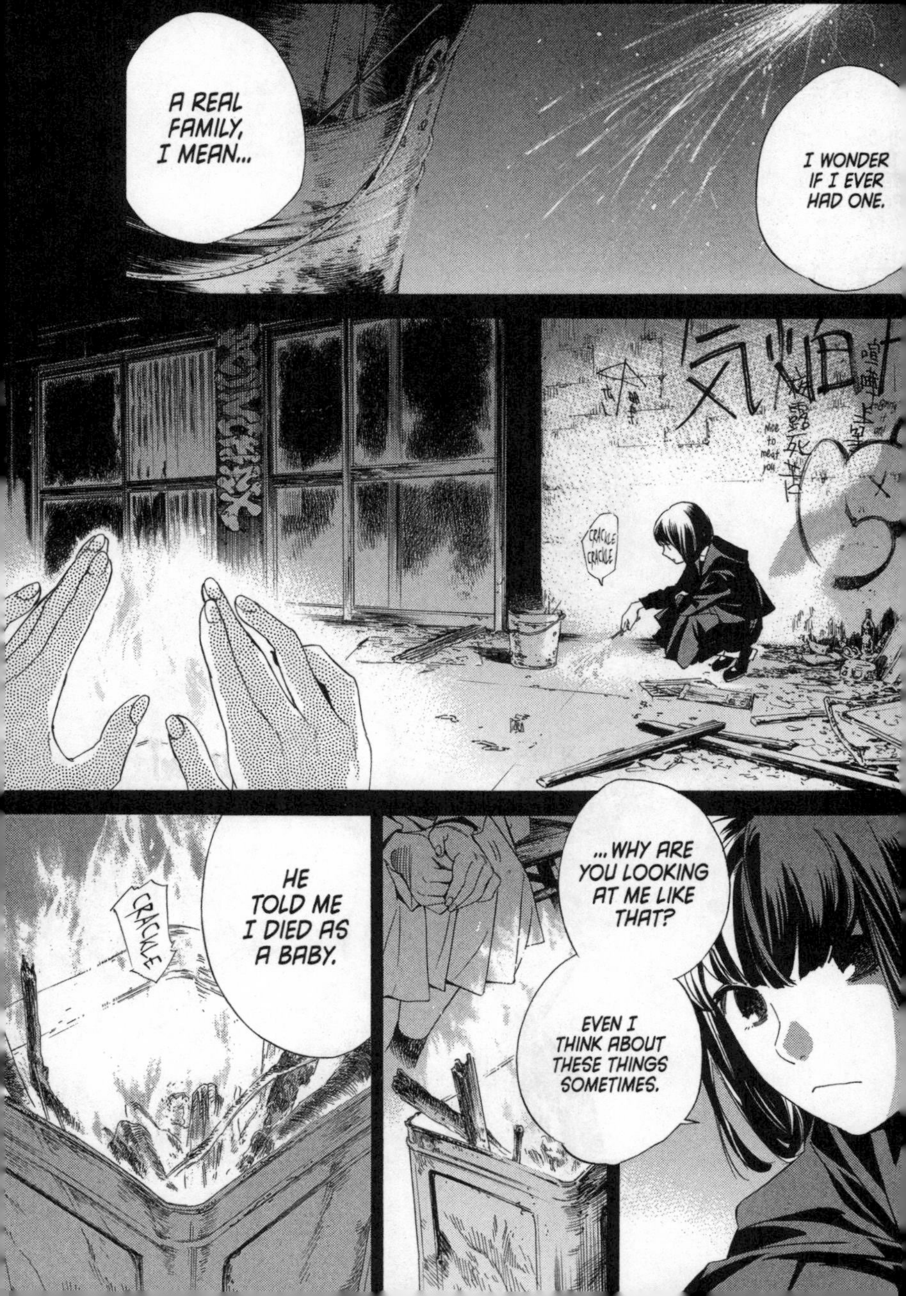
I WONDER IF I EVER HAD ONE.
A REAL FAMILY, I MEAN...
Nice to meat you
CRACKLE CRACKLE
...WHY ARE YOU LOOKING AT ME LIKE THAT?
EVEN I THINK ABOUT THESE THINGS SOMETIMES.
HE TOLD ME I DIED AS A BABY.
CRACKLE

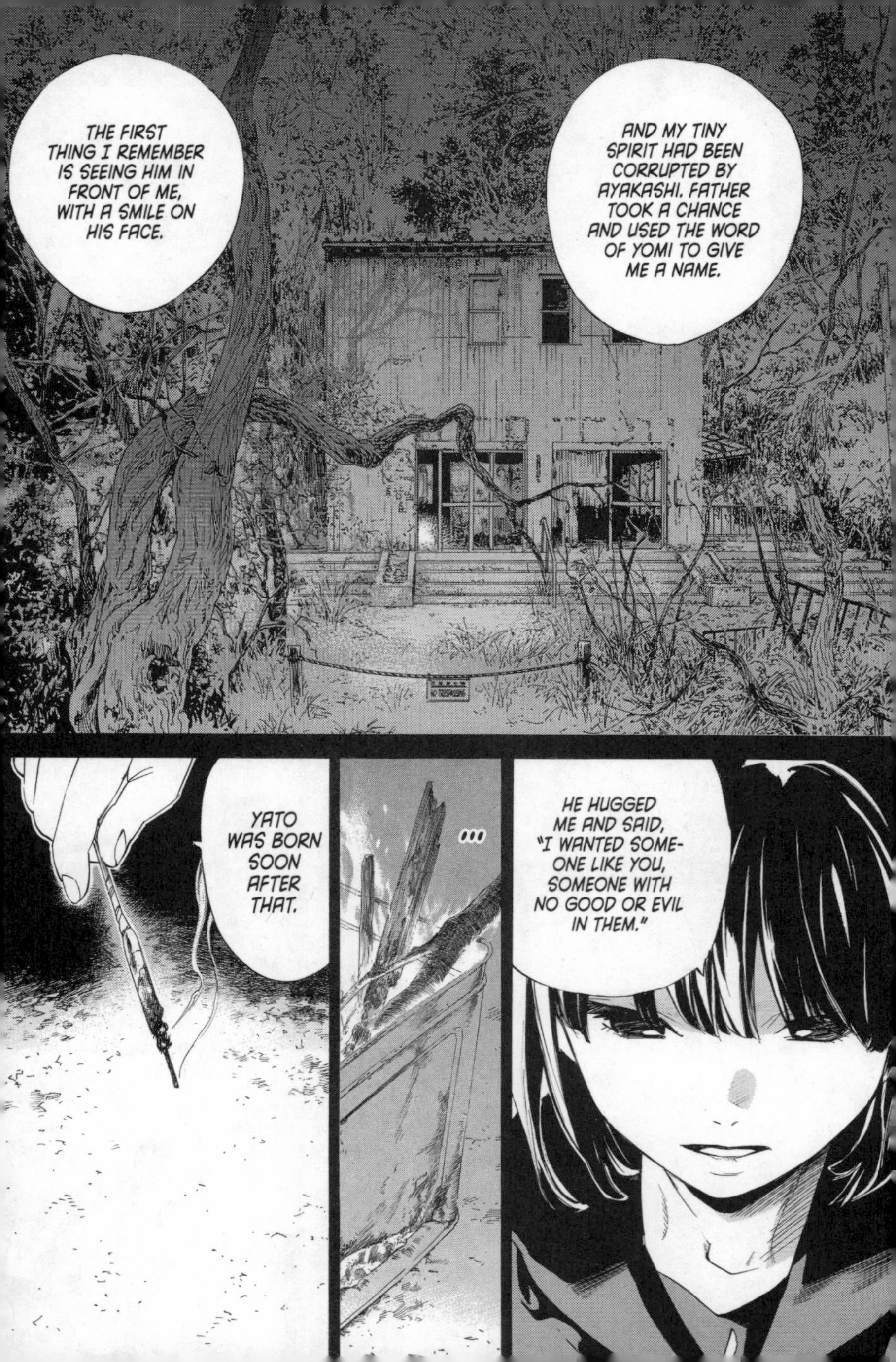
AND MY TINY SPIRIT HAD BEEN CORRUPTED BY AYAKASHI. FATHER TOOK A CHANCE AND USED THE WORD OF YOMI TO GIVE ME A NAME.
THE FIRST THING I REMEMBER IS SEEING HIM IN FRONT OF ME, WITH A SMILE ON HIS FACE.
HE HUGGED ME AND SAID, "I WANTED SOME-ONE LIKE YOU, SOMEONE WITH NO GOOD OR EVIL IN THEM."
...
YATO WAS BORN SOON AFTER THAT.

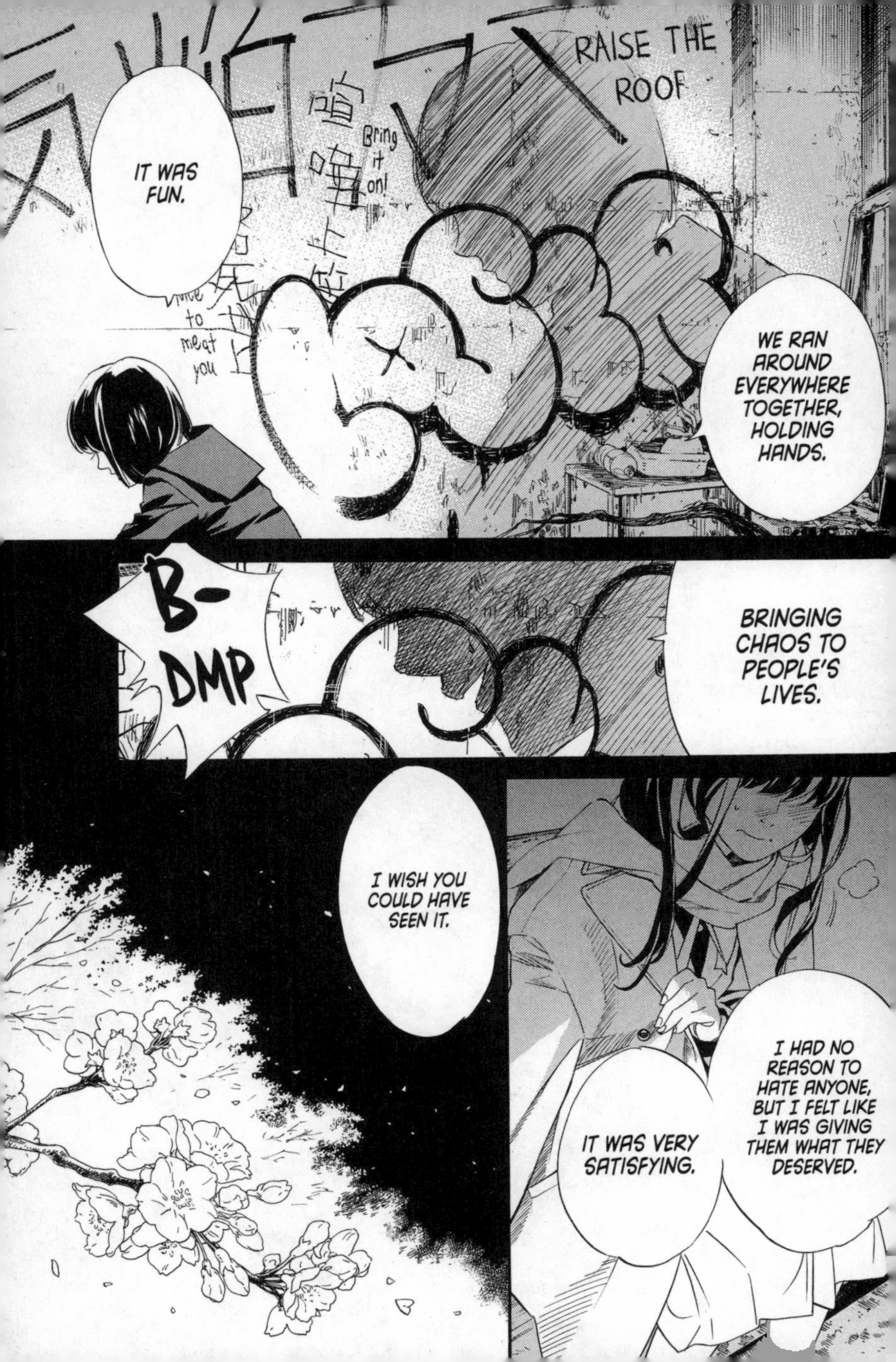
RAISE THE ROOF
WE RAN AROUND EVERYWHERE TOGETHER, HOLDING HANDS.
Bring it on!
IT WAS FUN.
Nice to meat you
BRINGING CHAOS TO PEOPLE'S LIVES.
B-DMP
I HAD NO REASON TO HATE ANYONE, BUT I FELT LIKE I WAS GIVING THEM WHAT THEY DESERVED.
IT WAS VERY SATISFYING.
I WISH YOU COULD HAVE SEEN IT.

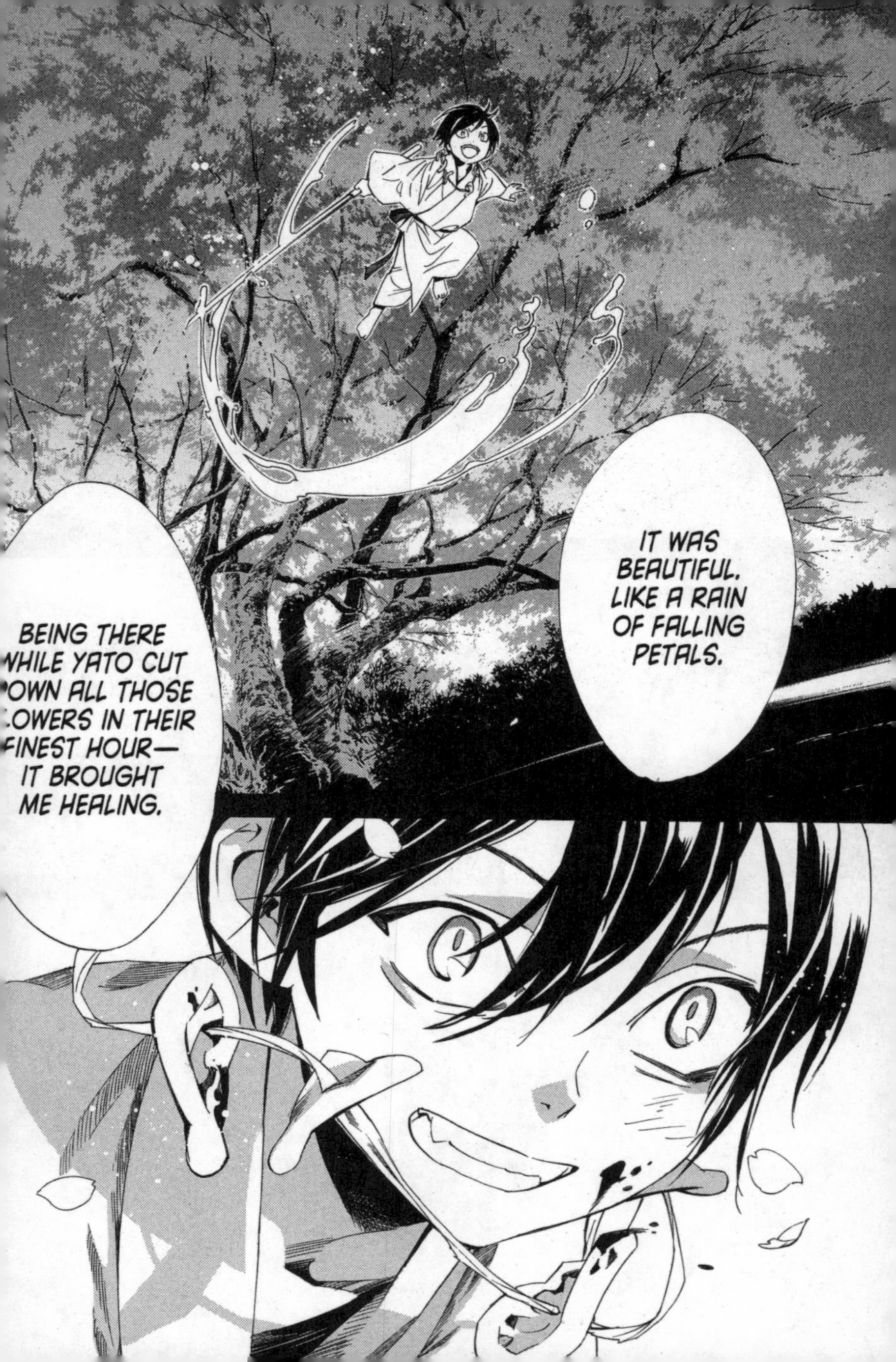
IT WAS BEAUTIFUL. LIKE A RAIN OF FALLING PETALS.
BEING THERE HILE YATO CUT OWN ALL THOSE OWERS IN THEIR FINEST HOUR— IT BROUGHT ME HEALING.

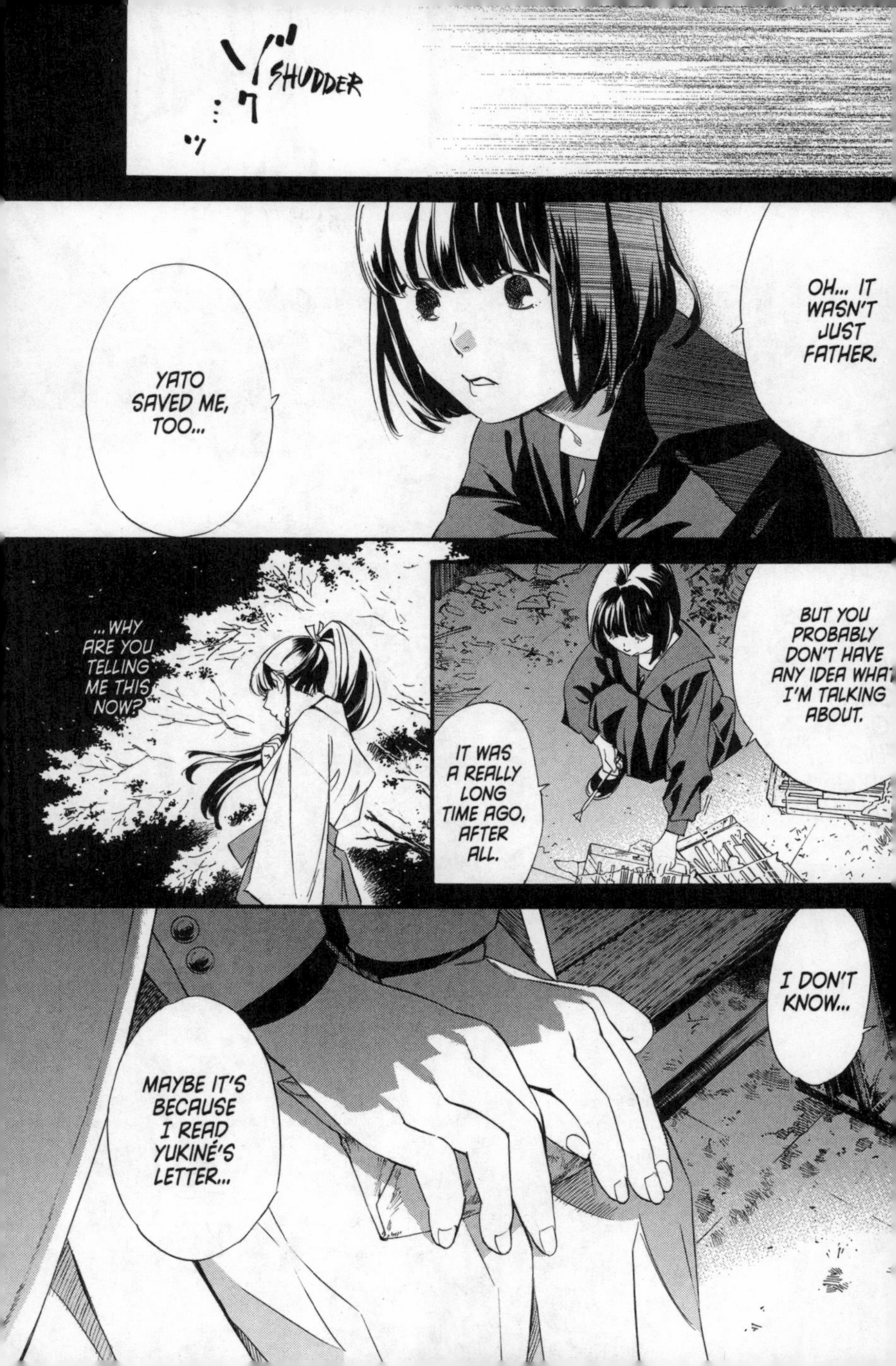
SHUDDER
OH... IT WASN'T JUST FATHER.
YATO SAVED ME, TOO...
BUT YOU PROBABLY DON'T HAVE ANY IDEA WHAT I'M TALKING ABOUT.
IT WAS A REALLY LONG TIME AGO, AFTER ALL.
...WHY ARE YOU TELLING ME THIS NOW?
I DON'T KNOW...
MAYBE IT'S BECAUSE I READ YUKINÉ'S LETTER...

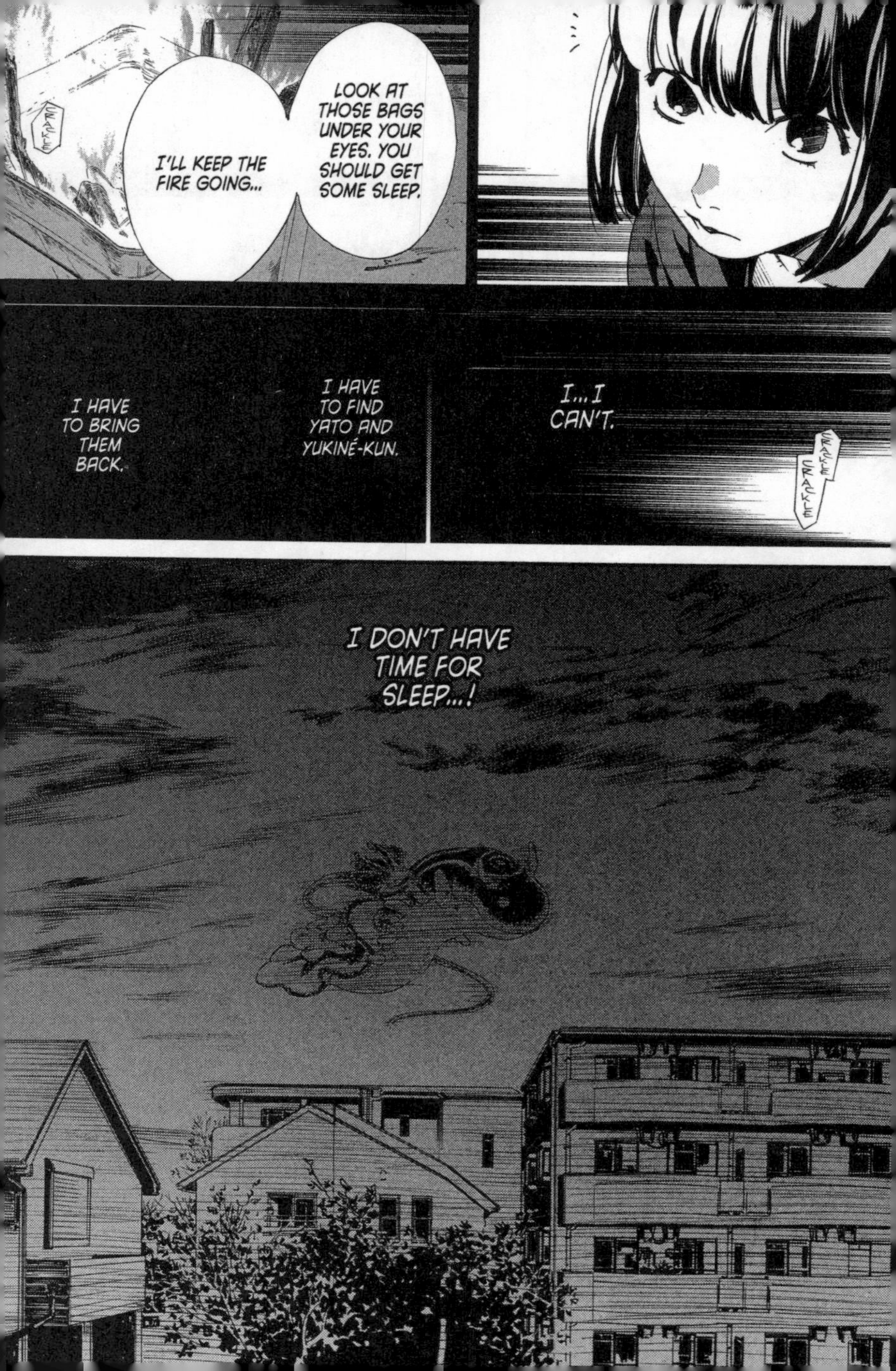
LOOK AT THOSE BAGS UNDER YOUR EYES. YOU SHOULD GET SOME SLEEP.
I'LL KEEP THE FIRE GOING...
CRACKLE
I...I CAN'T.
CRACKLE CRACKLE
I HAVE TO FIND YATO AND YUKINÉ-KUN.
I HAVE TO BRING THEM BACK.
I DON'T HAVE TIME FOR SLEEP...!

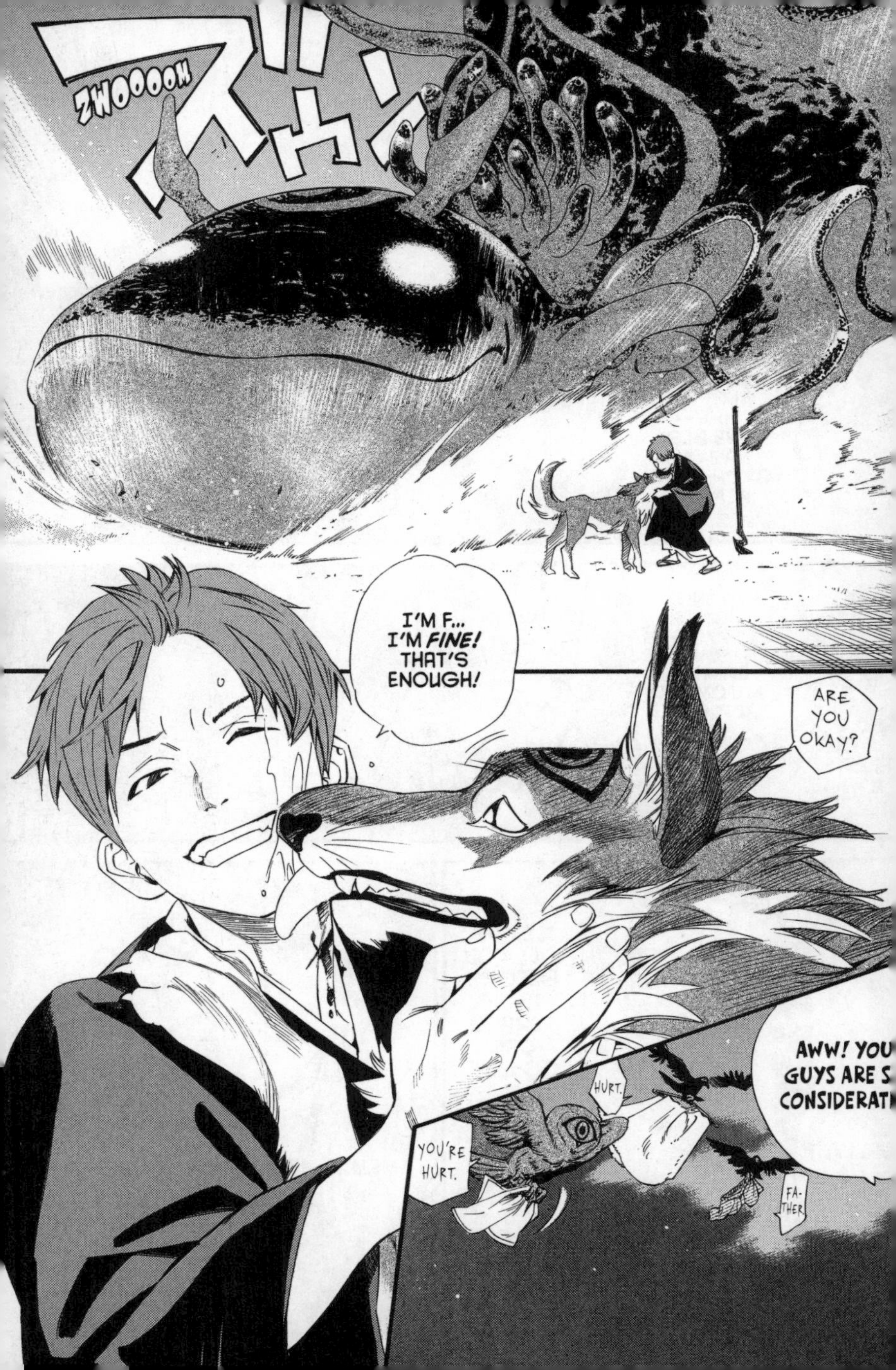
ZWOOOOM
ARE YOU OKAY?
I'M F... I'M FINE! THAT'S ENOUGH!
AWW! YOU GUYS ARE S CONSIDERAT
FA-THER
HURT.
YOU'RE HURT.

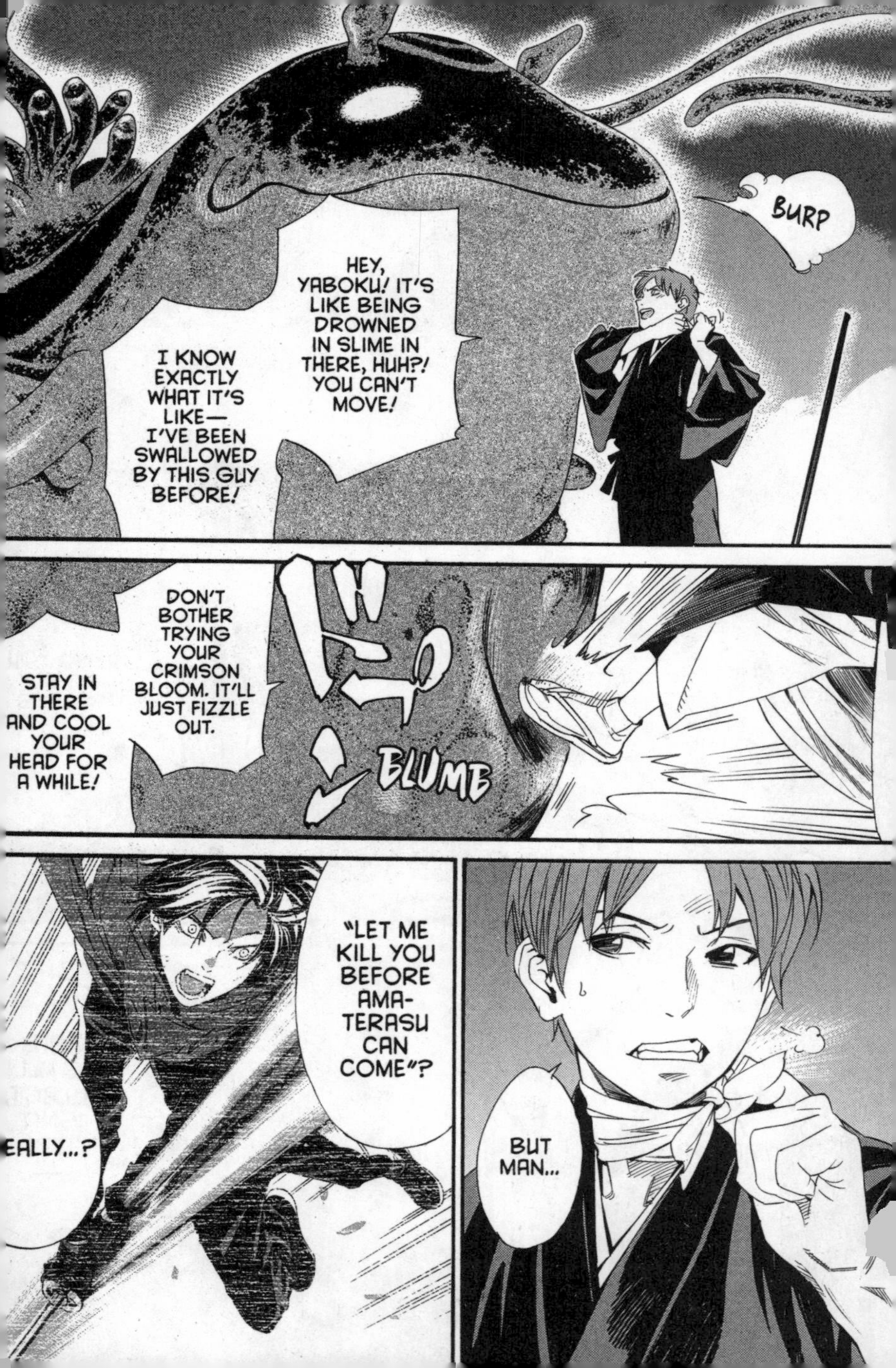
BURP
HEY, YABOKU! IT'S LIKE BEING DROWNED IN SLIME IN THERE, HUH?! YOU CAN'T MOVE!
I KNOW EXACTLY WHAT IT'S LIKE— I'VE BEEN SWALLOWED BY THIS GUY BEFORE!
BLUMB
DON'T BOTHER TRYING YOUR CRIMSON BLOOM. IT'LL JUST FIZZLE OUT.
STAY IN THERE AND COOL YOUR HEAD FOR A WHILE!
BUT MAN...
"LET ME KILL YOU BEFORE AMA-TERASU CAN COME"?
EALLY...?

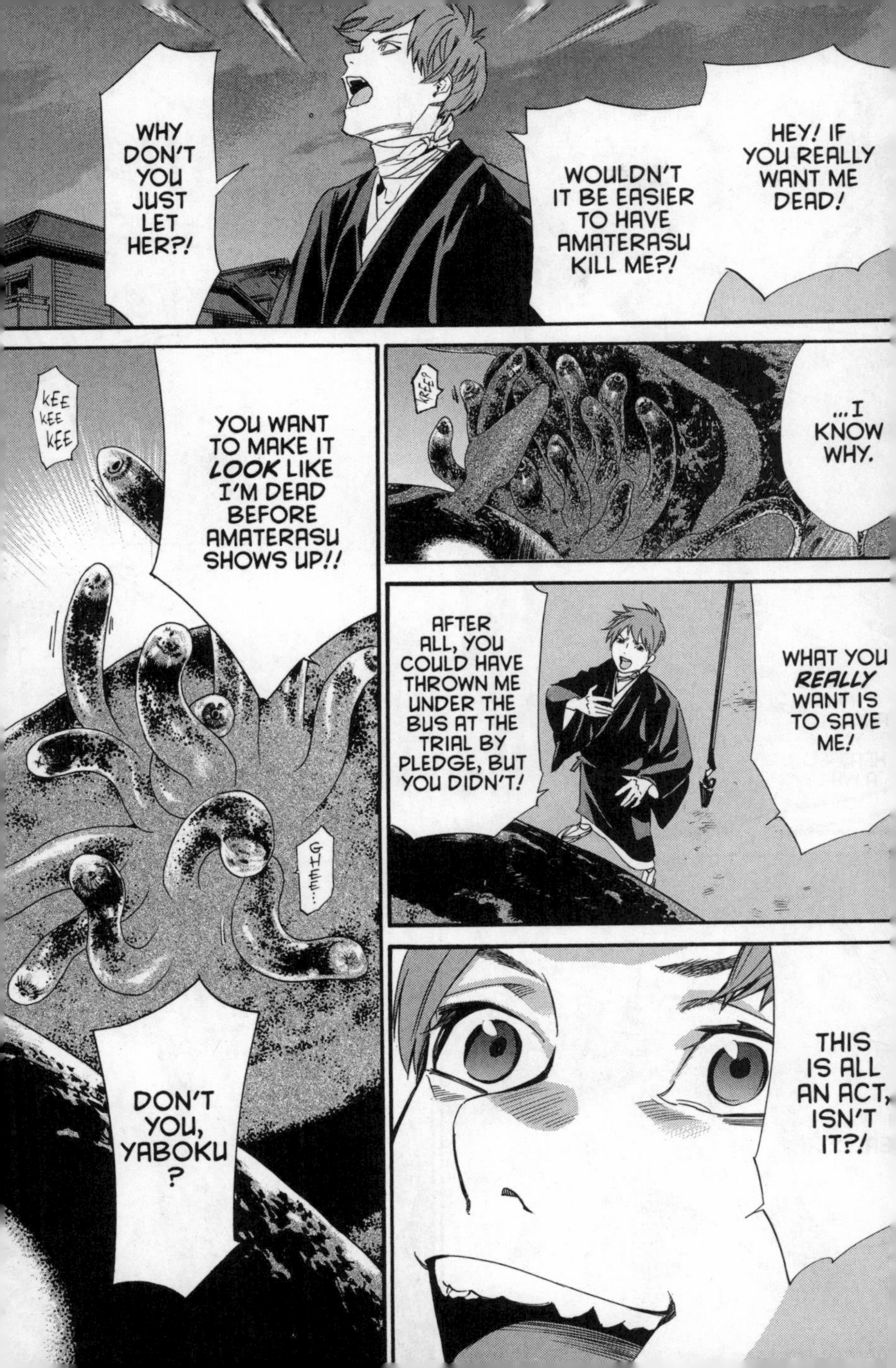

HEY! IF YOU REALLY WANT ME DEAD!
WOULDN'T IT BE EASIER TO HAVE AMATERASU KILL ME?!
WHY DON'T YOU JUST LET HER?!
...I KNOW WHY.
KREE?
WHAT YOU *REALLY* WANT IS TO SAVE ME!
AFTER ALL, YOU COULD HAVE THROWN ME UNDER THE BUS AT THE TRIAL BY PLEDGE, BUT YOU DIDN'T!
THIS IS ALL AN ACT, ISN'T IT?!
YOU WANT TO MAKE IT *LOOK* LIKE I'M DEAD BEFORE AMATERASU SHOWS UP!!
KEE KEE KEE
GHEE...
DON'T YOU, YABOKU?

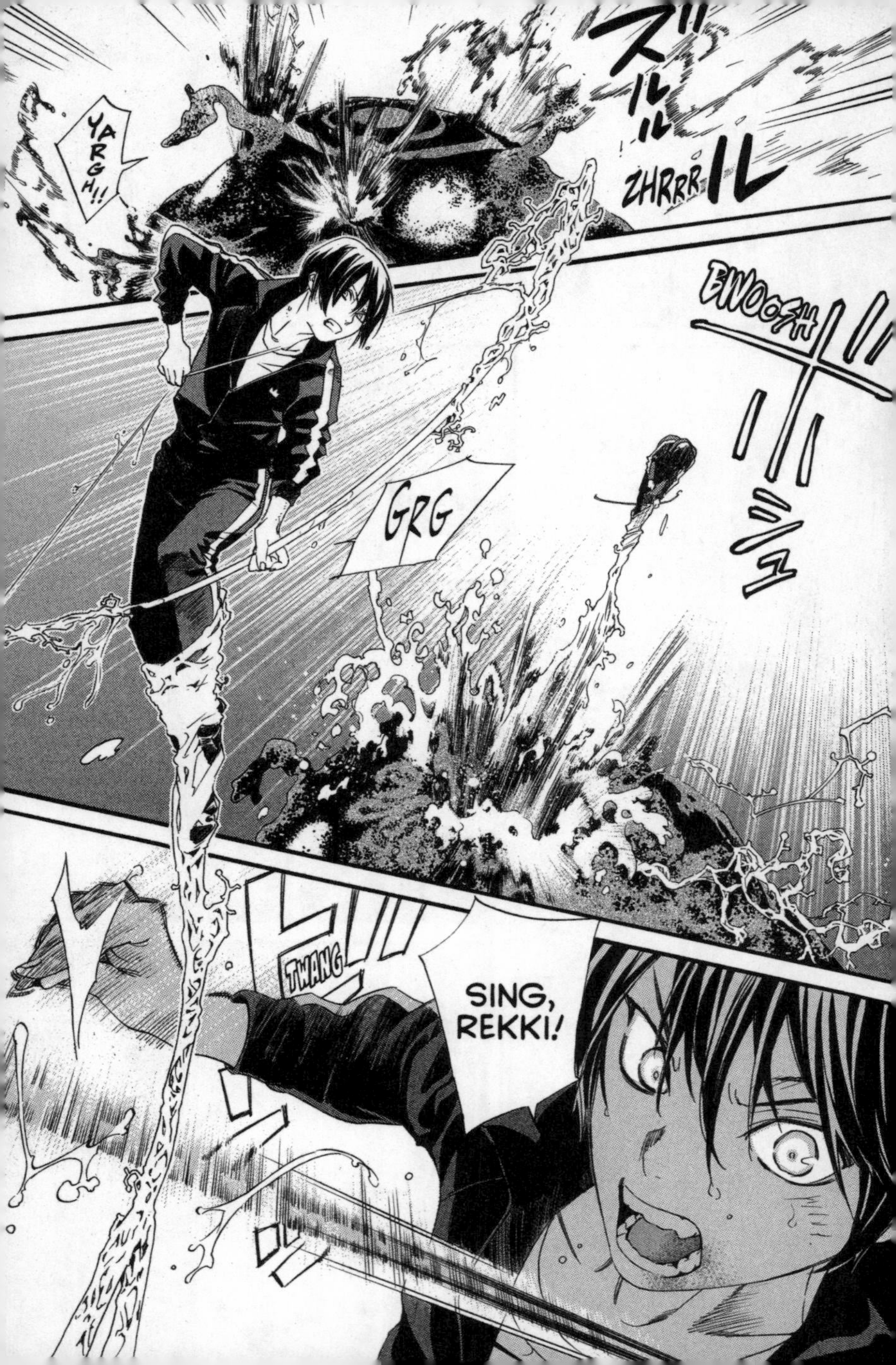
ズルルル
ZHRRRR
YARGH!!
ザシュ
BWOOSH
GRG
SING, REKKI!
TWANG

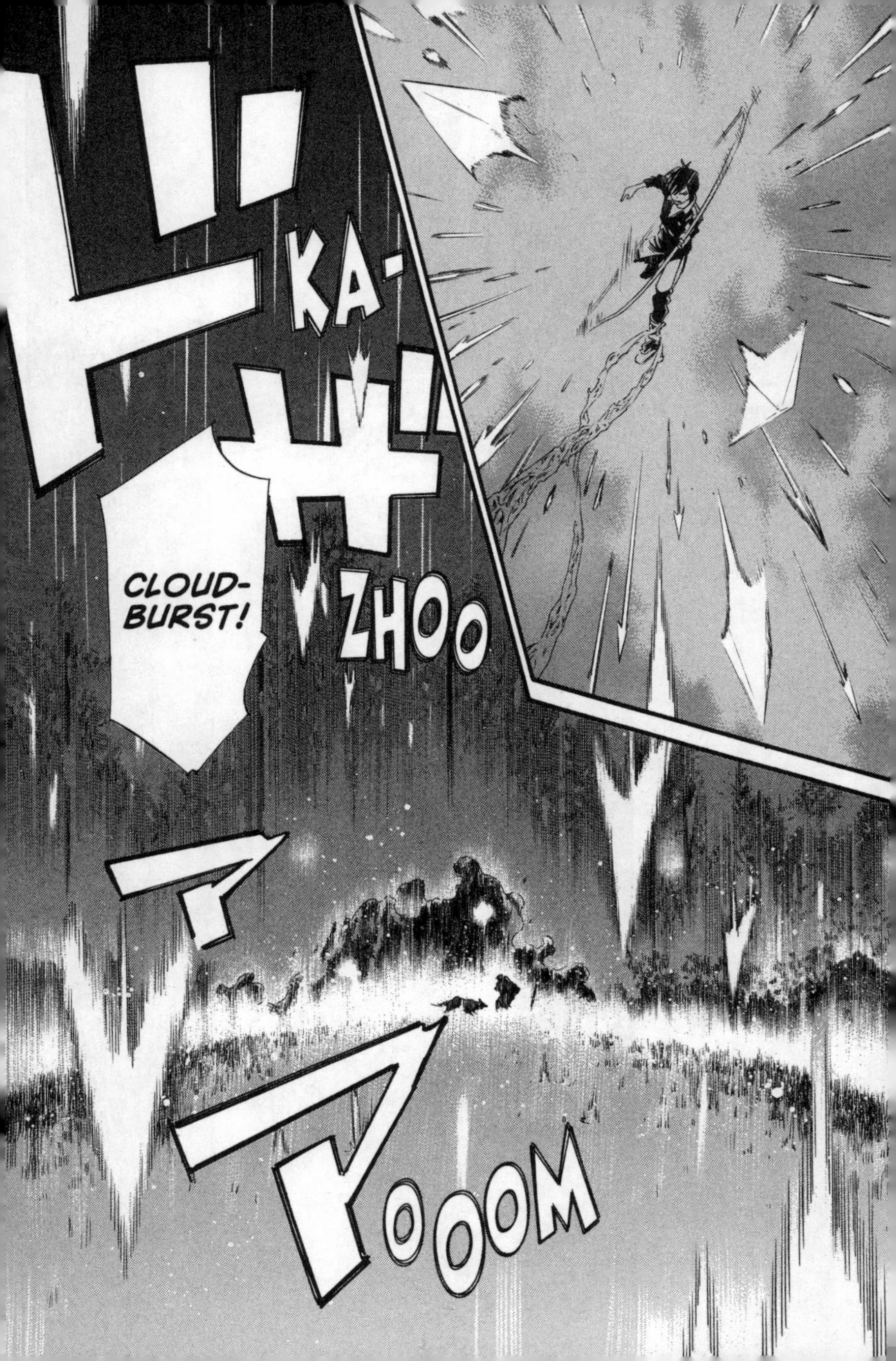
KA-
CLOUD-
BURST!
ZHOO
OOOM

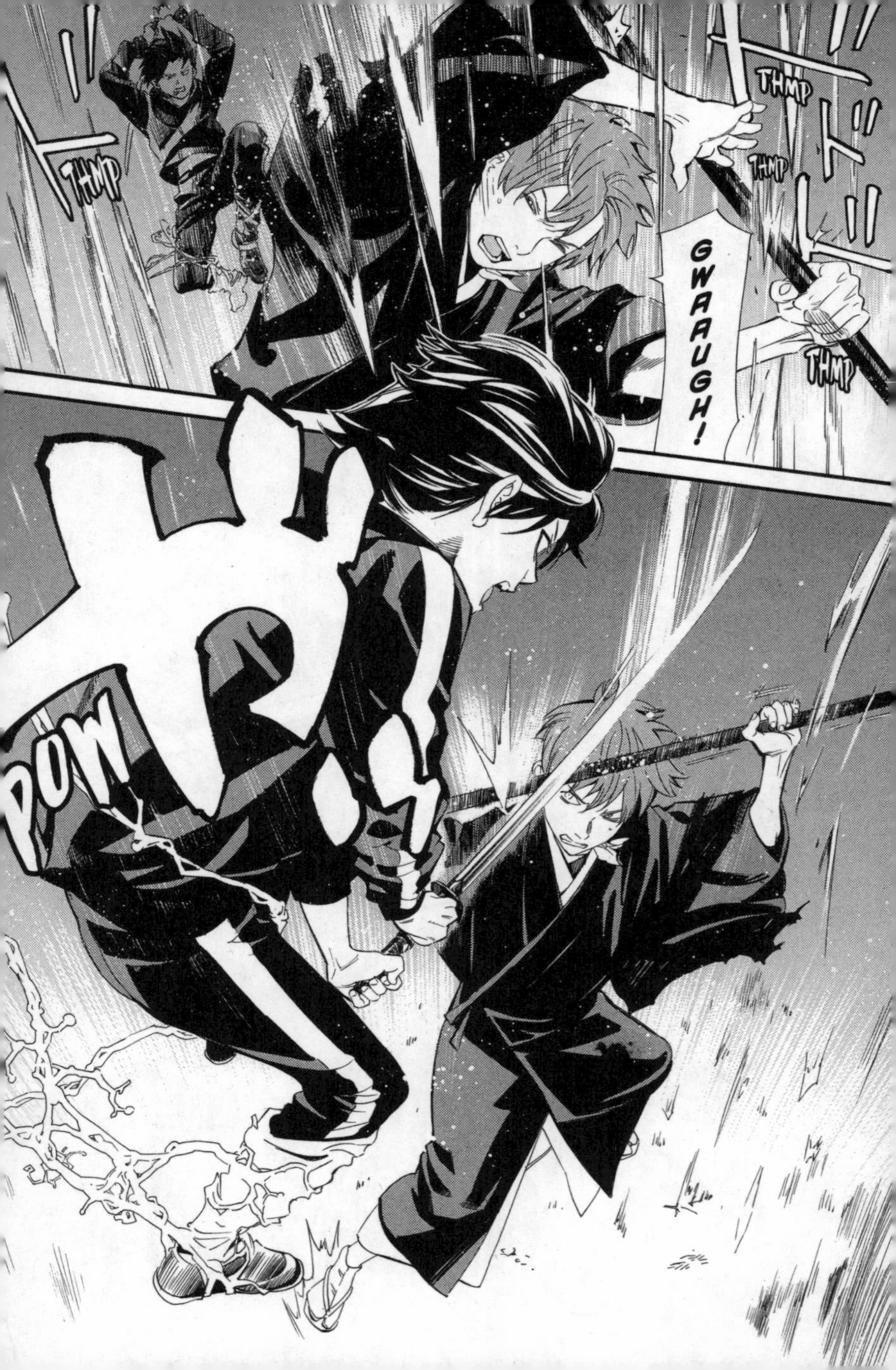
THMP
THMP
GWAAUGH!
THMP
THMP
POW

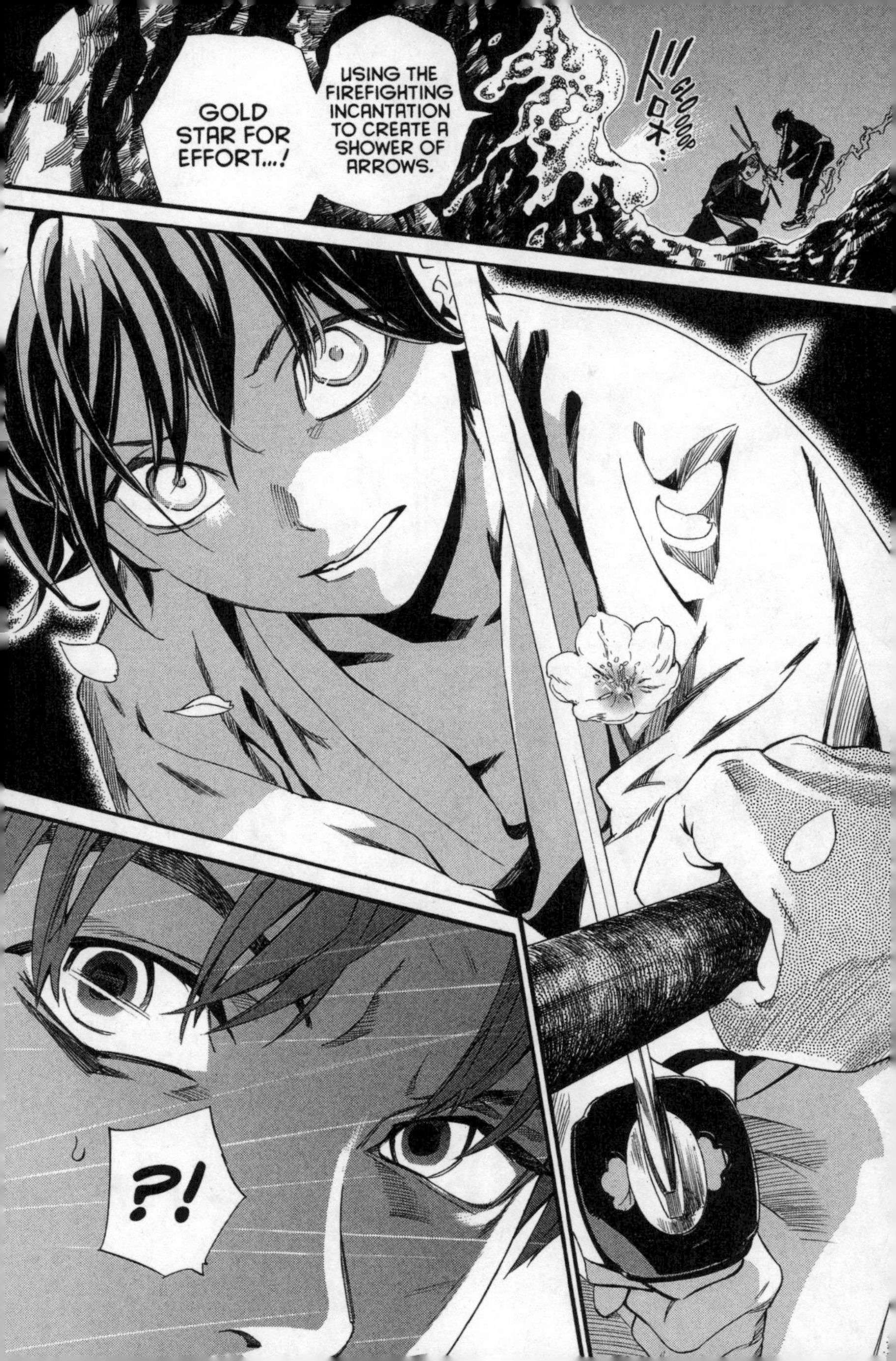
USING THE FIREFIGHTING INCANTATION TO CREATE A SHOWER OF ARROWS.
GOLD STAR FOR EFFORT...!
GLOOOOOP
?!

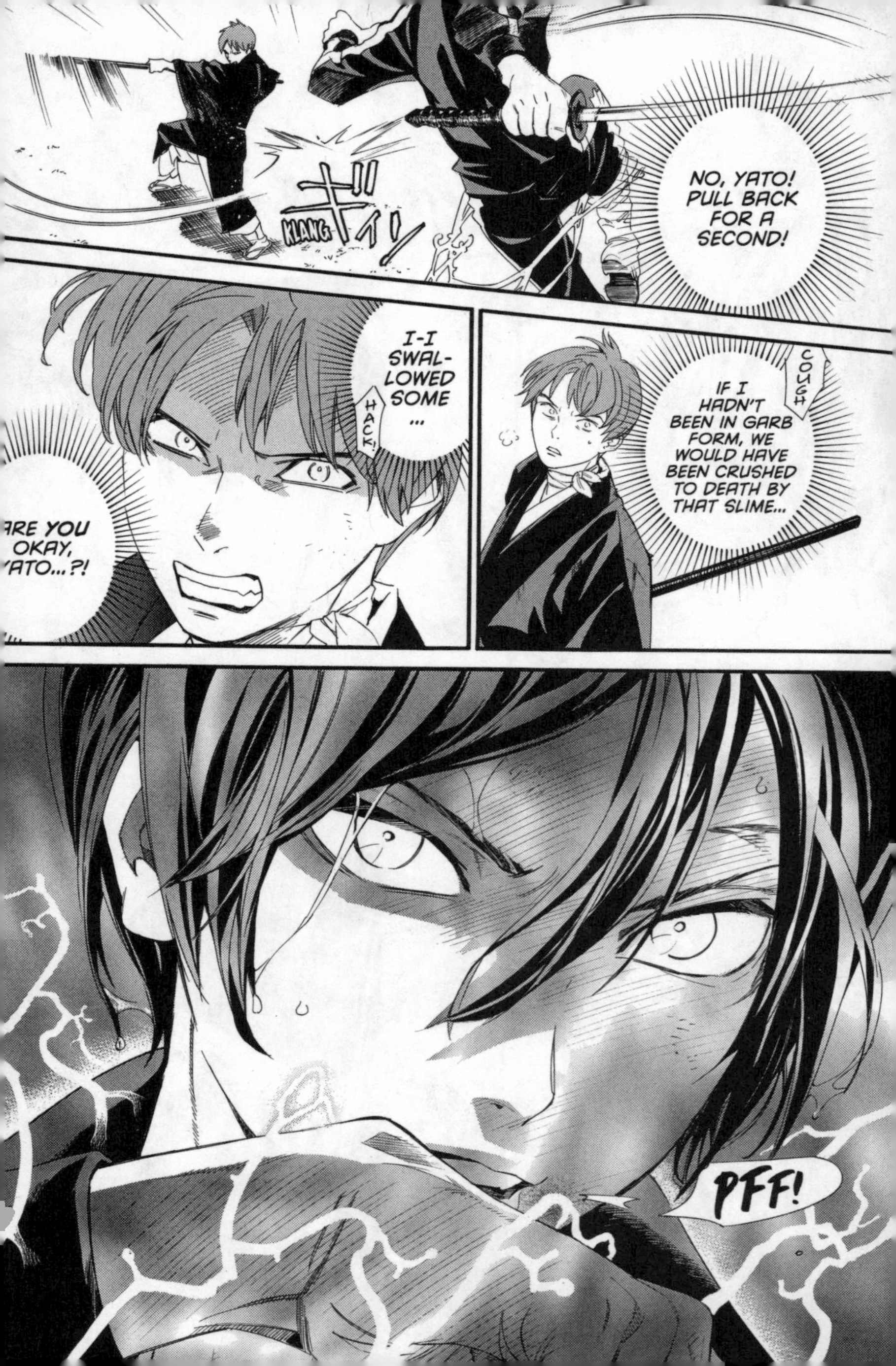
NO, YATO! PULL BACK FOR A SECOND!
KLANG
ギイン
COUGH
IF I HADN'T BEEN IN GARB FORM, WE WOULD HAVE BEEN CRUSHED TO DEATH BY THAT SLIME...
I-I SWAL-LOWED SOME ...
HACK!
ARE YOU OKAY, YATO...?!
PFF!

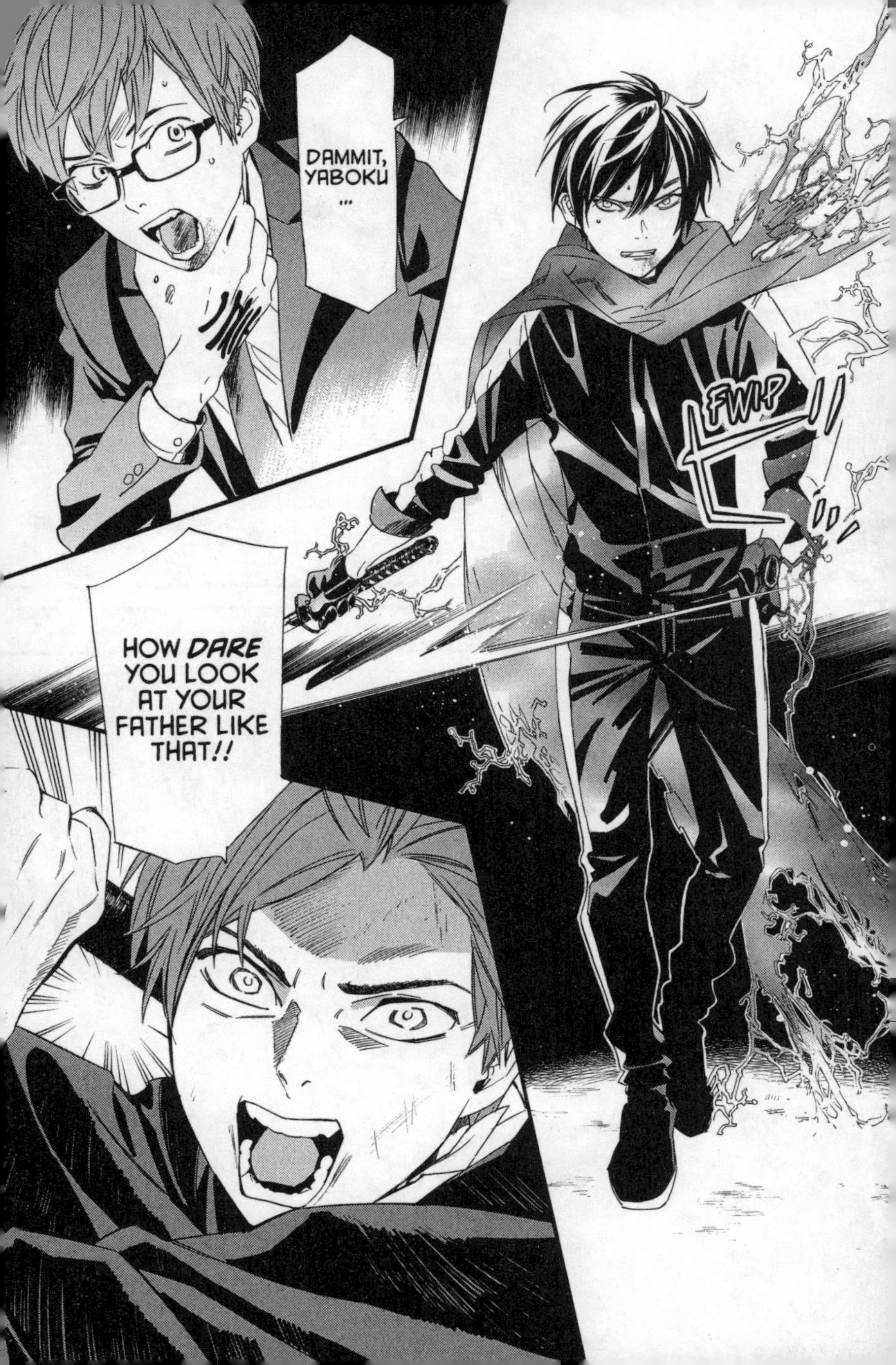
FWIP
DAMMIT, YABOKU ...
HOW DARE YOU LOOK AT YOUR FATHER LIKE THAT!!

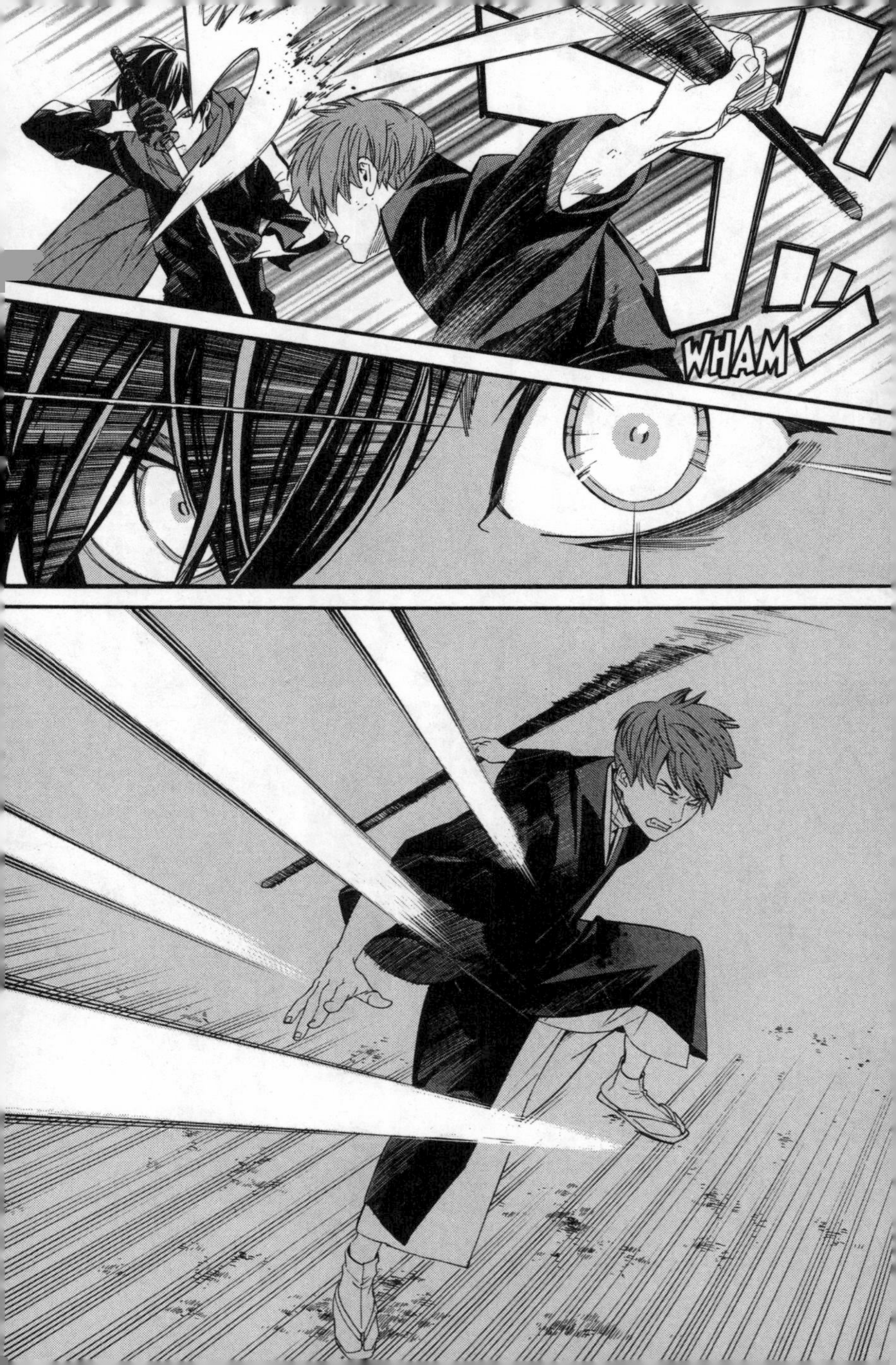
WHAM

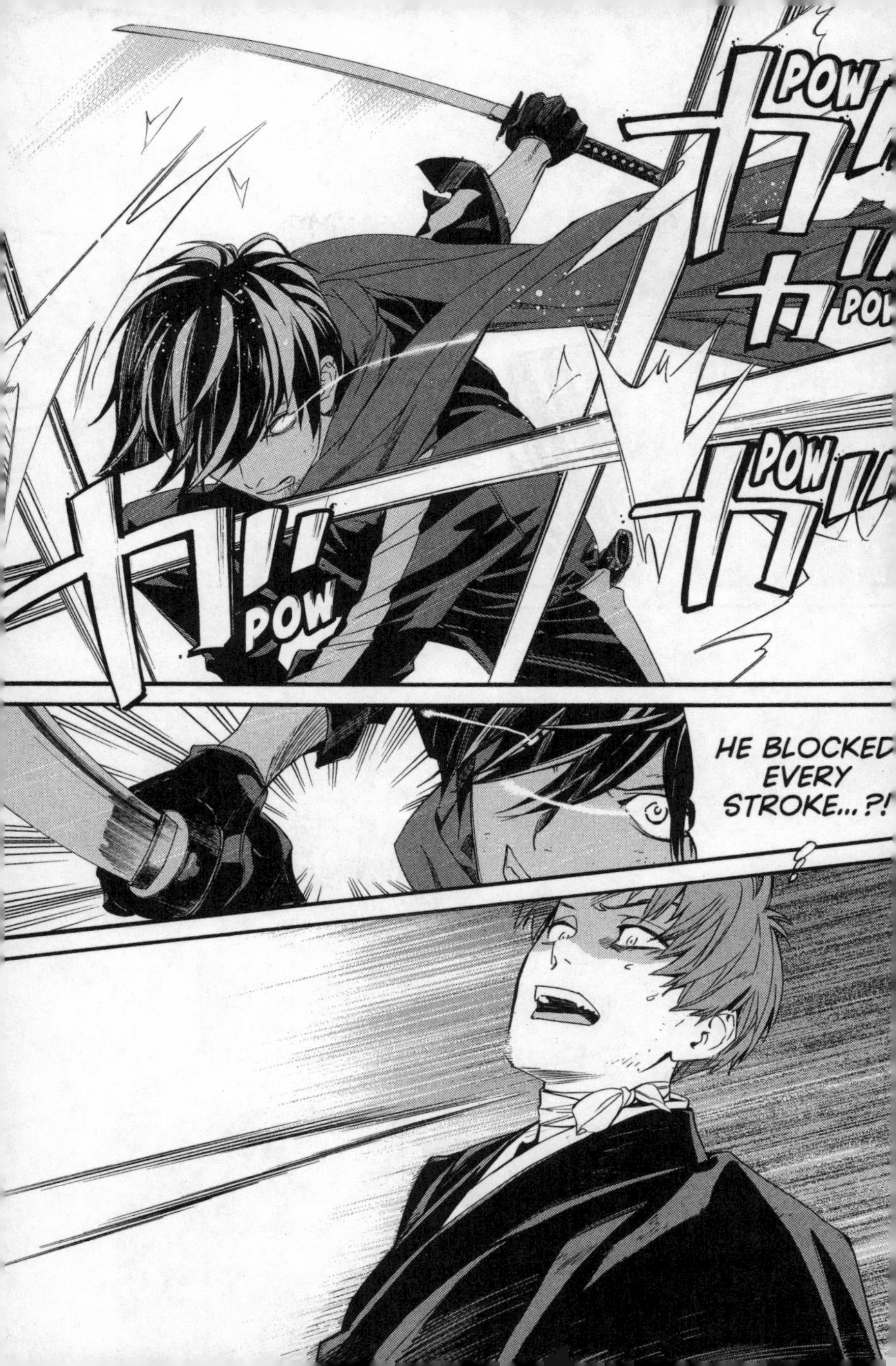
POW
POW
POW
POW
HE BLOCKED EVERY STROKE...?!

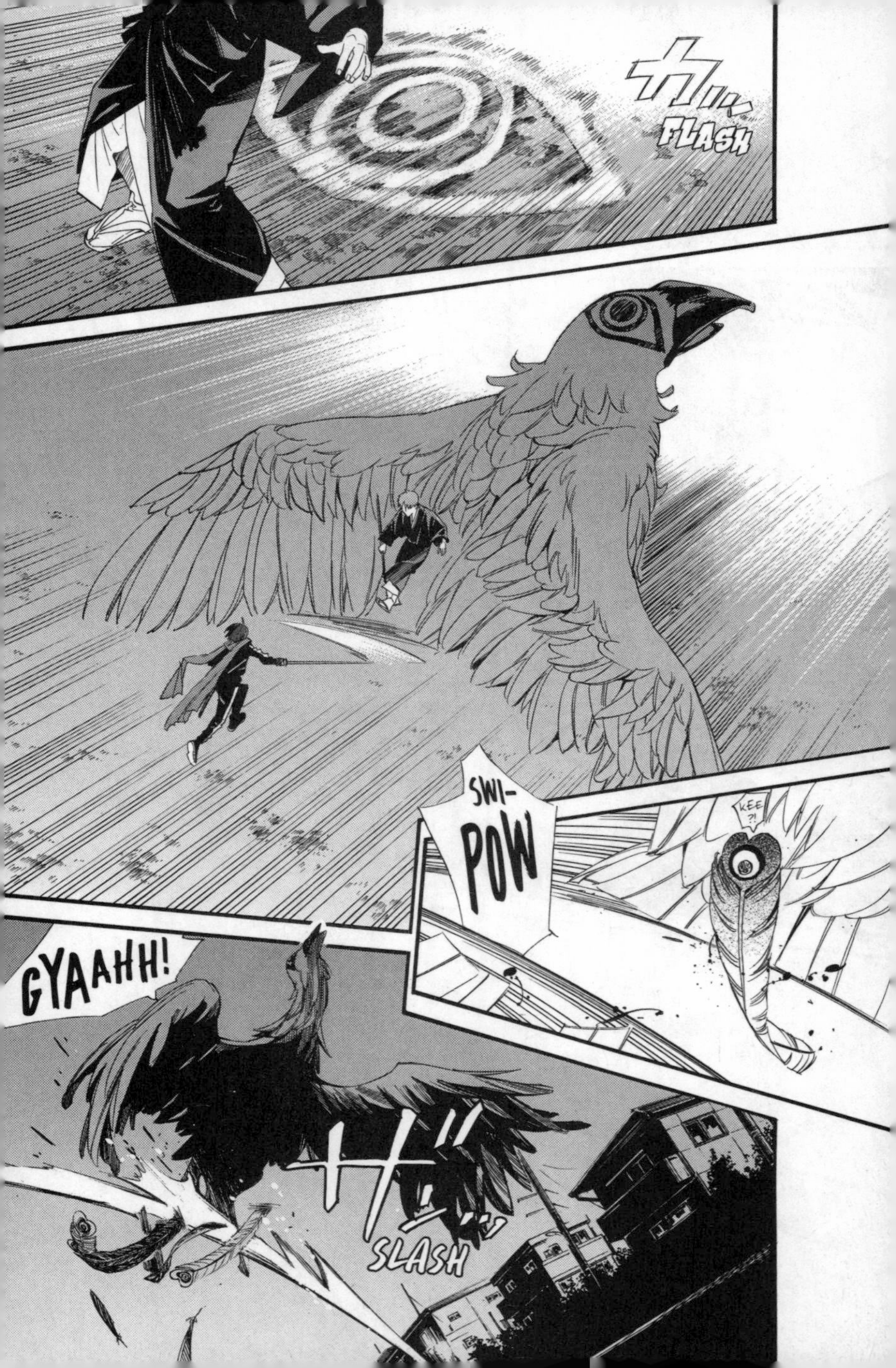
FLASH
SWI-
POW
KEE ?!
GYAAHH!
SLASH

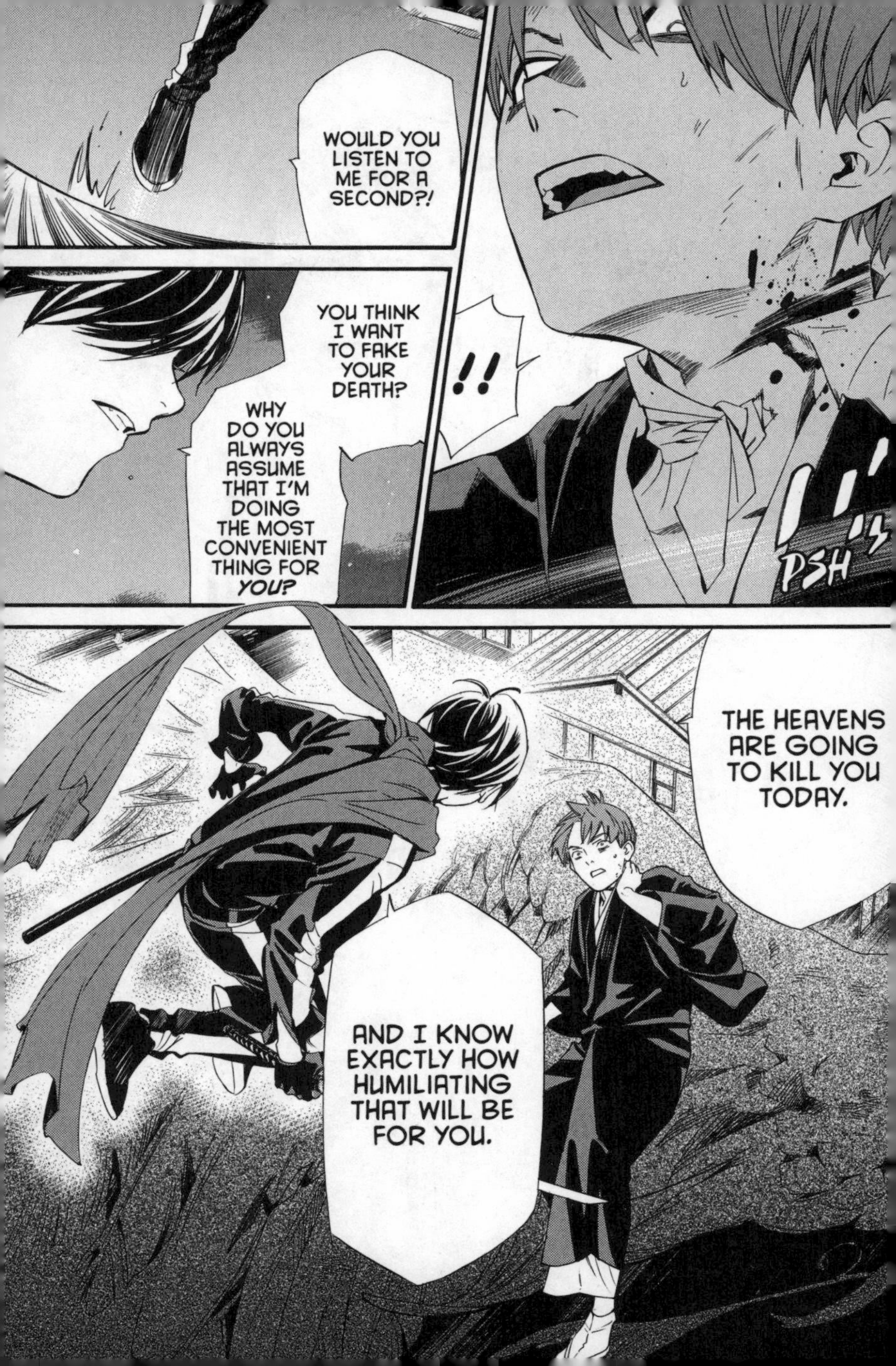
WOULD YOU LISTEN TO ME FOR A SECOND?!
YOU THINK I WANT TO FAKE YOUR DEATH?
WHY DO YOU ALWAYS ASSUME THAT I'M DOING THE MOST CONVENIENT THING FOR *YOU*?
!!
PSH
THE HEAVENS ARE GOING TO KILL YOU TODAY.
AND I KNOW EXACTLY HOW HUMILIATING THAT WILL BE FOR YOU.

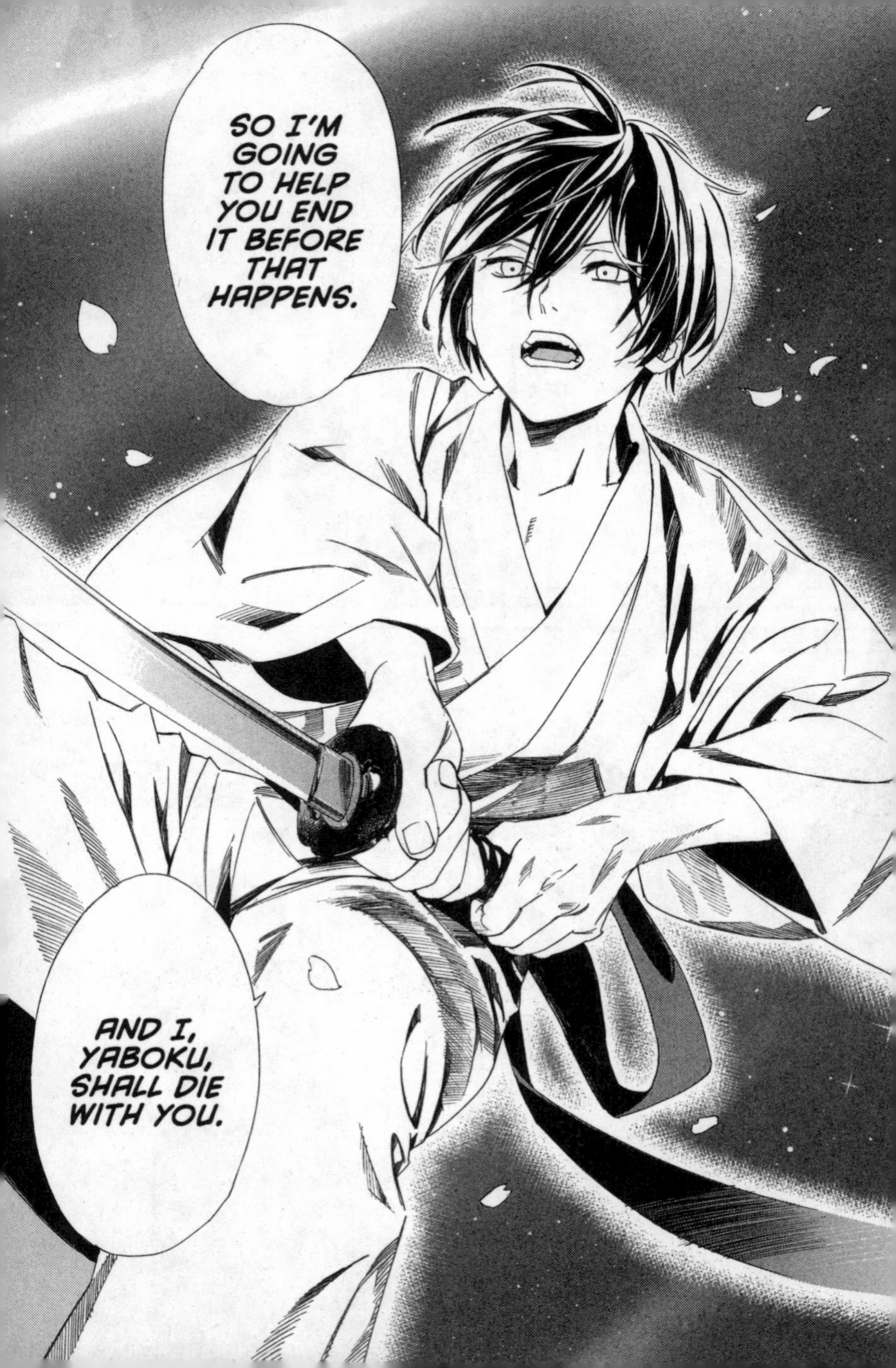
SO I'M GOING TO HELP YOU END IT BEFORE THAT HAPPENS.
AND I, YABOKU, SHALL DIE WITH YOU.

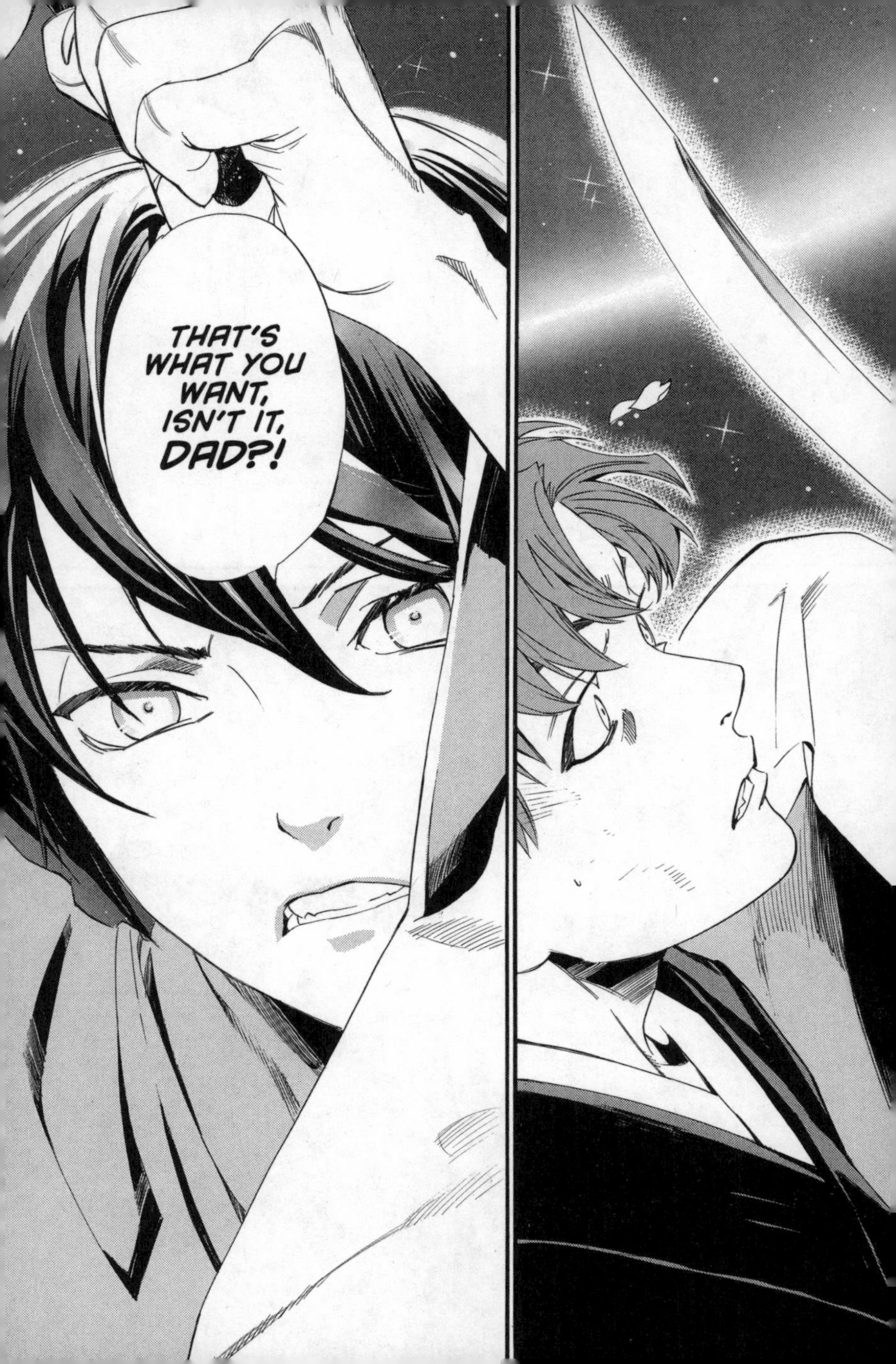
THAT'S WHAT YOU WANT, ISN'T IT, DAD?!

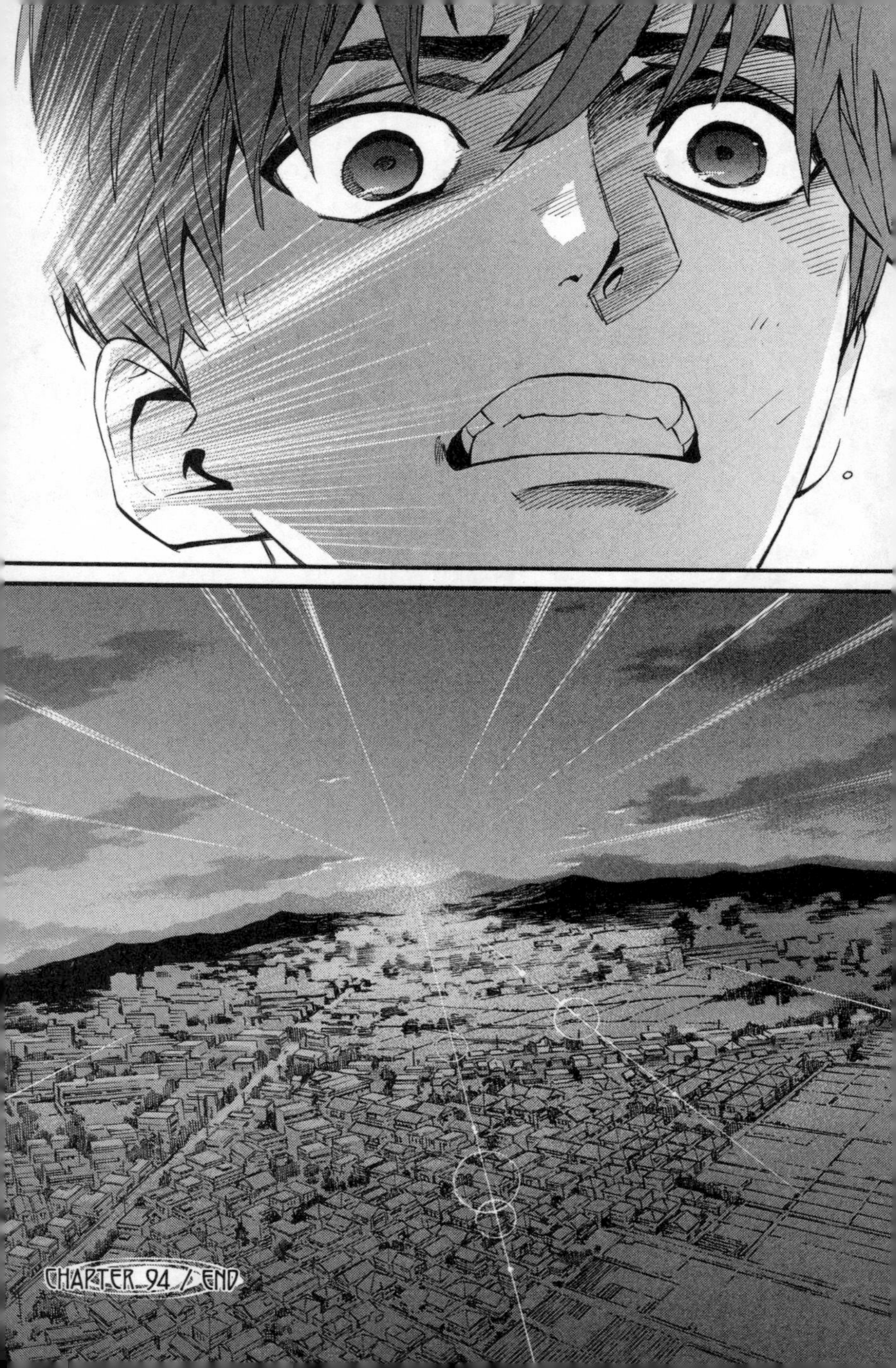
CHAPTER 94 / END

野良神

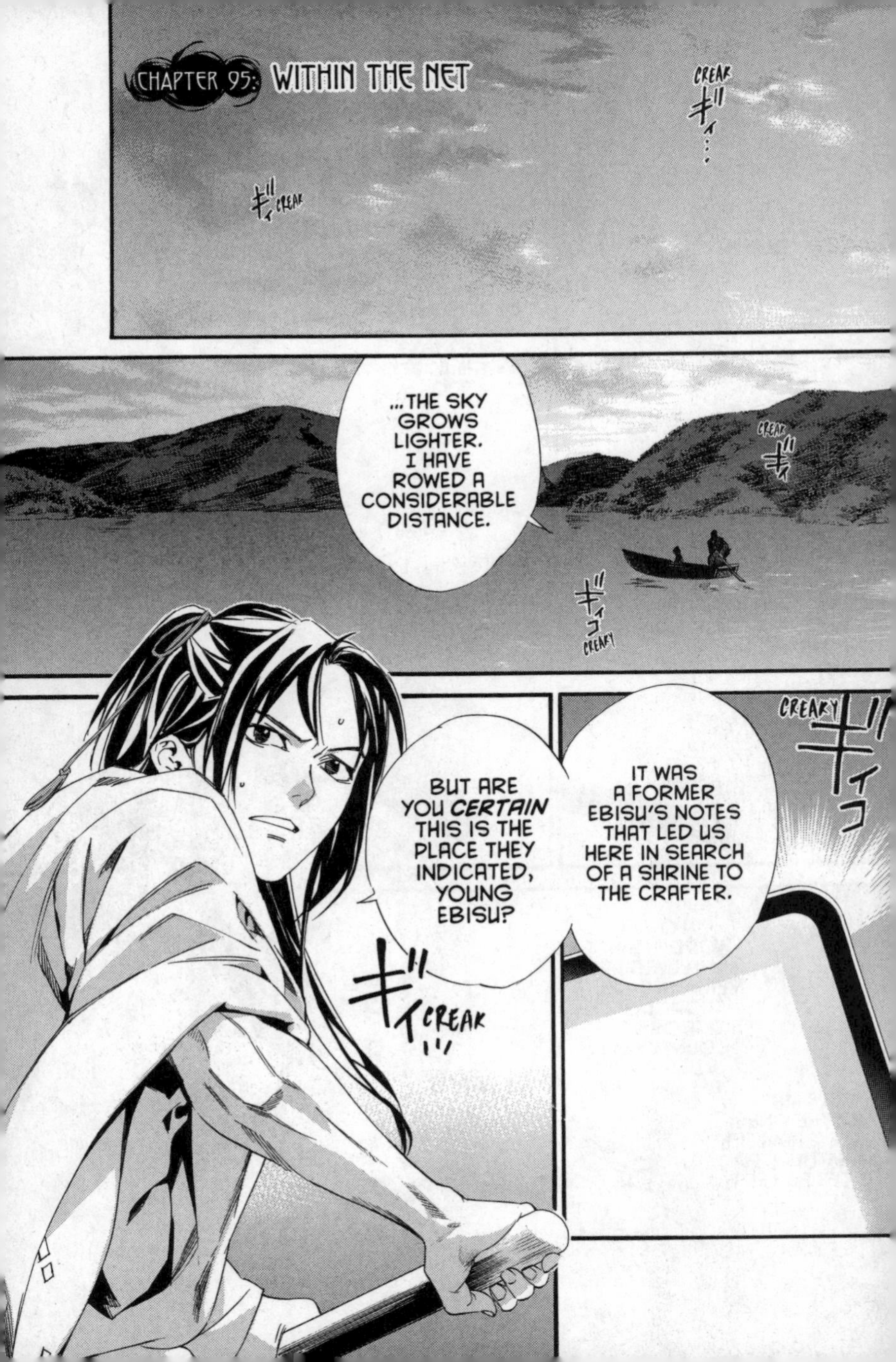
CHAPTER 95: WITHIN THE NET
CREAK ギィ…
ギィ CREAK
CREAK ギィ
...THE SKY GROWS LIGHTER. I HAVE ROWED A CONSIDERABLE DISTANCE.
ギィコ CREAKY
CREAKY ギィコ
IT WAS A FORMER EBISU'S NOTES THAT LED US HERE IN SEARCH OF A SHRINE TO THE CRAFTER.
BUT ARE YOU *CERTAIN* THIS IS THE PLACE THEY INDICATED, YOUNG EBISU?
ギィ CREAK

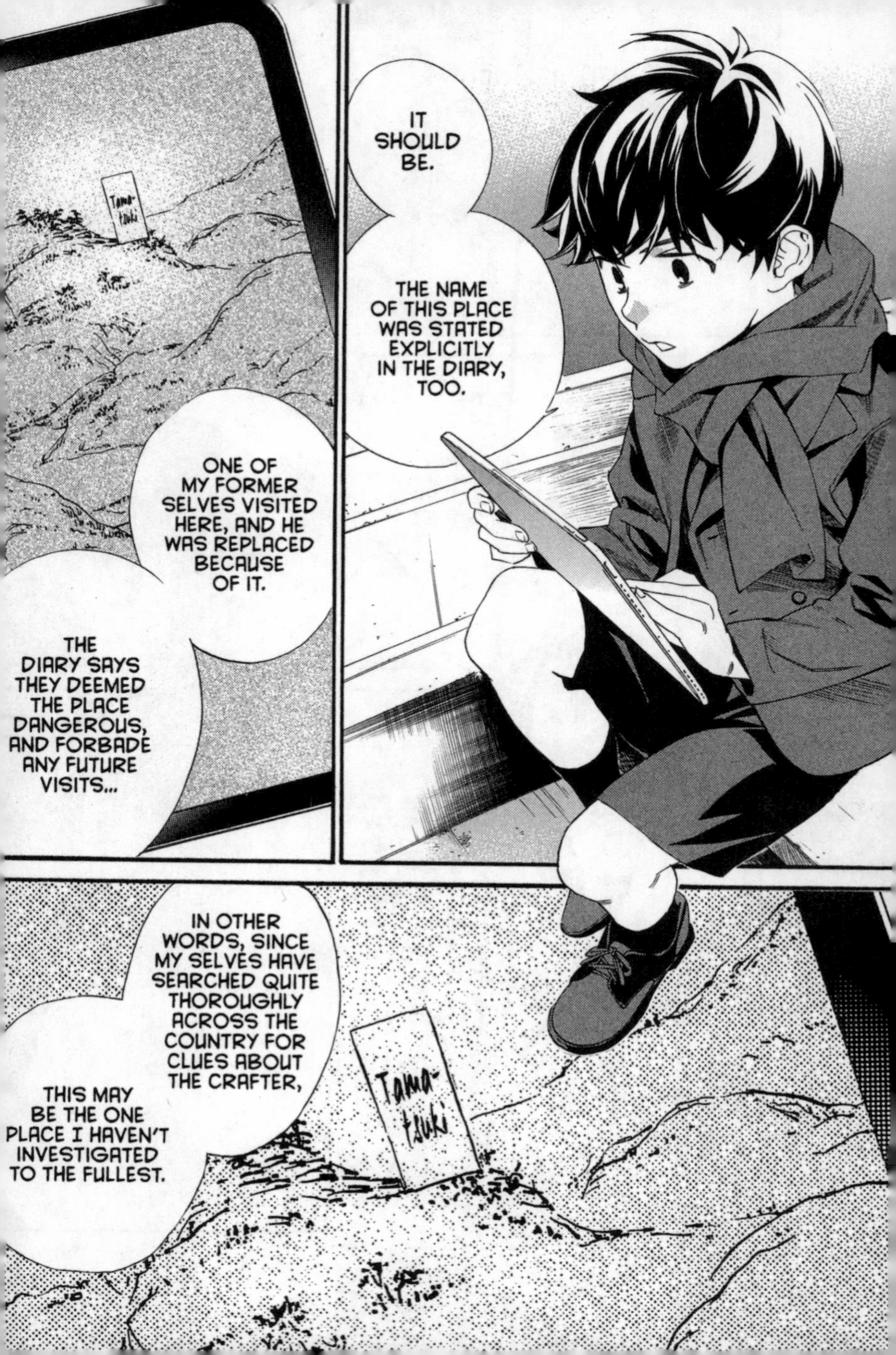
IT SHOULD BE.
THE NAME OF THIS PLACE WAS STATED EXPLICITLY IN THE DIARY, TOO.
Tama-tsuki
ONE OF MY FORMER SELVES VISITED HERE, AND HE WAS REPLACED BECAUSE OF IT.
THE DIARY SAYS THEY DEEMED THE PLACE DANGEROUS, AND FORBADE ANY FUTURE VISITS...
IN OTHER WORDS, SINCE MY SELVES HAVE SEARCHED QUITE THOROUGHLY ACROSS THE COUNTRY FOR CLUES ABOUT THE CRAFTER,
THIS MAY BE THE ONE PLACE I HAVEN'T INVESTIGATED TO THE FULLEST.
Tama-tsuki

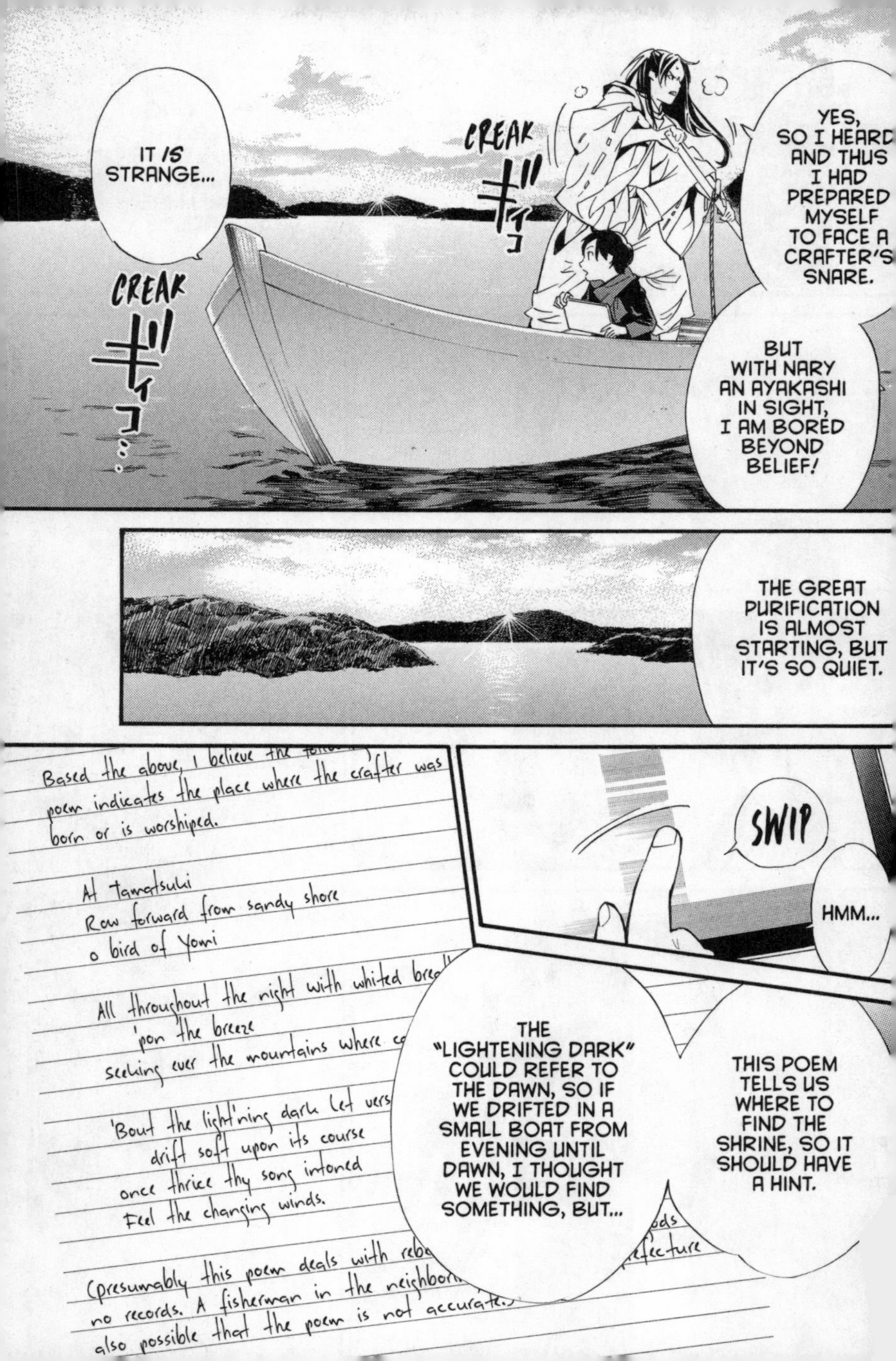
YES, SO I HEARD AND THUS I HAD PREPARED MYSELF TO FACE A CRAFTER'S SNARE.
BUT WITH NARY AN AYAKASHI IN SIGHT, I AM BORED BEYOND BELIEF!
CREAK ギィコ
IT IS STRANGE...
CREAK ギィコ…
THE GREAT PURIFICATION IS ALMOST STARTING, BUT IT'S SO QUIET.
SWIP
HMM...
THIS POEM TELLS US WHERE TO FIND THE SHRINE, SO IT SHOULD HAVE A HINT.
THE "LIGHTENING DARK" COULD REFER TO THE DAWN, SO IF WE DRIFTED IN A SMALL BOAT FROM EVENING UNTIL DAWN, I THOUGHT WE WOULD FIND SOMETHING, BUT...
Based the above, I believe the
poem indicates the place where the crafter was
born or is worshiped.
At Tamatsuki
Row forward from sandy shore
a bird of Yomi
All throughout the night with whited
'pon the breeze
seeking over the mountains where
'Bout the light'ning dark let
drift soft upon its course
once thrice thy song intoned
Feel the changing winds.
(presumably this poem deals with
no records. A fisherman in the
also possible that the poem is not accurate.)

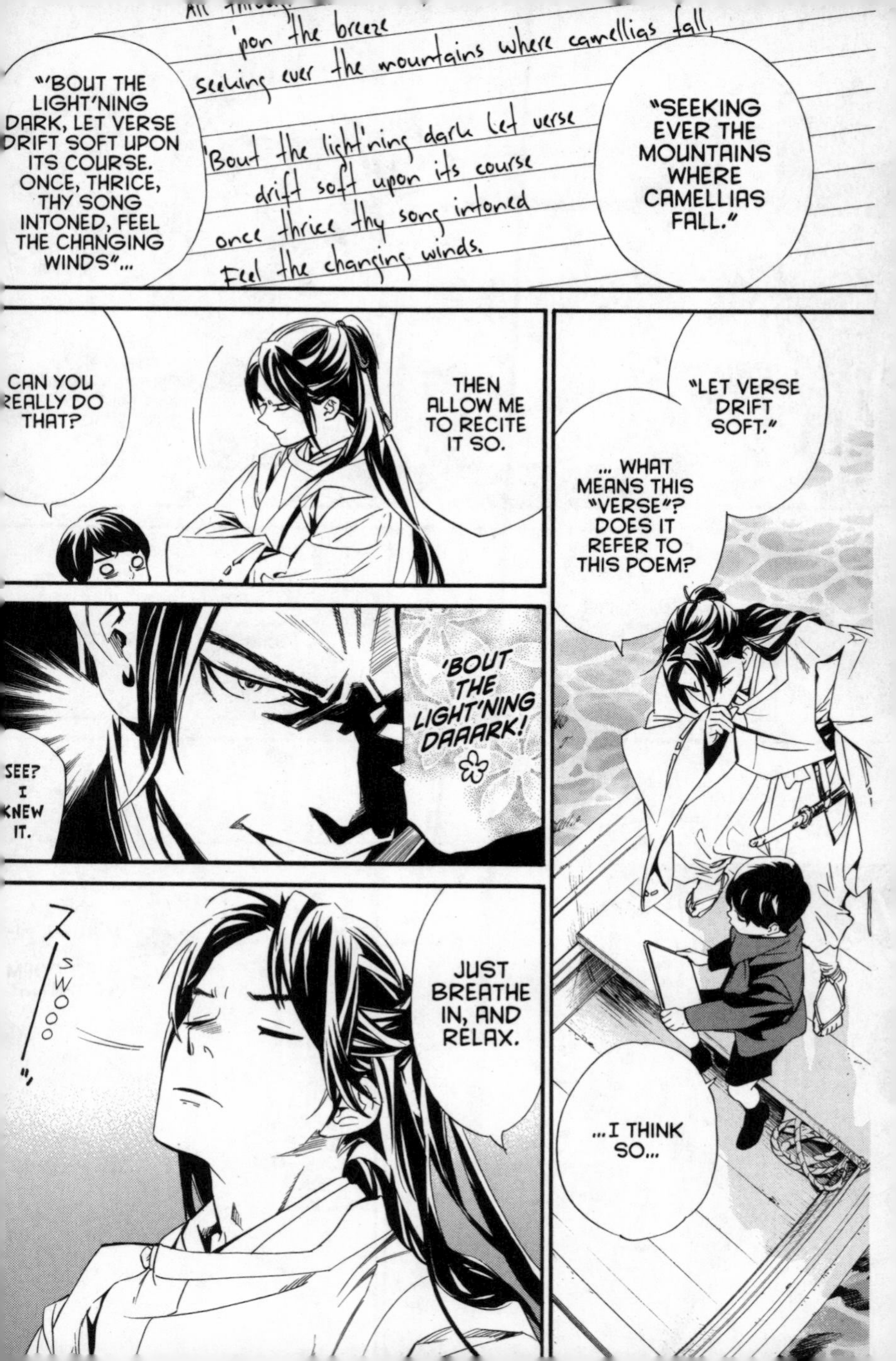
"SEEKING EVER THE MOUNTAINS WHERE CAMELLIAS FALL."
'pon the breeze
seeking ever the mountains where camellias fall,
'Bout the light'ning dark let verse
drift soft upon its course
once thrice thy song intoned
Feel the changing winds.
"'BOUT THE LIGHT'NING DARK, LET VERSE DRIFT SOFT UPON ITS COURSE. ONCE, THRICE, THY SONG INTONED, FEEL THE CHANGING WINDS"...
"LET VERSE DRIFT SOFT."
... WHAT MEANS THIS "VERSE"? DOES IT REFER TO THIS POEM?
...I THINK SO...
THEN ALLOW ME TO RECITE IT SO.
CAN YOU REALLY DO THAT?
'BOUT THE LIGHT'NING DAAARK!
SEE? I KNEW IT.
JUST BREATHE IN, AND RELAX.
ス SWOOO

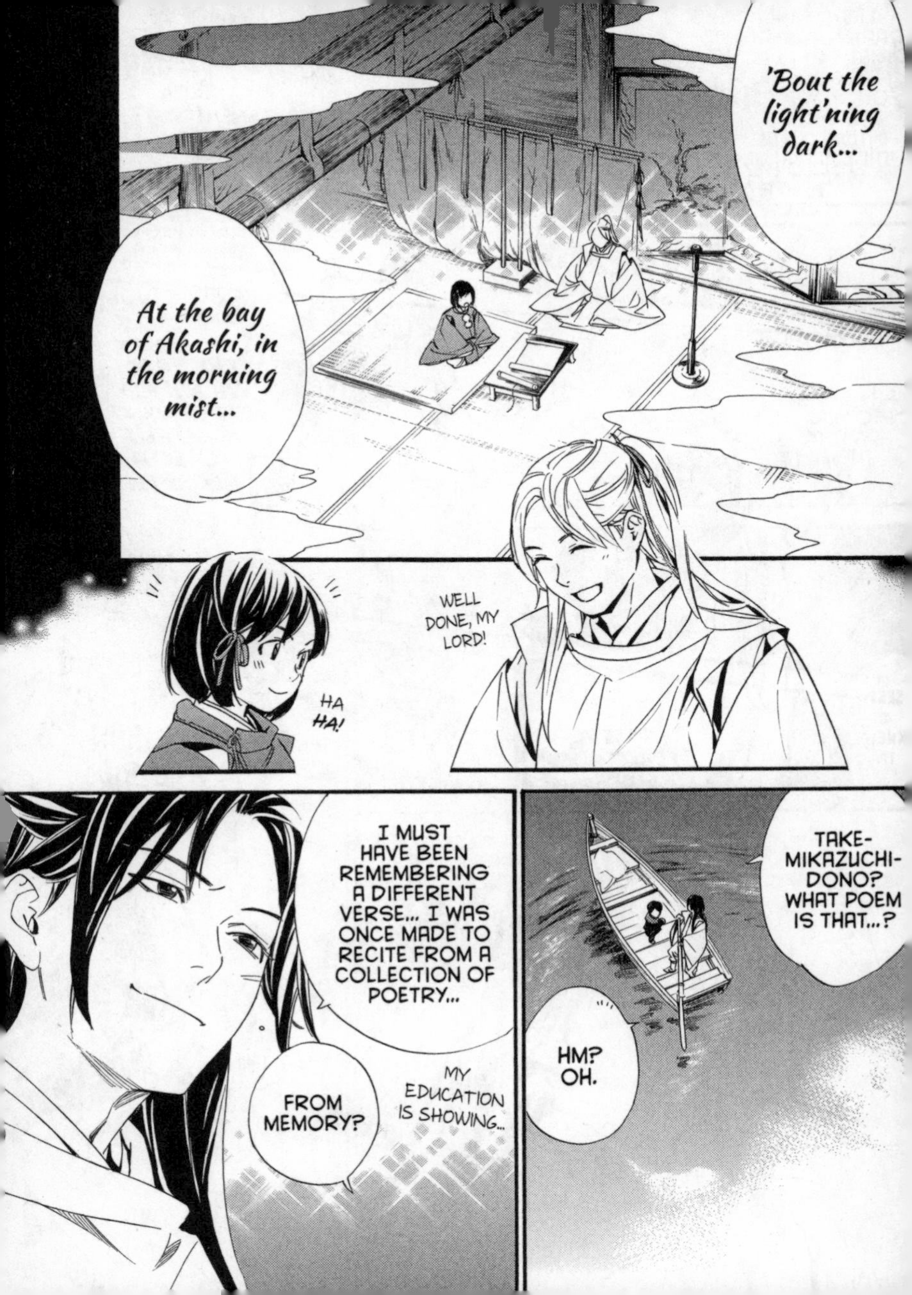
'Bout the light'ning dark...
At the bay of Akashi, in the morning mist...
WELL DONE, MY LORD!
HA HA!
TAKE-MIKAZUCHI-DONO? WHAT POEM IS THAT...?
HM? OH.
I MUST HAVE BEEN REMEMBERING A DIFFERENT VERSE... I WAS ONCE MADE TO RECITE FROM A COLLECTION OF POETRY...
FROM MEMORY?
MY EDUCATION IS SHOWING...

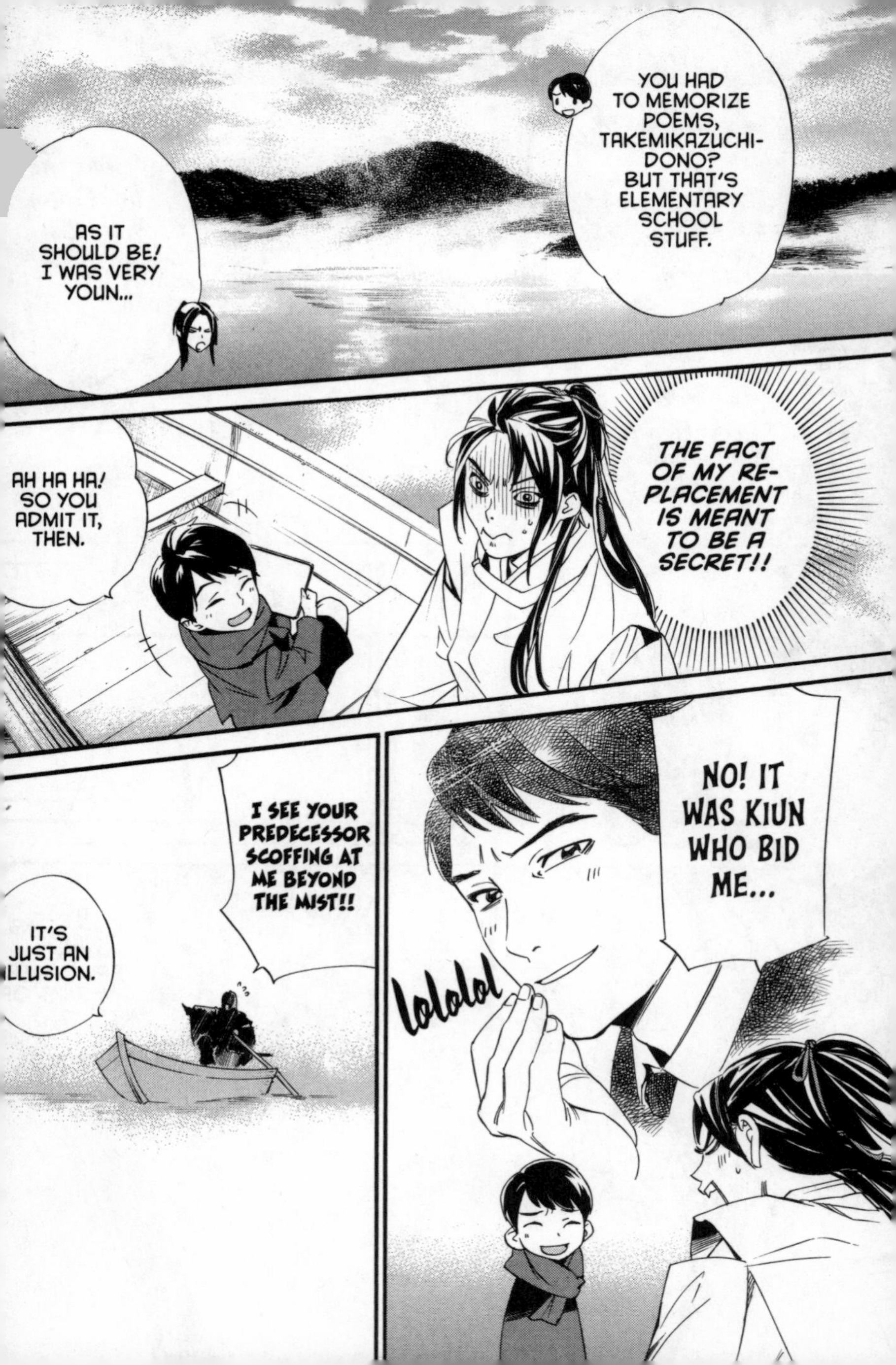
YOU HAD TO MEMORIZE POEMS, TAKEMIKAZUCHI-DONO? BUT THAT'S ELEMENTARY SCHOOL STUFF.
AS IT SHOULD BE! I WAS VERY YOUN...
THE FACT OF MY RE-PLACEMENT IS MEANT TO BE A SECRET!!
AH HA HA! SO YOU ADMIT IT, THEN.
NO! IT WAS KIUN WHO BID ME...
lololol
I SEE YOUR PREDECESSOR SCOFFING AT ME BEYOND THE MIST!!
IT'S JUST AN ILLUSION.

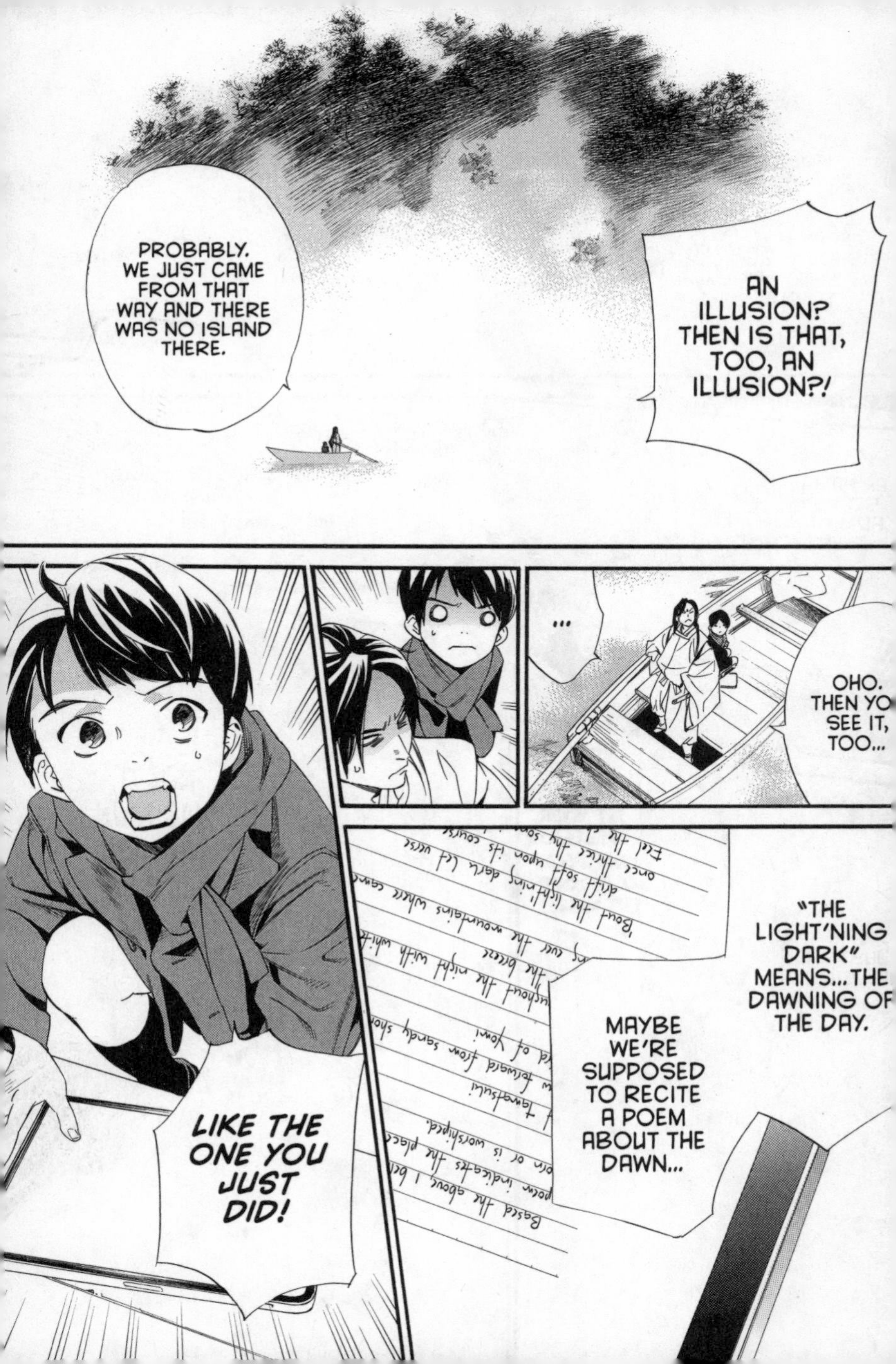
AN ILLUSION? THEN IS THAT, TOO, AN ILLUSION?!
PROBABLY. WE JUST CAME FROM THAT WAY AND THERE WAS NO ISLAND THERE.
OHO. THEN YO SEE IT, TOO...
...
"THE LIGHT'NING DARK" MEANS... THE DAWNING OF THE DAY.
MAYBE WE'RE SUPPOSED TO RECITE A POEM ABOUT THE DAWN...
LIKE THE ONE YOU JUST DID!

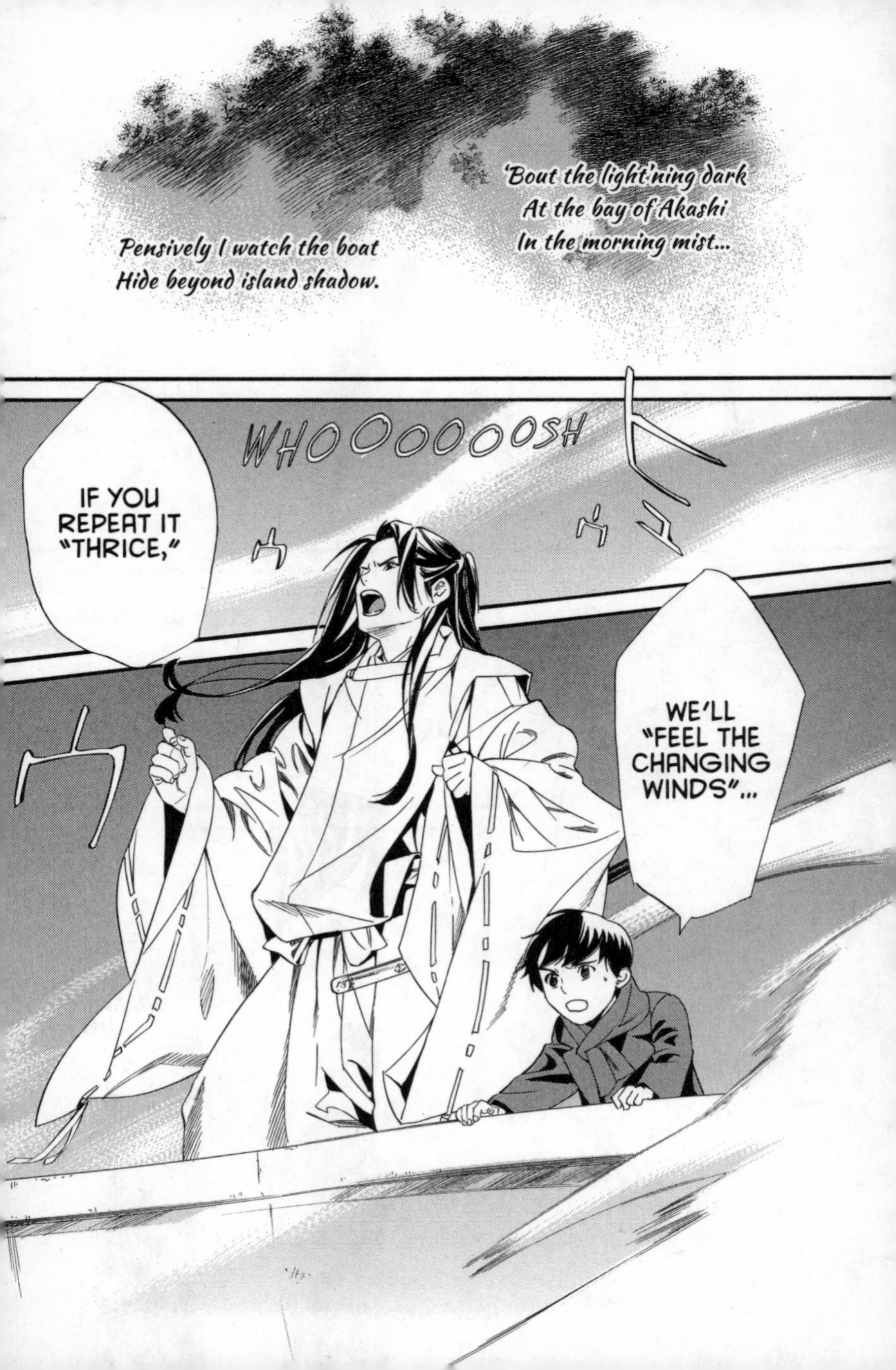
'Bout the light'ning dark
At the bay of Akashi
In the morning mist...
Pensively I watch the boat
Hide beyond island shadow.
WHOOOOOOOSH
IF YOU REPEAT IT "THRICE,"
WE'LL "FEEL THE CHANGING WINDS"...

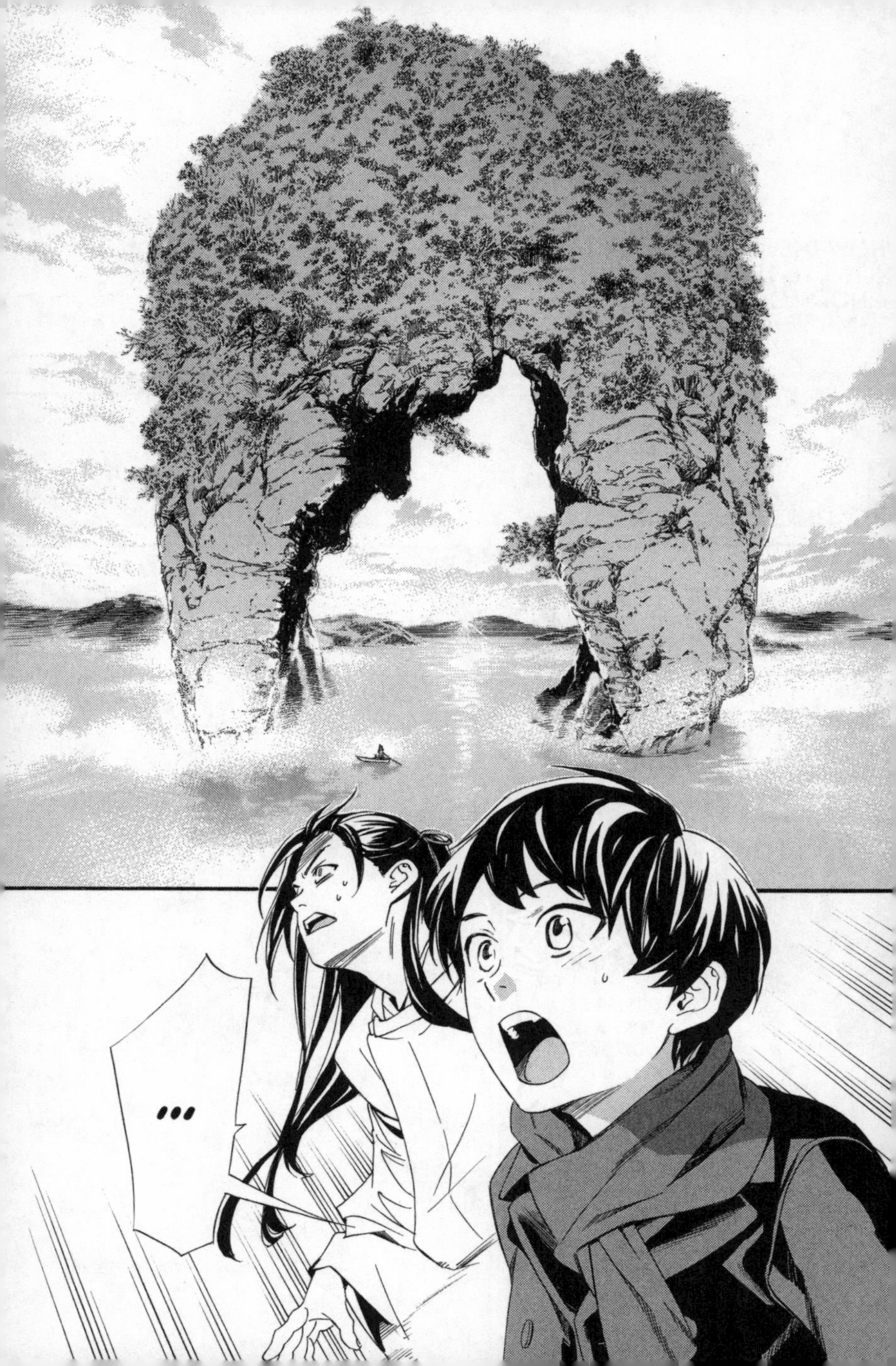
...

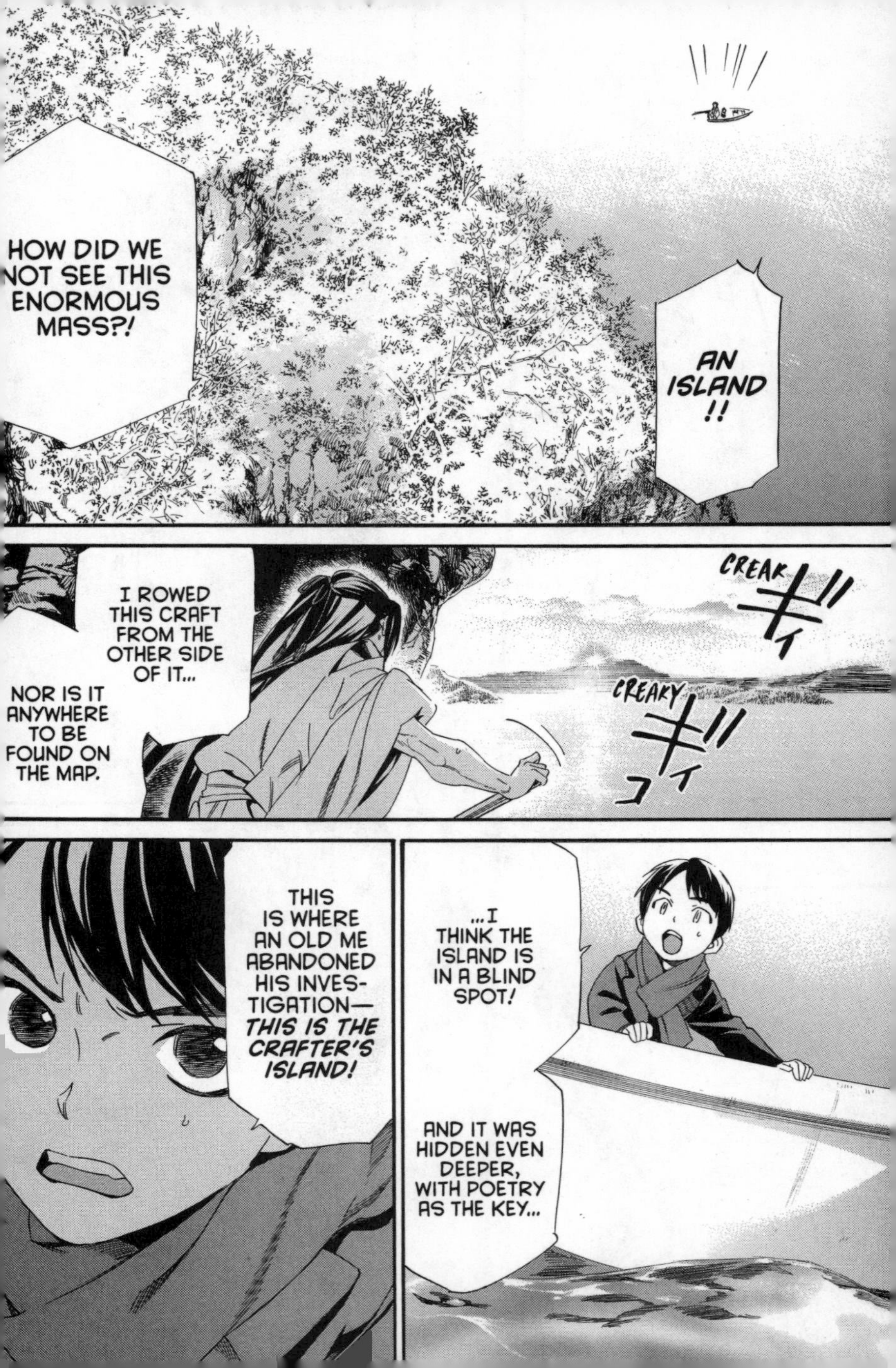
AN ISLAND !!
HOW DID WE NOT SEE THIS ENORMOUS MASS?!
CREAK
CREAKY
I ROWED THIS CRAFT FROM THE OTHER SIDE OF IT...
NOR IS IT ANYWHERE TO BE FOUND ON THE MAP.
...I THINK THE ISLAND IS IN A BLIND SPOT!
AND IT WAS HIDDEN EVEN DEEPER, WITH POETRY AS THE KEY...
THIS IS WHERE AN OLD ME ABANDONED HIS INVES-TIGATION—*THIS IS THE CRAFTER'S ISLAND!*

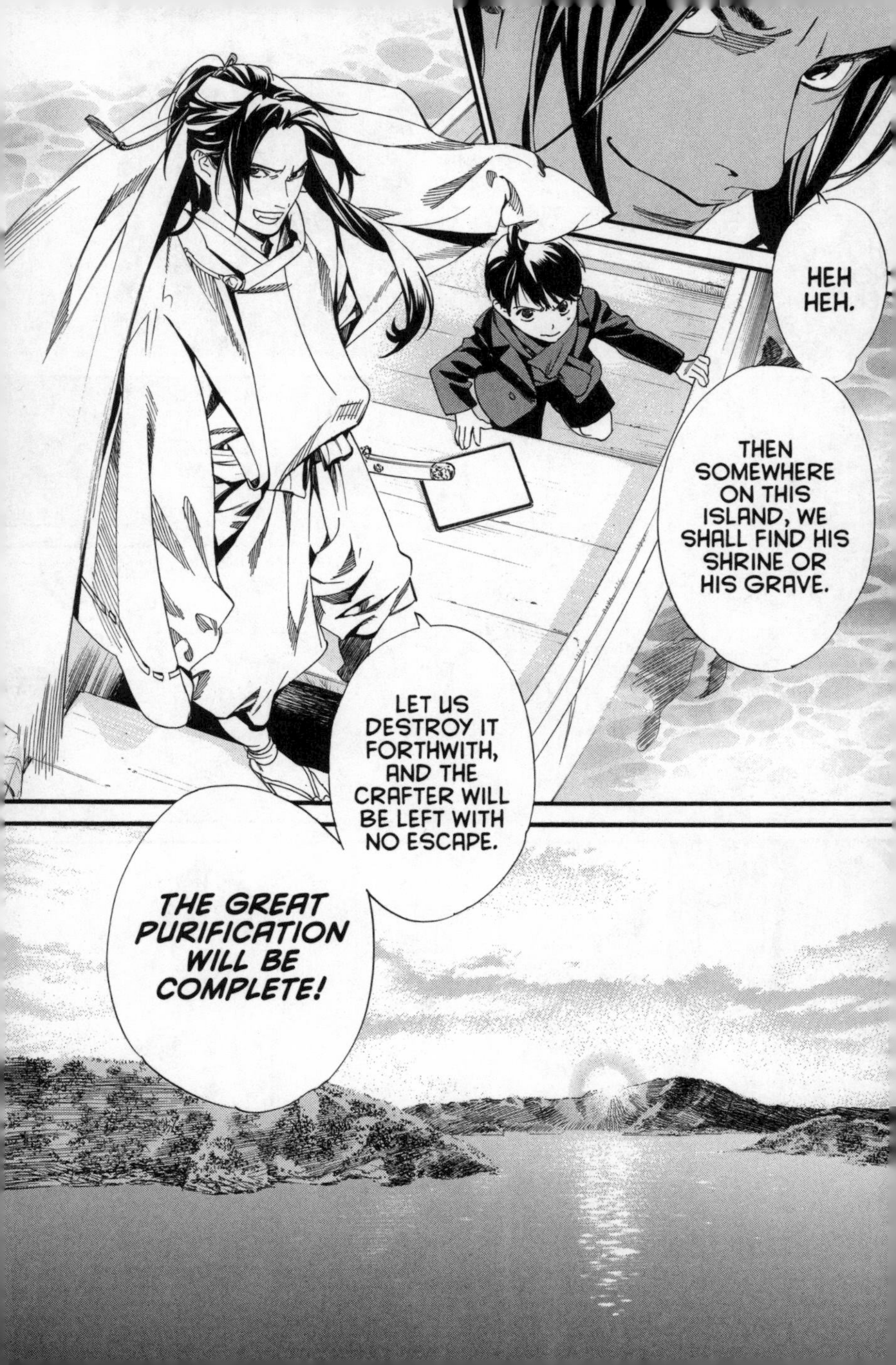
HEH HEH.
THEN SOMEWHERE ON THIS ISLAND, WE SHALL FIND HIS SHRINE OR HIS GRAVE.
LET US DESTROY IT FORTHWITH, AND THE CRAFTER WILL BE LEFT WITH NO ESCAPE.
THE GREAT PURIFICATION WILL BE COMPLETE!

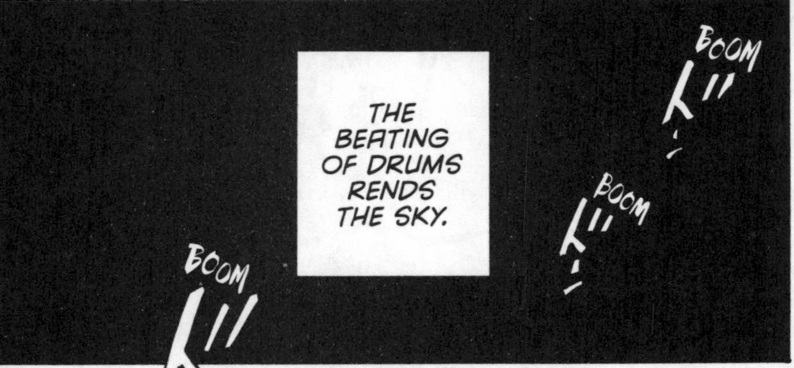
BOOM
BOOM
THE BEATING OF DRUMS RENDS THE SKY.
BOOM
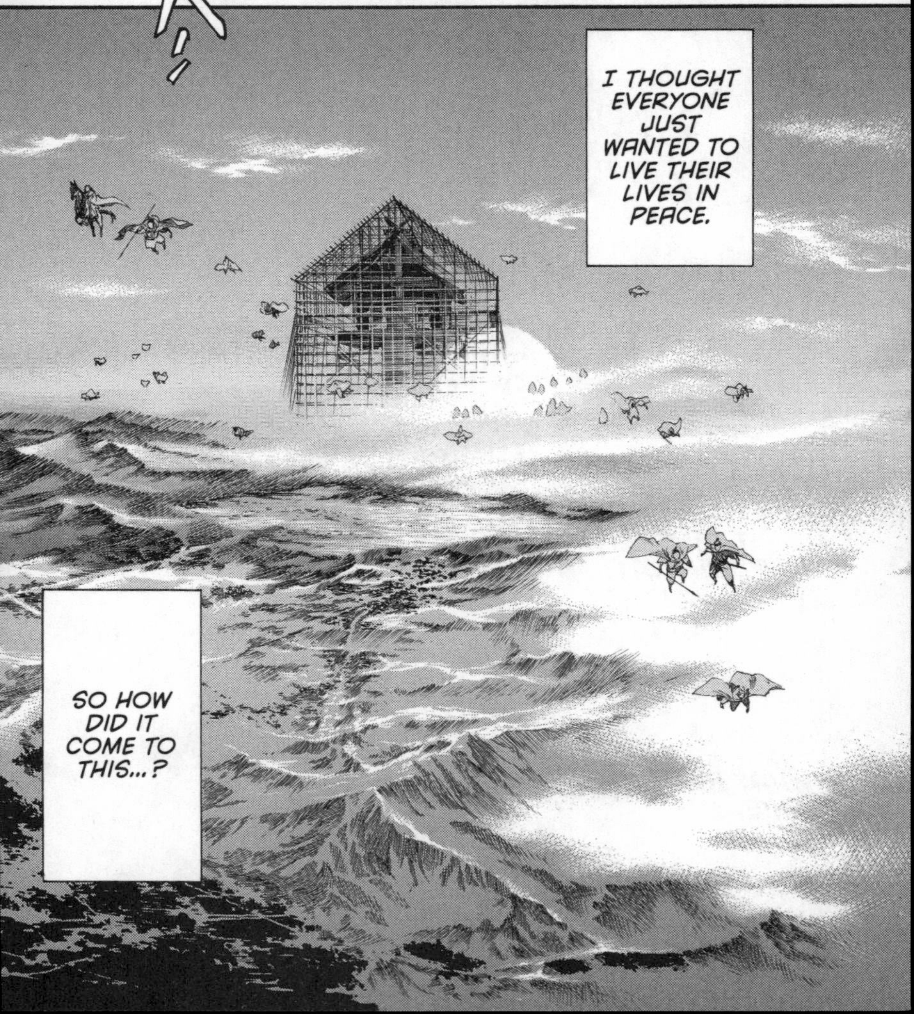
I THOUGHT EVERYONE JUST WANTED TO LIVE THEIR LIVES IN PEACE.
SO HOW DID IT COME TO THIS...?

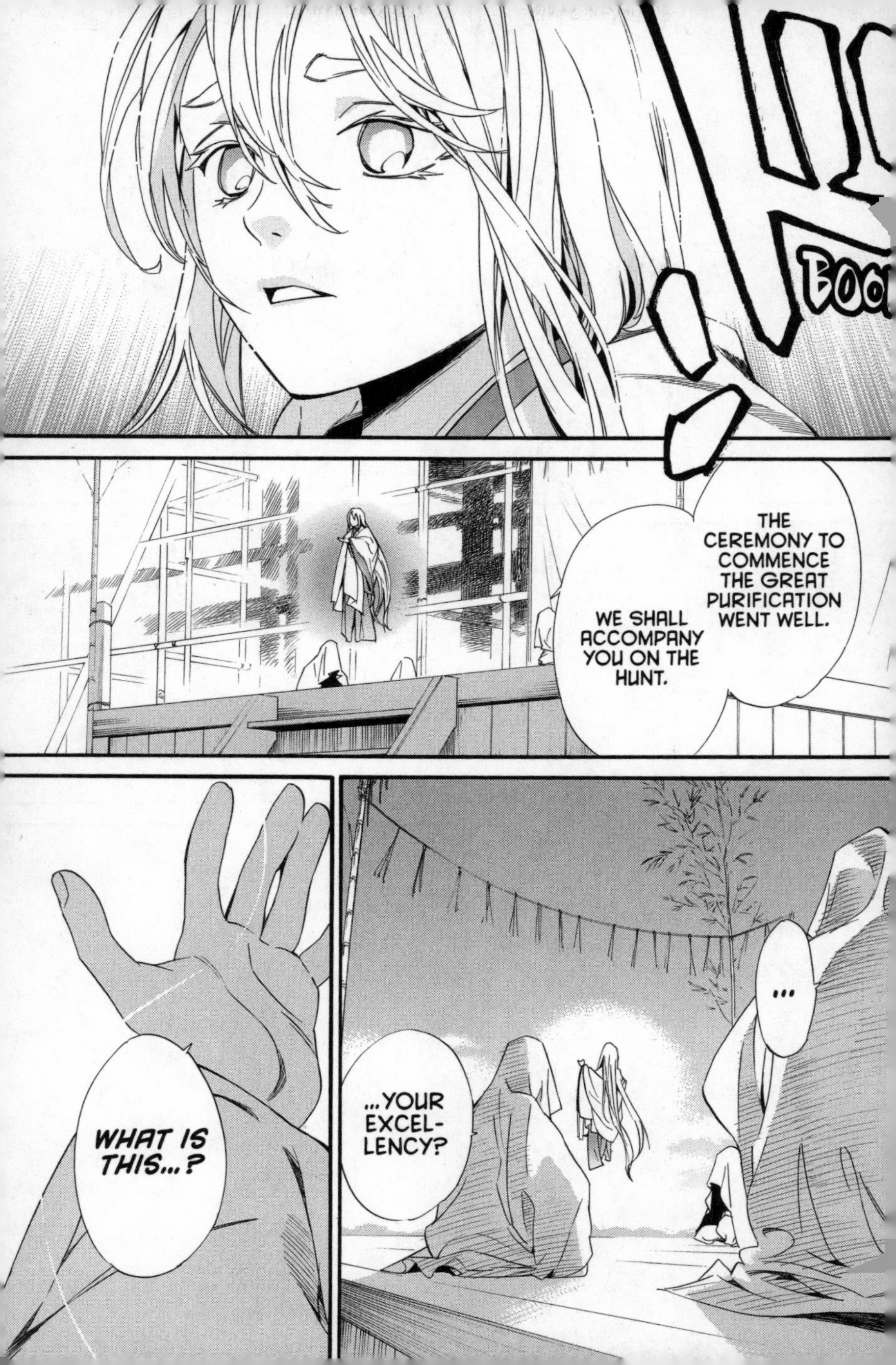
BOO
THE CEREMONY TO COMMENCE THE GREAT PURIFICATION WENT WELL.
WE SHALL ACCOMPANY YOU ON THE HUNT.
...
...YOUR EXCEL-LENCY?
WHAT IS THIS...?

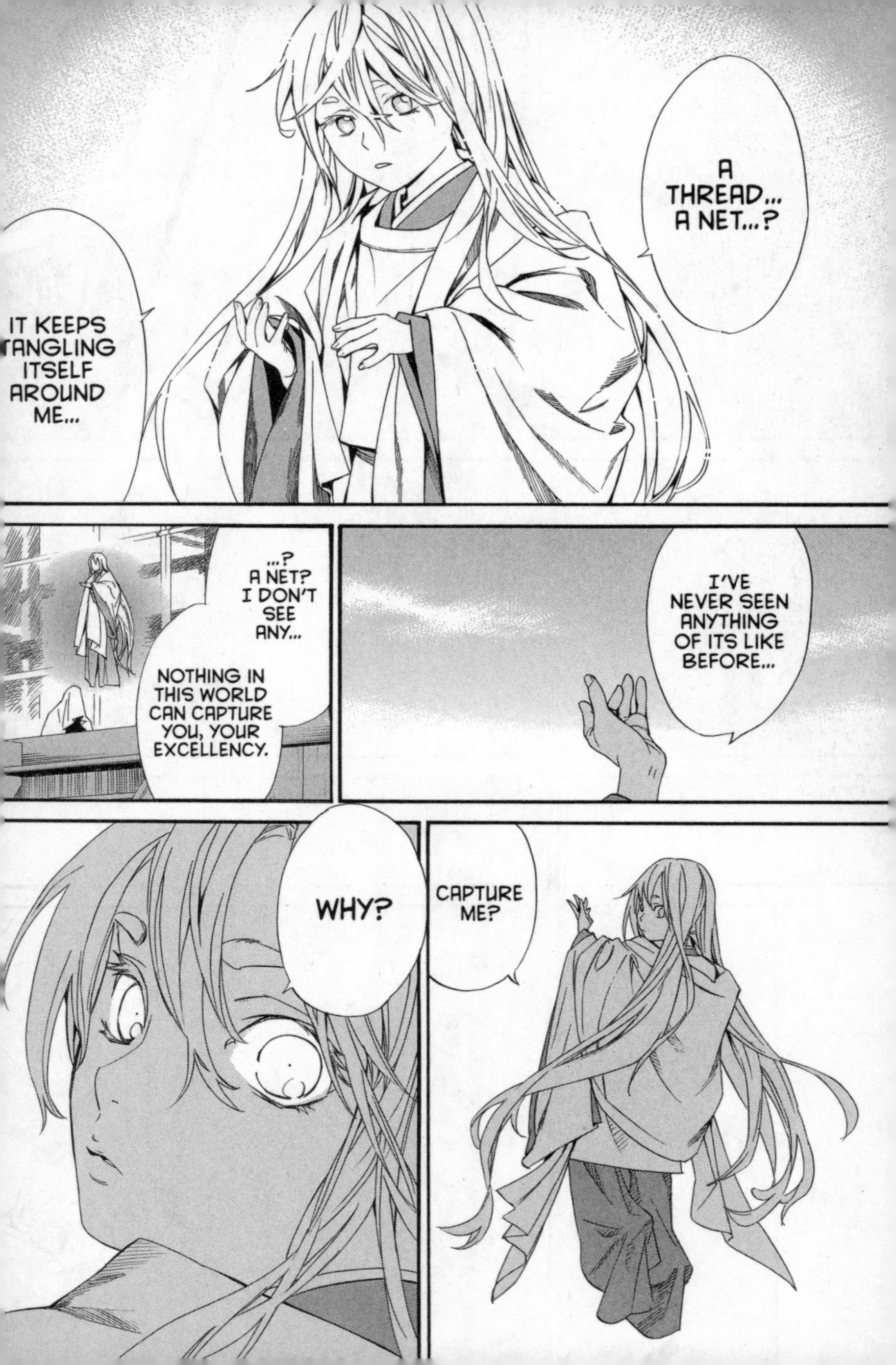
A THREAD... A NET...?
IT KEEPS TANGLING ITSELF AROUND ME...
I'VE NEVER SEEN ANYTHING OF ITS LIKE BEFORE...
...? A NET? I DON'T SEE ANY...
NOTHING IN THIS WORLD CAN CAPTURE YOU, YOUR EXCELLENCY.
CAPTURE ME?
WHY?

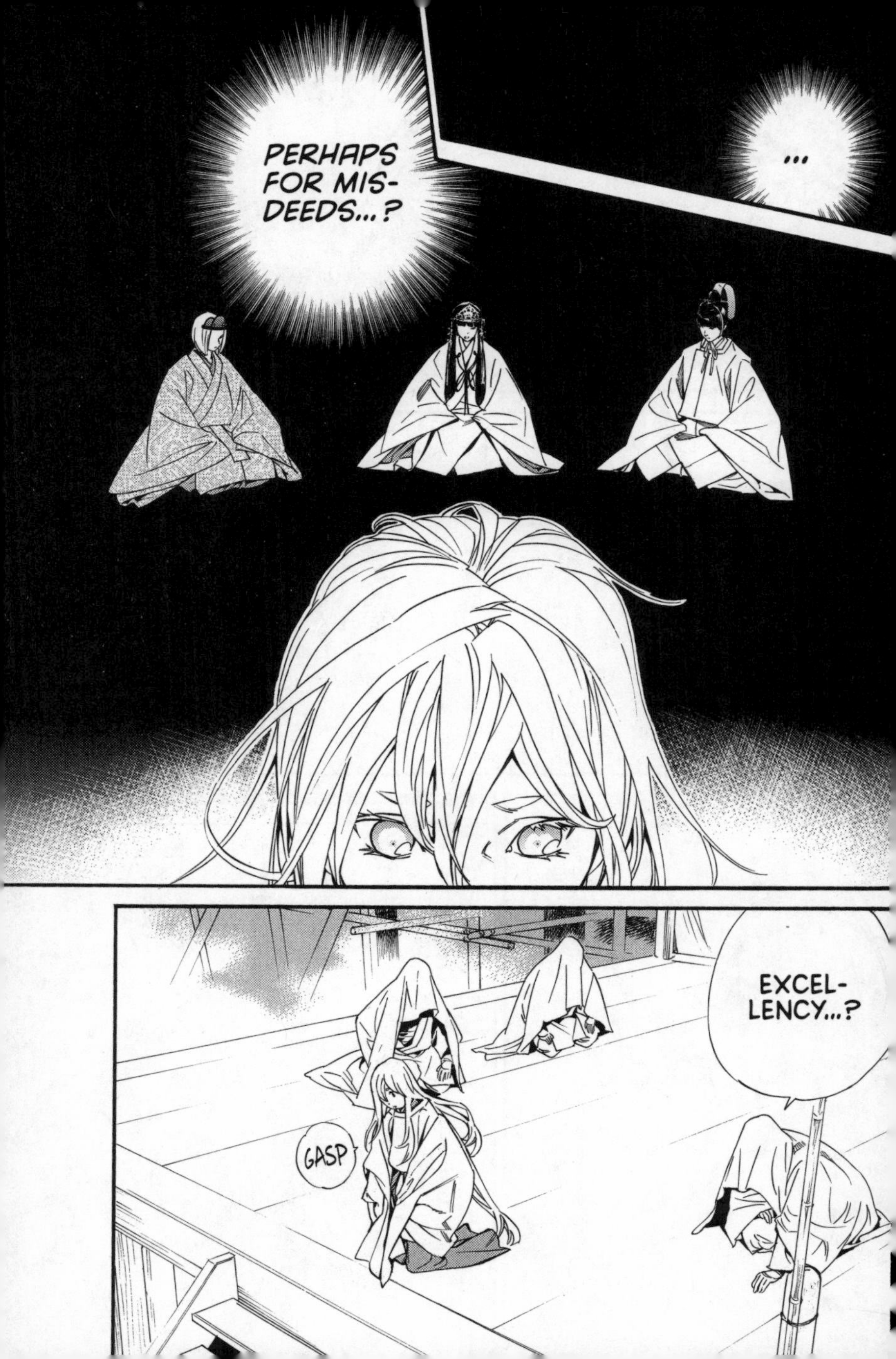
...
PERHAPS FOR MIS-DEEDS...?
EXCEL-LENCY...?
GASP

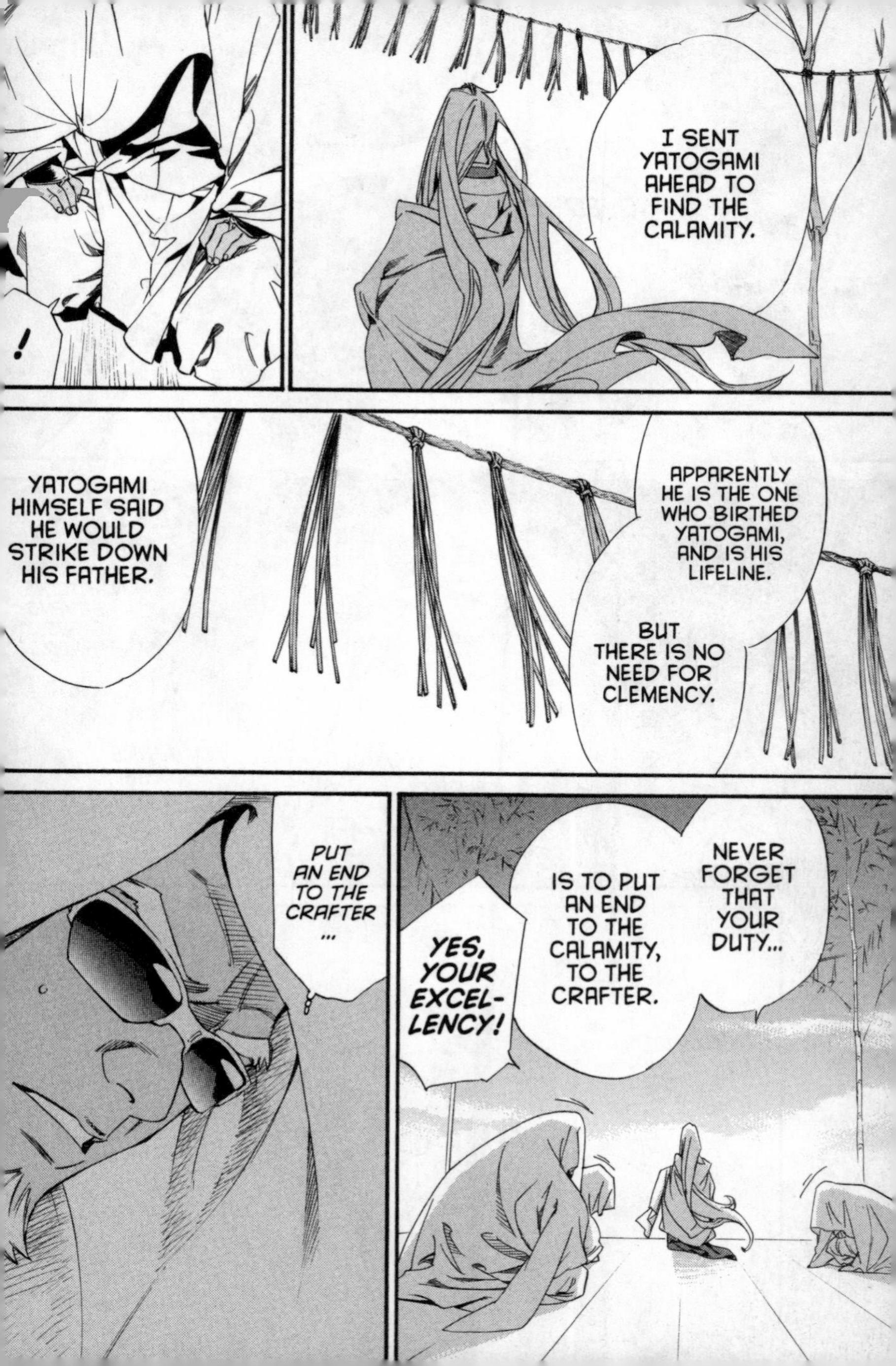
I SENT YATOGAMI AHEAD TO FIND THE CALAMITY.
!
APPARENTLY HE IS THE ONE WHO BIRTHED YATOGAMI, AND IS HIS LIFELINE.
BUT THERE IS NO NEED FOR CLEMENCY.
YATOGAMI HIMSELF SAID HE WOULD STRIKE DOWN HIS FATHER.
NEVER FORGET THAT YOUR DUTY...
IS TO PUT AN END TO THE CALAMITY, TO THE CRAFTER.
YES, YOUR EXCEL-LENCY!
PUT AN END TO THE CRAFTER...

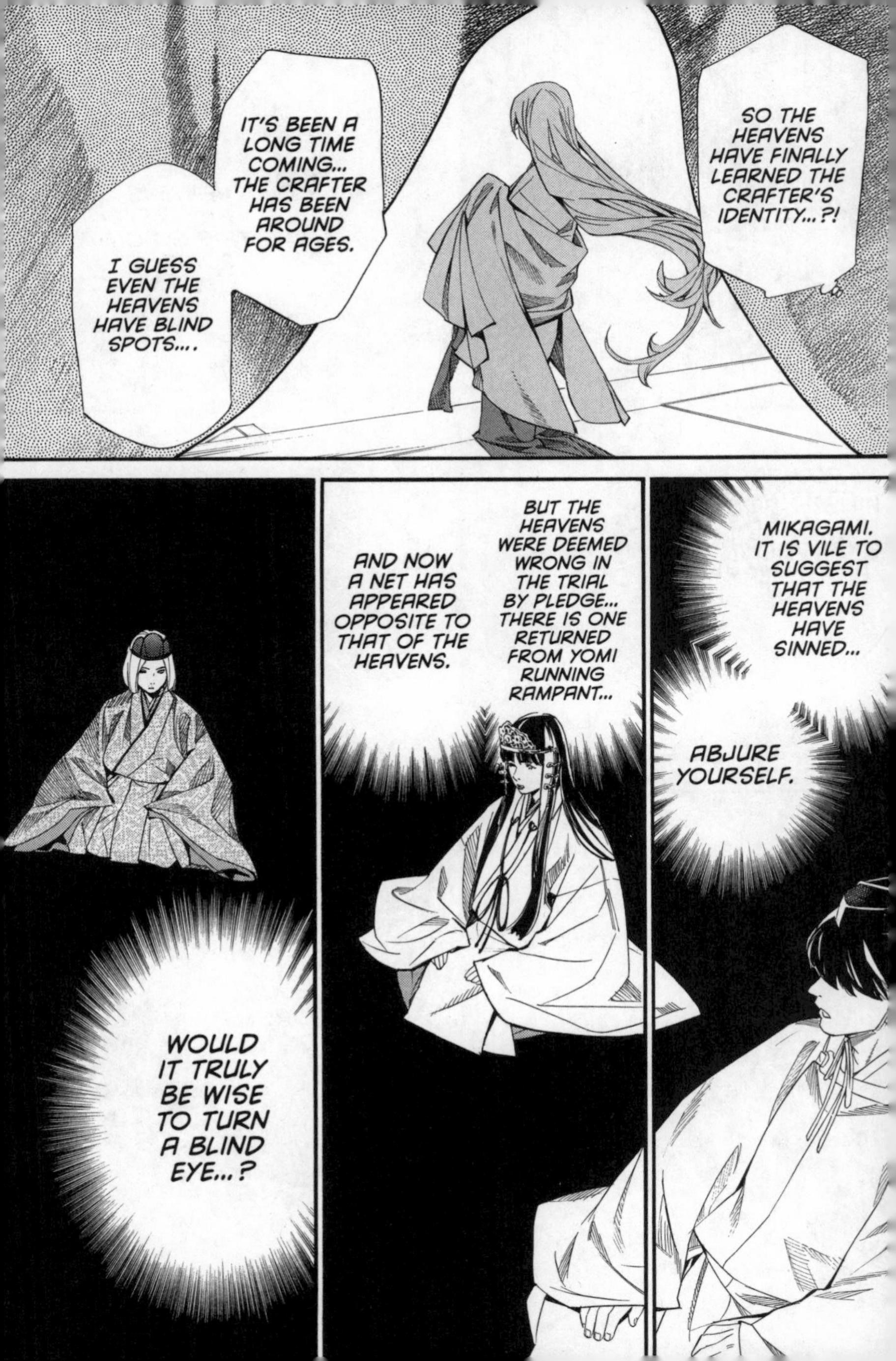
SO THE HEAVENS HAVE FINALLY LEARNED THE CRAFTER'S IDENTITY...?!
IT'S BEEN A LONG TIME COMING... THE CRAFTER HAS BEEN AROUND FOR AGES.
I GUESS EVEN THE HEAVENS HAVE BLIND SPOTS....
MIKAGAMI. IT IS VILE TO SUGGEST THAT THE HEAVENS HAVE SINNED...
ABJURE YOURSELF.
BUT THE HEAVENS WERE DEEMED WRONG IN THE TRIAL BY PLEDGE... THERE IS ONE RETURNED FROM YOMI RUNNING RAMPANT...
AND NOW A NET HAS APPEARED OPPOSITE TO THAT OF THE HEAVENS.
WOULD IT TRULY BE WISE TO TURN A BLIND EYE...?

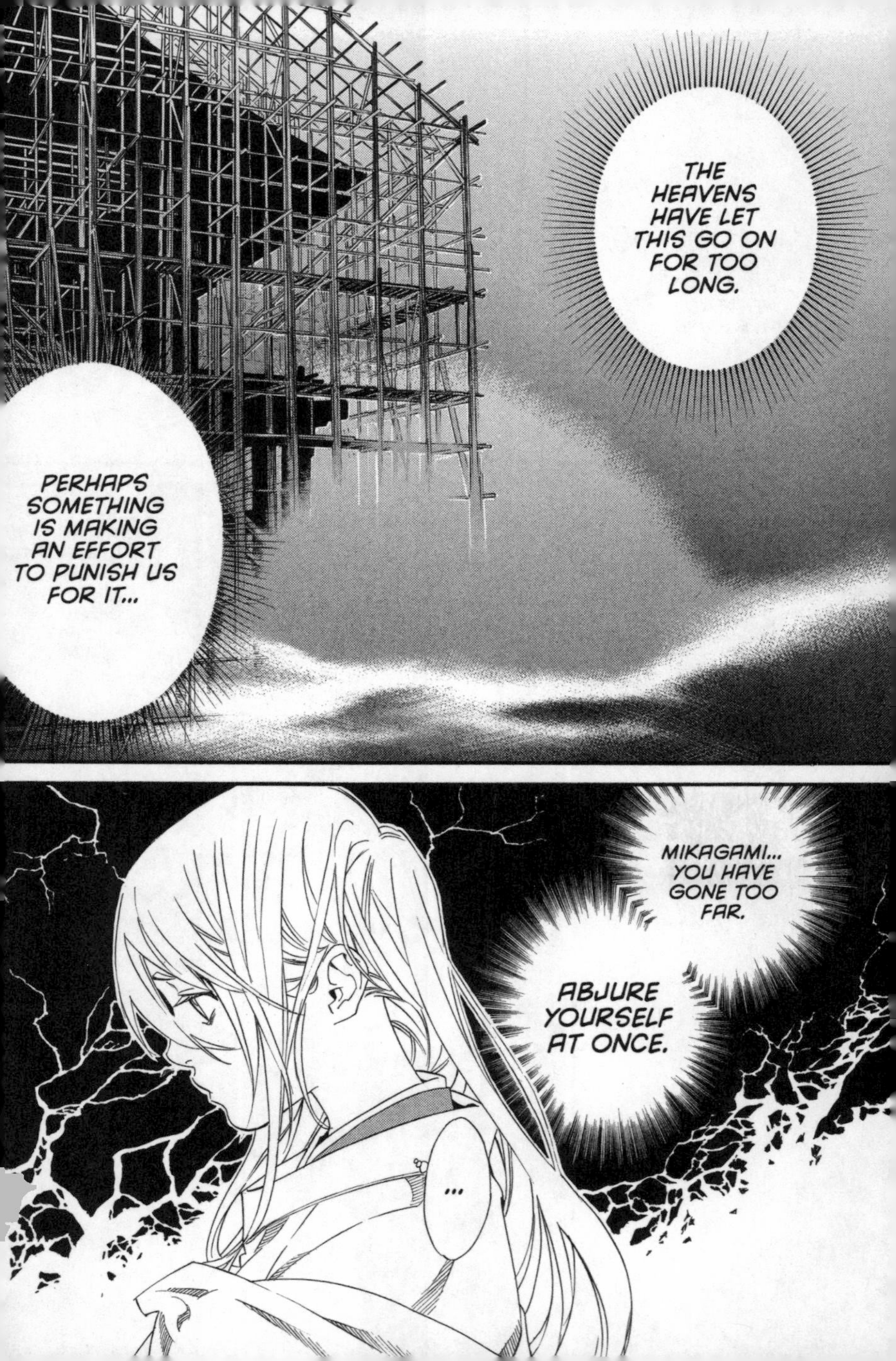
THE HEAVENS HAVE LET THIS GO ON FOR TOO LONG.
PERHAPS SOMETHING IS MAKING AN EFFORT TO PUNISH US FOR IT...
MIKAGAMI... YOU HAVE GONE TOO FAR.
ABJURE YOURSELF AT ONCE.
...

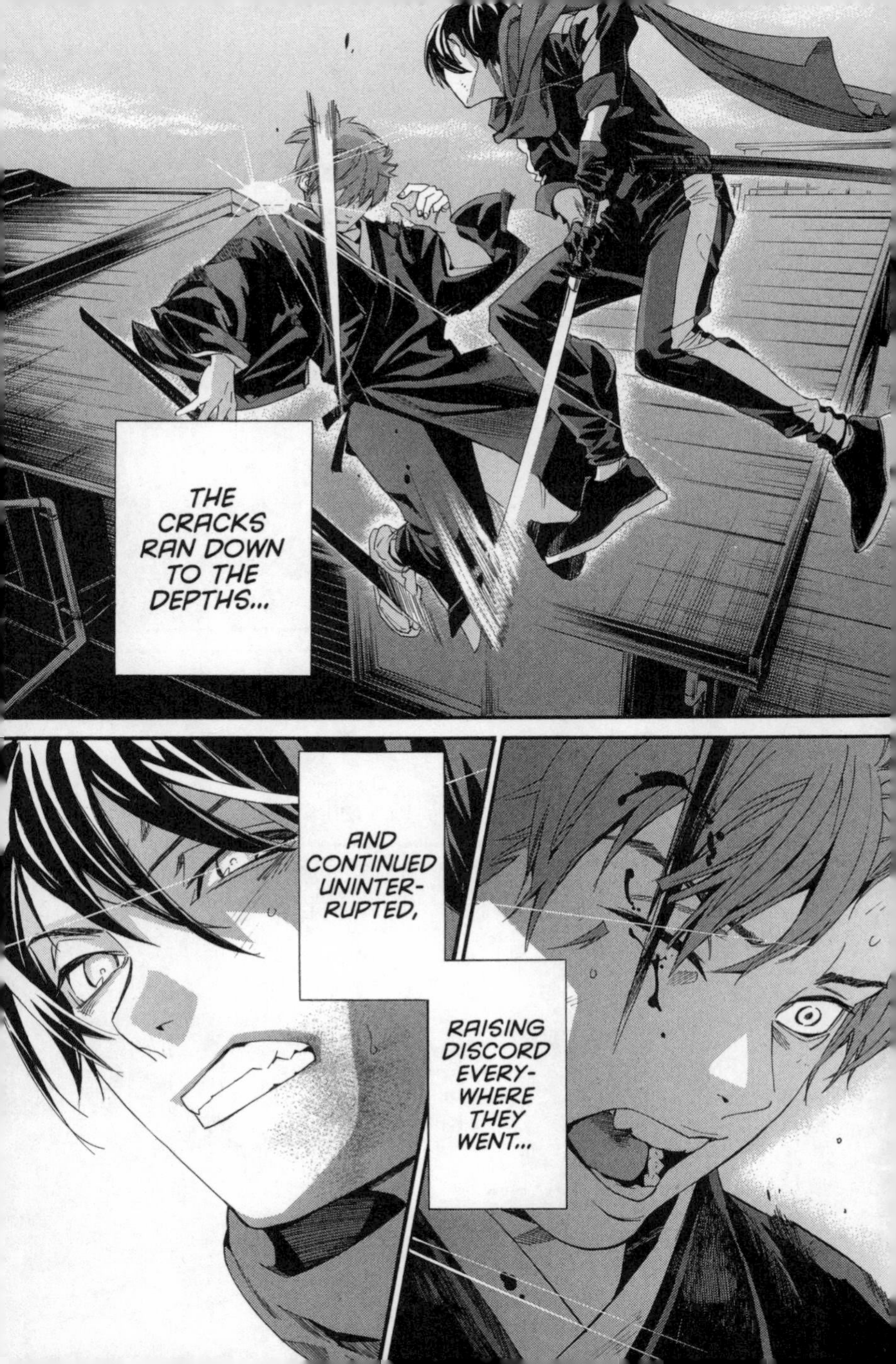
THE CRACKS RAN DOWN TO THE DEPTHS...
AND CONTINUED UNINTER-RUPTED,
RAISING DISCORD EVERY-WHERE THEY WENT...

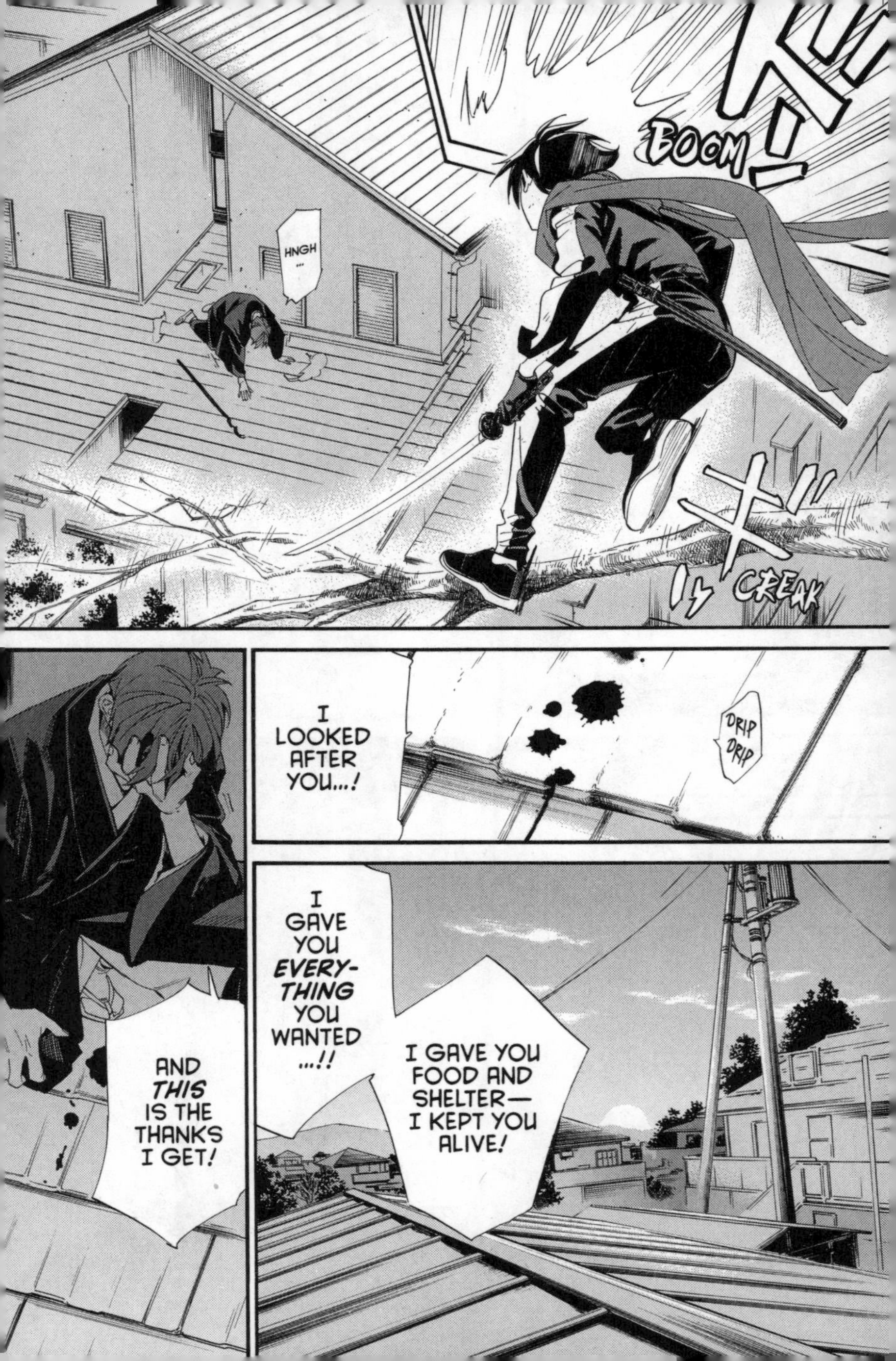
BOOM
HNGH ...
CREAK
I LOOKED AFTER YOU...!
DRIP DRIP
I GAVE YOU *EVERYTHING* YOU WANTED ...!!
I GAVE YOU FOOD AND SHELTER— I KEPT YOU ALIVE!
AND *THIS* IS THE THANKS I GET!

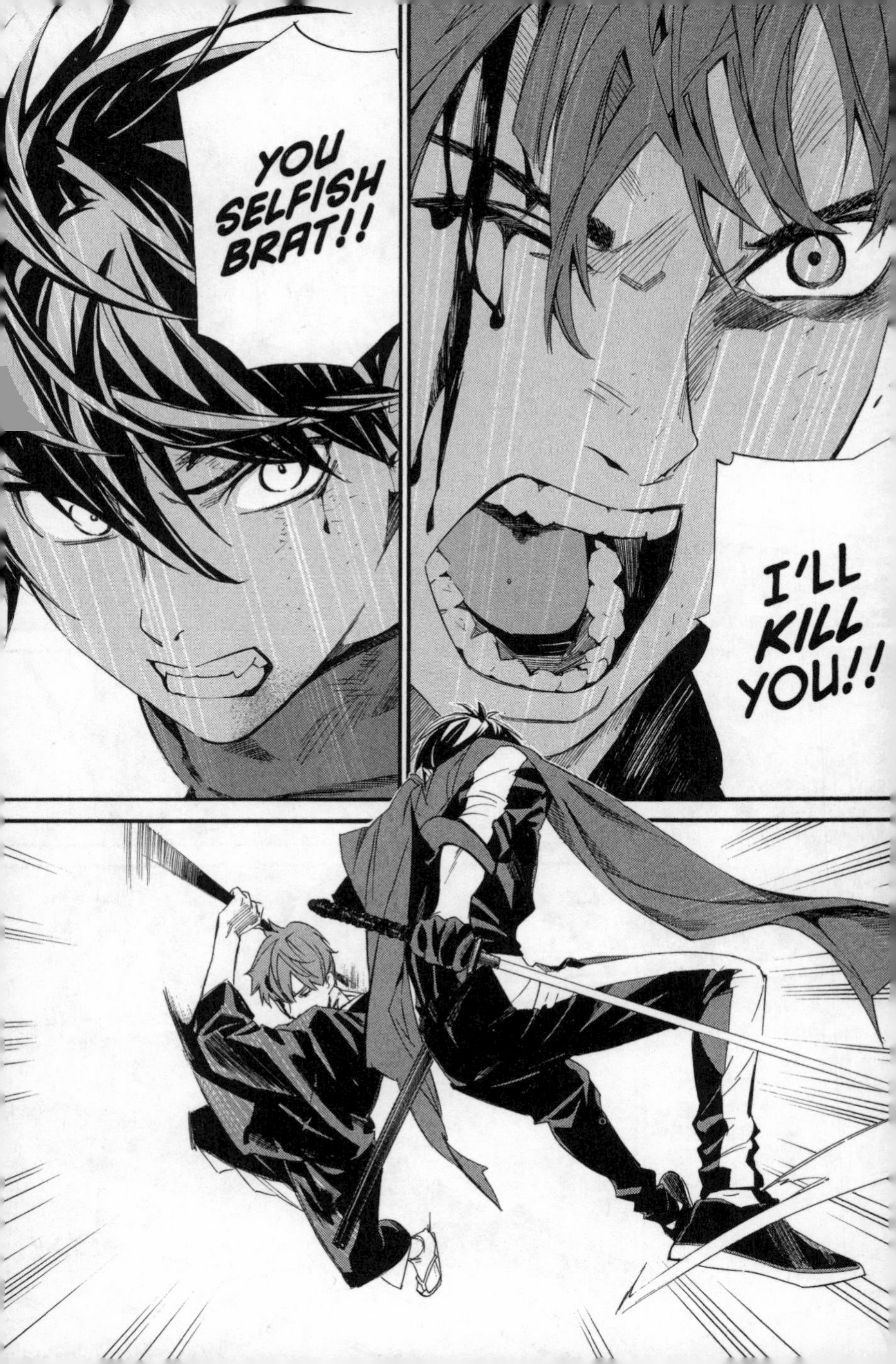
I'LL KILL YOU!!
YOU SELFISH BRAT!!

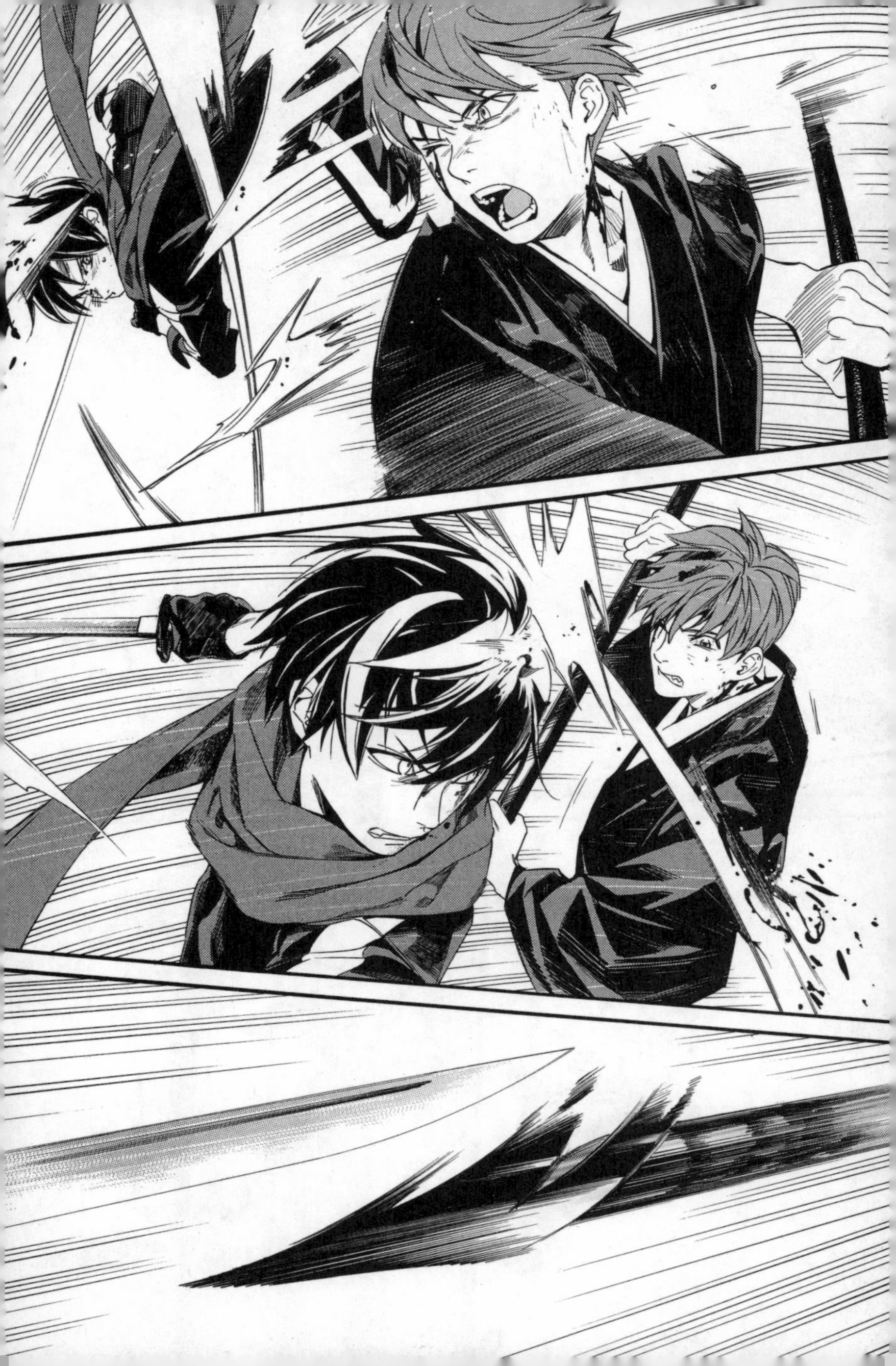

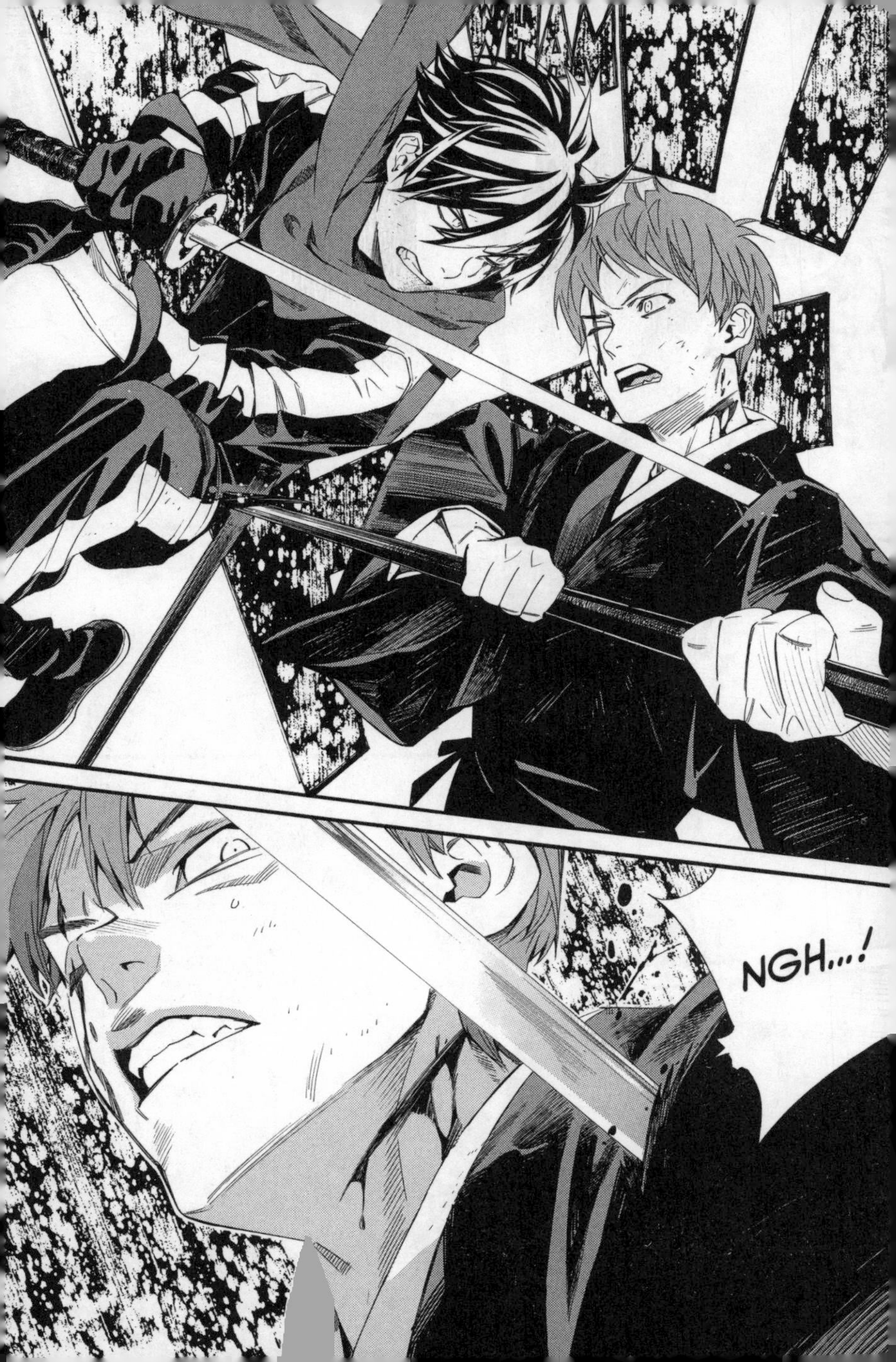
WHAM
NGH...!

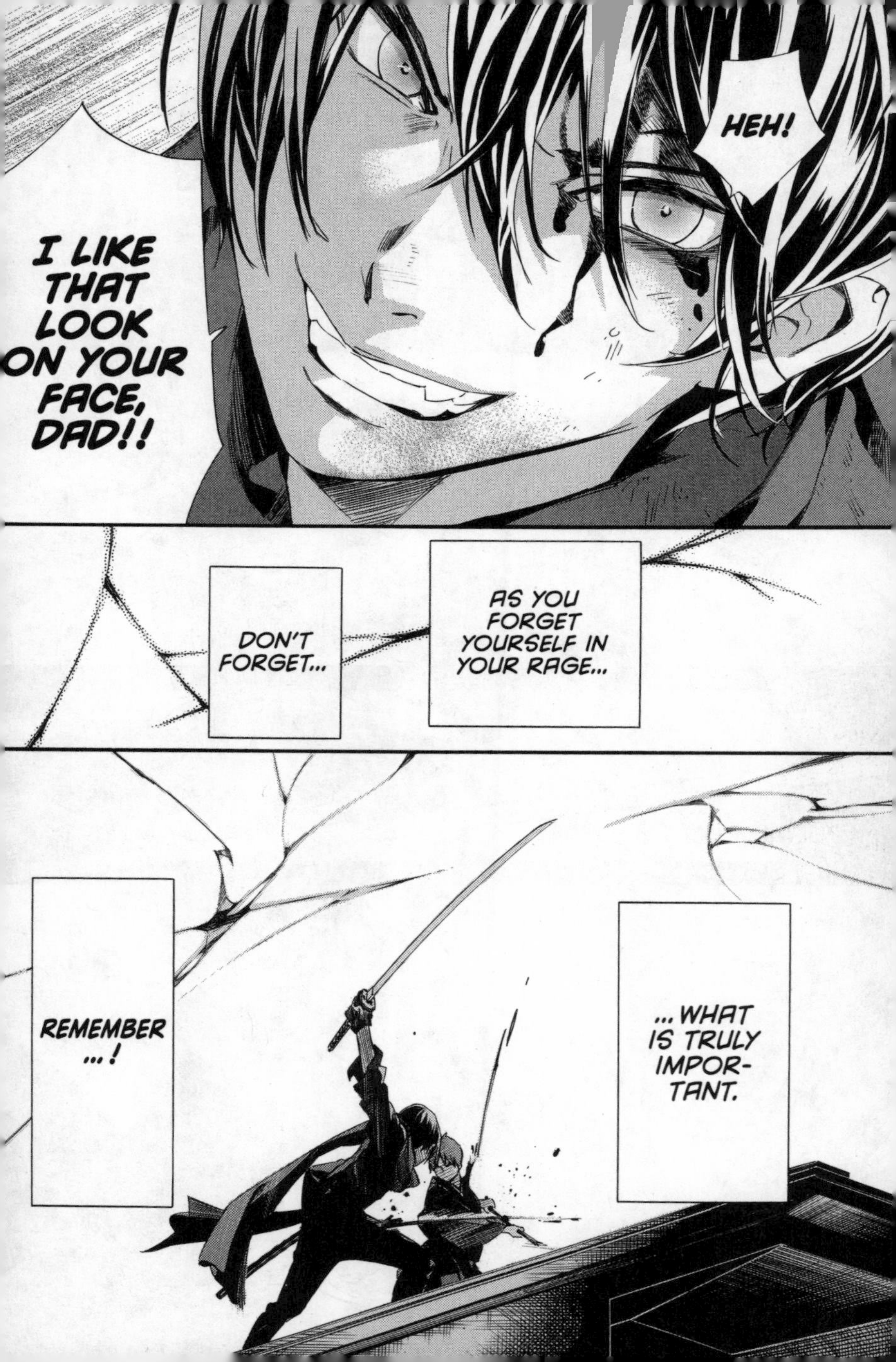
HEH!
I LIKE THAT LOOK ON YOUR FACE, DAD!!
AS YOU FORGET YOURSELF IN YOUR RAGE...
DON'T FORGET...
...WHAT IS TRULY IMPOR-TANT.
REMEMBER ...!

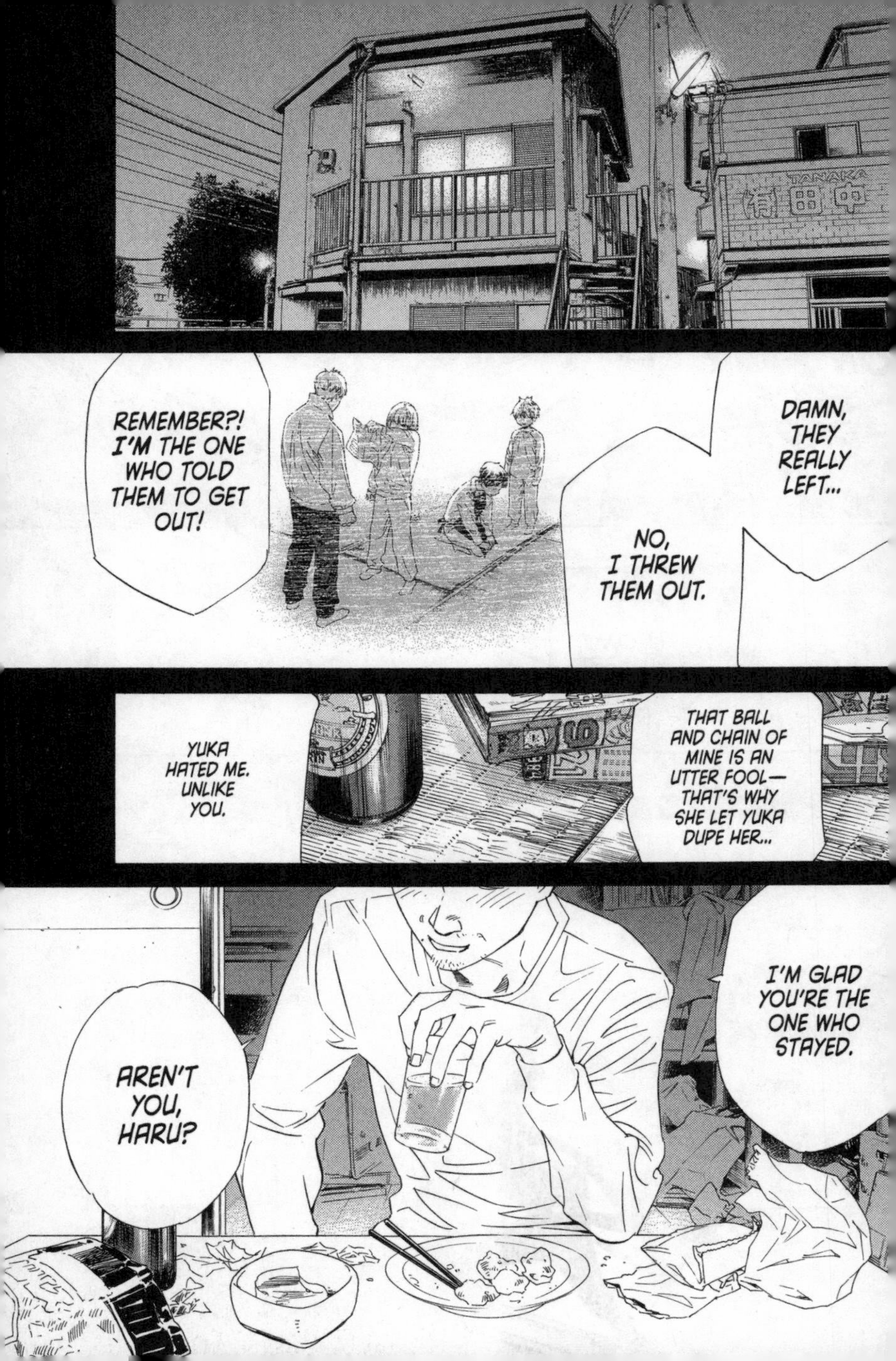
TANAKA
DAMN, THEY REALLY LEFT...
NO, I THREW THEM OUT.
REMEMBER?! I'M THE ONE WHO TOLD THEM TO GET OUT!
THAT BALL AND CHAIN OF MINE IS AN UTTER FOOL—THAT'S WHY SHE LET YUKA DUPE HER...
YUKA HATED ME. UNLIKE YOU.
I'M GLAD YOU'RE THE ONE WHO STAYED.
AREN'T YOU, HARU?

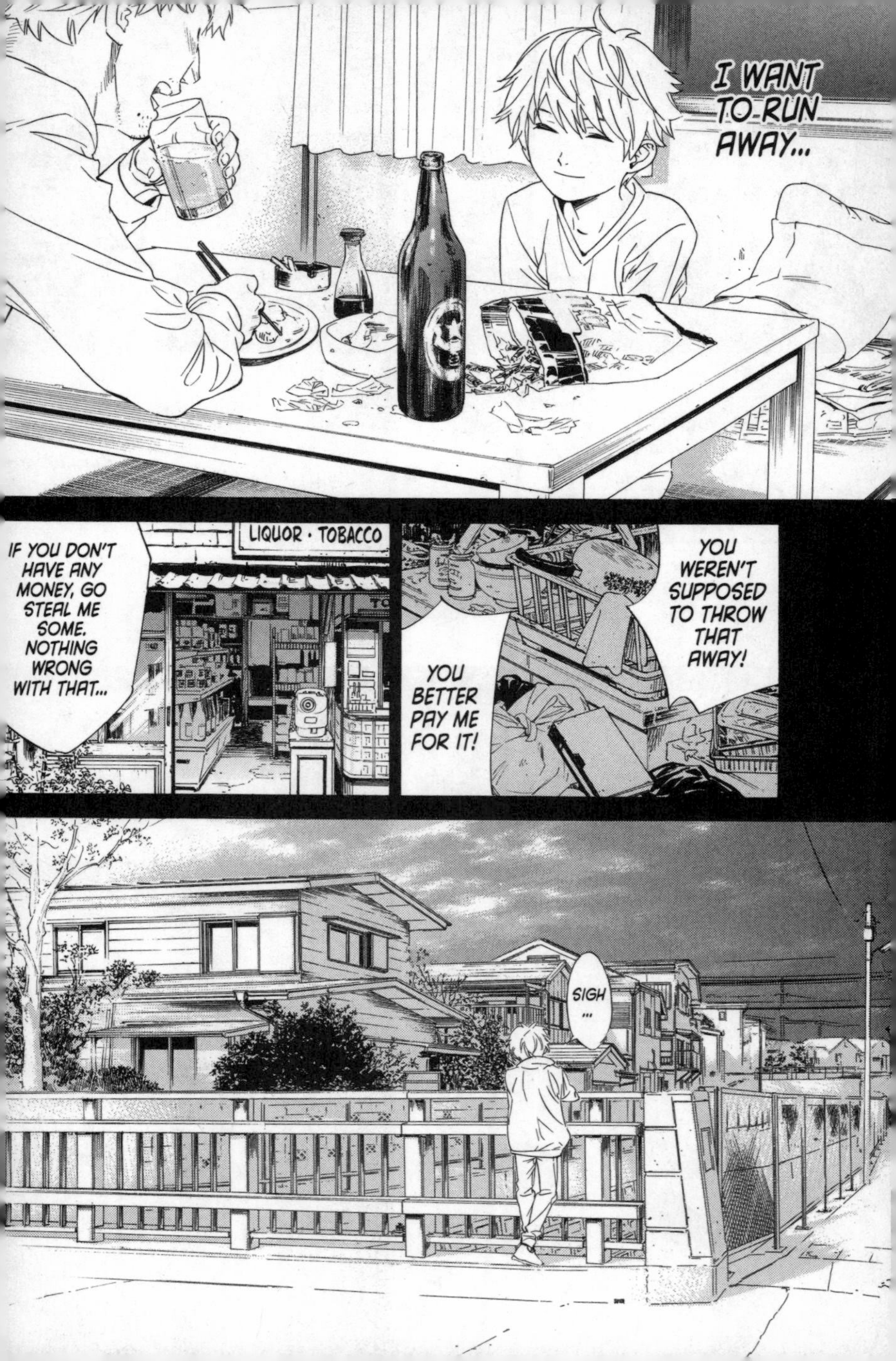
I WANT TO RUN AWAY...
YOU WEREN'T SUPPOSED TO THROW THAT AWAY!
YOU BETTER PAY ME FOR IT!
LIQUOR · TOBACCO
IF YOU DON'T HAVE ANY MONEY, GO STEAL ME SOME. NOTHING WRONG WITH THAT...
SIGH ...

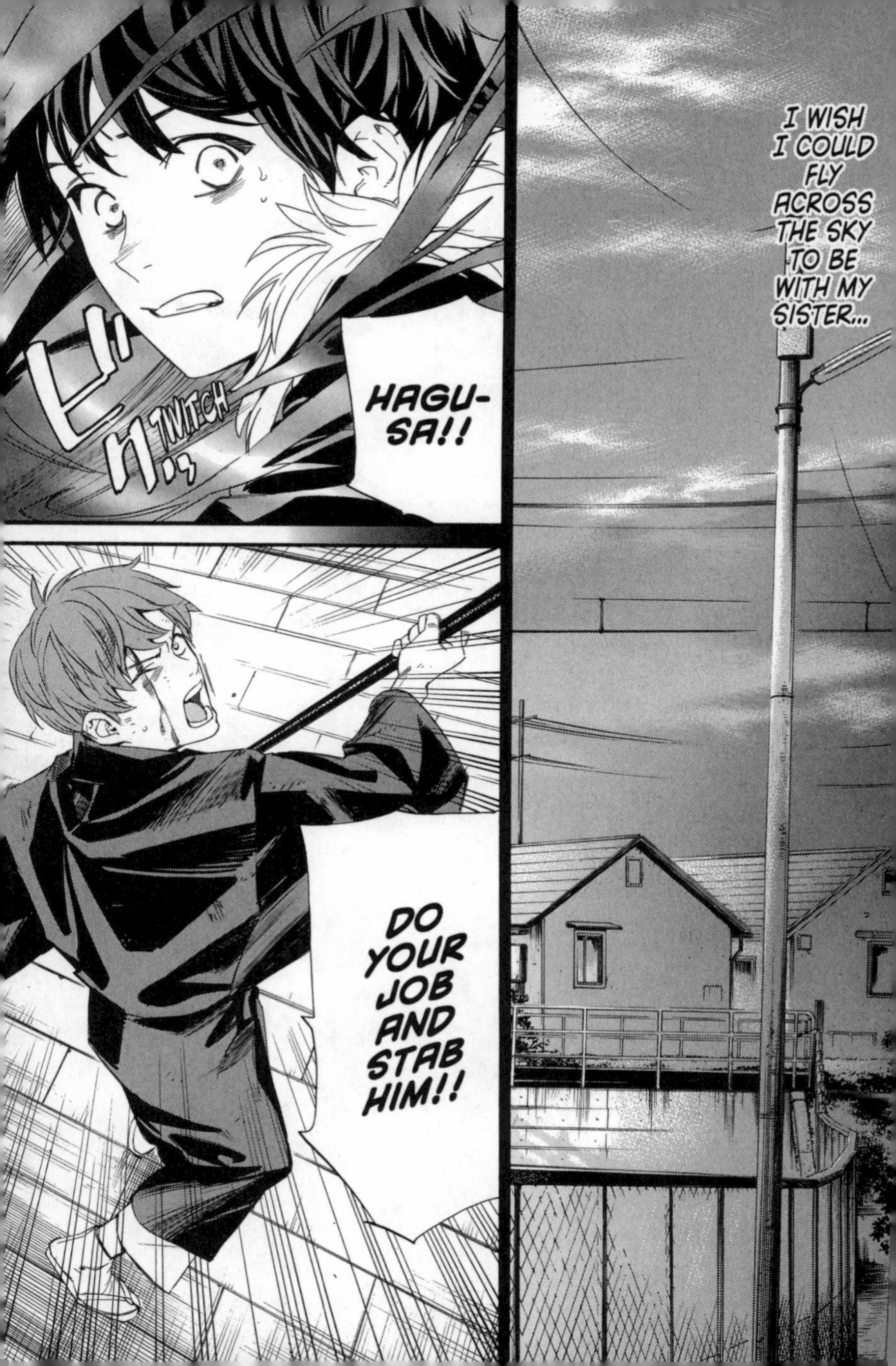
I WISH I COULD FLY ACROSS THE SKY TO BE WITH MY SISTER...
TWITCH
HAGU-SA!!
DO YOUR JOB AND STAB HIM!!

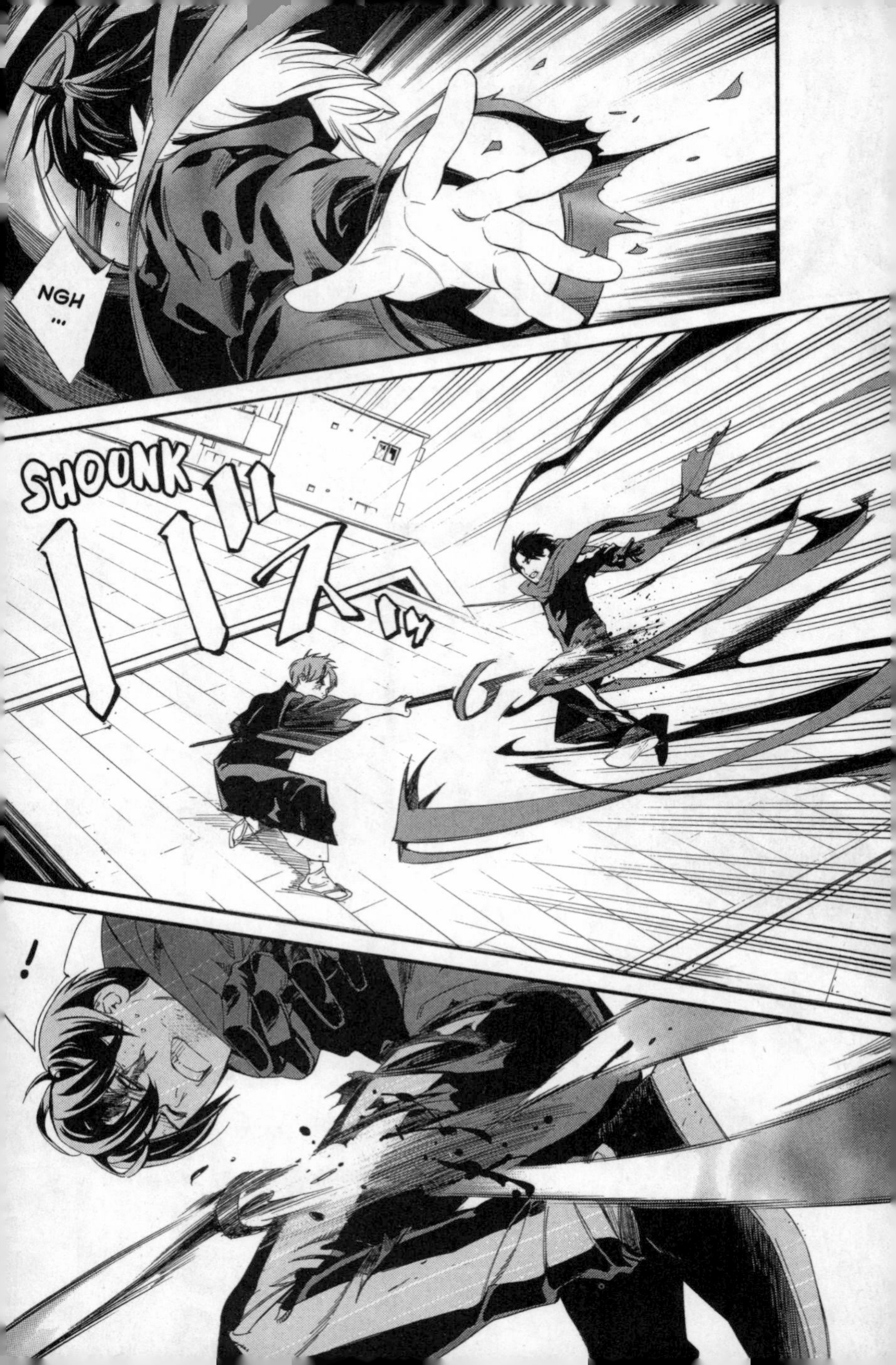
NGH ...
SHOONK
!

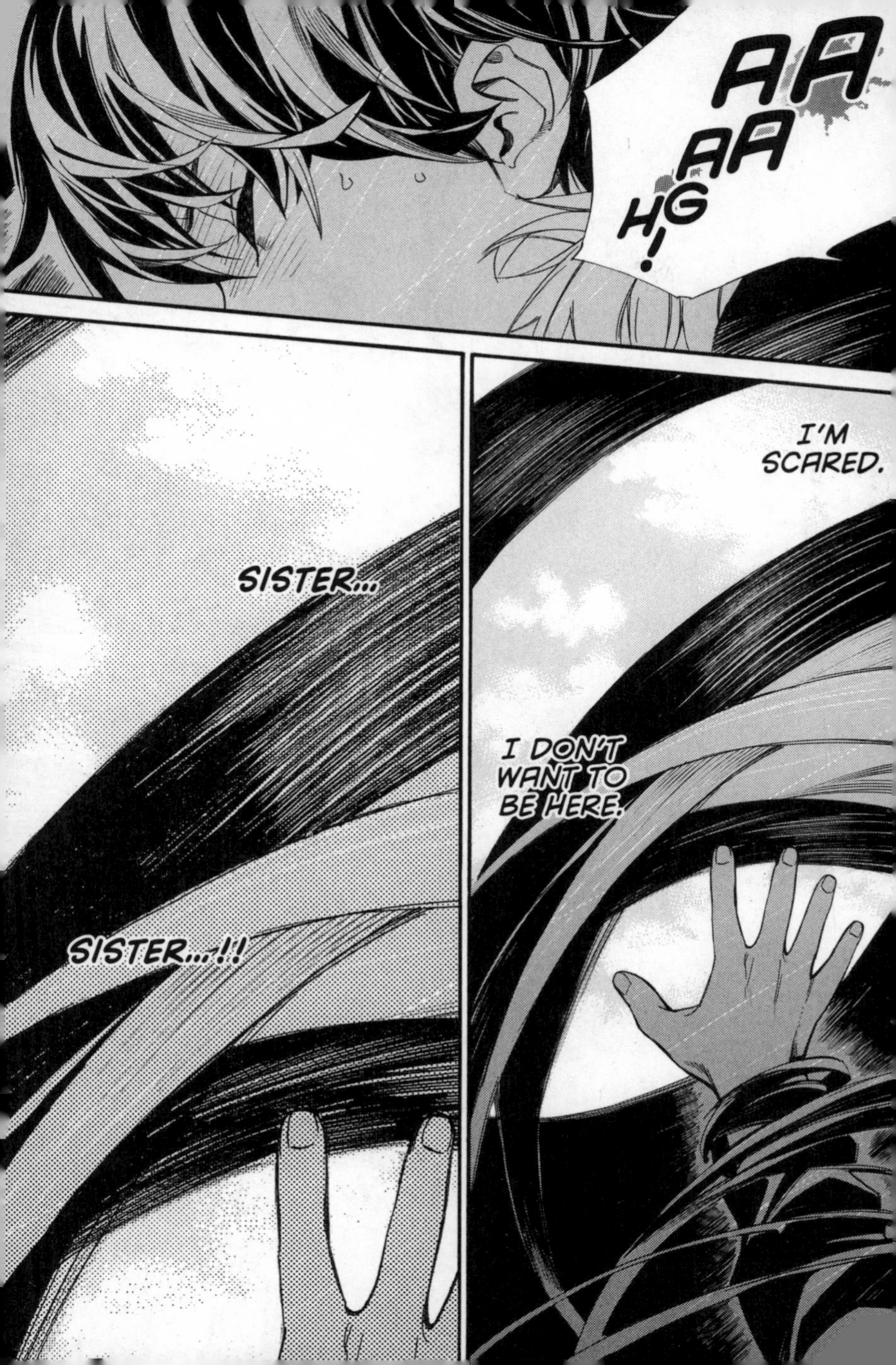
AAAAHG!
I'M SCARED.
I DON'T WANT TO BE HERE.
SISTER...
SISTER...!!

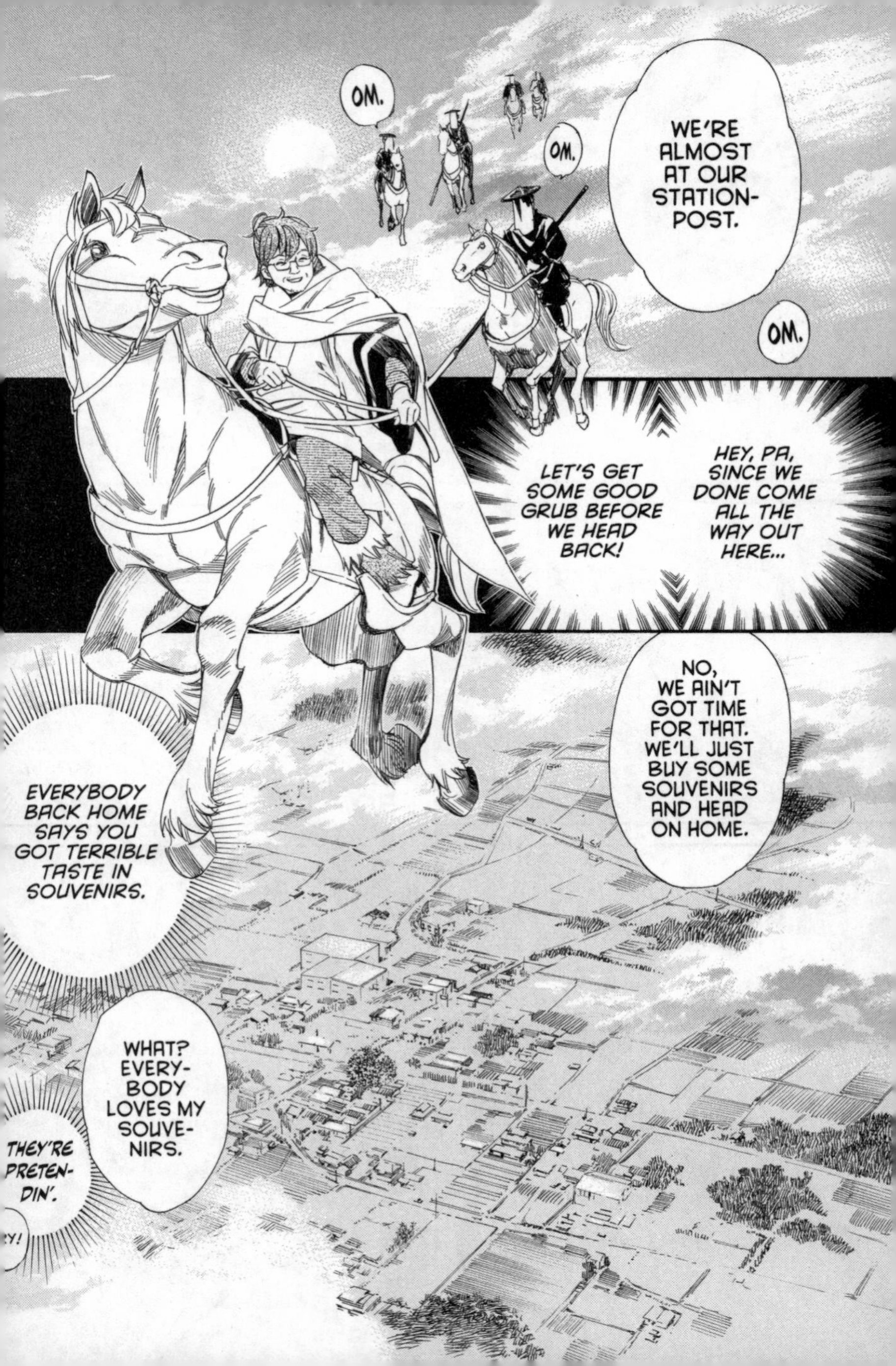
WE'RE ALMOST AT OUR STATION-POST.
OM.
OM.
OM.
HEY, PA, SINCE WE DONE COME ALL THE WAY OUT HERE...
LET'S GET SOME GOOD GRUB BEFORE WE HEAD BACK!
NO, WE AIN'T GOT TIME FOR THAT. WE'LL JUST BUY SOME SOUVENIRS AND HEAD ON HOME.
EVERYBODY BACK HOME SAYS YOU GOT TERRIBLE TASTE IN SOUVENIRS.
WHAT? EVERY-BODY LOVES MY SOUVE-NIRS.
THEY'RE PRETEN-DIN'.

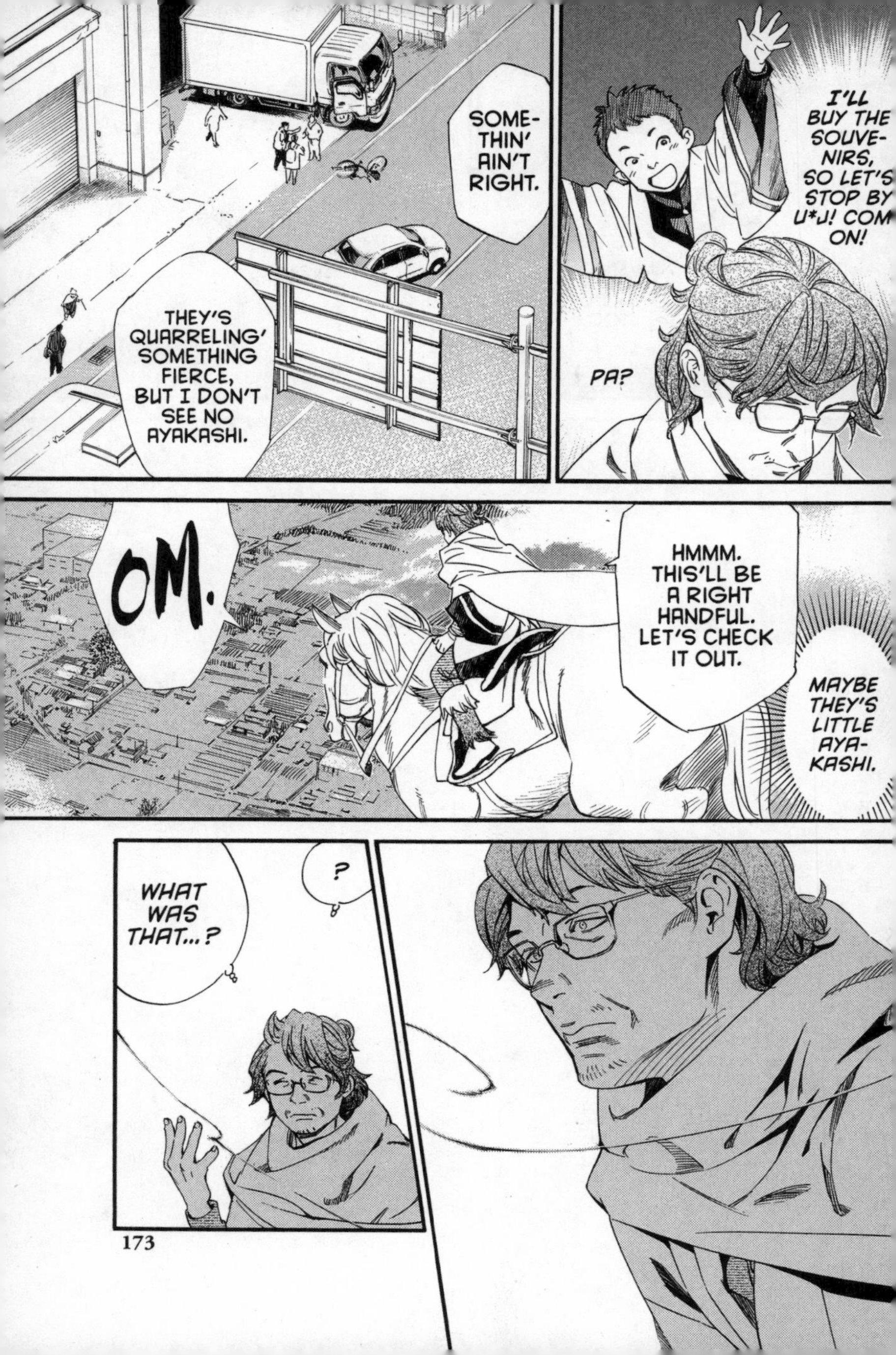
I'LL BUY THE SOUVE-NIRS, SO LET'S STOP BY U*J! COM ON!
PA?
SOME-THIN' AIN'T RIGHT.
THEY'S QUARRELING' SOMETHING FIERCE, BUT I DON'T SEE NO AYAKASHI.
MAYBE THEY'S LITTLE AYA-KASHI.
HMMM. THIS'LL BE A RIGHT HANDFUL. LET'S CHECK IT OUT.
OM.
?
WHAT WAS THAT...?

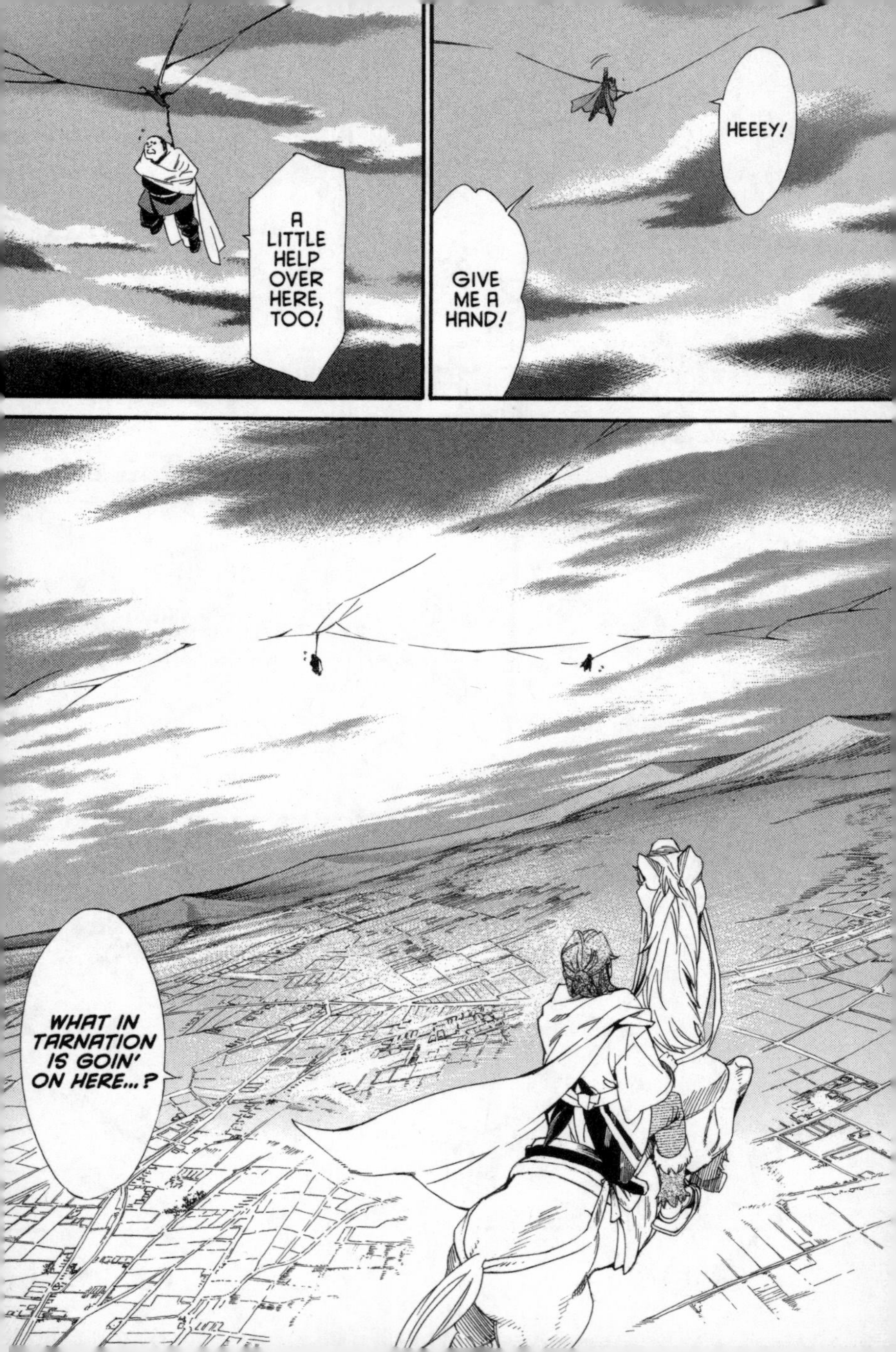
HEEEY!
GIVE ME A HAND!
A LITTLE HELP OVER HERE, TOO!
WHAT IN TARNATION IS GOIN' ON HERE...?

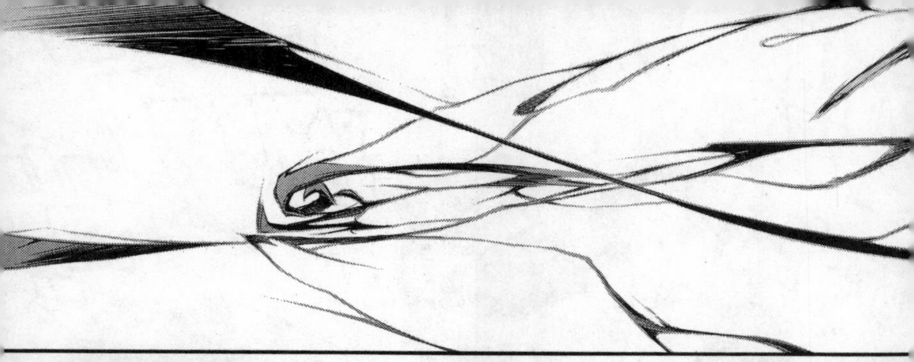
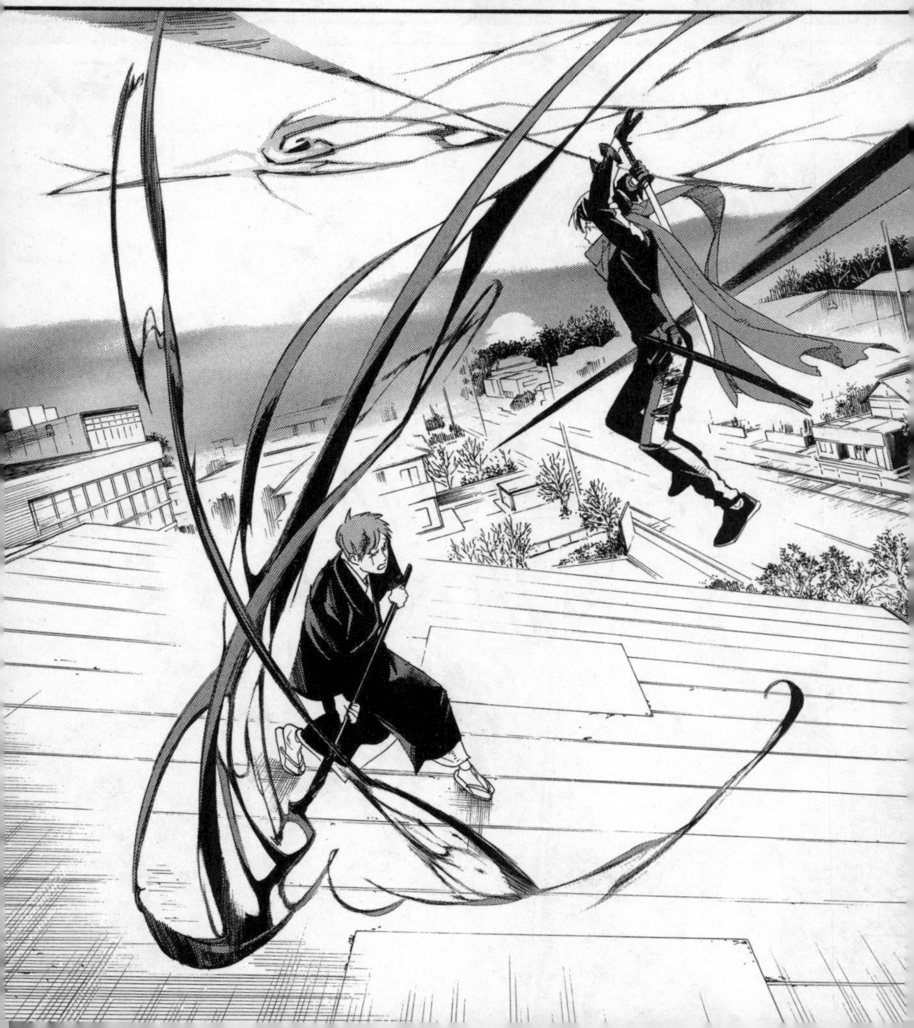

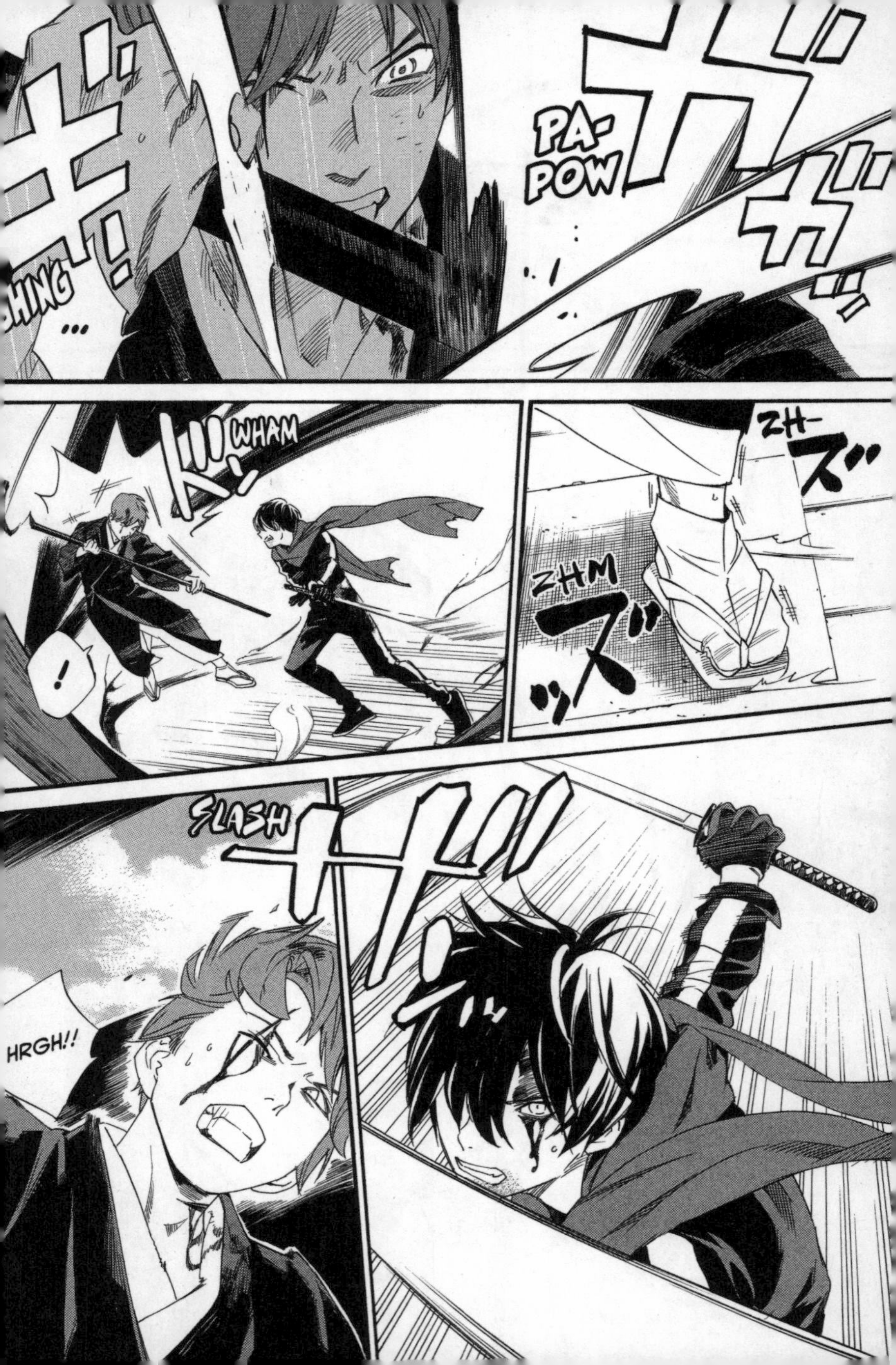
PA-POW
CHING
...
ZH-
ZHM
WHAM
!
SLASH
HRGH!!

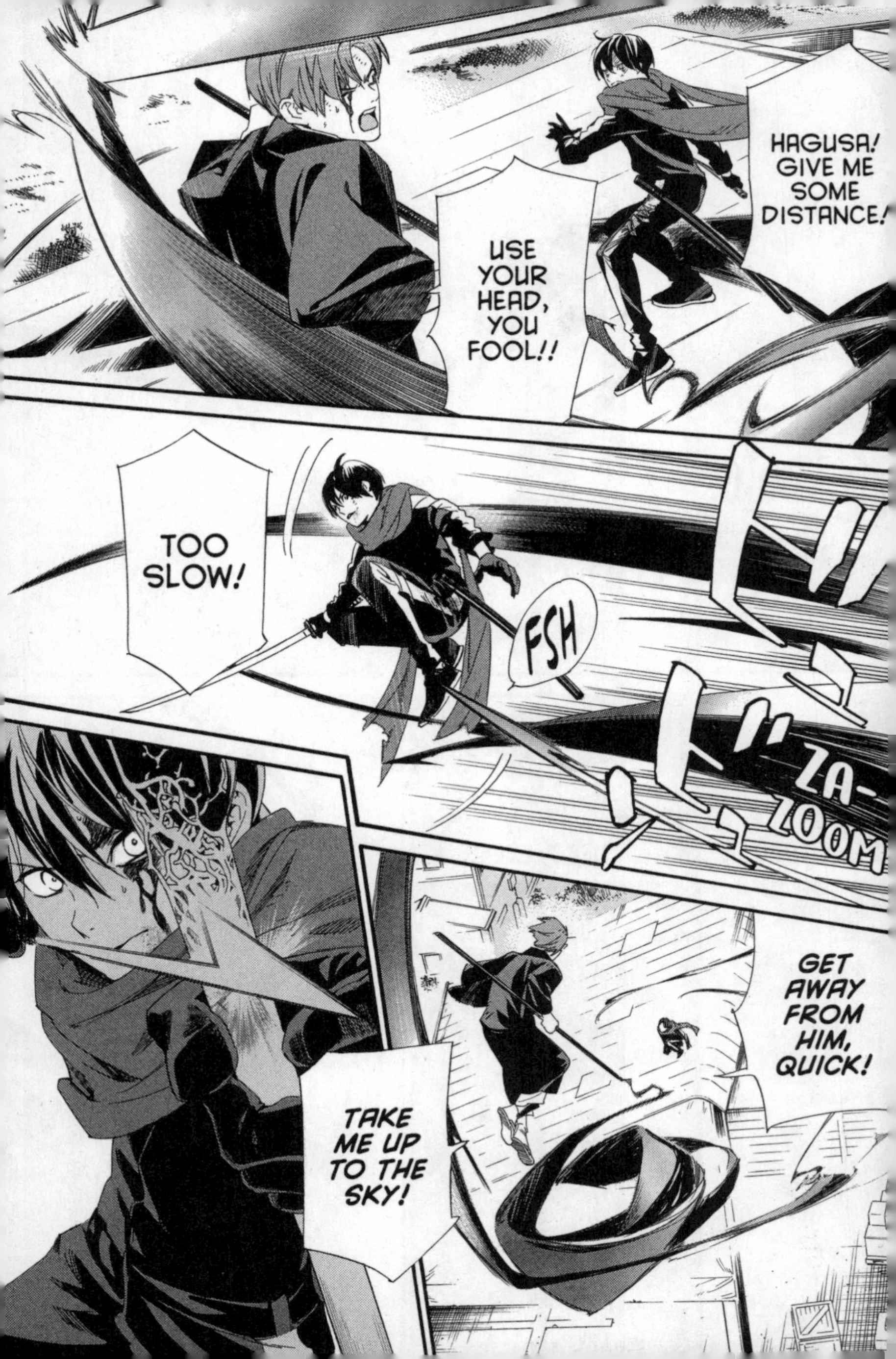
HAGUSA! GIVE ME SOME DISTANCE!
USE YOUR HEAD, YOU FOOL!!
ZA-ZOOM
FSH
TOO SLOW!
GET AWAY FROM HIM, QUICK!
TAKE ME UP TO THE SKY!

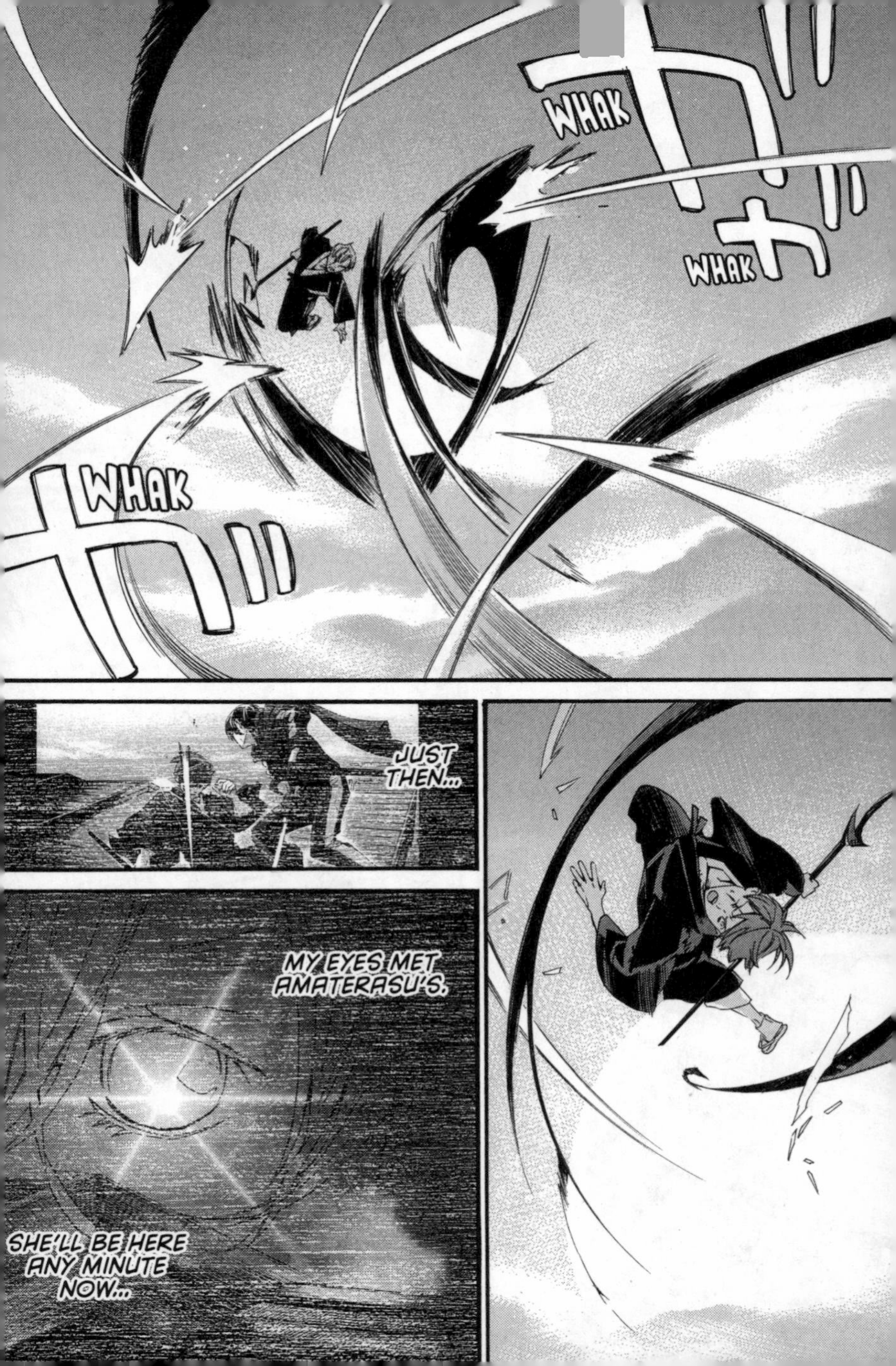
WHAK
WHAK
WHAK
JUST THEN...
MY EYES MET AMATERASU'S.
SHE'LL BE HERE ANY MINUTE NOW...

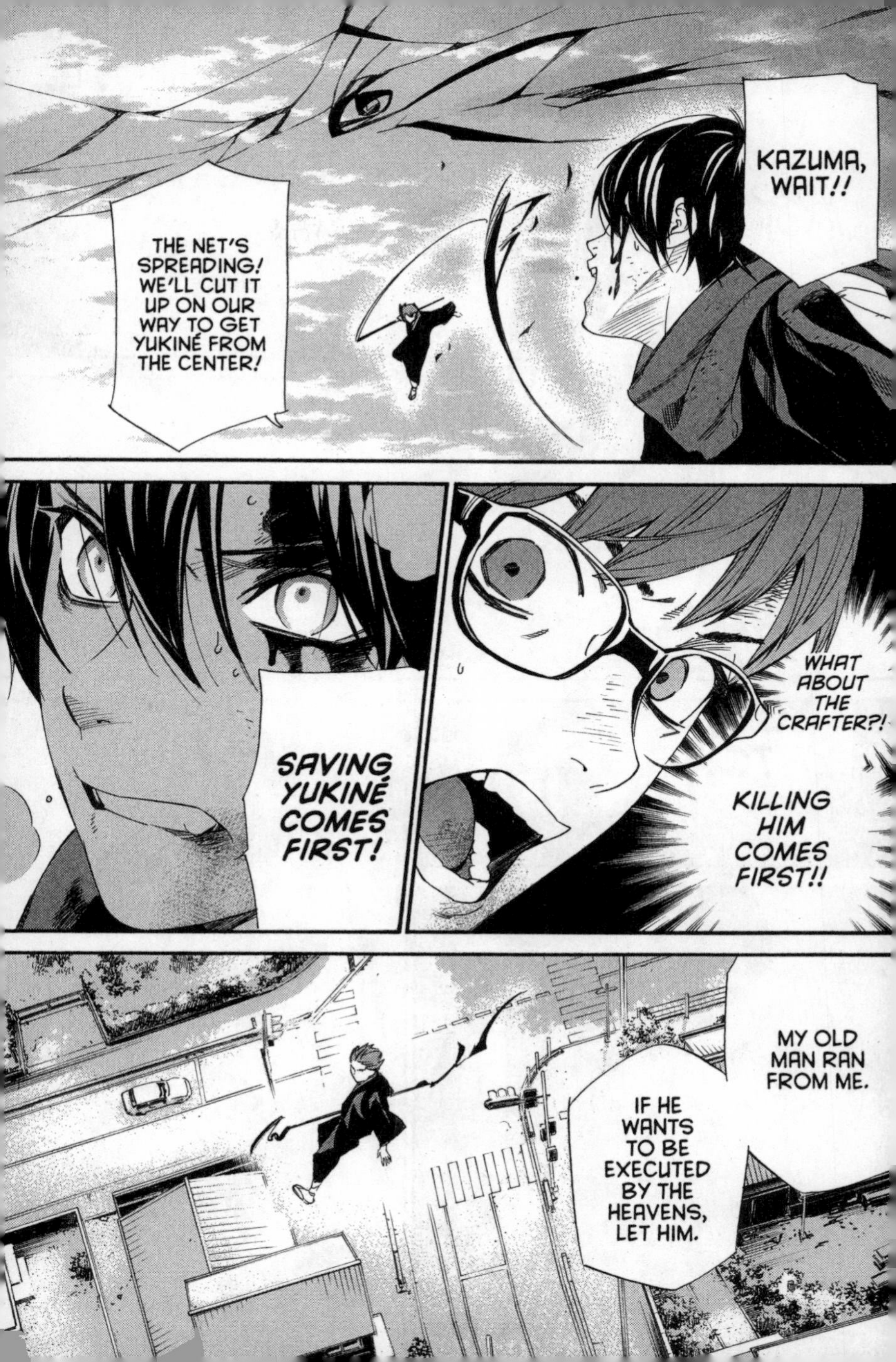
KAZUMA, WAIT!!
THE NET'S SPREADING! WE'LL CUT IT UP ON OUR WAY TO GET YUKINÉ FROM THE CENTER!
WHAT ABOUT THE CRAFTER?!
KILLING HIM COMES FIRST!!
SAVING YUKINÉ COMES FIRST!
MY OLD MAN RAN FROM ME.
IF HE WANTS TO BE EXECUTED BY THE HEAVENS, LET HIM.

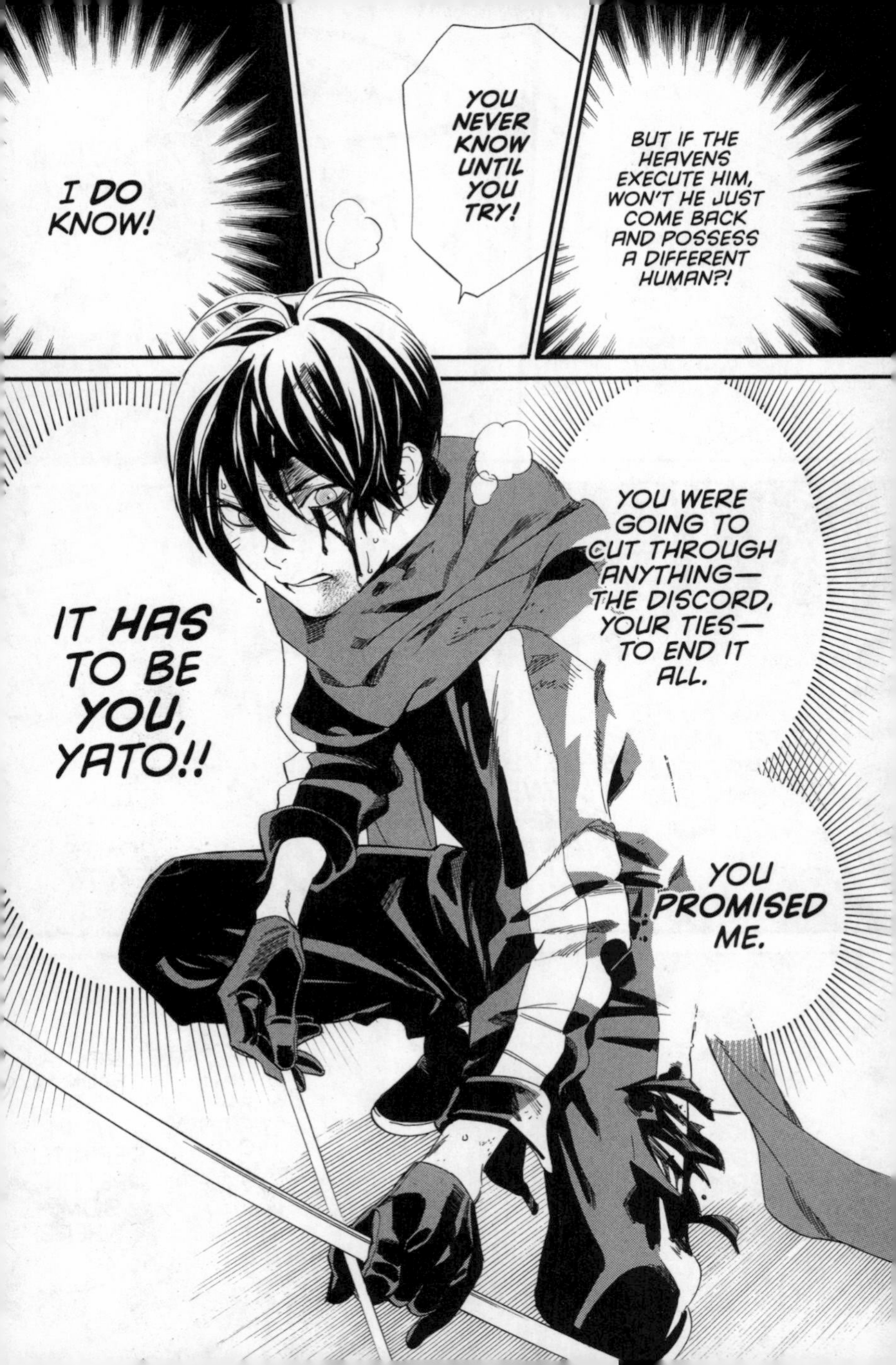
BUT IF THE HEAVENS EXECUTE HIM, WON'T HE JUST COME BACK AND POSSESS A DIFFERENT HUMAN?!
YOU NEVER KNOW UNTIL YOU TRY!
I DO KNOW!
YOU WERE GOING TO CUT THROUGH ANYTHING—THE DISCORD, YOUR TIES—TO END IT ALL.
YOU PROMISED ME.
IT HAS TO BE YOU, YATO!!

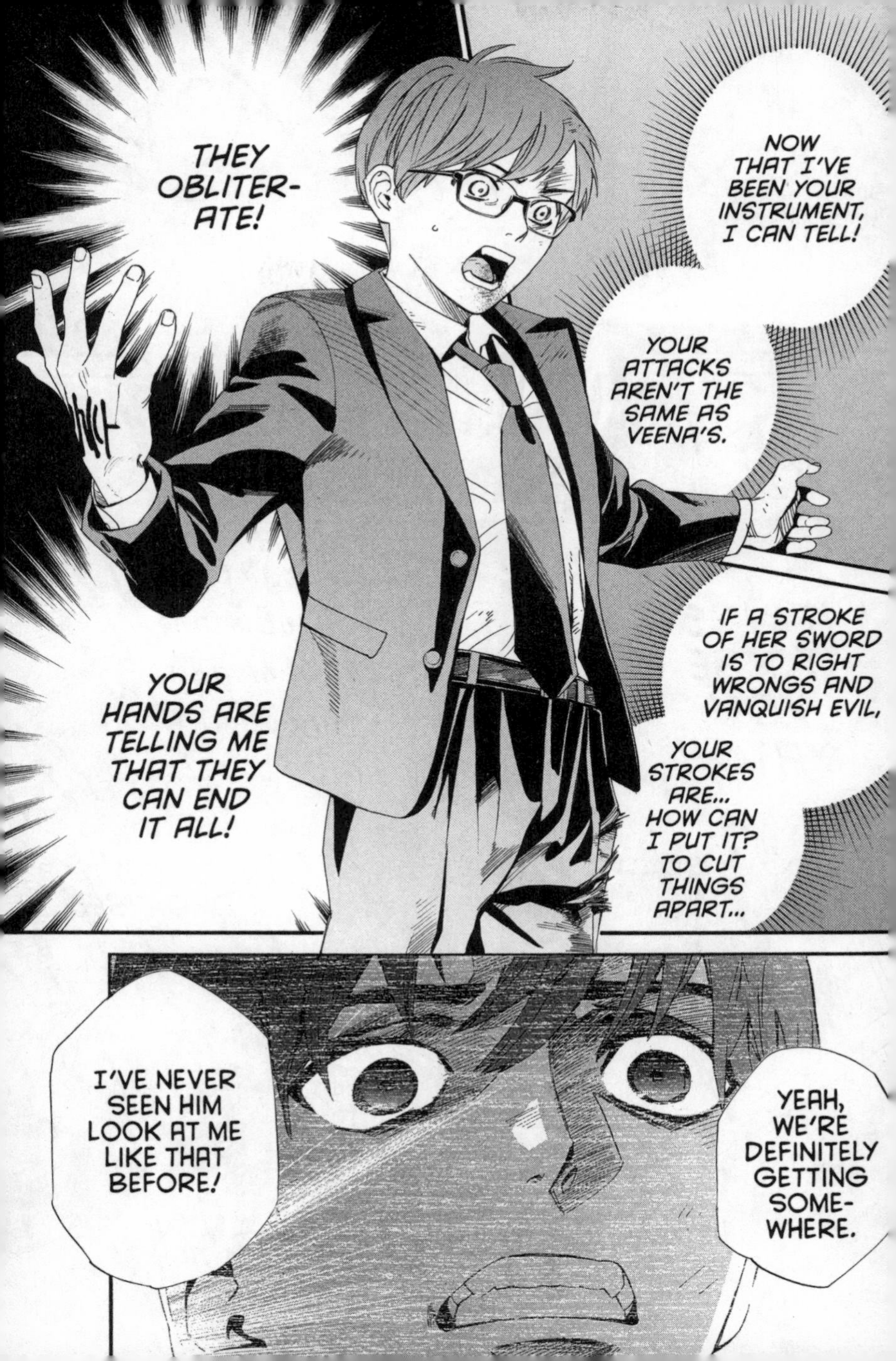
NOW THAT I'VE BEEN YOUR INSTRUMENT, I CAN TELL!
YOUR ATTACKS AREN'T THE SAME AS VEENA'S.
IF A STROKE OF HER SWORD IS TO RIGHT WRONGS AND VANQUISH EVIL,
YOUR STROKES ARE... HOW CAN I PUT IT? TO CUT THINGS APART...
YOUR HANDS ARE TELLING ME THAT THEY CAN END IT ALL!
THEY OBLITER-ATE!
YEAH, WE'RE DEFINITELY GETTING SOME-WHERE.
I'VE NEVER SEEN HIM LOOK AT ME LIKE THAT BEFORE!

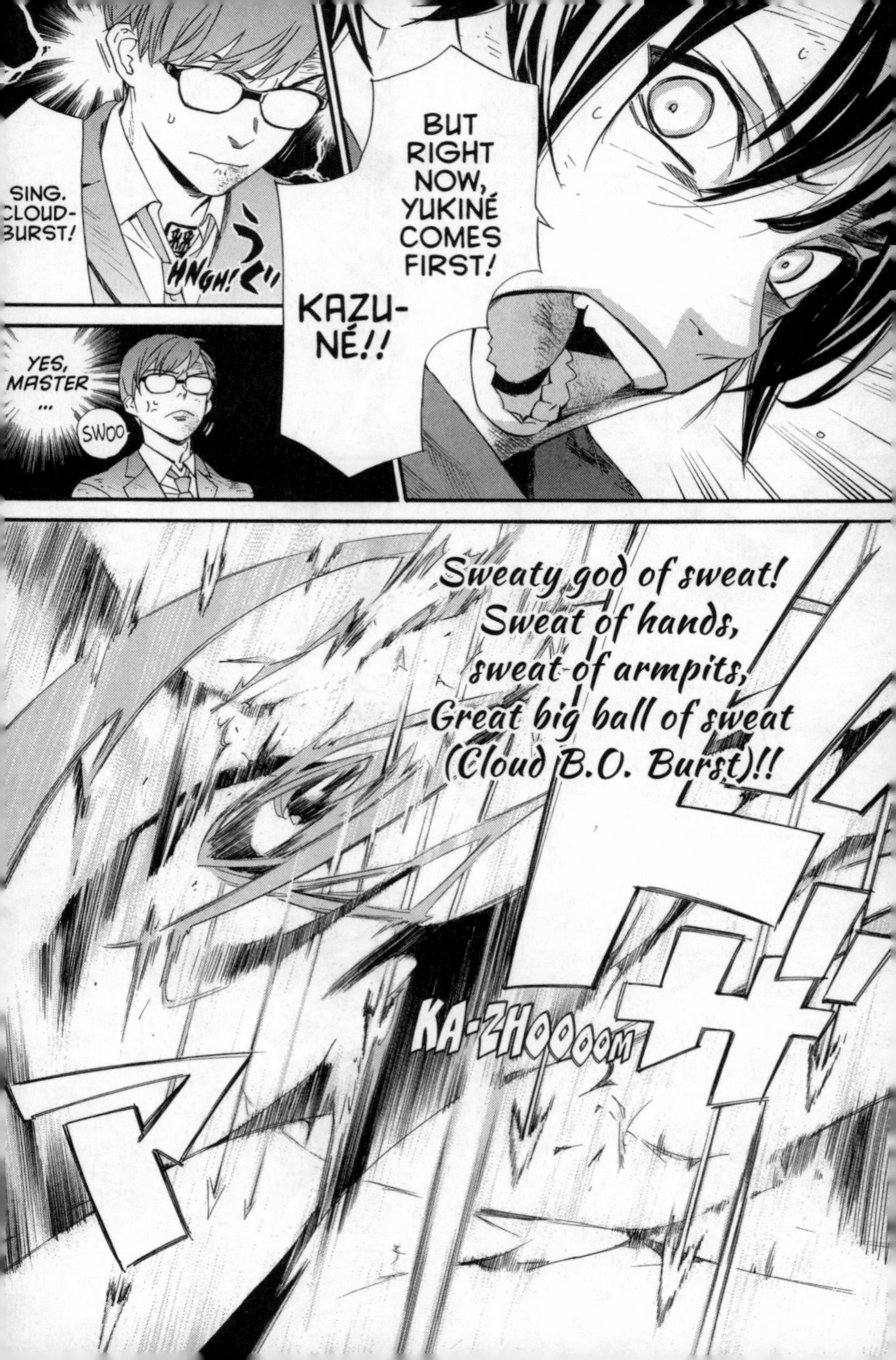
BUT RIGHT NOW, YUKINÉ COMES FIRST!
KAZUNÉ!!
SING. CLOUD-BURST!
HNGH!
YES, MASTER ...
SWOO
Sweaty god of sweat! Sweat of hands, sweat of armpits, Great big ball of sweat (Cloud B.O. Burst)!!
KA-ZHOOOOOM

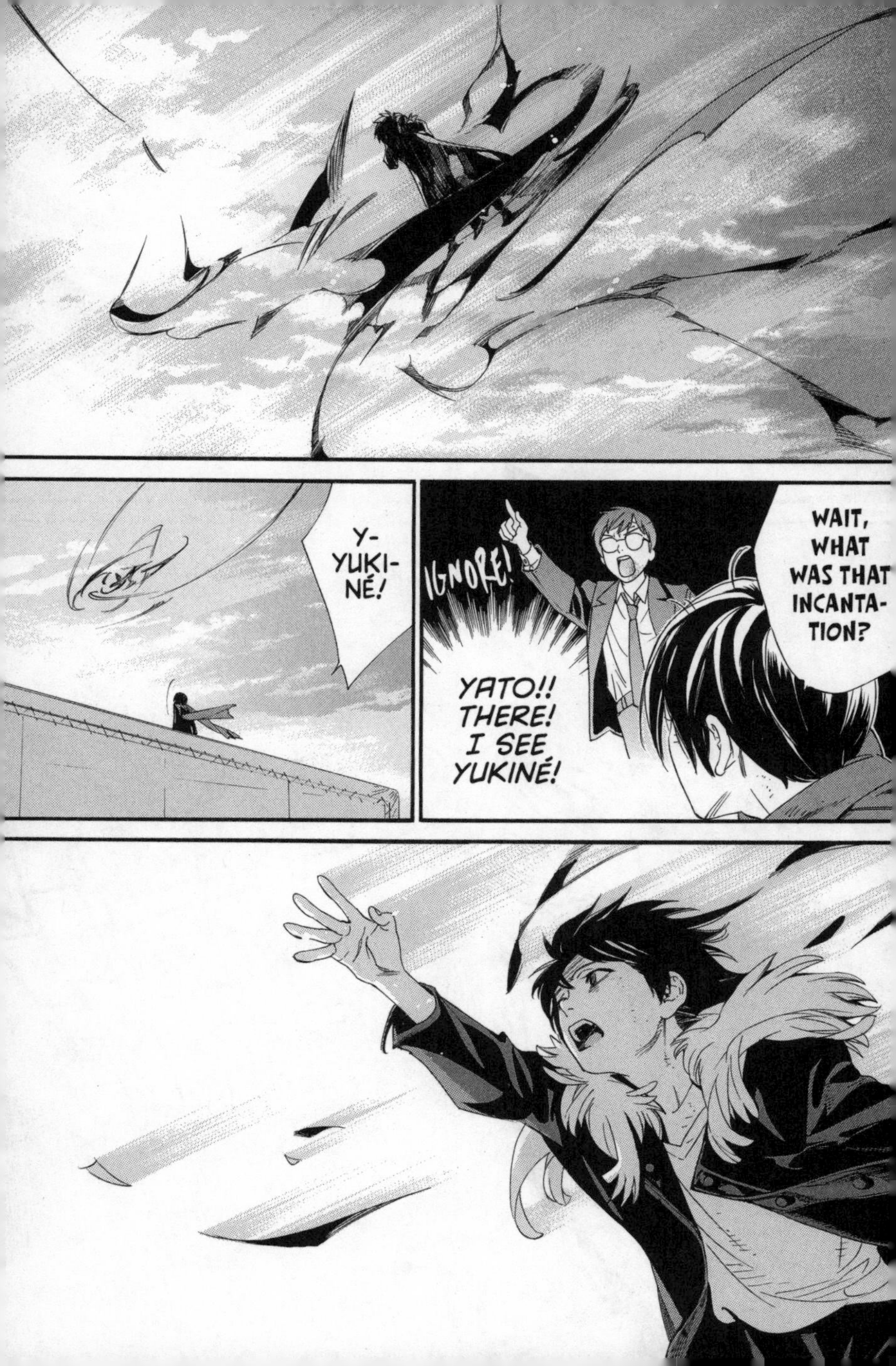
WAIT, WHAT WAS THAT INCANTATION?
IGNORE!
YATO!! THERE! I SEE YUKINÉ!
Y-YUKI-NÉ!

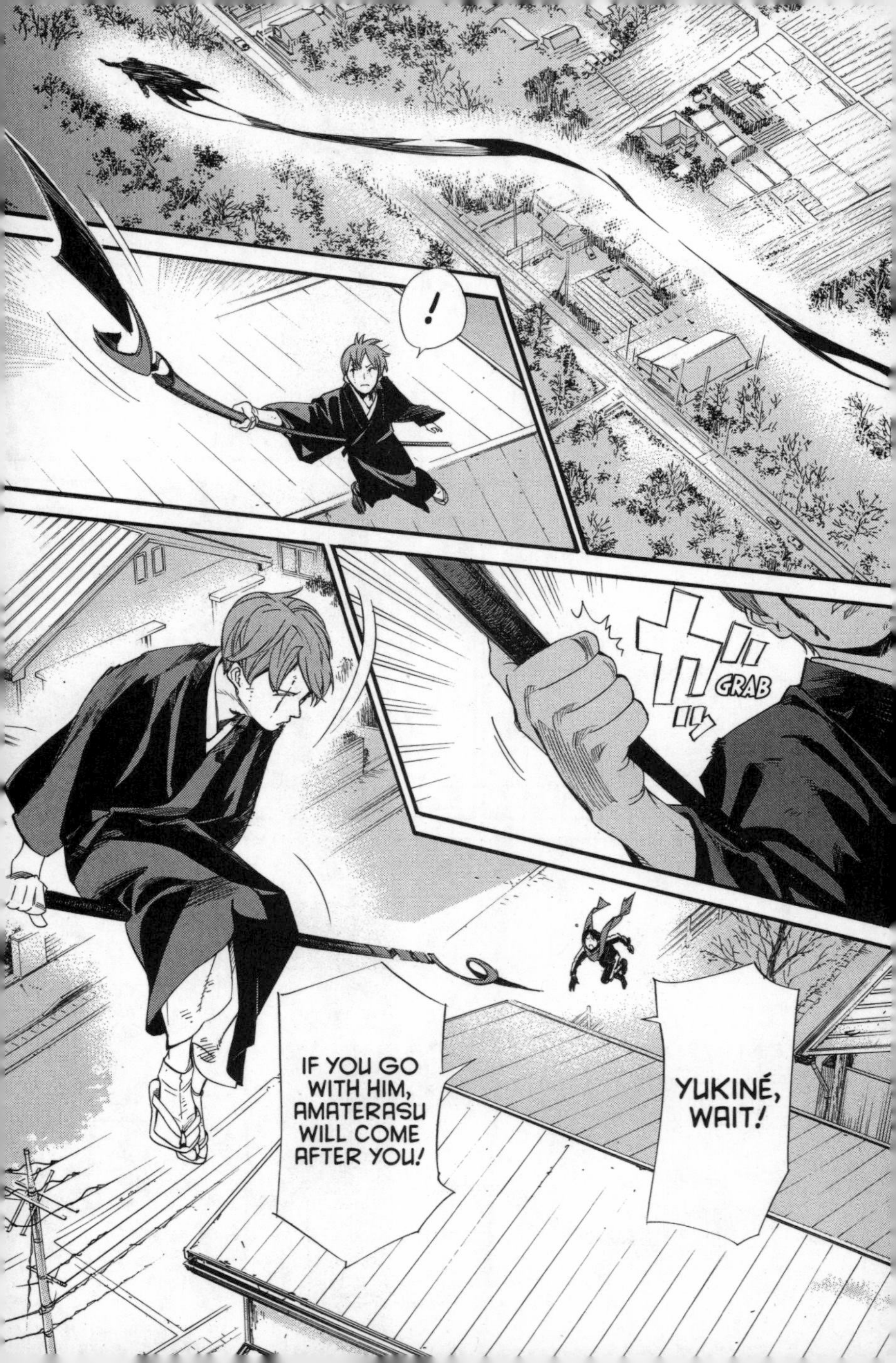
!
GRAB
YUKINÉ, WAIT!
IF YOU GO WITH HIM, AMATERASU WILL COME AFTER YOU!

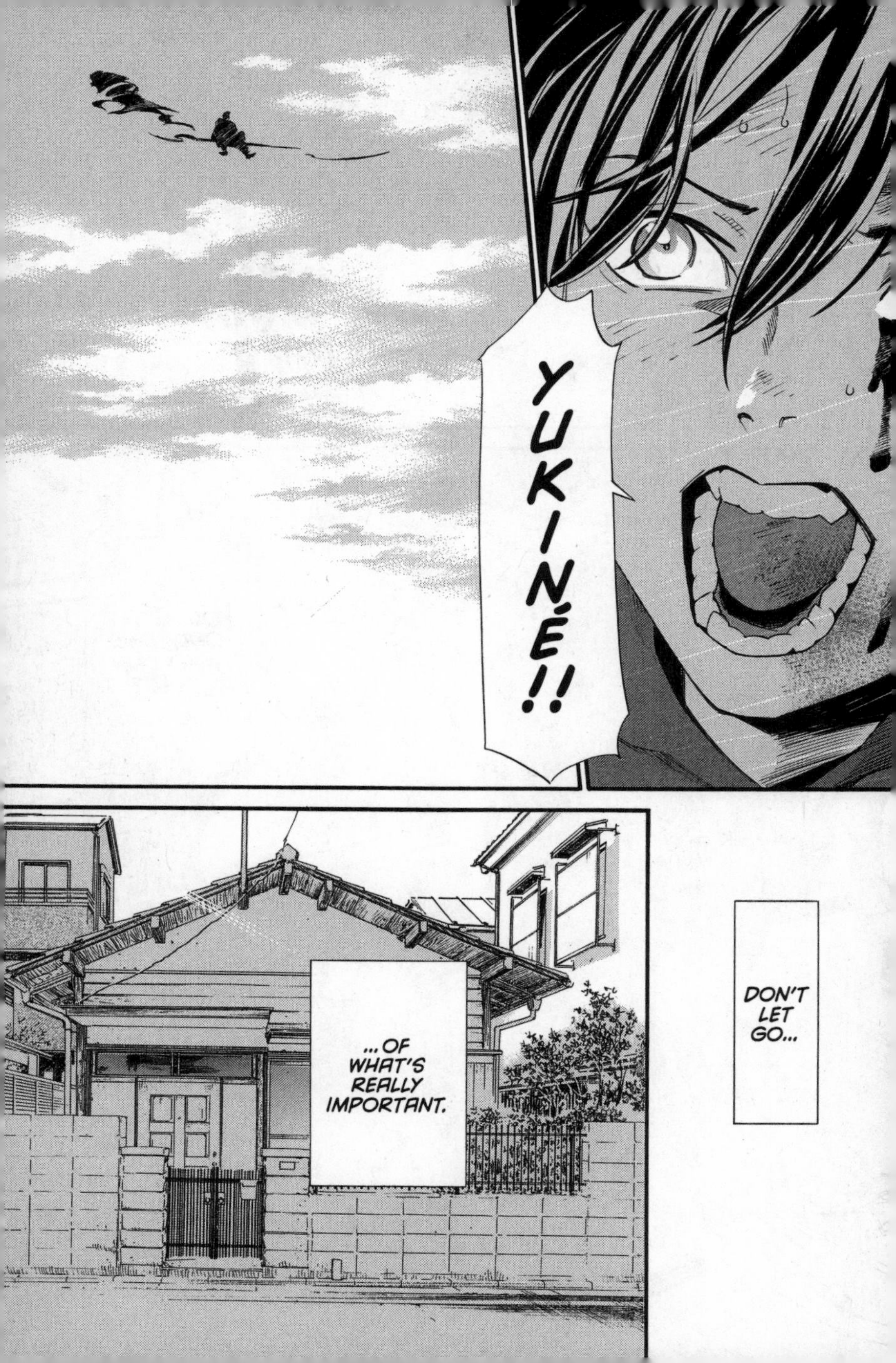
YUKINÉ!!
DON'T LET GO...
...OF WHAT'S REALLY IMPORTANT.

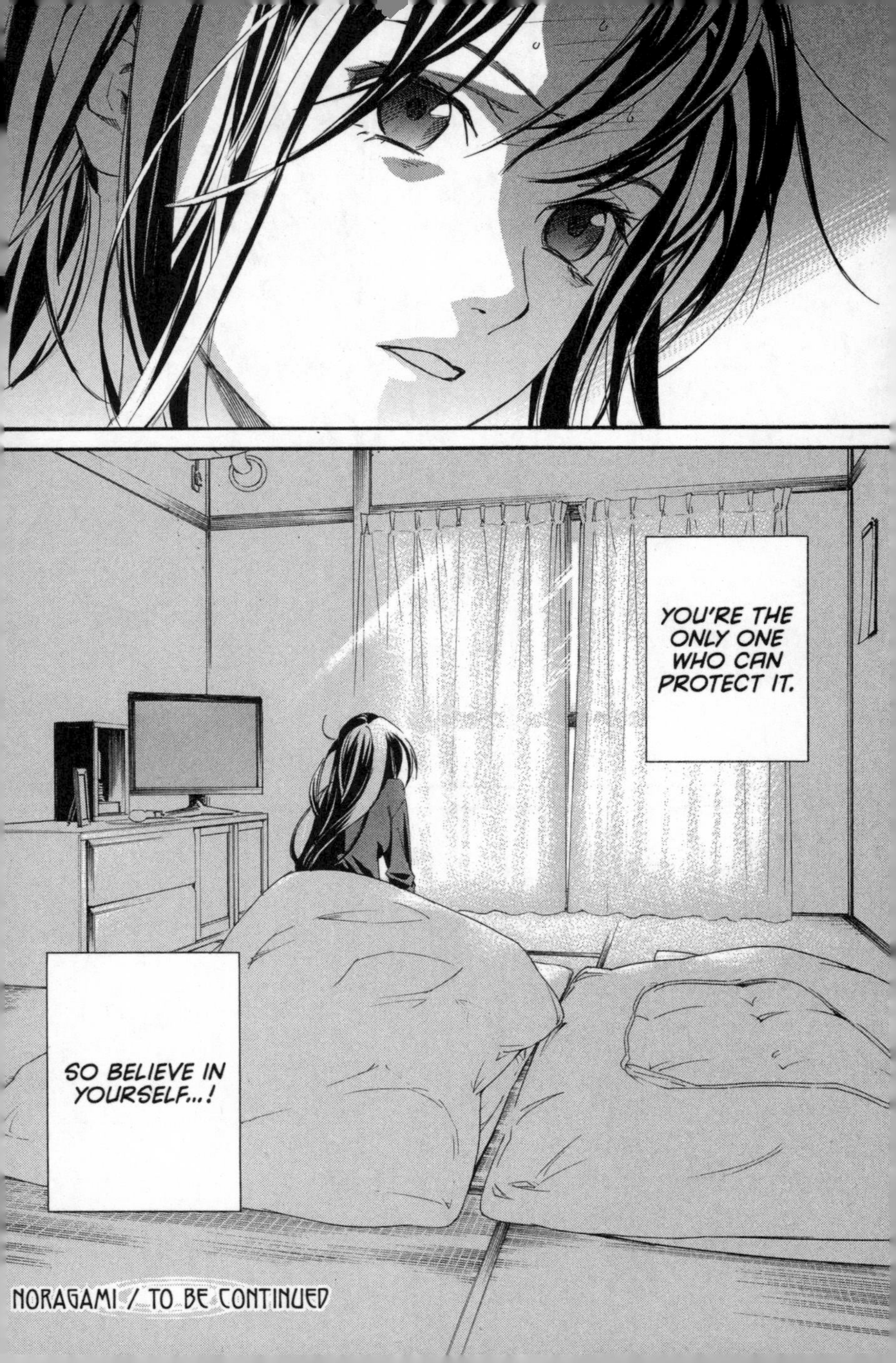
YOU'RE THE ONLY ONE WHO CAN PROTECT IT.
SO BELIEVE IN YOURSELF...!
NORAGAMI / TO BE CONTINUED

野良神

ATROCIOUS MANGA

SPUR OF THE MOMENT

MEW
MEW
12 ROLLS
CATS!
MEW
THIS IS AWFUL... SOMEONE'S ABANDONED THEM. ARE YOU OKAY? YOU'RE NOT HURT, ARE YOU?
WAIT! YOU CAN'T TOUCH THEM!
IT'S FINE. IT'S NOT LIKE THEY CAN MAKE ME SICK.
JUST SLOW DOWN...
AND TAKE A VIDEO!

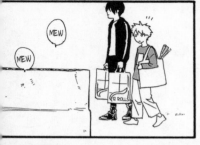

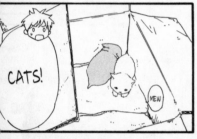

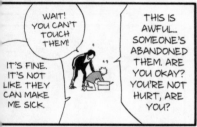

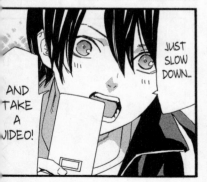

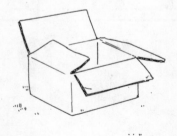

NONESSENTIAL

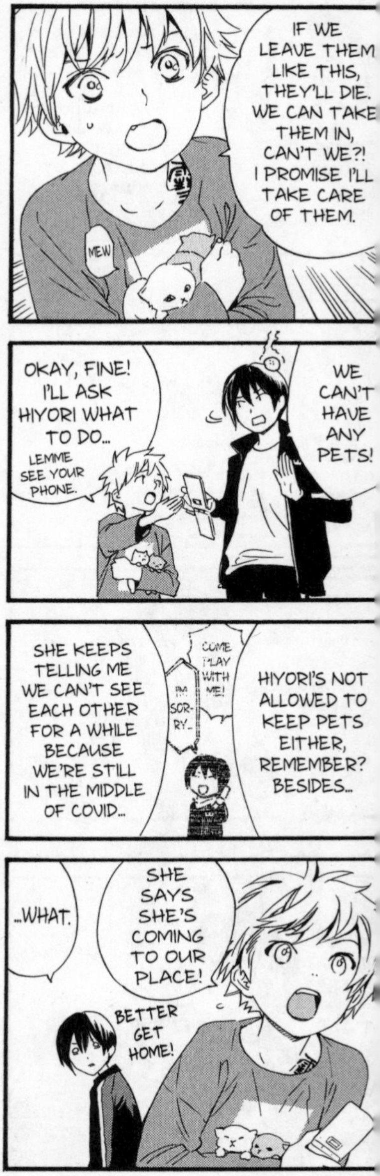
IF WE LEAVE THEM LIKE THIS, THEY'LL DIE. WE CAN TAKE THEM IN, CAN'T WE?! I PROMISE I'LL TAKE CARE OF THEM.
MEW
WE CAN'T HAVE ANY PETS!
OKAY, FINE! I'LL ASK HIYORI WHAT TO DO...
LEMME SEE YOUR PHONE.
HIYORI'S NOT ALLOWED TO KEEP PETS EITHER, REMEMBER? BESIDES...
COME PLAY WITH ME!
I'M SORRY...
SHE KEEPS TELLING ME WE CAN'T SEE EACH OTHER FOR A WHILE BECAUSE WE'RE STILL IN THE MIDDLE OF COVID...
SHE SAYS SHE'S COMING TO OUR PLACE!
BETTER GET HOME!
...WHAT.

WITH COVID

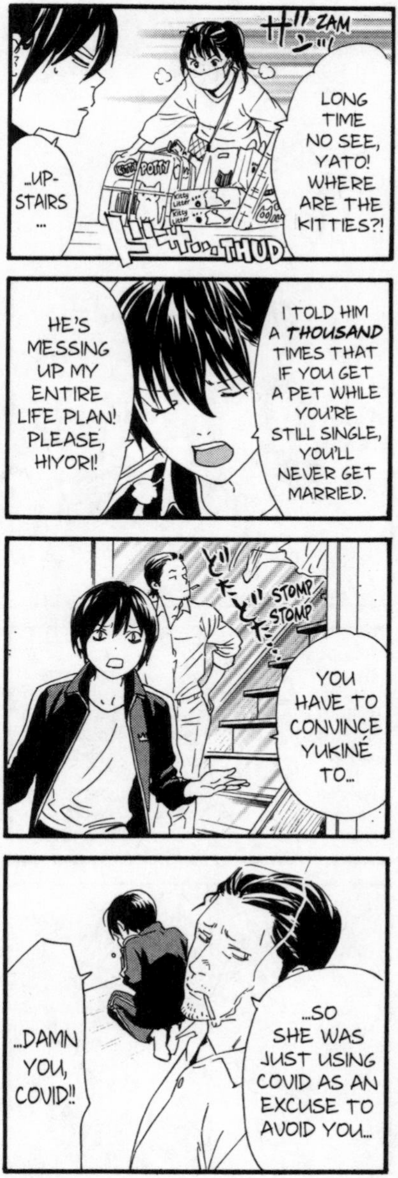
ZAM
LONG TIME NO SEE, YATO! WHERE ARE THE KITTIES?!
THUD
...UPSTAIRS...
I TOLD HIM A THOUSAND TIMES THAT IF YOU GET A PET WHILE YOU'RE STILL SINGLE, YOU'LL NEVER GET MARRIED.
HE'S MESSING UP MY ENTIRE LIFE PLAN! PLEASE, HIYORI!
STOMP STOMP
YOU HAVE TO CONVINCE YUKINÉ TO...
...SO SHE WAS JUST USING COVID AS AN EXCUSE TO AVOID YOU...
...DAMN YOU, COVID!!

ENLIGHTENED

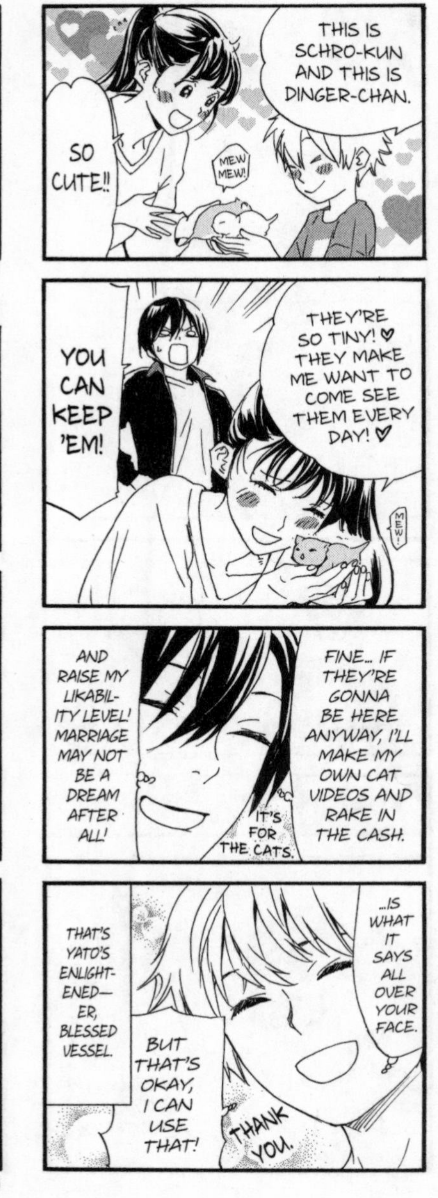
THIS IS SCHRO-KUN AND THIS IS DINGER-CHAN.
SO CUTE!!
MEW MEW!
THEY'RE SO TINY! ♥ THEY MAKE ME WANT TO COME SEE THEM EVERY DAY! ♥
YOU CAN KEEP 'EM!
MEW!
FINE... IF THEY'RE GONNA BE HERE ANYWAY, I'LL MAKE MY OWN CAT VIDEOS AND RAKE IN THE CASH.
IT'S FOR THE CATS.
AND RAISE MY LIKABIL-ITY LEVEL! MARRIAGE MAY NOT BE A DREAM AFTER ALL!
...IS WHAT IT SAYS ALL OVER YOUR FACE.
THAT'S YATO'S ENLIGHT-ENED— ER, BLESSED VESSEL.
BUT THAT'S OKAY, I CAN USE THAT!
THANK YOU.

SIDE JOB

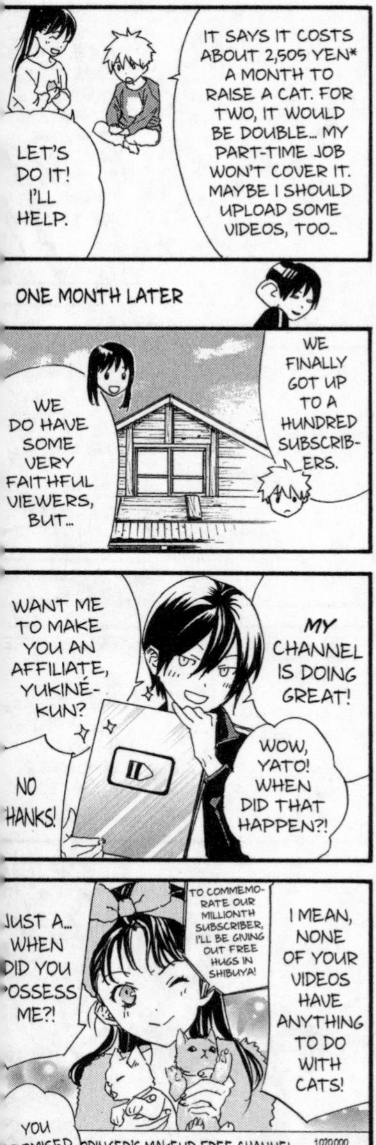
IT SAYS IT COSTS ABOUT 2,505 YEN* A MONTH TO RAISE A CAT. FOR TWO, IT WOULD BE DOUBLE... MY PART-TIME JOB WON'T COVER IT. MAYBE I SHOULD UPLOAD SOME VIDEOS, TOO...
LET'S DO IT! I'LL HELP.
ONE MONTH LATER
WE FINALLY GOT UP TO A HUNDRED SUBSCRIB-ERS.
WE DO HAVE SOME VERY FAITHFUL VIEWERS, BUT...
MY CHANNEL IS DOING GREAT!
WANT ME TO MAKE YOU AN AFFILIATE, YUKINÉ-KUN?
WOW, YATO! WHEN DID THAT HAPPEN?!
NO HANKS!
I MEAN, NONE OF YOUR VIDEOS HAVE ANYTHING TO DO WITH CATS!
TO COMMEMO-RATE OUR MILLIONTH SUBSCRIBER, I'LL BE GIVING OUT FREE HUGS IN SHIBUYA!
JUST A... WHEN DID YOU OSSESS ME?!
YOU ROMISED.
ODINGER'S MAKEUP-FREE CHANNEL
1,020,000 SUBSCRIBERS

*100 YEN = APPROX. $1

BUSINESS SAVVY

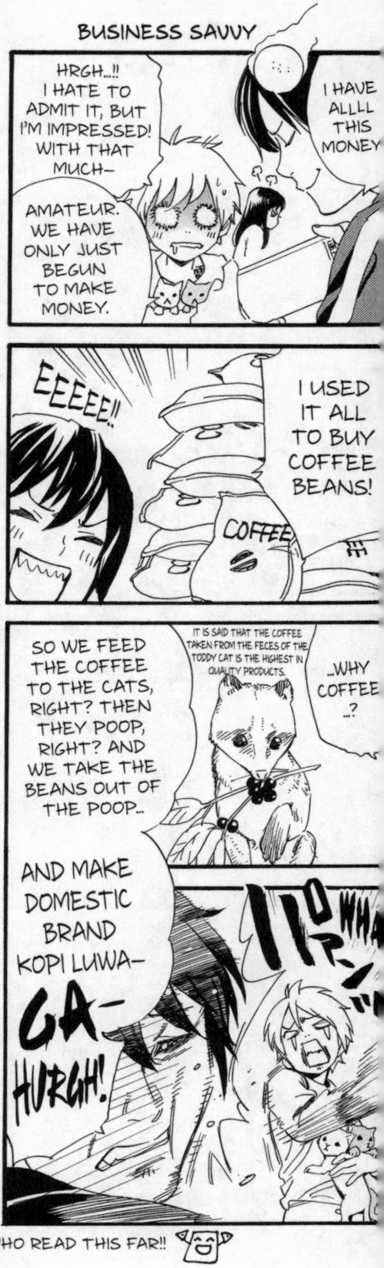
I HAVE ALLLL THIS MONEY
HRGH...!! I HATE TO ADMIT IT, BUT I'M IMPRESSED! WITH THAT MUCH—
AMATEUR. WE HAVE ONLY JUST BEGUN TO MAKE MONEY.
I USED IT ALL TO BUY COFFEE BEANS!
EEEEE!!
COFFEE
...WHY COFFEE...?
IT IS SAID THAT THE COFFEE TAKEN FROM THE FECES OF THE TODDY CAT IS THE HIGHEST IN QUALITY PRODUCTS.
SO WE FEED THE COFFEE TO THE CATS, RIGHT? THEN THEY POOP, RIGHT? AND WE TAKE THE BEANS OUT OF THE POOP...
AND MAKE DOMESTIC BRAND KOPI LUWA—
GA—HURGH!

SUPER SUPER RARE CHARACTER

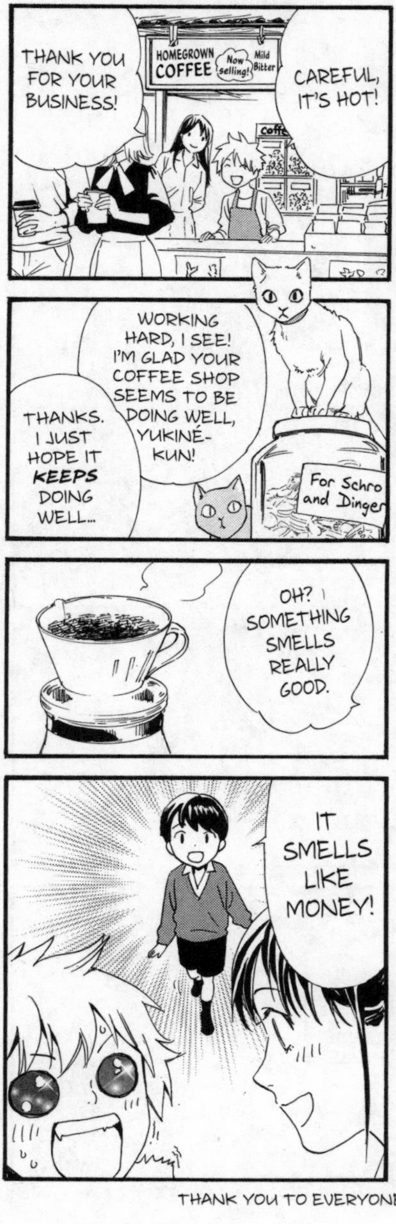
CAREFUL, IT'S HOT!
HOMEGROWN COFFEE
Now selling!
Mild
Bitter
THANK YOU FOR YOUR BUSINESS!
WORKING HARD, I SEE! I'M GLAD YOUR COFFEE SHOP SEEMS TO BE DOING WELL, YUKINÉ-KUN!
THANKS. I JUST HOPE IT **KEEPS** DOING WELL...
For Schro and Dinger
OH? SOMETHING SMELLS REALLY GOOD.
IT SMELLS LIKE MONEY!

THANK YOU TO EVERYONE WHO READ THIS FAR!!

TRANSLATION NOTES

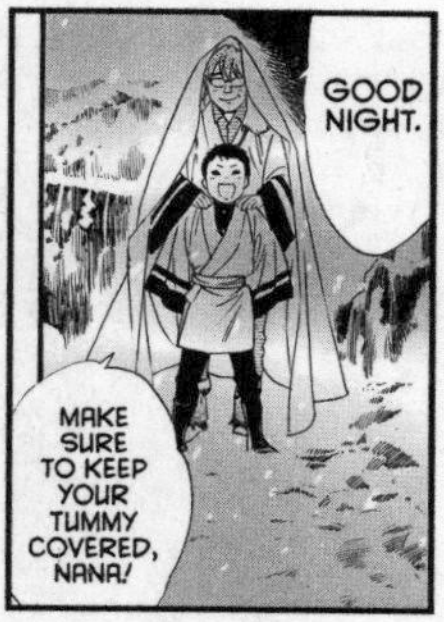
GOOD NIGHT.
MAKE SURE TO KEEP YOUR TUMMY COVERED, NANA!

Keep your tummy covered, page 16
Prevailing folk wisdom in Japan holds that sleeping with one's belly exposed is sure to result in catching a cold. This warning is more common in the summer months, when it's warm and people are less careful, but Shiiho insists on giving Nana this advice, even if it is unlikely in the middle of winter.

Kôhaku, page 52
The Kôhaku Uta Gassen, or Red and White Song Battle, is a New Year's Eve special shown on the NHK network every year. It features celebrity musical artists who are divided into a red team and a white team, who perform songs throughout the night. At the end, the judges and audience vote to decide which team performed better.

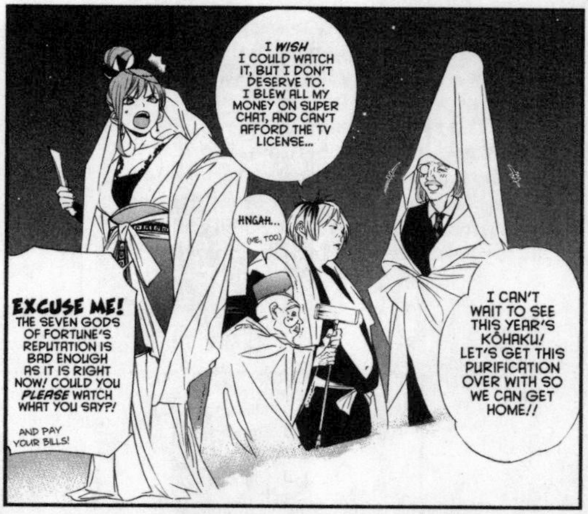
I CAN'T WAIT TO SEE THIS YEAR'S KÔHAKU! LET'S GET THIS PURIFICATION OVER WITH SO WE CAN GET HOME!!
I *WISH* I COULD WATCH IT, BUT I DON'T DESERVE TO. I BLEW ALL MY MONEY ON SUPER CHAT, AND CAN'T AFFORD THE TV LICENSE...
HNGAH... (ME, TOO)
EXCUSE ME! THE SEVEN GODS OF FORTUNE'S REPUTATION IS BAD ENOUGH AS IT IS RIGHT NOW! COULD YOU *PLEASE* WATCH WHAT YOU SAY?!
AND PAY YOUR BILLS!

TV license, Super Chat, page 52
In many countries, including Japan, public television is funded by a television license, which is like a tax paid for the reception of broadcasts. The annual license fee in Japan is around $140 for domestic broadcasts, but payment is not enforced. Technically, Hotei has the ability to watch Kôhaku, but his integrity will not allow him to do so. Super Chat is a YouTube feature that allows viewers to pay content providers to pin their comments to live streams, making them more visible.

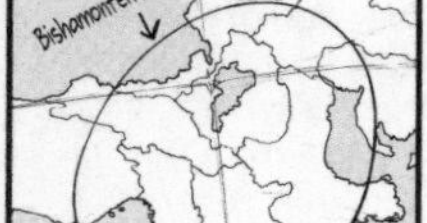
Bishamonten's Assignment

That ain't small, page 55
The area shown here represents part of the Chûbu region and the entire Kansai region. The area circled covers roughly six to eight prefectures, including Osaka, Kyoto, and Nara.

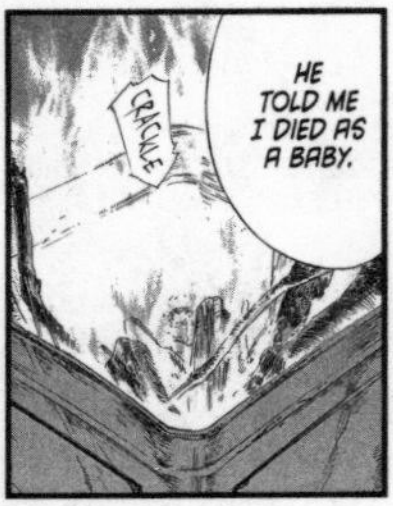
HE TOLD ME I DIED AS A BABY.
CRACKLE

I died as a baby, page 119

To be more precise, the stray was told that she was a *mizuko*, literally meaning "water child." This is a term applied to babies who died very shortly after birth, or possibly before birth. "Water child" is a reference to Hiruko, the leech child, who, the reader may recall, was born without bones and sent out to sea.

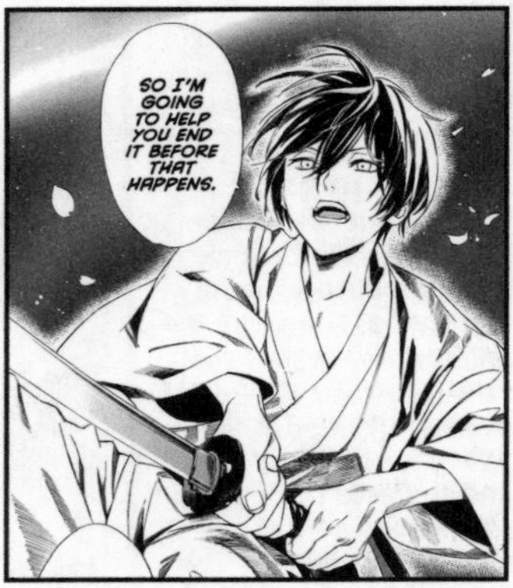
SO I'M GOING TO HELP YOU END IT BEFORE THAT HAPPENS.

Help you end it, page 138

In Japanese, Yato says he will *kaishaku* his father. Literally meaning "assist," *kaishaku* is the word used specifically in *seppuku* ritual suicide. In old times, a samurai would perform *seppuku* as a way to die honorably, rather than be disgraced by falling into the hands of his enemies. The samurai disembowels himself, and his assistant severs his spinal cord (usually by beheading) to end his suffering and finish his life. In other words, Yato is helping his father avoid the disgrace of being killed by his most hated enemies, by killing him himself.

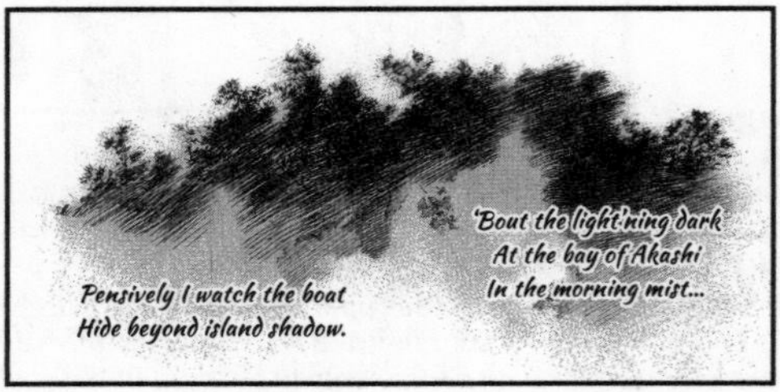
'Bout the light'ning dark
At the bay of Akashi
In the morning mist...
Pensively I watch the boat
Hide beyond island shadow.

Takemikazuchi's poem, page 150

The poem Takemikazuchi was forced to memorize back in the day is a poem written by an anonymous author, recorded in the *Kokin Wakashû*, or *Collection of Poems Ancient and Modern*, published around the year 905. Other English translations of it exist, but this particular translation is original to *Noragami*, largely so it can match the poem that serves as the clue to finding the crafter's shrine or grave.

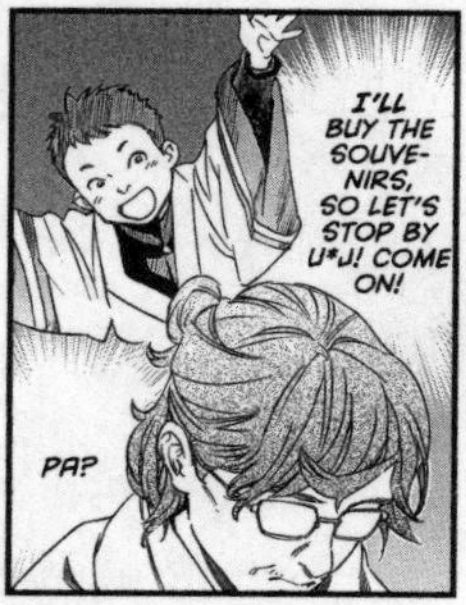
I'LL BUY THE SOUVE-NIRS, SO LET'S STOP BY U*J! COME ON!
PA?

U*J, page 173

Arahabaki and Shiiho are cleaning up the Kansai region of Japan, where USJ is located (short for Universal Studios Japan).

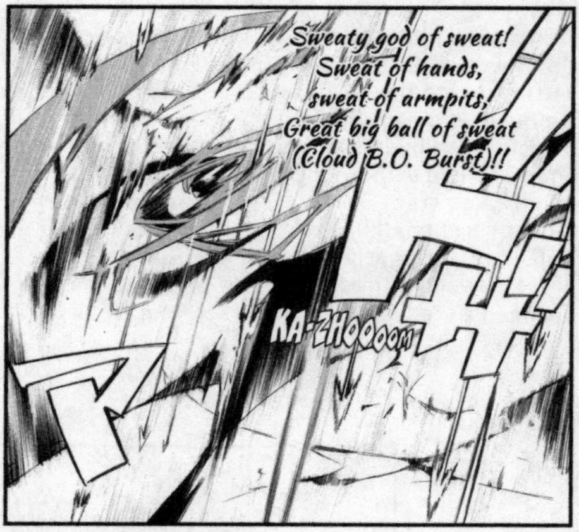
Sweaty god of sweat! Sweat of hands, sweat of armpits, Great big ball of sweat (Cloud B.O. Burst)!!
KA-ZHOOOOM

Cloud BO Burst, page 182

Yato had Kazuma use the Cloudburst, or *Shûu* song when they broke out of the giant fish ayakashi, but now Kazuma has added lyrics to the incantation, and changed the kanji characters of the song's title from "sudden shower" to "stinky shower." The terms are pronounced the same in Japanese.

Nyan-mage and *nekomata*, author's note

Nyan-mage is a mysterious resident of the Japanese theme park, Edo Wonderland. He is a white cat wearing a *chonmage* topknot, a hairstyle common among Edo samurai. As for why he would turn into a *nekomata*, according to Japanese folklore, if a cat lives long enough, its tail will split into two and it will become an ayakashi known as a *nekomata*. Perhaps the same applies to cat-shaped pens.

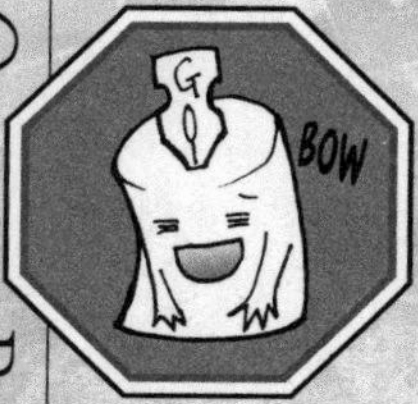
BOW

I love writing supplies, and I'm not happy unless I've used them until they're dead. The ball-point pen I most recommend is a Nyan-mage one I got from a friend. I've been using it on and off since my previous series *Alive*, and it still hasn't run out of ink. I think it might transform into a nekomata.

Adachitoka

Young characters and steampunk setting, like *Howl's Moving Castle* and *Battle Angel Alita*

Beyond the Clouds © 2018 Nicke / Ki-oon

A boy with a talent for machines and a mysterious girl whose wings he's fixed will take you beyond the clouds! In the tradition of the high-flying, resonant adventure stories of Studio Ghibli comes a gorgeous tale about the longing of young hearts for adventure and friendship!

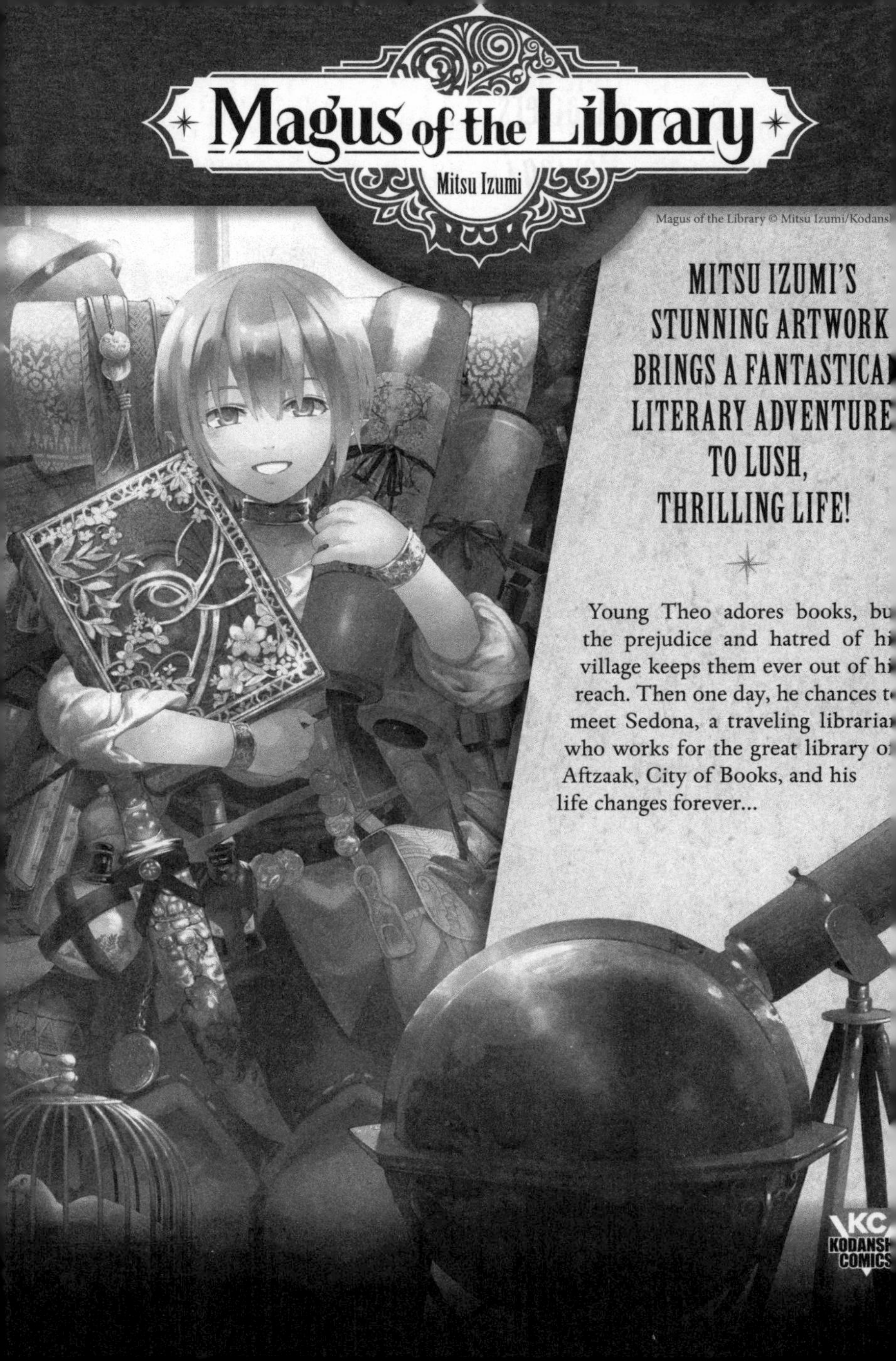
Magus of the Library
Mitsu Izumi
Magus of the Library © Mitsu Izumi/Kodansha
MITSU IZUMI'S STUNNING ARTWORK BRINGS A FANTASTICAL LITERARY ADVENTURE TO LUSH, THRILLING LIFE!
Young Theo adores books, but the prejudice and hatred of his village keeps them ever out of his reach. Then one day, he chances to meet Sedona, a traveling librarian who works for the great library of Aftzaak, City of Books, and his life changes forever...
KC
KODANSHA COMICS

The beloved characters from *Cardcaptor Sakura* return in a brand new, reimagined fantasy adventure!

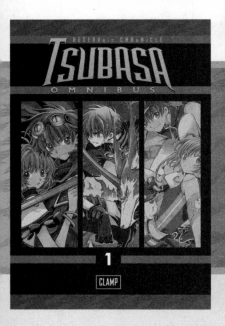

"[*Tsubasa*] takes readers on a fantastic ride that only gets more exhilarating with each successive chapter." —Anime News Network

In the Kingdom of Clow, an archaeological dig unleashes an incredible power, causing Princess Sakura to lose her memories. To save her, her childhood friend Syaoran must follow the orders of the Dimension Witch and travel alongside Kurogane, an unrivaled warrior; Fai, a powerful magician; and Mokona, a curiously strange creature, to retrieve Sakura's dispersed memories!

A SMART, NEW ROMANTIC COMEDY FOR FANS OF *SHORTCAKE CAKE* AND *TERRACE HOUSE!*

A romance manga starring high school girl Meeko, who learns to live on her own in a boarding house whose living room is home to the odd (but handsome) Matsunaga-san. She begins to adjust to her new life away from her parents, but Meeko soon learns that no matter how far away from home she is, she's still a young girl at heart — especially when she finds herself falling for Matsunaga-san.

PERFECT WORLD

Rie Aruga

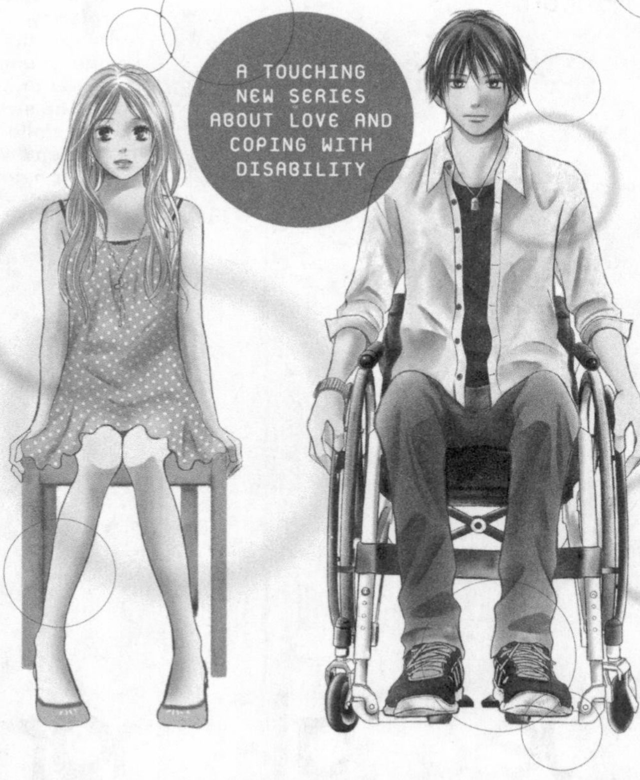
A TOUCHING NEW SERIES ABOUT LOVE AND COPING WITH DISABILITY

An office party reunites Tsugumi with her high school crush Itsuki. He's realized his dream of becoming an architect, but along the way, he experienced a spinal injury that put him in a wheelchair. Now Tsugumi's rekindled feelings will butt up against prejudices she never considered — and Itsuki will have to decide if he's ready to let someone into his heart...

"Depicts with great delicacy and courage the difficulties some with disabilities experience getting involved in romantic relationships... Rie Aruga refuses to romanticize, pushing her heroine to face the reality of disability. She invites her readers to the same tasks of empathy, knowledge and recognition."
—Slate.fr

"An important entry [in manga romance]... The emotional core of both plot and characters indicates thoughtfulness... [Aruga's] research is readily apparent in the text and artwork, making this feel like a real story."
—Anime News Network

KC KODANSHA COMICS

The adorable new odd-couple cat comedy manga from the creator of the beloved *Chi's Sweet Home*, in full color!

Praise for Chi's Sweet Home

"Nearly impossible to turn away... a true all-ages title that anyone, young or old, cat lover or not, will enjoy. The stories will bring a smile to your face and warm your heart."

—School Library Journal

Sue & Tai-chan
Konami Kanata

Sue is an aging housecat who's looking forward to living out her life in peace... but her plans change when the mischievous black tomcat Tai-chan enters the picture! Hey! Sue never signed up to be a catsitter! *Sue & Tai-chan* is the latest from the reigning meow-narch of cute kitty comics, Konami Kanata.

KC KODANSHA COMICS

Princess Jellyfish

Akiko Higashimura

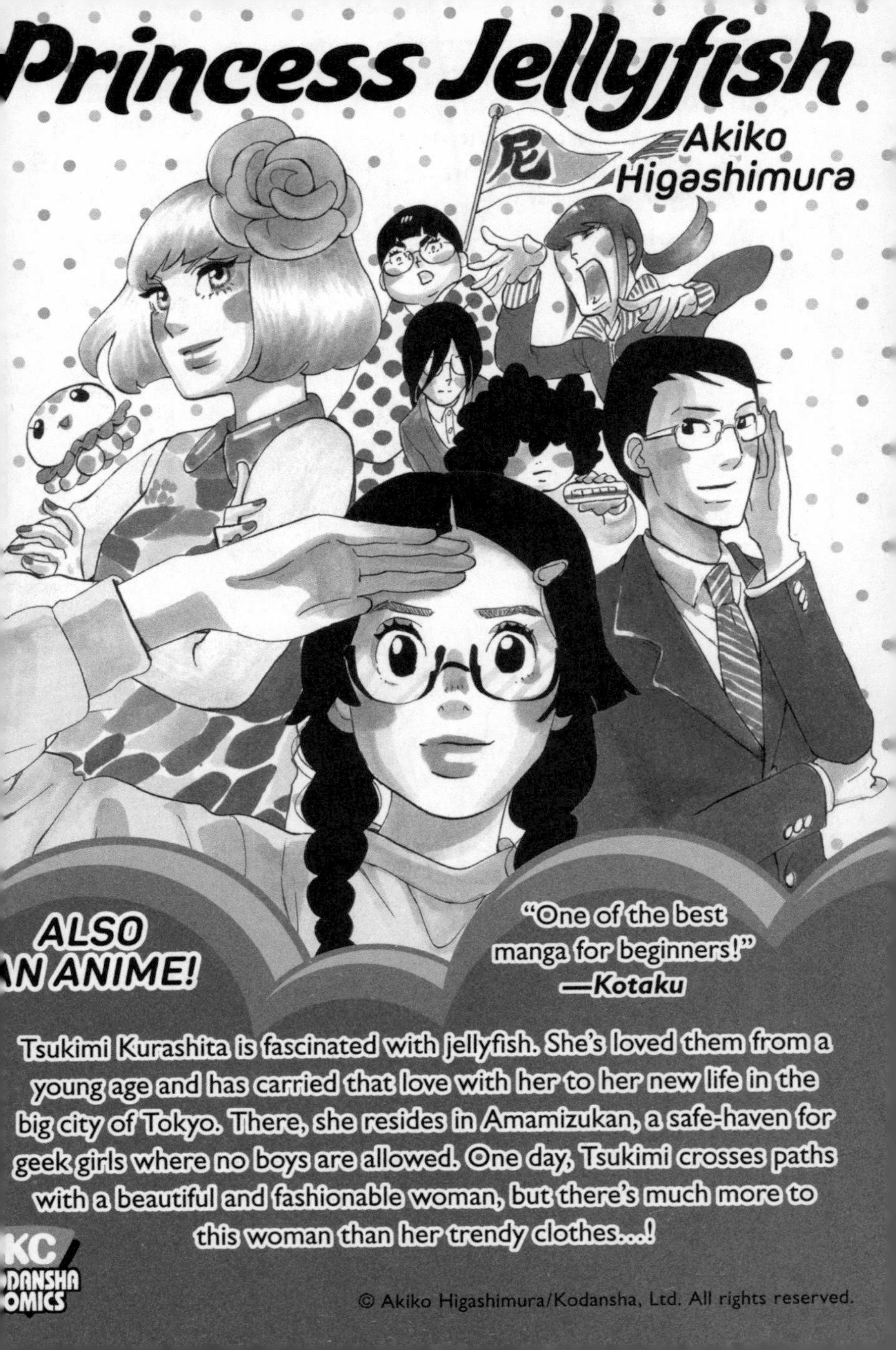

ALSO AN ANIME!

"One of the best manga for beginners!"
—*Kotaku*

Tsukimi Kurashita is fascinated with jellyfish. She's loved them from a young age and has carried that love with her to her new life in the big city of Tokyo. There, she resides in Amamizukan, a safe-haven for geek girls where no boys are allowed. One day, Tsukimi crosses paths with a beautiful and fashionable woman, but there's much more to this woman than her trendy clothes...!

Yuri Is My Job!

miman

JOIN US FOR AFTERNOON TEA WITH EQUAL PARTS YURI, ROM-COM, AND DRAMA!

Hime is a picture-perfect high school princess, so when she accidentally injures a café manager named Mai, she's willing to cover some shifts to keep her façade intact. To Hime's surprise, the café is themed after a private school where the all-female staff always puts on their best act for their loyal customers. However, under the guidance of the most graceful girl there, Hime can't help but blush and blunder! Beneath all the frills and laughter, Hime feels tension brewing as she finds out more about her new job and her budding feelings...

KC/ KODANSHA COMICS

"A quirky, fun comedy series... If you're a yuri fan, or perhaps interested in getting into it but not sure where to start, this book is worth picking up."
— Anime UK News

Noragami: Stray God 24 is a work of fiction. Names, characters, places, and incidents are the products of the author's imagination or are used fictitiously. Any resemblance to actual events, locales, or persons, living or dead, is entirely coincidental.

A Kodansha Comics Trade Paperback Original
Noragami: Stray God 24 copyright © 2021 Adachitoka
English translation copyright © 2022 Adachitoka

Published in the United States by Kodansha Comics, an imprint of Kodansha USA Publishing, LLC, New York.

Publication rights for this English edition arranged through Kodansha Ltd., Tokyo.

First published in Japan in 2021 by Kodansha Ltd., Tokyo.

ISBN 978-1-64651-425-0

Printed in the United States of America.

www.kodansha.us

9 8 7 6 5 4 3 2 1
Translation: Alethea Nibley & Athena Nibley
Lettering: Lys Blakeslee
Editing: Haruko Hashimoto
Kodansha Comics edition cover design by Phil Balsman

Publisher: Kiichiro Sugawara

Director of publishing services: Ben Applegate
Associate director, publishing operations: Stephen Pakula
Publishing services managing editors: Madison Salters, Alanna Ruse
Production managers: Emi Lotto, Angela Zurlo